PHIL EDMONSTON'S
LEMON-AID
USED CARS
AND MINIVANS
2005

PHIL EDMONSTON'S
LEMON-AID

USED CARS
AND MINIVANS
2005

PHIL EDMONSTON

PENGUIN
CANADA

PENGUIN CANADA

Penguin Group (Canada), a division of Pearson Penguin Canada Inc.,
     10 Alcorn Avenue, Toronto, Ontario, Canada M4V 3B2

Penguin Group (U.K.), 80 Strand, London WC2R 0RL, England
Penguin Group (U.S.), 375 Hudson Street, New York, New York 10014, U.S.A.
Penguin Group (Australia) Inc., 250 Camberwell Road, Camberwell, Victoria 3124, Australia
Penguin Group (Ireland), 25 St. Stephen's Green, Dublin 2, Ireland
Penguin Books India (P) Ltd, 11, Community Centre, Panchsheel Park, New Delhi – 110 017, India
Penguin Group (New Zealand), cnr Rosedale and Airborne Roads, Albany, Auckland 1310, New Zealand
Penguin Books (South Africa) (Pty) Ltd, 24 Sturdee Avenue, Rosebank 2196, South Africa

Penguin Group, Registered Offices: 80 Strand, London WC2R 0RL, England

First published 2004

(FR) 10 9 8 7 6 5 4 3 2 1

Copyright © Les Editions Edmonston, 2004

Manufactured in Canada.

NATIONAL LIBRARY OF CANADA CATALOGUING IN PUBLICATION

Edmonston, Louis-Philippe, 1944-
    Phil Edmonston's lemon-aid : used cars and minivans.

Annual
Imprint varies.
Continues: Lemon-aid used cars and minivans.
ISSN 1706-4317
ISBN 0-14-301631-8 (2005 edition)

1. Used cars—Purchasing—Periodicals. 2. Vans—Purchasing—Periodicals.
I. Title.

TL162.E3398   629.222'2'05   C2003-901021-X

Visit the Penguin Group (Canada) website at **www.penguin.ca**

CONTENTS

Honda	134	Nissan	152	Toyota/	
Civic, del Sol	134	Sentra	152	General Motors	167
				Corolla, Matrix/	
Hyundai	140	Subaru	154	Vibe	167
Accent	140	Impreza, Forester,			
Elantra	143	WRX	154	Toyota	173
		Legacy, Outback	160	Echo	173
Kia	146			Tercel, Paseo	175
Rio	147	Suzuki	165		
		Aerio, Esteem	165	Volkswagen	177
Mazda	149			Cabrio, Golf, Jetta	177
Protegé	149				

Medium Cars 182

Acura	184	Bonneville, Cutlass,		Mazda	248
1.6, 1.7L EL	184	Cutlass Supreme,		626, MX-6,	
CL-Series	185	Delta 88, Grand Prix,		Mazda6	248
Integra	189	Impala, Intrigue,			
		LeSabre, Lumina,		Nissan	252
DaimlerChrysler	191	Malibu, Monte		Altima	252
Breeze, Cirrus,		Carlo, Regal	219		
Stratus	191	Century, Ciera	231	Toyota	257
				Camry, Solara	257
Ford	196	Honda	236		
Contour, Mystique	196	Accord	236	Volkswagen	266
Sable, Taurus	199			New Beetle	266
		Hyundai	245	Passat	269
General Motors	212	Sonata	245		
Achieva, Alero					
Grand Am, Skylark	212				

Large Cars/Wagons 272

DaimlerChrysler	276	Ford	284	General Motors	294
300M, Concorde,		Cougar,		Caprice,	
Intrepid, LHS,		Thunderbird	284	Impala SS,	
New Yorker,		Crown Victoria,		Roadmaster	294
Vision	276	Grand Marquis	289		

Luxury Cars 294

Acura	300	Audi	306	BMW	312
RL	300	90, A4, A6 (100),		3 Series, 5 Series,	
TL	303	A8, S6, TT Coupe	306	M Series, Z3	312

KEY DOCUMENTS

Lemon-Aid Used Cars and Minivans 2005 is a feisty owner's manual that has no equal anywhere. We don't want you stuck with a lemon, or paying for repairs that are the automaker's fault and are covered by secret "goodwill" warranties. That's why we are the only book that includes many hard-to-find confidential and little-known documents that automakers don't want you to see.

In short, we know you can't win what you can't prove.

The following photos, charts, documents, memos, court filings and decisions, and service bulletins are included in this index so that you can stand your ground and be treated fairly. Photocopy and circulate whichever document will prove helpful in your dealings with automakers, dealers, service managers, insurance companies, or government agencies. Remember, most of the hundreds of summarized service bulletins outline repairs or replacements that should be done for free.

PART THREE 1970–2003 RATINGS

Minivans

SECRET WARRANTIES AND LUXURY LEMONS

Mercedes Hits a Pothole

Spend $25,000 on a car that doesn't run the way you expect it to, and you get pretty angry. Spend $50,000 or $100,000, and you get really angry. Just listen to the anguished howls of Mercedes-Benz owners on websites like *troublebenz.com, lemonmb.com,* and *mercedes problems.com,* as they vent about the latest mishap to afflict their Benzes. Depending on the model, the complaints range from faulty key fobs and leaky sunroofs to balky electronics that leave drivers and their passengers stranded. Regardless of the severity, a single sentiment runs through the gripes: This shouldn't be happening to a Mercedes.

Alex Taylor III

Fortune

October 13, 2003

How to Be a Millionaire

Thirty-seven percent of millionaires buy used cars, which is one reason why they're so well off.

Getting Rich in America

Dwight R. Lee and Richard B. McKenzie

Smart people buy used cars. That's why, after 32 years, *Lemon-Aid Used Cars and Minivans* is still going strong with over a million sales so far.

Lemon-Aid starts with the premise that the auto industry is fundamentally crooked and will lie and cheat to whatever degree is necessary to make a profit (think Ford/Firestone cover-up and Hyundai horsepower fibbing).

Europeans don't make better cars than Americans: VWs age poorly, and some Mercedes' models are luxury "lemons." Read their confidential service bulletins.

As a member of Parliament, I've seen automobile executives plead for corporate welfare and bailouts that went into executive bonuses instead of workers' pockets. I remember how GM closed its Camaro and Firebird plant in Quebec, after pocketing millions in grant money to keep it open. And, I'll never forget the time three decades ago when Ford goons threw me out of the Toronto auto show after I demanded that Ford extend its secret American rust repair warranty to Canadians. Three years later, the company relented and paid out almost $3 million in refunds.

Lemon-Aid knows most American cars are crap. We also know that Japanese cars have hit a quality plateau and are simply marking time as they search for maximum profits and market share. Imagine, Toyota Motor Corporation has already beaten Ford Motor Company in six-month sales to become the world's second-biggest automaker.

But, this isn't just a tale of fallen American car quality. We also know that European automakers' products aren't half as good as their hype and do well only because they spend millions of dollars on a fawning motoring press corps and market their vehicles to insecure social climbers with more money than brains.

Car buyers are fed up with failure-prone airbags and emissions systems, ABS brakes that don't brake, and secret warranties that pay engine and transmission repairs for only those owners who scream the loudest.

Take a look at the following two confidential service bulletins from General Motors, giving millions of car owners rights to significant repair refunds following engine and fuel gauge failures. Peruse carefully all the other bulletins concerning free repairs for you or your neighbours' cars found peppered throughout *Lemon-Aid*; you'll not find them published in any other consumer guide. Don't be shocked to see that automakers will lie through their teeth denying these bulletins exist—until you threaten to file your copy in small claims court (ouch!).

GM free fuel gauge repairs

Inaccurate fuel gauge readings

Bulletin No.: 01-06-04-008D   Date: April 2003
Inaccurate or Erratic Fuel Gauge Reading, Fuel Pump Related Driveability Concerns (Install New Fuel Tank Sender Sender)

2000–03	Chevrolet Cavalier, Malibu
2000–03	Oldsmobile Alero
2000–03	Pontiac Grand Am, Sunfire
2000–01	Toyota Cavalier
with plastic fuel tanks	

Condition

Some customers may comment about inaccurate or erratic fuel gauge readings. A typical comment might be that it appears from the gauge reading that there is fuel available, yet the tank is nearly empty.   ➤

> ### Cause
> This condition may be the result of the corrosive effect of certain fuel blends on the contact surfaces of the fuel tank sender sensor.

Another free fix that could save you close to $1,000. This fuel-level sender defect affects most of GM's car and truck lineup, and goes back to 1999 and earlier GM models not listed in the above bulletin (like Saturns and minivans). Use the 7-year/160,000-km benchmark in all claims and follow up in small claims court, if refused compensation (see Part Two, "Lawyers and Liars!").

GM free brake repairs

Front Disc Brakes – Pedal/Steering Wheel Pulsation

File In Section: 05 – Brakes   Date: December, 2001
Bulletin No.: 00-05-23-002A

Models:
1997–2002 Malibu
1997–99   Cutlass
1999–2002 Alero, Grand Am

Condition
Some customers may comment on a pulsation condition felt in the brake pedal and/or steering wheel during a brake apply. In some cases, it may be noted that the pulsation condition has reoccurred in 5,000–11,000 km (3,000–7,000 miles) after having had the brakes serviced, tires rotated, or any type of servicing that required wheel removal.

Cause
Pulsation is the result of brake rotor thickness variation causing the brake caliper piston to move in and out of the brake caliper housing. This hydraulic "pumping/pulsing" effect is transmitted through the brake system and may be felt in the brake pedal. In severe cases, this condition may also transmit through the vehicle structure and other chassis system components such as the steering column or wheel. The major contributor to rotor thickness variation is excessive lateral run-out of the rotor, causing the brake pads to wear the rotor unevenly over time.

Correction
Confirm that the brake pads have the number 1417 printed on the edge of the pad backing plate (refer to the illustration). This indicates the correct brake pads have been previously installed. The brake pads contained in Front Pad Kit, P/N 18044437, are the only brake pads that should be used on these vehicles. If the number 1417 is not present, or if the number is not legible, replace the brake pads. If the correct pads were previously installed, verify the brake pad thickness. If the brake pad friction material thickness is 4.6 mm (0.18 in) or greater, re-use the pads. If the friction material thickness is less than 4.6 mm (0.18 in), install new brake pads contained in Front Pad Kit P/N 18044437.

If the rotor thickness is less than 25 mm (0.98 in), install a new rotor. If rotor thickness is greater than 25 mm (0.98 in), refinish the rotor.

Replace existing front brake rotors and pads, if necessary, with new components indicated in the table following the applicable Service Manual procedures and the service guidelines contained in Corporate Bulletin Number 00-05-22-002.

At last, no more doubletalk or blaming the driver for faulty brakes. Here, GM puts the blame on its rotors, not the car owner.

Lemon-Aid Used Cars and Minivans 2005 exposes the lies, obfuscations, and deception to even the playing field. It's a uniquely Canadian owner's action manual that pulls no punches in disclosing what's a fair price, which cars and minivans are lemons, which repairs are the automakers' responsibility, and which scams you should avoid.

Paying a fair price is even more crucial this year now that low-percentage new-car financing, rebates, and subsidized three- and five-year leases have driven used prices to new lows. For the first time, fully loaded off-lease vehicles and used rentals can be veritable bargains (Budget is a good source)—if you know what to buy and how to use depreciation timing to your advantage (Ford Crown Vic, yes; Cadillac Catera, no).

My goal for over 32 years has been to keep ownership costs low and make automakers and dealers more honest and accountable—even as they hire lawyers and PR flacks to plead that wrong is right and that safety, like their own integrity, is relative. This guide continues a tradition of publicizing abusive auto industry practices and providing hard-to-get information that may save your life, or at least protect your wallet.

Lemon-Aid's information comes from owners who buy and drive these vehicles, not travel-junket-junkie, free-car-mongering car columnists. Our database includes Canadian and U.S. sources and is refined throughout the year with input from owner complaints, automaker whistleblowers, lawsuits, judgments, confidential technical service bulletins (TSBs), and independent garages.

Lemon-Aid arms you with internal service bulletins, memos, and confidential defect admissions you're not supposed to have. It is the first book to blow the whistle on the rising number of secret engine and transmission warranties used by Asian, European, and American automakers. We were also first off the mark in exposing secret warranty payouts for Chrysler, Ford, Lincoln, and GM mid-sized models equipped with melted or defective engine intake manifolds and head gaskets (a $1,000 repair); Saturn self-destructing engines; BMW M3's sustaining catastrophic engine failures; and Hyundai, Lexus, Toyota, and Honda engine and transmission defects (repaired for free for up to eight years).

Lemon-Aid is the only consumer guide to give Ford's Windstar minivan a "lemon" rating (see 2000 judgment in Windstar Section that awarded one owner $7,500 for "mental distress").

We also take on Alberta and British Columbia scumbag used-car dealers who pose as private sellers as they dispose of "junkers" imported from Eastern Canada.

We combine test results with owner feedback to provide a critical comparison of many cars and minivans sold during the past three decades. If improvements and additional safety features don't justify the higher costs of newer models (most don't), we say so. Safer, more reliable, and often cheaper alternatives are given for each vehicle, and reliability and crashworthiness ratings are shown for each model year. Finally, for frugal readers, this year's guide includes a helpful appendix that rates the best vehicles available for less than $1,000.

Phil Edmonston
February 2004

PART ONE

BARGAIN BUYS

1

Wake Up and Smell the Sake!
For too many years, Detroit companies' primary tactic for fighting back has been to shift consumers' attention to the future, while leveraging their past as a sentimental weapon to obscure the deficiencies of the present.

Micheline Maynard
The End of Detroit
Doubleday

Forbes' April 22, 2003 edition says it all: "What started out as a halo car (2002 Thunderbird) has turned into an embarrassment.... Quality was also a problem. The plastic top (for winter) scratched the body. And Ford dealers got an early reputation for ripping off customers by overcharging for the car...."

Chrysler is struggling with PT Cruiser sales and Ford says it will soon axe its $51,500 retro-styled T-Bird, along with the Taurus and several other models. Resale values, already in the basement, will likely go subterranean. But, no matter how cheap, these cars won't ever become used-car bargains or collectors' cars.

At their best, they're overpriced, mediocre cars. At their worst, they're junk.

Getting the best for less

So, what can you do to avoid buying junk? Simple.

Pick out a *Lemon-Aid*–recommended 3- to 5-year-old crashworthy, cheap, and reliable used car or minivan and keep it for at least another five to seven years. There's little difference in savings between the 8th and 10th year of ownership, says Toronto auto "number cruncher" Dennis DesRosiers. Sure, you'll lose a few thousand dollars in depreciation each ensuing year, but that'll be more than offset by the low price you paid initially.

There are lots of other reasons why now is a great time to buy a used car or minivan. Since 1996, new-car prices have moderated, creating a large reservoir of affordable used cars. And as we enter into 2005, used prices continue to decline principally in response to an uncertain economy, volatile fuel costs, new-car rebates, and low-percentage financing programs.

But prices are only one factor to consider. Vehicle quality and dependability are equally important.

Sure, you can prance around telling your friends how you "stole" that used Saturn or Caravan—until you have to spend $3,500 for engine or transmission work. Or, sometimes both. Granted, much of the junk has been cleared out and vehicles are safer, and loaded with extra convenience and performance features, but you've got to be careful in your choice and look beyond price.

Chrysler's minivans are lousy buys, unless you can get the automaker's 7-year powertrain warranty transferred to your vehicle. Then they are simply risky buys.

But, let's not just pick on GM and Chrysler. European automakers make their share of lemons as well.

J.D. Power and Associates rank Mercedes quality as much worse than average—in 26th place, behind Oldsmobile. However, if you were a steady reader of *Lemon-Aid* over the past 32 years, you would have been wary of Mercedes' poor quality and you likely saved money buying cheap and reliable used Japanese cars or rear-drive luxury American models.

It's incredible but true: There's no correlation between safe and dependable transportation and the amount of money a vehicle costs. In fact, almost the opposite conclusion can be reached: Cheap, simple vehicles, originally retailing for $10,000–$20,000, that have been on the market for a few years, are far better buys than most cars costing two or three times as much. Below are a few examples of what I mean.

Lemon-Aid best and worst buys

Smart buys

Acura Integra
Chrysler Colt, Sebring, and Avenger
Ford Crown Victoria, Escort, Grand Marquis, Mustang, and Probe
GM Camaro and Firebird
Honda Accord, Civic, CR-V, and Odyssey
Hyundai Accent, Elantra, and Tiburon
Lincoln Town Car
Mazda 323, 626, Miata, MPV, MX-6, and Protegé
Nissan Axxess, Maxima, and Sentra
Toyota Avalon, Camry, Corolla, Cressida, Echo, Sienna, and Tercel

Dumb buys

Cadillac Catera and Cimarron
Chrysler Concorde, Horizon, Intrepid, LHS, minivans, New Yorker, Neon, and Omni
Ford Sable, Taurus, and Windstar
GM Corvette, Fiero, Vega/Astre
Hyundai Excel, Pony, early Sonatas, and Stellar
Jaguar (all models)
Lincoln Continental (front-drive)
Mercedes-Benz 190, C-Class, and M series
Merkur (all models)
Kia (all models)
Nissan 240Z, 260Z, B210
Infiniti G20
Saab (all models)
Saturn Ion, L-series, S-series, and Vue
Suzuki Samurai and X-90
VW Eurovan and Passat (early models)

Note in the list above how frequently so-called "premium" luxury brands have fallen out of favour, are orphaned by shoppers, and then abandoned by the automakers themselves, leaving early purchasers with pseudo-luxo junk.

A short history of junk

I've spent almost 35 years battling automakers and dealers who lie through their teeth as they try to convince customers that their vehicles are well made, and that defects are caused mainly by the proverbial "nut behind the wheel," poor maintenance, or abusive driving. That's why the auto industry has such a lousy reputation—car owners know better. The average Canadian has personally (or knows someone who has) experienced the lying, cheating, and stealing that's so rampant at all levels of the automotive manufacturing and marketing process.

Firestone wasn't an aberration; it was a microcosm of what goes on throughout the industry. When the tires started shredding in other countries and injuries and deaths started to mount, Ford used a secret warranty program to pay off Explorer owners in Venezuela and Saudi Arabia. When the media discovered the cover-up, Ford lied to customers and officials alike, saying either that they weren't aware of the tire failures or that it was all Firestone's fault.

At first Ford and Firestone blamed their customers— then they turned on each other!

This dishonesty and poor quality control has always existed. When I founded the Automobile Protection Association (APA) in Montreal in the fall of 1969, American Motors was giving out free television sets with the purchase of its failure-prone Eagle sport-utility (actually, the television sets lasted longer than the Eagle); Volkswagen had a monopoly on hazardous, poorly heated, and sluggish Beetles; Ford was churning out biodegradable cars and trucks (and denying they had a secret "J-67" warranty to cover rust repairs); Firestone was dragged, kicking and screaming, into announcing the recall of 11 million tires for catastrophic tread separation (in the late '70s); and Chrysler's entire product line was "rain-challenged"—stalling and leaking in wet weather due to faulty ballast resistors, distributor caps, and rotors; and misaligned body panels.

Japanese and European cars imported into Canada during the '70s were unreliable rustbuckets. Yet they got a toehold in the North American car market because the Big Three's products were worse—and they still are. Seizing the opportunity, foreign automakers smartened up within a remarkably short period of time. They quickly built reliable and durable cars and trucks and offered them fully loaded and reasonably priced.

Meanwhile, American automakers continued pumping out dangerous and unreliable junk through the '90s—these included GM's Chevy Vega, Firenza, and Fiero, as well as early Saturns, Cavaliers, Sunbirds, and the Lumina/Trans Sport minivan; Chrysler's Omni, Horizon, Dynasty, Imperial, Concorde, Neon, and post-'90 minivans; and Ford's Pinto, Bobcat, Tempo, Topaz, Taurus, Sable, Contour, Mystique (mistake?), Merkur, Bronco, Explorer, and Windstar.

Not surprisingly, sales continued to nosedive.

Then, in the early '90s Detroit got a second chance to prove itself. The minivan carved out a new, popular marketing niche and American SUVs like the Ford Explorer were piling up profits. But, as Micheline Maynard makes crystal clear in *The End of Detroit,* the American auto industry's arrogance disconnected its products from reality, and by focusing mainly on high-profit trucks and SUVs, Detroit abandoned average car buyers to the Japanese and South Koreans.

"Foreign companies like Toyota and Honda," says Maynard, "solidified their dominance in family and economy cars, gained market share in high-margin luxury cars, and, in an ironic twist, soon stormed in with their own sophisticatedly engineered and marketed SUVs, pickups, and minivans. Detroit, suffering from a 'good enough' syndrome and wedded to ineffective marketing gimmicks like rebates and zero-percent financing, failed to give consumers what they really wanted: reliability, the latest technology, and good design at a reasonable cost."

Today, Detroit's Big Three quality control is still way below average when compared with Japanese and South Korean automakers. Where the gap is particularly noticeable is in engine, automatic transmission, airbag, and anti-lock brake reliability, as well as fit and finish.

Want proof not even your dealer's service manager can deny? Take a look at this Ford internal service bulletin depicting serious engine failures and Ford's half-hearted attempt to indemnify owners. Note how the same defect has been carried over a number of model years.

Coolant Loss/Engine Oil Contamination, 3.8L, 4.2L

Article No. 99 - 20 - 7
10/04/99
^ COOLING SYSTEM - 3.8L - UNDETERMINED LOSS OF COOLANT
^ COOLING SYSTEM - 4.2L - UNDETERMINED LOSS OF COOLANT
^ ENGINE - 3.8L - ENGINE OIL CONTAMINATED WITH COOLANT
^ ENGINE - 4.2L - ENGINE OIL CONTAMINATED WITH COOLANT

FORD:
1996–97   THUNDERBIRD
1996–98   MUSTANG, WINDSTAR
1997–98   E-150, E-250, F-150

MERCURY:
1996–97   COUGAR

This TSB article is being republished in its entirety to correct the front cover/water pump bolt torque values and the Front Cover Gasket Part Number.

ISSUE

Engine coolant may be leaking into the engine oil on some vehicles. The internal coolant leak may be difficult to identify. This may be caused by the lower intake manifold side gaskets and/or front cover gaskets allowing coolant to pass into the cylinders and/or the crankcase.

ACTION

Revised lower intake manifold side and front cover gaskets have been released for service.

WARRANTY STATUS

Eligible under the provisions of bumper to bumper warranty coverage and emissions warranty coverage.

Why Canadians Buy Used

There are almost 18 million cars on Canada's roads and they're all used—a transformation that occurs as soon as you drive off the dealer's lot. But we don't mind; we love used cars. Canadian car buyers are different from Americans: We are thrifty, unpretentious, and open-minded. We don't care where a car is made, as long as it's cheap and reliable. We are reluctant to trade in a vehicle that suits our needs just because it's old. In fact, almost 51 percent of Canadians keep cars and trucks nine years or more, says Dennis DesRosiers. We are also more conservative than Americans in our vehicle choice, with 86 percent of CAA's 2000 annual survey respondents stating they would buy the same vehicle again. And, confirming Canada's *société distincte* status, we love block heaters and minivans throughout Canada, and are particularly partial to downsized SUVs and AWD wagons in Quebec.

Through the '90s, the popularity of used vehicles went up substantially in Canada. Why? Because, according to the Royal Bank, the average Canadian's take-home pay didn't keep pace with the rising cost of purchasing and owning a new vehicle. And Canadians are wary of dealers selling used cars. Of the almost 20 percent of the vehicles on our roads that change hands each year, 70 percent are estimated to be private sales. Here are some of the main reasons why Canadians prefer buying used vehicles from each other:

1. Less initial cash outlay, slower vehicle depreciation, "secret" warranty repair refunds, and better and cheaper parts availability

New-vehicle prices have moderated somewhat over the past few years, but they're still quite high—Toronto-based auto consultant Dennis DesRosiers pegs the cost of the average new vehicle at almost $30,200. Insurance is another wallet buster, costing about $2,500 a year for young drivers. And once you add financing costs, maintenance, taxes, and a host of other expenses, CAA calculates the yearly outlay for a medium-sized car at over $8,252, or 36.7 cents/km; trucks or SUVs may run you about 10 cents/km more. For a comprehensive, though depressing, comparative analysis (cars vs. trucks, minivans, SUVs, etc.) of all the costs involved over a one- to 10-year period, access Alberta's consumer information website at *www1.agric.gov.ab.ca/app24/costcalculators/vehicle/getvechimpls.jsp.*

Used vehicles aren't sold with $700–$1,400 transport fees or $495 "administration" charges, either. And, you can legally avoid paying sales tax when you buy privately. That's right: You'll pay at least 10 percent less than the dealer's price and you may avoid the 7 percent federal Goods and Services Tax (GST) that applies in some provinces to dealer sales only.

Be practical. When buying a used car or minivan, keep in mind you're simply buying transportation and function. You want no-surprise handling; a comfortable ride; reliable performance; and interior, cargo, and passenger capacity. Because you only need about one-half the cash or credit required for a new vehicle, it's easy to see that you won't have to invest as much money in a depreciating investment. You may even be fortunate enough to forgo a loan.

Depreciation savings

If someone were to ask you to invest in stocks or bonds guaranteed to be worth less than half their initial purchase value after three to four years, you'd probably head for the door.

But this is exactly the trap you're falling into when you buy a new vehicle that will likely lose 60 percent of its value after three years of use (minivans and other specialty vehicles, like sport-utilities and trucks, depreciate more slowly). Here's how that would work out in Ontario:

Cost (new)

Purchase (1999 Honda Accord EX)	$28,000
Federal GST (7%)	$1,960
Provincial tax (8%)	$2,240
Total price	$32,200

When you buy used, the situation is altogether different. That same vehicle can be purchased four years later, in good condition, and with much of the manufacturer's warranty remaining, for less than one-half its original cost. Look at what happens to the price:

Cost (used)

Purchase price (four years old, 80,000 km)	$14,000
No GST (if sold privately)	—
Provincial tax (8%)	$1,120
Total price	$15,120

In this example, the Accord buyer saves $14,000 on the selling price, $1,960 in federal taxes, and $1,120 in provincial taxes, and gets a reliable, guaranteed set of wheels. Furthermore, the depreciation "hit" will be negligible in the ensuing years.

Secret warranty refunds

Almost all automakers use secret, "goodwill" warranties to cover factory-related defects, long after the original warranty has expired. This creates a huge fleet of used vehicles eligible for free repairs.

And, we're not talking about a few months' extension. In fact, some free repairs—like those related to Chrysler brakes and Nissan exhaust systems—are authorized up to 10 years as part of "goodwill" programs. Still, most secret warranty extensions hover around the 5- to 7-year mark and seldom cover vehicles exceeding 160,000 km or 100,000 miles. This benchmark includes engine and transmission defects affecting Detroit's Big Three, Honda, Hyundai, Lexus, and Toyota. Ford's 1995–98 Windstars carry a little-known 10-year warranty extension covering front coil spring breakage, and free tire replacement, if a tire is punctured.

NHTSA Campaign ID Number: 01I007000

Defect Summary:
This is not a safety defect in accordance with the safety act. However, it is deemed a safety improvement campaign by the agency. Vehicle description: 1995-1998 Ford Windstar Minivans. The front coil springs could potentially fracture due to corrosion.

Consequence Summary:
Some tires have deflated due to contact with a broken spring.

Corrective Summary:
Ford is extending the warranty for front coil spring replacement to a total of 10 years of service from the warranty start date, with unlimited mileage. This coverage is automatically transferred to subsequent owners at no charge. If either front coil spring fractures during the coverage period noted above, the dealer will replace both springs at no charge to the owner.

All, not just some of these springs should have been recalled. Don't want to put your family's life in danger? Take a copy of the NHTSA's defect report (above) and demand that the springs be changed before they fail, or you'll sue for their replacement in small claims court while holding the dealer and automaker responsible for any fatalities or injuries occurring in the interim.

Knowing which free repairs apply to your car will cut maintenance costs dramatically. Incidentally, automakers and dealers claim that there are no secret warranties, since they are all published in service bulletins. Although this is technically correct, have you ever tried to get a copy of a service bulletin? Or— if you did manage to get a copy—had the dealer or automaker say the benefits are only applicable in the States? Oh yeah!

Parts

Here we have to make a distinction between mechanical and body parts. Both categories are considerably cheaper when bought used; however, body panels have important advantages if they are purchased new, from the automaker.

Yes, we all know that original equipment (OEM) manufacturer parts prices are a huge rip-off that makes the apocryphal $800 Air Force toilet seat look like a Kmart "blue light" special. But, did you know that the Alliance of American Insurers has found that the cost to rebuild the average car or minivan with OEM parts would be three times its original selling price?

Take, for example, a 2002 Dodge Grand Caravan Sport, selling for $24,815 (U.S.). When totalled out and rebuilt entirely from car company parts, the cost soars to $71,631, not including the cost of labour and paint.

"The cost of repairing damaged automobiles accounts for between 40 and 50 percent of the insurance premium for most auto insurance consumers," said Kirk Hansen, Alliance director of claims.

"Therefore, the cost of crash parts has a significant, direct impact on the price consumers pay for auto insurance. Expensive parts result in more costly repairs, which in turn result in higher premiums. In addition, many vehicles that should be repaired must be totalled due to the high cost of car company parts."

Nevertheless, *Consumer Reports* concluded in a February 1999 study that car company body panels offer better crash protection, are more rust resistant, and fit better than generic parts. Although insurance appraisers often substitute cheaper, lower-quality aftermarket body parts in collision repairs, the study found that 71 percent of those policyholders who requested OEM parts got them with little or no hassle. *CR* suggests that consumers complain to their provincial Superintendent of Insurance if OEM parts aren't provided.

Parts are cheap and plentiful

Most vehicles are traded in before they have trouble. Generally, a new gasoline-powered car or minivan can be expected to run, relatively trouble-free, at least 200,000–240,000 km (125,000–150,000 mi.) in its lifetime, and a diesel-powered vehicle can easily triple those figures. Some repairs will crop up at regular intervals, and along with preventive maintenance, your yearly running costs should average about $700–$800. Buttressing the argument that vehicles get cheaper to operate the longer you keep them, the U.S. Department of Transportation points out that the average vehicle requires one or more major repairs after every five years of use. However, once these repairs are done, it can then be run relatively trouble-free for another five years or more. In fact, the further west you go in Canada, the longer owners keep their vehicles—an average of 10 years or more in some provinces.

Time is on your side in other ways, too. Three years after a model's launching, the replacement parts market usually catches up to consumer demand. Dealers stock larger inventories, and parts wholesalers and independent parts manufacturers expand their output. Used replacement parts are unquestionably easier to come by, through bargaining with local garages or through a careful search of auto wreckers' yards or the Internet. A reconditioned or used part usually costs one-third to one-half the price of a new part. There's generally no difference in the quality of reconditioned mechanical components, and they're often guaranteed for as long as, or longer than, new ones. In fact, some savvy shoppers use the ratings in Part Three of this guide to see which parts have a short life and then buy those parts from retailers that give lifetime warranties on their brakes, exhaust systems, tires, batteries, etc.

Also, buying from discount outlets or independent garages, or ordering through mail order houses, can save you big bucks (30–35 percent) on the cost of new parts and another 15 percent on labour when compared with dealer charges. Costco is another good example of savings realized through independent retailers. The retailer sells competitively priced replacement tires and sometimes throws in free tire rotation, balancing, and other inspections.

With some European models, you can count on a lot of aggravation and expense caused by the unacceptably slow distribution of parts and their high markup. Because these companies have a quasi-monopoly on replacement parts, there are few independent suppliers you can turn to for help. And junkyards, the last-chance repository for inexpensive car parts, are unlikely to carry foreign parts for vehicles more than three years old or manufactured in small numbers.

Finding parts for Japanese and domestic cars and vans is hardly a problem, though, due to the large number of vehicles produced, the presence of hundreds of independent suppliers, the ease with which relatively simple parts can be interchanged from one model to another, and the large reservoir of used parts stocked by junkyards. Redesigned vehicles, however, like the new Nissan Quest or Toyota Sienna, will likely have more difficulty with parts availability and higher costs, until independent suppliers heat up the competition.

Internet auto clubs and eBay Motors are often helpful sources for parts that are otherwise unobtainable. Club members trade and sell specialty parts, keep a list of where rare parts can be found, and are usually well informed as to where independent parts suppliers are located. Most car enthusiast magazines will put you in touch with auto clubs and suppliers of hard-to-find parts. eBay Motors at *www.ebaymotors.com* doesn't require any membership and serves shoppers from around the world.

2. Lower insurance rates

The price you pay for insurance can vary significantly, not only between insurance companies, but within the same company over time. But one thing does remain constant: the insurance for used vehicles is a lot cheaper than new-car coverage and through careful comparison shopping, insurance premium payouts can be reduced substantially. For example, the Ontario government has introduced cost-reduction initiatives that will create $1.2 to $1.3 billion in savings, which insurers will have to pass on to drivers.

One effective agency that tracks the lowest premiums is The Consumers Guide to Insurance at *www.insurancehotline.com*. It has created a "Watch Dog" service to alert drivers to the changes in their insurance rates. For $20 per year, the agency will automatically re-run members' profiles to ensure they always know which insurer has the lowest rate from its database of 30 insurance companies (representing over 80% of the written premiums in Canada).

Those auto owners looking for premium comparisons throughout Canada or insider tips on dealing with insurers should access *www.insurance-canada.ca/consquotes/onlineauto.php* or *www.autoinsurancetips.com*.

Some cars sustain lower collision costs than others. But you have to know which ones. For that you should visit the Insurance Bureau of Canada's Vehicle Insurance Information Centre (*www.vicc.com*; Tel.: 1-800-761-6703 or 416-445-5912). It provides a comprehensive look at the insurance claims experience of the most popular Canadian models of private passenger vehicles.

It includes collision, comprehensive, personal injury, and theft results for vehicles three or more years old.

One would expect the best-rated vehicles would cost less to insure; however, this isn't necessarily the case. Instead, use the figures as a guide to parts costs and the crashworthiness of different models.

Higher deductibles

Deductibles represent the amount of money you pay before you make a claim. By requesting higher deductibles on collision and comprehensive (fire and theft) coverage, you can lower your costs substantially. Auto insurance deductibles come in any amount, but generally range between $50 and $2,500. For example, increasing your deductible from $200 to $500 could reduce your collision and comprehensive costs by 15–30 percent.

No collision/comprehensive coverage

It may not be cost effective to have collision or comprehensive coverage on cars worth less than $1,000, because any claim you make would not substantially exceed annual cost and deductible amounts. Auto dealers and banks can tell you the worth of your car.

3. Fewer "hidden" defects

You can easily avoid any nasty surprises by having your choice checked out by an independent mechanic (for $75–$100) before paying for a used vehicle. This examination before purchase protects you against any hidden defects the vehicle may have. It's also a tremendous negotiating tool, since you can use the cost of any needed repairs to bargain down the purchase price.

It's easier to get permission to have the vehicle inspected if you promise to give the seller a copy of the inspection report, should you decide not to buy it. If you still can't get permission to have the vehicle inspected elsewhere, walk away from the deal, no matter how tempting the selling price. The seller is obviously trying to put something over on you. Ignore the standard excuses that the vehicle isn't insured, the licence plates have expired, or the vehicle has a dead battery.

4. You know the vehicle's history

Smart customers will want answers to the following questions before signing the contract: What did it first sell for and what is its present insured value? Who services it? How much of the original warranty or subsequent repair warranties are left? How many times has the vehicle been recalled for safety-related defects? Are parts easily available? Does the vehicle have a history of costly performance-related defects that can be corrected under a secret warranty, through a safety recall campaign, or with an upgraded part? (See Part Three).

Duelling Ratings

There are two major surveyors of automobile quality: J.D. Power and Associates, a private American automobile consulting organization, and Consumers Union, an American non-profit consumer organization that publishes *Consumer Reports*. J.D. Power and Associates publishes two quality reports: the first one, its Initial Quality Study, notes problems reported by owners during the first 90 days of ownership; and a more credible Long-term Quality Survey that highlights problems reported over several years. Often, vehicles that do poorly in one survey come out near the top on the other.

Just remember, don't look for 100 percent agreement among these groups' ratings; look instead for trends and general caveats that you can use to find the vehicle that best suits your needs and isn't costly to insure.

5. Litigation is quick, easy, and relatively inexpensive

Lawyers win, whether you win or lose. And you're likely to lose more than you'll ever get back, using the traditional court system in a used-car dispute.

But, if you're just a bit creative, you'll discover there are many federal and provincial consumer protection laws that go far beyond whatever protection may be offered by the standard new-vehicle warranty. Furthermore, buyers of used vehicles don't usually have to conform to any arbitrary rules or service guidelines to get this protection.

Let's say you do get stuck with a vehicle that's unreliable, has undisclosed accident damage, or doesn't perform as promised. Most small claims courts have a jurisdiction limit of $3,000–$10,000 (Alberta sets it at $25,000), which should cover the cost of repairs or compensate you if the vehicle is taken back. That way, any dispute between buyer and seller can be settled within a few months, without lawyers or excessive court costs. Furthermore, you're not likely to face a battery of lawyers standing in for the automaker and dealer in front of a stern-faced judge. Actually, you may not have to face a judge at all, since many cases are settled through court-imposed mediators at a pretrial meeting usually scheduled a month or two after filing.

Lemon-Aid *vs.* Consumer Reports

CR and *Lemon-Aid* ratings are often in agreement. Where they differ is in *Lemon-Aid*'s greater reliance upon National Highway Traffic Safety Administration (NHTSA) safety complaints, service bulletin admissions of defects, and owner complaints received through the Internet (rather than from a subscriber base, which may simply attract owners singing from the same hymnal).

In looking over *CR*'s best used-car picks for 2002 as published in its April 2002 edition, there are a number of vehicles that are recommended that defy all logic.

Foremost is the Ford Windstar, followed by the Taurus and Sable. It is inconceivable that *CR* isn't aware of the multiplicity of powertrain, body, and suspension failures affecting these vehicles. Then, there's the Chrysler Intrepid and its assorted minivans.

Now, you'd have to live on another planet to not know these vehicles are afflicted by chronic automatic transmission, body, brake, and AC defects. In fact, *Consumer Reports'* "Frequency of Repair" table in the same edition gives out plenty of black marks to the aforementioned models and components. Yet, sloppy research failed to pick up on these contradictions.

Choosing a Safe, Reliable, and "Green" Vehicle

Looking through Part Three and reading through the above-noted websites and magazines can help you find good, reliable used car buys.

Finding a safe car is a bit more difficult, though, since few used-car guides want to get into that kind of discussion.

First off, the best indicator of a car's overall safety is NHTSA's front, side, and rollover crashworthiness ratings, applicable to most vehicles made over the past several decades and sold in North America. Then you will want to compare NHTSA scores with ratings from the Insurance Institute for Highway Safety (IIHS), which crashes vehicles at a higher speed and at a more common offset angle, rather than head-on. Results from these two bodies are posted for each model rated in Part Three. However, there are many other national and international testing agencies that may be consulted and they can be found at *www.crashtest.com/netindex.htm.*

Of course no one expects to be in a collision, but NHTSA estimates that every vehicle, during its lifetime, will be in two accidents of varying severity. So why not put the averages on your side?

Most environmentally-friendly vehicles

Consider these important points when making your used-car choice:

- The 18 million cars and light-duty trucks Canada's roads today are responsible for 12 percent of the nation's greenhouse gas emissions.
- 5,000 deaths a year nationwide are attributed to smog pollutants. Smog pollutants cost the Ontario economy alone $9.9 billion in health care costs and business losses, according to the Ontario Medical Association.
- In buying a used vehicle, you are already doing a lot for the environment by not adding to the vehicle population. Nevertheless, in choosing a fuel-efficient, safe, small car, you are also protecting your life and wallet.

Following are the top 10 most environmentally-friendly 2003s, according to Environmental Defence Canada.

Honda Insight
Toyota Prius
Honda Civic Hybrid
Toyota Echo
Toyota Corolla
Honda Civic

Nissan Sentra
Pontiac Vibe/Toyota Matrix
Hyundai Accent
Toyota Celica

Note: All of the above vehicles have also been rated *Lemon-Aid* "Good Buys." The upgraded 2004 Prius hasn't been crash-tested, though it appears more refined and versatile than the Honda Insight and Hybrid.

Choosing the Right Seller

When to buy
In the fall, dealer stocks of good quality trade-ins and off-lease returns are at their highest level, and private sellers are moderately active. Prices will be higher, but there will be a greater choice of vehicles available. In winter, prices decline substantially. Dealers and private sellers are generally easier to deal with, because buyers are scarce and weather conditions don't present their wares in the best light. In spring and summer, prices go up a bit as private sellers become more active and dealers try to get full price for their diminishing stock.

Private sellers
Private sellers are your best source for a cheap and reliable used vehicle, because you're on an equal bargaining level with a vendor who isn't trying to profit from your inexperience. This translates into a golden opportunity to negotiate a fair price, which isn't common in many dealer transactions.

Apart from newspaper classified ads, you can track down deals and get a good idea of prices through the following:

- word of mouth
- grocery store bulletin boards
- specialty publications (e.g., *Auto Trader*, *Auto Mart*, or *Buy and Sell Bargain Hunter*)
- the *Canadian Red Book* or the Provincial Automobile Dealers Association *Black Book*
- Internet sellers such as eBay

The best way to determine the price range for a particular model is to read the publications or surf the websites listed in Appendix I before you buy the vehicle. This will give you a reasonably good idea of the top asking price. Remember, no seller expects to get his or her asking price, be it a dealer or private party. As with price reductions on home listings, a 10–20 percent reduction on the advertised price is common with private sellers. Dealers usually won't cut more than 10 percent off their advertised price.

Find out which published used-car guide is the accepted standard in your area of the country. The *Red Book* and *Black Book* serve Canadian dealers,

while the *Kelley Blue Book* and *Edmunds Price Guide* are two of the most popular American guides, offering comprehensive ratings and prices, gratis,
through the Internet. You can visit the *Kelley Blue Book* at *www.kbb.com* or
Edmunds at *www.edmunds.com*.

Don't be surprised to find that many national price guides have an Eastern
Ontario–Quebec price bias. They often list unrealistically low prices compared
with what you'll actually see in the eastern and western provinces and in rural
areas, where good used cars are often sold for outrageously high prices or
simply passed down through the family. Other price guides may list prices that
are much higher than those found in your region. Consequently, use
whichever price guide lists the highest value when selling your trade-in, or,
negotiating a write-off value with an insurer. When buying, use the guide with
the lowest values as your bargaining tool.

Promises and precautions

As a buyer, you should get a printed sales agreement, even if it's just hand-
written, that includes a clause stating there are no outstanding traffic violations
or liens against the vehicle. It doesn't make a great deal of difference whether
the car will be purchased "as is" or as certified under provincial regulation. A
vehicle sold as safety "certified" can still turn into a lemon or be dangerous to
drive. The certification process can be sabotaged if a minimal number of components are checked, the mechanic is incompetent, or the instruments are
poorly calibrated. "Certified" is not the same as having a warranty to protect
you from engine seizure or transmission failure. "Certified" means only that
the vehicle has met minimum safety standards on the day tested.

Make sure the vehicle is lien-free and has not been damaged in a flood
or written off after an accident. Flood damage can be hard to see.
However, it impairs ABS, power steering, and airbag functioning (making
deployment 10 times slower).

Canada has become a haven for rebuilt U.S. wrecks. Write-offs are also
shipped from provinces where there are stringent disclosure regulations to
provinces where there are lax rules—if rules exist at all.

If you suspect your vehicle is a rebuilt wreck from the States or was once a
taxi, use Carfax (*www.carfax.com*; Tel.:1-888-422-7329) to carry out a background check to see if the vehicle has been part of a fleet, wrecked, has flood
damage, is stolen, or shows incorrect mileage on the odometer. The $20 (U.S.)
fee by telephone is cut to $14.95 (U.S.) if the order is placed via the Internet.
A typical search takes only a few minutes and most Canadian provinces are
included in the database. The search will also turn up vehicles that were
trucked across the border as "parts" and then sold to resellers. An initial, free
search on the Internet will confirm whether or not your vehicle is listed in the
database.

In most provinces, you can do a lien and registration search yourself. If a
lien does exist, you should contact the creditor(s) listed to find out whether
any debts have been paid. If a debt is outstanding, you should arrange with the
vendor to pay the creditor the outstanding balance. If the debt is larger than

the purchase price of the car, it's up to you to decide whether or not you wish to complete the deal. If the seller agrees to clear the title personally, make sure that you receive a written relinquishment of title from the creditor before paying any money to the vendor. Make sure the title doesn't show an "R" for "restored," since this indicates the vehicle was written off as a total loss and may not have been properly repaired.

Even if all documents are in order, ask the seller to show you the vehicle's original sales contract and a few repair bills in order to ascertain how well it was maintained. The bills will show you if the odometer was turned back, and will also indicate which repairs are still guaranteed. If none of these can be found, run (don't walk!) away. If the contract shows that the car was financed, verify that the loan was paid. If you're still not sure that the vehicle is free of liens, ask your bank or credit union manager to check for you. If no clear answer is forthcoming, look for something else.

Repossessed vehicles

Repossessed vehicles are usually bad buys. They are often found at auctions, but they're sometimes sold by finance companies and banks as well. Fortunately, courts have held that these institutions are legally responsible for defects found in what they sell. Also, their deep pockets and abhorrence of bad publicity means you'll likely get your money back if you make a bad buy from a lending institution. The biggest problem with repossessions is that they were likely abused or neglected by their financially troubled owners, and these problems may not come to light until you've had the vehicle too long to make a successful claim. Although you rarely get to test-drive or closely examine these vehicles, a local dealer may be able to produce a vehicle maintenance history by running the Vehicle Identification Number (VIN) through its manufacturer's database.

Rental and leased vehicles

The second-best choice for getting a good used vehicle is a rental company or leasing agency. Due to a slumping economy, Budget, Hertz, Avis, and National are selling, at cut-rate prices, vehicles that have one to two years of service and approximately 80,000–100,000 km. These rental companies will gladly provide a vehicle's complete history and allow an independent inspection by a qualified mechanic of the buyer's choice, as well as arrange competitive financing.

Rental vehicles are generally well maintained, sell for a few thousand dollars more than privately sold vehicles, and come with strong guarantees, like Budget's 30-day money-back guarantee. Rental car companies also usually settle customer complaints without much hassle so as not to tarnish their image with rental customers.

Vehicles that have just come off a 3- or 5-year lease are much more competitively priced, generally have less mileage, and are usually as well maintained as rental vehicles. You're also likely to get a better price if you buy directly from the lessee rather than going through the dealership or an independent agency, but remember that you won't have the dealer's leverage to extract post-warranty "goodwill" repairs from the automaker.

New-car dealers

I bought my used 1995 fully-loaded GMC Vandura full-sized van from a new car dealer. It was a trade-in that had always been serviced by the selling dealer—who showed me the vehicle's complete repair history. Selling for $30,000 originally, it was $10,000 when I bought it four years later. The dealer probably made a couple thousand on the deal.

I know that most used-car buyers prefer to deal with private sellers. In fact, the Federation of Automobile Dealer Associations of Canada states that 20 years ago, 86 percent of used cars were sold by new-car dealers—today that number is less than 25 percent, due mainly to the GST, which has driven buyers into the arms of private sellers.

Nevertheless, I feel that new-car dealers aren't a bad place to pick up a good used car or minivan. Yes, prices can be 20 percent higher than those for vehicles sold privately, but zero percent financing plans are trimming used values dramatically. Plus, dealers are insured against selling stolen vehicles or vehicles with finance owing or other liens. They also usually allow prospective buyers to have the vehicle inspected by an independent garage, offer a much wider choice of models, and have their own repair facilities to do warranty work. Additionally, if there's a possibility of getting post-warranty "goodwill" compensation from the manufacturer, your dealer can provide additional leverage, particularly if he's a franchisee for the model you have purchased. Finally, if things do go terribly wrong, dealers have deeper pockets than do private sellers, so there's a better chance of getting paid should a court judgment be won against the firm.

"Certified" vehicles

Almost all automakers are providing "certified" used vehicles that have been refurbished by the dealer according to the manufacturer's guidelines. Sometimes, an auto association will certify a vehicle that has been inspected and had the designated defects corrected. In Alberta, the Alberta Motor Association (AMA) will perform a vehicle inspection at a dealer's request. On each occasion, the AMA gives a written report to the dealer that identifies potential and actual problems, required repairs, and serious defects.

Automaker-certified vehicles are guaranteed for mechanical fitness and carry a warranty according to the age of the vehicle. But these vehicles don't come cheap, mainly because manufacturers force their dealers to bring them up to better-than-average condition before certifying them. The higher price can be reduced by choosing an older certified model, or amortized by keeping the vehicle longer.

Used-car leasing

Not a good idea for new or used vehicles. Leasing has been touted as a method of making the high cost of vehicle ownership more affordable. Don't you believe it: Leasing is generally costlier than an outright purchase, and for most people the pitfalls far outweigh any advantages. If you must lease, do so for the shortest time possible and make sure the lease is close-ended (meaning that you walk away from the vehicle when the lease period ends). Also, make sure there's a maximum mileage allowance of at least 25,000 km a year and that the charge per excess kilometre is no higher than 8–10 cents.

Used-car dealers

Used-car dealers usually sell their vehicles for a bit less than what new-car dealers charge. However, their vehicles may be worth a lot less, because they don't get the first pick of top-quality trade-ins. Many independent urban dealerships are marginal operations that can't invest much money in reconditioning their vehicles, which are often collected from auctions and new-car dealers reluctant to sell the vehicles to their own customers. And used-car dealers don't always have repair facilities to honour what warranties they do provide. Often, their credit terms are easier (but more expensive) than those offered by franchised new-car dealers.

That said, used-car dealers operating in small towns are an entirely different breed. These small, often family-run businesses recondition and resell cars and trucks that usually come from within their community. Routine servicing is often done in-house, and more complicated repairs are subcontracted out to specialized garages nearby. These small outlets survive by word-of-mouth advertising and would never last long if they didn't deal fairly with local townsfolk. On the other hand, their prices will likely be higher than elsewhere, due to the better quality of used vehicles they offer and the cost of reconditioning and repairing what they sell under warranty.

Auctions

First of all, make sure it's a legitimate auction. Many are fronts for used-car lots where sleazy dealers put fake ads in complicit newspapers pretending to hold auctions that are no more than weekend selling sprees.

Furthermore, you'll need lots of patience, smarts, and luck to pick up anything worthwhile. Government auctions—places where the mythical $50 Jeep is sold—are fun to attend but highly overrated as places to find bargains. Look at the odds against you: It's impossible to determine the condition of the vehicles put up for bid; prices can be bid way out of control; and government employees, their relatives, and their friends usually pick over the good stuff long before you ever see it.

To attend commercial auctions is to swim with the piranhas. They are frequented by "ringers" who bid up the prices and by professional dealers who pick up cheap, worn-out vehicles unloaded by new-car dealers and independents. There are no guarantees, cash is required, and quality is apt to be as low as the price. Remember, too, that auction purchases are subject to provincial and federal sales taxes, the auction's sales commission (3–5 percent), and in some cases an administrative fee of $25–$50.

If you are interested in shopping at an auto auction, remember that certain days are reserved for dealers only, so call ahead. You'll find the vehicles locked in a compound, but you should have ample opportunity to inspect them and, in some cases, take a short drive around the property before the auction begins.

Paying the Right Price

Even though prices have become considerably more moderate, get ready for sticker shock when pricing minivans, SUVs, and pickups. These vehicles depreciate very little, and it's easy to get stuck with a cheap one that's been abused through hard off-roading or lack of care. Furthermore, even those vehicles with worse-than-average reliability ratings, like the Ford Focus and Chrysler minivans, still command higher-than-average resale prices for the simple reason that they're popular, though not as popular as they once were.

If you don't want to pay too much when buying used, you've got the following four alternatives.

- Buy an older vehicle. Choose one that's five years old or more and has a good reliability and durability record. Buy extra protection with an extended warranty. The money you save from the extra years' depreciation and lower insurance premiums will more than make up for the extra warranty cost.
- Look for off-lease vehicles sold privately by owners who want more than what their dealer is offering. If you can't find what you're looking for in the local classified ads, put in your own ad asking for lessees to contact you if they're not satisfied with their dealer's offer.
- Buy a vehicle that's depreciated more than average simply because of its bland styling, lack of high-performance features, or discontinuation. For example, many of the Japanese entry-level compacts like the Nissan Sentra cost less to own than their flashier American-made counterparts, yet are more reliable and equally functional for most driving chores.
- Buy a cheaper twin or re-badged model like a Mercury Villager, Plymouth Voyager, or Pontiac Vibe. They offer Japanese high quality and usually share the same basic design, appearance, dimensions, and mechanical components.

Prices and price scams

There are several price books, like the *Red Book* and *Black Book*, which are available for perusal at your local library, credit union, or bank. *Lemon-Aid's* prices are a synthesis of both guides, with auction figures thrown in. Remember, both buyers and sellers use the guide that will make them the most profit on each transaction. The most common price guide quoted is the *Red*

Book, which shows a used vehicle's retail and wholesale worth across the country, while the *Black Book* is more regionally oriented. Sellers quote the retail price, while buyers try to get as close to wholesale as they can.

In spite of what you'll be told, wholesale and retail prices leave considerable room for the dealer's profit margin and some extra padding—such as inflated preparation charges and administration fees that should be turned down flat.

> Your *Lemon-Aid* guide has levelled the playing field for the consumer when it comes to shopping for new or used vehicles. *Lemon-Aid* has also helped us consumers get the inside edge on how to protect ourselves from car manufactures, secret warranties, goodwill service, etc.
>
> I recently used your publication to help me in my decision to purchase a 1999 Toyota Tercel. Your *Lemon-Aid* guide also helped me avoid paying an "administration fee." I just walked out of the dealer's showroom. They must have thought I was crazy.
>
> I didn't even have time to take my shoes off when my wife called me and said the Toyota dealership was on the telephone. She had no idea what had happened.
>
> Suffice it to say, this wise consumer didn't pay an "administration fee" so someone could have dinner on me. If there is value in something I will pay it. If not, this customer walks. Here's to many years of carefree driving with my Toyota.
>
> Just an off note: After 17 years of working for General Motors I thought I knew it all about vehicles, making deals, problems, defects, warranties, etc.
>
> Was I wrong. You can never know it all. Keep publishing *Lemon-Aid* and I will keep reading it.
>
> I'm a long-time GM employee who bought his first foreign-made vehicle with the help of Phil Edmonston. Patriotism is one thing, but blowing your hard-earned money for junk is another, just so you can wave the flag.
>
> Sincerely,
> L.C.

Financing Choices

No one should spend more than 30 percent of his or her annual gross income on the purchase of a new or used vehicle. By keeping the initial cost low, the purchaser may be able to pay mostly in cash. This can be an effective bargaining tool to use with private sellers, but dealers are less impressed by cash sales because they lose their kickback from the finance and insurance companies.

Credit unions

Credit unions offer some of the cheapest loan rates around and are generally the preferred place to borrow money, due to their easy repayment terms. Of course, you'll have to join the credit union before the loan is approved and have to come up with a larger down payment than what other lending institutions require.

In addition to giving you reasonable loan rates, credit unions help car buyers in a number of other ways. Toronto's Metro Credit Union (*www.metrocu.com*), for example, has a CarFacts Centre, which provides free, objective advice on car shopping, purchasing, financing, and leasing. CarFacts advisors provide free consultations in person or by phone. This includes:

- fact sheets on all aspects of buying new or used vehicles
- a circulating library of vehicle buying and vehicle maintenance books and magazines
- computerized analysis of different buying, leasing, and borrowing options
- *Red Book* used-car price quotations
- dealer invoice price quotations on any make or model of new vehicle, at $20 each

Banks

Banks are a bit leery of financing used cars, because they fear you'll stop your payments if the vehicle turns out to be a dud. Nevertheless, with interest rates as high as 10 percent, they're not likely to turn you away.

In your quest for a bank loan, keep in mind that the loan officer will be impressed by a prepared budget and sound references. It also wouldn't hurt to have a vehicle already picked out at the local dealer, since banks like to encourage businesses in their area.

The Internet also offers help for people who need an auto loan and want quick approval, but don't like to face a banker. Used-car buyers can post a loan application on a bank's website, even if they don't have an account.

Dealers

Dealer financing isn't the rip-off it once was, but still be watchful for all the expensive little "extras" the dealer may try to pencil into the contract, because, believe it or not, dealers make far more profit on used-car sales than with new-car deals. Don't write them off for financing, though; they can finance your purchase at rates that compete with those of banks and finance companies. This is because they agree to take back the vehicle if the creditor defaults on the loan (one reason why Mitsubishi is behind the eight ball for 2004). Some dealers mislead their customers into thinking they can get financing at rates far below the prime rate. Actually, the dealer jacks up the base price of the vehicle to compensate for the lower interest charges.

Dealer Scams

Most dealer sales scams are so obvious, they're laughable. But like the Nigerian email "lost fortune" scam, there are enough stupid people to make these dealer deceptions profitable.

One of the more common tricks is to not identify the previous owner because the vehicle either was used commercially, was problem-prone, or had been written off as a total loss from an accident. It's also not uncommon to discover that the mileage has been turned back, particularly if the vehicle was part of a company's fleet. Your best defence? Demand the name of the vehicle's previous owner and run a VIN check through Carfax as a prerequisite to purchasing the vehicle.

It would be impossible to list all the dishonest tricks employed in used-vehicle sales. As soon as the public is alerted to one scheme, crooked sellers use other, more elaborate frauds. Nevertheless, under industry-financed provincial compensation funds, buyers can get substantial refunds if defrauded by a dealer.

Here are some of the more common fraudulent practices you're likely to encounter.

Failing to declare full purchase price

Here's where your own greed will do you in. A tactic used almost exclusively by small, independent dealers and some private sellers, the buyer is told that he or she can pay less sales tax by listing a lower selling price on the contract. But what if the vehicle turns out to be a lemon or the sales agent has falsified the model year or mileage? The hapless buyer is offered a refund on the fictitious purchase price indicated on the contract. If the buyer wanted to take the dealer to court, it's quite unlikely that he or she would get any more than the contract price. Moreover, both the buyer and dealer could be prosecuted for making a false declaration to avoid paying sales tax.

Phony private sales ("curbsiders")

Individuals sell about three times as many used vehicles as dealers, and crooked dealers get in on the action by posing as private sellers. They lure unsuspecting buyers through lower prices, cheat the federal government out of the GST, and routinely violate provincial registration and consumer protection regulations.

This scam is easy to detect if the seller can't produce the original sales contract or show some repair bills made out in his or her own name. You can usually identify a car dealer in the want ads section of the newspaper—just check to see if the same telephone number is repeated in many different ads. Sometimes you can trip up a curbsider by requesting information on the phone, without identifying the specific vehicle. If the seller asks you which car you are considering, you know you're dealing with a dealer.

Legitimate car dealers deplore the dishonesty of curbsider crooks, yet they are their chief suppliers. Dealership sales managers, auto auction employees, and newspaper classified ad sellers all know the names, addresses, and phone numbers of these thieves, but they don't act. Newspapers want the ad dollars, auctions want the action, and dealers want someplace they can unload their wrecked, rust-cankered, and odometer-tricked junkers with impunity. Talk about hypocrisy, eh?

Curbsiders are particularly active in Western Canada, importing vehicles from other provinces where they were sold by dealers, wreckers, insurance companies, and junkyards (after having been written off as total losses). They then place private classified ads in B.C. and Alberta papers, sell their stock, and import more. Writes one Vancouver *Lemon-Aid* reader:

> A 2-minute clip on TV is okay, but the story is not the curbers, or the Eastern wholesalers dumping "speedo'd" product on the West Coast....
>
> The story is the lack of sensitivity by the newspapers who turn a blind eye and let consumers get ripped off. The government agencies like ICBC who charge $20 to do a seach, which is useless if the car comes from out of province. The newspapers are making money, ICBC is making money, the cops acknowledge wide-scale dumping on the West Coast.... We need you to put the pressure squarely on newspapers to make sure every classified page in this country has information on how to trace a VIN number, how to check speedometers, and insurance declarations. Governments have no willpower to take on organized fraud....

If you get taken by one of these scam artists, don't hesitate to sue the publication carrying the ad through small claims court for allowing this rip-off artist to operate.

"Free-exchange" privilege

Dealers get a lot of sales mileage out of this deceptive offer. The dealer offers to exchange any defective vehicle for any other vehicle in stock. What really happens, though, is that the dealer won't have *anything else* selling for the same price and so will demand a cash bonus for the exchange...or you may get that dubious privilege of exchanging one lemon for another.

"Money-back" guarantee

Once again, the purchaser feels safe in buying a used car with this kind of guarantee, because what could be more honest than a money-back guarantee? Dealers using this technique often charge exorbitant handling charges, rental fees, or mechanical repair costs to the customer who's bought one of these vehicles and then returned it.

"50/50" guarantee

This means that the dealer will pay half the repair costs over a limited period of time. It's a fair offer if an independent garage does the repairs. If not, the dealer can always inflate the repair costs to double their actual worth and write up a bill for that amount (a scam sometimes used in "goodwill" settlements). The buyer winds up paying the full price of repairs that would probably have been much cheaper at an independent garage. The best kind of used-vehicle warranty is 100 percent with full coverage for a fixed term, even if that term is relatively short.

"As is" sales

Buying a vehicle "as is" usually means that you're aware of mechanical defects, you're prepared to accept the responsibility for any damage or injuries caused by the vehicle, and all costs to fix it shall be paid by you. However, the courts have held that the "as is" clause is not a blank cheque to cheat buyers and therefore must be interpreted in light of the seller's true intent. That is, was there an attempt to deceive the buyer by including this clause? Did the buyer really know what the "as is" clause could do to his or her future legal rights? It's also been held that the courts may consider oral representations ("parole evidence") that were never written into the formal contract. So, if a seller makes claims as to the fine quality of the used vehicle, these claims can be used as evidence. Courts generally ignore "as is" clauses when: the vehicle has been intentionally misrepresented; the dealer is the seller; or when the defects are so serious that the seller is presumed to have known of their existence. Private sellers are usually given more credibility than dealers or their agents.

Odometer fraud

The RCMP hate odometer complaints because rollbacks are a common crime that's hard to prove. In theory, sellers face hefty fines and even imprisonment if they're caught altering the mileage of any vehicle they sell, but in practice, few odometer tampering cases make it to court because intent to defraud is so difficult to prove. Usually, independent outfits are hired to pick up the vehicle or visit the dealership and "fix" the odometer, a practice allowed under Canadian federal and provincial laws.

Misrepresentation

Used vehicles can be misrepresented in a variety of ways. A used airport commuter minivan may be represented as having been used by a Sunday school class. A mechanically defective pickup that's been rebuilt after several major accidents may have plastic filler in the body panels to muffle the rattles or hide rust damage, heavy oil in the motor to stifle the clanks, and cheap retread tires to eliminate the thumps. Your best protection against these dirty tricks is to have the vehicle's quality completely verified by an independent mechanic before completing the sale. Of course, you can still cancel the sale if you only learn of the misrepresentation after taking the vehicle home, but your chances dwindle as time passes.

> I'm finding it difficult finding a reasonably priced used car in the Toronto area. Many of the ads for private sales here turn out to be dealers or mechanics selling cars pretending to be private persons. Also, the prices are ridiculously inflated. Your books are a great read and have made me at least slow down and ask questions. For

example, I almost got caught in a lease the other day and pulled out at the last minute. All this advertising had me believe there would be zero down, zero delivery, etc. until I found out there would be a $350 lease acquisition fee and a $250 admin. fee and all kinds of other charges, some legitimate such as licensing. However, my zero down turned into a whopping $1,200! I'm just now getting into your leasing section....

Private Scams

A lot of space in this guide has been used to describe how used-car dealers and scam artists cheat uninformed buyers. Of course, private individuals can be dishonest too. In either case, protect yourself at the outset by keeping your deposit small and getting as much information as possible about the vehicle you're considering. Then, after a test drive, you may sign a written agreement to purchase the vehicle and give a deposit of sufficient value to cover the seller's advertising costs, subject to cancellation if the automobile fails its inspection. After you've taken these precautions, watch out for the following private sellers' tricks.

Used vehicles that are stolen or have finance owing

Many used vehicles are sold privately without free title because the original auto loan was never repaid. You can avoid being cheated by asking for proof of purchase and payment from a private seller. Be especially wary of any individual who offers to sell a used vehicle for an incredibly low price. Check the sales contract to determine who granted the original loan and call the lender to see if it's been repaid. Place a call to the provincial Ministry of Transportation to ascertain whether the car is registered in the seller's name. Find out if a finance company is named as beneficiary on the auto insurance policy. Finally, call up the original dealer to determine whether there are any outstanding claims.

In Ontario, a Used Vehicle Information Package must be purchased by all private sellers at one of 300 provincial Driver and Vehicle License Issuing Offices or online at *www.mto.gov.on.ca/english/pubs/usedcar/usedcar.htm*. This package, which costs $20, contains the vehicle's registration history in Ontario; vehicle lien information (i.e. if there are any liens registered on the vehicle); the fair market value on which the minimum tax payable will apply; and other information such as consumer tips, vehicle safety standards inspection, retail sales tax information, and forms for bills of sale.

In other provinces, buyers don't have easy access to this information. Generally, you have to contact the provincial office that registers property and pay a small fee for a computer printout that may or may not be accurate. You'll be asked for the current owner's name and the car's VIN, which is usually found on the driver's side of the dashboard.

There are two high-tech ways to get the goods on a dishonest seller. First, have a dealer of that particular model run a "vehicle history" check through the automaker's online network. This will tell you who the previous owners and dealers were, what warranty and recall repairs were carried out, and what other free repair programs may still apply. Second, you could use Carfax (*www.carfax.com*; Tel.: 1-888-422-7329) to carry out a background check.

Wrong registration

Make sure the seller's vehicle has been properly registered with provincial transport authorities; if it isn't, it may be stolen or you could be dealing with a curbsider.

If you are selling a vehicle, protect yourself from legal liability by ensuring the registration has been transferred to the buyer. Normally, once you take the tags and give the buyer a bill of sale, you're no longer the registered owner. Nonetheless, go down to the registry office yourself to make sure the title has changed. As long as you're still listed as the owner of record, you could be sued for damages arising from an accident.

Summary to Saving Money and Keeping Safe

You *can* get a good used vehicle at a reasonable price—it just takes lots of patience and homework. You can further protect yourself by becoming thoroughly familiar with your legal rights as outlined in Part Two and buying a vehicle recommended in Part Three. Following is a summary of the steps to take to keep your risk to a minimum:

1. Buy a full-sized, rear-drive delivery van and convert it yourself, instead of opting for a more expensive, smaller, less powerful minivan.
2. Trade in your vehicle if this reduces another purchase's GST and PST by *more* than the potential profit of selling privately.
3. Sell privately for at least 15 percent more than what the dealer offered.
4. Buy from a private party, rental car outlet, or dealer (in that order).
5. Use an auto broker to save time and money.
6. Buy a *Lemon-Aid*-recommended vehicle for depreciation, parts, and service savings.
7. Buy a 3- or 4-year-old vehicle with lots of original warranty that can be transferred (35–50 percent savings over a new vehicle).
8. Choose a vehicle that's crashworthy and cheap to insure.
9. Carefully inspect front-drive vehicles that have reached their fifth year. Pay particular attention to the engine intake manifold and head gasket, CV joints, steering box, and front brakes.
10. Don't buy an extended warranty for a particular model year unless it's recommended you do so in *Lemon-Aid*.
11. Have repairs done by independent garages offering lifetime warranties.
12. Install used or reconditioned parts.
13. Keep all the previous owners' repair bills to facilitate warranty claims and to help mechanics know what's already been replaced or repaired.
14. Upon delivery, adjust mirrors to eliminate blind spots and adjust head

restraints to prevent your head from snapping back in the event of a collision. On airbag-equipped vehicles, move the seat backward more than half its travel distance and sit at least a foot away from the airbag housing. Ensure that the airbag, spare tire, and tire jack haven't been removed.

15. Make sure the dealer and automaker have your name in their computers as the new owner of record. Ask for a copy of your vehicle's history, stored in the same computers.

PART TWO

LAWYERS AND LIARS!

2

Ford's Engine Woes

A Technical Service Bulletin dated June 28, 1999, was circulated to Ford dealers. It dealt specifically with "undetermined loss of coolant" and "engine oil contaminated with coolant" in the 1996–98 Windstar and five other models of Ford vehicles. I conclude that Ford owed a duty of care to the Plaintiff to equip this vehicle [1996 Windstar] with a cylinder head gasket of sufficient sturdiness and durability that would function trouble-free for at least seven years, given normal driving and proper maintenance conditions. I find that Ford is answerable in damages for the consequences of its negligence.

Justice Tiernay, Superior Court of Justice, Ottawa Small Claims Court

John R. Reid and Laurie M. McCall v. Ford Motor Company of Canada

July 11, 2003

Detroit's "lemon" grove

Runzheimer Consultants says that 1 out of every 10 American vehicles produced by the Detroit Big Three is a "lemon." I would guess that owners of Ford Windstars, Chrysler Caravans, and GM Saturns with faulty automatic transmissions and engine head gaskets would put the number at a higher figure.

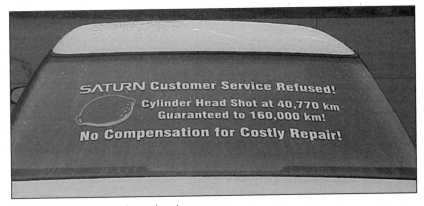

Saturn's ad campaigns are better than the car.

If you've bought an unsafe tire or a lemon, or if you've been forced to pay for repairs to correct factory-induced defects, this section's for you. It's intended to help you get your money back—without going to court or getting frazzled by the dealer's broken promises or "benign neglect." But if going to court is your only recourse, you'll find the jurisprudence you need to get an out-of-court settlement or to win your case without spending a fortune on lawyers and research.

Four Ways to Get Your Money Back

Remember the "money-back" guarantee? Well, automakers are reluctant to offer any warranty that requires them to take back a defective truck or van. Fortunately, our provincial consumer protection laws have filled the gap so that now, any sales contract for a new or used vehicle can be cancelled—or free repairs can be ordered—if the vehicle:

• is unfit for the purpose for which it was purchased
• is misrepresented
• is covered by a secret warranty, or a "goodwill" warranty extension
• hasn't been reasonably durable, considering how well it was maintained, the mileage driven, and the type of driving done (particularly applicable to engine, transmission, and paint defects)

Winning a claim on any one of the legal concepts enumerated above can lead to the contract's being cancelled, the purchase price refunded, and other costs ("damages") awarded.

For example, if the seller says a minivan can pull a 900 kg (2,000 lb.) trailer and you discover that it can barely tow half that weight, or won't reach a reasonable speed, you can cancel the contract for misrepresentation. The same principle applies to a seller's exaggerated claims concerning a vehicle's fuel economy or reliability, as well as to "demonstrators" that are in fact used cars with false (rolled-back) odometer readings.

All automakers use a system of secret warranties to pay for factory-related defects, but the refunds aren't always given out fairly and manufacturers deny such programs exist. Yet, big money is at play: $3,000–$5,000 bills for power-train repairs (engine and transmission) and new paint jobs (paint peeling or discolouring) are not uncommon.

Fortunately, small claims court judges take a dim view of these secret programs and have forced car manufacturers and their dealers to reimburse customers for repairs under the legal doctrine of *implied* warranty long after the manufacturer's *expressed* warranty has expired. Any vehicle component that fails prematurely is in violation of the implied warranty's reasonable durability.

Detroit's Big Three, as well as Japanese automakers like Honda, are often successfully challenged in small claims court—as the jurisprudence in this section attests.

Unfair contracts

Sales contracts aren't fair, nor are they meant to be. Lawyers spend countless hours making sure their clients are well protected with iron-clad standard-form contracts. Called "contracts of adhesion," judges look upon these agreements with a great deal of skepticism. They know these loan documents, insurance contracts, and automobile leases grant the buyer/leaser little or no bargaining power. So when a dispute arises over terms or language, provincial consumer protection statutes require that judges interpret these contracts in the way most favourable to the consumer. Simply put, ignorance can be a good defence.

"Hearsay" can't be heard

It's essential that printed evidence and/or witnesses (relatives are not excluded) are available to confirm that a false representation actually occurred, that a part is failure-prone, or that its replacement is covered by a secret warranty. Stung by an increasing number of small claims court defeats, automakers are now asking small claims court judges to disallow evidence from *Lemon-Aid*, service bulletins, or memos on the pretext that it's hearsay (not proven), unless confirmed by an independent mechanic or unless the document is recognized by the automaker or dealer's representative at trial. This is why you should bring in an independent garage mechanic or body expert to buttress your allegations. Sometimes, though, the service manager or company representative will make key admissions if questioned closely by you, a court mediator, or the trial judge. Some questions to ask: Is this a common problem? Do you recognize this service bulletin? Is there a case-by-case "goodwill" plan covering this repair? That questioning can be particularly effective if you call for the exclusion of witnesses until they're called (let them mill around outside the courtroom wondering what their colleagues have said).

Automakers often blame owners for having pushed their vehicle beyond its limits. Therefore, when you seek to set aside the contract or get a repair reimbursed, it's essential that you get the testimony of an independent mechanic and co-workers in order to prove that the vehicle's poor performance isn't caused by negligent maintenance or abusive driving.

The reasonable durability claim is your ace in the hole. It's probably the easiest allegation to prove, since all automakers have benchmarks as to how long body components, trim and finish, and mechanical and electronic parts should last (see the durability chart on pages 59–60). Vehicles are expected to be reasonably durable and merchantable. What is reasonably durable depends on the price paid, kilometres driven, the purchaser's driving habits, and how well the vehicle was maintained by the owner. Judges carefully weigh all these factors in awarding compensation or cancelling a sale.

Whatever the reason you use to get your money back, don't forget to conform to the "reasonable diligence" rule that requires you to file suit within a reasonable time after purchase or after you've discovered the defect. If there have been no negotiations with the dealer or automaker, this period cannot exceed a few months. If either the dealer or the automaker has been promising to correct the defects for some time or has carried out repeated unsuccessful repairs, the delay for filing the lawsuit can be extended.

General refunds

Unless you can quote a court decision for support and have your receipts handy, it's hard to get refunds for hotel and travel costs, or compensation for general inconvenience. Nevertheless, the following British Columbia court decision could be helpful in backing up your demand for general compensation and inconvenience. It gives $2,257 to a motorist fed up with his lemon Cadillac:

Wharton v. Tom Harris Chevrolet Oldsmobile Cadillac Ltd. and General Motors of Canada Limited, B.C. Supreme Court, Date: 19991202, Docket: C982104, Registry: Vancouver.

In his decision, Judge Leggatt threw the book at GM and the dealer:

(a) Hotel accommodations: $217.17
(b) Travel to effect repairs at 30 cents/km: The plaintiff claims some 26 visits from his home in Ucluelet to Nanaimo. Some credit should be granted to the defendants since routine trips would have been required in any event. Therefore, the plaintiff is entitled to be compensated for mileage for 17 trips (approximately 400 km from Ucluelet to Nanaimo return) at 30 cents/km.

                                                           $2,040.00

TOTAL: $2,257.17

[20] The plaintiff is entitled to non-pecuniary damages for loss of enjoyment of their luxury vehicle and for inconvenience in the sum of $5,000.

Automakers and dealers hate to pay these kinds of consequential expenses because they can't control the amount of the refund. Courts are more generous, having ruled that all expenses, inconvenience, and even mental distress flowing from a problem covered by a warranty or service bulletin are the manufacturer's/dealer's responsibility under both common law (all provinces except Quebec) and Quebec civil law (see pages 432–436, where a 2000 Windstar owner got $7,500—for mental distress). Fortunately, when legal action is threatened—usually through small claims court—automakers quickly back down from their refusal to pay consequential damage claims.

Warranties

The manufacturer's or dealer's warranty is a written legal promise that a vehicle will be reasonably reliable, subject to certain conditions. Regardless of the number of subsequent owners, this promise remains in force as long as the warranty's original time/kilometre limits haven't expired. Unfortunately, these warranties are full of so many loopholes ("You abused the car; it was poorly maintained; it's normal wear and tear") that they may be useless when a vehicle breaks down.

Thankfully, car owners get another kick at the can. As clearly stated in *Frank v. GM*, every vehicle sold new or used in Canada is also covered by an *implied* warranty—a collection of federal and provincial laws and regulations that protect you from hidden defects, misrepresentation, and a host of other scams. Furthermore, Canadian law presumes that car dealers, unlike private sellers, are aware of the defects present in the vehicles they sell. That way, they can't just pass the ball to the automakers and walk away from the dispute.

Treacherous tires

Tires aren't usually covered by car manufacturers' warranties (except for GM and Ford), and are warranted instead by the tiremaker on a pro-rated basis. This isn't such a good deal, because the manufacturer is making a profit by charging you the full list price. If you were to buy the same replacement tire from a discount store, you'd likely pay less, without the pro-rated rebate.

But consumers have gained additional rights following Bridgestone/Firestone's massive recall in 2001 of its defective ATX II and Wilderness tires. Due to the confusion and chaos surrounding Firestone's handling of the recall, Ford's 575 Canadian dealers stepped into the breach and replaced the tires for any equivalent tires dealers had in stock. No questions asked.

This is an important precedent that tears down the traditional wall separating tire manufacturers from automakers in product liability claims. In essence, whoever sells the product can now be held liable for damages. In the future, Canadian consumers will have an easier time holding the dealer, automaker, and tire manufacturer liable, not just for recalled products, but for any defect that affects the safety or reasonable durability of that product.

This is particularly true now that the Supreme Court of Canada (*Winnipeg Condominium v. Bird Construction* [1995] 1S.C.R.85) has ruled that defendants are liable in negligence for any designs that resulted in a risk to the public for safety or health. The Supreme Court reversed a long-standing policy and provided the public with a new cause of action that had not existed before in Canada.

Other warranties

Safety restraints such as airbags and safety belts have warranty coverage extended for the lifetime of the vehicle, following an informal agreement made between automakers and the National Highway Traffic Safety Administration (NHTSA). In Canada, though, many automakers try to dodge this responsibility, alleging that they are separate entities, their vehicles are different, and no U.S. agreement or service bulletin binds them. That distinction is both disingenuous and dishonest, and wouldn't likely hold up in small claims court—probably the reason why most automakers relent when threatened with legal action.

Aftermarket products and services—such as gas-saving gadgets, rustproofing, and paint protectors—can render the manufacturer's warranty invalid, so make sure you're in the clear before purchasing any optional equipment or services from an independent supplier.

How fairly a warranty is applied is more important than how long it remains in effect. Once you know the normal wear rate for a mechanical component or body part, you can demand proportional compensation when you get less than normal durability—no matter what the original warranty said.

Some dealers tell customers that they need to have original equipment parts installed in order to maintain their warranty. A variation on this theme requires that routine servicing—including tune-ups and oil changes (with a certain brand of oil)—be done by the selling dealer, or the warranty is invalidated.

Nothing could be further from the truth.

Canadian law stipulates that whoever issues a warranty cannot make that warranty conditional on the use of any specific brand of motor oil, oil filter, or any other component, unless it's provided to the customer free of charge.

Sometimes dealers will do all sorts of minor repairs that don't correct the problem, and then after the warranty runs out they'll tell you that major repairs are needed. You can avoid this nasty surprise by repeatedly bringing in your vehicle to the dealership before the warranty ends. During each visit, insist that a written work order include the specific nature of the problem as *you* see it and that the work order carry the notation that this is the second, third, or fourth time the same problem has been brought to the dealer's attention. Write it down yourself, if need be. This allows you to show a pattern of non-performance by the dealer during the warranty period and establishes that it's a serious and chronic problem. When the warranty expires, you have the legal right to demand that it be extended on those items consistently reappearing on your handful of work orders. *Lowe v. Fairview Chrysler* (see pages 86–87) is an excellent judgment that reinforces this important principle. In another lawsuit, *François Chong v. Marine Drive Imported Cars Ltd. and Honda Canada Inc.* (see page 86), a Honda owner forced Honda to fix his engine seven times—until they got it right.

A retired GM service manager gave me another effective tactic to use when you're not sure a dealer's warranty "repairs" will actually correct the problem for a reasonable period of time after the warranty expires. Here's what he says you should do:

> When you pick up the vehicle after the warranty repair has been done, hand the service manager a note to be put in your file that says you appreciate the warranty repair, however, you intend to return and ask for further warranty coverage if the problem reappears before a reasonable amount of time has elapsed—even if the original warranty has expired. A copy of the same note should be sent to the automaker.... Keep your copy of the note in the glove compartment as cheap insurance against paying for a repair that wasn't fixed correctly the first time.

Extended (supplementary) warranties

Supplementary warranties providing extended coverage may be sold by the manufacturer, dealer, or an independent third party, and are automatically transferred when the vehicle is sold. They cost between $1,000 and $1,500, and should be purchased only if the vehicle you're buying is off its original warranty, if it has a reputation for being unreliable or expensive to service (see Part Three), or if you're reluctant to use the small claims courts when factory-related trouble arises.

Don't let the dealer pressure you into deciding right away. Generally, you can purchase an extended warranty anytime during the period in which the manufacturer's warranty is in effect, or, in some cases, shortly after buying the vehicle from a used-car dealer. An automaker's supplementary warranty is the best choice, but will likely cost about a third more than warranties sold by independents. And in some parts of the country, notably British Columbia, dealers have a quasi-monopoly on selling warranties, with little competition from the independents.

Because up to 60 percent of the warranty's cost represents dealer markup, dealers love to sell extended warranties, whether you need them or not. Out of the remaining 40 percent comes the sponsor's administration costs and profit margin, calculated at another 15 percent. What's left to pay for repairs is a minuscule 25 percent of the original amount. The only reason why automakers and independent warranty companies haven't been busted for operating this warranty Ponzi scheme is because only half of the car buyers who purchase extended service contracts actually use them.

It's often difficult to collect on supplementary warranties because independent companies frequently go out of business or limit the warranty's coverage through subsequent mailings. Both situations are covered by provincial laws. If the bankrupt warranty company's insurance policy won't cover your claim, take the dealer to small claims court and ask for the repair cost and the refund of the original warranty payment. Your argument for holding the dealer responsible is a simple one: By accepting a commission for acting as an agent of the defunct company, the dealer took on the obligations of the company as well. As for limiting the coverage after you have bought the warranty policy, this is illegal—and it allows you to sue both the dealer and the warranty company for a refund of both the warranty and repair costs.

Emissions control warranties

These little-publicized warranties can save you big bucks if major engine or exhaust components fail prematurely. They come with all new vehicles and cover major components of the emissions control system for up to 8 years/130,000 km, no matter how many times the vehicle is sold. Unfortunately, although owners' manuals vaguely mention the emissions warranty, most don't specify which parts are covered. Fortunately, the U.S. Environmental Protection Agency has intervened on several occasions with hefty fines against Chrysler and Ford and ruled that all major motor and fuel-system components are covered. These include fuel metering, ignition spark advance, restart, evaporative emissions, positive crankcase ventilation, engine electronics (computer modules), and catalytic converters, as well as hoses, clamps, brackets, pipes, gaskets, belts, seals, and connectors. Canada, however, has no government definition, and it's up to each manufacturer and the small claims courts to decide which components are covered.

Many of the confidential technical service bulletins (TSBs) listed in Part Three show parts failures that are covered under the emissions warranty, even though motorists are routinely charged for their replacement. The following example, applicable to Ford's 1996–98 cars, minivans, vans, and trucks, shows the automaker will pay for major repairs to correct the loss of engine coolant or engine oil contaminated with coolant. Unfortunately, few owners will ever see these bulletins, and will end up paying for repairs that are really Ford's responsibility.

Coolant Loss/Engine Oil Contamination, 3.8L, 4.2L

Article No. 99 - 20 - 7
10/04/99
˄ COOLING SYSTEM - 3.8L - UNDETERMINED LOSS OF COOLANT
˄ COOLING SYSTEM - 4.2L - UNDETERMINED LOSS OF COOLANT
˄ ENGINE - 3.8L - ENGINE OIL CONTAMINATED WITH COOLANT
˄ ENGINE - 4.2L - ENGINE OIL CONTAMINATED WITH COOLANT

FORD:
1996–97   THUNDERBIRD
1996–98   MUSTANG, WINDSTAR
1997–98   E-150, E-250, F-150

MERCURY:
1996–97   COUGAR

This TSB article is being republished in its entirety to correct the front cover/water pump bolt torque values and the front cover gasket part number.

ISSUE:
Engine coolant may be leaking into the engine oil on some vehicles. The internal coolant leak may be difficult to identify. This may be caused by the lower intake manifold side gaskets and/or front cover gaskets allowing coolant to pass into the cylinders and/or the crankcase.

ACTION:
Revised lower intake manifold side and front cover gaskets have been released for service.

WARRANTY STATUS:
Eligible under the provisions of bumper-to-bumper warranty coverage and emissions warranty coverage.

Make sure you get your emissions system checked out thoroughly by a dealer or independent garage before the emissions warranty expires and before having the vehicle inspected by provincial emissions inspectors. In addition to ensuring you pass provincial tests, this precaution could save you up to $1,000 if both your catalytic converter and other emissions components are faulty.

Tracking secret warranties

Few vehicle owners know that secret warranties exist. Automakers are reluctant to make these free repair programs public because they feel it would weaken confidence in their product and increase their legal liability. The closest they come to an admission is sending a "goodwill policy," "product improvement program," or "special policy" TSB to dealers or first owners of record.

Consequently, the only motorists who find out about these policies are the original owners who haven't moved or leased their vehicles. The other motorists who get compensated for repairs are the ones who read *Lemon-Aid* each year, wave TSBs, and yell the loudest.

This year's *Lemon-Aid* updates all of these secret warranties and reprints confidential TSBs and automaker memoranda that allow car owners to stand toe-to-toe with automakers and service managers. An up-to-date listing of TSBs for free repairs under secret warranties and other service programs can be found in Part Three under the heading "Secret Warranties/Service Tips/TSBs." Some may be less secret than others, as secret warranties go through the four stages enumerated below.

1st Stage—Reports of problems from regional service managers and possible solutions are posted on the automaker's internal computer network. This info is never shared with the customer and doesn't appear on ALLDATA's TSB database. It can sometimes be found on NHTSA's service bulletins site, or in various car forums.

2nd Stage—If the defect grows in scope and a more involved solution is needed (for example, one requiring upgraded parts), automakers then draw up a formal TSB and distribute it to dealers and U.S. and Canadian government agencies. The TSB is only issued after the manufacturer thinks it has a solution for the defect. And, even then, better remedies are often found much later. TSBs issued by Chrysler, Ford, and GM will usually spell out clearly which base warranty will cover the repair (emissions warranty, bumper-to-bumper, etc.). Interestingly, Asian and European automakers are vague in describing their warranty obligations. Honda, for example, uses the term "goodwill" as a euphemism to describe its warranty extensions and Toyota advises dealers to carry out the free repairs only if the owner complains. Of course, many owners don't know a free repair program exists that covers their problem, so they endure, rather than pay.

Rear Brake Drum – Rusted/Frozen

NUMBER: 05-001-01   DATE: Feb. 9. 2001
SUBJECT: Snow/Water Ingestion Into Rear Brake Drum
OVERVIEW:
This bulletin involves installing a revised rear drum brake support (backing) plate and possible replacement of the rear brake shoes and drums.
MODELS:
2001   (RS) Town & Country/Caravan/Voyager
1996–2000 (NS) Town & Country/Caravan/Voyager

SYMPTOM/CONDITION:

While driving through deep or blowing snow/water, the snow/water may enter the rear brake drums, causing rust to develop on the rear brake drum and shoe friction surfaces. This condition can lead to temporary freezing of the rear brake linings to the drums. This symptom is experienced after the vehicle has been parked in below freezing temperatures long enough for the snow/water to freeze inside of the rear brake drums. If the parking brake has been applied, the symptom is more likely to occur.

"No sir, we have never heard of that bulletin; snow is a maintenance item, ya know?" It's not likely your dealer will say that $300 brake problem is due to a factory defect described in the "for dealers' eyes only" bulletin shown above.

97-060   September 22, 1997

Applies To: 1994–97 Accord four-door - All

Front door glass comes out of run channel

SYMPTOM

When operating a front window (power or manual), the rear edge of the glass comes out of the B-pillar run channel.

PROBABLE CAUSE

The window regulator is out of adjustment.

CORRECTIVE ACTION

Adjust the window regulator, the front channel, and the glass.

WARRANTY CLAIM INFORMATION

In warranty:

The normal warranty applies.

Failed part:	P/N 72250-SV-A11, H/C 4272282
Defect Code:	030
Contention Code:	B01
Skill level:	Repair Technician

Out of warranty:

Any repair performed after warranty expiration may be eligible for goodwill consideration by the District Service Manager or your Zone Office. You must request consideration, and get a decision, before starting work.

Honda's admission that it will offer goodwill consideration to affected vehicles is a fair response to what the company's own bulletin calls a "failed part." But, since these TSBs aren't publicly disclosed, how many owners know they can get this financial help?

3rd Stage—More and more customers hear through *Lemon-Aid*, ALLDATA, friends, and relatives that some TSBs recognize that a common factory-related defect exists, and find that the base warranty is clearly inadequate to deal with the scope of the problem. Dealers and customers exert pressure for additional after-warranty assistance. This, in turn, results in a second TSB, sent only to dealers, extending the warranty coverage to correct the defect and usually leaving the amount of the customer's refund to the dealer's discretion. Ford calls this second TSB a Special Service Instruction and assumes the full cost of the adjustment, repair, or replacement of the defective part. Take note: Ford says owners are *not* to be notified of SSI free fixes (see Special Service Instruction #00T04).

Now, customer dissatisfaction builds to a crescendo, since the dealers and automakers keep the extended guidelines to themselves, and customers get widely divergent refunds. This only angers the owners more, brings in the media, and leads to a proliferation of Internet gripe sites and lawsuits (small claims and class actions).

4th Stage—Finally, the aggravation is too great and the automaker decides to mail out an owner notification letter (sent to first owners only, at their last known address) that clearly spells out what all owners will get and which vehicles are involved. A special bulletin or letter is also sent out to dealers to ensure they follow the guidelines 100 percent. Ford calls these Owner Notification Programs, GM calls them Special Policies, and Chrysler calls them Owner Satisfaction Notifications. No matter the euphemism, they are all an extension of the original warranty and apply to vehicles purchased new or used.

Director		Ford Motor Company
Vehicle Services and Programs		P.O. Box 1904
Ford Customer Service Division		Dearborn, MI 48121-1904

March, 1999

To: All Ford and Lincoln-Mercury Dealers

Subject: Owner Notification Program 99M01 - Certain 1997 and 1998 Crown Victoria Police Interceptor Vehicles with 4.6L SOHC Engines - Intake Manifold Additional Coverage

OASIS

- Yes

OWNER LIST

- Yes

PARTS RETURN

- Yes, Return Removed Intake Manifold Assembly (Read Your Overnight Messages for Instructions)

PROGRAM TERMS

- 7 Years from Warranty Start Date, Regardless of Mileage

AFFECTED VEHICLES

Certain 1997 and 1998 Crown Victoria Police Interceptor vehicles with 4.6L SOHC engines built at the St. Thomas Assembly Plant from January 29, 1997 through November 22, 1997.

REASONS FOR THIS PROGRAM

Fatigue cracks may develop in some of the compostite intake manifolds used on the 4.6L SOHC engines installed in the affected cars. This condition may result in engine coolant leakage which, if not detected or ignored, will cause engine overheating. Complete loss of coolant may result in engine damage or engine failure.

SERVICE ACTION

Owners of the affected cars are being notified that additional coverage for this specific condition is being provided for 7 years from the vehicle's warranty start date (no mileage limitation). This additional coverage is automatically transferred to subsequent owners.

REFUNDS

Ford will refund for owner-paid repairs directly caused by this condition which were made before the date of the Owner Letter (or after the date of the Owner Letter if an <u>emergency</u> repair was made away from the servicing dealer).

Under the above Owner Notification Program, 1997–98 Crown Victoria owners will get free engine intake manifolds up to seven years without any mileage limitation. But Ford will only apply the ONP to police vehicles.

Intake Manifold – Crossover Channel Coolant Seepage

Article No. 02-2-2

^ COOLANT - COOLANT SEEPAGE AT INTAKE MANIFOLD CROSSOVER - VEHICLES EQUIPPED WITH 4.6L 2V ENGINE ONLY

^ ENGINE - 4.6L 2V - COOLANT SEEPAGE AT INTAKE MANIFOLD CROSSOVER

FORD:

1996–97 THUNDERBIRD

1996–2001 CROWN VICTORIA, MUSTANG

2002 EXPLORER

LINCOLN:

1996–2001 TOWN CAR

MERCURY:

1996–97 COUGAR

1996–2001 GRAND MARQUIS

ISSUE

Some vehicles may exhibit an Intake Manifold crossover (first runner) coolant seepage condition. This may be caused by a crack in the Intake Manifold coolant crossover.

ACTION

Inspect the suspect Intake Manifold for a coolant leak at the first runner crossover area (Figure 1). If coolant seepage is found in this area, order the appropriate Service kit and install parts, by referring to the appropriate Model Year Workshop Manual (Section 303-01).

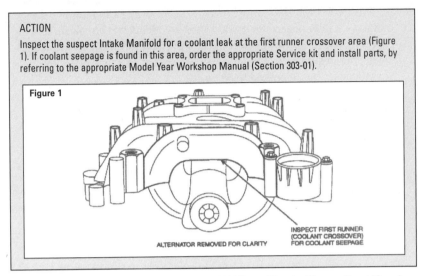

Figure 1

INSPECT FIRST RUNNER (COOLANT CROSSOVER) FOR COOLANT SEEPAGE

ALTERNATOR REMOVED FOR CLARITY

Here, Ford admits to faulty manifolds on the 1996–2001 Crown Victoria, Mercury Grand Marquis, and Lincoln Town Car and the 1996–97 Ford Thunderbird and Mercury Cougar. Owners get zilch!

Canadian consumers don't have to take this abuse. Read the following email I received recently from a *Lemon-Aid* reader who threatened Ford with litigation if it didn't apply the same refund program to him that it gave police officers:

> My 1997 Mercury Grand Marquis lost most of its coolant during my commute home from work on the evening of Wednesday, 24 September, 2002. I immediately stopped the car and switched off the engine, and (after a long wait) had it towed to an independent repair service, which diagnosed a cracked inlet manifold.
>
> This defect is a known problem on Ford Crown Victorias, as described in *Lemon-Aid Used Cars and Minivans 2003*, page 39, and according to the diagnostician who located the crack in the manifold.

The Grand Marquis and Crown Victoria are fundamentally the same car. I understand that the engines are identical. I am aware of a manufacturer's warranty covering this problem on Crown Victorias, under the designation "ONP #01M02", restricted to seven years from manufacture, but unlimited mileage.

I telephoned Ford Canada (1-800-565-3673), speaking to "Ayeesha" (ext. 2103), Ford Service Centre representative, at 14:30, 25 September. It was confirmed to me that the warranty (ONP #01M02) does indeed exist but, amazingly, is applied only to Crown Victorias. I complained that this was an arbitrary distinction, since the design of both cars is fundamentally the same, and the engines are identical. This means that the same design flaws will be present, and certainly the inlet manifolds will have the same qualities and problems. This warranty restriction appears to be based on the number of complaints logged by the Ford call centre, and the subsequent advice of the engineering department. Since I understand that there are more Crown Victorias on the road than Grand Marquis, it is inevitable that there will be a greater frequency of complaints relating to Crown Victorias.

I requested referral through Ayeesha to a manager, but there was nobody available at the time; I was told that I would be called back within 24–48 hours. I complained that my car is currently sitting in a repair shop awaiting repair at an estimated repair cost of $1,395.53. Ayeesha then clearly stated that if it is determined that the warranty will apply to the Grand Marquis model at a later date, Ford would reimburse me the full cost of repair, even if it is carried out by an independent dealer. Based on these comments, I have now authorized the repair.

I am surprised and upset that my arguments that the Grand Marquis is fundamentally of the same design as the Crown Victoria fell on deaf ears. I commented that it had been determined that failure of the inlet manifold on the Crown Victoria within seven years of manufacture constituted failure of the product to be fit for the purpose for which it is manufactured and purchased. This same concept must, therefore, apply equally to the Grand Marquis since it is fundamentally the same vehicle....

...As indicated to Ayeesha, I intend to pursue this matter through the various options open to me. Although I trust and anticipate that you will see that my argument is sound, I must state that if reimbursement is not forthcoming, I may take the matter up through a small claims court. I have already sought some advice in this regard, and if I am forced to pursue recompense through court, I also intend to claim costs and damages based on hardship caused by the fact that I lost an entire evening arranging to have the vehicle towed, and am now without the car for at least five days while waiting for repairs to be effected—causing serious problems in getting to and from work....

The above owner got a confidential refund from Ford shortly after sending a copy of his email to *Lemon-Aid.*

Remember, second owners and repairs done by independent garages are included in these secret warranty programs, even though you may be turned away at first. Large, costly repairs—such as blown engines, burned transmissions, and peeling paint—are usually covered, but, even mundane little repairs, which can still cost you a hundred bucks or more, are frequently included in these programs. Take, for example, the elimination of foul, musty, or mildew odours emitted by your air conditioning unit. Despite what the dealer may say, it's covered by the base warranty provided by all automakers.

If you have a TSB but you're still refused compensation, keep in mind that secret warranties are an admission of manufacturing negligence. Try to compromise with a pro rata adjustment from the manufacturer. If polite negotiations fail, challenge the refusal in court on the grounds that you should not be penalized for failing to make a reimbursement claim under a secret warranty you never knew existed!

Here are a few examples of the latest, most comprehensive secret warranties that have come across my desk in the last several years.

Acura/Honda

1994–97 Acura CL and Honda Accord, Prelude, and Odyssey models equipped with 4-cylinder engines

Problem: Defective engine oil seals can slip, causing the engine to drain of oil and eventually seize. **Warranty coverage:** Honda has backed away from this free repair, claiming it's for Americans only, but the company usually relents when the customer refuses to go away. Dealer is expected to install a clip to ensure the seal cannot move.

1998–2003 Honda Accord, Odyssey, and Pilot models equipped with 6-cylinder engines

Problem: Defective aluminum engine block. **Warranty coverage:** Repair or replace engine under a "goodwill" program.

Honda: V6 Engine Oil Leaks   01-009

September 10, 2002

Applies To:
1998–2002 Accord V6 - ALL
1999–2003 Odyssey - ALL
2003 Pilot - ALL

SYMPTOM: An oil leak from the front, middle, or rear of the engine.

PROBABLE CAUSE: The cast aluminum engine block may be porous at the front, middle, or rear.

CORRECTIVE ACTION: Depending on the location of the leak, seal it with JB Weld or with 3-Bond-coated sealing bolts. ➤

In warranty: The normal warranty applies.

Out of warranty: Any repair performed after warranty expiration may be eligible for goodwill consideration by the District Parts and Service Manager or your Zone Office. You must request consideration, and get a decision, before starting work.

1995 Acura 2.5 TL, NSX, and Accord V6; all 1996–97 Acuras and Hondas (except Integra Type R and Passport)

Problem: Engine malfunctions could cause emissions to exceed federal norms. **Warranty coverage:** In a U.S. EPA settlement, Honda paid fines totalling $17.1 million and extended its emissions warranty on 1.6 million 1995–97 models to 14 years/240,000 km (150,000 mi.) (page 6 of the June 15, 1998, edition of *Automotive News*). Costly engine and exhaust system parts like catalytic converters will be replaced free of charge, up to 14 years/240,000 km (150,000 mi.). Additionally, Honda will provide a full engine check and emissions-related repairs at 80,000–120,000 km (50,000–75,000 mi.) and will give free tune-ups at 120,000–240,000 km (75,000–150,000 mi.). Environment Canada (EC) has a commitment from Honda Canada to apply the settlement terms to Canadian owners, says EC spokesman Leif Stephanson (Oil, Gas and Energy Branch Air Pollution Prevention Directorate, 351 St. Joseph Blvd., 10th Floor, Gatineau, QC, K1A 0H3; Fax: 819-953-8903; Email: *ogeb@ec.gc.ca*) in the following November 20, 2003 email:

> The judgment to which you refer was a Consent Decree between Honda and the U.S. Justice Department, the U.S. Environmental Protection Agency (U.S. EPA), and the California Air Resources Board. As a matter of contract between Honda and these U.S. government officials, as set forth in the Consent Decree, Honda agreed to implement certain actions that extended beyond the U.S. EPA's regulations. As a result, these actions had no direct legal bearing on Canadian requirements. Nevertheless, prior to the date of the indicated U.S. EPA press release, members of the Canadian government met with officials from Honda, who committed to implement certain measures from the Consent Decree in Canada.

Mr. Stephenson doesn't spell out which free repairs or tune-ups await Canadian Honda/Acura owners; however, I don't think any small claims court judge would accept Canadian Acura/Honda owners getting less.

1999–2003 Acura CL and TL; Honda Accord, Prelude, and Odyssey models

Problem: Defective automatic transmission and torque converter. **Warranty coverage:** This "goodwill" warranty extension was confirmed in the August 4,

2003 edition of *Automotive News*. Honda will fix or replace the transmission free of charge up to 7 years/100,000 miles (160,000 km) whether owners bought their vehicle new or used. The company will also reimburse owners who already paid for the repair.

Audi/VW

2001–03 cars equipped with 1.8 L engines, which includes the Audi TT and A4; and the VW Golf/GTI, Jetta, New Beetle, and Passat. The companies also included the Passat W8 engine, all VWs equipped with the 2.8 L VR6; as well as the Audi 3.0 L V6 engine. In total, approximately 530,000 cars are affected by this action.

Problem: Defective ignition coils. When these coils fail, the vehicle suddenly stalls and won't start. **Warranty coverage:** VW will fix every single car by replacing the coils whether they are broken or not. There is no mileage or time limit on this warranty extension. Owners complain that a backlog of parts has resulted in long waits and repeat dealer visits.

1998–2002 New Beetles and 1999–2002 Golfs, GTIs and Jettas. 850,000 vehicles are affected

Problem: If window clamp malfunctions, it prevents the window from being raised or lowered. **Warranty coverage:** The new clamp and the work to install it will be covered free of charge under this special warranty.

Chrysler

1991–2001 models with A604, 41TE, and 42LE automatic transmissions

Problem: Faulty automatic transmissions that shift erratically, gear down to "limp mode," are slow to shift in or out of Reverse, and self-destruct. This is an A604 (and its spin-offs) software and hardware problem that has bedevilled Chrysler owners for over a decade. **Warranty coverage:** Without a court threat, Chrysler usually denies any problem or refund program exists. If you have the assistance of your dealer's service manager, expect an offer of 50 percent (about $1,500). File the case in small claims court and Chrysler will sweeten the offer considerably. Be warned, though, you may need to repeatedly repair the transmission, as this *Lemon-Aid* reader recounts:

> I've just been told that I need my *fourth transmission* on my '96 Town & Country minivan, with 132,000 miles [212,000 km] on it. I've driven many cars well past that mileage with only *one* transmission. The dealer asked Chrysler, who said they would not help me. My appeals to Chrysler's customer service department yielded me the same result.... Chrysler split some of the costs with me on the previous rebuilt replacements.

1995–99 models equipped with 4-cylinder engines

Problem: Faulty engine head gaskets will cause the engine to overheat, lose power, burn extra fuel, and possibly, self-destruct. **Warranty coverage:** Without a court threat, Chrysler usually denies any problem or refund program exists. If you have the assistance of your dealer's service manager, expect an offer of 50 percent (about $1,500). File the case in small claims court and Chrysler will sweeten the offer considerably.

Your small claims court filing likely won't go beyond the pretrial mediation stage: Chrysler reps are loath to defend the cases in front of independent garage testimony. However, if you must go to court, arm yourself with the following consumer's court story.

> Phil, I sued DaimlerChrysler for $2,000 (the cost of repairs for the head gasket, and the resulting ruined cylinder head), and won.... Chrysler sent a letter refusing to reimburse me, after I sent the first request for goodwill warranty coverage (my car had 90,000 miles [144,000 km] when the head gasket blew). I filed the court case just against DaimlerChrysler (not including the used car dealership where I bought the car—this was unintended, I just forgot to put them on the case too), and they let it go to court without contacting me and trying to offer a deal. The Chrysler district manager for my area, and the service manager from the dealership where I had the car serviced (not where I bought it) showed up to fight for Chrysler, and the only evidence they brought was a copy of my car's original warranty. Their argument was that there had been no recall on the part, my car was out of warranty, and thus they were not responsible for the costs.
>
> The district manager even said "Yeah, some of the gaskets in these Neons have failed, but not all of them!"
>
> My argument was that this was a faulty product (evidenced by multiple websites discussing the matter); it had been redesigned because it was faulty (I included a copy of the TSB for the new head gasket); it failed in my car; ruined my head; and they were responsible for the cost of repairs. I discussed the secret warranty at length, and in my evidence included a copy of an invoice I printed off of *www.geocities.com/norman_neon*, which states "goodwill warranty assistance" covered the cost of repairs.
>
> I mentioned this part of my submitted evidence right after the Chrysler guy said "There is no goodwill warranty on this part." It was all just great! Thanks for all your help....
>
> Sincerely, T.W.

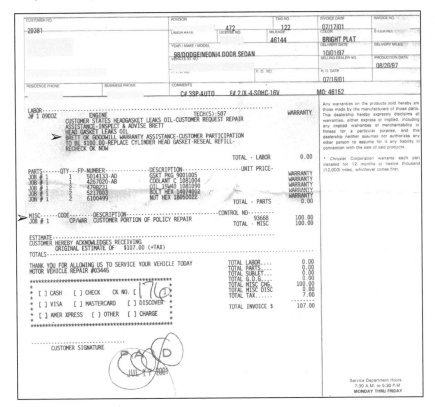

Chrysler/Jeep

1989–93 Cherokee and Wagoneer; 1990–93 Dynasty, New Yorker, Fifth Avenue, and Imperial; 1991–92 Eagle Premier; 1991–93 minivans

Problem: ABS brakes that fail or malfunction. **Warranty coverage:** Piggybacking a service campaign onto a recall, Chrysler extended the warranty to 10 years/160,000 km on a number of costly ABS components. Owners will also be reimbursed for previous ABS repairs—not applicable to calipers, pads/shoe linings, or other maintenance items. Two other ABS components, piston seals (excessive wear) and the pump motor (deterioration), will be repaired free of charge at any time during the life of the vehicle.

Don't worry about the '93 cut-off date. This warranty extension is useful mainly as a benchmark as to how long these components should last and how much you should pay on a pro-rated basis. Let's say you have a 1999 model with an ABS braking system that had a major failure of the above components in 2003. Since the system only lasted 5 years, instead of 10, you should ask for 50 percent off your bill.

> Hi Phil. I thought I should let you know that Chrysler sent me a cheque
> to cover the full cost of the repair of my ABS brakes. I appreciate your
> book providing the copy of Safety Recall 685 as it sure makes things a
> whole lot easier when you have a document like that to refer to.
>
> Fred K.

1993–99 Concorde, Intrepid, New Yorker, LHS, Vision, and Grand Cherokee

Problem: AC evaporator failure or malfunction. **Warranty coverage:** 7 years/ 115,000 km. Although this "goodwill" extension has expired, it sets a benchmark for what Chrysler considers the normal durability of its ACs.

ADDENDUM TO BASIC WARRANTY

The following applies to 1993 through 1997 New Yorker, LHS, Concorde, Intrepid, Vision and Grand Cherokee vehicles equipped with factory-installed air conditioning:

The Basic Warranty coverage for the air conditioner evaporator has been extended to 7 years or 115,000 kilometres, whichever occurs first, from the vehicle's warranty start date.

This extended coverage applies to all owners of the vehicle. All of the other warranty terms apply to this extension.

Chrysler, Ford, and General Motors

All years, all models

Problem: Premature wearout of key front- and rear-brake components. **Warranty coverage: Calipers and pads**: Goodwill settlements confirm that brake calipers and pads that fail to last 2 years/40,000 km will be replaced for 50 percent of the repair cost; components not lasting 1 year/20,000 km will be replaced for free. Rotors: If they last less than 3 years/60,000 km, rotors will be replaced at half price; replacement is free up to 2 years/40,000 km. Interestingly, premature brake component wearout is quite common among all automobile manufacturers, although only Chrysler, Ford, and GM have standardized their policies for goodwill refunds.

Apparently, brake suppliers are using cheaper calipers, pads, and rotors that can't handle the heat generated by normal braking. Consequently, drivers find routine braking causes rotor warpage that produces excessive vibrations, shuddering, noise, and pulling to one side when braking.

Chrysler, Ford, General Motors, and Hyundai

1994–2003 engine head gasket and intake manifold failures; 1998–99 Hyundai Accent

Problem: A serious engine defect from 1994–2003 caused by irrational price-cutting, these automakers have serious problems with poor-quality engine head gaskets and plastic intake manifolds failing at 60,000–100,000 km. The engine may overheat, lose power, burn extra fuel, and, possibly, self-destruct. Under the best of circumstances, the repair will take a day and cost about $800–$1,000. **Warranty coverage:** Without a court threat or a copy of a warranty extension or service bulletin, these companies usually deny any problem or refund program exists. If you have the assistance of your dealer's service manager, expect a 50 percent offer up to 5 years/ 100,000 km (about $1,500, if other parts are damaged). 1996 and later Windstars will be covered up to 7 years/160,00 km if you threaten to cite the *Dufour* or *Reid* Windstar judgments (see pages 82 and 33).

No matter which automaker you are dealing with, filing your claim in small claims court always sweetens the company's settlement offer. Furthermore, you won't likely have to step inside a courtroom to get your refund, since most small claims court filings are settled at the pretrial mediation stage.

Engine claims are entering a second phase where the original free repair has to be repaired, again. Car owners are told they had one kick at the can and that's it, but, once again, small claims court judges don't always see it that way. Courts have held that the company's first repair was an admission that the product was faulty, its correction must last a reasonable period of time, or be redone.

> Phil, I thought you might be interested to know, I sued Saturn in small claims court and wound up settling before trial for 75 percent of the total repair for the repair of my '95 Saturn's engine head gasket.

Chrysler, Ford, General Motors, and Honda

Various years, all models

Problem: A common problem for over two decades, faulty paint jobs may cause paint to turn white or peel off horizontal panels.

A paint-delaminated Ford Taurus. Chrysler, Ford, and GM will repaint their vehicles for free, if threatened with a small claims lawsuit.

In *Frank v. GM*, the Saskatchewan small claims court (see pages 76–78) set a 15-year benchmark for paint finishes, and three other Canadian small claims judgments have extended the benchmark to seven years, second owners, and pickups. **Warranty coverage:** Automakers will offer a free paint job or partial compensation up to 6 years/no mileage limitation. Thereafter, all three manufacturers offer 50–75 percent refunds on the small claims courthouse steps.

Chris Ekstrom, an Edmonton owner of a 1992 Dodge Caravan, formed a Chrysler Lemon Owners Group (CLOG) in 2002 to pressure the automaker to settle its paint and automatic transmission complaints. Nancy Frith, a Nova Scotia owner of a 1992 Dodge Shadow, filed suit and was awarded $2,000 for the paint delamination/peeling of her car. CBC TV *Marketplace* interviewed both owners and you can capture that program at *www.cbc.ca/consumers/ market/files/cars/paintpeel/index.html.*

Ford

1994–2001 models equipped with automatic transmissions

Problem: Hardware and software components may fail prematurely. This problem is usually indicated by erratic shifting, delayed shifting, harsh engagement, and a tendency for the transmission to "hunt" for the proper gear. Barely noticeable at first, it will worsen progressively, until the transmission breaks down completely. **Warranty coverage:** Ford has repaired or replaced transmissions at no charge up to 7 years/160,000 km, no matter if the vehicle was bought new or used. The company's initial offer is usually 50 percent of the estimated $3,000 repair cost, unless an "implied warranty" small claims court action is threatened—then it may jump up to 100 percent.

1996–99 Taurus SHO

Problem: Frequent failures of engine cam sprockets, resulting in ruined engines. Because engines are so expensive and in short supply, they can cost $8,000–$20,000 to repair. As more of these cars move into the 60,000+ km mileage range, more will experience this failure. Estimates are that 5–10 percent of V8-equipped vehicles will experience this problem. Reasons for this defect, its cause, correction, internal bulletins, claims procedures, and class action filing are found on *www.v8sho.com/SHO/96shohome.html*. **Warranty coverage:** Insiders tell me Ford will cover repairs when threatened with small claims suits on cars that haven't passed 7 years/160,000 km. Without the court threat, owners are offered 50 percent up to 100,000 km.

1995–98 Windstar

Problem: Defective front coil springs may suddenly break, puncturing the front tire, leading to loss of steering control. **Warranty coverage:** Under a "Safety Improvement Campaign," negotiated with NHTSA, Ford will replace *broken* coil springs at no charge up to 10 years/unlimited mileage (Transport Canada has no record of this free repair on its website). The company won't replace the springs until they have broken—if you're alive to submit a claim. 1997–98 models that are registered in rust-belt states and Canada have been recalled for the installation of a protective shield (called a spring *catcher* bracket in the Canadian recall) to prevent a broken spring from shredding the front tire.

1996–97 Mustang, Cougar, and Thunderbird; 1997 F-Series trucks equipped with 3.8L or 4.2L engines

Problem: These vehicles may experience engine coolant leaks at the front cover gasket; this could cause severe engine damage from overheating if not corrected. This is the defect cited in Judge Tiernay's decision found at the beginning of Part Two. **Warranty coverage:** At no charge to the owner, the dealer will replace the engine front cover gasket with a redesigned gasket and— now get this—*replace the engine oil and filter!* This is a generous special warranty extension because: 1) It also covers lower intake side gaskets; 2) The free repair is still applicable, even if there is a repeat failure; 3) There is no engine test required to get the new, more durable components installed; 4) Costs for previous repairs will be paid in full; and 5) It includes vehicles purchased used, and there is no mileage limitation. Although this program expired March 21, 2001, it has been extended on a case-by-case basis.

Owners whose cars already have been repaired should take their original receipt to a Ford or Lincoln-Mercury dealer. However, Ford has acknowledged that some of those consumers may have had their gaskets replaced with the older, troublesome gasket. That gasket could leak, too, and those consumers are eligible not only for the reimbursement but for a new repair, say Ford spokespeople.

The easiest way to tell if a new, improved gasket was used is to check the part number on the receipt or to call the dealer who did the work. An "early upgraded" gasket had this part number: F8ZZ-6020-AA. However, since the middle of 1999, an even newer design was used. Its part number is YF2Z-6020-AA. Ford engineers believe that the "early upgraded" gasket will be fine, but consumers who worry that it is not good enough are eligible for a second repair.

My only gripe about this warranty extension is that it leaves out the 1996–98 Windstar and Econoline E-150 and E-250, the 1998 Mustang, and 1998 F-Series trucks, which are all included in service bulletin #99-20-7 (see page 440), detailing the failure that Ford is correcting. If you are the owner of one of these excluded vehicles, send the dealer and Ford a claim letter under the implied warranty and emissions warranty, as well. If refused compensation, subpoena Ford's bulletin and owner letter as proof that you should have been included.

2000–01 Focus

Problem: Premature corrosion of the rear wheel bearings may cause the wheel to wobble. **Warranty coverage:** Under ONP #01B85, Ford said it would replace the rear wheel bearings at no charge until December 31, 2002, as long as you live right—that is, as long as you live in the right part of the country. This regional extended warranty is clearly illogical and Ford's cut-off date is arbitrary and unfair. Focus owners may ask for a pro rata refund from Ford or simply claim a complete refund in small claims court.

Director Ford Motor Company
Vehicle Services and Programs   P.O. Box 1904
Ford Customer Service Division   Dearborn, MI 48121-1904

December 2001

To: All Ford and Lincoln-Mercury Dealers

Subject: Customer Satisfaction Program 01B85 — Supplement 1: Revised Technical Instructions and Parts Information

OASIS

- Yes

OWNER LIST

- Yes

PROGRAM TERMS

- This program will be in effect unti December 31, 2002 regardless of mileage.

REASONS FOR THIS SUPPLEMENT

The Technical Instructions and Parts Ordering Information have been revised to:

- Eliminate damage to the double-lip seal during installation by clarifying spindle preparation.
- Remove the requirement to replace the spindle if the double-lip seal is deformed during installation
- Revise the parts ordering procedure for the disc brake kit (Attachement II). ➤

AFFECTED VEHICLES

Certain 2000 and 2001 model year Focus vehicles built at the Wayne
Assembly Plan from July 19, 1999 through February 20, 2001 and the
Hermosillo Assembly Plant from October 4, 1999 through June 18, 2001,
originally sold in or currently registered in the following U.S. states and
Canadian provinces:

U.S. States:	Connecticut	Kentucky	Minnesota	Ohio
	Delaware	Maine	Missouri	Pennsylvania
	Illinois	Maryland	New Hampshire	Rhode Island
	Indiana	Massachusetts	New Jersey	Vermont
	Iowa	Michigan	New York	West Virginia
				Wisconsin

Canadian	Quebec	Nova Scotia	New Brunswick
Provinces:	Ontario	Newfoundland	Prince Edward Island

REASON FOR PROGRAM

In high corrosion areas, where salt is used on roadways in the winter,
the rear wheel bearing seal race may experience surface corrosion. If
this condition occurs, the wheel bearing seals may become damaged
and allow contamination to enter the wheel bearings. As a result, the
wheel bearings may prematurely wear and cause a noticeable noise. If
not repaired, this condition could progress to the point where the wheel
begins to wobble.

How's this for weird? Ontarians get the free corrosion repairs, but cars registered in Manitoba or
elsewhere, but driven on Ontario roads (I'm thinking students, here), are out of luck. And what
about all those used units exported to Alberta and British Columbia? Makes no sense
whatsoever, and this policy would never hold up in court.

Ford/Lincoln

1996–2001 Crown Victoria and Lincoln Town Car fleet vehicles

Problem: Intake manifolds may crack at the coolant crossover, resulting in
engine coolant leakage. **Warranty coverage:** ONP #01M02 will pay for the
intake manifold's replacement up to seven years, regardless of mileage. Ford
has refunded repair costs to non-fleet vehicles when threatened with small
claims court action.

1998–2000 Crown Victoria and Lincoln Town Car fleet vehicles

Problem: Rear suspension upper control arm brackets may crack and allow
the bracket to separate from the frame. This will cause a clunking noise and
cause the rear suspension to feel loose. **Warranty coverage:** ONP #00B60 paid
for the crack repair and the installation of a reinforcement bracket until
January 31, 2002. Affected owners who drive non-fleet cars should demand a
refund, using small claims court action for leverage.

1998 Cavalier/Sunfire

Problem: Excessive oil consumption. **Warranty coverage:** Customer Satisfaction Campaign will cover all the cost incurred to eliminate the problem. Service bulletin number: 98017; Date of bulletin: 08/98; NHTSA Item Number: SB615103.

1999 Cavalier/Sunfire

Problem: Defective throttle valve cable produces erratic engine performance. **Warranty coverage:** Customer Satisfaction Campaign will cover the cost of replacing the throttle valve cable. Service bulletin number: 99039; Date of bulletin: 07/99; NHTSA Item Number: SB606219.

2001 Alero

Problem: Transmission bearing failure. **Warranty coverage:** Customer Satisfaction Campaign for 4T40-E transaxle converter bearing failure inspection/replacement. Service bulletin number: 01031; Date of bulletin: 04/01; NHTSA Item Number: SB619400.

2001 DeVille

Problem: Engine crankshaft pulley failure. **Warranty coverage:** Customer Satisfaction Campaign allows for a rebuilt crankshaft or engine replacement. Service bulletin number: 01012; Date of bulletin: 02/01; NHTSA Item Number: SB619207.

Honda

1996–2000 Honda Civic and 1997–99 CR-V

Problem: Harsh-shifting automatic transmission and torque converter. **Warranty coverage:** Honda will fix or replace the transmission free of charge up to 7 years/160,000 km (100,000 mi.) under a "goodwill" program, whether owners bought their vehicle new or used (see bulletin #00-012, published June 26, 2001 found on page 93).

Toyota

1988–95 compact pickups, T100 pickups, and 4Runner sport-utilities with 3.0L and 3.6L 6-cylinder engines; engine sludge afflicts 1997 through 2002 Toyota and Lexus vehicles with 2.2L 4-cylinder, or 3.0L, V-6 engines.

Problem: Defective head gaskets may cause loss of engine coolant, engine overheating, or destruction of the engine's short block. Sludge buildup may require a rebuilt engine. **Warranty coverage:** Toyota will replace the defective gasket and other affected components at no charge up to 8 years/160,000 km (100,000 mi.). The sludge fix has no mileage limitation and, following *Lemon-Aid* and owner protests, the onerous requirement that owners produce proof of every oil change has been dropped.

Incidentally, there have been a lot of 1996 model head gasket failures reported to the NHTSA; resulting in Toyota extending this warranty's parameters to include '96 and later models on a case-by-case basis.

The 8-year extended engine warranty is one of the longest in the auto industry and should be used as a benchmark when arguing for after-warranty assistance from other automakers.

How Long Should a Part or Repair Last?

How do you know when a part or service doesn't last as long as it should and whether you should seek a full or partial refund? Sure, you have a gut feeling based on the use of the vehicle, how you maintained it, and the extent of work that was carried out. But, you'll need more than emotion to win compensation from garages and automakers.

You can definitely get a refund if a repair or part lasts longer than its guarantee, but not as long as is generally expected. But you'll have to show what the auto industry considers to be reasonable durability.

Automakers, mechanics, and the courts have their own benchmarks as to what's a reasonable period of time or amount of mileage one should expect a part or adjustment to last. Consequently, I've prepared the following table to show what most automakers consider is reasonable durability, as expressed by their original and "goodwill" warranties.

ACCESSORIES

Air conditioner	7 years
Cellular phone	5 years
Cruise control	5 years/ 100,000 km
Power antenna	5 years
Power doors, windows	5 years
Radio	5 years

BODY

Paint (peeling)	7 years
Rust (perforations)	7 years
Rust (surface)	5 years
Water/wind/air leaks	5 years

BRAKE SYSTEM

Brake drum	120,000 km
Brake drum linings	35,000 km
Brake rotor	60,000 km
Disc brake calipers	30,000 km
Disc brake pads	30,000 km

Master cylinder, rebuild	100,000 km
Wheel cylinder, rebuild	80,000 km

ENGINE AND DRIVETRAIN

Constant velocity joint	6 years/ 160,000 km
Differential	7 years/ 160,000 km
Engine (gas)	7 years/ 160,000 km
Radiator	4 years/ 80,000 km
Transfer case	7 years/ 150,000 km
Transmission (auto.)	7 years/ 150,000 km
Transmission (man.)	10 years/ 250,000 km

Transmission oil cooler	5 years/ 100,000 km

Seatbelts	life of vehicle

EXHAUST SYSTEM

Catalytic converter	5 years/ 100,000 km or more
Muffler	2 years/ 40,000 km
Tailpipe	3 years/ 60,000 km

IGNITION SYSTEM

Cable set	60,000 km
Electronic module	5 years/ 80,000 km
Retiming	20,000 km
Spark plugs	20,000 km
Tune-up	20,000 km

SAFETY COMPONENTS

Airbags	life of vehicle
ABS brakes	7 years/ 160,000 km
ABS computer	10 years/ 160,000 km

STEERING AND SUSPENSION

Alignment	1 year/ 20,000 km
Ball joints	80,000 km
Power steering	5 years/ 80,000 km
Shock absorber	2 years/ 40,000 km
Struts	5 years/ 80,000 km
Tires (radial)	5 years/ 80,000 km
Wheel bearing	3 years/ 60,000 km

VISIBILITY

Halogen/fog lights	3 years/ 60,000 km
Sealed beam	2 years/ 40,000 km
Windshield wiper motor	5 years/ 80,000 km

Much of the preceding guidelines were extrapolated from Chrysler and Ford payouts to thousands of dissatisfied customers over the past decade, in addition to Chrysler's original 7-year powertrain warranty applicable from 1991–95 and re-applied since 2001. Other sources for this chart were the Ford and GM transmission warranties outlined in their secret warranties; Ford, GM, and Toyota engine "goodwill" programs laid out in their internal service bulletins; and court judgments where judges have given their own guidelines as to what is reasonable durability.

Safety features generally have a lifetime warranty—with the exception of ABS—which is usually considered part of normal maintenance. Nevertheless, the Chrysler 10-year "free-service" program portion of its ABS recall announced five years ago can serve as a handy benchmark as to how long one can expect these components to last.

Airbags are a different matter. Those that are deployed in an accident—and the personal injury and interior damage their deployment will likely have caused—are covered by your accident insurance policy. However, if there is a sudden deployment for no apparent reason, the automaker and dealer should be held jointly responsible for all injuries and damages caused by the airbag.

You can prove their liability by downloading your vehicle's data recorder data. This will likely lead to a more generous settlement from the two parties and prevent your insurance premiums from being jacked up. Inadvertent deployment may occur after passing over a bump in the road, slamming the car door, or, in some Chrysler minivans, simply putting the key in the ignition. This happens more often than you might imagine, judging by the hundreds of recalls and thousands of complaints recorded on NHTSA's website (*www.nhtsa.dot.gov/cars/problems/complain/Index.cfm*).

Use the manufacturer's emissions warranty as your primary guideline for the expected durability of high-tech electronic and mechanical pollution control components, such as powertrain control modules (PCM) and catalytic converters. Look first at your owner's manual for an indication of which parts on your vehicle are covered. If you come up with few specifics, ask the auto manufacturer for a list of specific components covered by the emissions warranty. If you're stonewalled, ask your local MP to get the info from Transport Canada or Environment Canada, and invest $25 (U.S.) in an ALLDATA service bulletin subscription.

Recall repairs

Vehicles are recalled for one of two reasons: They may be unsafe or they don't conform to federal pollution control regulations. Whatever the reason, recalls are a great way to get free repairs—if you know which ones apply to you and you have the patience of Job.

More than 450 million unsafe vehicles have been recalled by automakers for the free correction of safety-related defects since American recall legislation was passed in 1966 (a weaker Canadian law was enacted in 1971). During that time, about one-third of the recalled vehicles never made it back to the dealership for repairs because owners were never informed, or they just didn't consider the defect that hazardous, or they gave up waiting for corrective parts.

Subsequent American legislation targets automakers who drag their feet in making recall repairs. Owners on both sides of the border may wish to cite the following NHTSA guidelines for support:

Dealer Recall Responsibility – For U.S. and IPC (U.S. States, Territories, and Possessions)

The U.S. National Traffic and Motor Vehicle Safety Act provides that each vehicle that is subject to a recall must be adequately repaired within a reasonable time after the customer has tendered it for repair. A failure to repair within 60 days after tender of a vehicle is *prima facie* evidence of failure to repair within a reasonable time. If the condition is not adequately repaired within a reasonable time, the customer may be entitled to an identical or reasonably equivalent vehicle at no charge or to a refund of the purchase price less a reasonable allowance for depreciation. To avoid having to provide these burdensome remedies, every effort must be made to promptly schedule an appointment with each customer and to repair their vehicle as soon as possible. In the recall notification letters, customers are told how to contact the U.S. National Highway Traffic Safety Administration if the recall is not completed within a reasonable time....

Incidentally, the above NHTSA guidelines were part of a service bulletin sent by GM to its dealers, outlining an 11-year Special Warranty and recall on its 1994–2000 trucks with faulty 6.5L fuel injection pumps (Bulletin No.: 00064C; September, 2002).

If you've moved or bought a used vehicle, it's smart to pay a visit to your local dealer, give him your address, and get a "report card" on which recalls, free-service campaigns, and warranties apply to your vehicle. Simply give the service advisor your Vehicle Identification Number (VIN)—found on the dash just below the windshield on the driver's side, or on your insurance card—and have the number run through the automaker's computer system Ask for a computer printout of the vehicle's history (have it faxed to you, if you're so equipped) and make sure you're listed in the automaker's computer as the new owner. This ensures that you'll receive notices of warranty extensions and emissions and safety recalls.

Still, don't expect to be welcomed with open arms when your vehicle develops a safety- or emissions-related problem that's not yet part of a recall campaign. Automakers and dealers generally take a restrictive view of what constitutes a safety or emissions defect and frequently charge for repairs that should be free under federal safety or emissions legislation. To counter this tendency, look at the following list of typical defects that are clearly safety related. If you experience similar problems, insist that the automaker fix the problem at no expense to yourself, including a car rental:

- airbag malfunctions
- corrosion affecting safe operation
- disconnected or stuck accelerators
- electrical shorts
- faulty windshield wipers
- fuel leaks
- problems with original axles, drive shafts, seats, seat recliners, or defrosters
- seatbelt problems
- stalling or sudden acceleration
- sudden steering or brake loss
- suspension failures
- trailer coupling failures

In the U.S., recall campaigns force automakers to pay the entire cost of fixing a vehicle's safety-related defect for any vehicle purchased up to eight years before the recall's announcement. A reasonable period beyond that time is usually a slam dunk in small claims court. Recalls may be voluntary or ordered by the U.S. Department of Transportation and can be nationwide or regional. In Canada, all recalls are considered voluntary. Transport Canada can only order automakers to notify owners that their vehicles may be unsafe; it can't force them to correct the problem. Fortunately, most U.S.-ordered recalls are carried out in Canada, and when Transport Canada makes a defect determination on its own, automakers generally comply with an owner notification letter and a recall campaign.

Safety defect information

If you wish to report a safety defect or want recall info, you may access Transport Canada's website. You can get recall information in French or English, as well as general information relating to road safety and importing a vehicle into Canada. The web page can be accessed at *www.tc.gc.ca/roadsafety/ recalls/search_e.asp*. Cybersurfers can now access the recall database for 1970–2003 model vehicles but, unlike the U.S. government's NHTSA website, owner complaints aren't listed, defect investigations aren't disclosed, voluntary warranty extensions (secret warranties) aren't shown, and service bulletin summaries aren't provided. You can also call Transport Canada at 1-800-333-0510 (toll-free within Canada) or 613-993-9851 (within the Ottawa region or outside Canada) to get additional information.

If you're not happy with Ottawa's treatment of your recall inquiry, try NHTSA's website. It's more complete than Transport Canada's (NHTSA's database is updated daily and covers vehicles built since 1952). You can search the database for your vehicle or tires at *www.nhtsa.dot.gov/cars/problems*.

You'll get immediate access to four essential database categories applicable to your vehicle and model year: the latest recalls, current and closed safety investigations, defects reported by other owners, and a brief summary of TSBs. NHTSA's fax-back service provides the same info through a local line that can be accessed from Canada—although long-distance charges will apply. (Most calls take 5–10 minutes to complete.) The following local numbers get you into the automatic response service quickly and can be reached 24 hours a day: Tel.: 202-366-0123 (202-366-7800 for the hearing impaired).

Black boxes: forget privacy rights

If your car has an airbag, it's probably spying on you.

Event data recorders (EDRs) are the size of a VCR tape and have been hidden under the seat or in the centre consoles of about 25 million airbag-equipped Ford and GM vehicles sold in North America since the early 1990s. Presently, about 20 percent of all domestic and imported cars carry them.

The data recorders operate in a similar fashion to flight data recorders used in airplanes: They record data during the last five seconds before impact, including the force of the collision, the airbag's performance, when the brakes were applied, engine and vehicle speed, gas pedal position, and whether the driver was wearing a seat belt.

Apart from the "invasion of privacy" aspect of hiding recorders in customers' vehicles, Ford and GM have systematically hidden their collected data from U.S. and Canadian vehicle safety researchers that are investigating thousands of complaints relating to airbags that don't deploy when they should (or deploy when they shouldn't) and anti-lock brakes that don't brake.

This refusal to share data with customers and researchers is unfortunate, because the recorders are collecting critical information that could lead to better-functioning safety devices. In fact, experts say that highway safety could be vastly improved if black boxes that record information about car crashes were installed in all cars, just as similar devices are placed in all airplanes. To find out if your car or truck carries an EDR go to: *www.cbc.ca/consumers/ market/files/cars/blackboxes*.

Fortunately, it has become impossible for automakers to hide recorder data now that Vitronix Corp sells a $2,500 (U.S.) portable download device that accesses the data and stores it in any PC. It's presently marketed to accident reconstructionists, safety researchers, law enforcement agencies, and insurance companies.

Car owners who wish to dispute criminal charges, oppose their insurer's decision, or hold an automaker responsible for a safety device's failure (airbags, seat belts, or brakes) will find this data invaluable.

Safety benefits

Enthusiastically promoted by government and law enforcement agencies around the world, these data recorders have actually had a positive effect in accident prevention: European studies show that drivers who know their vehicles are equipped with the device have 20–30 percent less accidents and drive more slowly.

The recorders are also sending people to jail, helping accident victims reap huge court awards, and prompting automaker recalls of unsafe vehicles.

- In January 2004, South Dakota Congressman Bill Janklow was convicted of manslaughter for speeding through a stop sign after using his EDR (event data recorder) readout to prove he was driving slower than police estimated.
- In October 2003, Montreal police won their first dangerous driving conviction using EDR data (*R. c. Gauthier*, [2003-05-27] QCCQ 500-01-013375-016, source: *www.canlii.org/qc/jug/qccq/2003/2003qccq17860.html*).
- In June 2003, Edwin Matos of Pembroke Pines, Fla., was sentenced to 30 years in prison for killing two teenage girls, after crashing into their car at more than 160 km/h (100 mph). The recorder's speed data convicted him.
- Two months earlier, an Illinois police officer received a $10 million (U.S.) settlement after data showed the driver of an empty hearse, who was supposedly unconscious from a diabetes attack, actually accelerated and braked in the moments before slamming into the officer's patrol car.
- In July 2002, New Brunswick prosecutors sent a dangerous driver to jail for two years based on his car's EDR data. (*R. v. Daley*, 2003 NBQB 20 Docket(s): S/CR/7/02, source: *www.canlii.org/nb/cas/nbqb/2002/2003nbqb20.html*.
- Data recorders showed GM that its airbags were deploying inadvertently, forcing a recall of more than 850,000 Cavaliers and Sunfires.

Incidentally, California is the only jurisdiction where EDR data cannot be downloaded unless the car owner agrees or a court order is issued.

The TREAD Act (2000)

Angered by the Ford/Firestone tire scandal, where it was shown both companies hid warranty claims data and Ford carried out a secret warranty campaign to pay off claimants in Venezuela, the U.S. Congress passed the Transportation Recall Enhancement, Accountability, and Documentation (TREAD) Act in November 2000. The Act came into full force in 2004 and forces additional disclosure to NHTSA by automakers and equipment manufacturers. They must report, on a quarterly basis, incidents involving death or injury, the aggregate number of property damage claims, warranty claims, consumer complaints, and field reports, and provide copies of internal field reports generated within the manufacturer's system.

Three Steps to a Settlement

Step 1: Informal negotiations

If your vehicle was misrepresented, has major defects, or wasn't properly repaired under warranty, the first thing you should do is give the seller (the dealer and automaker or a private party) a written summary (by registered mail or fax) of the outstanding problems and stipulate a time period in which they will need to be corrected or your money will be refunded. Keep a copy for yourself, along with all your repair records. Be sure to check all of the sales and warranty documents you were given to see if they conform to provincial laws. Any errors, omissions, or violations can be used to get a settlement with the dealer in lieu of making a formal complaint.

At the beginning, try to work things out informally and, in your attempt to reach a settlement, keep in mind the cardinal rule: Ask only for what is fair and don't try to make anyone look bad.

Speak in a calm, polite manner and try to avoid polarizing the issue. Talk about how "we can work together" on the problem. Let a compromise slowly emerge—don't come in with a hard-line set of demands. Don't demand the settlement offer in writing, but make sure that you're accompanied by a friend or relative who can confirm the offer in court if it isn't honoured. Be prepared to act upon the offer without delay so your hesitancy won't be blamed for its withdrawal.

Dealer/service manager

Service managers have more power than you may have realized. They make the first determination of what work is covered under warranty or through post-warranty "goodwill" programs and are directly responsible to the dealer and manufacturer for that decision (dealers hate manufacturer audits that force them to pay back questionable warranty decisions). Service managers are paid to save the dealer and automaker money and to mollify irate clients—almost an impossible balancing act. Nevertheless, when a service manager agrees to extend warranty coverage, it's because you've raised solid issues that neither the dealer nor automaker can ignore. All the more reason to present your argument in a confident, forthright manner with your vehicle's service history and *Lemon-Aid*'s "How Long Should Parts/Repairs Last?" chart. Also bring as many technical service bulletins and owner complaint printouts as you can find, from websites like NHTSA's. It's not important that they apply directly to your problem; they establish parameters for giving out after-warranty assistance or "goodwill."

Don't use your salesperson as a runner, since the sales staff are generally quite distant from the service staff and usually have less pull than you do. If the service manager can't or won't set things right, your next step is to convene a mini-summit with the service manager, the dealership principal, and the automaker's rep. By getting the automaker involved, you run less risk of having the dealer fob you off on the manufacturer and you can often get an agreement where the seller and automaker pay two-thirds of the repair cost.

Independent dealers and dealers who sell a brand of used vehicle that they don't sell new give you less latitude. You have to make the case that the vehicle's defects were present at the time of purchase or should have been known to the seller, or that the vehicle doesn't conform to the representations made when it was purchased. Emphasize that you intend to use the courts if necessary to obtain a refund—most independent sellers would rather settle than risk a lawsuit with all the attendant publicity. An independent estimate of the vehicle's defects and cost of repairs is essential if you want to convince the seller that you're serious in your claim and stand a good chance of winning your case in court. Come prepared with an estimated cost of repairs to challenge the dealer who agrees to pay half the repair costs and then jacks up the costs 100 percent so that you wind up paying the whole shot.

Step 2: Sending a registered letter, fax, or email

This is the next step to take if your claim is refused. Send the dealer and manufacturer a polite registered letter or fax that asks for compensation for repairs that have been done or need to be done; insurance costs while the vehicle is being repaired; towing charges; supplementary transportation costs like taxis and rented cars; and damages for inconvenience.

Specify 5 days (but allow 10) for either party to respond. If no satisfactory offer is made, file suit in small claims court. Make the manufacturer a party to the lawsuit, especially if the emissions warranty, a secret warranty extension, a safety-recall campaign, or extensive chassis rusting is involved.

**Used Vehicle Complaint Letter/Fax/Email
Without Prejudice**

Date: _____
Name: _____

Please be advised that I am dissatisfied with my used vehicle, a (state model), for the following reasons:

1. _____
2. _____
3. _____
4. _____
5. _____

In compliance with the provincial consumer protection laws and the "implied warranty" set down by the Supreme Court of Canada in *Donoghue v. Stevenson, Wharton v. GM,* and *Sharman v. Ford Canada,*

➤

I hereby request that these defects be repaired without charge. This vehicle has not been reasonably durable and is, therefore, not as represented to me.

Should you fail to repair these defects in a satisfactory manner and within a reasonable period of time, I shall get an estimate of the repairs from an independent source and claim them in court, without further delay. I also reserve my right to claim up to $1 million for punitive damages, pursuant to the Supreme Court of Canada's February 22, 2002, ruling in *Whiten v. Pilot*.

I have dealt with your company because of its honesty, competence, and sincere regard for its clients. I am sure that my case is the exception and not the rule.

A positive response within the next five (5) days would be appreciated.

Sincerely,

Secret Warranty Claim Letter/Fax/Email
Without Prejudice

Date: _____
Name: _____

Please be advised that I am dissatisfied with my vehicle, a _____, bought from you on _____.
It has had the following recurring problems that I believe are factory-related defects, as confirmed by internal service bulletins sent to dealers, and are covered by your "goodwill" policies:

1. _____
2. _____
3. _____

If your "goodwill" program has ended, I ask that my claim be accepted nevertheless, inasmuch as I was never informed of your policy while it was in effect and should not be penalized for not knowing it existed.

I hereby formally put you on notice under federal and provincial consumer protection statutes that your refusal to apply this extended warranty coverage in my case would be an unfair warranty practice within the purview of the above-cited laws.

Your actions also violate the "implied warranty" set down by the Supreme Court of Canada (*Donoghue v. Stevenson* and *Longpre v.*

St. Jacques Automobile) and repeatedly reaffirmed by provincial consumer protection laws (*Lowe v. Chrysler, Dufour v. Ford du Canada*, and *Frank v. GM*).

I have enclosed several estimates (my bill) showing that this problem is factory related and will (has) cost $_____ to correct. I would appreciate your refunding me the estimated (paid) amount, failing which, I reserve the right to have the repair done elsewhere and claim reimbursement in court without further delay. I also reserve the right to claim up to $1 million for punitive damages, pursuant to the Supreme Court of Canada's February 22, 2002, ruling in *Whiten v. Pilot*.

A positive response within the next five (5) days would be appreciated.

Sincerely,

(signed with telephone number, fax number, or email address)

Step 3: Mediation and arbitration

If the formality of a courtroom puts you off or you're not sure that your claim is all that solid and don't want to pay legal costs to find out, consider using mediation or arbitration. These services are sponsored by the Better Business Bureau, Automobile Protection Association, Canadian Automobile Association, the Canadian Automobile Manufacturers Vehicle Arbitration Program at *camvap.ca* (if you bought your vehicle new), small claims court (mediation is often a prerequisite to going to trial), and consumer mediation services set up by provincial and territorial governments.

CAMVAP arbitration hearings often result in a vehicle being repaired or replaced, as this Toronto owner of a 2001 Nissan Maxima discovered:

> At 10,000 km, my steering wheel would shimmy when the brakes were applied. I brought the car in to the dealership and they turned the rotors. The problem went away only to reappear at 18,000 km. At this time the dealership replaced the rotors. At 30,000 km, the problem returned.
>
> Once again the rotors were turned down and the problem went away. At 36,000 km, the problem returned for the fourth time. This time around, Nissan Canada refused to fix the brakes. I got nowhere with Nissan Canada Customer Service. They were extremely rude and confrontational with me.
>
> I demanded CAMVAP arbitration.
>
> The result of the hearing was that Nissan had to reimburse my costs for brake repairs. They have also been given one last chance to fix the problem (they will replace pads and rotors). If, within the next 20,000 km, the brake problem reappears, upon examination of the car

by my mechanic (indicating the car has not been driven hard), Nissan will have to buy the car back at the odometer reading at the hearing. We had to come to the agreement at the hearing since buybacks can not be ordered after 60,000 km on the car. As we had 49,000 km on the car at the hearing, the car will likely go over 60,000 km before any problem would first appear.

Getting outside help

Don't lose your case due to poor preparation. Ask government or independent consumer protection agencies to evaluate how well you're prepared before going to your first hearing. Also, use the Internet to ferret out additional facts and gather support (*www.lemonaidcars.com* is a good place to start).

Online services/Internet/websites

America Online is a good online service provider with active consumer forums that use experts to answer consumer queries and to provide legal and technical advice. The Internet offers the same information using a worldwide database. If you or someone you know is able to create a website, you might consider using this site to attract attention to your plight and arm yourself for arbitration or court. You may wish to follow the example of some existing websites I've listed in Appendix I.

Classified ads and television exposés

Put an ad in the local paper describing your plight and ask for data from others who may have experienced a problem similar to your own. This alerts others to the potential problem, helps build a base for a class action or group meeting with the automaker, and puts pressure on the local dealer and manufacturer to settle. Sometimes the paper's news desk will assign someone to cover your story after your ad is published.

Television producers and their researchers need articulate consumers with issues that are easily filmed and understood. If you want media coverage, you must summarize your complaint and have visual aids that will hold the viewer's interest. Paint delamination? Show your car. Bought a lemon car? Show your bills along with the car. Holding a demonstration? Make it a "lemon" parade: Target one of the largest dealers; give your group a nifty name, like CLOG or FFLOG (Chrysler Lemon Owners Group or Ford Focus Lemon Owners Group); and make sure the vehicles are decorated with signs and lemons.

In tailoring your story for TV, keep in mind that the viewers should be able to understand the issues with the sound turned off.

Federal and provincial consumer affairs

The wind left the sails of the consumer movement in the late-'80s, leaving consumer agencies understaffed and ignored. This has created a passive mindset among many staffers, who are tired of getting their heads kicked in by businesses, deadwood bosses, and budget-cutters.

Consumer affairs offices can still help with investigation, mediation, and some litigation. Strong and effective consumer protection legislation still exists in most of the provinces, and resourceful consumers can use these laws in conjunction with media coverage to prod provincial consumer affairs offices into action. Furthermore, provincial bureaucrats aren't as well shielded from criticism as their federal counterparts. A call to your MPP or MLA, or to their executive assistant, can often get things rolling.

Federal consumer protection is a government-created PR myth. Don't expect the staffers in the reorganized Office of Consumer Affairs to be very helpful—they've been de-fanged and de-gummed through budget cuts and a succession of ineffective ministers. Although the beefed-up Competition Act has some bite with regards to misleading advertising and a number of other illegal business practices, the federal government has been more reactive than proactive in applying the law.

Nevertheless, when used creatively, the revised Competition Act can be a powerful tool for forcing a formal government investigation and prosecution, attracting media attention, and obtaining individual and collective compensation. Industry Canada has provided a user-friendly complaint form at *strategis.ic.gc.ca/sc_mrksv/competit/complaint/form.html* where consumers can easily lodge misleading advertising or price-fixing complaints under the Competition Act statutes. An online complaint sent to the above address above made Toyota cease its ACCESS price-fixing practices (though rumour has it, the company's dealers may try it on their own).

Invest in protest

You can have fun and put additional pressure on a seller or garage by putting a lemon sign on your car and parking it in front of the dealer or garage; creating a "lemon" website; or forming a self-help group like those mentioned earlier.

Use your website to gather data from others who may have experienced a problem similar to your own. As with placing a newspaper ad, this can help you set the foundation for a meeting with the automaker or even a class action, and pressures the dealer or manufacturer to settle. Websites are often the targets of news stories, so yours may be picked up by the media.

One other piece of advice from this consumer advocate with hundreds of picketing and mass demonstrations under his belt over the past 33 years: keep a sense of humour and never break off negotiations.

Finally, don't be scared off by threats that it's illegal to criticize a product or company. Unions, environmentalists, and consumer groups do it regularly (informational picketing) and the Supreme Court of Canada in *R. v. Guinard* reaffirmed this right in February 2002. In that judgment, an insured posted a sign on his barn claiming the Commerce Insurance Company was unfairly refusing his claim. The municipality of St-Hyacinthe told him to take the sign down. He refused, maintaining that he had the right to state his opinion. The Supreme Court agreed.

This judgment means that consumer protests, signs, and websites that criticize the actions of corporations cannot be shut up or taken down simply because they say unpleasant things.

Fighting Back

Sudden acceleration, chronic stalling, and ABS and airbag failures

Incidents of sudden acceleration or chronic stalling are quite common. However, they are very difficult to diagnose and are treated quite differently by federal safety agencies.

Sudden acceleration is considered to be a safety-related problem—stalling isn't. Never mind that a vehicle's sudden loss of power on a busy highway puts everyone's lives at risk (2001–03 VW and Audi ignition coil failures). The same problem exists with engine and transmission powertrain failures, which are only occasionally considered to be safety related. ABS and airbag failures are universally considered to be life-threatening defects. If your vehicle manifests any of these conditions, here's what you need to do:

1. Get independent witnesses to the fact that the problem exists. This includes verification by an independent mechanic, passenger accounts, downloaded data from your vehicle's data recorder and lots of Internet browsing using *www.lemonaidcars.com* and Google's browser as your primary tools. Notify the dealer/manufacturer by fax, email, or registered letter that you consider the problem to be a factory-induced, safety-related defect. Make sure you address your correspondence to the manufacturer's product liability or legal affairs department. At the dealership's service bay, make sure that every work order clearly states the problem, as well as the number of previous attempts to fix it. (This should result in you having a few complaint letters and a handful of work orders, confirming that this is an ongoing deficiency.) If the dealer won't give you a copy of the work order because the work is a warranty claim, ask for a copy of the order number "in case your estate wishes to file a claim, pursuant to an accident." (This will get the service manager's attention.) Leaving this kind of "paper trail" is crucial for any claim you may have later on, because it shows your fear and persistence, and clearly indicates that the dealer and manufacturer had ample time to correct the defect. In California, for example, the state's recently revamped Lemon Law requires that car owners clearly show they made two attempts to have a safety defect corrected (other states require three or four attempts) before the court will grant a refund, order the car taken back, or impose punitive damages.

2. Note on the work order that you expect the problem to be diagnosed and corrected under the emissions warranty or a "goodwill" program. It also wouldn't hurt to add the phrase on the work order or in your claim letters that any deaths, injuries, or damage caused by the defect will be the dealer's and manufacturer's responsibility since this work order (or letter, fax, or email) constitutes you putting them on "formal notice."

3. If the dealer does the necessary repairs at little or no cost to you, send a follow-up confirmation that you appreciate the assistance. Also, emphasize that you'll be back if the problem reappears, even if the warranty has expired, because the repair renews your warranty rights applicable to that

defect. In other words, the warranty clock is set back to its original position. Understand that you won't likely get a copy of the repair bill, either, because dealers don't like to admit that there was a serious defect present. Keep in mind, however, that you can get your complete vehicle file from the dealer and manufacturer by issuing a subpoena (cost: about $25), if the case goes to small claims or a higher court. This request has produced many out-of-court settlements when the internal documents show extensive work was carried out to correct the problem.

4. If the problem persists, send a letter, fax, or email to the dealer and manufacturer saying so, look for ALLDATA service bulletins to confirm your vehicle's defects are factory related, and call Transport Canada or NHTSA or log onto NHTSA's website to report the failure. Also, call the Nader-founded Center for Auto Safety in Washington, D.C. (202-328-7700) for a lawyer referral and an information sheet covering the problem. For tire complaints, also notify researchers at the Strategic Safety website (*www.strategicsafety.com*).

5. Now come two crucial questions: repair the defect now or later; use the dealer or an independent? Generally it's smart to use an independent garage if you know the dealer isn't pushing for free corrective repairs from the manufacturer; weeks or months have passed without any resolution of your claim; the dealer keeps repeating it's a maintenance item; and you know an independent mechanic who will give you a detailed work order showing the defect is factory related and not due to poor maintenance. Don't mention that a court case may ensue, since this will scare the dickens out of your only independent witness. An added bonus is that the repair charges will be about half of what a dealer would demand. Incidentally, if the automaker later denies warranty "goodwill" because you used an independent repairer, use the argument that the defect's safety implications required emergency repairs, carried out by whomever could see you first.

6. Dashboard-mounted warning lights usually come on prior to airbags suddenly deploying, ABS brakes failing, or engine glitches causing the vehicle to stall out. (Sudden acceleration usually occurs without warning.) Automakers consider these lights to be critical safety warnings and generally advise drivers to *immediately* have the vehicle serviced to correct the problem (advice found in the owner's manual) when any of the above lights come on. This bolsters the argument that your life was threatened, emergency repairs were required, and your request for another vehicle or a complete refund isn't out of line.

7. Sudden acceleration can have multiple causes, isn't easy to duplicate, and is often blamed on the driver mistaking the accelerator for the brakes or failing to perform proper maintenance. Yet NHTSA data shows that with the 1992–2000 Explorer, for example, a faulty cruise control or PCV valve and poorly mounted pedals are the most likely causes of the Explorer's sudden acceleration. So how do you satisfy the burden of proof showing the problem exists and is the automaker's responsibility? Use the legal doctrine called "the balance of probabilities" by eliminating all of the possible dodges the dealer or manufacturer may employ. Show that

proper maintenance has been carried out, you're a safe driver, and the incident occurs frequently and without warning.

8. If any of the above defects causes an accident, the airbag fails to deploy, or you're injured by its deployment, ask your insurance company to have the vehicle towed to a neutral location and clearly state that neither the dealer nor automaker should touch the vehicle until your insurance company and Transport Canada have completed their investigation. Also, get as many witnesses as possible and immediately go to the hospital for a check-up, even if you're feeling okay. You may be injured and not know it because the adrenalin coursing through your veins is masking your injuries. Plus, a hospital exam will easily confirm that your injuries are accident related, which is essential in court or for future settlement negotiations.

9. Peruse NHTSA's online accident database to find reports of other accidents caused by the same failure.

10. Don't let your insurance company settle the case if you're sure the accident was caused by a mechanical failure. Even if an engineering analysis fails to directly implicate the manufacturer or dealer, you can always plead the aforementioned balance of probabilities. If the insurance company settles, your insurance premiums will probably be increased.

Defective tires

Tire companies are far easier to deal with than automobile manufacturers because, under the legal doctrine of *res ipsa loquitor* (liability is shown by the failure), tires aren't supposed to fail. It's for this reason that tire companies try to avoid liability by imputing blame to someone or something else, like punctures, impact damage, overloading, over-inflating, or under-inflating. If you have a premature tire failure, consider the 10 steps outlined previously, plus include the following:

1. Access NHTSA and Strategic Safety websites (see Appendix I) for current data on which tires are failure-prone and which companies are under investigation, conducting recalls, or carrying out "silent recalls."

2. Keep the tire. If the tiremaker says an analysis must be done, permit only a portion of the tire to be taken away.

3. Plead the balance of probabilities, using friends and family to refute the tire company's contention that you caused the failure.

4. Ask for damages that are adequate for the replacement of all the tires on your vehicle, including mounting costs.

5. Include in your damage claim any repairs needed to fix body damage caused by the tire's failure.

Paint and body defects

The following settlement advice applies mainly to paint defects, but you can use these tips for any other vehicle defect that you believe is the automaker's or dealer's responsibility. If you're not sure that the problem is a factory-related deficiency or a maintenance item, have it checked out by an independent garage or get a technical service bulletin summary for your vehicle. The summary may include specific bulletins relating to the diagnosis, correction, and ordering of upgraded parts needed to fix your problem.

1. If you know your vehicle's paint problem is factory related, take your vehicle to the dealer and ask for a written, signed estimate. When you're handed the estimate, ask if the paint job can be covered by some "goodwill" assistance. (Ford's euphemism for this secret warranty is "Owner Notification Program" or "Owner Dialogue Program," GM's term is "Special Policy," and Chrysler simply calls it an "Owner Satisfaction Notice." Don't use the term "secret warranty" yet; you'll just make everyone angry and evasive.)

2. Your request will probably be met with a refusal, an offer to repaint the vehicle for half the cost, or (if you're lucky) an agreement to repaint the vehicle free of charge. If you accept half-cost, make sure that it's based on the original estimate you have in hand, since some dealers jack up their estimates so that your 50 percent is really 100 percent of the true cost.

3. If the dealer/automaker has already refused your claim and the repair hasn't been done yet, get an additional estimate from an independent garage that shows the problem is factory related.

4. Again, if the repair has yet to be done, mail or fax a registered claim to the automaker (send a copy to the dealer), claiming the average of both estimates. If the repair has been done at your expense, mail or fax a registered claim with a copy of your bill.

5. If you don't receive a satisfactory response within a week, deposit a copy of the estimate or paid bill and claim letter/fax before the small claims court and await a trial date. This means that the automaker/dealer will have to appear, no lawyer is required, and costs should be minimal (under $100). Usually, an informal pretrial mediation hearing with the two parties and a court clerk will be scheduled in a few months, followed by a trial a few weeks later (the time varies among different regions). Most cases are settled at the mediation stage.

Things that you can do to help your case: collect photographs, maintenance work orders, previous work orders dealing with your problem, and technical service bulletins; and speak to an independent expert (the garage or body shop that did the estimate or repair is best, but you can also use a local teacher who teaches automotive repair). Remember, service bulletins can be helpful, but they aren't critical to a successful claim.

Other situations

• If the vehicle has just been repainted but the dealer says that "goodwill" coverage was denied by the automaker, pay for the repair with a certified cheque and write "under protest" on the cheque. Remember, though, if the dealer does the repair, you won't have an independent expert who can affirm that the problem was factory related or that it was a result of premature wearout. Plus, the dealer can say that you or the environment caused the paint problem. In these cases, technical service bulletins can make or break your case.

- If the dealer/automaker offers a partial repair or refund, take it. Then sue for the rest. Remember, if a partial repair has been done under warranty, it counts as an admission of responsibility, no matter what "goodwill" euphemism is used. Also, the repaired component/body panel should be just as durable as if it were new. Hence, the clock starts ticking from the beginning until you reach the original warranty parameter—again, no matter what the dealer's repair warranty limit says.
- It's a lot easier to get the automaker to pay to replace a defective part than it is to be compensated for a missed day of work or a ruined vacation. Manufacturers hate to pay for consequential expenses apart from towing bills, because they can't control the amount of the refund. Fortunately, Canadian courts have taken the position that all expenses (damages) flowing from a problem covered by a warranty or service bulletin are the manufacturer's or dealer's responsibility under negligence and product liability provisions found in provincial consumer protection statutes, common law jurisprudence, Quebec civil law, and federal consumer protection legislation. Nevertheless, don't risk a fair settlement for some outlandish claim of "emotional distress," "pain and suffering," etc. If you have invoices to prove actual consequential damages, then use them. If not, don't be greedy.

Very seldom do automakers contest these paint claims before small claims court, opting instead to settle once the court claim is bounced from their customer relations people to their legal affairs department. At that time, you'll probably be offered an out-of-court settlement for 50–75 percent of your claim.

Stand fast and make reference to the service bulletins you intend to subpoena in order to publicly contest in court the unfair nature of this "secret warranty" program. (Automaker lawyers cringe at the idea of trying to explain why consumers aren't made aware of these bulletins.) One hundred percent restitution will probably follow.

Three good examples of favourable paint judgments are *Shields v. General Motors of Canada, Bentley v. Dave Wheaton Pontiac Buick GMC Ltd. and General Motors of Canada,* and, the most recent, *Maureen Frank v. General Motors of Canada Limited.*

Shields v. General Motors of Canada, No. 1398/96, Ontario Court (General Division), Oshawa Small Claims Court, 33 King Street West, Oshawa, Ontario L1H 1A1, July 24, 1997, Robert Zochodne, Deputy Judge. The owner of a 1991 Pontiac Grand Prix purchased the vehicle used with over 100,000 km on its odometer. Commencing in 1995, the paint began to bubble and then flake and eventually peel off. Deputy Judge Robert Zochodne awarded the plaintiff $1,205.72 and struck down every one of GM's environmental/acid rain/UV rays arguments. Other important aspects of this 12-page judgment that GM did not appeal:

1. The judge admitted many of the technical service bulletins referred to in *Lemon-Aid* as proof of GM's negligence.

2. Although the vehicle had 156,000 km when the case went to court, GM still offered to pay 50 percent of the paint repairs if the plaintiff dropped his suit.
3. Deputy Judge Zochodne ruled that the failure to protect the paint from the damaging effects of UV rays is akin to engineering a car that won't start in cold weather. In essence, vehicles must be built to withstand the rigours of the environment.
4. Here's an interesting twist: the original warranty covered defects that were present at the time it was in effect. The judge, taking statements found in the GM technical service bulletins, ruled the UV problem was factory related, and therefore it existed during the warranty period and thereby represented a latent defect that appeared once the warranty expired.
5. The subsequent purchaser was not prevented from making the warranty claim, even though the warranty had long since expired from a time and mileage standpoint and he was the second owner.

Bentley v. Dave Wheaton Pontiac Buick GMC Ltd. and General Motors of Canada, Victoria Registry No. 24779, British Columbia Small Claims Court, December 1, 1998, Judge Higinbotham. This small claims judgment builds upon the Ontario *Shields v. General Motors of Canada* decision and cites other jurisprudence as to how long paint should last on a car. If you're wondering why Ford and Chrysler haven't been hit by similar judgments, remember that they usually settle.

Maureen Frank v. General Motors of Canada Limited, No. SC#12 (2001), Saskatchewan Provincial Court, Saskatoon, Saskatchewan, October 17, 2001, Provincial Court Judge H.G. Dirauf.

On June 23, 1997, the Plaintiff bought a 1996 Chevrolet Corsica from a General Motors dealership. At the time the odometer showed 33,172 km. The vehicle still had some factory warranty. The car had been a lease car and had no previous accidents.

During June of 2000, the Plaintiff noticed that some of the paint was peeling off from the car and she took it to a General Motors dealership in Saskatoon and to the General Motors dealership in North Battleford where she purchased the car. While there were some discussions with the GM dealership about the peeling paint, nothing came of it and the Plaintiff now brings this action claiming the cost of a new paint job.

During 1999, the Plaintiff was involved in a minor collision causing damage to the left rear door. This damage was repaired. During this repair some scratches to the left front door previously done by vandals were also repaired.

The Plaintiff's witness, Frank Nemeth, is a qualified auto body repairman with some 26 years of experience. He testified that the peeling paint was a factory defect and that it was necessary to completely strip the car and repaint it. He diagnosed the cause of the peeling paint as a separation of the primer surface or colour coat from the electrocoat primer. In his opinion no primer surfacer was applied at all. He testified that once the peeling starts, it will continue. He has seen this problem on General Motors vehicles. The defect is called delamination.

Mr. Nemeth stated that a paint job should last at least 10 years. In my opinion most people in Saskatchewan grow up with cars and are familiar with cars. I think it is common knowledge that the original paint on cars normally lasts in excess of 15 years and that rust becomes a problem before the paint fails. In any event, paint peeling off, as it did on the Plaintiff's vehicle, is not common. I find that the paint on a new car put on by the factory should last at least 15 years.

General Motors acknowledge that the Plaintiff had a General Motors Warranty of 36 months or 60,000 km, whichever comes first. The Plaintiff was not given a GM booklet at the time she bought the car. She knew of the 36 months but was unaware of the 60,000 km. At the time the Plaintiff noticed the delamination, a service invoice D-2 shows that on June 18, 1999 the odometer showed 72,504 km.

Invoice P-6 shows that on August 4, 2000, the odometer reading was 92,043 km. It is therefore clear that in June 2000, when the Plaintiff noticed the delamination problem, her car had exceeded the 60,000 km warranty limit. The warranty booklet was not placed into evidence and I do not have the benefit of the exact wording of the warranty. I do not know if the 60,000 km limit applies to the whole car or only to the moving parts. On the evidence presented, I find the warranty coverage for the delamination has expired. However, the Consumer Protection Act also gives the Plaintiff a warranty that the paint is of acceptable quality and that it is durable for a reasonable period: Sections 48 (d), 48 (g), 50 (2).

It is clear from the evidence of Frank Nemeth (independent body shop manager) that the delamination is a factory defect. His evidence was not seriously challenged. I find that the factory paint should not suffer a delamination defect for at least 15 years and that this factory defect breached the warranty that the paint was of acceptable quality and was durable for a reasonable period of time.

I accept the testimony of Frank Nemeth that the whole car needs to be stripped and painted.

The Defendant did not call any witnesses. (I note section 51 (1) of the Consumer Protection Act with respect to the onus of proof.)

Counsel for the defendant submitted that any award I should make should be reduced because of betterment. While betterment was discussed at trial, I am not persuaded that any award for damages should be reduced in this case. See *Scheeler v. C. M. Holdings Inc.* (1997) 183 Sask R (Q.B.) and *Nan v. Black Pine Manufacturing Ltd.* (1991) 5WWR172 (B.C.C.A.). I have reviewed *Pitch Snyder, Damages for Breach of Contract*, 2nd edition, pages 2-14.3 to 2-22 and read

Betterment Before Canadian Common Law Courts by J. Berryman, (1993) 72 Canadian Bar Review.

It is clear that the onus to show and calculate any betterment is on the Defendant. He has not done so. In any event, I doubt that any betterment in this case would be significant.

The repair cost given by Mr. Nemeth of Superior Auto Body Ltd., Exhibit P-7 shows the repair cost (including minor dents) to be $3,679.90. I reduce the sum by $267.52 for the repair cost of the dents.

There will be judgment for the Plaintiff in the amount of $3,412.38 plus costs of $81.29.

Some of the important aspects of the *Frank* judgment are:

1. The judge accepted that the automaker was responsible, even though the car was bought used. The subsequent purchaser was not prevented from making the warranty claim, even though the warranty had long since expired from a time and mileage standpoint and she was the second owner.
2. The judge stressed that the provincial warranty can kick in anytime the automaker's warranty has expired or isn't applied.
3. By awarding full compensation to the plaintiff, the judge didn't feel there was a significant "betterment" or improvement added to the car that would warrant reducing the amount of the award.
4. The judge decided that the paint delamination was a factory defect.
5. The judge also concluded that without this factory defect, a paint job should last up to 15 years.
6. GM offered to pay $700 of the paint repairs if the plaintiff dropped the suit; the judge awarded five times that amount.
7. Maureen Frank won this case despite having to confront GM lawyer Ken Ready, who has argued other paint cases for GM and Chrysler.

Other paint/rust cases

Martin v. Honda Canada Inc., March 17, 1986, Ontario Small Claims Court (Scarborough), Judge Sigurdson. The original owner of a 1981 Honda Civic sought compensation for the premature "bubbling, pitting, cracking of the paint and rusting of the Civic after five years of ownership." Judge Sigurdson agreed and ordered Honda to pay the owner $1,163.95.

Thauberger v. Simon Fraser Sales and Mazda Motors, 3 B.C.L.R., 193. This Mazda owner sued for damages caused by the premature rusting of his 1977 Mazda GLC. The court awarded him $1,000. Thauberger had previously sued General Motors for a prematurely rusted Blazer truck and was also awarded $1,000 in the same court. Both judges ruled that the defects could not be excluded from the automaker's expressed warranty or from the implied warranty granted by ss. 20, 20(b) of the B.C. Sale of Goods Act.

Whittaker v. Ford Motor Company (1979), 24 O.R. (2d), 344. A new Ford developed serious corrosion problems in spite of having been rustproofed by the dealer. The court ruled that the dealer, not Ford, was liable for the damage for having sold the rustproofing product at the time of purchase. This is an important judgment to use when a rustproofer or paint protector goes out of business or refuses to pay a claim, since the decision holds the dealer jointly responsible.

See also:

- *Danson v. Chateau Ford* (1976) C.P., Quebec Small Claims Court, No. 32-00001898-757, Judge Lande
- *Doyle v. Vital Automotive Systems*, May 16, 1977, Ontario Small Claims Court (Toronto), Judge Turner
- *Lacroix v. Ford*, April 1980, Ontario Small Claims Court (Toronto), Judge Tierney
- *Marinovich v. Riverside Chrysler*, April 1, 1987, District Court of Ontario, No. 1030/85, Judge Stortini

Going to Court

When to sue

If the seller you've been negotiating with agrees to make things right, give him or her a deadline and then have an independent garage check the repairs. If no offer is made within 10 working days, file suit in court. Make the manufacturer a party to the lawsuit only if the original, unexpired warranty was transferred to you; your claim falls under the emissions warranty, a TSB, a secret warranty extension, or a safety recall campaign; or there is extensive chassis rusting due to poor engineering.

Choosing the right court

You must decide what remedy to pursue; that is, whether you want a partial refund or a cancellation of the sale. To determine the refund amount, add the estimated cost of repairing existing mechanical defects to the cost of prior repairs. Don't exaggerate your losses or claim for repairs that are considered routine maintenance.

A suit for cancellation of sale involves practical problems. The court requires that the vehicle be "tendered" or taken back to the seller at the time the lawsuit is filed. This means that you are without transportation for as long as the case continues, unless you purchase another vehicle in the interim. If you lose the case, you must then take back the old vehicle and pay storage fees. You could go from having no vehicle to having two, one of which is a clunker.

Generally, if the cost of repairs or the sales contract amount falls within the small claims court limit (discussed later), file the case there to keep costs to a minimum and get a speedy hearing. You will need to know the correct legal name and representatives of the other parties. Small claims court judgments aren't easily appealed, lawyers aren't necessary, filing fees are minimal (about $125), and cases are usually heard within a few months.

Mr. Edmonston, I emailed you earlier in the year seeking help on my small claims case against Ford. I'm happy to report that I won my case and received a $1,900 settlement check from Ford in the mail yesterday! As you may recall I have a 1991 Explorer that has a significant paint peel problem.

I followed all the steps recommended by your website—ultimately I ended up in small claims court. Ford had indicated in court documents that they were going to send a representative to the hearing, but nobody showed. The judge made a quick ruling in my favour and I was out the door. I didn't even get a chance to show the load of material I had brought to make my case.

Mark G.

Watch what you ask for. If you ask for more than the small claims court limit, you'll have to go to a higher court—where costs quickly add up and delays of a few years or more are commonplace.

Small claims courts

Small claims courts are scary to most businesses. Not because they can issue million-dollar judgments, or force litigants to spend millions in legal fees (they can't), but because they can award sizeable sums to small plaintiffs and make jurisprudence that other judges on the same bench are likely to follow.

Interestingly, small claims court is quickly becoming a misnomer, now that Alberta allows claims of up to a limit of $25,000 and most other provinces permit $10,000 claims.

There are small claims courts in most counties of every province, and you can make a claim in the county where the problem happened or where the defendant lives and conducts business. The first step is to make sure that your claim doesn't exceed the dollar limit of the court. (The limits differ from province to province.) Then, you should go to the small claims court office and ask for a claim form. Instructions on how to fill it out accompany the form. Remember, you must identify the defendant correctly. It's a practice of some dishonest firms to change a company's name to escape liability; for example, it would be impossible to sue Joe's Garage (1999) if your contract is with Joe's Garage Inc. (1984).

At this point, it would be a smart idea to hire a lawyer or a paralegal for a brief walk-through of small claims procedures to ensure that you've prepared your case properly and that you know what objections will likely be raised by the other side. If you'd like a lawyer to do all the work for you, there are a number of law firms around the country that specialize in small claims litigation. Small claims doesn't means small legal fees, however. In Toronto, some law offices charge a flat fee of $1,000 for the basic small claims lawsuit and trial.

Remember that you're entitled to bring to court any evidence relevant to your case, including written documents, such as a bill of sale or receipt, contract, or letter. If your car has developed severe rust problems, bring a photograph (signed and dated by the photographer) to court. You may also have witnesses testify in court. It's important to discuss a witness's testimony prior to the court date. If a witness can't attend the court date, he or she can write a report and sign it for representation in court. This situation usually applies to an expert witness, such as an independent mechanic who has evaluated your car's problems.

If you lose your case in spite of all your preparation and research, some small claims court statutes allow cases to be retried, at a nominal cost, in exceptional circumstances. If a new witness has come forward, additional evidence has been discovered, or key documents (that were previously not available) have become accessible, apply for a retrial. In Ontario, this little-known provision is Rule 18.4 (1).B.

Key Court Decisions

The following Canadian and U.S. lawsuits and judgments cover typical problems that are likely to arise. Use them as leverage when negotiating a settlement or as a reference should your claim go to trial. Legal principles applying to Canadian and American law are similar; however, Quebec court decisions may be based on legal principles that don't apply outside that province.

Additional court judgments can be found in the legal reference section of your city's main public library or at a nearby university law library. Ask the librarian for help in choosing the legal phrases that best describe your claim.

Two useful Internet sites for legal research are LexisNexis (*www.lexis-nexis.com*) and Findlaw (*www.findlaw.com*). Their main drawback, though, is you may need to subscribe or use a lawyer's subscription to access jurisprudence and other areas of the sites.

An excellent reference book that will give you plenty of tips on filing, pleading and collecting your judgment is Judge Marvin Zuker's *Ontario Small Claims Court Practice 2002–2003*, Carswell, 2002. Judge Zuker's book is easily understood by non-lawyers and uses court decisions from across Canada to help you plead your case successfully in almost any Canadian court.

Product Liability

Almost three decades ago, the Supreme Court of Canada in *Kravitz v. GM* clearly affirmed that automakers and their dealers are jointly liable for the replacement or repair of a vehicle if independent testimony shows it is afflicted by factory-related defects that compromise its safety or performance. The existence of a secret warranty extension or technical service bulletins also help prove that the vehicle's problems are the automaker's responsibility. For example, in *Lowe v. Fairview Chrysler* (see pages 86–87) technical service bulletins were instrumental in showing an Ontario small claims court judge that Chrysler had a history of automatic transmission failures since 1989!

In addition to replacing or repairing the vehicle, an automaker can also be held responsible for any damages arising from the defect. This means that loss of wages, supplementary transportation costs, and damages for personal inconvenience can be awarded. However, in the States, product liability damage awards often exceed millions of dollars, while Canadian courts are far less generous.

Before settling any claim with GM or any other automaker, download the latest information from dissatisfied customers who've banded together and set up their own self-help websites. Follow the links at *www.lemonaidcars.com.*

Implied Warranty ("Reasonable" Durability)

This is that "other" warranty they never tell you about. It applies during and after the expiration of the manufacturer's or dealer's expressed or written warranty and gives you the assurance that a part or repair will last a "reasonable" period of time. What is reasonable depends in large part to benchmarks used in the industry, the price of the vehicle, and how it was driven and maintained. Look at the reasonable durability chart on pages 59–60 for some guidelines as to what you should expect.

Judges usually apply the implied or legal warranty when the manufacturer's expressed warranty has expired and the vehicle's manufacturing defects remain uncorrected. In the following decision, the implied warranty forced Ford to pay for a 1996 Windstar's engine failure (a common defect).

Dufour v. Ford Canada Ltd., April 10, 2001, Quebec Small Claims Court (Hull), No. 550-32-008335-009, Justice P. Chevalier. Ford was forced to reimburse the cost of engine head gasket repairs carried out on a 1996 Windstar 3.8L engine—a vehicle not covered by the automaker's Owner Notification Program, which cut off assistance after the '95 model year.

COUR DU QUÉBEC
Division petites créances

QUÉBEC
DISTRICT DE HULL

NO: 550-32-008335-009

Hull, le 10 avril 2001

SOUS LA PRESIDENCE DE:
L'HONORABLE PIERRE
CHEVALIER
Juge de la Cour du Québec

BASTIEN DUFOUR

Partie requérante,

-c.-

FORD DU CANADA LTÉE, 7800, route Transcanadienne à Pointe-Claire (Québec) H9H 1C6

Partie intimée

JUGEMENT

Les parties essentielles de la requête se lisent comme suit :

I am hereby claiming from Ford Canada expenses and collateral expenses incurred for the repair of the 3.8 litter engine of a Ford Windstar GL 1996, VIN 2FMDA5147TBA95586.

The said engine had to have the head gasket and thermostat replaced on 02 June 2000, after a total of 116,892 kms indicated on the vehicle odometer. This repair was deemed necessary by my hometown Ford dealership (Mont-Bleu Ford in Gatineau, Que.) after I observed inadequate performance of the interior heating system and abnormal engine coolant temperature indications, and after a leak down test performed by the Mont-Bleu Ford dealership.

I consider such a defect to be abnormal as components such as an engine should have a life expectancy of at least 160,000 kms of 7 years without major repairs such as head gasket repair or replacement.

2

I have enclosed a copy of my bill showing that this problem is factory related and has cost $1364.35 to correct; this amount includes the cost for the engine head gasket repair and appropriate provincial and federal sales taxes

L'ensemble de la preuve satisfait le Tribunal par prépondérance de preuve que la détérioration impliquée est survenue prématurément par rapport à un bien identique et que cette détérioration n'est pas due à un défaut d'entretien.

L'article 1729 C.c.Q. stipule qu'en cas de vente par un vendeur professionnel, l'existence d'un vice au moment de la vente est présumée, lorsque la détérioration du bien survient prématurément par rapport à des biens identiques. De plus, les intimés n'ont pas repoussé la présomption en établissant que le défaut serait dû à une mauvaise utilisation du bien par l'acheteur. Selon l'art. 1730, le fabricant est soumis à cette même garantie.

Vu les articles 1729 et 1730 du Code civile du Québec, le Tribunal fait droit à la réclamation et condamne la partie intimée à payer à la partie requérante la somme de 1 364,35 $ avec intérêts au taux légal de 5% depuis la requête, soit le 19 septembre 2000 et les frais de 72 $.

PIERRE CHEVALIER
Juge de la Cour du Québec

Use the above judgment as leverage in your negotiations to get compensation for premature engine or automatic transmission repairs involving any automaker. If you have to go to court, cite the decision in your filing.

Kravitz v. General Motors, January 1979, Supreme Court of Canada, I.R.C.S., No. 393. This owner of a new Oldsmobile was never able to have it properly repaired under warranty. When the warranty period was over, General Motors and the dealer refused to do further free work or to give him another vehicle. The presiding judge awarded the car owner damages and a refund of the purchase price. This Quebec precedent is based on articles 1522–1530 of the Quebec Civil Code (hidden defects), but it applies in common-law provinces as well. The Supreme Court ruled that both the dealer and the manufacturer can be held jointly or separately responsible and that the manufacturer's warranty does not negate the implied legal warranty of fitness.

Used-Vehicle Defects

Fissel v. Ideal Auto Sales Ltd. (1991), 91 Sask. R. 266. Shortly after the vehicle was purchased, the car's motor seized and the dealer refused to replace it, even though the car was returned on several occasions. The court ruled that the dealer had breached the statutory warranties in s. 11 (4) and (7) of the Consumer Products Warranties Act. The purchasers were entitled to cancel the sale and recover the full purchase price.

Friskin v. Chevrolet Oldsmobile, 72 D.L.R. (3d), 289. A Manitoba used-car buyer asked that his contract be cancelled because of a chronic stalling problem. The garage owner did his best to correct it. Despite the seller's good intentions, the Manitoba Consumer Protection Act allowed for cancellation.

Graves v. C&R Motors Ltd., April 8, 1980, British Columbia County Court, Judge Skipp. The plaintiff bought a used car on the condition that certain deficiencies be remedied. They never were, and he was promised a refund, but it never arrived. The plaintiff brought suit, claiming that the dealer's deceptive activities violated the provincial Trade Practices Act. The court agreed, concluding that a deceptive act that occurs before, during, or after the transaction can lead to the cancellation of the contract.

Hachey v. Galbraith Equipment Company (1991), 33 M.V.R. (2d) 242. The plaintiff bought a used truck from the dealer to use in hauling gravel. Shortly thereafter, the steering failed. The plaintiff's suit was successful because expert testimony showed that the truck wasn't roadworthy. The dealer was found liable for damages for being in breach of the implied condition of fitness for the purpose for which the truck was purchased, as set out in s. 15 (a) of the New Brunswick Sale of Goods Act.

Henzel v. Brussels Motors (1973), 1 O.R., 339 (C.C.). The dealer sold this used car while brandishing a copy of the mechanical fitness certificate as proof that the car was in good shape. The plaintiff was awarded his money back because the court held the certificate to be a warranty that was breached by the car's subsequent defects.

Johnston v. Bodasing Corporation Limited, February 23, 1983, Ontario County Court (Bruce), No. 15/11/83, Judge McKay. The plaintiff bought a used 1979 Buick Riviera, for $8,500, that was represented as being "reliable." Two weeks after purchase, the motor self-destructed. Judge McKay awarded the plaintiff $2,318 as compensation to fix the Riviera's defects.

One feature of this particular decision is that the trial judge found the Sale of Goods Act applied, notwithstanding the fact that the vendor used a standard contract that said there were no warranties or representations. The judge also accepted the decision in *Kendal v. Lillico* (1969), 2 Appeal Cases, 31, which indicates that the Sale of Goods Act covers not only defects that the seller ought to have detected, but also latent defects that even his utmost skill and judgment could not have detected. This places a very heavy onus on the vendor and it should prove useful in actions of this type in other common-law provinces with laws similar to Ontario's Sale of Goods Act.

Kelly v. Mack Canada, 53 D.L.R. (4th), 476. Kelly bought two trucks from Mack Sales. The first, a used White Freightliner tractor and trailer, was purchased for $29,742. It cost him over $12,000 in repairs during the first five months, and another $9,000 was estimated for future engine repairs. Mack Sales convinced Kelly to trade in the old truck for a new Mack truck. Kelly did this, but shortly thereafter, the new truck had similar problems. Kelly sued for the return of all his money, arguing that the two transactions were really one.

The Ontario Court of Appeal agreed and awarded Kelly a complete refund. It stated, "There was such a congeries of defects that there had been a breach of the implied conditions set out in the Sale of Goods Act."

Although Mack Sales argued that the contract contained a clause excluding any implied warranties, the court determined that the breach was of such magnitude that the dealer could not rely upon that clause. The dealer then argued that since the client used the trucks, the depreciation of both should be taken into account in reducing the award. This was refused on the grounds that the plaintiff never had the product he bargained for and in no way did he profit from the transaction. The court also awarded Kelly compensation for loss of income while the trucks were being repaired, as well as the interest on all of the money tied up in both transactions from the time of purchase until final judgment.

Morrison v. Hillside Motors (1973) Ltd. (1981), 35 Nfld. & P.E.I.R. 361. A used car advertised to be in A-1 condition and carrying a 50/50 warranty developed a number of problems. The court decided that the purchaser should be partially compensated because of the ad's claim. In deciding how much compensation to award, the presiding judge considered the warranty's wording, the amount paid for the vehicle, the year of the vehicle, its average life, the type of defect that occurred, and how long the purchaser had use of the vehicle before its defects became evident. Although this judgment was rendered in Newfoundland, judges throughout Canada have used a similar approach for more than a decade.

Neilson v. Maclin Motors, 71 D.L.R. (3d), 744. The plaintiff bought a used truck on the strength of the seller's allegations that the motor had been rebuilt and that it had 210 hp. The engine failed. The judge awarded damages and cancelled the contract because the motor had not been rebuilt, it did not have 210 hp, and the transmission was defective.

Parent v. Le Grand Trianon and Ford Credit (1982), C.P., 194, Judge Bertrand Gagnon. Nineteen months after paying $3,300 for a used 1974 LTD, the plaintiff sued the Ford dealer for his money back because the car was prematurely rusted out. The dealer replied that rust was normal, there was no warranty, and the claim was too late. The court held that the garage was still responsible, for the following reasons:

- When purchased, the car had been repainted by the dealer to camouflage rust and perforations.
- During the 19 months, the plaintiff and the dealer continued to explore ways in which the rusting could be stopped.
- It wasn't until just before the lawsuit that the plaintiff found out how bad the rust was.
- Ford and its dealers admitted they knew that many of their 1970–74 cars had serious premature corrosion problems.

The plaintiff was awarded $1,500 for the cost of rust repairs.

"As is" clauses

Since 1907, Canadian courts have ruled that a seller can't exclude the implied warranty as to fitness by including such phrases as "there are no other warranties or guarantees, promises, or agreements than those contained herein." *Sawyer-Massey Co. v. Thibault* (1907), 5 W.L.R. 241.

Adams v. J&D's Used Cars Ltd. (1983), 26 Sask. R. 40 (Q.B.). Shortly after purchase, the engine and transmission failed. The court ruled that the inclusion of "as is" in the sales contract had no legal effect. The implied warranty set out in Saskatchewan's Consumer Products Warranties Act was breached by the dealer. The sale was cancelled and all monies were refunded.

Repairs

Faulty diagnosis

Davies v. Alberta Motor Association, August 13, 1991, Alberta Provincial Court, Civil Division, No. P9090106097, Judge Moore. The plaintiff had a used 1985 Nissan Pulsar NX checked out by the AMA's Vehicle Inspection Service prior to buying it. The car passed with flying colours. A month later, the clutch was replaced and numerous electrical problems ensued. At that time, another garage discovered that the car had been involved in a major accident, had a bent frame and a leaking radiator, and was unsafe to drive. The court awarded the plaintiff $1,578.40 plus three years of interest. The judge held that the AMA set itself out as an expert and should have spotted the car's defects. The AMA's defence—that it was not responsible for errors—was thrown out. The court held that a disclaimer clause could not protect the association from a fundamental breach of contract.

Secret Warranties

It's common practice for manufacturers to secretly extend their warranties to cover components with a high failure rate. Customers who complain vigorously get extended warranty compensation in the form of "goodwill" adjustments.

François Chong v. Marine Drive Imported Cars Ltd. and Honda Canada Inc., May 17, 1994, British Columbia Provincial Small Claims Court, No. 92-06760, Judge C.L. Bagnall. Mr. Chong was the first owner of a 1983 Honda Accord with 134,000 km on the odometer. He had seven engine camshafts replaced—including four under Honda "goodwill" programs, one where he paid part of the repairs, and one via a small claims court judgment. Please note that the Honda no longer has serious engine problems.

In his ruling, Judge Bagnall agreed with Chong and ordered Honda and the dealer to each pay half of the $835.81 repair bill, for the following reasons:

> The defendants assert that the warranty which was part of the contract for purchase of the car encompassed the entirety of their obligation to the claimant, and that it expired in February 1985. The replacements of the camshaft after that date were paid for wholly or in part by Honda as a "goodwill gesture." The time has come for these gestures to cease, according to the witness for Honda. As well, he pointed out to me that the most recent replacement of the camshaft was paid for by Honda and that, therefore, the work would not be covered by Honda's usual warranty of 12 months from date of repair. Mr. Wall, who testified for Honda, told me there was no question that this situation with Mr. Chong's engine was an unusual state of affairs. He said that a camshaft properly maintained can last anywhere from 24,000 to 500,000 km. He could not offer any suggestion as to why the car keeps having this problem.
>
> The claimant has convinced me that the problems he is having with rapid breakdown of camshafts in his car is due to a defect, which was present in the engine at the time that he purchased the car. The problem first arose during the warranty period and in my view has never been properly identified nor repaired.

Automatic transmission failures (Chrysler)

Lowe v. Fairview Chrysler-Dodge Limited and Chrysler Canada Limited, May 14, 1996, Ontario Court (General Division), Burlington Small Claims Court,

No. 1224/95. The following judgment, in the plaintiff's favour, raises important legal principles relative to Chrysler:

- Technical service bulletins are admissible in court to prove that a problem exists and certain parts should be checked out.
- If a problem is reported prior to a warranty's expiration, warranty coverage for the problematic component(s) is automatically carried over after the warranty ends.
- It's not up to the car owner to tell the dealer/automaker what the specific problem is.
- Repairs carried out by an independent garage can be refunded if the dealer/automaker unfairly refuses to apply the warranty.
- The dealer/automaker cannot dispute the cost of the independent repair if they fail to cross-examine the independent repairer.
- Auto owners can ask for and win compensation for their inconvenience, which in this judgment amounted to $150.

Court awards quickly add up. Although the plaintiff was given $1,985.94, with the addition of court costs and prejudgment interest, plus costs of inconvenience fixed at $150, the final award amounted to $2,266.04.

False Advertising

Misrepresentation

Goldie v. Golden Ears Motors (1980) Ltd, Port Coquitlam, June 27, 2000, British Columbia Small Claims Court, Case No. CO8287, Justice Warren. The court awarded plaintiff Goldie $5,000 for engine repairs on a 1990 Ford F-150 pickup in addition to $236 for court costs. The dealer was found to have misrepresented the mileage and sold a used vehicle that didn't meet Section 8.01 of the provincial motor vehicle regulations (unsafe tires, defective exhaust, and headlights).

In rejecting the seller's defence that he disclosed all information "to the best of his knowledge and belief," as stipulated in the sales contract, Justice Warren stated:

> The words "to the best of your knowledge and belief" do not allow someone to be willfully blind to defects or to provide incorrect information. I find as a fact that the business made no effort to fulfill its duty to comply with the requirements of this form. The defendant has been reckless in its actions. More likely, it has actively deceived the claimant into entering into this contract. I find the conduct of the defendant has been reprehensible throughout the dealings with the claimant.

This is an important judgment because it closes a loophole that sellers have used to justify their misrepresentation, and it allows for rescission of the sale and damages if the vehicle doesn't meet highway safety regulations.

Vehicle not as ordered

Whether you're buying a new or used vehicle, the seller can't misrepresent it. Anything that varies from what one would commonly expect, or from the seller's representation, must be disclosed prior to signing the contract. Typical scenarios are odometer turnbacks, accident damage, used or leased cars sold as new, new vehicles that are the wrong colour and the wrong model year, or vehicles that lack promised options or standard features.

Lasky v. Royal City Chrysler Plymouth, February 18, 1987, Ontario High Court of Justice, 59 O.R. (2nd), No. 323. The plaintiff bought a 4-cylinder 1983 Dodge 600 that was represented by the salesman as being a 6-cylinder model. After putting 40,000 km on the vehicle over a 22-month period, the buyer was given her money back, without interest, under the provincial Business Practices Act.

Damages (Punitive)

Punitive damages (also known as exemplary damages) allow the plaintiff to get compensation that exceeds his or her losses, as a deterrent to those who carry out dishonest or negligent practices. These kinds of judgments, common in the U.S., sometimes reach hundreds of millions of dollars.

Punitive damages are rarely awarded in Canadian courts and are almost never used against automakers. When they are given out, it's usually for sums less than $100,000. The most recent award, in *Prebushewski v. Dodge City Auto (1985) Ltd. and Chrysler Canada Ltd.* (2001 SKQB 537; Q.B. No. 1215), was for $25,000 and was handed down December 6, 2001, in Saskatoon, Saskatchewan. It followed testimony from Chrysler's expert witness that the company was aware of many cases where daytime running lights shorted and caused 1996 Ram pickups to catch fire. The plaintiff's truck had burned to the ground and Chrysler refused the owner's claim, in spite of its knowledge that fires were commonplace.

Angered by Chrysler's stonewalling, Justice Rothery rendered the following judgment:

> Not only did Chrysler know about the problems of the defective daytime running light modules, it did not advise the plaintiff of this. It simply chose to ignore the plaintiff's requests for compensation and told her to seek recovery from her insurance company. Chrysler had replaced thousands of these modules since 1988. But it had also made a business decision to neither advise its customers of the problem nor to recall the vehicles to replace the modules. While the cost would have been about $250 to replace each module, there were at least one million customers. Chrysler was not prepared to spend $250 million even though it knew what the defective module might do....
>
> Counsel for the defendants argues that this matter had to be resolved by litigation because the plaintiff and the defendants simply

had a difference of opinion on whether the plaintiff should be compensated by the defendants. Had the defendants some dispute as to the cause of the fire, that may have been sufficient to prove that they had not wilfully violated this Part of the Act. They did not. They knew about the defective daytime running light module. They did nothing to replace the burned truck for the plaintiff. They offered the plaintiff no compensation for her loss. Counsels' position that the definition of the return of the purchase price is an arguable point is not sufficient to negate the defendants' violation of this Part of the Act. I find the violation of the defendants to be willful. Thus, I find that exemplary damages are appropriate on the facts of this case.

In this case, the quantum ought to be sufficiently high as to correct the defendants' behaviour. In particular, Chrysler's corporate policy to place profits ahead of the potential danger to its customer's safety and personal property must be punished. And when such corporate policy includes a refusal to comply with the provisions of the Act and a refusal to provide any relief to the plaintiff, I find an award of $25,000 for exemplary damages to be appropriate. I therefore order Chrysler and Dodge City to pay:

1. Damages in the sum of $41,969.83;
2. Exemplary damages in the sum of $25,000;
3. Party and party costs.

Vlchek v. Koshel (1988), 44 C.C.L.T. 314, B.C.S.C., No. B842974. The plaintiff was seriously injured when she was thrown from a Honda all-terrain cycle on which she had been riding as a passenger. The Court allowed for punitive damages because the manufacturer was well aware of the injuries likely to be caused by the cycle. Specifically, the Court ruled that there is no firm and inflexible principle of law stipulating that punitive or exemplary damages must be denied unless the defendant's acts are specifically directed against the plaintiff. The Court may apply punitive damages "where the defendant's conduct has been indiscriminate of focus, but reckless or malicious in its character. Intent to injure the plaintiff need not be present, so long as intent to do the injurious act can be shown."

See also:
- *Granek v. Reiter*, Ont. Ct. (Gen. Div.), No. 35/741.
- *Morrison v. Sharp*, Ont. Ct. (Gen. Div.), No. 43/548.
- *Schryvers v. Richport Ford Sales*, May 18, 1993, B.C.S.C., No. C917060, Judge Tysoe.
- *Varleg v. Angeloni*, B.C.S.C., No. 41/301.

Provincial business practices acts cover false, misleading, or deceptive representations, and allow for punitive damages should the unfair practice toward the consumer amount to an unconscionable representation. (See C.E.D. (3d) s. 76, pp. 140–45.) "Unconscionable" is defined as "where the consumer is not reasonably able to protect his or her interest because of physical infirmity, ignorance, illiteracy, or inability to understand the language of an agreement or similar factors."

- Exemplary damages are justified where compensatory damages are insufficient to deter and punish. See *Walker et al. v. CFTO Ltd. et al.* (1978), 59 O.R. (2nd), No. 104 (Ont. C.A.).
- Exemplary damages can be awarded in cases where the defendant's conduct was "cavalier." See *Ronald Elwyn Lister Ltd. et al. v. Dayton Tire Canada Ltd.* (1985), 52 O.R. (2nd), No. 89 (Ont. C.A.).
- The primary purpose of exemplary damages is to prevent the defendant and all others from doing similar wrongs. See *Fleming v. Spracklin* (1921).
- Disregard of the public's interest, lack of preventive measures, and a callous attitude all merit exemplary damages. See *Coughlin v. Kuntz* (1989), 2 C.C.L.T. (2nd) (B.C.C.A.).
- Punitive damages can be awarded for mental distress. See *Ribeiro v. Canadian Imperial Bank of Commerce* (1992), Ontario Reports 13 (3rd) and *Brown v. Waterloo Regional Board of Comissioners of Police* (1992), 37 O.R. (2nd).

In the States, punitive damage awards have been particularly generous. Do you remember the Alabama fellow who won a multi-million dollar damages award because his new BMW had been repainted before he bought it and he wasn't told so by the seller?

The case was *BMW of North America, Inc. v. Gore*, 517 U.S. 559, 116 S. Ct. 1589 (1996). In this case, the Supreme Court cut the damages award and established standards for jury awards of punitive damages. Nevertheless, million-dollar awards are still quite common. For example, an Oregon dealer learned that a $1 million punitive damages award was not excessive under Gore and under Oregon law.

The Oregon Supreme Court determined that the standard it set forth in *Oberg v. Honda Motor Company*, 888 P.2d 8 (1996), on remand from the Supreme Court, survived the Supreme Court's subsequent ruling in Gore. The court held that the jury's $1 million punitive damages award, 87 times larger than the plaintiff's compensatory damages in *Parrott v. Carr Chevrolet, Inc.*, (2001 Ore. LEXIS 1 January 11, 2001) wasn't excessive. In that case, Mark Parrott sued Carr Chevrolet, Inc. over a used 1983 Chevrolet Suburban under Oregon's Unlawful Trade Practices Act. The jury awarded Parrott $11,496 in compensatory damages and $1 million in punitive damages because the dealer failed to disclose collision damage to a new car buyer.

See also:

- *Grabinski v. Blue Springs Ford Sales, Inc.*, 2000 U.S. App. LEXIS 2073 (8th Cir. W.D. MO, February 16, 2000).

Now that you know how to get the best deal and protect your rights, let's take a look at which used cars and minivans are the best buys.

PART THREE

1970–2003 RATINGS:
The Good, the Bad, and the Awful

3

Who Can You Trust?

From the PR point of view, the most ignorant and pliable journalists are often preferred to their more talented colleagues. Many of the least informed and least capable automotive journalists I know enjoy the best access to car company products and personnel. They work at getting it.

In today's automotive journalism, knowledge of the industry, personnel, and products has become secondary to skill in "greasing" its PR contacts for access and good times.

This is not to say that there is no honest, independent, informed, and perceptive automotive reporting, but it is becoming the exception to a tainted general run of mediocrity.

Matt Joseph
blueovalnews.com
June 30, 2003

Who You Can't Trust

GM, which makes twice as much money from its finance arm as from making cars, is probably better understood as a first-rate bank with a third-rate car company attached.

James Arnold
BBC News Online
September 5, 2003

Chrysler's PT Cruiser (2001–04) has fallen upon hard times. New models aren't selling well, and a 2001 that once sold for $23,665, now sells for $14,000.

Cherries and Lemons

A good used car or minivan must first meet your everyday driving needs. Secondly, the vehicle must be crashworthy and be reasonably durable, enough to last at least 10 years. Annual maintenance should be no more than the CAA-surveyed average of $800 and depreciation should be between 50 and 60 percent after three years of use. Parts should also be reasonably priced and easily available, customizing should be easy and inexpensive, and servicing shouldn't be given with a shrug or a snarl (sorry, Mercedes and VW).

Depreciation bargains

During the past decade, rebates, cut-rate financing, subsidized leases, and a reputation for poor quality have depressed the residual values of Detroit Big Three cars and trucks. According to Automotive Lease Guide, 3-year-old Detroit-made vehicles that came off lease this year kept only 39 percent of their sticker value; 1997 models returned after three years were valued at 45 percent. If the residual value of a leased vehicle falls below expectations, the dealer must absorb the loss when the customer returns it. This makes for heavy new-car losses, a reluctance by dealers to write new leases, and used-car bargains.

Falling Values

These average residual values are based on vehicles returned in 2003 after a 36-month lease.

COMPANY	TRADE-IN VALUES
Acura, Honda	52.00%
Lexus, Toyota, VW	49.00%
Infiniti, Nissan	45.00%
GM	40.00%
Chrysler, Ford	39.00%

Land Rover Jaguar, Saab, and Volvo aren't included; Canadian values are about 10% higher.

Source: U.S. *Automotive Lease Guide* and *Canadian Red Book*

Definitions of Terms

Ratings

It would be impossible to rate vehicles that go back to 1970 (grouped in Appendix II) if *Lemon-Aid* hadn't been rating cars and trucks for over 32 years.

This edition makes use of owner complaints, confidential technical service bulletins (TSBs), and test-drives to expose serious factory-related defects, design deficiencies, or servicing glitches and to give owners ammo to get their money back. It should be noted that customer complaints alone do not make a scientific sampling, and that's why they are used in conjunction with other sources of information. On the other hand, owner complaints and comments, combined with inside information found in TSBs, are a good starting point to cut through the automakers' hyperbole and get a glimpse of reality.

A/T – Harsh Shifts/Stays in First Gear

Bulletin No.: 00-012

Date: June 26, 2001

1996–2000 Civic
1997–99 CR-V

Harsh Shifting Automatic Transmission

SYMPTOM: The transmission shifts harshly, or it may stay in First gear. The harsh shifting is more noticeable on the 1–2 and 2–3 upshifts under light throttle. It is not affected by operating temperature. The MIL may be on with DTC P0730 or P0715 stored.

PROBABLE CAUSE: Contamination of the linear solenoid and its associated passages inside the transmission, or a broken spring internal to the transmission.

Out of warranty: Any repair performed after warranty expiration may be eligible for goodwill consideration by the District Service Manager or your Zone Office. You must request consideration, and get a decision, before starting work.

Take a good look at this confidential Honda service bulletin. It admits that an extensive range of Civics and CR-Vs have serious transmission failures coverecd by "goodwill" payouts. *Lemon-Aid* is the only publication that gives this info to consumers.

Models are rated on a scale from Recommended to Not Recommended, with the most recent year's rating reflected by the number of stars beside the vehicle's name. Recommended vehicles are those that will give their owners relatively trouble-free service. This doesn't mean that only luxury Japanese models get a good rating. In fact, Chrysler's Sebring and PT Cruiser, Ford's Escort, GM's Camaro and Firebird, and Hyundai's Elantra and Tiburon, get postitive ratings because they are easy to find, fairly reliable, and reasonably priced—not the case with many overpriced Hondas and Toyotas.

Vehicles that are given an Above Average or Average rating are good second choices if a Recommended vehicle isn't your first choice or is too expensive. A Below Average vehicle will likely be troublesome; however, a low price and reasonably priced servicing may make it an acceptable buy. Vehicles given a Not Recommended rating are best avoided, no matter how low the price. They may be attractively styled and loaded with convenience features (early Ford Windstar and Chrysler minivans, for example), but they're likely to suffer from so many durability and performance problems that you will never stop paying for them. Sometimes, however, a Not Recommended model will improve over several model years and garner a better rating (as the GM Astro and Safari minivans have done).

Incidentally, for those owners who wonder how I can stop recommending model years I once recommended, let me be clear: As vehicles age, their ratings always change to reflect new information from owners, service bulletins, etc., relating to durability and the automaker's warranty performance. Unlike Enron and Nortel stock analysts, I warn shoppers of changes in subsequent editions of *Lemon-Aid* or in updates to my website, *www.lemonaidcars.com*.

I do more than simply write about bad cars; I also try to get refunds for buyers who made the wrong choice. Throughout the year, I lobby automakers to compensate out-of-warranty owners through formal warranty extension programs or on an individual case-by-case basis. I also publish in *Lemon-Aid* little-known court judgments to help car owners win their cases or get a fair settlement.

Some enterprising readers of *Lemon-Aid* use the Not Recommended rating as a buying opportunity. Dave Ingram, a friend and well-known B.C. broadcaster, uses my Not Recommended list as a shopping guide for cheap vehicles: he buys them up at depressed prices and refurbishes them, using garages that offer lifetime warranties on major components that I rate as weak. He's done that with several used Cadillacs and Jeep Wagoneers and seems happy with the system. Personally, I don't think he would have done so well without the complicity of his independent garage contacts in North Vancouver.

Reliability data is compiled from a number of sources: confidential technical service bulletins; owner complaints sent to the author each year by *Lemon-Aid* readers; vehicle owners' comments posted on the Internet; and survey reports and tests done by auto associations, consumer groups, and government organizations. Some auto columnists feel this isn't a scientific sampling, and they're quite right. Nevertheless, it seems to have been mostly on the mark over the past three decades.

Not all vehicles sold since the '70s are profiled; those that are new to the market or relatively rare may receive only an abbreviated mention until sufficient owner or service bulletin information becomes available. Best and worst buys for each model category (e.g., "Small Cars" or "Medium Cars") are listed in a summary at the beginning of each rating section. Also, don't forget to look up the cheap alternative choices profiled in Appendix II.

Strengths and weaknesses

Every automaker has quality shortcomings: With the Detroit Big Three, it's engine head gaskets and automatic transmissions; South Korean vehicles have weak transmissions; and Japanese makes are mostly noted for their electrical system, brake, door, and window glitches, though powertrain failures are appearing more frequently. Unlike other auto guides, *Lemon-Aid* pinpoints potential parts failures, explains why those parts fail, and advises you as to your chances of getting a repair refund. We also give parts numbers for upgraded parts (why replace poor-quality brake pads with the same ones, for example?) and offer troubleshooting tips direct from the automakers' bulletins, so your mechanic won't replace parts unrelated to your troubles before coming upon the defective component that is actually responsible.

Parts supply can be a real problem. It's a myth that automakers have to keep a sufficient supply of parts to service what they sell, as any buyer of a Chrysler Colt, Chevrolet Corsica/Beretta/Tempest, Lincoln Continental, or Renault 5 will quickly tell you. Plus, apart from *Lemon-Aid*, there's no consumer database that warns prospective purchasers as to which models are "parts-challenged."

The "Secret Warranties/Service Tips/TSBs" and vehicle "Profile" tables show a vehicle's overall reliability and safety, providing details as to which specific model years pose the most risk. This helps an independent mechanic check out the likely trouble spots before you make your purchase.

Safety summary

Ongoing safety investigations, safety-related complaints, and safety probes make up this section. National Highway Traffic Safety Administration (NHTSA) complaints are summarized by model year, even though they aren't all safety related. The summary will help you spot a defect trend before a recall or bulletin is issued (like cracked Ford and GM engine intake manifolds or Corvette steering failures). Another advantage is that you can prove a part failure is widespread and factory related, and use that information for free "goodwill" repairs or in litigation involving accident damage, injuries, or death. NHTSA records indicate that ABS and airbag failures represent the most frequent complaints from car and van owners. Other common safety-related failures concern sudden acceleration, the vehicle rolling away with the transmission in Park, and minivan sliding doors not opening when they should or opening when they shouldn't.

If *Lemon-Aid* doesn't list a problem you have experienced, go to the NHTSA website's database at *www.nhtsa.dot.gov/cars/problems* for an update. Your vehicle may be currently under investigation or may have been recalled since this year's guide was published.

Recalls aren't listed in this guide because there are so many and the info can be easily obtained from either NHTSA or Transport Canada by telephone or on Internet websites listed in Appendix I. Furthermore, most dealers willingly give out recall info when they run a "vehicle history" search through their computer, since they hope to snag the extra service.

Secret warranties/Service tips/TSBs

It's not enough to know which parts on your vehicle are likely to fail. You should also know which repairs will be done for free by the dealer and automaker, even though you aren't the original owner and the manufacturer's warranty has long since expired.

Welcome to the hidden world of secret warranties, found in confidential technical service bulletins or gleaned from owner feedback. Over the years, I've grown tired of having service managers deny that service bulletins exist to correct factory-related defects free of charge. That's why I pore over thousands of bulletins each year and summarize or reproduce in *Lemon-Aid* the important ones for each model year, along with selected diagrams. These bulletins target defects related to safety, emissions, and performance that service managers would have you believe don't exist or are your responsibility. If you photocopy the exact service bulletin included in *Lemon-Aid*, you'll have a better chance of getting the dealer or automaker to cover all or part of the repair cost. Bulletins taken from *Lemon-Aid* have also been instrumental in helping claimants win in small claims court mediation and trials (remember to have the bulletins validated by an independent mechanic).

Service bulletins cover repairs that may be eligible for warranty coverage in one or more of the following five categories:

- emissions warranty (5–8 years/80,000–130,000 km)
- safety component warranty (this covers seat belts, ABS, and airbags, and usually lasts 8 years—the lifetime of the vehicle)
- body warranty (paint: 6 years; rust perforations: 7 years)
- secret warranty (coverage varies)
- factory defect/implied legal warranty (depends on mileage, use, and repair cost)

Use these bulletins to get free repairs—even if the vehicle has changed hands several times—and to alert an independent mechanic about which defects to look for. They're also great tools for getting compensation from automakers and dealer service managers after the warranty has expired, since they prove that a failure is factory related and therefore not part of routine maintenance or an environmental anomaly (like bird droppings and acid rain).

Their diagnostic shortcuts and lists of upgraded parts make these bulletins invaluable in helping mechanics and do-it-yourselfers troubleshoot problems inexpensively and replace the right part the first time. Auto owners can also use the TSBs listed here to verify that a repair was diagnosed correctly, the right upgraded replacement part was used, and the labour costs were fair.

Getting your own bulletins

Summaries of service bulletins relating to 1982–2004 vehicles can be obtained for free from the ALLDATA or NHTSA websites (listed in Appendix I, "Internet Hot Spots"). If you want individual bulletins for your car, they can be ordered from ALLDATA; $25 (U.S.) will get you a DVD or Internet download containing all the bulletins applicable to your vehicle (BMW, Acura, and Honda excepted).

Vehicle profile tables

These tables cover the various aspects of vehicle ownership at a glance. Included for each model year are the vehicle's original selling price (the manufacturer's suggested retail price, or MSRP), the wholesale and retail price you can expect to pay, reliability ratings (specific defective parts are listed in the "Strengths and weaknesses" section), which model years have secret warranties, and details on crashworthiness.

Prices

Dealer profit margins on used cars vary considerably—giving lots of room to negotiate a fair price if you take the time to find out what the vehicle is really worth. Three prices are given for each model year: the vehicle's selling price when new as suggested by the manufacturer; its maximum used price (▲), which is often the starting price with dealers, and its lowest used price (▼), more commonly found with private sellers.

The original selling price (MSRP) is also given as a reality check for greedy sellers who inflate prices on some vehicles (mostly Japanese imports, minivans, and sport-utilities) in order to get back some of the money *they* overpaid in the first place. This is particularly true in the Prairie provinces and British Columbia.

Used prices are based on sales recorded as of February 2004. Prices are for the lowest-priced standard model that is in good condition with a maximum of 20,000 km for each calendar year. Be watchful for price differences reflecting each model's equipment upgrades, designated by a numerical or alphabetical abbreviation. For example, L, LX, and LXT usually mean more standard features are included. Numerical progression usually relates to engine size.

Prices reflect the auto markets in Quebec and Ontario, where the majority of used-vehicle transactions take place. Residents in Eastern Canada should add 10 percent, and Western Canadians should add at least 15–20 percent to the listed price. Why the higher cost? Less competition and inflated new-vehicle prices in these regions. Don't be too disheartened, though; some of what was overpaid will be recouped when you resell the vehicle down the road.

Why are *Lemon-Aid*'s prices sometimes lower than the prices found in dealer guides (like the *Red Book*)? The answer is simple: Dealer guides inflate their prices (much like homeowners in real estate transactions) so that you can bargain the price down and wind up convinced that you made a great deal.

I use newspaper classified ads from Quebec, Ontario, and B.C., as well as auction reports, for my used values. I then check these figures with the *Red Book* and *Black Book*. I don't start with the *Red Book*'s retail or wholesale figures (prices are inflated about 10 percent for wholesale-private sales and almost 20 percent for retail-dealer sales—compare the two and you'll see what I mean). I then project what the value will be by mid-model year, and that lowers my prices further. I'll almost always fall way under the *Red Book*'s value, but not far under the *Black Book*'s prices.

I print a top and bottom price to give the buyer some margin for negotiation, as well as to account for regional differences in prices, the sudden popularity of certain models or vehicle classes, and the generally depreciated value of used vehicles.

Most new cars depreciate 50–60 percent during the first three years of ownership, despite the fact that good-quality used cars are in high demand. On the other hand, some minivans and most vans, pickups, and sport-utilities lose barely 40 percent of their value, even after four years of ownership.

Since no evaluation method is foolproof, check dealer prices with local private classified ads and add the option values listed below to come up with a fairly representative offer. Don't forget to bargain down the price further if the odometer shows a cumulative reading of more than 20,000 km per calendar year. Interestingly, the value of anti-lock brakes in trade-ins has plummeted in the last few years as they became a standard feature on many entry-level vehicles.

It will be easier for you to match the lower used prices if you buy privately. Dealers rarely sell much below the maximum prices. They inflate their prices to cover the costs of reconditioning or paying future warranty claims and to make you feel better. If you can come within 5–10 percent of this guide's price, you'll have done well.

Value of Options by Model Year								
Option	1996	1997	1998	1999	2000	2001	2002	2003
Air conditioning	$200	$300	$300	$400	$500	$600	$800	$900
AM/FM radio & CD player	100	100	100	150	175	200	300	500
Anti-lock brakes	0	50	100	125	150	175	300	300
Automatic transmission	150	200	250	275	300	400	500	700
Cruise control	0	50	50	75	100	125	225	300
Electric six-way seat	0	50	100	125	150	175	200	400
Leather upholstery	50	100	200	225	325	400	500	800
Level control (suspension)	0	50	75	100	125	150	250	350
Paint protector	0	0	0	0	0	0	0	0
Power antenna	0	0	0	0	0	75	75	75
Power door locks	0	50	100	125	150	175	200	250
Power windows	0	50	100	125	150	175	225	275
Rustproofing	0	0	0	0	25	25	50	50
Sunroof	0	50	50	75	125	150	300	500
T-top roof	150	200	300	400	500	700	1,000	1,200
Tilt steering	0	50	50	75	75	100	175	250
Tinted windows	0	0	0	0	25	50	50	50
Tires (Firestone)	-100	-100	-100	-100	-100	-150	-150	-150
Traction control	50	100	125	150	175	275	400	500
Wire wheels/locks	50	75	100	125	150	175	275	350

In the table above, take note that some options—like paint protection, rust-proofing, and tinted windows—have little worth on the resale market, though they may make your vehicle easier to sell.

Extended warranties and secret warranties

Usually, but not always, an extended warranty is advised for those model years that aren't rated Recommended. But don't buy too much warranty. For example, if the vehicle has a history of powertrain problems, only buy the cheaper powertrain warranty—not the bumper-to-bumper product. Also, only invest in enough extra warranty to get you through the critical fifth year of ownership. In shopping for an extended warranty, don't be surprised to discover that dealers have the market practically sewn up. You can bargain the price down by getting competing dealers to bid against each other, contacting them by fax or through their websites. Be wary of extended-warranty companies that aren't backed by the major automakers.

Model years that are eligible for free repairs under a secret warranty are listed in the "Secret Warranties/Service Tips/TSBs" section.

Reliability

The older a vehicle, the greater the chance that major components like the engine and transmission will fail as a result of high mileage and environmental wear and tear. Surprisingly, there's a host of other expensive-to-repair failures that are just as likely to occur in a new vehicle as in an older one. Air conditioning, electronic computer modules, electrical systems, and brakes are the most troublesome components, manifesting problems early in a vehicle's life. Other deficiencies that will appear early, due to sloppy manufacturing and a harsh environment, include failure-prone body hardware (trim, finish, locks, doors, and windows), water leaks, wind noise, and paint peeling/discoloration.

The following legend is used to show a vehicle's relative degree of overall reliability; the numbers lighten as the rating becomes more positive.

❶	❷	③	④	⑤
Unacceptable	Below Average	Average	Above Average	Excellent

Crash data

Front and side impact protection figures and rollover resistance ratings are taken from NHTSA's New Car Assessment Program. The Insurance Institute for Highway Safety (IIHS) supplies data on offset crash and head restraint protection. The frontal collision test crashes a vehicle into a fixed barrier, head-on, at 57 km/h (35 mph), in order to evaluate the effects of the consequent forces exerted on the specially constructed dummies placed in the front seat. *Lemon-Aid* gives the crash score for the driver.

NHTSA shows a vehicle's level of crashworthiness by the likelihood, expressed as a percentage, of the belted occupants being seriously injured. The higher the number, the greater the protection:

NHTSA Front Collision Ratings

⑤	10 percent or lower chance of serious injury
④	11–20 percent chance of serious injury
③	21–35 percent chance of serious injury
❷	36–45 percent chance of serious injury
❶	46 percent or greater chance of serious injury

Vehicles that are identical but carry different nameplates from the same manufacturer can be expected to perform similarly in these crash tests. On the other hand, sometimes the same vehicle will post dramatically different results when tested from one year to the next, even though the model has remained relatively unchanged. Safety experts admit that this happens occasionally and that consumers should look at the trend established over three or more model years.

NHTSA Side Collision Ratings

⑤   5 percent or lower chance of serious injury
④   6–10 percent chance of serious injury
③   11–20 percent chance of serious injury
❷   21–25 percent chance of serious injury
❶   26 percent or greater chance of serious injury

SMALL CARS

The proverbial "econobox," this size of car is for city dwellers who want economy at any price. Small cars offer excellent gas economy, easy manoeuvrability in urban areas, and a low retail price.

One of the more alarming characteristics of a small car's highway performance is its extreme vulnerability to strong lateral winds, which may make the car difficult to keep on course. Most of these cars can carry only two passengers in comfort—rear seating is limited—and there is insufficient luggage capacity. As well, engine and road noise are fairly excessive.

Year 2000 and later small cars broke ranks with traditional stylists. The Toyota Echo (above) and Ford's Focus use similar aerodynamic designs that provide a surprising amount of interior space, better-than-average crashworthiness, and a commanding view of the road. Of course, you'll have to get used to gauges mounted to the right of the steering wheel (Echo).

Crash safety may be compromised by the small size and light weight of some older small vehicles. Nevertheless, if they incorporate a body structure that deflects crash forces away from occupants, these small cars can be more crashworthy than some larger vehicles. Always check out NHTSA and IIHS crash ratings.

SMALL CAR RATINGS

Recommended

Hyundai Elantra (2001–03)
Mazda Protegé (1996–2003)
Nissan Sentra (1995–2003)
Subaru Forester (2001–03)

Suzuki Aerio (2003)
Suzuki Esteem (1996–2002)
Toyota Echo (2000–03)
Toyota Tercel (1993–99)

Above Average

General Motors Cavalier, Sunfire
  (2002–03)
General Motors/Suzuki Firefly,
  Metro, Sprint/Swift (1998–2001)
Honda Civic, del Sol (1992–2003)
Hyundai Accent (2001–03)
Hyundai Elantra (1996–2000)
Mazda 323, Protegé (1991–95)

Nissan Sentra (1991–94)
Subaru Forester (1998–2000)
Subaru Impreza (1997–2003)
Subaru Legacy, Outback (1997–2003)
Toyota Corolla, Matrix/Vibe (1991–2003)
Toyota Paseo (1992–99)
Toyota Tercel (1991–92)

Average

DaimlerChrysler Neon (2003)
Ford Escort, ZX2 (1998–2000)
General Motors Cavalier, Sunfire
  (1996–2001)
General Motors/Suzuki Firefly,
  Metro, Sprint/Swift (1995–97)
Honda Civic, del Sol (1972–91)
Hyundai Accent (1995–2000)
Hyundai Elantra (1991–95)

Mazda 323, Protegé (1985–90)
Nissan Sentra (1988–90)
Subaru Impreza, Loyale
  (1994–96)
Subaru Legacy, Outback (1989–96)
Toyota Corolla (1985–90)
Toyota Tercel (1987–90)
Volkswagen Cabrio, Golf, Jetta
  (1999–2003)

Below Average

DaimlerChrysler Neon (2000–02)
Ford Escort, ZX2 (1997)
General Motors/Suzuki Firefly,
  Metro, Sprint/Swift (1987–94)

Saturn Ion (2003)
Saturn L-series (2000–03)
Saturn S-series (1998–2002)
Volkswagen Cabrio, Golf, Jetta
  (1993–98)

Not Recommended

Daewoo (2001–03)
DaimlerChrysler Neon (1995–99)
Ford Escort (1981–96)
Ford Focus (2000–03)
General Motors Cavalier, Sunfire
  (Sunbird) (1984–95)

Kia Rio (2001–03)
Nissan Sentra (1983–87)
Saturn S-series (1992–97)
Subaru WRX (2002–03)
Volkswagen Cabrio, Golf, Jetta
  (1985–92)

Daewoo not recommended

South Korean automaker Daewoo marketed three cars in Canada from 2000–02: the Lanos subcompact, the Nubira compact sedan and wagon, and the Leganza luxury sedan. All of these cars are Not Recommended because Daewoo sold its car division to GM and neither company will service these models, let alone respect the original warranty. By the way, Daewoo depreciation is mind-boggling: A 2002 Leganza that originally sold for $25,495 is now worth about $10,000—if you can find a buyer!

DaimlerChrysler

NEON   ★★★

RATING: Average (2003); Below Average (2000–02); Not Recommended (1995–99). A low-quality econobox that eats engine head gaskets for breakfast and wallets for lunch. The best of a bad lot would be a 2003 model covered by Chrysler's 7-year powertrain warranty. The Highline and Sport versions are more feature-laden. Incidentally, if you have to choose between a Ford Focus or a Neon, go for the Chrysler. **Maintenance/Repair costs:** Higher than average. **Parts:** Easily found and relatively inexpensive. However, Chrysler is particularly slow in distributing parts needed for safety recall campaigns; waits of several months are commonplace. **Best alternatives:** Other cars worth considering are the Ford Escort/Tracer (post-'91); Geo Metro; Honda Civic; Hyundai Accent; Mazda Protegé; Suzuki Esteem; and Toyota Echo, Tercel, or Corolla. **Online help:** *www.neons.org; www.carsurvey.org/model_Dodge_ Neon.html; www.geocities.com/norman_neon/; www.allpar.com/fix/ secret-warranties.html;* and *www.autosafety.org/autodefects.html.*

Strengths and weaknesses: A small, noisy car with big quality problems, the Neon does offer a spacious interior and responsive steering and handling. Nevertheless, through the 2001 model, it uses an antiquated 3-speed automatic gearbox, a DOHC 150-hp power plant that has to be pushed hard to do as well as the SOHC 132-hp engine, and a mushy base suspension.

But the worst news is that these cars have a plethora of serious factory-related powertrain defects affecting primarily the 1995–99 model years. Foremost is a biodegradable 2.0L 4-cylinder engine head gasket that's covered by a 7-year/160,000 km secret warranty. This has been confirmed by anecdotal feedback from successful claimants.

Many other owners have complained of an abrupt-shifting and unreliable automatic transmission, an air conditioning system that often requires expensive servicing, following condenser and compressor failures (covered by a secret 7-year warranty), a multitude of electrical glitches, lots of interior noise and water leaks, uneven fit and finish, and poor-quality trim items that break or fall off easily. The finish is not as good as on most other subcompacts; the thickness of the coat varies considerably and can chip or fade easily (another defect eligible for a "goodwill" fix).

Year 2000–03 models continue to have engine and transmission glitches that are mostly caused by poorly calibrated computer modules (an 8-year/130,000 km emissions warranty item). Writes one owner of a 2002 Neon SXT:

> After 2,000 miles [3,200 km] my power windows began to stick and wouldn't roll down. I took it to the dealer to get serviced and was told something was spilled, such as a soda, which was the cause of the problem. I was told I needed to be more careful. After three days, they decided to correct the problem.

Like so many other reviews, the Neon began to idle really rough at about 3,000 miles [4,800 km]. The car idled more roughly in the winter months than warm weather. The car would knock off every morning when the temperature was around 40 degrees. At this point, the car was a little over 6 months old. I feel like I am driving a 4X4 with this car. I have tried to sell this car and I can't give it away! I wouldn't wish this nightmare on anyone.

Engine – Roughness With AC ON, Below Normal Idle Speed

NUMBER: 18-017-01 REV A
DATE: Dec. 7, 2001
SUBJECT: Engine Idle Undershoot/Performance
OVERVIEW: This bulletin involves selectively erasing and reprogramming the Powertrain Control Module (PCM) with new software.
MODELS: 2000–01 (PL) Neon

Transaxle – Delayed Engagement

NUMBER: 21-07-00
DATE: August 25, 2000
SUBJECT: Delayed Engagement
OVERVIEW: This bulletin involves diagnosing delayed engagement and if necessary, replacing the front pump assembly with a revised part.
MODELS: 2000 (NS) Caravan/Voyager; 2000 (PL) Neon

Some 2002 and later performance defects add some new wrinkles. For example, when passing through puddles, water is ingested into the engine though the air intake port (Chrysler will replace the engine when threatened with court action); AC fails to cool vehicle adequately; no-start due to early starter rust-out; rear brake squeaks; engine noticeably loses power when windows are lowered, sunroof is opened, or AC is engaged; and overall poor fuel economy (18–19L/100 km [15–16 mpg]).

Vehicle history: The Neon remained basically unchanged until the '99 models got de-powered airbags. Year 2000 versions were completely redesigned, gaining increased interior room and trunk space. The manual transmission and stereo were also upgraded, traction control was offered, and redesigned doors reduced wind noise and water leaks. 2002s got an upgraded automatic transmission (same reliability problems, though) and 2003 Neons were renamed the SX 2.0 and came in three trim levels: base ($14,995), Sport ($17,895), and R/T ($20,795). They have new front and rear fascias, a new steering wheel, revised engine mounts to smooth out engine roughness, and a taller Fifth gear for the manual transmission.

Safety summary: All years/models—Fires. • "Inappropriate" airbag deployment or failure to deploy. • Sudden acceleration. • Chronic stalling. • No-start due to rusted-out starter. • Throttle system failures. • Faulty cruise control. • Steering loss. • Steering locks up every time it rains. • Chronic transmission failures and slippage. • Transmission suddenly downshifts to First gear when accelerating at 90 km/h. • ABS brake failures. • Defective brake master cylinder. • Premature front brake pad/rotor wearout. • Excessive vibration. • Small horn buttons are hard to find in an emergency. • Trunk lid or hood may fall. • Headlight switch is a "hide and go seek" affair. • Axle shafts may suddenly collapse. **1995–96**—Electrical short in dashboard. • Seat belt failed to restrain driver. • Driver-side seat belt pulled out from buckle during collision. • Sticks in idle. • Door hinge failures. • Premature wheel bearing and steering knuckle wear. • Chronic light and gauge failures. **1995–99**—Chronic engine head gasket failures. • Engine camshaft seal leaks oil • Engine motor mount and exhaust donut gasket failures. **1995–2000**—NHTSA probe of seat belt latch. **1997**—Cruise control won't disengage when braking. • Gas tank leaks fuel. • O-ring in the fuel rail leaks fuel. • Sudden steering lock-up after passing over speed bump. • Window seal failures. • Fuel pump failures. • Seat belt failed to restrain occupant. • Catalytic converter failure. **1998**—Driver-side window exploded in warm weather. • Front right wheel bolt fell out, causing wheel to bend. • Engine surging and stalling. • Engine loses speed rapidly when going uphill. • Excessive engine carbon buildup. • Timing belt broke, causing extensive engine damage. • There is a partial steering hang-up when making a right turn. **1999**—Vehicle suddenly "jumps" out of gear. • In rainy weather, vehicle makes loud noise, sometimes stalls, or loses steering power. • Defective ignition switch fuse causes sudden shutdown. **2000**—Over 352 safety complaints as of January 2003 indicate that the 2000 refinements haven't improved overall reliability or safety. Main problem areas: airbag, automatic transmission (see bulletin above for delayed shifting diagnosis), power steering, tires, and brake failures; engine fires; premature brake rotor and pad wear, signalled by excessive vibrations and squealing when brakes are applied; steering lock ups; stalling and stumbling; interior/exterior light dimming; seat belts failing to retract; and an inoperative horn. Snapping noises from the front suspension may be caused by loose front crossmember mounting bolts. • An upgraded right-side motor mount may reduce steering wheel or chassis shaking. **2000–01**—Poor engine idle (see bulletin above). **2001**—Over 131 safety complaints as of January 2003. Engine stalling and stumbling, and airbags failing to deploy are the most frequent problems reported. Other incidents include electrical shorts (lights and gauges), Eagle low-profile tire blowouts, engine damage caused by water ingested through the air intake system, loss of steering, weak trunk lid springs, and an annoying reflection in the front windshield. **2002**—Stalling due to water ingestion into engine when it rains. • Transmission slips between First and Second gear. • Vehicle pulls when cruising or upon acceleration, and tends to wobble side to side at low speed. • Excessive steering wheel vibration makes it hard to maintain control. • Brakes fail to "catch" when first applied. • Airbag light stays lit. • Tailpipe melted part of the rear bumper. **2003**—Engine manifold failure. •

Burnt spark plug wires (especially with #4 plug). • Poor braking. • Power-steering failure. • Tire blew because rim peeled off. • Suspension bottoms out when passing over a dip in the road.

Secret Warranties/Service Tips/TSBs

All models/years: Paint delamination, peeling, or fading (see Part Two for info on making a claim). **1995–97**—If water drips into the vehicle from the roof-rail weather stripping channel, install an anti-drip roof-rail retainer channel. **1995–99**—A new Multi-Layer Steel engine head gasket provided superior sealing characteristics for the above-noted models, which is an admission that the previous head gaskets were poorly designed (the following Chrysler bulletin can be quite useful in getting a head gasket repair refund on any Chrysler engine with a faulty head gasket).

Cylinder Head Gasket: Technical Service Bulletins

Multi-Layer Steel Head Gasket Installation Procedures
No.: 09-09-98   Group: Engine   Effective Date: Nov. 6, 1998
Subject: Multi-Layer Steel (MLS)

Head Gasket installation

Procedures

MODELS:

1995–99	(JA)	Cirrus/Stratus/Breeze
1996–99	(JX)	Sebring Convertible
1996–99	(NS)	Town & Country/Caravan/Voyager
1995–99	(PL)	Neon
1997–99	(GS)	Chrysler Voyager (International Market)

NOTE:

THIS INFORMATION APPLIES TO MODELS WITH A 2.0L SOHC/DOHC OR 2.4L ENGINE

DISCUSSION:

A new Multi-Layer Steel (MLS) head gasket has been developed and is being implemented into production vehicles. Additionally, it has been approved for service applications. This new gasket will provide superior sealing characteristics, but will require extra care in its installation where a composite gasket was previously in place.

• Oil leakage at the cam position sensor is often mistaken for an engine head gasket failure. Chrysler says the cam seal should always be replaced whenever the head gasket is changed. • Smooth road steering wheel vibration is likely caused by a faulty bushing that should be replaced by Chrysler on a pro rata basis. It's a three-hour repair. **1995–2000**—Eliminating a steering column clunk or rattle.

NO: 90-07-98   GROUP: Engine   DATE: Dec. 11, 1998
SUBJECT: Oil Seepage at Cam Position Sensor/Misinterpreted
Head Gasket Leak

MODELS:

1995–99	(JA)	Cirrus/Stratus/Breeze
1996–99	(JX)	Sebring Convertible (Export Market)
1995–99	(PL)	Neon
1997–99	(GS)	Caravan/Voyager (Export Market)
1996–99	(NS)	Town & Country/Caravan/Voyager

NOTE:

THIS INFORMATION APPLIES TO MODELS WITH A 2.0L SOHC/DOHC OR A 2.4L ENGINE.

DISCUSSION:

Whenever performing oil leak diagnosis on one of these models, carefully inspect the cam sensor area to determine if the leak originates from the seal of from other sources. A leak in this area can be misinterpreted as a leaking head gasket. Additionally, whenever a head gasket is replaced, the cam seal should always be replaced to prevent the possibility of the vehicle returning with oil seepage.

1996—Cold-start hesitation, engine misfiring, and erratic idling. • Excessive engine vibration and exhaust noise. • Transmission slippage from Second to Third gear during light acceleration. • Speed control overshoots or under-shoots. • Rear brake chirps or howls. • AC evaporator produces a high-pitched whistle. • Fuel tank won't fill or is slow to fill. • Interior window film buildup. • Water leaks at cowl cover seam. Water could enter the air cleaner housing, be ingested into the engine, and cause serious engine damage. To prevent this from occurring, the dealer will drill a hole in the housing and seal the cowl-to-head weather stripping. This 30-minute correction is free of charge under Chrysler Customer Satisfaction Notice #660. It's not a safety recall, so you may have a hard time getting Chrysler to acknowledge the problem. Recent model Neons have a similar defect, but no formal program has been announced. Still, the company has been replacing water-damaged engines for free on a case-by-case basis. **1996–99**—Troubleshooting a sunroof that makes a ratcheting noise when engaged. **1997**—Rear brake howl. • Front footwell creak/rattle. • Scratched door glass. • Improper AC compressor engagement. • Loss of power steering in heavy rain or when passing through puddles. • Poor radio reception. • Warning that premium fuel may cause stalling, long cold-start times, hesitation, and warm-up sags. • Front suspension popping/creaking noise. **1998**—AC compressor lock-up at low mileage. • Sag, hesitation, harsh AC operation, and headlight flickers. • Steering wheel/column rattles and clunks. • Cold-start power-steering noise. • Front brake squeal, creep, or groan. • Paint fogging. • Warning that premium fuel may cause stalling, long cold-start times, hesitation, and warm-up sags. • Popping noise when passing over bumps or making turns. • Sunroof shade rattles in open position. • Vehicle overheats or radiator fan runs continuously. **1998–99**— How to fix a water leak in the left side of the trunk. **1999–2000**—Low mileage AC lock-up. **2000**—Erratic engine performance may be fixed by recalibrating the PCM (powertrain control module). • Delayed automatic transmission engagement likely caused by a faulty front pump. • Harsh AC engagement and clunk noise. • Front suspension creaking. • Front door water leaks. • Power steering moan. • Shake in steering wheel and/or seat at idle. • Poorly seated instrument panel top cover. • Instrument panel creaks. • Rear door glass won't roll down all the way. • High window cranking effort or slow power window operation. • Blower motor noise or vibration. • Front suspension snapping noise. • Deck-lid rattle and water/dust intrusion past the deck-lid seal. • Difficulty moving front seats forward. • Discoloured B-pillar appliqué. • Water enters the horn assembly. **2000–01**—Poor performance of AC and engine. • Power steering moan. • Remedy for AC honking. • Rattling wheel covers. **2001**—AC expansion valve noise. • Engine hesitation. • Delamination may require the replacement of the accessory drive belt for the power steering pump and AC compressor. • Excessive AC compressor or expansion valve noise. • Front seat rattling. • No-start problem in cold weather. • Rear window may not go all the way down. **2002**—Poor engine and AC performance caused by miscalibrated or faulty computer modules. • Low-speed power steering moan. • Wheel cover rattling when passing over bumps. • If the odometer reading is inaccurate, dealer will reprogram instrument cluster module free of charge under Customer Satisfaction Program #93. • AM radio station static. • Defective fuel filler cap. **2003**—Water leaks onto the right front seat floor (see following bulletin).

Body – Water Leaks to Passenger Front Floor

NUMBER: 23-008-03
DATE: Apr. 11, 2003
SUBJECT: Right Side Cowl Water Leak
OVERVIEW: This bulletin involves sealing a right side cowl seam.
MODELS: 2003 Neon/SX 2.0
SYMPTOM: Water on the right front passenger floor.

Neon, SX 2.0 Profile

	1996	1997	1998	1999	2000	2001	2002	2003
Cost Price ($)								
Base	12,835	14,750	15,350	15,215	17,995	18,375	18,505	—
Sport/SX 2.0	15,515	16,900	17,500	—	—	—	—	14,995
Used Values ($)								
Base ʌ	3,500	4,000	5,000	5,500	6,500	8,000	9,000	—
Base v	3,000	3,500	4,000	5,000	6,000	7,000	8,000	—

Sport/SX 2.0 ▲	4,500	5,500	6,000	—	—	—	—	10,000
Sport/SX 2.0 ▼	4,000	4,500	5,500	—	—	—	—	9,000

Reliability	❶	❶	❶	❶	❶	❷	③	③
Crash Safety (F)	④	④	③	③	—	④	④	④
Side	—	—	❷	❷	—	③	③	③
Offset	❶	❶	❶	❶	❷	❷	❷	❷
Rollover Resistance	—	—	—	—	—	④	④	④
Head Restraints (F)	—	❶	—	❷	❶	④	④	④
Rear	—	—	—	—	—	③	③	③

Ford

ESCORT, ZX2 ★★★

RATING: Average (1998–2000); Below Average (1997); Not Recommended (1981–96). Although there are lots of cheap 2000 Escorts coming off lease now, the car has been down-rated due to its many powertrain deficiencies and Ford's lack of parts and servicing support. **Maintenance/Repair costs:** Higher than average. Repairs can be done by independents or Ford or Mazda dealers. **Parts:** Expensive, and getting harder to find. **Best alternatives:** The Geo Metro; Honda Civic; Hyundai Accent; Mazda Protegé; Suzuki Esteem; and Toyota Tercel, Echo, or Corolla. **Online help:** *www.tgrigsby.com/views* (The Anti-Ford Page) and *www.autosafety.org/autodefects.html.*

Strengths and weaknesses: These front-drive small cars are usually reasonably priced and economical to operate, and they provide a comfortable though busy ride and adequate front seating for two adults. However, they have a "Dr. Jekyll and Mr. Hyde" disposition, depending on which model year you buy. From 1982 through 1990, these subcompacts were dull performers with uninspiring interiors. Worse, they had a nasty reputation for being totally unreliable and expensive to repair.

Vehicle history: 1991—The 1991 model's changeover to more reliable Mazda components gave it a longer wheelbase, making for a more comfortable ride and a bit roomier interior. **1994**—ABS added to the GT, and all models got a driver-side airbag; motorized seat belts harass front passengers. **1995**—Dual airbags were installed and motorized seat belts remained (ugh). **1997**—Highlights are fresh styling, a new 110-hp 2.0L 4-cylinder engine, a standard 5-speed manual transmission and optional 4-speed automatic, dual airbags and optional ABS with rear discs. **1998**—Debut of a sporty Escort ZX2 coupe in the States, a year later in Canada. **2000**—Wagons axed and the ZX2 coupe got a firmer suspension and a 130-hp engine.

Owner complaints relating to the 1991–96 model years concern primarily seat belts and airbags, fuel tanks, coil spring and tie-rod failures; automatic transmission and engine (premature timing belt replacement around 90,000 km) breakdowns; and cooling system, brakes, electrical, air conditioning, fuel pump, and ignition system failures. Quality control and reliability improved a bit with the 1997 and 1998 models, but many of the earlier powertrain deficiencies remained.

The 1999 and 2000 models continue to have lots of engine and transmission failures, plus steering vibration, and electrical, fuel, and brake system problems (excessive wear of front brake pads and rotors around 10,000 km).

Safety summary: 1995–2000—An incredibly high number of safety-related complaints were recorded for these years. The following problems return continually: no airbag deployment; inadvertent airbag deployment; airbag-induced injuries; electrical and engine wiring fires; brake failures, and premature rotor and pad replacement; snapped front and rear coil springs damage tire; sudden tie-rod failure leading to steering loss; automatic transmission that slips, jumps out of gear, leaks, or fails early; unanticipated acceleration; seat belt malfunctions; horn that blows inadvertently, won't blow, or is hard to access; faulty door locks; and speedometer failures ($400 repair). **1996**—Many complaints that the fourth cylinder piston self-destructs, destroying engine. • Early steering assembly replacement. • Fuel line failures. • Doors stick shut. • Rear quarter panel water leaks. **1997**—Engine head gasket failures. • Chronic stalling caused by faulty fuse connection. • Heater core leak may cause a fire in the airbag assembly. • Crankshaft pulley failure results in steering loss. **1998**—Faulty fuel pump/pressure regulator, CV joints, and wheel bearings. • Delayed shifts. • Steering lock-up. • Defective engine mounts cause excessive vibration. **1999**—Chronic surging and stalling. • Headlight socket melts. • Hood flew open. • Faulty motor mounts cause excessive vibration. • Poor structural integrity (broken welds, distorted sheet metal, and extensive flexing throughout vehicle). • Suspension and alignment problems. • Poor defrosting. **2000**—Chronic stalling. • Vehicle suddenly jumps forward or rearward when the accelerator is only slightly depressed. • Excessive vibration. • Slips in and out of gear when coming to a stop. • Transmission coolant line clamp came apart. • Delayed transmission engagement, or slippage. • Power-steering loss due to snapped serpentine belt:

> While driving about 30 mph [48 km/h] power steering went out. Dealer found serpentine belt had snapped, causing bracket to water pump housing to break. Tension rod and water pump housing were replaced at consumer's cost.

• Brake pedal slowly creeps to the floor when applied. • Shock absorber rubbed against tire, causing a blowout. • Sunroof shattered while vehicle was parked. • Windshield suddenly shattered. • Seat belts jam in the retracted position. • Intermittent failure of the power door locks and windows.

Secret Warranties/Service Tips/TSBs

All models/years: Radio whining or buzzing noise can be eliminated by following the service tips found in TSB #01-7-3. • Repeated heater core failures have also been a frequent problem, covered in TSB #01-15-6. **1993–2001**—Paint delamination, peeling, or fading (see Part Two). **1994–98**—Tips on eliminating wind noise around doors are given in TSB #97-15-1. **1997–99**—PCV (positive crankcase ventilation) system may freeze, resulting in a serious oil leak through the dipstick tube. • A front brake grinding noise, pulling or drag, and uneven brake pad wear are all signs of corrosion affecting the caliper slide pins. • Excessive vibration at idle may be corrected by replacing the engine support crossmember bushings. This repair cost should be covered by Ford up to 7 years/160,000 km. • Tips on silencing a variety of squeaks and rattles. • No restart in cold weather, the cooling fan won't shut off, or the battery going dead all signal the need to change the integrated relay control module. **1997–2002**—Reduced engine power and stalling.

Engine – Low Power/Stalling/DTC's PO300-PO304 Set

Article No. 02-9-1   05/13/02

FORD:

1997–2002 Escort

2000–02

MERCURY:

1997–99 Tracker

ISSUE

Some vehicles equipped with the 2.0L SPI engine may exhibit a Malfunction Indicator Lamp (MIL) illuminated and Diagnostic Trouble Codes (DTCs) PO300 through PO304 stored in memory. The vehicle may also have a rough idle or reduced power condition, and/or may stall at an idle. This may be caused by sticking exhaust valves due to excessive carbon buildup.

ACTION

Check for faulty fuel injectors and ignition wires. One or more exhaust valves may be temporarily sticking due to carbon build-up between the valve stem and guide. If the diagnostic checks point to a sticking exhaust valve, the cylinder head assembly may need to be replaced with a new level cylinder head assembly that includes revised valve guides and exhaust valves to help prevent carbon buildup.

This is a major engine head gasket repair that could easily cost over $1,000. It is obviously a manufacturing defect that should be covered by Ford's benchmark 7-year warranty applied in its 1994–95 3.8L engine head gasket ONP covering the Taurus, Sable, and Windstar. Stand your ground.

1997–2003—Excessive vibration countermeasures:

Engine – Vibration While Idling

Article No.: 03-15-15

Date: 08/04/03

1997–2002 ESCORT
1998–2003 ESCORT ZX2
1997–99 TRACER

ISSUE: This TSB article is being republished to assist in diagnosing idle vibration.

ACTION: Diagnose and repair idle vibration conditions.

OTHER APPLICABLE ARTICLES: 99-11-1

WARRANTY STATUS: Eligible under the provisions of bumper-to-bumper warranty coverage.

OPERATION	DESCRIPTION	TIME
031515A	Neutralize engine mounts	0.3 hr.
2003 Escort ZX2		
031515B	Perform service procedure to diagnose and repair idle vibration concerns 1997–2002 Escort, Escort ZX2, and Tracer	2.3 hrs.
DEALER CODING		
	CONDITION	
BASIC PART NO.	CODE	
6028	07	

1998—An erratic transaxle shift may simply be caused by a pinched wire. • Erratic fuel gauge operation or slow fill-ups may be corrected by installing a slosh module fuel gauge kit. **1999**—Tips on reducing noise, vibration, and harshness. **2000**—Delayed transmission engagement; MIL light comes on. • Troubleshooting intake manifold air leaks. **2000–01**—Exhaust system buzzing or rattling (a problem for almost a decade). • Fuel fill nozzle clicks off too soon when fuelling up. • Positive crankcase ventilation (PCV) freezes up. • Inoperative CD player. • Tips on properly adjusting the transmission range sensor. • Remedy for a burning oil smell. • Troubleshooting poor engine performance at idle and excessive gas consumption. • Remedies for an engine that won't start or shut down properly. • Engine oil leak at the oil pan, front cover, or the front and rear crankshaft oil seal. • Engine oil pan gasket and oil filter leaks. • Vehicle may not start in freezing weather, due to moisture freezing in the fuel pump relay. • Fuel delivery malfunctions. • Eliminating a high idle condition when starting or decelerating. • Improved parking brake cables and rear brake linings are available to reduce rear brake drag. • Light to moderate rear axle whine. • Squeak, creak from driver's area. • Possible causes of a thump or clunk coming from the suspension. • Improved rear shock absorbers are available to reduce suspension noise. • Front seat cushion sagging. • Cause and correction of vinyl dash abrasions and premature wear. • Diagnostic tips to eliminate wind noise around doors. • Revise hood seal to reduce wind whistle. • AC goes into defrost mode when vehicle goes uphill. • Repeated heater core failures.

Escort, ZX2 Profile

	1994	1995	1996	1997	1998	1999	2000
Cost Price ($)							
Escort Base/LX	12,195	12,995	13,595	14,595	14,895	14,895	—
GT	13,995	14,295	15,295	—	—	—	—
ZX2	—	—	—	—	—	15,895	17,995
Used Values ($)							
Base/LX ⋀	2,000	2,500	3,000	4,000	5,000	5,500	—
Base/LX ⋁	1,500	2,000	2,500	3,500	4,500	5,000	—
GT ⋀	2,500	3,000	3,500	—	—	—	—
GT ⋁	2,000	2,500	3,000	—	—	—	—
ZX2 ⋀	—	—	—	—	—	6,000	7,500
ZX2 ⋁	—	—	—	—	—	5,500	7,000
Reliability	❷	❷	③	③	③	④	④
Crash Safety (F)	⑤	④	④	④	③	③	③
Side	—	—	—	—	③	③	③
Offset	—	—	—	③	③	③	③
Head Restraints	—	❶	—	❶	—	❶	—

Note: Ratings and prices are also applicable to the Mercury Tracer.

FOCUS   ★

RATING: Not Recommended (2000–03). How stupid can Ford be? Consider this: The Focus can't be driven through puddles because its low-mounted air intake hose ingests water into the engine ($5,000 repair). Chronic stalling is also a major problem, but Ford's secret warranty doesn't cover afflicted 2002 and 2003 models. **Maintenance/Repair costs:** Predicted to be higher than average once warranty expires. **Parts:** Expensive and sometimes hard to find. **Best alternatives:** The Geo Metro; GM Cavalier or Sunfire; Honda Civic (it's softer riding, quieter, and has a smoother-running engine); Hyundai Accent; Mazda Protegé; Suzuki Esteem; and Toyota Corolla, Echo, or Tercel. **Online help:** *www.autosafety.org/article.php?scid=&did=309.*

Strengths and weaknesses: Hailed as Europe's 1999 Car of the Year (yikes, that should be your first warning sign), Ford's sleek 2000 Focus came to North America shortly thereafter as an uplevel, premium small car. The Escort's base engine, a 110-hp 2.0L 4-cylinder, was carried over to the Focus LX and SE, while the 130-hp twin-cam 2.0L (also used on the Escort ZX2 coupe) became the standard power plant on the ZTS and ZX3 and optional on the SE.

Vehicle history: 2002—Debut of a high-performance, 170-hp SVT Focus with sport suspension and 17-inch wheels; and the ZX5, a four-door hatchback that looks like a shortened version of the Focus wagon. **2003**—A standard 5-year warranty came on the scene (should be at least seven years).

The 130-hp 2.0L engine is barely sufficient for highway cruising, where passing and merging require a bit more power. The Focus isn't a quiet car, either. Any decent speed is accompanied by constant engine buzz and some hard shifting with the automatic gearbox. Brakes add to the Focus' symphony of sound by emitting a grinding sound when applied, and the front suspension creaks when the car is put through its paces. There is some vibration felt when driving over smooth highways, and uneven terrain causes the car to bounce about.

The Focus does handle well in city traffic, thanks to its tight turning radius and nimble steering. The small back corner windows are also handy for keeping the rear visibility unobstructed. The car's unusually tall roofline gives ample headroom and allows for a higher, more upright riding position than what you'll see with traditional small cars. Front and rear legroom is impressive, as well, as long as the front passengers don't push their seats too far back.

This is one of the most unreliable and dangerously defective cars that Ford has built in recent memory. Powertrain, fuel, electrical, and brake system failures are commonplace. Service bulletins are replete with special instructions telling dealers how to practically rebuild the car to make it tolerably driveable. Powertrain problems include chronic stalling (covered up to 10 years by a secret warranty), excessive vibration, and poor engine and transmission performance. 2003 SVT flywheel, pressure plate, and clutch assembly failures. Other problems: ignition switch; seatback bar digs into driver's back; power window failure; excessive engine, brake, steering column, suspension, and wheel noise; trunk latch sticks or suddenly opens; trunk leaks water; AC leaks coolant; driver's door won't open from the inside; fuel door lid broke in half; hood latch broke off when closing hood; right rear door moulding fell off; and poor-fitting interior panels.

Safety summary: All models: 2000—NHTSA probes rear wheel-bearing defects. **2000–01**—NHTSA probes airbag burns, vehicle fires. • Ford admits to chronic stalling and extends engine computer warranty to 10 years (see Secret Warranties below). **2000–02**—NHTSA continues to investigate complaints of chronic stalling (*www.autosafety.org/EA02-022-OpeningMemo.pdf*), while Ford attempts different fixes outlined in confidential service bulletins. • Chronic stalling, with loss of brakes and steering, believed to be caused by faulty fuel pump. • Airbag deploys for no apparent reason or after vehicle hits a pothole. • Sudden brake loss. • Differential fluid leaks on brake components (right side), causing brake loss. • Defective speed control causes sudden acceleration in spite of corrective recall. • Other sudden acceleration incidents ascribed to faulty power control module (PCM) and driver's shoe being caught under the plastic console. • Sudden acceleration in Reverse. • Collapse of tie-rod and axle, leading to loss of control. • Defective axle wheel bearing. • Sudden pull to the left when turning left. • Clutch pedal spring pops out, injuring driver. • Pedal fell on floorboard. • Transmission slippage and failure. •

Inaccurate fuel gauge (sender and fuel pump replaced). • Windshield cracks for no reason. • AC condensation drips on accelerator pedal. • Exhaust fumes enter passenger compartment. • Smoking electrical wiring in dash. • Under-hood fire ignited after AC engaged. • Driver-side seat belt won't deploy. • Emergency brake often fails to engage because button on handle stays depressed. • Vehicle was cruising at 110 km/h when gas pedal fell off its mounting. • Frayed accelerator throttle cable snapped; cable also kinks, causing hesitation, acceleration, and surging. • Stabilizer bar suddenly broke. • Car left in Park, rolled downhill. • Rear end is very unstable in snow, feels "wobbly" under normal conditions, and throws rear passengers about. • Sudden, unintended acceleration, then engine cuts out. • Engine shuts down while cruising on the highway. • New engine needed because roadway rain-water ingested into engine due to low air intake valve. • Transmission hard to shift into Second and Reverse in cold weather. • Fuel tank leak due to cracked filler pipe. • No brakes. • No steering. • Steering wheel locks while driving. • Broken rack and pinion. • Airbags didn't deploy. • Tie-rod suddenly broke off. • Front and rear wheels buckle. • Collapsed front wheel:

> My father owns this vehicle, but he bought it for me for safety rea-sons. I am a 16-year-old female. Travelling at normal highway speed on a dry, two-lane highway with no traffic at night, my 2002 Ford Focus lost control due to the front control arm fracturing. My right front tire ended up totally unattached to the control arm and only staying attached to the vehicle by the hold of the tie-rod. My vehicle swerved into the median and into the oncoming traffic (thankfully no traffic was around).

• Rear hatch opens on its own. • Faulty rear wheel bearings cause wheel to wobble and wander. • Original Firestone tires wear out prematurely. • Child restraint bracket puts dents in the rear seat. • Inaccurate fuel gauge sender and fuel pump replaced. • Windshield cracks or shatters for no reason. • AC con-densation drips on accelerator pedal. • Exhaust fumes enter passenger compartment. • Dash lights flicker, then quit. **2003**—Chronic stalling. • Airbags failed to deploy. • Reports of severe back trauma from seatback failure in rear-enders. • Transmission and axle failures. • Sudden brake loss. • Excessive vibration. • Trunk latch suddenly releases. • Sunlight washes out speedometer reading. • Windshield cracks for no reason.

Secret Warranties/Service Tips/TSBs

All models: 2000—Ford Campaign No.: 03M02 allows for the free replace-ment of front coil springs that fracture up to 10 years or 150,000 miles (24,000 km).

Director   Ford Motor Company
Service Engineering Operations      P.O. Box 1904
Ford Customer Service Division   Dearborn, MI 48121-1904

May 2003

TO: All U.S. Ford and Lincoln Mercury Dealers

SUBJECT: Customer Satisfaction Program 03M02: Certain 2000 Model Year Focus Vehicles – Additional Coverage for Front Coil Springs

OASIS:

- Yes

OWNER LIST:

- No

PROGRAM TERMS:

This program extends the coverage on the front coil springs to 10 years of service or 150,000 miles from the vehicle's warranty start date, whichever occurs first. This coverage will automatically transfer to subsequent owners. If a vehicle already has more than 150,000 miles, this coverage will last until December 31, 2003.

VEHICLES COVERED BY THIS PROGRAM

Certain 2000 model year Focus vehicles built at Wayne Assembly Plant from March 5, 1999 through December 23, 1999 and at Hermosillo Assembly Plant from May 21, 1999 through December 30, 1999.

REASON FOR PROVIDING ADDITIONAL COVERAGE

In some of the affected vehicles, portions of the front coil springs may not have received adequate corrosion protection during the manufacturing process. Inadequate corrosion protection eventually may lead to a fracture of the spring. A spring fracture may result in suspension noice, possibly accompanied by saggiing of one side of the vehicle. This is most likely to occur on vehicles operated for extended periods of time in high-corrosion areas of North America. Only a small percentage of the affected vehicles are expected to experience this concern.

SERVICE ACTION

If a front coil spring should fracture, the dealer technician will replace both front coil springs, check front wheel alignment and, if necessary, adjust toe angle at no charge to the owner of the vehicle.

Take note that both coils must be replaced.

• Under Special Service Instruction 00204, Ford will reprogram the power-train computer module to correct poor engine performance on vehicles equipped with a manual transmission. • ONP 99B21 will replace the fuel pulse damper free of charge and ONP 99B22 will pay the costs associated with the replacement of the side engine mount. • Vehicles equipped with a manual transmission will have their clutch master cylinder and pedal return spring replaced, free of charge, under ONP 00B59. • Ford also announced in Special Field Action 0012 that it will henceforth guarantee all original equipment tires for 3 years/36,000 miles (58,000 km). • Defective Sony subwoofer speakers will be replaced for free under ONP 01B73. **2000–01**—Chronic stalling fix. Reuters News Service reported on November 20, 2003 that a faulty fuel delivery module linked to chronic engine stalling would be replaced free of charge by Ford up to 10 years, without any mileage limitation (Campaign No.: 03N01). Ford spokesman Glenn Ray told Reuters, "It's a product improvement program. There is nothing fundamentally wrong with the quality of the fuel delivery module. It doesn't fail instantaneously or suddenly." • Replace rear wheel bearings through December 31, 2003, regardless of mileage under Ford Campaign No.: 01B85. **2000–02**—AC evaporator case/cowl leaks water into the interior. • Whistling from the heater plenum. • AC fluttering noise. • Repeated heater core failure. • Low power and stalling (see 1997–2002 Escort section on page 111). **2000–03**—Troubleshooting rear end water leaks:

Trunk/Liftgate Area Water Leaks

Article No.: 02-15-6

Date: 08/05/02

WATER LEAK FROM TRUNK/LIFTGATE AREA

2000–03 FOCUS

ISSUE: Some vehicles may exhibit a difficult to diagnose or difficult to repair water leak condition in the trunk/liftgate area. This may be caused by panel sealing, panel adjustments, weatherstrips, etc.

2001—Shifter difficult to shift out of Park. • 2.0L Zetec engines may hesitate, surge, or idle roughly in cold weather. • Intermittent stalling, hesitation, or lack of power. • Engine may produce higher-than-normal idle speed, or run roughly at idle. • Slight engine vibration at idle. • Troubleshooting the Check Engine light. • Eliminating a burning oil smell. • Rear brake squeal may be caused by the composition of the lining material. • Power steering pump pulley may squeak or chirp upon start-up. • A squeaking may emanate from the door check strap area. • Ignition key may be difficult to turn in cylinder. • Seat seams may split.

Focus Profile

	2000	2001	2002	2003
Cost Price ($)				
LX	14,995	16,015	15,970	16,275
ZX3	16,697	16,690	17,390	17,550
Wagon SE	17,695	17,271	18,995	19,165
Used Values ($)				
LX ▲	6,000	7,500	9,000	10,000
LX ▼	5,000	6,000	7,500	9,000
ZX3 ▲	7,000	8,000	10,000	11,000
ZX3 ▼	6,000	7,500	9,000	10,000
Wagon SE ▲	8,000	10,000	11,000	12,500
Wagon SE ▼	7,000	9,000	10,500	11,500
Reliability	❶	❷	❷	③
Crash Safety (F)	⑤	⑤	④	④
4d	④	④	⑤	⑤
Wagon	—	—	⑤	⑤
Side	④	④	④	④
4d	③	③	③	③
Offset	④	④	④	④
Head Restraints	③	④	④	④
Rollover Resistance	—	④	④	④

General Motors

CAVALIER, SUNFIRE ★★★★

RATING: Above Average (2002–03); Average (1996–2001); Not Recommended (1984–95). One of the better American small cars, which isn't saying much; engine or brake repair bills will run you bankrupt if you get a pre-1996 model or if maintenance schedules aren't followed to the letter. Try to get a 2001–02 model with a 4-speed automatic transmission; it will be a bit more reliable, reduce engine noise, and make for more responsive performance. Mediocre crash protection. The base Sunbird changed its name to the Sunfire in 1995. The Cavalier Z24 convertible was replaced by the LS in 1995. **Maintenance/Repair costs:** Average. Repairs aren't dealer dependent; however, ABS troubleshooting is a real head-scratcher. **Parts:** Reasonably priced; often available for much less from independent suppliers. **Best alternatives:** The Geo Metro; Honda Civic; Hyundai Accent or Elantra; Mazda Protegé; Nissan Sentra; Suzuki Esteem; and Toyota Corolla, Echo, or Tercel. Also take a look at the slightly more upscale Hyundai Tiburon. **Online help:** *www.autosafety.org/article.php?did=41&scid=46* and *www.autooninfo.info/RelPerChevroletCharts.htm.*

Strengths and weaknesses: These twins are two of the lowest-priced cars to come equipped with standard ABS and dual airbags. In fact, GM claims it loses $1,000 on every one it sells. These small cars are attractively styled (especially the coupe), come with lots of interior room, and offer a nicely tuned suspension. The ride and handling have also improved markedly since 1999, with power rack-and-pinion steering, a longer wheelbase, and a wider track. The Sunfire is identical to the Cavalier, except for its more rakish look. The Cavalier Z24 and Sunfire GT are performance versions of the compacts introduced five years ago. They use a more refined version of the less-than-reliable Quad 4 2.4L DOHC 16-valve 4-cylinder power plant.

Vehicle history: 1995—Wider and taller than previous models; standard dual airbags and ABS; a stiffer structure; and an improved suspension. **1996**—LS sedan and convertible got standard traction control, and the Z24 picked up a new dual-camshaft 2.2L engine. **1998**—The base engine lost five horses. **1999**—2.4L twin-cam engine and front brake lining upgrades. **2000**—A slightly restyled front and rear end; an improved storage area; standard AC and PASSLOCK security system; upgraded standard ABS; and a smoother-shifting 5-speed manual transmission. **2003**—Re-styled and lengthened; a new 140-hp 2.2L engine; a stiffer suspension; larger wheels and rear brakes; three-point centre seat belts; optional front side airbags; and ABS.

Snappy road performance (with the right engine and transmission hookup), though, has been marred by abysmally poor powertrain reliability. The early 2.0L versions are lacklustre performers—overwhelmed by the demands of passing and merging. On top of that, major reliability weaknesses afflict many mechanical and body components through the 1998 model year, where engine, transmission, electronic module, and brake failures are particularly common. Specifically, owners report engine blocks crack, cylinder heads leak, and the turbocharged version frequently needs expensive repairs.

For 1990–94 versions, the Cavalier's base 2.2L 4-cylinder and optional 3.1L engines replaced the failure-prone 2.0L and 2.8L power plants. Unfortunately, the newer engines also have a checkered reputation, highlighted by reports of chronic head gasket failures afflicting the 4-cylinder power plant. Air conditioning and hood latch failures, seat belt defects, and a plethora of body deficiencies are also commonplace. Door bottoms and wheel housings are particularly vulnerable to rust perforation. Premature paint peeling and cracking, discoloration, and surface rust have been regular problems through 1997.

Since 1999, these vehicles have become more reliable and durable. Nevertheless, owners are still plagued by troublesome engines, faulty brakes, airbags that continue to malfunction and injure occupants, chronic stalling, and transmission and fuel pump failures. The Getrag manual gearbox isn't very reliable, nor is it easily repaired, and faulty computer modules, fuel injection, and cooling systems cause stalling and a shaky idle. The power steering may lead or pull, and the steering rack tends to deteriorate quickly, usually requiring replacement some time shortly after 80,000 km. The front MacPherson struts also wear out rapidly, as do the rear shock absorbers. Many owners complain of rapid front brake wear and warped brake discs after a year or so. One owner reported the following brake repairs to NHTSA:

> Front brake rotors are warping and had to be turned at 1,600 miles [2,560 km] and 1,800 miles [2,880 km]. They then were replaced at 2,800 miles [4,480 km]. They would cause the vehicle to jump when braking.

Owner-reported problems for the past four model years: front vacuum leak causes vehicle to lose power; lots of electrical system glitches; hard starts; chronic stalling; slipping transmission; grinding noise when shifting gear; rattling noise when shifting from First to Second gear; frequent steering failures and noisy steering; excessive pulsation when braking; airbag warning lamp coming on continuously; a symphony of interior noises; and window that may fall off its track and slide between the door panels. Fit and finish quality is still quite variable, often leading to poor paint application, inside and outside body panel gaps, and lots of exposed screw heads. Most body hardware is fragile (like the bumper coming apart).

Safety summary: Although complaints have been separated according to model and year, there is considerable overlap since these two vehicles are practically identical. **All years**: Engine head gasket and intake manifold failures. • Transmission slippage or breakdown. • Owners report complete brake failure and lock-up, extended stopping distances, ABS that self-activates, premature rotor warpage and pad wear, and a grinding and knocking noise when braking. • Airbags fail to deploy or deploy accidentally. • Sudden acceleration, stalling. • Weak door hinges. • Inoperative horn. **1997**—Engine fires. • During a collision, driver sustained serious leg injuries when the seat pushed her lower body under the instrument panel. • Premature oil pump failure. • Faulty fuel pump relay provokes stalling. • Failure of the engine mounts and ignition switch. • Cruise control failure. • Sudden loss of power. • Steering wheel locked up. • Faulty master cylinder and modulator assembly led to brake failure. • Cracked water pump. • Dashboard cracking, rattling, and popping. • Defective instrument panel control module. • Low beam switch failure. • Inoperative lighting due to rotted-out wiring harness. • Door hinges don't hold door open. • Door came ajar while driving. • Windshield wiper failure. • When turned off, windshield wiper stops in the field of vision. • Lug nuts are easily broken when changing tire. **1998**—Fire in the trunk area. • Airbag-induced burns and fractures are common. • Loose or broken engine mounts. • Chronic engine overheating. • Steering wheel locks up after a cold start. • Steering shaft sheared off when turning. • Inaccurate fuel gauge. • One Saskatchewan *Lemon-Aid* reader reports that the rear bumper will crack extensively in cold weather if hit only slightly. • Windshield glare from the dash. • Driver seat lever interferes with entry/exit. **1999–2000**—The trunk lid remains open at such a low angle that it's easy to hit your head. **2000–01**—NHTSA engine stalling probe. **2001**—Fire caused by shorted wire in the back seat area. • Chronic stalling (fuel pump suspected) and hard starting. • Vehicle loses power due to a vacuum leak. • Gears slip and grind when shifting automatic transmission. • Steering loss; steering column creaking. • Reports of windshield and sunroof suddenly shattering. • Windshield constantly fogs up. **2002**—Driver injured when seatback failed after vehicle was rear-ended. • Springs suddenly pushed out of the seatback. • Premature failure of Goodyear tires. • Vehicle may roll away with gearshift lever in Park and key removed from the ignition. • Frequent stalling due to faulty PCM module. • Transmission suddenly slipped into Neutral while cruising on the highway. **Cavalier: 1999–2001**—Engine fires. • Leaking fuel tank. • Plastic fuel tank is easily punctured. • Right wheel axle twisted off vehicle. • Chronic hesitation, stalling, and surging. • Clutch will not disengage, causing sudden acceleration. • Brake failure due to leaking master cylinder fluid. • ABS locked up, causing vehicle to go into a skid. • Seat belt failed to retract. • Transmission wouldn't go into Reverse, transmission failed to engage upon start-up, automatic transmission locks up in Second gear, and vehicle rolled away even though parked with parking brake engaged. • When vehicle is in Drive with foot on the brake, it lurches forward, stalls, and produces a crashing sound. • During highway driving, the vehicle suddenly accelerated without steering control. • Rear leaf spring U-bolts broke, causing entire rear end to drop. • Front right side of the vehicle collapsed due to wheel bolts shearing off, causing the wheel to detach completely. • Springs are too weak, causing poor stability and control. • Floor mat impedes clutch pedal travel. • Sudden brake cable breakage while driving, brake grinding noise, and early warping of the front and rear brakes. • When driving with door locked, door came ajar. • Hood flew up while driving. • Misaligned driver's door. • Windshield water leaks. **2002**—Reverse tail light bulb exploded, causing light assembly to catch on fire. • Considerable fuel spillage when refuelling. • Left rear axle fell off. • Plastic bumper fell off while driving. • Headlights often go out. **2003**—Tire jack collapsed. • Transmission allows vehicle to roll backward when parked. • Inoperative fuel gauge. • Stalling caused by defective fuel pump. • Burnt electrical wires and light sockets. • Excessive driver's side mirror vibration. **Sunfire: 1999–2001**—Brake master cylinder leaks. • When brakes are applied, all the interior lights go out. • Dash warning light indicating time to upshift comes on at the wrong time. • Fuel tank leakage. • AC fumes enter the interior at idle. **2002**—Sudden brake failure. • At highway speeds, vehicle will suddenly shut down.

Secret Warranties/Service Tips/TSBs

All models/years: GM has a new kit that it says will eliminate AC odours. • A rotten-egg odour coming from the exhaust is probably caused by a malfunctioning catalytic converter; this repair may be covered by GM's emissions warranty. • Paint delamination, peeling, or fading (see Part Two). • Plastic wheel nut covers tend to fall off. GM will replace them for free on a case-by-case basis, says TSB #01-03-10-009. **All models: 1985–2000**—Snow may intrude into the rear brake drum assembly and interfere with braking, says TSB #00-05-24-001, April 2000. **1992–97**—Inspect the timing chain every 100,000 km to make sure the front oil passage plug isn't blocked by debris. **1995–97**—Axle seal leakage may be caused by a pinched transaxle vent hose. •

Delayed automatic transmission engagement after a cold soak signals the need to install a revised forward clutch housing assembly. • Rear brakes that heat up or drag may need the brake lamp switch adjusted or new parking brake cables. • Repair tips are offered for scuffed interior quarter-trim panels on convertibles. • A sticking deck lid may need an upgraded lid release cable. • A dome light that won't shut off probably has a corroded door jamb switch. • The left-hand mirror may not adjust if the lever has become disengaged. • A popping noise originating from the engine compartment may mean that the torque strut-mount attaching bolts are loose. • Rear shock noise can be silenced by installing upgraded upper shock mounts. • Troubleshooting tips on silencing rear shock noise and rear seatback rattles and squeaks are available. • Door rattles when the window is lowered may be silenced by replacing the door glass downstop or front guides. **1995–98**—A bulge in the front bucket seatback requires additional bracing to correct. • Install a drain path in convertibles to prevent water from collecting in the rear footwell area. **1995–99**—A faulty rear lid (trunk) latch may only need a new cable. **1995–2000**—Instrument panel squeak or rattle, scratched right front door trim panel, or right-side end of instrument panel contacting door trim panel can be fixed by removing the instrument panel assembly and realigning the tie bar. This two-hour repair will be covered under GM's base warranty or through its "goodwill" policy. • GM will install upgraded rear brake backing plates to prevent snow intrusion freezing the brake shoes to the drums. **1995–2003**—Engine head gasket failures that include overheating, loss of coolant, coolant odour, coolant leaks around the cylinder head, and white smoke from the exhaust. Sometimes the heater won't work, or a film (from the coolant) will be deposited on the inside glass surfaces. If the coolant leaks inside the engine, it can cause severe engine damage from overheating. GM "goodwill" covers head gasket problems for 7 years/100,000 miles (160,000 km), whichever comes first. Remember, if you have an engine head gasket failure on a GM vehicle or engine not included in the above-noted programs, don't despair. Simply use the same benchmarks for your own vehicle and threaten small claims action on those grounds. Make sure you cite TSB #98054A, "Campaign: Cylinder Head Gasket Failure, Coolant Leakage," published September 1998. Incidentally, some *Lemon-Aid* readers say minor head gasket leaks can be plugged by a $30 (U.S.) sealer called "Cracked Leak Cure" that's available at *www.detsco.com/clc*. • Automatic transmission delay and surging (flare) (see following bulletin).

A/T – Shift Flare/SES Lamp ON/DTC's Set

Bulletin No.: 03-07-30-021

Date: May 2003

Neutral flare and/or rpm flare while in Drive, no 1–2 upshift, Service Engine Soon (SES) light illuminated, diagnostic trouble codes (DTCs) P1810, DTC P1815 set (replace transmission fluid pressure (TFP) manual valve position switch)

1995–2003	Chevrolet Cavalier
1997–2003	Chevrolet Malibu
1999–2003	Oldsmobile Alero
1995–2003	Pontiac Sunfire
1998–2003	Pontiac Grand Am

➤

with 4T40E Transmission (RPO MN4) or 4T45E Transmission (RPO MN5)

Some customers may comment on a neutral flare and/or rpm increase while in Drive or no 1–2 upshift and/or the Service Engine Soon (SES) telltale may be illuminated. On 1995–2002 model vehicles, the Powertrain Control Module (PCM) may set a DTC P1810 while on 2003 model vehicles, the PCM may set a DTC P1815. The cause may be the transmission fluid pressure (TFP) switch (also known as the pressure switch manifold [PSM]). It will be referred to as the TFP switch in this bulletin.

1996–97—Coolant odour or leakage may occur at the joint where the radiator outlet pipe is connected to the coolant pump cover or at the joint between the cooling system air-bleed pipe and the coolant outlet. • Coolant loss, leakage, coolant lamp on, or coolant odour can be corrected by installing a new thermostat gasket. **1996–2002**—Coolant leakage from the water pump weep hole will be plugged by installing a free coolant collector, says TSB #01-06-02-012. **1997**—A Low Engine Coolant light may come on to signal that the cooling system surge tank is defective. **1997–2002**—A clunk noise from the front of the vehicle when turning may be fixed by simply lubricating the intermediate shaft, says TSB #01-02-032-001A. **1998**—A delayed, slow, or no 2–3 upshift may require a new transmission case cover or assembly. • A 2.2L cold engine hesitation, sag, or stall may be corrected by recalibrating the power control module (PCM). **1999–2000**—No Third and Fourth gear may require a new direct clutch piston assembly. **1999–2002**—Problems opening the fuel-filler door can be fixed by installing a free fuel-filler pocket, says TSB #01-08-65-001. **2000**—Premature connecting rod failure if engine is run at high rpms with low mileage. • Rough engine idle, misfire, or Check Engine light coming on are all due to a poorly calibrated computer module. • Possibility of engine coolant leaks caused by the upper radiator hose rubbing against the battery tray. • Automatic transmission may not go into Third or Fourth gear. • Mismachined sealing surface on forward clutch housing (4T40-E transmission). • Grinding or growling from transmission when in Park on an incline. • Vehicles equipped with a 2.2L engine may produce an annoying engine or transmission whine. • Door rattles. • Driver-side manual mirror doesn't adjust when the adjusting lever is moved. **2000–02**—Harsh transmission shifts accompanied by the Service Engine Soon lamp warning is caused by a short in the input speed sensor wiring, says TSB #00-06-04037A. • Manual transmission rattle. • A wet road "sizzle" noise coming from the rear of the vehicle requires the installation of free wheelhouse liners, says TSB #01-08-58-005. • Inaccurate fuel gauge readings can be corrected for free by installing a new fuel tank sender sensor kit under Customer Satisfaction Campaign #00101 (see "Inaccurate fuel gauge readings" TSB on page 3). **2000–03**—Troubleshooting engine problems (see following bulletin).

Engine – Overheating/Coolant Consumption/Smoke

Bulletin No.: 03-06-01-022

Date: July 29, 2003

Guidelines for Cylinder Bore Liner Replacement on the L4 Ecotec Engine
2002–03 Chevrolet Cavalier
2002–03 Oldsmoblie Alero
2002–03 Pontiac Grand Am, Sunfire
with 2.2L Engine (VIN F - RPO L61)

Replacement of the cylinder bore liner is now a validated service repair process and an alternative to engine block or engine assembly replacement. Conditions for engine cylinder bore liner replacement are somewhat difficult to determine and may initially appear as other common customer concerns. Customer may comment on conditions such as:

^Engine overheating

^Engine coolant consumption

^White smoke from vehicle exhaust

^Poor heater performance

^Excessive engine oil consumption

^Unusual engine knocking noises

Drivetrain – Clunk Noise During Low Speed Turns

Bulletin No.: 03-07-29-005

Date: June 2003
Clunk noise from front end during low speed turns or manoeuvres
(Replace side transmission mount)
2000–03 Chevrolet Cavalier
2000–03 Pontiac Sunfire with 5-speed manual transmission (RPO MM5)

Some customers may comment on a clunk noise from the front of the vehicle. This condition is most common during a hard left or right turn when starting from a complete stop.

2001–02—If the vehicle fails to crank or start, the battery cable connection may be at fault. • Inoperative cigarette lighter will be replaced for free, says TSB #01-08-49-016. **2002**—ABS light comes on when transmission is placed in Second or Fourth gear. • 4-speed automatic transmission fluid leakage. • Faulty automatic transmission converter pump. • Customer Satisfaction Campaign inspection for transaxle converter bearing failure are detailed in TSB #01031. • Windshield glass distortion. • Inaccurate fuel gauge readings. • Exterior lamp condensation. • MIL warning lamp stays on. • Hoot or whistling upon start-up in cold weather. • CD can't be inserted or ejected. **2003**—Troubleshooting erratic shifting (see following bulletin).

SES Lamp ON/Firm Shifts/No Downshifts/Shudder

Bulletin No.: 02-07-30-039C

Date: June 12, 2003

Firm transmission shifts, shudder/chuggle, transmission won't downshift on deceleration, Service Engine Soon light illuminated, DTC P0742 set (perform diagnostics and replace TCC PWM solenoid)

2003 Buick Century, LeSabre, Park Avenue, Regal, Rendezvous
2003 Cadillac DeVille, Seville
2003 Chevrolet Cavalier, Impala, Malibu, Monte Carlo, Venture
2003 Oldsmobile Alero, Aurora, Silhouette
2003 Pontiac Aztek, Bonneville, Grand Prix, Grand Am, Montana, Sunfire

• Correcting transmissions that won't shift, or shift erratically (replace driven sprocket support assembly).

Cavalier, Sunfire Profile

	1996	1997	1998	1999	2000	2001	2002	2003
Cost Price ($)								
Cavalier	13,030	14,390	14,765	15,365	15,765	14,260	14,500	15,785
Z24	17,643	19,000	19,295	20,035	20,515	21,165	22,475	21,550
Z24 Conv./LS	22,925	24,285	25,880	26,450	27,200	—	—	—
Sunfire	13,380	15,340	15,960	16,135	16,165	14,755	14,790	15,485
Used Values ($)								
Cavalier △	3,000	4,000	4,500	5,000	6,000	7,000	8,000	9,500
Cavalier ▽	2,500	3,500	4,000	4,500	5,000	6,000	7,000	8,500
Z24 △	4,500	5,500	6,500	8,000	9,000	11,000	13,000	14,000
Z24 ▽	3,500	4,500	5,000	7,000	8,000	10,000	11,500	13,000
Z24 Conv. /LS △	6,500	7,500	9,000	10,000	11,000	—	—	—
Z24 Conv. /LS ▽	5,500	6,500	8,000	9,000	10,000	—	—	—
Sunfire △	3,500	4,500	5,000	5,500	6,500	7,500	9,000	10,000
Sunfire ▽	3,000	3,500	4,500	5,000	5,500	6,500	8,000	9,000
Reliability	❶	❷	❷	③	③	③	③	③
Crash Safety (F)								
Cavalier 2d	—	—	③	③	③	③	③	④
Cavalier 4d	③	③	④	④	④	④	④	④
Side								
Cavalier 2d	—	—	❶	❶	❶	❶	❶	❶
Cavalier 4d	—	—	❶	❶	❶	❶	❶	❶
Offset	❷	❷	❷	❷	❷	❷	❶	❶
Head Restraints	—	❷	—	❷	—	❷	❶	❶
Rollover Resistance	—	—	—	—	—	④	④	④

Note: NHTSA says the Sunfire safety ratings should be identical to the Cavalier's score.

SATURN S-SERIES, L-SERIES, ION   ★★

RATING: *S-series coupe:* Below Average (1998–2002); Not Recommended (1992–97). *L-series:* Below Average (2000–03); *Ion:* Below Average (2003). Japanese and South Korean competitors have been proven to offer far better quality at a competitive cost. Even GM's less pretentious models, like the Cavalier and Sunfire or the miniscule Metro and Firefly, offer better quality and value for your money. Don't go anywhere near a used Saturn unless you're armed to the teeth with a comprehensive extended warranty or have thoroughly perused this Saturn owners' forum: *www.pedsweb.com/saturn.* Owners wishing to customize their cars or get inexpensive parts should contact *www.6thplanetusedparts.com/links2.html.* As bizarre as it may appear, the Saturn division has a better reputation than the car it sells. **Maintenance/Repair costs:** Average; repairs aren't dealer dependent, unless you're seeking some Saturn "goodwill" refunds. **Parts:** Higher-than-average cost, but not hard to find through independent suppliers. **Best alternatives:** The Honda Civic LX, Hyundai Elantra, and Toyota Corolla perform well and are more refined and reliable. **Online help:** *www.geocities.com/saturn_hate/index.html*; *fixmysaturn.netfirms.com*; *www.geocities.com/lafire000/*; and *koenigland.com/saturn.*

Strengths and weaknesses: The entry-level S-series is far from high-tech and has remained virtually unchanged, except for the addition of a larger L-series for the 2000 model year, a minor face-lift, and a bit more legroom (phased in since it was launched in 1991). The base model provides a comfortable driving position, adequate instrumentation and controls, unobstructed visibility, good braking, dent-resistant body panels, and better-than-average crashworthiness scores. But, balancing these advantages, buyers have to contend with excessive engine noise, limited rear seat room, optional ABS and traction control, the coupe's third-door window that doesn't roll down, and serious factory-related deficiencies.

L-series

In an attempt to save money by adapting a European car to the American market, Saturn brought out the LS sedan and LW wagon, derivatives of GM's Opel Vectra. Some major differences, however, include a lengthened body, a standard ignition theft-deterrent system, a re-engineered chassis to give a more comfortable ride, and the use of a homegrown 137-hp 2.2L 4-banger constructed with aluminum components (remember the Vega?). Other components lifted directly from the European parts bin are the Opel's 3.0L V6 engine, a manual transmission from Saab, and German-made braking systems.

The more-expensive L-series models provide a more comfortable driving position and a roomy interior with a full range of convenience features, instruments, and controls. The 2002 L-series got standard head curtain airbags, ABS brakes, four-wheel disc brakes on all but the base model, and traction control. The V6 powertrain matchup, firm ride, impressive high-speed stability, and impressive braking all point to the L-series' European heritage. Additionally, there's better soundproofing and lots of storage areas, including a large, accessible trunk.

Vehicle history: Coupe: 1992—Returns with upgrades to reduce engine noise and vibration. **1993**—A standard driver-side airbag. **1994**—A recalibrated transmission. **1995**—A standard passenger-side airbag, 15 more horses for the base engine, and minor styling changes. **1996**—An upgraded 4-speed automatic. **1999**—An innovative third half-door on the driver's side. **2000**—Front seats were given more travel. **2002**—Replaced by the 2003 Ion. **Saturn L-series: 2002**—Standard curtain side airbags. **2003**—A restyled front end and four-wheel disc brakes.

Saturns have exhibited a plethora of serious body and mechanical problems, which GM has masked by generously applying its base warranty to original buyers. Owners of used Saturns are treated like they're from some other planet, however, and frequently complain that they had to pay dearly for GM's powertrain and body mistakes. Servicing quality has been spotty, too, and will likely become more problematic as GM takes the division off life-support in an effort to make it profitable.

The loud, coarse, standard single-cam engine gives barely adequate acceleration times with the manual transmission. This time is increased with the 4-speed automatic gearbox, which robs the engine of what little power it produces. Other generic problems affecting all model years are rough running, stalling, hard starting, and very poor gas mileage.

GM has been more upfront in admitting its vehicles' failures, like its announcement to extend its "goodwill warranty" to six years on 1994–96 Saturns that overheat and blow their engine head gaskets. Nevertheless, in some cases, the engine repair only lasts for a little while, as other powertrain problems soon appear:

> My '96 SW1 suffered a cracked cylinder head, which was repaired under a "goodwill" policy. Subsequently, four weeks later my engine seized and had to be replaced.
>
> I have gone all the way up the line with Saturn and their "experts" are claiming there is no relation to the two incidents, but are refusing to explain why. I will be taking them to court to get the $3,000 back for the repairs.
>
> The irony of this all, is as I was trying to sell the vehicle (I will never buy a Saturn again), my transmission failed, as did the clutch disc. This is another $3,000 worth of repairs. I bought the car for $13,000 in June of 2000 with only 67,000 km on it. Since January 27, 2002, when it had 144,000 km on it, I have had $9,000 in repairs to it. Please, please tell your readers, public, and whoever you can to stay away from Saturn! They make terrible vehicles and are even worse in customer service.

How ironic that a company ranked number one in dealer service according to the J.D. Power and Associates 2002 Customer Service Index Study can't assume its responsibilities when the original warranty expires.

Technical service bulletins and other owner complaints indicate that a variety of major quality problems are likely to crop up. These include self-destructing engines; chronically malfunctioning automatic transmissions; failure-prone brake, ignition, fuel, and electrical systems (flickering, dimming lights your cup of tea?); alternator and AC compressor failures; a host of body defects, led by paint delamination, rattles, wind and water leaks; poorly welded exhaust systems; and failure-prone Firestone tires (mostly the Affinity brand).

Ion

A larger, more comfortable, and more powerful vehicle than its S-series predecessor, the Ion is powered by a 140-hp 2.2L 4-cylinder engine, and gives buyers the choice of either a four-door coupe or sedan. Other features include power steering, a 5-speed manual transmission, speed-sensitive windshield wipers, split folding rear seatbacks, and plastic body side panels.

Safety summary: All models/years: Reports of stuck accelerators. • Airbag failed to deploy. • Seat belt failed to restrain driver in collision. • Gear lever slips out of gear and is hard to put into Reverse. • Manual transmission jumps out of Third and Fifth gear. • Frequent brake failures. • Brake rotor warpage and frequent pad replacement. • Sudden head gasket failure causes other engine components to self-destruct. • Chronic stalling. • Loss of steering control. • Poor horn performance. **1996–97**—Steering wheel came apart while car was being driven. • In a rear-end collision, driver's seatback broke, causing serious injuries. **L-series: 2000–01**—Transmission can't be shifted into a forward gear. • Location of power seat button allows it to be accidentally activated, causing seat to suddenly recline. • Power door locks short out. **2000–02**—Inoperative rear door glass (see following bulletin).

BULLETIN NO.: 02-T-27   ISSUE DATE: May 2002

CATEGORY TYPE: Body – 04

CATEGORY: Doors/Windows/Mirrors

CORPORATION NO.: 02-08-64-010

SUBJECT:

Rear Door Glass Inoperative or Operates Erratically due to Window Regulator becoming Disengaged from Door Glass (Adjust Front and/or Rear Door Glass Run Channels, and Re-engage Window Regulator to Door Glass)

MODELS AFFECTED:

2000–02 L-Series vehicles

CONDITION:

Some customers may comment the rear door glass is inoperative or displays erratic operation.

CAUSE:

The condition may be caused by excessive fore and aft movement of the door glass between the window run channels.

CORRECTION:

To correct this condition refer to service procedure in this bulletin to adjust the front and/or rear door glass window run channels.

• Electrical short causes all lights and gauges to suddenly come on. • Seat belt won't lock up at sudden stops. **2002**—Headlights and interior lights go out, flicker or dim intermittently when foot is taken off accelerator, or clutch or cooling fan is engaged. • Tire rims broke off. • Door handles don't go back into place after being used. **SC1: 2000–01**—When applying brakes, there's excessive noise coming from the rear end. • Fuel sloshing sound when fuel tank is half full. • Brake pedal makes a loud popping noise or drops to the floor, without warning. **2002**—Stabilizer bar actually causes excessive vibration. **SC2: 2000–01**—Seat belt tightens on any sudden movement, however slight. • The small, recessed horn buttons make it hard to find and activate the horn without looking down. **SC2: 2002**—Ineffective, noisy brakes. **SL: 2000–01**—Steering wheel came apart while driving. • Total loss of steering when the retaining clip was omitted during assembly. **SL1: 2000–01**—Windshield wipers fail to adequately clean the windshield. • Defrosting system doesn't work properly, causing moisture damage and poor visibility. **2002**—Seat belt suddenly unlatched when vehicle was rear-ended. Engine makes a ticking noise and then suddenly stalls in traffic. • In a rear-ender, seat lever released, causing seatback to suddenly recline. • Unable to shift to a lower gear when going downhill. • Inaccurate fuel gauge. **SL2: 2000–01**—Sudden acceleration. • Seat belts are hard to engage. • When driving at night, one sees multiple lights when looking through the rear view mirror at the vehicle in back, as well as the reflection of the defroster lights. • During rainy weather, rear windshield view is distorted or wavy. **2002**—Faulty throttle position sensor (TPS) causes vehicle to maintain speed when braking. **SW2: 2000–01**—Automatic transmission slippage caused collision. • Film collects on interior of windshield.

Secret Warranties/Service Tips/TSBs

All models: 1991–97—SOHC engines that run hot or have coolant mixed in the engine oil probably have a defective engine cylinder—a factory-related goof, according to TSB #96-T-65A. As a partial response to angry Saturn owners, GM has set up a "goodwill" warranty to pay for head gasket repairs for 6 years/ 160,000 km. Owners of Saturns that have exceeded this limitation may seek refunds from small claims court.

BULLETIN NO.: 96-T-65A   **ISSUE DATE: February 1997**

GROUP/SEQ. NO. Engine-15   **CORPORATION NO.: 686204R**

SUBJECT:

Engine Runs Hot and Engine Oil Mixed with Engine Coolant in Engine Coolant Recovery Resevoir (Replace Cylinder Head Assembly)

This bulletin is revised to replace an incorrect part number for the one gallon container of DEX-COOL (TM) and supersedes bulletin 96-T-65, which should be discarded.

MODELS AFFECTED:

1991–97 Saturns equipped with SOHC (LKO-1991–1994, L24-1995°1997) ENGINES

CONDITION:

Engine may run hot and/or have engine oil mixed with engine coolant. This condition may be noticeable when checking coolant recovery reservoir level.

CAUSE:

Some 1991–97 SOHC engines may develop a crack on or near the camshaft journals and surrounding casting areas allowing engine oil to mix with engine coolant. These cracks may be caused "folds" in the aluminum that occur during the head casting process.

CLAIM INFORMATION

Case Type	Description	Labour Operation Code	Time
VW	Replace Cylinder Head Assembly	T9715	11.2 hrs
Add:	with AC		0.8 hrs
	with power steering		0.3 hrs

To receive credit for this repair during the warranty coverage period, submit a claim through the Saturn Dealers System as shown.

Imagine over 12 hours being needed to repair GM's factory mistake. Take special note that the problem is carried forward in the TSB to the 1997 model, whereas the official "goodwill" warranty stops with the 1996 models.

• Paint delamination, peeling, or fading (see Part Two). **1991–2001**—GM admits in TSB #01-T-07 that a cracked engine coolant temperature sensor may be the culprit behind hard starts, poor engine performance, engine over-heating, and leaking or low coolant. **1996–97**—If your Saturn runs out of fuel while the fuel gauge reads one-quarter full, it's likely you have a plugged EVAP canister vent, which should be repaired free of charge under the emissions war-ranty. • Water leaks into the headliner on cars equipped with a sunroof require new drain hoses or better sealing. **1996–2001**—Water leaks into headliner are likely caused by a faulty sunroof or plugged drain hole grommets. **1996–2003**—A rotten-egg odour coming from the exhaust is likely the result of a malfunctioning catalytic converter, which you can have replaced free of charge under GM's emissions warranty. **1998**—Dozens of bulletins target a plethora of rattles, whistles, pops, clicks, knocking, and grinding noises. • Sunroof, footwell, and trunk water leaks are also common problems addressed in a variety of service bulletins. • Excessive vehicle vibration. • Noisy window regulator. • Premature corrosion near door weather strip. • Loss of AC vent air-flow. • Reducing AC odours. • Power steering pump drive shaft seal leak. • Intermittent no-start. • Transaxle whine in Second gear. • Rear brake noise and pulsation countermeasures. **1999**—Harsh shifting. • Steering column pop-ping. • Rattle, pop, or clicking noise from front of vehicle. • AC noise (hissing). • Clunking noise in front side door when windows are operated. • Troubleshooting chronic short circuits. • Water leak onto headliner and/or left footwell area and rear luggage compartment. • Excessive vibration at cruising speed. **1999–2002**—GM says in TSB #01-T-35 that it may replace the wind-shield washer pump seal and affected nozzle if the spray pattern is unacceptable. **2000**—In a March 2000 Customer Satisfaction Campaign letter (No: 00-C-09) sent to dealers, GM admits that the Saturn 2.2L 4-cylinder engines "were produced with internal engine components that may fail prema-turely. The most likely symptom you may experience is an engine miss accompanied by an engine noise." GM says it will replace the engine at no charge with no mileage or time limitations, in addition to providing a loaner vehicle or paying rental costs. **2000–01**—Delayed, harsh engagement into Reverse or Drive, erratic shifting between First and Second gear, or no Second or Third gears. • AC odours upon start-up. • Steering wheel shake or vibration at highway speeds. • Inoperative power windows and sunroof. **2000–02**—If the engine produces a whistling noise, GM suggests you replace the engine intake manifold gasket in TSB #02-T-22. Of course, this should be a free repair, under J025-1. • GM has a quick fix for headliner sagging at rear of sun-roof opening. • Water leaks into the interior will be fixed under warranty, says TSB #00-T-41A. **2002**—Transmission fluid leakage is likely from a faulty transaxle temperature sensor. **L-series: 2000–01**—No Third and Fourth gear (replace direct clutch piston assembly). • Steering wheel shake or vibration at highway speeds. • Front doors re-lock after being unlocked with key. • Rattle from behind the right-hand side of the instrument panel. • Wind whistle from the front door glass area and from the outside rear-view mirror. • Inoperative rear door glass. **2000–02**—A free revised intake manifold gasket will cure engine whistle. • Troubleshooting the most common water leaks into the interior. • Headliner sagging. • Misaligned rear bumper. **2000–03**—Poor AC automatic temperature control performance. **2002**—Inadequate horn performance. **2002–04**—A defective or contaminated fuel sender is the likely cause of inaccurate fuel readings. GM will adjust or replace the sender under a secret "goodwill" warranty (see TSB #03-08-49-022). **Ion: 2003–04**—Intermittent no-start. • Low-speed grinding noise or hesitation requires the installation of a new TCM calibration, says TSB #03-07-30-051. • Automatic transmission delay, surging requires the replacement of the control valve body and recalibration of the ECM (TSB #03-07-30-052). • Clutch chatter; won't release. • Coolant leak from water pump plug; upgraded water pump. • Fuel system buzzing or growling from rear of vehicle. • Water leaks into the interior. • Rear door cracking. • Faulty blower motor.

Saturn S-series, L-series, Ion Profile

	1996	1997	1998	1999	2000	2001	2002	2003
Cost Price ($)								
SL	12,998	13,948	14,188	13,488	13,588	14,358	14,245	—
SC	15,348	16,028	16,418	16,618	16,743	16,763	16,765	—
LS/L100	—	—	—	—	19,255	20,065	21,125	—
LW/LW200	—	—	—	—	24,400	25,235	23,325	25,355
Ion	—	—	—	—	—	—	—	15,495
Used Values ($)								
SL ⋀	2,500	3,000	4,000	5,000	6,000	7,000	10,500	—
SL ⋁	3,000	2,500	3,500	4,500	5,500	6,000	10,000	—
SC ⋀	4,000	4,500	5,500	6,500	7,500	8,500	11,500	—
SC ⋁	3,500	4,000	4,500	6,000	7,000	8,000	11,000	—
LS/L100 ⋀	—	—	—	—	8,500	10,000	12,500	—
LS/L100 ⋁	—	—	—	—	7,500	9,000	11,000	—
LW/LW200 ⋀	—	—	—	—	11,000	12,500	15,500	17,500
LW/LW200 ⋁	—	—	—	—	10,000	12,000	14,500	16,500
Reliability	❶	❶	❶	❶	❷	❷	❷	③
Crash Safety (F)	④	④	⑤	⑤	—	—	⑤	⑤
L-series	—	—	—	—	—	④	⑤	④
Ion	—	—	—	—	—	—	—	⑤
Side	—	③	③	③	—	—	③	③
L-series	—	—	—	—	—	❷	③	③
Ion	—	—	—	—	—	—	—	③
Offset	③	③	③	③	③	③	③	—
L-series	—	—	—	—	③	③	③	③
Head Restraints	❶	❶	❶	❶	❶	❶	❶	❶
Ion	—	—	—	—	—	—	—	⑤
Rollover Resistance	—	—	—	—	—	④	④	④

Note: Poor head restraint rating includes both S- and L-series.

General Motors/Suzuki

FIREFLY, METRO, SPRINT/SWIFT   ★★★★

RATING: Above Average (1998–2001); Average (1995–97); Below Average (1987–94). Stay away from AC-equipped versions, unless you want to invest in an AC repair facility. Look at the redesigned 1998 version for better quality, a new body style, standard dual airbags, and a peppier 4-cylinder engine. Convertibles pack plenty of fun and performance into a reasonably priced subcompact body. The Suzuki Swift carried on alone after the 2000 model year. **Maintenance/Repair costs:** Average. **Parts:** Expensive; sometimes drivetrain and body components are back ordered several weeks. **Best alternatives:** The Honda Civic LX, Hyundai Accent, Suzuki Esteem, and Toyota Tercel perform well and offer better quality. **Online help:** *www.autosafety.org/.*

Strengths and weaknesses: Cheap to buy and run, providing better-than-average quality control and crashworthiness, these tiny, 3- and 4-cylinder front-drive hatchbacks offer good performance and impressive economy for urban dwellers. In fact, these little squirts should be considered primarily city vehicles due to their small size, small tires, low ground clearance, and average high-speed handling. Interior garnishing is decent but plain, and there's plenty of room for two passengers, with four fitting in without too much discomfort. The turbocharged convertible model is an excellent choice for high-performance thrills in an easy-to-handle ragtop.

On the downside, owners will face an anemic, noisy engine that makes these cars the antithesis of "swift"; a harsh, choppy ride; lots of interior noise; a spartan interior; poorly performing original equipment tires; and inadequate braking.

Vehicle history: Suzuki Swift: 1992—Slight front end and dash restyling. **1995**—Redesign saw more horsepower, dual airbags, and optional anti-lock brakes; the two-door hatchback got a bit longer wheelbase. **1998**—Nine more horses, de-powered airbags, additional cabin space, and an upgraded interior. **2001**—Last year on the market.

Mechanically speaking, the GM/Suzuki partnership has kept factory-related defects to a tolerable level, particularly following the '95 model's redesign. Trouble spots on pre-'95 models: excessive oil consumption; automatic transmission and differential failures around 80,000 km; electrical system shorts; a faulty AC and cooling system (fogging of the side windows and windshield due to inadequate heat distribution is a common complaint); premature brake, clutch, and exhaust system wearout; and minor fuel-supply malfunctions. Body construction is subpar on these models.

The redesigned 1995s were built with more care. Additionally, they transmitted more road feel and gave a more comfortable ride.

Remaining problems on the 1995–2001 models have been premature front brake wear; electrical system and AC malfunctions; and subpar body assembly, highlighted by paint peeling and discoloration, early rusting, and poorly fitted body panels, leading to rattles and air and water leaks.

Safety summary: All models/years: Side window defogging is slow and sometimes inadequate. • Driver's window continually pops out of its mount. **1999**—Airbags failed to deploy. • Airbags deployed in very low speed collision. • Loose fuel hose caused fuel leak. • Cracked engine head gasket. • Premature wearout of front brake pads. • Defective suspension strut and mount caused premature tire wear, vibration, and pulling. Tires aren't very durable. • Inaccurate speedometer; dealer says it can't be repaired. • Key is hard to insert into doors, often jams. **2000**—Sudden, unintended acceleration accompanied by brake failure. • Loss of steering control. • Excessive vibration/shimmying when underway. • Chronic stalling when shifting from Park to Drive or when the AC is engaged. • AC and electrical components failures. • Airbag warning light stays lit. • Inoperative defroster. • Swift seatbacks collapsed from a rearender. • Rainwater leaks into interior. **2001**—Intermittent stalling problem. • Applied brakes and vehicle suddenly pulled sharply to the left. • Hatchback latch opens while driving.

Secret Warranties/Service Tips/TSBs

All models: 1993–99—Troubleshooting tips on correcting condensation in exterior lights. **1993–2001**—Paint delamination, peeling, or fading (see Part Two). • GM has a special kit that will reduce AC odours. **1994–98**—GM outlines which conditions require new or refaced brake rotors. **1997–2000**—Reasons why speedometer gives inaccurate readings. **1998–2000**—Outside rear mirror housing turns chalky/dull. **1999–2000**—Engine overheating and/or loss of coolant may be due to a faulty radiator filler neck or cap.

Firefly, Metro, Sprint/Swift Profile

	1994	1995	1996	1997	1998	1999	2000	2001
Cost Price ($)								
Firefly	9,145	10,395	10,995	11,495	11,680	10,690	11,410	—
Metro	8,995	10,395	10,995	11,495	11,680	10,690	11,410	—
Swift	8,995	10,495	10,995	10,995	11,495	11,595	11,595	11,595
Used Values ($)								
Firefly ʌ	3,000	3,000	3,000	3,000	3,500	4,000	5,000	—
Firefly v	2,500	3,000	3,000	3,000	3,000	3,500	4,500	—
Metro ʌ	3,000	3,000	3,000	3,000	3,500	4,000	5,000	—
Metro v	2,500	3,000	3,000	3,000	3,000	3,500	4,500	—
Swift ʌ	2,000	2,000	2,500	2,500	3,000	3,500	4,500	5,500
Swift v	2,000	2,000	2,000	2,500	2,500	3,000	4,000	5,000
Reliability	❷	❷	③	③	④	④	④	④
Crash Safety (F)	③	③	④	④	—	—	—	—
Head Restraints	—	❶	—	—	—	—	—	—

Honda

CIVIC, DEL SOL   ★★★★

RATING: Above Average (1992–2003); Average (1972–91). If you want to get a good buy at a fair price, the 1992–96 models are your best bet for their lighter weight and tighter handling. Any CRX represents a good buy, as well. The Civic has been downgraded due to the increasing number of safety- and performance-related defects reported by owners. Defects include airbags that fail to deploy or deploy with such force that they cause severe injuries, ABS brake failures and constant rotor and pad maintenance, sudden acceleration, original equipment tire failures, and considerable instability on wet roads. **Maintenance/Repair costs:** Average. Repairs can be carried out by independent garages, but the 16-valve engine's complexity means that dealer servicing is a must. To avoid costly engine repairs, owners must check the engine timing belt every 3 years/60,000 km and replace it every 100,000 km ($300). **Parts:** Parts are a bit more expensive than most other cars in this class; airbag control modules and body panels may be back ordered for weeks. **Best alternatives:** GM Firefly or Metro, Hyundai Accent or Elantra, Mazda Protegé, Nissan Sentra, Suzuki Esteem, and Toyota Echo or Corolla. The CRX's '93 del Sol replacement was a cheapened spin-off that carried over the CRX's faults, without its high-performance thrills. Si models are Honda's factory hot rods (the Acura 1.6 EL is an Si clone), which provide lots of high-performance thrills, without the bills. Despite this four-wheel disc brakes, the Si's mediocre braking and its lack of low-end torque are the car's main performance flaws. **Online help:** *www.cartrackers.com/Forums/ live/Honda; www.carsurvey.org/model_Honda_Civic.html;* and *www.epinions.com/ auto_Make-Honda.*

Strengths and weaknesses: The quintessential econobox, Civics have distinguished themselves by providing sports-car acceleration and handling with excellent fuel economy and quality control that is far better than what American, European, or other Asian automakers can deliver. Other advantages: a roomy, practical trunk; smooth-shifting automatic transmission; a comfortable ride; good front and rear visibility; high-quality construction; bulletproof reliability; and simple, inexpensive maintenance.

Some Civic disadvantages: the Si's suspension may be too firm for some, and its spoiler may block rear visibility. It's hard to modulate the throttle without having the car surge or lurch. The base engine loses its pep when the Overdrive gear on the automatic transmission engages in city driving, and the VTEC variant is noisy. Seats lack sufficient padding, rear access is difficult, rear seat room is limited to two adults, there's lots of engine and road noise, and an unusually large number of safety-related complaints include airbag malfunctions, sudden acceleration, and complete brake failure.

The 1984–95 Civics suffered from failing camshafts, crankshafts, and head gaskets, as well as prematurely worn piston rings.

What are minor body faults with recent models turn into major rust problems with older Civics, where simple surface rust rapidly turns into perforations. The underbody is also prone to corrosion, which leads to severe structural damage that compromises safety. The fuel tank, front suspension, and steering components, along with body attachment points, should be examined carefully in any Civic more than a decade old.

The 1996 redesign improved overall reliability and handling and increased interior room, but engine head gasket failures on non-VTEC engines continued to be a problem through the 2000 model year.

Year 2001 and later models are marginally better performers, yet quality control still needs improvement. Heading the list of owner complaints are engine crankshaft failures; transmission malfunctions; weak front springs and shocks; frequent brake repairs (rotor warpage and pad replacement); AC failures; suspension knocks and squeaks; a subpar stereo system; erratic fuel gauge readings; delaminated paint; and chronic water leaks.

Owners also complain of a constantly lit Check Engine light; faulty engine computer module and oxygen sensor; early replacement of the crankshaft pulley and timing belt; and fuel and electrical system failures. Other common problems: windshield air leaks and noise; warped windshield mouldings (see service bulletin below); hard-to-access horn buttons; windows that fall off their tracks; side mirrors that vibrate excessively; headlights that can't be focused properly and are prone to water leaks; gas-tank fumes that leak into the interior; and premature rusting, uneven paint application, chalky spots, and paint delamination. Here's what this owner of a 2001 Civic discovered:

> Paint is developing crow's feet in four separate places...body shop said it was due to bird droppings or sap. I believe this to be impossible and believe it to be a defect in the paint. Blemishes and loss of gloss continue to develop in the paint.

Vehicle history: 1992—A driver-side airbag, a base 102-horsepower, 1.5L 4-cylinder, plus a frugal CX and VX with 70- and 92-hp 4-cylinder engines, and a sporty Si with ABS. **1994**—A standard passenger-side airbag. **1996**—ABS for EX sedans, longer and better soundproofed, upgraded engines, and split folding rear seatbacks. **1999**—The Si is upgraded; and new front and rear styling. **2001**—More interior room, additional horsepower, and fresh styling; no more hatchback. **2002**—Debut of a 160-hp SiR sporty hatchback, improved fit and finish, a firmer suspension, and a rear stabilizer bar (except on the base model). Front suspension uses MacPherson struts, which increases interior space while watering down the car's sporty performance.

Safety summary: All models: 1995–2003—Spoiler restricts rear visibility, and large rear-view mirror restricts forward visibility for tall drivers. • Civic owners report numerous safety defects that include sudden acceleration, engine and transmission malfunctions, and airbags that fail to deploy, deploy inadvertently, or deploy with such force they cause severe injuries:

My '98 Civic was totalled by another driver's negligence; I was told by
a lawyer that because my son and I were not killed in the accident we
could not file a claim against the manufacturer for the airbags not
deploying even though it was a head-on collision.

• Ball joints on these vehicles don't have a castilated nut to secure the ball in
position; the nut can back off, and the ball pulls out of the steering arm. •
Other safety-related complaints: dangerous instability on wet roads, sudden
acceleration or stalling, faulty cruise control, ABS brake failures and constant
rotor and pad replacement, defective automatic transmission, transmission
that suddenly jumps into Reverse, original equipment tire failures, hood and
trunk lids that come crashing down, inoperative door locks, cracked windshields, and headlights and interior lights that suddenly go out.
2000—Accelerator pedal sticks; cables mounted too tight. • Accelerator cable
got hung up in the cruise control, causing the vehicle to suddenly accelerate. •
While driving, vehicle suddenly accelerated due to the throttle sticking open,
and brakes couldn't stop the car. • Car suddenly accelerated when passing
another vehicle. • Gas pedal keeps sticking while driving at a low speed. •
Transmission popped out of gear and brake pedal went right to the floor,
without any braking effect. • Brakes locked up and vehicle pulled to the left
when coming to an emergency stop. • Sudden steering loss while driving. •
Excessive vibration due to engine main bearing failure. • Transmission sometimes fails to change gear. • Vehicle suddenly went into Reverse although shift
lever was put into Drive. • While stopped at a light on a hill, vehicle suddenly
shifted into Reverse. • Another driver had the same thing happen, except this
time the transmission shifted into Neutral. • Transmission was stuck in
Reverse. • Faulty power door lock makes it impossible to open door from the
inside or outside. • Dome light won't work when doors are open. • Tail lights
don't work when the headlights and dash lights are on. • Rear-view mirror is
poorly located and is non-adjustable, creating a large forward blind spot for tall
drivers. • Sheet metal fatigue on both front fenders. • Faulty hood support rod
causes the hood to come crashing down. • Exterior rear-view mirror becomes
loose, despite dealer efforts to tighten it. **2001**—Car caught on fire near where
the oxygen sensor wires are located. • Child became entangled in rear-seat
shoulder belt; had to be cut free. • Car hesitates or stalls when decelerating. •
Vehicle surged forward when put into Reverse and engaged Reverse when put
into Drive:

While shifting the gear in Reverse the car went forward, and when I
shifted it to Drive, the car went backward. When I stepped on the gas
pedal lightly, it accelerated really fast and when I lightly step on the
brake, it abruptly stops.

The Honda service department is trying to fix this car. The first
problem reported was the "power switch," secondly they reported that
it's a "transmission problem," but still couldn't figure out what else is
the problem. Lastly, they notified me that the problem is the "transmission solenoid."

• Transmission may suddenly pop out of Second gear while underway or refuse to shift into Third or Fourth gear. • Transmission leaks. • Vehicle rolls back when stopped on an incline. • Sudden brake failure (master cylinder replaced). • When brakes are applied first thing in the morning, they don't "grab," resulting in extended stopping distance. • Leaking front strut causes poor handling and front-end noise. • Incorrect fuel gauge and speedometer readings. • Airbag warning light is constantly lit (heating coil or core is suspected). • Loose door latches. • Interior lights dim when AC is engaged. • Water leaks into trunk through tail lights, onto driver's side carpet through door or firewall, or wets front passenger-side carpet (AC condensate suspected). **2002**—Airbags fail to deploy:

> My 2002 Honda Civic EX hit another vehicle squarely in the rear end while travelling approximately 15 mph [24 km/h]. Neither of the front airbags deployed!
>
> The collision repair centre could find nothing wrong with my air bags. The tow truck operator and the collision repair centre told me that there was some sort of alert out for 2001 and 2002 Honda Civics where the airbags didn't deploy after a front-end collision.

• Cellular phone (Nokia) electromagnetic signals may cause sudden acceleration. • Vehicle continues to accelerate when brakes are applied. • Cracked engine block causes oil leakage. • Car rolls backward on an incline with an automatic transmission. • Car was in Park on an incline and rolled away. • Vehicle downshifts on its own. • Sudden failure of the front tie-rod. • Complete loss of steering. • Seat belt doesn't fully retract. • Windshield cracked for no apparent reason. **2003**—Vehicle accelerated when brakes were applied. • Sudden steering lock-up. • Transmission jumps into Neutral. • Power window failure. • Faulty Firestone tires. • Loose driver's seat.

Secret Warranties/Service Tips/TSBs

All models/years: Most Honda TSBs allow for special warranty consideration on a "goodwill" basis even after the warranty has expired or the car has changed hands. Referring to this euphemism will increase your chances of getting some kind of refund for repairs that are obviously related to a factory defect. **1988–2000**—A rear suspension clunk can be silenced by replacing the rear trailing arm bushing. **1992–97**—An abnormally long crank time before the car starts may be caused by a leaking check valve inside the fuel pump. • Water leaking into the footwell from under the corner of the dash can be stopped by applying sealer to the seam where the side panel joins the bulkhead. **1994–97**—If the AC doesn't blow cold air, you may need to replace both the evaporator and the receiver/dryer. • When operating a manual or power-assisted front window, the rear edge of the glass comes out of the channel. **1995–97**—A wind whistle at the top of the windshield can be silenced by applying additional sealer. **1996–98**—A poorly performing AC may need a new condenser fan motor and shroud. **1996–2000**—Poor AC performance. • Harsh shifts. **1996–2001**—Oil pressure switch Product Update Campaign (secret warranty). Another free fix if the dealer is on your side. **1998–2003**—Deformed windshield moulding (see following bulletin).

Deformed Windshield Moulding

Bulletin No.: 00-064

August 12, 2003

1998–2002 Accord; 1998–2003 Civic; 1999–2003 Odyssey; 1998–2001 Prelude; and 2000–03 S2000

CAUSE: The inner lip is folded, causing a poor fit against the body.

CORRECTIVE ACTION: Remove the entire inner lip, and fill the channel between the moulding and the body with silicone sealant.

2000—Steering pull or drifting. • Whistling or howling noise coming from the top middle of the windshield at highway speeds. • Moon roof seal sticks up or leaks. • Key is difficult to remove from the ignition switch; rear door lock tab is hard to open. **2001**—Product Update Campaign for the inspection or replacement of the engine control module/PCM. • Delayed upshift after a cold start. • Stiff manual transmission shifter; pops out of gear. • Rear main seal leak troubleshooting tips. • Separation of the lower control arm ball joints. • Noisy or stiff steering; fluid leakage. • Troubleshooting tips for front-brake groan or squeal. • Engine vibration and under-hood rattling; rattling when passing over rough roads; headliner may rattle from hitting the frame. • Creaking sound heard coming from the right side of the dash when passing over rough terrain. • Front suspension noise. • Clutch pedal squeaks or clicks when pressed. • Erratic fuel gauge readings, especially when parked on an incline; fuel gauge won't read full. • Sticking speedometer and tachometer needles. • Windshield cracking at the lower corners. • Damaged or cracked foglight lens. • Audio Update Campaign (secret warranty). • AC condensate drips onto passenger-side carpet. • Water leaks into trunk. • Driver's seat rocks back and forth. • Seat belt slow to retract. **2001–02**—Engine hesitation when accelerating is often caused by low oil pressure. • A growling noise from the engine area is likely caused by a worn alternator bearing. • Troubleshooting front brake groan or squeal. • Rear suspension squeak (replace the rear knuckle bushing under a "goodwill" warranty). • Trunk lid is difficult to close. **2001–03**—Dashboard creaking. • Clicking noise when turning (manual transmission). **2002**—Automatic transmission slippage. • Shift lever may be difficult to move. • Troubleshooting a noisy clutch. • Creaking or ticking from the dash or front strut; clean and install shims.

Creaking/Ticking Noises

Bulletin No.: 02-045

Date: October 29, 2002

2001–02 Civics

SYMPTOM: A creaking or ticking comes from the dashboard or front fender area. The noise occurs when driving over bumps, and sometimes when braking or turning.

PROBABLE CAUSE: Paint from the front damper mounting base is sticking to the body or burrs from a body spot weld are contacting the front damper mounting base.

CORRECTIVE ACTION: Install shims to the damper mounting base and/or remove the front damper/spring assembly, grind off the body spot weld burrs, and refinish the surface.

Out of warranty: Any repair performed after warranty expiration may be eligible for goodwill consideration by the District Parts and Service Manager or your Zone Office. You must request consideration, and get a decision, before starting work.

• Hard-to-turn seatback lock. • Driver's seat rocks back and forth. • Front windows won't fully roll down.

Civic Profile

	1996	1997	1998	1999	2000	2001	2002	2003
Cost Price ($)								
Base Civic	12,995	13,495	14,000	14,200	14,200	15,800	15,900	16,000
Si	17,495	17,895	17,995	18,800	18,800	19,800	19,902	20,700
SiR	—	—	—	—	—	—	—	25,500
del Sol	20,495	20,995	—	—	—	—	—	—
Used Values ($)								
Civic Λ	4,500	5,500	6,500	7,500	8,500	10,000	11,500	13,500
Civic V	4,000	5,000	5,500	6,500	7,500	9,000	10,500	12,500
Si Λ	5,500	7,000	8,000	9,000	10,500	12,000	14,000	16,500
Si V	5,000	6,000	7,000	8,000	9,500	11,000	13,000	15,500
SiR Λ	—	—	—	—	—	—	—	20,500
SiR V	—	—	—	—	—	—	—	19,500
del Sol Λ	6,000	7,500	—	—	—	—	—	—
del Sol V	5,500	6,500	—	—	—	—	—	—
Reliability	③	③	③	④	④	④	④	④
Crash Safety (F)	—	④	④	④	④	⑤	⑤	⑤
4d	④	④	④	④	④	⑤	⑤	⑤
Side	—	—	③	❷	❷	⑤	③	③
4d	—	③	③	③	③	④	④	④
Offset	③	③	③	③	③	④	⑤	⑤
Head Restraints	—	❷	—	❷	—	❷	③	—
4d	—	—	—	—	—	⑤	③	⑤
del Sol	—	④	—	—	—	—	—	—
Rollover Resistance	—	—	—	—	—	④	④	④

Hyundai

ACCENT   ★★★★

RATING: Above Average (2001–03); Average (1995–2000). Having lived through its Pony, Stellar, and Excel abominations, I can't believe I'm giving a Hyundai product such a high rating. But just like the early Honda and Nissan rustbuckets imported in the '70s and '80s, Hyundai has admitted its mistakes and brought out more refined, better-warranteed products—at bargain prices. Think of the Accent as a more refined Metro/Sprint from South Korea with more standard features. **Maintenance/Repair costs:** Average. **Parts:** Reasonably priced and easily found. **Best alternatives:** GM Firefly or Metro, Honda Civic (a decade-old Honda CRX in good condition would be a master stroke), Hyundai Elantra, Mazda Protegé, Nissan Sentra, Suzuki Esteem, and Toyota Echo or Corolla. **Online help:** *www.carsurvey.org/model_Hyundai_Accent.html.*

Strengths and weaknesses: Launched as a '95 model, the early Accents were basically Excels that had been substantially upgraded to provide decent performance and reliability at a phenomenally low price. Of course, with its small 4-cylinder engine, it's no tire-burner, but it will do nicely for urban commuting and grocery-getting.

Vehicle history: Until the redesigned 2000 models arrived, the Accent hadn't changed much over the years. **1996**—Height-adjustable seat belts and a 105-hp GT hatchback. **1997**—Models saw the debut of a GS hatchback and a GL sedan. **1998**—New engine mounts to cut down vibration, in addition to restyled front and rear ends. **1999**—Power steering and longer warranties. **2000**—A smoother-shifting automatic transmission; a stiffer, better-performing suspension; a stronger and quieter-running engine; and a more comfortable driving position with good visibility. **2001**—Engine got 16 additional horses. **2003**—A slightly larger engine and restyled front and rear end.

Problem areas include the engine cooling system and cylinder head gaskets (engine overheating), engine sputtering, a Check Engine light that constantly comes on, and chronic automatic transmission failures (an extended transmission warranty is suggested for models no longer under warranty). Owners also frequently complain of excessive front-end vibration; wheel bearings, fuel system, and electrical component failures; premature front brake wear; and excessive noise when braking.

Safety summary: All models/years: Horn controls may be hard to find in an emergency. • Rear head restraints appear to be too low to protect occupants. • Rear seat belt configuration complicates the installation of a child safety seat (pre-2001 models). **All models: 1995**—NHTSA probe of front suspension lower control arms. **1995–97**—NHTSA believes airbags may deploy with too much force; seven children have been killed. **1998–99**—Airbags failed to deploy, or deploy inadvertently. • Complete brake failure. • Sudden transmission failure. • Headlights flicker when turning and high beam is inadequate. • Engine control monitor melted. • Fuel gauge failures. **2000**—Fire erupted in the dashboard area. • Accelerator sticks. • Hood flew up and smashed through the windshield. • Left and right axles broke while vehicle was underway. • Transmission sticks between First and Second gear and pops out of Fifth gear. • No-shifting, due to a failure of the control shaft assembly. • Premature transmission clutch replacement. • In snowy, icy, or wet road conditions, there's an unpredictable loss of rpms and powertrain response, making for difficult hand-ling and control. • Headlight failures caused by defective relay switch. • Windshield wipers fail, due to the wiper linkage disconnecting from the wiper motor. • Seat belts tighten uncomfortably. **2001**—Gas pooled underneath the rear seat. • Airbags fail to deploy. • Steering shook so badly that driver lost control of vehicle. • Transmission jumps from Drive to Neutral. • Gearshift jumps out of Reverse. • Seat belts unlatch during impact; passenger seat belt tightens uncomfortably. • Windshield and rear window suddenly shattered. • Early ignition coil replacement. **2002**—Airbags failed to deploy. • Throttle body sensor failure causes car to accelerate on its own; intermittent high engine revs. • Chronic stalling. • Automatic transmission failures characterized by slippage, free-wheeling, jerky shifts, and a clunking noise. • Rear brake drums may be out of round. • When stopped, brake pedal sinks slowly to the floor and car rolls away (possibly faulty brake master cylinder). • Manual windows fall down. **2003**—Under-hood fire. • Airbags failed to deploy.

Secret Warranties/Service Tips/TSBs

All models/years: Tips on troubleshooting excessive brake noise. • Apparent slow acceleration upon cold starts is dismissed as normal. • A new AC "refresher" will control AC odours. **All models: 1995–98**—Harsh shifting may be fixed by installing an upgraded transaxle control module (TCM). • Clutch drag may be caused by a restriction in the hydraulic line from grease used during the assembly of the clutch master assembly. **1995–2001**—In the following bulletin, Hyundai says a faulty transaxle oil temperature sensor could be the cause of poor automatic transmission performance on Accent, Elantra, Tiburon, and Sonata models.

A/T – MIL ON DTCs P0712/P0713 Set

Group: Transaxle   Number: 00-40-10   Date: August 2000   Model: All
Subject: Automatic Transaxle Oil Temperature Sensor Diagnosis

Description:
An automatic transaxle oil temperature sensor with an OPEN circuit may result in the following symptoms:
^ Harsh P-R or P-D engagement
^ No Fourth gear engagement (1996–2000 Elantra & Tiburon1, 1995–2001 Accent)
^ Second gear hold (1999–2001 Sonata)
^ Damper clutch not engaged
^ MIL illuminated
^ Diagnostic Trouble Code: P0713—Fluid temperature sensor—open circuit   ➤

An automatic transaxle oil temperature sensor with a SHORT circuit may result in the following symptoms:
^ 2–3 shift flare (Accent, Elantra, Tiburon)
^ MIL illuminated
^ Diagnostic Trouble Code: P0712—Fluid temperature sensor—short circuit

1996–2003—The following TSB, published in April 2001, says many automatic transmission breakdowns can be traced to faulty transaxle solenoids.

A/T – Erratic Shifts/Slipping/MIL ON/DTCs Set

Group: Transaxle   Number: 00-40-011   Date: April 2001
Model: 1996–2000 Elantra, 1997–2001 Tiburon, 1996–2003 Accent

Description:

Incorrect operation of the transaxle solenoids for the 1996–2000 Elantra, 1997–2001 Tiburon, and the 1996–2003 Accent may result in the following symptoms:

^ Erratic shift or slipping
^ Transaxle held in Third gear Fail-Safe
^ Diagnostic Trouble Codes - P0740, P0742, P0743, P0745, P0747, P0748, P0750, P0752, P0753, P0755, P0757, P0758, P0760, P0765 (see DTC information).
^ MIL illuminated

This bulletin shows Hyundai's transmission problems are factory related and affect many models and model years. Don't let the service manager convince you the failure is your responsibility.

1998–99—Defective exhaust manifolds will be replaced for free on a case-by-case basis under Hyundai Campaign #03-01-004. **2000–01**—Hyundai has a free kit that will free up stiff manual transmission shifting. **2000–02**—Free bracket reinforcement:

"A"-Pillar Reinforcement Bracket Installation

Bulletin Number: 02-01-010

Date: October 2002

2000–02 Accent three-door front "A"-pillar brackets (campaign 055)

DESCRIPTION: Some 2000–02 MY Accent three-door vehicles may require installation of a bracket at the mid-position of the "A"-pillar and replacement of the upper "A"-pillar bracket assembly to further support the trim cover on both "A"-pillars.

2002—Harsh or delayed automatic transmission shifting.

Accent Profile								
	1996	1997	1998	1999	2000	2001	2002	2003
Cost Price ($)								
L/GS	10,495	10,995	11,295	11,565	11,565	11,995	12,395	12,395
GL 4d	12,695	12,995	12,995	13,245	13,595	13,595	13,795	13,795

Used Values ($)

L/GS ⋀		2,500	3,500	4,000	4,500	5,500	6,500	7,500	8,500
L/GS ⋁		2,000	3,000	3,500	4,000	5,000	6,000	7,000	8,000
GL 4d ⋀		3,500	4,500	5,000	6,000	7,000	7,500	8,500	9,500
GL 4d ⋁		3,000	4,000	4,500	5,500	6,500	7,000	8,000	9,000
Reliability		③	③	④	④	⑤	⑤	⑤	⑤
Crash Safety (F)		③	③	③	—	—	—	④	④
Side		—	—	—	—	—	—	③	⑤
Head Restraints		—	❶	—	❶	—	③	③	③
Rollover Resistance		—	—	—	—	—	④	④	④

ELANTRA ★★★★★

RATING: Recommended (2001–03); Above Average (1996–2000); Average (1991–95). Hyundai quality is the best of the South Korean automakers and generally much better than what Detroit offers. Another advantage is that the Accent, Elantra, and Tiburon fly under most buyers' radar, making them more available and much more reasonably priced than better-known brands. There's only a $1,000–$3,500 difference between the high-end and entry-level models. Try to find a 2001–03 model with an unexpired comprehensive 5-year/100,000 km base warranty, or buy any post-1996 version, but give up some of your savings to buy an extended powertrain warranty to protect your wallet from the occasional transmission failure. **Maintenance/Repair costs:** Average. Dealer servicing has improved considerably and independent garages find the Elantra's simple mechanical layout quite easy to diagnose and service. **Parts:** Reasonably priced and easily found. **Best alternatives:** GM Firefly or Metro; Honda Civic; Hyundai Accent; Mazda Protegé; Nissan Sentra; Suzuki Esteem or Swift; and Toyota Echo, Tercel, or Corolla. **Online help:** *www.autosafety.org* and *www.carsurvey.org*.

Strengths and weaknesses: This conservatively styled "high-end" front-drive sedan was launched as a 1992 model, carrying a 113-hp 1.6L 4-cylinder engine. It's only marginally larger than the failure-prone Hyundai Excel, but its overall reliability is much better, making it a credible alternative to the Mazda Protegé, Nissan Sentra, Saturn, and Toyota Corolla. The redesigned 1996 and later versions actually narrow the handling and performance gap with the segment leader, Honda's Civic.

Elantra's 1993 4-cylinder gained 11 more horses and is fairly smooth and efficient when mated to the 5-speed manual transmission. On all model years, though, the 4-speed automatic transmission cuts power by at least 10 horses and is a bit noisy. Adding to the horsepower gap, Hyundai admits it fudged horsepower numbers by about four percent on its entire model lineup for the last decade. The lesser power isn't easily discernible in city driving, but can be worrisome when merging with high-speed traffic.

There is some excessive body lean when cornering, but overall handling is fairly good, due mainly to a relatively long wheelbase and sophisticated suspension. Brakes are adequate, though sometimes difficult to modulate. Conservative styling makes the Elantra look a bit like an underfed Accord, but there's plenty of room for four average-sized occupants. Tall drivers might find the driver's seat rearward travel insufficient, which makes headroom a bit too tight.

Vehicle history: 1996—Totally redesigned with additional interior room, improved performance and handling, and a quieter-running engine; a wagon and 130-hp 1.8L engine were added, along with dual airbags and upgraded seat belts. **1999**—Mildly revised styling. **2001**—Another revision saw the wagon disappear, increased interior and engine size (now a 140-hp 2.0L 4-cylinder), and added four-wheel disc brakes and ABS. **2002**—Debut of a GT version, which is a bargain when one totes up the cost of its standard features.

Post-'96 models' passing power with the automatic gearbox is perpetually unimpressive, and the trunk's narrow opening makes for a relatively small trunk. The power problem is attenuated with the revamped 2001 versions.

Owners of 1996–2000 model Elantras report few serious defects; however, as with most Hyundai products, transmission failures are commonplace and have been the object of numerous service bulletins (see the Accent "Secret Warranties/Service Tips/TSBs") and recalls. Airbag failures are another frequent complaint. Other problem areas: body deficiencies (fit, finish, and assembly), a leaking sunroof, paint cracking, engine misfire and oil leaks (some oil burning), hard starting, and warped brake rotors. This having been said, the above-noted problems are in no way as severe or as frequent as what you would find with the Detroit Big Three competition.

The 2001–03 models are noted for chronic stalling; excessive brake noise and chassis vibration (see Service Tips below); a passenger-side scraping noise when underway; wind howling in the interior when encountering a crosswind; a humming noise emanating from the corners of the windshield; tire thumping; delayed window defrosting; and rainwater seeping in under the door.

Safety summary: All models/years: Airbags failed to deploy. • Chronic stalling. • Erratic transmission shifting and excessive noise. • Sudden brake loss. • Warped front brake rotors and master cylinder failure. • Passenger seat belt retracts and locks so that passengers are unable to move. **1998–99**— Faulty speed sensor. • Cracked transmission case. • Low beam headlights give poor illumination. • Poorly designed jack. **1999**—AC makes a grinding noise. • Defective heater fan and motor assembly. • Trunk lid doesn't close properly. • Loose driver's seat. • Defective door handle. • Paint/clearcoat cracking. **2000**—Vehicle rolled forward even though emergency brake was applied. • Clutch slave cylinder failure. • Vehicle pulls left continuously. • Sudden steering failure; loose steering. • Low beam doesn't light up driver's view— instead, the light reflects outward to the left or right. • AC circulates bad air. • Tire jack is too small and weak. • Defective side moulding. **2001**—Driver-side airbag deployed for no reason. • Sudden, unintended acceleration. • Check Engine light remains lit. • Child had to be cut from jammed rear centre seat belt. • Seat belt failed to lock up in a collision. • Brakes randomly engage by themselves and overheat/pulsate. • Rear doors freeze shut in cold weather. **2002**—Seatback failure when car was rear-ended. • Brake and gas pedals are set too close together. • While driving in rainstorm, all interior and exterior lights shut off. **2003**—Engine surging while on the highway. • Vehicle suddenly lost all power. • Complete loss of brakes. • Headlights will read "dim" but will actually be on high. • Distracting windshield glare. • Seat belts fail to lock.

Secret Warranties/Service Tips/TSBs

All models/years: Hyundai has a new brake pad kit (#58101-28A00) that the company says will eliminate squeaks and squeals during light brake application. Hyundai also suggests that you replace the oil pump assembly if the engine rpm increases as the automatic transmission engages abruptly during a cold start. • A harsh downshift when decelerating may require a free transmission replacement, says bulletin #98-40-001. • Poor shifting may be caused by an inhibitor switch short circuit. TSB #98-50-001 provides information regarding some brake noises and appropriate services for each condition. • Intermittent slippage in Fourth gear. • Troubleshooting vibration and ride harshness. **All models: 1995**—The exhaust system releases a rotten-egg odour. • Rear suspension squeaking noises. • An inaccurate fuel gauge. • Trunk water leaks and troubleshooting tips for locating and plugging other interior water leaks. **1996**—A cold exhaust system buzz can be silenced by installing a sub-muffler resonator. • Improved shifting into all gears can be accomplished by installing an upgraded transaxle control module (TCM). **1996–97**—Automatic transmission won't engage Overdrive. • Clutch pedal squeaking. • Tapping noise coming from the passenger-side dash panel/engine compartment area. • Exhaust system buzz. • Improved shifting into all gears. • Improved shifting into Reverse. • Clutch drag. **1996–98**—DOHC engine timing chain noise repair. **1996–99**—Transmission oil leakage likely caused by a defective oil pump housing seal. **1996–2000**—Erratic shifting. **1999–2002**—Harsh or delayed Park–Reverse or Park–Drive engagement. **2001–02**—Troubleshooting 2–3 shift flaring usually requires a simple updating of the transaxle control module (TCM), says TSB #02-40-001. **2002**—Troubleshooting engine rpm fluctuation. **2002–03**—Excessive chassis vibration when cruising. According to one Hyundai staffer, the problem is presently being resolved through a secret warranty campaign that pays for a wheel exchange:

> Only Elantra model years 2002–03 are affected; there is a different steel wheel design on others. Therefore, Tiburons are not affected at all as they all have alloys, either 16 inch or 17 inch. Also, my thought was that everybody at one time or another gets up to highway speed and would experience this shimmy at one point or another, but I have only had the complaint from two to three individuals at my location. It could possibly be that only a certain "batch" of wheels that were manufactured could have this problem or ones that were created during

[a] specific timetable. Another possibility is that often companies sub-contract out the manufacture of some parts (and later regret it) due to increased pressure of attaining a certain level of production.

2003—Automatic transmission sticks in Second gear. • Harsh shifts into Drive or Reverse. • Rough running engine may require an upgraded fuel pump. • Corrosion in the front door wiring connector.

Elantra Profile

	1996	1997	1998	1999	2000	2001	2002	2003
Cost Price ($)								
GL	13,495	13,995	14,295	14,595	14,875	14,875	15,295	15,295
GLS/VE	16,745	17,245	17,545	17,695	17,475	17,075	16,995	16,995
GT	—	—	—	—	—	—	18,495	18,495
Used Values ($)								
GL ⋀	3,500	4,500	5,000	5,500	6,500	8,000	9,500	11,000
GL ⋁	3,000	3,500	4,500	5,000	5,500	6,500	8,000	9,500
GLS/VE ⋀	4,500	5,500	6,000	6,500	8,000	9,500	10,500	12,500
GLS/VE ⋁	4,000	4,500	5,500	6,000	7,000	8,000	9,500	11,500
GT ⋀	—	—	—	—	—	—	11,500	13,500
GT ⋁	—	—	—	—	—	—	10,500	12,000
Reliability	③	④	④	④	④	⑤	⑤	⑤
Crash Safety (F)	④	③	③	③	—	④	④	④
Side	—	—	③	—	—	⑤	⑤	⑤
Offset	③	③	③	③	③	—	❶	❶
Head Restraints	—	❶	—	③	—	④	④	④

Kia

After going bankrupt in 1998, Kia was bought by Hyundai (it's also partly owned by Ford through its Mazda affiliation) and now sells two small cars, a mid-sized sedan, a minivan, and a sport-utility. Unlike on-the-ropes Daewoo, Kia has the money and backing to build a solid, stable dealer organization in Canada, but it'll take a great deal of time.

Despite Kia's impressive sales over the past few years, thanks to low prices and a comprehensive base warranty, all of the consumer and government feedback I've seen paints a very poor picture of Kia's quality control, particularly when it comes to automatic transmission performance and durability (a Daewoo bugaboo, too). Add in that this is only the company's fifth year in Canada, it's continually beset by labour unrest, and that few dealers can be found outside of large urban areas, and you have all the ingredients to make any Kia purchase a long-term risky buy. And if Hyundai finds that warranty costs for Kia defects threaten its overall profits, customers will be abandoned in a heartbeat (remember the Pony and Stellar?).

RIO ★

RATING: Not Recommended (2001–03). Try, instead, a Hyundai Accent, or a Toyota Echo. **Maintenance/Repair costs:** Average. **Parts:** Average cost, and parts are easily found, despite the small dealer network. **Best alternatives:** The GM Firefly or Metro; Honda Civic; Hyundai Accent or Elantra; Mazda Protegé; Nissan Sentra; and Toyota Echo, Tercel, or Corolla. **Online help:** *www.autosafety.org* and *www.carsurvey.org.*

Strengths and weaknesses: A bit smaller than the Sephia and Spectra, the Rio is a spin-off of the Aspire, marketed from 1995 to 1997 under the Ford nameplate. It's one of the cheapest cars on the market and offers both a sedan and wagon version. Both have a 4-cylinder engine that increased from 1.5L and 96 hp to 1.6L and 104 hp for 2003. Functional styling and limited standard features reflect the fact that these cars put fuel economy and a low base price before performance and convenience. Base Rios are equipped with a puny 104-hp 1.6L 4-cylinder engine teamed with a 5-speed manual transmission. Options available include a 4-speed automatic transaxle; ABS; air conditioning; power steering, door locks, and windows; and foglights. Side airbags aren't offered. Fuel economy: 6.8–8.6L/100 km.

Vehicle history: 2003—Subtle styling changes, a slightly larger engine, and extra standard and optional features. Kia claims engineering updates reduce noise and vibration, suspension alterations improve ride comfort, and that larger front brakes increase stopping power.

Highly manoeuvrable in city traffic and quite fuel efficient, this small car is, nevertheless, poorly suited for highway cruising or driving situations that require quick merging with traffic. Kia's horsepower ratings may be just as suspect as Hyundai's, and reports of chronic stalling sap owner confidence even more:

> My 2002 Rio has been towed on 9/2 and 9/6 due to the car shutting down. They said first it was the alternator and fuel pump, now they say it is the battery cable. Today is the 15th of September. And I still do not have the new car I bought.
> Please help before it shuts down in highway traffic and I get killed.

Other areas of complaint: weak and noisy engine performance; busy, harsh ride; slow and imprecise highway handling; limited passenger room and problematic entry/exit; tire thumping; small audio controls and missing remote trunk release; low-budget interior materials; small door openings and limited rear headroom and legroom; trunk's small opening doesn't take bulky items and doesn't offer a pass-through for large objects; optional tilt steering wheel doesn't tilt much; poor body construction; and a small dealer network that may complicate servicing and warranty performance.

Owners report problems with the automatic transmission, seat belts, and electrical and fuel systems; frequent front-end alignments; unreliable tires; and weak, prematurely worn, and noisy brakes. Writes this owner of a 2002 Rio:

> I had the front brakes replaced due to a clip that fell off and got between the brake pad and drum, and the rear brakes replaced due to brake dust and glazing of drums. Now less than two weeks later, I'm starting to have the same grinding noise in the rear brakes again.

Kia's products, unlike Daewoo's, do have a track record—and it's not good. In fact, *Consumer Reports* says in its April 1999 New Car edition, "You'd have to search far and wide to find a car that's worse than this small Korean model." *CR*'s conclusion is confirmed by the proportionally large number of safety-related complaints recorded by NHTSA below.

Safety summary: All models: 2001—NHTSA probes airbag non-deployment. **2001–02**—Defective fuel line ignited an under-hood fire. • Hood flew up and broke front windshield. • Side airbag failed to deploy. • Vehicle disengages from Overdrive due to a missing transmission control modulator. • Transmission jumps out of gear when brakes are applied. • Brakes stick and pedal goes to the floor without vehicle stopping. • Brakes are noisy. • Excessive shaking and vibration; vehicle swerves all over the road. • Chronic stalling. • Rear seat belt shreds or jams. • Steering binds and grinds when turned; on other occasions it's too loose. • Premature tire wear. • Vehicle assembled without a horn. • Various electrical problems, including clock spring failure, cause the Check Engine light and airbag warning lamp to remain lit. • Fuel light constantly stays lit. • Bent wheel rims.

Secret Warranties/Service Tips/TSBs

All models: 2001—Revised transmission shift lever and bushing spacer. • Reinforced fuse box cover latch. • Troubleshooting automatic transmission concerns. **2001–02**—Special Service Campaign addresses premature transmission failures.

Rio Profile

	2001	2002	2003
Cost Price ($)			
S	11,995	12,095	12,351
RS	12,995	13,095	13,251
Used Values ($)			
S ʌ	5,000	6,500	8,000
S v	4,500	6,000	7,500
RS ʌ	5,500	7,500	8,500
RS v	5,000	7,000	8,000

Reliability	③	③	③
Crash Safety (F)	—	④	④
Side	❷	③	❷
Head Restraints	③	③	③
Rollover Resistance	—	④	④

Mazda

PROTEGÉ ★★★★★

RATING: Recommended (1996–2003); Above Average (1991–95); Average (1985–90). The redesigned 1996–2003 Protegé offers fresh styling, a larger wheelbase, standard dual airbags, and a new 4-banger. Plus, they should be plentiful at bargain prices as they come off their 3-year leases. The best buy of all, though, is the totally revamped 1999 and later models. **Maintenance/Repair costs:** Higher than average. Repairs are dealer dependent. **Parts:** Expensive, but easily found. **Best alternatives:** GM Firefly or Metro, Honda Civic, Hyundai Accent or Elantra, Nissan Sentra, Suzuki Esteem or Swift, and Toyota Echo or Corolla. **Online help:** *www.autosafety.org* and *www.carsurvey.org*.

Strengths and weaknesses: These Mazdas are peppy performers with a manual transmission hooked to the base engine. The automatic gearbox, however, produces lethargic acceleration that makes highway passing a bit chancy. Handling and fuel economy are fairly good for a car design this old. However, overall durability is not as good as that of more recent Mazda designs, beginning with the 1991 Mazda 323 and Protegé, both of which were also sold as Ford Escorts. Catalytic converters plug up easily, and other pollution-control components have been troublesome. Automatic transmission defects, air conditioner breakdowns, and engine oil leaks are also commonplace. Oil leaks in the power-steering pump may also be a problem.

The fuel-injected 1.6L engine is a better performer than the 1.5L, but you also get excessive engine and exhaust noise. Stay away from the harsh-shifting and fuel-thirsty 3-speed automatic transmission.

The 1985–90 models aren't very reliable at all. Owners report hard starting in cold weather, in addition to automatic transmission problems and electrical system failures. The engine camshaft assembly and belt pulley often need replacing around 120,000 km. Clutch failures are also common. Other areas of concern are frequent constant velocity joint replacement and rack-and-pinion steering wearout. The front brakes wear quickly due to poor-quality brake pads and seizure of the calipers in their housings. Check for disc scoring on the front brakes. Stay away from models equipped with a turbocharger—few mechanics want to bother repairing it or hunting for parts.

Vehicle history: 1991–95—Reasonably reliable and inexpensive. **1995–98**—Redesigned versions are better buys for cheapskate shoppers looking for more reliability with a dash of additional performance at an affordable price. Powered by a standard, fuel-efficient, 1.5L engine mated to a manual 5-speed transmission, these econoboxes are among the most responsive and roomiest small cars around. **1999**—A restyled interior and exterior and a more powerful engine lineup. **2000**—Premium models received front-seat side airbags and an improved ABS system. **2002**—The introduction of the Protegé5 four-door hatchback sport wagon and the MP3, a higher-performing sedan variant. **2003**—A turbocharged 170-hp MazdaSpeed Protegé debuted and sold in small quantities.

Although 1996–2003 Protegés are far more reliable than most American-made small cars, their automatic transmissions are the pits (a problem also seen to a lesser extent with Ford's Escort and Hyundai's lineup), with erratic shifting and locking up in Fifth gear. Owners report that fuel system and electrical problems return year after year, and the front brakes (excessive noise, vibration, rotor warping, and premature pad wear) are a continual annoyance. Other generic deficiencies: weak rear defrosting; chronic engine stalling (secret warranty applies up to seven years); engine rattling around 2800 rpm upon a cold start-up; noisy suspension; AC failures; and body defects, including wind and water leaks into the interior.

Safety summary: All models/years: Airbags failed to deploy. • Transmission failures and malfunctions. • Poor headlight illumination. **1995–99**—Cracked fuel line caused fire. • Sudden tire tread separation (Firestone). • Chronic stalling. • Excessive brake fade. • Metal rods in driver's seat could cause severe back injuries in a rear-end collision. • Driver's seat belt buckle wouldn't unlatch. • Brake pedal pad is too narrow and should be coated with non-skid material. • Severe static electricity shock when exiting vehicle. **1999–2002**—Delayed braking. • Check Engine light activation is your first warning sign that automatic transmission is faulty. • Car rolled backward and hit a tree, despite being parked with brakes applied. • Vehicle constantly pulls to the right. • Passenger unable to disengage seat belt. • Bucket seat seatbacks contain metal support bars that are extremely uncomfortable. **2001**—Loss of brakes. • Gear shift lever jumped from Drive to Neutral while vehicle was underway. • Defective steering column coupling. Broken rear axle causes severe pulling to one side. • Windows take a long time to defrost. • **2002**—Continual stalling. • Brake line split, leading to rear-ender. **2003**—Nauseating fumes entered the vehicle. • Brake pedal pushed almost to the floor before brakes work, and they produce excessive noise. • Passenger seat belt won't disengage. • Passenger seat belt broke; seat belt case and release button broke while trying to release belt.

Secret Warranties/Service Tips/TSBs

All models: 1995–98—Poor engine performance may require a new intake valve. • Excessive vibration in gear or at idle may mean the engine mount material has hardened or cracked. • Erratic shifting may signal that the valve body harness is defective. • If the gear selector lever is hard to operate, it's likely that the lower manual shaft in the transfer case has excessive rust. • An inoperative AC may have a corroded pressure switch terminal assembly. **1996–98**—A noisy driveshaft can be silenced by installing a countermeasure dynamic damper. **1997–98**—A 1–2 upshift shock at light throttle may require the replacement of the large and small accumulator spring with a single spring. • If the brake warning light is constantly lit, even though the brakes check out okay, it's likely the speedometer assembly transistor has been damaged. **1998–2003**—Dealing with musty, mildew-type AC odours:

AC – Musty/Mildew Odours

Bulletin No.: 07-001/03

1998–2002 626; 1998–2003 Protegé; 2000–03 Protegé5; 2000–03 MPV; 1998 MPV; 1998–2002 Millenia; and 1999–2003 Miata.

This odour is the result of mould growth in the AC evaporator/cooling unit, which is caused by condensation, dust, and pollen within the cooling unit. This condition is usually worse during high humidity conditions. "Mazda Air Cooling Coil Coating" is available to encapsulate the mould to reduce odours. If the product is properly applied, it can effectively reduce the musty/mildew odour for up to three years.

1999—No shift from Second to Third gear. • Manual transmission jerking or hesitation. • Inoperative wiper motor. • Weather stripping comes off rear doors. • Door key may jam in locks. • Excessive exhaust resonance noise. • Engine rattling. • Clutch squealing. • Off-centre steering wheel. **1999–2000**—Mazda will replace the mass airflow sensor free of charge up to 7 years/70,000 miles (112,000 km). Problems with this component include a lack of power, hesitation, or a poor idle. Don't argue, simply tell the dealer you are aware of the replacement campaign, and anyway, it's a part covered by the more comprehensive emissions warranty. **2000**—Excessive exhaust resonance noise. **2000–01**—Clutch squealing. • Inoperative wiper motor. • Off-centre steering wheel. **2002**—Tips on eliminating AC odour. **2003**—Cold engine rattling. • Wind noise around doors. • Eliminating a "rotten-egg" exhaust smell.

Protegé Profile								
	1996	1997	1998	1999	2000	2001	2002	2003
Cost Price ($)								
Protegé	13,895	14,685	14,675	14,970	15,095	15,795	15,795	15,795
Used Values ($)								
Protegé ⋏	4,000	4,500	5,000	6,000	8,000	9,000	11,000	12,000
Protegé ⋎	3,500	4,000	4,500	5,000	7,000	8,000	9,500	11,000
Reliability	④	④	④	④	④	⑤	⑤	⑤
Crash Safety (F)	—	③	③	—	④	⑤	⑤	⑤
Side	—	—	—	—	③	③	③	③
Offset	③	③	③	③	③	③	③	③
Head Restraints	—	❶	—	❷	❷	③	③	③
Rear	—	—	—	—	—	❷	❷	❷

Nissan

SENTRA   ★ ★ ★ ★ ★

RATING: Recommended (1995–2003); Above Average (1991–94); Average (1988–90); Not Recommended (1983–87). The redesigned 1995 version offers fresh styling, a longer wheelbase, a peppier power plant, standard dual airbags, and side door beams. **Maintenance/Repair costs:** Higher than average on early models, but anybody can repair these cars. **Parts:** Reasonably priced and easily obtainable. **Best alternatives:** A GM Firefly or Metro, Honda Civic, Hyundai Elantra, Mazda Protegé, Suzuki Esteem or Swift, and Toyota Echo or Corolla. **Online help:** *www.autosafety.org* and *www.carsurvey.org.*

Strengths and weaknesses: Until the 1991 models arrived, early Sentras were a crapshoot: they're cheap, generally reliable, inexpensive to repair; and give good fuel economy.

So what's not to like?

Rudimentary ride and handling, and subpar build quality. Quality improved considerably with the 1991 version, yet the vehicle's base price rose only marginally, making these later model years bargain buys for consumers looking for a reliable "beater."

The 1991–94s are a bit peppier and handle better, although some quality problems remain. These include faulty fuel tanks, leaking manual and automatic transmissions, a persistent rotten-egg smell, and noisy engine timing chains and front brakes. With the exception of electronic component failures, repairs are still relatively simple to perform.

Vehicle history: 1995—Larger, and better performing. **1998**—New front and rear ends and a new 140-hp SE sedan. **2000**—Underwent a major redesign, offering more powerful engines, a better ride, and enhanced handling. It's well worth the $1,000–$2,000 increase from the '99 version and is basically identical to the costlier 2001 version. **2002**—The 145-hp SE model was replaced at the top of the line by the SE-R and SE-R Spec V; the latter offering a 180-hp engine, a limited-slip differential, and a sport-tuned suspension, to compete against the Honda Civic SiR and Mazda's high-performance spin-offs. Four-wheel disc brakes also become a standard feature.

The 1995–2002 owner complaints concern stalling and hard starting; engine rattles; electrical glitches; premature brake wear and excessive brake noise; automatic transmission whine; AC solenoid failures and AC that blows hot air or freezes up; and accessories that malfunction. Owners have also had to contend with a recurrent steering clunk noise, clutch, clutch switch, suspension strut, wheel bearing, and catalytic converter failures. Crank position sensor malfunction may prevent vehicle from being started. Body assembly is also targeted with some complaints of loose windshield mouldings, poor body fit, paint defects, and air and water leaks into the interior through the trunk and doors.

Year 2003 models are slightly improved, but owners are still plagued by clutch, exhaust, fuel system, and electrical problems. Front brake pads and rotors wear out quickly; there's excessive bouncing and vibration caused by prematurely worn struts; doors vibrate noisily; passenger-side windows leak; rear bumpers may fall off; and some incidents of excessive wind noise around the windshield moulding.

Safety summary: All models/years: Brake and accelerator pedals set too close together. • Airbags fail to deploy, or deploy inadvertently. • Steering lock-up. • Chronic stalling. • Sudden acceleration. • Premature tire wear. • Horn blows on its own. **1996**—Airbag deployment caused severe injuries. • Airbag ruptured. • Premature automatic transmission failures. • Rusty rear coil springs broke in two. • Hubcaps frequently fall off. **1997**—Sudden failure of the brake lights, headlights, and dash lights. **1998–99**—ABS failures. • Defective brake master cylinder. • Excessive stopping distance. • Sticking throttle. • Ignition key breaks off in the ignition. • Faulty power door locks. • Vehicle leaks when it rains. • Windshield wiper washer leaks, and washer produces acrid fumes that enter the cabin. • Front seats jam when moved back. **1999**—Loss of braking; extended braking distance. • Fuel filler flap fell into fuel filler tube. **2000**—Suspension attachment bolts broke off. **2001**—Brakes easily lock up at all speeds. • Warped brake rotors. **2002**—Fire ignited in the headlight assembly:

> I am a professional fire investigator. This vehicle fire originated with the headlight assembly. The burn patterns clearly indicate this to be the area of origin and the supporting burn patterns indicate the fire originated in the headlight assembly. Even though this recall does not specifically address a possible fire hazard, I believe the fire is related to the recall problem.

• Fire erupted in the engine compartment. • Sudden acceleration and frequent stalling. **2003**—ABS brake failure; brakes lock up at low speed, particularly on wet roads. • Windshield wipers, turn signals, headlights, horn, and hazard lights may suddenly fail. • Continental tire tread separation. • The gas and brake pedals may be set too far apart for some.

Secret Warranties/Service Tips/TSBs

All models/years: Predicted life of timing belt. • Flashing lights when signal lights are engaged. • Faulty master cylinder causes brake pedal to slowly drop to the floor. • Engine pinging on light acceleration. **1995–96**—An engine that cranks but won't start may need TSB #96-032 for the correct repair. • An engine malfunction light that is constantly lit may be fixed by installing a new rear heated oxygen sensor. • An automatic transmission that won't shift out of Park may need a countermeasure interlock cable. • TSB #NTB96-001 gives lots of troubleshooting tips on finding and correcting various squeaks and rattles. **1995–99**—Harsh shifts and low power with the automatic transmission may be due to reduced movement of the A/T throttle wire cable inside the cable housing. • A self-activating horn can be fixed by replacing the horn springs and spring insulators. **1997–99**—Harsh shifts and low power with the automatic transmission. • Horn self-activates. • More tips on silencing squeaks and rattles. • Diagnosing causes of brake judder and steering wheel shimmy. • Extended-life pads for the front brakes. • Curing sulfur odour. • Slow retraction of the front seat belt. **1999–2001**—Hard starting in cold weather or at high altitude. • Engine pings with light-to-moderate acceleration. • Exhaust manifold heat shield rattle. • Automatic transmission won't upshift. • Tips to improve downshifting (modified downshift spring). • Brake pedal slowly drops to floor (master cylinder check). • Vehicle wanders or pulls to one side. • Horn activates randomly. • Noisy, vibrating speedometer. • Water condensation from AC. • Rotten-egg exhaust odour. • Anti-theft system prevents starting. **2000**—Vehicle lacks power; transmission sticks in Third gear. • Slow fuel fill; pump nozzle clicks off continually. • Erratic AC vent flow. • Front suspension squeak, rattling. • Windshield hum or whistle. **2001–02**—Low power or poor running. • Water leak in trunk area. • Rear brake caliper knock, clunk, or rattle. **2003**—Anti-theft system may make for hard starts or no-starts. • Troubleshooting tips for a lit MIL light. • Turn signals may be too fast. • AC may operate erratically and have a sticking case door.

Sentra Profile

	1996	1997	1998	1999	2000	2001	2002	2003
Cost Price ($)								
Sentra	13,448	13,698	14,498	15,398	15,398	15,298	15,598	15,598
Used Values ($)								
Sentra ▲	3,500	4,500	5,500	6,500	7,500	9,000	10,000	12,000
Sentra ▼	3,000	4,000	5,000	6,000	6,500	8,000	9,500	11,500
Reliability	④	④	④	④	⑤	⑤	⑤	⑤
Crash Safety (F)	—	④	③	—	—	④	④	④
Side	—	—	③	—	—	—	—	❷
Offset	—	—	③	③	③	③	③	③
Head Restraints	—	❷	❷	❷	❷	❷	❷	③

Subaru

IMPREZA, FORESTER, WRX   ★★★★

RATING: *Impreza:* Above Average (1997–2003); Average (1994–96); *Forester:* Recommended (2001–03); Above Average (1998–2000); *WRX:* Not Recommended (2002–03). **Maintenance/Repair costs:** Higher than average. Mediocre, expensive servicing is hard to overcome because independent garages can't service key AWD components. Only buy a Subaru if you must have AWD and you're confident you can get dependable service from your local Subaru dealer. **Parts:** Expensive and hard to find. Emissions components are often back ordered for months, but cheap aftermarket components can be found outside the dealer network. **Best alternatives:** If you don't need the AWD capability, you're wasting your money. Here are some front-drives worth considering: the GM Firefly or Metro, Honda Civic, Hyundai Elantra, Mazda Protegé, Nissan Sentra, Suzuki Esteem or Swift, and Toyota Echo or Corolla. Some recommended small vehicles with 4X4 capability that are set on a car, not a truck, frame (providing more car-like handling), include the GM Vibe, Honda CR-V, and the Toyota Matrix or RAV4. **Online help:** *techinfo.subaru.com/html/shoppingHome.jsp*; *www.autosafety.org*; *www.carsurvey.org*; and *www.i-club.com*.

Strengths and weaknesses: These well-equipped small cars have one of the most refined and reliable AWD drivetrains you'll find (prior to 1996, they were mostly front-drive economy cars). With their four-wheel traction, Subarus provide excellent handling without any torque steer, good braking, lots of storage space with the wagons, nice control layout, and better-than-average quality control.

On the other hand, Subaru makes you pay dearly for the AWD capability, small doors and entryways restrict rear access, the coupe's narrow rear window and large rear pillars hinder rear visibility, heat and air distribution is inadequate, and front and rear seat legroom may be insufficient for tall drivers.

The full-time 4X4 Impreza is essentially a shorter Legacy with additional convenience features. It comes as a four-door sedan, a wagon, and an Outback Sport wagon, all powered by a 135-hp 2.2L or a 165-hp 2.5L 4-cylinder engine. The 2.5L performs much better with the Impreza and Forester than with the Legacy Outback. It is smooth and powerful, with lots of low-end torque for serious off-road use. The automatic transmission shifts smoothly. The manual transmission's "hill holder" clutch prevents the car from rolling backward when starting out.

These Subarus hurtle through corners effortlessly with a flat, solid stance and plenty of grip. Tight cornering at highway speeds is done with minimal body lean and no loss of control, and steering is precise and predictable.

Vehicle history: Impreza: 1995—A coupe and an Outback model were sold with optional AWD. **1996**—A mix of front-drives and all-wheel drives, along with a new sport model, a new Outback wagon (for light off-roading), and larger engines. **1997**—Additional power and torque, a re-styled front end, and a new Outback Sport wagon. **1998**—A revised dash and door panels, the Brighton was dropped, and the high-end 2.5 RS was added. **1999**—Stronger engines, more torque, and upgraded transmissions. **2002**—The 2.2L 4-cylinder was dropped, along with Subaru's pretensions for making affordable entry-level cars. Totally redesigned models include the 2.5 TS Sport Wagon, 2.5 RS Sedan, Outback Sport Wagon, the sporty WRX Sedan, and Sport Wagon. There is no longer a two-door version available.

Another Subaru spin-off, the Forester, was launched as a 1998 model and is a cross between a wagon and a sport-utility. Based on the shorter Impreza, the Forester uses the Legacy Outback's 2.5L 165-hp engine coupled to a 5-speed manual transmission or an optional 4-speed automatic. Its road manners are more subdued, and its engine provides more power and torque for off-roading. **Forester: 1999**—A quieter, torquier engine, a smoother-shifting transmission, and a more solid body. **2000**—Standard cruise control (L) and a limited-slip differential (S). **2003**—Improved interior materials, upgraded suspension, enhanced handling and ride quality, larger tires and fenders, and revised head restraints and side-impact airbags.

All post-'95 Subarus are noted for better-than-average quality control and above-average-quality mechanical components; nevertheless, servicing quality is spotty, and recent models have shown serious automatic transmission and brake deficiencies. There's also a history of premature clutch failures and shuddering, particularly after a cold start-up. Owners also report poor engine idling; frequent cold-weather stalling; manual transmission malfunctions; rear wheel bearing failures; excessive vibration caused by the alloy wheels; premature exhaust system rust-out and early brake caliper and rotor scoring and wear; minor electrical short circuits; catalytic converter failures; body panel and trim fit and finish deficiencies characterized by water leaks and condensation problems from the top of the windshield or sunroof; windshield cracking and scratching too easily; and paint peeling. In addition to the paint peeling from delamination, owners report that Subaru paint chips much too easily. Says the Alberta owner of a 2001 Impreza:

> I have a chipping 2001 Subaru Impreza Outback Sport and have been trying to get the dealership to deal with it. The car is now one year old and has over 50 rock chips on the hood alone. I barely touched the car when putting in the gas and the paint fell off. I spent the extra money on paint protection when I got the car and I am afraid of what might be left after I pay this car off. We use the car for skiing so it does see a little gravel (it's Alberta!) and I bought it because it was backed by the Ski Association.

Owners of 2002 and 2003 WRXs are particularly affected by poor braking that runs counter to the high-performance hype found in Subaru's ads:

> I have experienced multiple occurrences of ABS problems. If a wheel hits a bump when the brakes are applied the brakes let go completely for 2–3 seconds. It's as if the system is sensing a loss of grip at whatever wheel has hit the bump and instead of releasing pressure on that wheel for a fraction of a second it releases pressure on all four brakes for 2–3 seconds.
>
> This can occur not only under hard braking but also when slowing down gradually from a low speed. This is at best discomforting and at

worst dangerous. I know that NHTSA is aware of the thread in the brake forum of *www.i-club.com*. Additionally the problem has been documented in the April 2002 issue of *Sport Compact Car* magazine, page 16. Article is titled "Picking Nits." Section of the article is "Ambitious ABS."

Here's a quote: "It takes only the slightest bump, pavement irregularity or suggestion of lost traction to send the WRX's ABS into convulsions." Another one: "What makes most Subarus uncommonly safe and stable in severe conditions makes the usually confidence-inspiring WRX feel frighteningly unpredictable charging into bumpy corners. Our long-term WRX is getting an off switch for the ABS."

Safety summary: All models: 1994–2001—Airbags are a serious problem with all Subarus: either they fail to deploy in an accident, or they deploy inadvertently while parked, when turning, if the underside of the car scrapes the road, or if the car drives over a dip in the road, hits a pothole, is stuck in a ditch, or is being washed—or the key is simply put into the ignition. • Sudden acceleration. • Brake malfunctions and ABS brake failures. • Two other common problems are the premature replacement of brake sensors, pads, and rotors, and wheel hubcaps that constantly fall off due to their poor design. • Front shoulder belts are uncomfortable and rear seat belts are hard to buckle up. **1996**—Short seatback and absence of head restraint could cause severe neck injuries in a collision. • Sudden acceleration. • When the vehicle is being driven, transmission may suddenly jump out of Drive into Neutral. • Seat belt failed to retract in an accident. • Floor carpet prevented brake pedal application. • Complete engine failure at 18,000 km. • Chronic stalling. • Computer sensor control unit failure. • Intermittent brake loss. • Excessive shaking at highway speeds. • Windshield wiper bolt failure. • Left turn signal fails intermittently. • AC seizure. • O-ring failure causes AC to leak freon. • Bridgestone tires frequently blow out. • New-design headlights give poor illumination. **1997**—Airbags deployed in an accident and a brown liquid burned driver's arms. • Seat belts failed to tighten in accident. • Sudden engine shutdown on the highway and won't restart. • Sudden acceleration. • Cruise control failed to disengage when brakes were applied. • Igniter failed, allowing unburned fuel to flow into catalytic converter. • AC blew fumes into interior, causing driver to black out. • Complete engine failure due to defective valves and pistons. • Sudden loss of steering. • Transmission surges when cold, or shifts into Neutral at low speed or when descending a small hill. • Transmission failures. • Frequent electronic control unit failures. • Rear seat belts are too long to properly secure child safety seat, and the locking mechanism doesn't lock properly. • Shorted hazard switch drained battery. • Alternator belt snapped, causing battery and brake warning lights to come on and making car hard to steer. • Alternators frequently quit while vehicle is under power. • Brake lights often fail. • Headlights are mistakenly turned off when turn signal lever is engaged. **1998**—Oil leak from oil filter seam caused fire. • Front strut assembly failure. • Cruise control failed to disengage when brakes were applied. • Excessive shaking at highway speeds. • Seatback collapsed when vehicle was rear-ended.

• Subaru told car owner that tendency to pull to the right was a design feature. • Sudden brake loss after linings, calipers, and master cylinder had been replaced. **1999**—Chronic cold engine hesitation, stalling. • Engine failure due to cracked #2 piston. • When accelerating or decelerating, vehicle will begin to jerk due to excessive play in the front axle. • Wheel bearing failures. • Transmission plug fell out. • Tire blowout; air slowly escapes. • Front bumper skirt catches on parking blocks, resulting in bumper twisting and being ripped off. • The centre rear seat belt's poor design prohibits the installation of many child safety seats. **2000–01**—Driver burned from airbag deployment. • Clunking noise when brakes are applied. **2000–03**—Soft pedal and late brake engagement—pedal goes almost to the floor. **WRX: 2002**—Erratic transmission performance:

> First gear is a major issue in my vehicle. I can only engage First gear if I'm at a complete stop. So if I've slowed down to 5–10 mph [8–16 km/h] I'm forced to go into Second gear, which not only wears out my clutch prematurely, but could also cause an accident if I needed to build speed quickly. The transmission overall seems to be a big issue with WRX owners. Please go to *www.i-club.com* and under forums. Do a search for tranny and also First gear. You will see a slew of issues.

• Poor ABS braking performance, resulting in extended stopping distance, related to bad design and premature component wearout:

> The brakes that come standard on this vehicle are nowhere near sufficient for a vehicle with this level of performance. My brakes are scored, have grooves, and have chips and burrs. During my hour commute to work I experience brake fade and brake shudder in the steering wheel. The dealer tells me these problems are "normal."
>
> Well, if you're going to sell me a car that accelerates and handles like a race car, it should be able to stop like one as well. Or at least stop at all! This vehicle requires larger, more performance-oriented brakes right from the factory.

• Exhaust shows heat damage after only 6,400 km (4,000 mi.). **Forester: 2000**—The following comments apply to the Forester but can be relevant to Impreza owners, too. Sudden acceleration. • Driver burned from airbag deployment. • Sudden loss of transmission fluid. • Driver's seatback may suddenly recline because seat belt gets tangled up in the recliner lever. • Frequent wheel bearing failures. • Clunking noise when brakes are applied. • Fuel filler cap design is too complicated for gas station attendants to put on properly. Driver, therefore, has to pay dealer to reset Check Engine light. **2001**—Airbags failed to deploy. • Sudden, unintended acceleration and surging. • Chronic stalling. • Breakage of rear wheel bearings. • Brake and accelerator pedals are too close together. • In a collision, airbags failed to deploy and seat belt didn't restrain occupant. • In a similar incident, shoulder belt allowed driver's head to impact the windshield. • Water leaks through moon roof and top of windshield. • Headlights don't illuminate the edge of the road and are either too bright on High or too dim on Low. • Alarm system self-activated, trapping baby inside of car until fire rescue arrived. **Forester: 2001**—Airbags failed to deploy. • Drivetrain rattles and grinds when shifted into Second or Third gear. • Brakes can fail when braking over bumps at moderate speeds. • Sudden, unintended acceleration and surging, especially when parking. • Dangerous delay, then surging when accelerating in forward or Reverse. • Surging at highway speeds and stalling at lower rpms. • Transmission failure; gears lock in Park intermittently. • Open wheel design allows snow and debris to pack in the area and throw wheel out of balance, creating dangerous vibration. • High hood allows water into the engine. **2003**—Intermittent stalling. • When backing into a parking space the Hill Holder feature activates forcing the driver to use excessive throttle in Reverse. • Heater, defroster failure. • Front seats move fore and aft. **WRX: 2003**—Windshield cracking. • Chronic ABS brake failures.

Secret Warranties/Service Tips/TSBs

All models/years: Troubleshooting tips on a sticking anti-lock brake relay are offered. This problem is characterized by a lit ABS warning light or the ABS motor continuing to run/buzz when the ignition is turned off. • Diagnostic and repair tips are offered on transfer clutch binding and/or bucking on turns. • A rotten-egg smell could be caused by a defective catalytic converter. It will be replaced, after a bit of arguing, free of charge, up to five years under the emissions warranty. **All models: 1997–99**—Excessive driveline vibration is covered in TSB #05-33-98R. Subaru's fix requires modifying the differential. **2000–01**—Likely reasons why the automatic transmission light comes on. • Concerns with brake rotor scoring. • Subpar catalytic converter performance. **Forester: 2000–01**—Front oxygen air/fuel sensor cracking.

Forester, Impreza, WRX Profile

	1996	1997	1998	1999	2000	2001	2002	2003
Cost Price ($)								
Forester	—	—	26,695	26,695	26,895	28,395	28,395	28,395
Base/Brighton	17,995	16,991	16,240	17,795	—	—	—	—
Sedan 4X4	17,995	21,395	21,395	21,995	21,995	22,196	21,995	22,995
WRX	—	—	—	—	—	—	34,995	34,995
Used Values ($)								
Forester ⋏	—	—	10,000	11,000	14,500	17,000	20,000	24,000
Forester ⋎	—	—	9,000	10,000	13,500	16,500	19,500	22,000
Base/Brighton ⋏	5,000	6,000	6,500	8,500	—	—	—	—
Base/Brighton ⋎	4,500	5,500	6,000	8,000	—	—	—	—
Sedan 4X4 ⋏	6,000	7,500	9,000	10,500	12,000	14,000	15,500	17,000
Sedan 4X4 ⋎	5,000	6,500	8,000	9,500	11,000	13,000	14,500	16,500
WRX ⋏	—	—	—	—	—	—	23,500	28,000
WRX ⋎	—	—	—	—	—	—	23,000	26,000

Reliability	3	4	4	4	5	5	4	4
Crash Safety (F)	4	4	—	—	—	—	—	4
Forester	—	—	—	4	4	4	4	5
Side	—	—	3	3	—	—	5	4
Forester	—	—	3	3	—	5	5	5
Offset	—	—	—	—	—	—	4	5
Forester	—	—	—	5	5	5	5	5
Head restraints	—	2	—	—	—	2	3	—
Forester	—	—	—	2	—	3	3	5
Rollover Resistance								
Forester	—	—	—	—	—	3	3	3

Note: Budget an extra $500 or more for an extended powertrain warranty to protect you from premature and repeated clutch failures.

LEGACY, OUTBACK ★★★★

RATING: Above Average (1997–2003); Average for AWD (1991–96); Average for front-drives (1989–96). A competent, full-time 4X4 performer for drivers who want to move up in size, comfort, and features. Available as a four-door sedan or five-door wagon, the Legacy is cleanly and conventionally styled, with even a hint of the Acura Legend in the rear end. The AWD is what this car is all about. It handles difficult terrain without the fuel penalty or clumsiness of many truck-based SUVs. **Maintenance/Repair costs:** Higher than average. Repairs are dealer dependent. **Parts:** Parts aren't easily found and can be costly. **Best alternatives:** The Honda CR-V, Hyundai Santa Fe, Suzuki Grand Vitara, and Toyota RAV4. **Online help:** *techinfo.subaru.com/html/shoppingHome.jsp*; *www.autosafety.org*; and *www.carsurvey.org*.

Strengths and weaknesses: Costing a bit more than the Impreza, these Subarus are well appointed, provide a comfortable ride with acceptable handling, and have lots of cargo room. On the downside, owners report problematic automatic transmission performance when hooked to the base engine; the 2.5L is a sluggish performer, due undoubtedly to the car's heft; excessive engine noise; mediocre handling on base models; excessive 4-cylinder engine noise; power window and lock switches aren't easily accessible; there's a tight fit for the middle rear-seat passenger; cramped back seat; limited rear headroom for tall passengers; trunk hinges can damage cargo and cut into storage space; seat belts may be too short for large occupants; and servicing is very dealer-dependent.

The Outback is a marketing coup that stretches the definition of sport-utility by simply customizing the all-wheel-drive Legacy to give it more of an outdoorsy flair. American Motors tried the same marketing approach with the Eagle in the '70s and failed miserably, due to poor quality control, lousy marketing, and a passive public whose concept of off-road thrills was watching James Dean at the drive-in.

First launched in 1989 as front-drives, these compacts are a bit slow off the mark. The 5-speed is a bit notchy, and the automatic gearbox is slow to downshift, has difficulty staying in Overdrive, and is failure-prone. Early Legacys are noisy, fuel-thirsty cars with bland styling that masks their solid, dependable AWD performance. Actually, the availability of a proven 4X4 powertrain in a compact family sedan and wagon makes these cars appealing for special use. In spite of their reputation for dependability, though, Subarus are not trouble-free—engine, clutch, turbo, and driveline defects are common on the early models through to the 1998 versions.

Vehicle history: 1995–98—These redesigned models have sleeker styling, additional interior room (though legroom is still at a premium), a bit more horsepower with the base engine, and a new 2.5L 4-cylinder driving the 1996 AWD GT and LSi. The Outback, a Legacy/Madison Avenue spin-off, was transformed into a sport-utility wagon with a taller roof. Even with the improvements noted above, acceleration is still only passable (if you don't mind the loud engine), but highway handling and ride are remarkably good. The 1997 models marked a return to the company's 4X4 roots, with the repackaging of its Legacy and Impreza 4X4 lineup as Outbacks. A Legacy 2.5L GT all-wheel-drive sporting sedan, or wagon variant, also joined the group that year. In addition to these re-designated models—and the squeezing out of a bit more horsepower from its limited range of engines—Subaru continued to tap the sport-utility craze by offering a greater variety of AWD vehicles. **1999**—Debut of an upgraded 2.2L engine. **2000**—Longer and carrying a new 2.5L engine. **2001**—Two new Outback wagons, featuring a more powerful 3.0L engine, joined the lineup. **2002**—The addition to the lineup of the H6-3.0 VDC Outback sedan, equipped with a standard 3.0L engine. **2003**—New front end styling, GT gets an upgraded engine and a semi-manual Sport Shift; Outback suspension is upgraded to improve cornering and reduce front-end plow.

The 2.5L engine is a competent performer only with a manual gearbox. The 4-cylinder engine is noisy and rough-running. It's tuned more for low-end torque than for speedy acceleration. The 6-cylinder is adequate, but doesn't feel like it has much in reserve. The automatic transmission shifts into too high a gear to adequately exploit the engine's power and is reluctant to downshift into the proper gear. The manual transmission's shift linkage isn't suitable for rapid gear changes.

Base models don't handle well. They bounce around on uneven pavement, the rear end tends to swing out during high-speed cornering, and there's too much body lean in turns at lesser speeds. Higher-end models handle well, though there's some excessive lean when cornering. The GT's firmer suspension exhibits above-average handling.

Legacys and Outbacks have had more than their share of reliability problems over the years. Powertrain defects can sideline the car for days. Engine and transmission problems keep showing up. One owner of a '98 Legacy Outback has replaced his engine twice, at 800 km and 4,000 km. There are several reports of the transmission jumping out of gear when using First gear to slow down or to descend a steep grade. From 1999 through 2003, servicing can be awkward because of the crowded engine compartment, particularly on turbocharged versions.

Other problems: automatic transmission (front seals, especially) and clutch breakdowns are most common, the transmission sometimes downshifts abruptly while descending a long grade or travelling on snow-packed high-ways, and the front brakes require frequent attention. Check Engine and ABS warning lights come on constantly for no reason. Shock absorbers, constant velocity joints, and catalytic converters also often wear out prematurely. Other problems that appear over most model years include chronic electrical and fuel system malfunctions; hard starting, surging and stalling in cold weather; starter and ignition relay failures; and snow packed inside the wheelwells, binding steering. Misadjusted door strikers make for hard closing/opening.

Safety summary: All models/years: Many reports of ABS brake failure and premature wearout of brake components. • Small horn buttons may be hard to find in an emergency. **All models: 1996**—Car suddenly fishtails out of control when making a lane change. • Electrical system fire. • Cruise control won't disengage. • Premature tire failures (Bridgestone). • Hood flew up while driving. • Engine replaced at 18,000 km. • AC condenser and alternator fail-ures. • Sudden electrical shutdown. • Chronic hesitation, high-speed miss, and stalling. • Fuse blew out five times, causing stall. • Faulty gas gauge. • Low rear bench seat and no head restraints. • Sudden acceleration. • When the vehicle is being driven, transmission may suddenly jump out of Drive into Neutral. • Inadvertent airbag deployment. • Floor carpet prevented brake pedal application. • Complete engine failure at 18,000 km. • Chronic stalling. • Computer sensor control unit failure. • Excessive shaking at highway speeds. • Windshield wiper bolt failure. • Alternator failures while driving. • Left turn signal fails intermittently. • Climate control button sticks. • AC seizure. • O-ring failure causes AC to leak freon. • Bridgestone tires frequently blow out. • Keyless entry failed due to pinched wire in driver's door. • New-design headlights give poor illumination. **1997**—Sudden acceleration. • Cruise control failed to disengage when brakes were applied. • Igniter failed, allowing unburned fuel to flow into catalytic converter. • AC blew fumes into interior, causing driver to black out. • Stalling caused by igniter failure. • Complete engine failure due to defective valves and pistons. • Sudden loss of steering. • Transmission surges when cold, or shifts into Neutral at low speed or when descending a small hill. • Transmission failures. • Frequent electronic control unit failures. • Rear seat belts are too long to properly secure child safety seat, and the locking mechanism doesn't lock properly. • Brake and engine lights continually on. • Three alternators replaced by one owner. • Shorted hazard switch drained battery. • Alternator belt snapped, causing bat-tery and brake warning lights to come on and making car hard to steer. • Alternators frequently quit while vehicle is under power. **1998**—Oil leak from oil filter seam caused fire. • Sudden brake loss after linings, calipers, and master cylinder had been replaced. • Cruise control failed to disengage when brakes were applied. • Excessive shaking at highway speeds. • Seatback collapsed when vehicle was rear-ended. • Subaru told car owner that tendency to pull to the right was a design feature. **1999**—Sudden acceleration. • Chronic cold engine hesitation, stalling. • Engine failure due to cracked #2 piston. • When accelerating or decelerating, vehicle will begin to jerk due to excessive play in the front axle. • Tire blowout; air slowly escapes. • Front bumper skirt catches on parking blocks, resulting in bumper twisting and being ripped off. • The centre rear seat belt's poor design prohibits the installation of many child safety seats. **2000–01**—Igniter failure allowed unburned gasoline to flow into catalytic converter and resulted in chronic stalling. • Sudden, unintended acceleration in forward gear and in Reverse. • Vehicle suddenly veers to the right when accelerating or braking. • Cruise control failed to disengage when brake pedal was depressed. • Fuel sloshes in fuel tank due to the absence of baffles. • During a collision, airbags deployed but failed to inflate. • The suspension's design causes severe pulling to one side. • Excessive steering and vehicle vibration when passing over uneven pavement. • Steering lock-up while driving. • Knocking and clunking noise heard when turning. • Vehicle's rear end bounces about when passing over bumps. • Engine failure due to a cracked #2 piston. • Frequent surging from a stop. • Hard to shift from Park to Reverse. • Cracked seat belt buckle. • Seat belts are too short for large occupants. • Rear centre seat belt prevents the secure attachment of child safety seats. • Misadjusted door strikers make for hard closing/opening. • Snowstorm ice builds up in the wheelwell, making turning difficult. • Sudden tire blowout. **2002**—Sudden acceleration. • While idling in Park, vehicle suddenly jumped into Drive. **2003**—Chronic stalling in forward gear and in Reverse, particularly with 6-cylinder-equipped models:

> On multiple occasions, and with multiple drivers, I have had two 2003 Outbacks with frequent stalling when moving from Neutral to First, or to Reverse. This is potentially dangerous when moving out into traffic. Subaru denies receiving prior complaints (despite the material on your site) and in general denies that there is any problem. They also compelled me to sign a "gag" clause as part of a deal whereby they exchanged car #1 for car #2. I have arbitrarily put in a specific month, day, and year, but it has happened on multiple occasions. Also car #1 had two incidents of the engine running too rough to be driven, progressively losing power and then quitting— when restarted, ran fine. Also, car #1 had one episode of turning over well but refusing to start.

Secret Warranties/Service Tips/TSBs

All models/years: Troubleshooting tips on a sticking anti-lock brake relay are offered. This problem is characterized by a lit ABS warning light or the ABS motor continuing to run/buzz when the ignition is turned off. • Diagnostic and repair tips are offered on transfer clutch binding and/or bucking on turns. • A rotten-egg smell could be caused by a defective catalytic converter. It will be replaced, after a bit of arguing, free of charge, up to five years under the emissions warranty. **1995**—Tips are provided on silencing excessive front strut noise and engine oil pump leaks. **1995–96**—If the antenna won't fully retract, Subaru suggests cleaning the antenna mast and replacing the dress nut. **1997–99**—Excessive driveline vibration is covered in TSB #05-33-98R. Subaru's fix requires modifying the differential. **2000–01**—Loose bolts on the front seat belt retractor. • Inlet heater hose leaks engine coolant. • Probable causes for the automatic transmission temperature light flashing. • Measures that will eliminate brake squeal. **2002**—Excessive blower motor noise. • Countermeasures to reduce brake squeal. **2003**—Defective engine water pump. • Improved Sport Shift cold weather operation. • Defective transmission parking pawl rod. • Roof rack wind noise. • Premature suspension corrosion (see bulletin excerpt below):

> Certain rear suspension subframe components were produced with poor paint quality which, after continued exposure to corrosive road salts for a period of several years, could result in rust-out of the component and possible breakage of the subframe. If such breakage occurs while the vehicle is being operated, control of the vehicle could be affected, increasing the risk of a crash.
>
> Remedy: Dealers will clean and rustproof the rear suspension subframe.

Legacy, Outback Profile

	1996	1997	1998	1999	2000	2001	2002	2003
Cost Price ($)								
Legacy	23,195	—	—	—	—	—	—	—
Legacy 4X4	25,195	19,995	19,995	20,495	23,595	24,295	27,395	27,295
Used Values ($)								
Legacy ∧	4,500	—	—	—	—	—	—	—
Legacy ∨	4,000	—	—	—	—	—	—	—
Legacy 4X4 ∧	5,500	7,000	8,000	10,000	12,000	13,500	17,000	22,000
Legacy 4X4 ∨	5,000	6,000	7,000	9,000	11,000	12,500	15,500	21,000
Reliability	③	③	③	③	④	④	④	④
Crash Safety (F)								
Legacy 4d	④	④	④	④	—	④	④	④
Side	—	—	③	③	—	④	④	③
Wagon	—	—	—	—	—	—	—	④
Offset	③	③	③	③	⑤	⑤	⑤	⑤
Head Restraints	❷	❷	❷	❷	❷	③	③	③

Note: Consider an extended powertrain warranty to protect you from premature and repeated clutch and transmission failures.

Suzuki

AERIO, ESTEEM	★★★★★

RATING: *Aerio:* Recommended (2003); *Esteem:* Recommended (1996–2002). Suzuki's Aerio entry-level front-drive sedan and wagon replace the Esteem and offer optional all-wheel drive, making them among the lowest-priced AWD vehicles available in Canada. Both models come with a 145-hp 4-cylinder engine that's among the most-powerful standard engines in this class. Every Aerio comes with AC, power windows and mirrors, tilt steering wheel, CD player, and split folding rear seats. The GS sedan and SX use 15-inch alloy wheels, the S uses 14-inch steel rims. With the Esteem, getting the most horse-power bang for your buck means shopping for an Esteem sport model or looking over the upgraded year 2000 versions. Wagons are especially versatile and reasonably priced for the equipment provided. Both the base GL and upscale GLX come loaded with standard features that cost extra on other models. The GL, for example, comes with power steering, rear window defroster, remote trunk and fuel-filler door releases, tinted glass, and a fold-down rear seat (great for getting extra cargo space). GLX shoppers can look forward to standard ABS, power windows and power door locks, and a host of other interior refinements. **Maintenance/Repair costs:** Average. **Parts:** Average cost, and parts are easily found. **Best alternatives:** The GM Firefly or Metro; Honda Civic; Hyundai Accent or Elantra; Mazda Protegé; Nissan Sentra; and Toyota Echo, Tercel, or Corolla. **Online help:** *www.autosafety.org* and *www.carsurvey.org.*

Strengths and weaknesses: The Esteem is a small four-door sedan that is a step up from the Swift (see General Motors/Suzuki). Smaller than the Honda Civic and Chrysler Neon, it has a fairly spacious interior, offering rear accommodation (for two full-sized adults) that is comparable to or better than most cars in its class. It stands out with its European-styled body and large array of such standard features as AC, a fold-down back seat, and remote trunk and fuel-door releases. The roomy cabin has lots of front and rear headroom and legroom for four adults. Cargo space is fairly good with the sedan; exceptional with the wagon's rear seats folded.

The small 95-hp engine delivers respectable acceleration and overall performance is acceptable, thanks to the Esteem's four-wheel independent suspension, which gives just the right balance between a comfortable ride and no-surprise handling. For a bit more power, look for a '96 or later sport variant that carries a 125-hp power plant.

Vehicle history: 1998—A wagon version joined the lineup. **1999**—New front-end styling, 14-inch wheels, and an upgraded sound system. **2000**—More power provided by a 122-hp 1.8L engine. **2003**—Esteem was replaced by the Aerio.

Some of the drawbacks to owning one of these econoboxes: small tires compromise handling, and power steering doesn't transmit much road feedback. The Esteem's automatic transmission also may shift harshly and vibrate excessively between gear changes. Braking is mediocre for a car this light.

During the relatively short time the Esteem has been on the market, it has proven to be a high-quality, reliable small car. In this respect, it competes well with its Detroit-built rivals like the Chevrolet Cavalier, Dodge Neon, and Ford Escort, while being outclassed by the Honda Civic, Mazda Protegé, and Toyota Corolla. Problems reported by owners: premature front brake wear, noisy front brakes, occasional electrical short circuits, wind and water intrusion into the passenger compartment, and fragile body panels and trim items.

Safety summary: All models: 1996—Airbag failed to deploy. • ABS failure. • Engine crankshaft pulley broke while driving. • Transmission failure. **1997**— Sudden brake failure. • Seat belts failed to secure occupants in a collision. • Sudden, total electrical shutdown. • Plastic outside door handles break easily. • Horn doesn't work. **1998**—Airbag failed to deploy. • Seat belt failed to lock up in a collision. • Vehicle is unstable at high speed. • Door handle failures. **1999**—Engine oil leak sprays oil throughout the engine compartment. • Stuck accelerator. • Loss of power when accelerating. • Stuck accelerator pedal. • Chronic stalling. • Transmission and brake failures. • Brakes continue to squeal even after installing new rotors and pads. **2000**—No airbag deployment. • Sudden acceleration from a stop. • Automatic transmission bangs into gear. • Gear shift lever fell from Drive to Neutral and is hard to move. • Excessive steering wheel vibration and noise. • Windshield seal vibrates and cracks in cold weather. **2001**—Automatic transmission stuck in lower gear. • Brake failure. • Complete electrical failure fixed temporarily by lifting the hood and jiggling the master control fuse.

Secret Warranties/Service Tips/TSBs

All models: 1996–97—Uneven wear of the front disc brake pads can be corrected by modifying the upper bushing tolerance, says TSB #TS 5-03-04126. **1998–99**—Remote-entry battery failure due to defective fob diode. **1999–2002**—Voluntary emissions recall to replace the vapour control valve.

Esteem Profile

	1996	1997	1998	1999	2000	2001	2002	2003
Cost Price ($)								
Aerio	—	—	—	—	—	—	—	15,785
Aerio SX (AWD)	—	—	—	—	—	—	—	19,785
GL	13,495	13,495	13,895	13,995	15,495	15,695	16,195	—
GLX	14,495	15,495	16,895	17,195	18,491	18,795	19,795	—
Used Values ($)								
Aerio ▲	—	—	—	—	—	—	—	11,500
Aerio ▼	—	—	—	—	—	—	—	11,000

Aerio SX (AWD) ⋀	—	—	—	—	—	—	—	14,000
Aerio SX (AWD) ⋁	—	—	—	—	—	—	—	13,500
GL ⋀	3,000	3,500	4,500	5,500	7,000	8,500	9,500	—
GL ⋁	2,500	3,000	4,000	5,000	6,500	7,000	9,000	—
GLX ⋀	4,000	4,500	5,500	6,500	8,500	9,500	11,000	—
GLX ⋁	3,000	4,000	5,000	6,000	7,500	8,500	9,500	—
Reliability	④	④	④	④	④	⑤	⑤	—
Head Restraints	—	—	—	❷	—	❷	❷	—

Note: The Esteem wasn't crash-tested.

Toyota/General Motors

COROLLA, MATRIX/VIBE ★★★★

RATING: *Corolla:* Above Average (1991–2003); Average (1985–90). Be wary of serious safety deficiencies that include airbag malfunctions, airbag-induced injuries, seat belt failures, and poorly designed headlights that misdirect the light beam. Since the 1997 model was de-contented (less soundproofing, fewer standard features, etc.), there has been a noticeable reduction in quality control. The 1995–96 models combine the best array of standard features, quality control, and "reasonable" (for a Toyota) used prices. 1998–2001 models are good second choices with their horsepower-enhanced engine. *Matrix/Vibe:* Above Average (2003). Aimed at the youth market, these versatile and relatively reliable spin-offs don't provide enough horsepower to justify their "sporty" pretensions. **Maintenance/Repair costs:** *Corolla:* Lower than average, and repairs can be done anywhere; *Matrix/Vibe:* Powertrain and body part supply is a bit problematic. **Parts:** Corolla parts are reasonably priced and easily found. **Best alternatives:** The GM Firefly or Metro, Hyundai Accent or Elantra, Mazda Protegé, Nissan Sentra, and Suzuki Esteem or Aerio. **Online help:** *www.matrixowners.com*; *www.autosafety.org*; and *www.carsurvey.org*.

Strengths and weaknesses: A step up from the Tercel/Echo, the Corolla has long been Toyota's standard-bearer in the compact sedan class. Over the years, however, the car has grown in size, price, and refinement to the point where it can now be considered a small family sedan. All Corollas ride on a front-drive platform with independent suspension on all wheels.

   Post-1987 models are much improved over earlier versions and many are on our roads after 15 years. The two-door models provide sporty performance and good fuel economy, especially when equipped with the 16-valve engine. The base engine, however, lacks power and is agonizingly slow merging and passing on the highway. Owners report problems with premature front suspension strut and brake wear; brake vibration; faulty defrosting that allows the windows to fog up in winter; and rusting of body seams, especially door bottoms, side mirror mounts, trunk and hatchback lids, and wheel openings.

The 1990–94 Corolla's problems are limited to harsh automatic shifting, early front brake pad and strut/shock wearout, AC high-pressure tube leaks, electrical glitches, ignition problems, windshield wiper linkage failures, and some interior squeaks and rattles. They do, however, still require regular valve adjustments to prevent serious engine problems. Less of a problem with these later models, rusting is usually confined to the undercarriage and other areas where the mouldings attach to sheet metal.

The 1995–99 models have chronic seat belt retractor glitches and airbag malfunctions. Additionally, owners report powertrain, brake, and electrical problems; poor rear windshield defrosting; vibrations, squeaks, and rattles afflicting the brakes, steering, and suspension; and body trim imperfections that include water leaking through the doors.

The 2000–02 models have fewer deficiencies reported by owners, partly because they're still under warranty and haven't been on the market that long. Nevertheless, owners report that fenders are easily dented, the windshield and windshield frame may suddenly crack, the engine may leak oil, and the seat belt shoulder strap is mounted too high, cutting across the driver's neck.

Year 2003 Corolla, Matrix/Vibe owners report the following problems: engine surging; excessive steering wander; transmission clutch failures; with transmission in Park, vehicle can roll away; defective crankshafts; power-steering pump failures; a clicking sound emanates from the driver-side dashboard; a rotten-egg smell comes from the exhaust or through the vents; the CD player makes a grinding noise when braking; excessive vibration felt in the interior during acceleration after start-up; excessive dashboard vibration; headlight condensation, driver's seat fabric tears easily; hood popped up while car was underway; black tape covering the window frame tends to bubble; paint blisters quite easily; and gas mileage may not be up to expectations.

Vehicle history: 1993—Redesigned model is larger and equipped with a driver-side airbag and optional ABS. **1994**—A passenger-side airbag and improved seat belt retractors. **1995**—A torquier 1.8L engine that had 10 fewer horses than the '94 (105). **1996**—Five fewer horses (100), new front and rear ends, and an upgraded manual transmission. **1997**—An upscale CE version debuts, while the wagon is axed. **1998**—Another redesign produced a slightly more powerful engine (120 horses), two inches more in length, and optional front passenger side-impact airbags. **1999**—Addition of a front stabilizer bar to improve handling. **2000**—Five additional horses and tilt steering on the CE and LE. **2001**—A slight face-lift and the addition of a new sport-oriented variant called the Corolla S. The VE was dropped and the formerly mid-level CE replaced it, carrying fewer standard features. The LE dropped to the CE's former level and was also de-contented, losing its standard AC and power windows, locks, and mirrors. **2003**—Redesigned to be taller, wider, and longer; adds a new 4-speed automatic transmission; gets five more horses; and the launch of the Matrix/Vibe.

Matrix/Vibe

These small front-drive, or all-wheel-drive sporty wagons are a cross between a mini SUV and a station wagon, packaged like a small minivan. Vibe is built in Fremont, California, at GM's NUMMI factory, while the nearly identical Toyota Matrix is manufactured in Toyota's Cambridge, Ontario plant, alongside the Corolla, whose platform it shares, though it provides a larger interior volume.

The front-drive Matrix/Vibe is equipped with a 130-hp engine, 5-speed manual overdrive transmission, and lots of standard features; however, the weak, buzzy base engine can be felt throughout the car; 4X4 models are about 10 percent heavier and get seven fewer horses (123) than the already power-challenged 130-hp front-drive. Says *Forbes* magazine:

> [B]oth all-wheel-drive cars are saddled with a really wretched 4-speed automatic that almost has to be shifted manually to get the car moving. To put it bluntly, the AWD Vibe and Matrix are so pokey, they feel like they're towing Winnebagos. To boot, the 1.8L engine doesn't hit its paltry torque peak...until a screaming 4200 rpm, at which point the vibration—did somebody say Vibe?—in the cabin is worse than a little off-putting.

The Matrix XRS and Vibe GT are the top-of-the-line performance leaders, with a 180-hp 4-cylinder engine and a high-performance 6-speed manual gearbox, plus ABS, premium six-speaker stereo, anti-theft system, 17-inch alloy wheels, and unique exterior cladding.

These vehicles hail from factories that have garnered high-quality ratings and also come with similar warranties. If you really need additional horsepower, get either the XRS or GT. But keep in mind that there are better high-performance choices out there, like the Honda Civic Si, Mazda Protegé5, or a base Acura RSX. Other front-drives worth considering are the Chrysler PT Cruiser, Hyundai Elantra or Tiburon, Honda Civic, Nissan Sentra, or the Toyota Corolla. Of course, the Subaru Impreza or Forester would be other good choices for the 4X4 variant.

Safety summary: All models/years: No airbag deployment during collisions. **1996**—Fires originating in the fuel tank, dash, and engine compartment areas. • Airbag deployed for no reason. • Brake failures and high maintenance costs. • Driver headrest too wide for adequate rear visibility. • Seat belt failures and malfunctioning retractors. • Hood flew up while vehicle was underway. • Inoperative door locks. **1997**—Fires reportedly caused by faulty seat belt wiring. • Brake failures. • Sudden acceleration. • Inadvertent airbag deployment (when the ignition is turned on). • Steering column grinding. • Interior water leaks. • Malfunctioning door locks. • Windshield wipers suddenly quit. • Poor visibility due to film on windshield interior and lack of an adequate rear defroster. • Frequent reports that the seat belt retractors won't release or retract. • Researchers are looking into 20 incidents where the turn signal failed after the hazard warning light activated. **1998**—Engine compartment fires, gas fumes in the interior, brake and power-steering failures, and excessive steering column noise. • Excessive drifting and high-speed instability, due to lack of a stabilizer bar. • Sudden acceleration. • Premature control arm failure. • Seat belt released in accident. • Rear wheel broke at the axle. • Random honking. **1998–2000**—Brakes lock up. • Vehicle continues to wander and sway at moderate speeds; side winds increase the vehicle's instability. • Gearshift dropped from Drive to Neutral while driving. • Floor mat jams the accelerator. • Engine stalls after refuelling. • Front strut assembly failure. • Inadequate headlight illumination; one side will be aimed too high, other side, too low. **1999**—Inadvertent airbag deployment. • Engine compartment fire. • Loss of braking ability. • Defective tires (Firestone). • Sudden acceleration. • Cruise control self-activates. • Automatic transmission locked up while driving. • Vehicle went out of control after rear control arm failure. • At cruising speed, vehicle tends to wander all over the road. • Windshield shattered when door was closed. • Poor headlight design causes blind spot and poor visibility. • Defective engine camshaft gets inadequate oil lubrication and loses compression. • Rear seat belts aren't compatible with many child safety seats. **2001**—Sudden acceleration. • Stuck accelerator pedal. • Headlight illumination problem continues; high beam shoots skyward and is especially hazardous in rain or fog. • Rear driver-side axle sheared in half; vehicle rolled over. • Excessive front brake pad wear; premature failure of the brake proportioning valve and rear brake shoes. • Hole in the oil pan. • Failure of all four Goodyear Integrity tires. • Inside trunk release handle doesn't glow as advertised. **2002**— Fuel leakage:

> On 04/29/02 consumer discovered that vehicle was leaking fuel. Vehicle was repaired by dealer who advised consumer that the fuel lines had come loose. On 07/29/02 while driving, engine compartment caught on fire as a result of fuel leaking.

• In one deployment, airbag ripped and allowed child to be seriously injured. • Unable to shift out of Park. • While using cruise control, gas pedal suddenly went to the floor. • Left rear tire fell off while driving. • Vehicle tends to wander at highway speeds:

> Vehicle wanders and sways back and forth. Vehicle was taken to dealership, and mechanic stated that all four wheels were bent. Vehicle came from factory that way. Goodyear, Integrity, P185/65R14. Right front tire had a bulge on outside.

• Early fuel pump replacement led to rotten-egg smell. • Strong sulfur smell in the interior. • Weak climate control system. • Both headlights have stray beams that project upward at a 45-degree angle; very distracting, particularly in mist. • Poor quality wiper blade. **Matrix: 2003**—Engine surges when braking with AC engaged. • Excessive steering wander; feels a bit vague, with too much play; some torque steer (twisting) evident, especially on wet roads. • The manual shift lever's upward and forward position is counterintuitive and feels a bit ragged. • Instrument panel lights are dimmed by automatic sensor to a point where they can't be read in twilight hours and the automatic headlights come on and go off for no apparent reason.

Secret Warranties/Service Tips/TSBs

All models/years: Improved disc brake pad kits are described in TSB #BR94-004. • Brake pulsation/vibration, another generic Toyota problem, is fully addressed in TSB #BR94-002, "Cause and Repair of Vibration and Pulsation." • Complaints of steering column noise may require the replacement of the steering column assembly, a repair covered under Toyota's base warranty. • AM static noise on all vehicles with power antennas usually means the antenna is poorly grounded. • Toyota has developed special procedures for eliminating AC odours and excessive wind noise. These problems are covered in TSBs #AC00297 and #BO00397, respectively. **All models: 1990–2001**—Toyota has developed a special grease to eliminate clicking when the vehicle goes into Drive or Reverse. **1998**—Tips on reducing excessive engine V-belt noise. • Delayed upshift to Overdrive with cruise control engaged can be fixed by changing the cruise control ECU logic. • Water leakage into the rear cab can be plugged by installing an improved C-pillar moulding clip. • If the rear door glass malfunctions when temperatures dive, install an upgraded mounting channel insert bar. • Toyota will replace the airbag computer under a service campaign. **1998–99**—A front suspension squeaking noise can be silenced by replacing the steering rack end shaft under warranty, but Toyota tell dealers to do the repair only if the customer demands it. **1998–2000**—In an attempt to reduce brake vibration complaints, Toyota will install a new front disc brake pad kit, says TSB #BR002-00, issued March 10, 2000. This fix is covered by Toyota's base warranty, but, again, the customer must demand the repair (it also might help if you show the service manager the following bulletin).

Front Brake Vibration

Bulletin: BR002-00   Group: Brakes   Date: March 10, 2000

Introduction

A new Front Disc Brake Pad kit is available and a procedure has been developed for applying Disc Brake Grease to the brake cylinder mountings, brake pads, and pad support plates to reduce the possibility of front brake vibration under certain operating conditions.

Applicable Vehicles

1998–2000 model year Corolla

Parts Information

Previous Part Number	Current Part Number	Part Name
04465-12520	04465-02050	Pad Kit, Front Disc Brake
04945-02020	Same	Shim Kit (if needed*)
08887-80409	Same	Grease, Disc Brake Shim
04947-02020	Same	Fitting kit, Front Disc Brake (if needed**)

* Visually inspect shims for heat discolouration. If discoloured, replace the shims.   ➤

* Visually inspect pad support plates for damage. If damaged, replace the pad support plates.

OPCODE	DESCRIPTION	TIME	OPN	T1	T2
473025	Grind Front Discs and Replace Pads, Shims (if needed), and Apply Grease to Front Disc Brake	1.3	43512-12550	21	99
Combo A	Cylinder Mountings, Brake Pads, and Pad Support Plates for Vibration (both sides).	0.8			

Warranty Information

Applicable Warranty*:

This repair is covered under the Toyota Basic Warranty. This warranty is in effect for 36 months or 36,000 miles [57,600 km], whichever occurs first, from the vehicle's in-service date.

* Warranty application is limited to correction of a problem based upon a customer's specific complaint.

Brake pulsation has been a recurring Toyota problem, affecting its entire model lineup over the past decade. Many "goodwill" programs cover its diagnosis and correction.

1999—A single-cylinder misfire that causes a rough idle or the activation of the malfunction indicator light (MIL) will be fixed under Toyota's base warranty. **1999–2002**—Accessory drivebelt/belt tensioner assembly noise is addressed in TSB #EG015-01, published December 7, 2001. The service bulletin claims the squeak or rattle noise will be corrected free of charge up to 3 years/58,000 km (36,000 mi.), if the owner complains. • Vibration troubleshooting tips. • Sulfur exhaust odour remedies. • Countermeasures for vehicle pulling to one side. **2003**—The following items may affect the Corolla, as well. **Matrix:** Upper suspension tapping noise. • No airflow from centre vents. • Loose, or deformed front or rear glass door run. • AC doesn't put out sufficient cool air. • Headlights come on, when turned off. • Sulfur odour in the interior. • Discoloured wheelhouse moulding. **Vibe:** Engine lacks performance after 7000 rpms. • Transmission shifts too early when accelerating at full throttle when the engine is cold. • Harsh shifting. • Grinding or growling while in Park on an incline. • Water leak from the A-pillar or headliner area. • Upper suspension tapping noise. • Low voltage display or dim lights.

Corolla Profile

	1996	1997	1998	1999	2000	2001	2002	2003
Cost Price ($)								
Base Corolla	13,508	13,968	14,928	15,090	15,625	15,625	15,765	15,290
Matrix	—	—	—	—	—	—	—	16,745
XR AWD	—	—	—	—	—	—	—	24,210
Vibe	—	—	—	—	—	—	—	20,995
GT AWD	—	—	—	—	—	—	—	27,000
Used Values ($)								
Base Corolla ⋀	5,000	5,500	6,500	7,500	9,000	10,000	11,000	12,500
Base Corolla ⋁	4,000	5,000	6,000	7,000	7,500	9,000	10,000	11,500
Matrix ⋀	—	—	—	—	—	—	—	13,500
Matrix ⋁	—	—	—	—	—	—	—	13,000
XR AWD ⋀	—	—	—	—	—	—	—	20,000
XR AWD ⋁	—	—	—	—	—	—	—	19,000

Vibe ▲	—	—	—	—	—	—	—	15,000
Vibe ▼	—	—	—	—	—	—	—	14,000
GT AWD ▲	—	—	—	—	—	—	—	19,000
GT AWD ▼	—	—	—	—	—	—	—	18,000
Reliability	③	③	③	③	③	④	④	⑤
Crash Safety (F)	④	④	④	—	④	④	④	⑤
Side	—	③	③	—	④	④	③	⑤
Offset	—	—	③	③	③	③	③	⑤
Head Restraints	—	❶	③	③	—	❷	④	⑤
Rollover Resistance	—	—	—	—	—	④	④	④

Toyota

ECHO ★★★★★

RATING: Recommended (2000–03). An incredibly practical small car, if you can get by the tall, function-over-form styling. It represents an excellent alternative to the similarly styled, glitch-ridden Ford Focus. **Parts:** Should be easily obtainable from the Tercel parts bin. Body panels may be back ordered. **Maintenance/Repair costs:** Extraordinarily low. **Best alternatives:** A GM Firefly or Metro; Honda Civic; Hyundai Accent; Mazda Protegé; Nissan Sentra; and Suzuki Swift, Esteem, or Aerio. **Online help**: *www.autosafety.org* and *www.carsurvey.org*.

Strengths and weaknesses: Toyota scrapped its stripped-down Tercel in favour of the year 2000 Echo, an entry-level five-passenger model that uses some of the same engine technology as the Lexus to give great fuel economy without sacrificing performance.

Both two- and four-door models are available, and the car costs substantially less than the Corolla. The Echo also offers about the same amount of passenger space as the Corolla, thanks to a high roof and low floor height.

Cockpit controls and instrumentation are particularly user-friendly, located high on the dash and more toward the centre of the vehicle, rather than directly in front of the driver, where many gauges and controls would be hidden by the steering column.

The Echo is powered by a 108-hp 1.5L DOHC 4-cylinder engine featuring variable valve timing cylinder head technology. Normally, an engine this small would provide wimpy acceleration, but thanks to the Echo's light weight, acceleration is more than adequate with a manual gearbox and acceptable with the automatic.

Standard safety features: five three-point seat belts (front seat belts have pretensioners and force limiters), two front airbags (side airbags are not available), four height-adjustable head restraints, rear child seat tether anchors, and rear child door locks.

Vehicle history: 2003—A major restyling adds 4 cm (1.6 in.) to overall length via new front and rear sheet metal and revised bumpers, hood, front fenders, headlights, tail lights, trunk lid, and grille.

The Echo has more usable power than the Tercel and provides excellent fuel economy and lots of interior space. There's plenty of passenger room, along with an incredible array of storage areas, including a huge trunk and standard 60/40 split folding rear seats. All models are reasonably well equipped, with good-quality materials, well-designed instruments and controls, comfortable seating, easy rear access, and excellent fore and aft visibility. It's quite nimble when cornering, very stable on the highway, and surprisingly quiet for an economy car. The car hasn't changed much since its 2000 model debut.

What's there not to like? Try the tall profile and light weight, which make the Echo vulnerable to side-wind buffeting; base tires that provide poor wet traction; excessive torque steer that makes for sudden pulling to one side when accelerating; and the narrow body width, which limits rear bench seating to two adults.

Safety summary: All models: 2001—Toyota should reposition the Overdrive switch; the right thigh may bump against it. • At 100 km/h, the engine jumps to higher rpms and causes a bit of a surprise. • Vehicle drifted off the highway at 110 km/h. **2002**—Airbag failed to deploy. • Several incidents of sudden, unintended acceleration:

> While driving, the Echo will accelerate to 60 mph [96 km/h] without hitting the gas pedal. I have to put the vehicle in Neutral to stop it. I contacted dealer, but he cannot locate the cause.
>
> The sudden acceleration incident occurred three times. The dealer was unable to duplicate the problem in test driving, but removed the cruise control. The problem was not corrected by removing the cruise control.

Secret Warranties/Service Tips/TSBs

All models: 2000—Toyota has a Special Service Campaign (secret warranty) that allows for the free replacement of the brake booster and front brake pads on vehicles equipped with an automatic transmission. Confirmation of this campaign can be found in Toyota Service Bulletin Number TC01027, Bulletin Sequence Number 625, published 10/01, and recorded in the NHTSA database as Item Number SB625616. • MIL light may indicate a single-cylinder misfire (modify the ECM). • Probable causes for interior squeaks and rattles. • Wheel covers may click or squeak. • Excessive wind noise. • Fuel gauge and speedometer malfunctions. • Brake clicking countermeasures. • Defective airflow rotary control knob. **2000–02**—Improved carpet design. **2001**—Special Service Campaign to inspect the rear brake tubes free of charge. • Roof moulding may come loose or become deformed. **2002**—Countermeasures for vehicle pulling to one side. **2003**—Hood lock assembly will be replaced free of charge to prevent snow entry/cable rusting (see TSB #BO018-03).

Echo Profile	2000	2001	2002	2003
Cost Price ($)				
Base	13,835	13,980	14,084	13,690
Used Values ($)				
Base ∧	7,000	8,000	9,500	11,000
Base ∨	6,500	7,000	8,500	10,000
Reliability	⑤	⑤	⑤	⑤
Crash Safety (F)	—	④	④	④
Side	—	③	③	③
Head Restraints	—	⑤	⑤	⑤
Rollover Resistance	—	④	④	④

TERCEL, PASEO ★★★★★

RATING: *Tercel:* Recommended (1993–99); Above Average (1991–92); Average (1987–90). *Paseo:* Above Average (1992–99). 1999 was the last model year for both the Tercel and the Paseo. **Maintenance/Repair costs:** Inexpensive. Repairs can be done anywhere. **Parts:** Reasonably priced and easily obtainable. **Best alternatives:** A GM Firefly or Metro, Honda Civic, Hyundai Accent or Elantra, Mazda Protegé, Nissan Sentra, Suzuki Esteem, and Toyota Echo or Corolla. **Online help:** *www.autosafety.org* and *www.car-survey.org.*

Strengths and weaknesses: Don't buy a Toyota on reputation alone, because many early models (1985–90) can have serious braking, electrical, carburetor (stalling), and rusting problems, and they may be overpriced to boot. Also, stay away from the troublesome 4X4 versions made from 1984 to 1987.

All Tercels should be checked for door panel and underbody rust damage. 1987–90 Tercels are prone to rust around the rear wheels and side mirror mounts, and along the bottoms of doors, hatches, and rear quarter panels. Early models suffer from extensive corrosion of rear suspension components.

Vehicle history: 1991–94—This generation dropped the wagon and hatchback in favour of two- and four-door sedans; was the first to be fuel injected; and had potentially unsafe (due to poor anchoring), unreliable, and uncomfortable door-mounted front-shoulder belts. **1993**—Driver's side airbag. **1995**—Dual airbags, three-point seat belts, and side-door beams; a bit more horsepower (93); aero styling and a redesigned interior. **1997**—Only a bare-bones CE model remains. **2000**—Both the Tercel and Paseo were replaced by the Echo.

Tercels are extraordinarily reliable, and the first generation improvements provided livelier and smoother acceleration and made the interior space feel much larger than it was. Owners report these early models had hard-shifting automatic transmissions, premature brake and suspension component wearout, brake pulsation, leaking radiators, windshield whistling, and myriad squeaks and rattles.

Updated 1995–99 Tercels are noted for sporadic brake, electrical system, suspension, and body/accessories problems.

Paseo

This 1996–99 baby Tercel's main advantages are a peppy 1.5L 4-cylinder engine, a smooth 5-speed manual transmission, good handling, a supple ride, great fuel economy, and above-average reliability. On the other hand, this light little sportster is quite vulnerable to side winds; there's lots of body lean in turns; there's plenty of engine, exhaust, and road noise; front headroom and legroom are limited; and there is very little rear seat space. Generally, safety problems and defects affecting the Tercel were also likely to affect the Paseo.

Safety summary: Interestingly, there are far fewer safety-related Tercel and Paseo complaints recorded over the years than those listed for the Corolla, Camry, or Sienna. **All models/years:** Airbag failing to deploy. • Seat belt lock-up. • Windshield seal leaks. • Brake failures. • Inadequate defrosting. • Chronic stalling. • Vehicle jumping out of gear. • Engine failure due to defective oil indicator. **1996**—Fuel line explosion. • Fire caused by an overheated heater fan motor. • Inadequate defrosting. • Light rear end makes car unstable at higher speeds. **1997**—Front ball joints snapped while car was underway.

Secret Warranties/Service Tips/TSBs

All models/years: TSB #B0003-97 recommends the use of a new wind noise repair kit. • Interior squeaks and rattles can be fixed with Toyota's kit (#08231-00801). • TSB #AC002-97 gives lots of troubleshooting tips on eliminating AC odours. • Older Toyotas with stalling problems should have the engine checked for excessive carbon buildup on the valves before any other repairs are done. • Improved disc brake pad kits are described in TSB #BR94-004. • Brake pulsation/vibration, another generic Toyota problem, is fully addressed in TSB #BR94-002, "Cause and Repair of Vibration and Pulsation." • A damaged power antenna or poor grounding due to corrosion are the most likely causes of AM radio static. • The company will make available seat belt extensions. **1998**—Diagnostic tips for eliminating vehicle vibration. • Front door belt moulding wind noise.

Tercel, Paseo Profile

	1992	1993	1994	1995	1996	1997	1998	1999
Cost Price ($)								
Tercel	8,798	9,098	9,618	10,998	11,948	12,498	12,498	12,625
Paseo	13,338	14,398	14,698	16,878	17,215	17,608	15,998	16,150

Used Values ($)

Tercel ⋀	3,000	3,000	3,500	4,000	4,500	5,000	5,500	5,500
Tercel ⋁	2,000	2,500	3,000	3,500	4,000	4,500	5,000	5,000
Paseo ⋀	3,500	3,500	4,000	4,500	5,000	5,500	6,000	7,000
Paseo ⋁	3,000	3,000	3,500	4,000	4,500	5,000	5,500	6,000

Reliability	③	③	③	④	⑤	⑤	⑤	⑤
Crash Safety (F)	❷	❷	④	④	③	④	—	—
Paseo	③	③	—	—	—	④	—	—
Side	—	—	—	—	—	③	③	—
Head Restraints	—	❷	—	❶	—	❶	—	—
Paseo	—	—	—	❶	—	❷	—	—

Volkswagen

CABRIO, GOLF, JETTA   ★★★

RATING: Average (1999–2003); Below Average (1993–98); Not Recommended (1985–92). These small cars are much more expensive than the competition and they age particularly badly. Plus, VW, with its Canadian headquarters located in the States, is not very generous with "goodwill" repairs. A Jetta is a Golf with a trunk; a Cabrio is a Golf without a roof. Interestingly, the early convertibles (Cabriolets) are real bargains, inasmuch as they depreciate steeply after their first five years on the market. **Maintenance/Repair costs:** Higher than average. Repairs are very dealer dependent. **Parts:** Expensive, but generally available from independent suppliers. Recall campaign parts may be back ordered for months. **Best alternatives:** The Honda Civic, Hyundai Elantra or Tiburon, Mazda Protegé, Nissan Sentra, and Toyota Corolla. **Online help:** *www.autosafety.org; www.carsurvey.org;* and *64.255.13.120/index.php (MyVWLemon.com).*

Strengths and weaknesses: On the positive side, these small imports are fun to drive and provide great fuel economy. The 1.8L gasoline engine is very peppy, and the diesel engines are very reliable and good all-around performers. Both engines are easily started in cold weather. But here's the rub: Golfs and Jettas, like the failure-prone Rabbit they replaced, aren't reliable once the warranty expires. What you save in fuel, you lose in the car's high retail price, which is carried over into the used-car market, and the ever-mounting maintenance costs as the vehicle gains years and mileage will easily wear you down.

Reliability is impressive—for the first three years. Then the brake components and fuel and electrical systems start to self-destruct as your wallet gets lighter. Exhaust system components aren't very durable, body hardware and dashboard controls are fragile, the paint often discolours and is easily chipped, and window regulators constantly fail:

I bought my '96 Jetta GLS in 1999. I have replaced eight window regulators in three years, one power window motor, and I can't get the Check Engine light off for the life of me. I have also had to put the door moulding on the driver's side back door three times.

I found that the windows falling into the door is always due to a broken window regulator, which are less than half the price if you order them from anyone other than the VW dealer, and are not hard to put in yourself.

Volkswagen has terrible quality problems that can't be repaired at the corner garage. Owners report electrical short circuits; heater/defroster resistor and motor failures; leaking transmission and stub axle seals; and defective valve-pan gaskets, head gaskets, timing belts, steering assemblies, suspension components, alternator pulleys, and brake and electrical systems. Body problems are legion, with air and water leaks, faulty catalytic converters, inoperative locks and latches, poor-quality body construction and paint, and cheap, easily broken accessories and trim items.

The redesigned 1994–96 models are a bit safer and a tad more reliable. Nevertheless, problems disclosed in service bulletins for these model years show that serious defects continue to accumulate along with the years. Powertrain failures, poor driveability, water leaks, trim defects, and premature rear tire wear are all addressed. Owners also report the following: electric door locks that take a long time to lock; paint that is easily nicked, chipped, and marked; a variety of trim defects; premature rear tire wear; and poor-quality seat cushions.

Factory defects on 1990–96 Golfs and Jettas are so numerous that they make these models very risky buys. Problems include automatic transmission, engine, suspension component, and catalytic converter failures; electrical short circuits; AC malfunctions; and fragile trim items. Body assembly and paint are second-class, leading to rattles and air leaks as the vehicles age.

Vehicle history: 1985—Both the Golf hatchback and the Jetta's two-door and four-door sedans have more interior space. **1991**—Debut of the 2.0L 134-hp Golf GTI 16V and mandatory 5-speed manual transmission. **1992**—Upgraded diesel engine gets seven more horses (59). **1994**—Dual airbags and the top-line GLX model got a 172-horsepower V6. **1995**—Golf GTI VR6, plus two other Golf models make their debut, height-adjustable manual front seat belts with emergency tensioners, and side impact door beams. **1996**—Dashboard-mounted glove box returns and improved seat belt retractors and door locking system. **1997**—The 116-hp 4-cylinder engines got a redesigned cylinder head that cuts engine noise; the Golf GTI VR6 rides lower, thanks to new shocks, springs, and anti-roll bars; the Cabrio Highline received standard AC and a few other amenities; and a cheapened base convertible lost its standard ABS and a few other goodies. **1999**—Updated interior and exterior styling and a more powerful engine; Cabrios were given new European styling. **2001**—A 150-hp 1.8L turbo four became available for the GLS and was standard in the base GTI; and a Jetta wagon was added along with steering-mounted audio controls (on some models). **2002**—Debut of a more powerful 1.8L 4-cylinder engine, a 5-speed automatic transmission, and an optional 6-speed manual transmission; 2.8L V6 horsepower boosted to 200.

Jettas provide slightly more comfort and better road performance than their Golf hatchback counterparts. The 1.6L 4-cylinder found on early Jettas was surprisingly peppy, and the diesel engine is very economical, although quite slow to accelerate. Diesels have a better overall reliability record than gasoline models. These cars suffer from rapid body deterioration and some mechanical problems after their fourth year in service. For example, starters often burn out because they are vulnerable to engine heat; as well, sunroofs leak, door locks jam, window cranks break, and windows bind. Owners also report engine head gasket leaks, as well as water pump and heater core breakdowns. It's axiomatic that all diesels are slow to accelerate, but VW's Fourth gear can't handle highway speeds above 90 km/h. Engine noise is deafening when shifting down from Fourth gear.

The 1996–2003 models are more reliable, but, nevertheless, owners still report chronic automatic transmission, brake, and electrical system problems, in addition to subpar body construction and paint, leaky sunroofs, malfunctioning gauges and accessories, fragile locks and latches, bumpers that become brittle and crack as the temperature falls, defective security systems, and disagreeable interior odours. The following Toronto VW owner had this to say:

> Hi Phil, I recently purchased a used 1999 VW Jetta (one of the new model types) and after talking to some co-workers there seems to be a problem with the AC in both Jettas and Golfs. The problem is that condensation builds up on one of the filters and after a little while bacteria will start to grow and then when you turn on the fan for the AC the air being pumped out starts to stink. One of my co-workers said it was so bad in her VW Jetta that she thought her husband had left his old hockey equipment in the car!

Safety summary: The NHTSA database shows the following problems are reported repeatedly: fires; airbags that fail to deploy or cause severe injuries when they go off; airbag light stays on for no apparent reason; transmission and wheel bearing failures; transmission pops out of gear; electrical malfunctions leading to chronic stalling; self-activating alarms; lights going out; erratic cruise control operation; brake, tire, and AC failures; inadequate defrosting; AC mould and mildew smell; poor-quality body components; window regulator failure; power windows inoperable. Also, doors may open suddenly; locks jam shut, fall out, or freeze; power window motors and regulators self-destruct; hood suddenly flies up; cigarette lighter pops out of holder while lit; the seat heater may burn a hole in the driver's seat; and battery acid can leak onto the power steering reservoir and cause sudden steering loss. **1996**—Rear wheel and axle may separate. **1997**—Fire caused by faulty driver's seat wiring. • Battery exploded. **1998**—Engine damaged after water was ingested through the air intake system. • Transmission locked into Third gear. • ABS brake failures. •

Head restraints suddenly drop down. • Inaccurate fuel gauge. **1999**—Plastic fuel line fails in cold weather. • Vehicle may suddenly spin out of control. • Chronic stalling in traffic with engine warning light lit. • Headlight failure; no low beam. **2000**—Sudden acceleration. • Cracked axle. • Early replacement of the rear brake pads. • There also seems to be a problem with either the airflow meter or some sort of sensor relating to the airflow. • Dashboard causes excessive windshield glare. **2000–03**—Airbag cover pops off while driving. • Cracked oil pan. • Engine burns oil. • Chronic stalling in traffic. • Hard starting. • Noisy, prematurely worn brakes. • Sudden headlight failure; poor headlight illumination. • Faulty power window regulators cause windows to fall down into door panels. **2001**—Timing chain exploded. • Frequent stalling due to defective airflow sensor. • Premature constant velocity joint replacement. **2001–02**—Faulty ignition coils:

> Ignition coils failed three times. Car has been in repair shop for a month, no replacement parts are being delivered.

2002—Fires under the bumper and in the engine compartment. • Sudden, unintended acceleration. • Many reports that the front/side airbags deployed for no reason; driver burned:

> Driving on the turnpike, the driver-side airbag deployed without any sort of impact. There is no visible damage to the vehicle, which was only two months old at the time. Fortunately the only injury was a burn from the airbag on the side of my arm.
>
> My biggest fear is knowing relatives and friends who drive Jettas and who have young children in their car. This incident could have easily been fatal.

• Brake failure. • Vehicle hesitates upon acceleration. • Engine warning light is constantly lit. • Broken window regulator; window falls into the door panel:

> On three separate occasions the driver-side front window (twice) and the passenger-side front window (once) has fallen down into the door. On the first occasion the window shattered inside the door and had to be replaced.

Secret Warranties/Service Tips/TSBs

All models: 1996–97—A shifter that's hard to move side-to-side or won't go into Reverse may signal that the selector shaft is binding in the selector shaft housing bearing. **1997**—Erratic electrical functions may be caused by a loose ground at one of two grounding studs located under the battery tray. • If the transmission pops out of gear, check for a hairline crack on the selector shaft shift detent sleeve. **1998–99**—Noisy, vibrating blower motor. • Defective instrument cluster. • Radio volume control malfunction. **1999**—Humming noise from front of vehicle when turning may be caused by the differential spider gear. • Sunroof binding or noise will be fixed with replacement slides. **1999–2000**—An engine rapping noise or throttle pedal vibration. **1999–2001**—Inoperative window regulator. • Malfunctioning instrument cluster. **2000**—Automatic transmission may go into limp mode without malfunction indicator light (MIL) activated. • Vibrating shifter. **2000–01**—Troubleshooting prematurely worn rear brake pads. **2001**—Leaking intake hoses. • Inoperative secondary air pump (blown fuse). • Troubleshooting "defective control module" indication. • Leaking transmission pan gasket. **2002**—Inoperative fresh air blower. • Broken armrest lid. • Defective VI radio controls.

Cabrio, Golf, Jetta Profile

	1996	1997	1998	1999	2000	2001	2002	2003
Cost Price ($)								
Cabrio	26,495	25,230	25,300	25,300	25,300	28,530	28,530	—
Golf	14,325	14,690	16,765	15,610	18,950	19,040	19,230	17,950
Jetta	17,650	18,050	18,620	18,620	21,170	21,280	21,490	24,260
Used Values ($)								
Cabrio ▲	9,000	11,000	12,000	13,500	15,000	18,000	20,000	—
Cabrio ▼	8,000	9,500	11,000	12,500	14,500	17,000	19,000	—
Golf ▲	5,500	6,500	7,500	8,500	9,500	11,000	12,000	13,000
Golf ▼	4,500	5,500	6,500	7,500	9,000	10,000	11,000	12,500
Jetta ▲	7,000	8,000	9,000	9,500	10,500	12,500	15,500	18,000
Jetta ▼	6,000	7,000	8,000	9,000	9,500	11,000	14,500	17,000
Reliability	❷	❷	③	③	③	③	④	④
Crash Safety (F)								
Golf	—	③	③	—	—	⑤	⑤	⑤
Jetta	③	③	③	—	—	⑤	⑤	⑤
Side (Jetta)	—	—	③	③	—	④	④	④
Offset	❷	❷	❷	③	③	④	③	⑤
Head Restraints (F)	—	❷	—	❷	—	❷	⑤	⑤
Rear	—	—	—	❶	—	—	③	⑤
4d	—	—	—	—	—	—	—	③
Jetta	—	—	—	—	—	—	④	③
Rear	—	—	—	—	—	—	—	③
Rollover Resistance	—	—	—	—	—	④	④	④

MEDIUM CARS

Medium-sized cars, often referred to as "family" cars, are a trade-off between size and fuel economy, offering more room and convenience features but a bit less fuel economy (9.5–11.5L/100 km) than a small car. These cars are popular because they combine the advantages of smaller cars with those of larger vehicles. As a result of their versatility, as well as both upsizing and downsizing throughout the years, these vehicles shade into both the small and large car niches. The trunk is usually large enough to meet average baggage requirements, and the interior is spacious enough to meet the needs of the average family (seating four people in comfort and five in a pinch). These cars are best for combined city and highway driving, with the top three choices traditionally dominated by Japanese automakers: the Honda Accord, Mazda 626, and Toyota Camry. VW's Passat has taken top honours in *Consumer Reports'* annual listing of Best Buys; however, its high resale value is a real budget buster and its safety-related factory-induced defects are worrisome.

The Honda Accord has a slight performance edge over Toyota's Camry—the Japanese equivalent of your father's Oldsmobile.

Ford's Taurus and Sable are in a sales death spiral following persistent owner complaints of drivetrain deficiencies and generally poor quality control. Chrysler's Breeze, Cirrus, and Stratus have improved in quality over the past several years and generally offer the most interior space and competitive used prices, despite the fact they've been off the market for the past two years. GM is the best of the Detroit Big Three. Its models may be bland and a bit overpriced, but quality control is better than both Ford and Chrysler and there are more models from which to choose.

Nissan's Altima has become quite popular since its 2001 model was redesigned to combine sharp-looking, aerodynamic styling with a sizzling high-performance engine and sophisticated handling features. Unfortunately, the car's on-road performance is hobbled by poor quality control, leading many owners to regret their purchase.

Nissan's Altima is a strikingly styled performer that has disappointed many with its poor reliability- and safety-related defects.

MEDIUM CAR RATINGS

Recommended
Acura 1.6, 1.7L EL (1997–2003)
Acura Integra (1994–2001)
Honda Accord (2000–02)

Mazda 626 (1999–2003)
Toyota Camry (2003; 1995–96)

Above Average
Acura CL-Series (1998–2003)
Acura Integra (1986–93)
General Motors Bonneville, Cutlass,
  Cutlass Supreme, Delta 88, Grand
  Prix, LeSabre, Regal (1984–87)
Honda Accord (2003; 1990–99)

Hyundai Sonata (1999–2003)
Mazda 626, MX-6 (1996–98)
Nissan Altima (1998–2001)
Toyota Camry, Solara (1997–2002;
  1985–94)

Average
Acura CL-Series (1997)
DaimlerChrysler Breeze, Cirrus,
  Stratus (1999–2000)
General Motors Bonneville, Cutlass,
  Cutlass Supreme, Delta 88, Grand
  Prix, Impala, Intrigue, LeSabre,
  Lumina, Malibu, Monte Carlo, Regal
  (2000–03)

General Motors Century (1998–2003)
General Motors Grand Am, Alero,
  Skylark (2000–03)
Honda Accord (1985–89)
Hyundai Sonata (1995–98)
Mazda 626, MX-6 (1994–95)
Nissan Altima (2002–03; 1993–97)
Volkswagen New Beetle (1998–2003)

Below Average

DaimlerChrysler Breeze, Cirrus,
  Stratus (1995–98)
Ford Sable, Taurus (2000–03)

General Motors Achieva, Grand Am,
  Skylark (1995–99)
General Motors Century (1997)
Volkswagen Passat (1998–2003)

Not Recommended

Ford Contour, Mystique (1995–99)
Ford Sable, Taurus (1986–99)
General Motors Achieva (Calais),
  Grand Am, Skylark (1985–94)
General Motors Bonneville, Cutlass,
  Cutlass Supreme, Delta 88, Grand
  Prix, Intrigue, LeSabre, Lumina,
  Malibu, Monte Carlo, Regal
  (1988–99)

General Motors Century, Ciera
  (1982–96)
Hyundai Sonata (1986–93)
Mazda 626, MX-6 (1985–93)
Volkswagen Passat (1989–97)

Acura

1.6, 1.7L EL   ★★★★★

RATING: Recommended (1997–2003). The Honda equivalent for the revised 2001 1.7L EL is the Civic EX Sedan. The 2001 EL Premium commanded a $2,000 premium over the base version. **Maintenance/Repair costs:** Average. Repairs aren't dealer dependent. **Parts:** Average parts cost, thanks to the use of generic Honda Si parts sold through independent suppliers. **Best alternatives:** The Honda Civic EX or Si; Hyundai Elantra wagon, Sonata, or Tiburon; Mazda 626 or Protegé; Nissan Sentra or Stanza; and Toyota Camry or Corolla.

Strengths and weaknesses: The first Japanese automobile built exclusively in and for the Canadian market, the EL is essentially an all-dressed Civic sedan, sold under the Acura moniker. It came about as an answer to Canadian Acura dealer pleadings for a more affordable Acura. **Online help:** For the latest owner reports, service bulletins, and money-saving tips, look at *www.autosafety.org.*

Vehicle history: 1997—Since its '97 model launch, the EL has been immensely popular—and hard to find on the used-car market. **2001**—The 1.7L 2001 model was an all-new incarnation (as is the 2001 Civic) that is roomier, better equipped, and more fuel efficient, even though horsepower remains the same.

Based on the top-line Civic Si, the EL comes with a peppy 127-hp VTEC 1.6L 4-banger that's both reliable and economical to run. Add to this the Civic's chassis and upgraded suspension components and you have outstanding performance, as good as or better than that of the Civic Si. Some of the 1.6 EL's weak points: a narrow interior, with seats and seatbacks not to everyone's liking; emergency braking that's only average; head restraints rated "Poor" by IIHS; and excessive engine noise intruding into the passenger compartment despite upgraded soundproofing.

Over the years on the market, the EL has done quite well, even though it hasn't changed much. No safety complaints have been reported, and the few owner complaints recorded have mostly concerned wind noise, easily dented body panels, malfunctioning accessories (AC, audio system, electrical components, etc.), and fragile trim items. Some minor turn-offs with the 2001 model: car loses power when the AC is activated; there are no stereo controls on the steering wheel; and the driver's seat armrest can interfere with the gearshift lever.

Secret Warranties/Service Tips/TSBs

All models/years: Most Honda/Acura TSBs allow for special warranty consideration on a "goodwill" basis even after the warranty has expired or the car has changed hands. Referring to this euphemism will increase your chances of getting some kind of refund for repairs that are obviously related to a factory defect. Keep in mind that many Honda bulletins often apply to Acuras as well. So check out the Civic and Accord's TSBs and safety complaints before assuming a particular Acura problem doesn't exist or is your responsibility. • Acura says it will replace any seat belt's tongue stopper button for the life of the vehicle. • Interestingly, the automatic transmission failures afflicting 2000–03 Acuras and Hondas don't seem to be a problem with this entry-level Acura. Still, should you have a tranny breakdown within 7 years/160,000 km, don't hesitate to cite Honda's latest transmission extended warranty to back up your claim.

1.6 EL Profile

	1997	1998	1999	2000	2001	2002	2003
Cost Price ($)							
1.6 EL	17,800	18,800	19,800	20,005	21,500	21,700	22,000
Used Values ($)							
1.6 EL ʌ	7,500	8,500	9,500	11,500	13,500	15,500	18,000
1.6 EL ν	6,500	7,500	9,000	11,000	13,000	15,000	17,500
Reliability	⑤	⑤	⑤	⑤	⑤	⑤	⑤

Note: These vehicles have not been crash-tested.

CL-SERIES   ★★★★

RATING: Above Average (1998–2003); Average (1997). Overpriced and hard to find; be wary of the failure-prone automatic transmission on all model years, which is one reason the CL doesn't get a five-star rating like its little brother. **Maintenance/Repair costs:** Lower than average. Repairs can be done practically anywhere. **Parts:** Cost is a bit higher than average, but they're not hard to find. **Best alternatives:** BMW 318, Honda Accord, Lexus SC 300, Nissan Maxima, and Toyota Camry. **Online help:** For the latest owner reports, service bulletins, and money-saving tips, look at *www.autosafety.org.*

Strengths and weaknesses: The only difference between the 2.2L CL and the 3.0L CL is the 3.0L CL's larger engine, different wheels, and larger exhaust tip. The 2.2L CL's engine was upgraded to 2.3L on the 1998 models.

These cars are stylish, front-drive, five-passenger luxury coupes that are American designed and built. They have a flowing, slanted back end and no apparent trunk lock (a standard remote keyless entry system opens the trunk from the outside and a lever opens it from the inside). And while other Japanese automakers are taking content out of their vehicles, Acura has put content into the CL, making it one of the most feature-laden cars in its class.

Sure, we all know that the coupe's mechanicals and platform aren't that different from the Accord's, but when you add up all of its standard bells and whistles, you get a fully loaded medium-sized car that costs thousands of dollars less than such competing luxury coupes as the BMW 318 and the Lexus SC 300.

Vehicle history: 1998—These cars have changed little since they were launched as 1997 models. **1998**—Debut of the 2.3L engine. **2003**—CL soldiers on with the two-door coupe and Type S coupe, equipped with stronger base 3.2L V6s.

Recent model CLs get plenty of power from the smooth-running and quiet 3.2L V6. Handling is better than average, thanks to an upgraded suspension, variable-assisted steering, and 16-inch wheels. The ride is comfortable and well controlled. Braking is first-class (100–0 km/h: 35 m).

Front and rear bucket seats are supportive and easily adjusted. There's plenty of room up front, controls and most gauges are user-friendly (the navigation system and tachometer placement are the only exceptions), and the climate controls are efficient and within easy reach. Owners appreciate the large trunk with its low liftover and a locking ski pass-through that enhances the CL's cargo space.

On the minus side, this is not a car for passengers in the rear. Adults will likely find their heads pressed against the top of the backlight glass, and legroom and footroom are at a premium. Rear access is a crouch-and-crawl affair. Trunk lid hinges intrude into the trunk area and risk damaging cargo when the trunk is closed.

Here are some of the problems reported with the 1997–99 models: faulty transmission control unit; transmission downshift problems; chronic brake rotor pulsation and other brake problems, leading to resurfacing of brake rotors and early replacement of brake pads, rotors, calipers, and springs; repeated front-end realignments; door and wind noise leading to replacement of door; and a sunroof that won't stop at closed position, requiring replacement of sunroof switch and controller.

Owners have reported that the 2002s also have serious automatic transmission problems leading to complete failure, as the following owner relates:

> Car started free revving and erratically upshifting and downshifting with hard jerks. All malfunction indicators lit up. Almost lost control on the freeway. Was told transmission is shot on a car that is a bit over a year old.

Even if the transmission remains intact, its erratic performance creates a serious safety hazard, says another 2002 3.2 CL owner:

> The transmission downshifted by itself to a lower gear, causing the vehicle to decelerate in a dangerous manner. Sooner or later someone is going to get killed if this problem is not corrected.

Sudden, unintended acceleration and hesitation complaints are also thought to be transmission-related (see "Secret Warranties/Service Tips/TSBs").

Safety summary: All models: 1997—Complete brake failure; vehicle hit a wall. • Frequent brake rotor replacement. • Chronic hesitation and stalling. • When accelerating, vehicle will appear to stall, and then suddenly accelerate. • Inadvertent airbag deployment. • Passenger front seat belt locks up and won't retract. • Leaky oil pan seals. • Premature catalytic converter failure. • Subframe out of alignment, causing vehicle to pull to one side. • Complete automatic transmission failure, or transmission locks in Fourth gear. • Main computer failure. **1998**—When driving on a flat surface at 45 km/h, or 1500 rpm, vehicle will jerk and pull for about 30 seconds. • Transmission seals failed. • Chronic electrical shorts. • Premature shock failure. • Sudden power steering loss. • Excessive steering play due to faulty steering column coupling. • Vehicle will sometimes accelerate when slowing for a stop. **1999**—Airbags didn't deploy. • Transmission failure; inoperative gearshift due to water on the horn. • Steering locks up intermittently. • Short-statured drivers may be seriously injured by the front airbag's deployment. **2002**—Transmission slips out of gear, suddenly downshifts, and engine surges. • Sudden, unintended acceleration, accompanied by loss of braking ability. • Window slides down into door.

Secret Warranties/Service Tips/TSBs

All models/years: Most Honda/Acura TSBs allow for special warranty consideration on a "goodwill" basis even after the warranty has expired or the car has changed hands. Referring to this "goodwill" will increase your chances of getting some kind of refund for repairs that are obviously related to a factory defect. • Acura says it will replace any seat belt's tongue stopper button for the life of the vehicle. **All models: 1997**—Under a Product Update Campaign (secret warranty), Acura will re-route the hood cable so it doesn't cause a coolant leak from rubbing against the radiator. • Remedy for front seat that won't slide forward or backward. • Freeing up seatback adjustment lever •

Silencing a dash pop or creak. • Fix for incorrect fuel gauge and speedometer readings. • Correction for brake fluid leaking from the ABS modulator. • Fix for wind noise from front side windows. **1997–98**—Power seat noise. • Power windows don't work. • Window rattling. **1998–99**—Steering wheel remote audio switches may not work properly. **2001–03**—In September 2002, Honda extended its warranties to 7 years/160,000 miles (256,000 km) on automatic transmissions on about 1.2 million cars and minivans because the components may fail or wear out early. The new retroactive warranty includes 2000 and 2001 Accords, Preludes, and Odysseys; 2000–02 Acura 3.2 TLs; 2001–02 Acura 3.2 CLs; and some 2003 models of both Acura models, spokesman Kurt Antonius said. He admitted about 25,000 vehicles have experienced transmission problems, which include slow or erratic shifting. What's most disappointing about Honda's warranty extension is that it doesn't go back to the 1997 model years, where transmission breakdowns are also quite common. Prediction: If Acura/Honda doesn't extend this extension, they'll be causing themselves unnecessary grief from multiple class actions and small claims court filings. **2002**—Airbag light may remain lit. • Windshield wiper smearing and streaking. • Faulty Delphi Freedom Group batteries will be taken back. • Moon roof squeaks. • Seatback panel may loosen. • Missing speed sensor plug. • Troubleshooting engine oil leaks. **2.2L: 1997**—Front balancer shaft oil seal may back out of the oil pump housing, resulting in the oil rapidly pumping out of the engine without warning. **1999**—Coolant leak from the engine block. **3.0L: 1997–99**—A Product Update Campaign calls for the re-routing of the PCV hose to prevent the intake manifold EGR port from clogging. This is especially applicable to vehicles using fuel sold in the United States. • V6 engine oil leaks. **1998–99**—Troubleshooting the inadvertent activation of the MIL (malfunction indicator light).

CL-Series Profile

	1997	1998	1999	2002	2003
Cost Price ($)					
2.2L/2.3L CL	27,800	30,000	30,900	36,000	37,800
3.0L CL	30,650	34,000	35,000	—	—
Type S CL	—	—	—	40,000	41,800
Used Values ($)					
2.2L/2.3L CL ʌ	8,500	10,500	13,500	25,000	29,000
2.2L/2.3L CL v	8,000	9,500	13,000	24,000	28,000
3.0L CL ʌ	10,500	12,500	15,500	—	—
3.0L CL v	10,000	11,500	15,000	—	—
Type S CL ʌ	—	—	—	27,000	31,000
Type S CL v	—	—	—	25,000	29,000
Reliability	④	④	④	④	④
Crash Safety					
Head Restraints	❶	—	❶	❶	①

Note: These vehicles have not been crash-tested.

INTEGRA   ★★★★★

RATING: Recommended (1994–2001); Above Average (1986–93). The Integra rating is unusually high due to the few owner complaints recorded and the car's all-around competent performance. Interestingly, there's little price difference between a used entry-level and high-end model, despite a $4,000 premium when new. **Maintenance/Repair costs:** Lower than average. Repairs can be done practically anywhere. **Parts:** Cost is a bit higher than average, but they can be bought from cheaper independent Honda suppliers. **Best alternatives:** The Honda Accord; Mazda 626; Hyundai Elantra wagon, Sonata, or Tiburon; and Toyota Camry. **Online help:** For the latest owner reports, service bulletins, and money-saving tips, look at *www.autosafety.org.*

Strengths and weaknesses: A Honda spin-off, early Integras (1986–89) came with lots of standard equipment and are a pleasure to drive, especially when equipped with a manual transmission. The 4-speed automatic saps the base engine's power considerably, but there is usually sufficient reserve power to accomplish most tasks. Surprisingly, these early models corner better and are more agile than later 1990–93 models. Its hard ride can be reduced a bit by changing the shocks and adding wide tires. The front seats are very comfortable, but they're set a bit low, and the side wheelwells leave little room for your feet. Rear-seat room is very limited, especially on the three-door version.

Vehicle history: 1986–89—Redesigned; in 1989, engines became smoother running and picked up 12 more horsepower (130). **1990**—Four-door sedan replaced the four-door hatchback, adding a bit more interior room; and the GS debuted. **1992**—140-hp engine. **1994**—142-hp engine added variable valve timing for extra power and smoothness. **1997**—The G-SR gained a 170-hp engine and a high-performance 195-hp Type R debuted. **1998**—A slight front-end restyling. **1999**—RS version dropped. **2000**—Return of the Type R and the addition of an upgraded 4-speed automatic transmission to the general lineup. **2001**—Emergency trunk release. **2002**—Replaced by the RSX.

For model years 1990–93, the high-revving 1.7L power plant growls when pushed and lacks guts (read, torque) in the lower gears. The 1.8L engine runs more smoothly but delivers the same maximum horsepower as the 1.7L it replaced, until the '94 model year, when it gained 10 extra horses. Surprisingly, overall performance has been toned down and is compromised by the 4-speed automatic gearbox. Interior design is more user-friendly, with the front seating roomier than in previous years, but reduced rear seating is still best left to small children.

Mechanical reliability is impressive, but that's the case with most Hondas, which sell for far less, and many mechanical components are so complex that self-service can pretty well be ruled out. The Integra's front brakes may require more attention than those of other Hondas. Surprisingly, what Integras give you in mechanical reliability and performance, they take away in poor quality control on body components and accessories. Water leaks, excessive wind noise, low-quality trim items, and plastic panels that deform easily are all commonplace. Owners also report severe steering shimmy, excessive brake noise, premature front brake pad wearout, and radio malfunctions.

The 1994–2001 models offer a smoother ride than previous versions. On the other hand, the powerful VTEC engine requires lots of shifting, and interior room is still problematic. Overall, there are too few improvements to justify the high prices that post-1999 models command; therefore, target cars in the 1997–99 model range for optimum savings and performance.

Owners report that some steering wheel shimmy, fit and finish deficiencies, and malfunctioning accessories continue to be problematic on later models. Only a smattering of automatic transmission defects have been mentioned, though any glitches within 7 years/160,000 km should be fixed free of charge (see Acura CL section). Premature front brake wear is also an ongoing concern, often fixed for free if the client is the least bit threatening. Squeaks and rattles frequently crop up in the door panels and hatches, and the sedan's frameless windows often have sealing problems.

Safety summary: All models/years: No airbag deployment or inadvertent deployment, sudden acceleration, automatic transmission defects, poor headlight illumination, and chronic brake failures are common to all model years. **1996**—Engine wiring fire. • Prematurely warped rotors are the cause of excessive vibration and pulling. • Power-steering pump failure. • Clutch spring failure. • Vehicle surges forward, as if cruise control suddenly engaged at a higher speed; brakes failed. • Gas pedal jams open. **1997**—Key can be removed from ignition without putting transmission in Park. • Moon roof motor failure. • Passenger seat belt releases inadvertently. • Ignition interlock failed. **1998**—Sudden steering lock-up. • Battery leak could have caused fire by burning hole in charcoal canister. • Driver's seat belt won't loosen. • Horn failure. • Sunroof malfunctions. • Window motor inoperative. • Windshield wipers suddenly stopped working; resumed operation when car was restarted. **1999**—Front windshield distorts vision. • Check Engine light comes on constantly. **2000**—Small horn buttons are difficult to activate in an emergency. • Check Engine light stays on. • Seat belts fail to release when unbuckled. • Steering wheel obstructs view of speedometer. **2001**—Sudden steering wheel lock-up while driving.

Secret Warranties/Service Tips/TSBs

All models/years: Most Honda/Acura TSBs allow for special warranty consideration on a "goodwill" basis even after the warranty has expired or the car has changed hands. • Vehicle cranks but won't start. • Severe and persistent steering wheel shimmy is likely due to an imbalanced wheel/tire/hub/rotor assembly. • Check Engine light constantly lit. • Headlight fogging. • Debris in blower motor (install protective screen). • Window guide channel comes loose. Front-brake squeal countermeasures. • Reducing rattles from the rear shelf area. • Noisy power steering. **All models: 1990–97**—Rear trailing arm bushing noise can be corrected by installing plastic shims. **1992–99**—A defective seat belt tongue stopper will be replaced free of charge with no ownership, time, or mileage limitations. **1994–97**—Rear seatback rattles mean the latch needs to be readjusted. • Exhaust system buzzing can have two sources: the flexible joint connections may have insufficient spring tension or the inner exhaust pipe is vibrating against the outer pipe. **1996–97**—A squeaking steering wheel heard when turning signals the need to grease the pinion shaft and grommet. **RSX: 2002–04**—A sulphur smell in the interior can be eliminated by replacing the catalytic converter, sealing open body seams, and installing flaps on the tailgate drain holes; all free fixes under the emissions warranty (see TSB #03-031).

Integra Profile

	1995	1996	1997	1998	1999	2000	2001
Cost Price ($)							
RS	18,595	18,795	19,500	21,000	—	—	—
LS/SE	23,095	23,245	23,800	23,800	21,800	22,000	22,500
Used Values ($)							
RS ⋀	5,000	6,500	7,500	8,500	—	—	—
RS ⋁	4,500	6,000	7,000	8,000	—	—	—
LS/SE ⋀	6,500	7,500	8,500	9,500	10,500	13,000	15,000
LS/SE ⋁	6,000	6,000	8,000	10,500	10,000	12,000	14,000
Reliability	④	④	④	④	⑤	⑤	⑤
Crash Safety	—	④	—	—	—	—	—
Head Restraints (F)	❷	—	③	—	③	—	③
Rear	—	—	—	—	❷	—	—
Rollover Resistance	④	—	—	—	—	—	—

DaimlerChrysler

BREEZE, CIRRUS, STRATUS ★★★

RATING: Average (1999–2000); Below Average (1995–98). Stay away from any model carrying the anemic and failure-prone 4-cylinder engine. If it does fail, make Chrysler recognize its secret warranty. Believe it or not, these cars have fewer mechanical and safety problems than found on the Ford competition. Nevertheless, be prepared to experience a number of nasty safety-related failures such as airbags that don't deploy, sudden acceleration, a jerky automatic transmission that suddenly drops out of gear, and loss of braking. The Breeze has a higher-than-average resale value that beats the heck out of the Cirrus and Stratus. **Maintenance/Repair costs:** Higher than average, but repairs aren't dealer dependent. **Parts:** Higher-than-average cost (independent suppliers sell for much less), but they are not hard to find. Recall parts, though, tend to dribble in; a month's wait isn't unusual (as has been the case with the transaxle oil cooler hose campaign for 2001 models). Don't even think about buying any one of these cars without a 3- to 5-year supplementary warranty. **Best alternatives:** The Acura Integra, Hyundai Elantra wagon or Sonata, Mazda 626, Nissan Altima or Stanza, and Toyota Camry. **Online help:** For the latest owner reports, safety reports, complaint strategies, and money-saving tips, look at *www.autosafety.org/autodefects.html*; *www.wam.umd.edu/~gluckman/Chrysler/* (Chrysler Products' Problem Web Page); *www.daimlerchryslervehicleproblems.com*; and *www.allpar.com/fix/secret-warranties.html*.

Strengths and weaknesses: Roomy and stylish, well appointed, and comfortable, the Chrysler Cirrus and Dodge Stratus were 1996 mid-sized sedan replacements for the LeBaron. The Breeze, launched as a 1996 model and dropped after its 2000 model run, is essentially a "de-contented" version of the more expensive Cirrus.

For 2001, the Avenger coupe and sedan were dropped and the Stratus and the Cirrus coupe, sedan, and convertible fell under the Sebring moniker. Other improvements for the renamed models: a smoother ride and the addition of a 2.7L engine.

Most components have been used for some time on other Chrysler models, particularly the Neon subcompact and the Avenger and Sebring sports coupes. Power is supplied by one of four engines: a 2.0L 4-cylinder engine (shared with the Neon), a 2.4L 4-banger, or the recommended 2.5L and 2.7L V6. Carrying Chrysler's "cab-forward" design a step further up the evolutionary ladder, these cars have short rear decks, low noses, and massive sloping grilles. A wheelbase that's two inches longer than the Ford Taurus makes these cars comfortable for five occupants, with wide door openings and plenty of trunk space.

Judged by their styling and roominess alone, these cars would appear to be great buys. But they aren't.

They are, in fact, high-risk choices from both a performance and a quality control standpoint. Problems reported by owners include the following: chronic automatic transmission failures; early and frequent engine head gasket failures, through 1998 models (no doubt part of the Neon engine legacy), and erratic engine operation; ABS malfunctions and sudden brake and steering loss; paint delamination and peeling; electrical short circuits; weak headlights; underperforming AC; water leaks into the trunk area and interior; easy-to-break trim items; lots of squeaks and rattles; and head restraints that are set too far back. Incidentally, in 1999 the manual seat height adjuster was dropped, making it difficult for short drivers to distance themselves safely from the airbag deployment. Additionally, this complicates both forward and rearward visibility, which is already seriously compromised by the cars' styling.

Vehicle history: 1995—Avenger and Sebring coupe launched. **1996**—Horsepower boosted to 163 on the 2.5L engine. **1997**—Sebring convertible launched on Cirrus sedan platform (see "Sports Cars"). **2000**—Stratus, Avenger, and Breeze nameplates dropped. **2001**—4-cylinder engine and manual transmission are no longer available; Cirrus nameplate dropped.

Safety summary: All models/years: 1995–96—Frequent reports of engine fires. • Chronic engine oil leaks and oil galley plug failures. • Repeated engine head gasket failures, some resulting in engine compartment fires. • Timing belt failure after recall correction. • Chronic stalling or loss of engine power blamed on timing belt tensioner and pulley failure. • Engine sometimes loses power, then quickly accelerates. At other times, while at highway speeds, vehicle won't slow down when foot is taken off the gas pedal; instead, it speeds up. • Engine warning light often alight for no reason. • Reports of sudden acceleration in Drive and Reverse. • Owner claims that sudden acceleration is caused by a design flaw in cable to throttle body. • Airbags often fail to deploy. • Frequent ABS failures and prematurely worn rotors, calipers, and pads. • Rear brake failures also reported. • Floormat can catch the steering shaft clamp and jam the steering column assembly, causing the steering to lock up. • Steering components worn out prematurely. • Main computer failed seven times. • Oxygen sensor prone to early failure and fluid leakage. • Child was able to take parked vehicle out of gear without applying brake. • Vehicle jumped out of Third gear. • Defective electrical switch causes transmission to stick in Second gear. • Transmission won't engage or upshift to Third or Fourth gear. • Leaking transmission front pump seal. • Prematurely worn strut links and wheel bearings. • Heat is unevenly distributed, causing front and rear passengers to be cold. • AC fails to cool interior unless vehicle is travelling at high speed. • Dash reflection into windshield hampers view. • Inadequate headlight illumination. • Windshield wipers don't run fast enough to clear windshield in a heavy downpour. • Rear brake lights and brake switch failure. • Sloping hood design creates poor visibility for parking. • Fuel tank gauge indicates empty when tank is half-full. • Trunk lid closes on its own. • Seatbacks collapsed when vehicle was rear-ended. • Seat frame and anchor broke as driver sat down. • Power window motor failures. • Door locks work intermittently. • Binding door hinges make for difficult closing. • Door handle design pinches fingers. • Key sticks in the ignition when vehicle is shut off. **1995–99**—Upgraded engine head gasket. • Cam position sensor oil seepage. **1997**—Engine compartment fire ignited while car was parked in garage. • Reports of sudden acceleration in Drive and Reverse. • Chronic stalling at highway speeds. • Vehicle rolled away while parked with shifter in Park position and keys pulled from ignition. • Shifter came off in hand when shifting. • Airbags fail to deploy. • Floormat can catch the steering shaft clamp and jam the steering column assembly, causing the steering to lock up. • Frequent engine head gasket failures. • It's common for the engine timing belt idler pulley to fail and damage the timing belt. • Sudden brake and power-steering loss. • Brake pads and rotors fail prematurely. • Seat buckle design is too short, causing difficulty in latching. • Driver-side shoulder belt failed to restrain driver in a collision. • Starter short caused fuse to blow. • Fuel sender for dash gauge often defective. • Inoperative power door lock motor. **1997–98**—NHTSA is looking into complaints of steering shaft binding. **1998**—Airbag exploded rather than inflated. • Airbags fail to deploy. • Frequent complaints of ABS failures. • Floormat jammed the steering column assembly, causing the steering to lock up. • Automatic transmission (floor console design) throw from Drive to

Reverse to Park is too long, resulting in consumer thinking vehicle is in Park when it's really in Reverse. • Floor shift indicator on the dash doesn't give a true reading of which gear is engaged. • Gearshift lever can be moved into Drive without putting foot on brakes to engage the transmission/brake interlock system. • High trunk lid makes it impossible to see directly behind the vehicle. **1999**—Several trunk fires reported from a too-intense trunk-mounted light bulb. • Airbags failed to deploy in a collision. • Airbag deployed inadvertently, knocking driver out and causing an accident. • Sudden acceleration; stuck throttle. • Stalling upon acceleration and when foot is taken off of the gas pedal. • Steering locks up when making left-hand turns. • Automatic transmission has a short lifespan; sensors are the first to go. • Transmission lever can be shifted into Drive without first depressing brake pedal. • Cracked axle. • Dash reflects onto front windshield. • Many incidents reported of sudden brake failure without any prior warning. • While driving, brake vacuum hose separated, causing complete brake failure. • Chronic brake rotor warpage around 8,000 km (5,000 mi.), resulting in severe brake vibrations, noise, and extended stopping distance. • Engine fumes invade the cabin, causing driver drowsiness. • Frequent electrical shorts cause gauges, wipers, and windows to function erratically. • Engine, ABS, and airbag warning light often come on for no reason. • Seat belts fail to tighten. **2000**—Electrical system fire. • Brake lock-up; no airbag deployment in resulting collision. • Low-speed gear whine. • Automatic transmission has a hard 3–2 shift. • Transmission drops out of gear at 75 km/h. • Brake system failures due to loss of vacuum. • Warped brake drums and rotors; very noisy braking. • Wheel lug nuts loosen on their own. • Gas pedal sticks. • Excessive rear window fogging. • Windshield wiper doesn't clear snow adequately from driver-side windshield. • Excessive dashboard reflection onto windshield. • Driver's door jams due to faulty door panel. • Seat belts too tight. • Chronic dead battery. • Hot trunk light will burn items stored in trunk. • Space-saver spare tire is only good for a few miles and at slow speeds.

Secret Warranties/Service Tips

All models/years: Anecdotal reports confirm Chrysler has a 7-year/160,000 km secret warranty covering engine head gasket failures and paint delamination, peeling, and fading (see Part Two). • Chrysler will replace AC evaporators up to 7 years/115,000 km. **All models: 1995–96**—Water leaks into the passenger compartment from behind the door trim panel. Correct the leakage by installing new door panel clips, door watershields, and additional tape to seal the watershield. **1995–97**—Troubleshooting tips are available to correct poor AC performance. • A powertrain "bump" when the AC engages is normal, according to Chrysler. • Transmission shudder could be caused by using the wrong transmission fluid. **1995–98**—Repair procedure for the evaporator failure. **1995–99**—Intermittent loss of speed control. **1995–2000**—A steering wheel rattle or clunk can be silenced by replacing the steering gear.

NO: 24-04-98   GROUP: Air Conditioning DATE: Apr. 17, 1998
SUBJECT: AC Systems Performance

MODELS:

1995–98 (JA) Breeze/Cirrus/Stratus
1996–98 (JX) Sebring Convertible

SYMPTOM/CONDITION:

AC performance complaints and/or AC compressor failure (seized) in high ambient temperatures (90°+F). This condition is aggravated by start and stop city driving and/or extended periods of idling with the AC running.

DIAGNOSIS:

If the vehicle operated in high ambient temperatures or AC compressor has failed (seized) or system passes the Performance Test Procedure as described on page 24–5 of the Breeze/Cirrus/Stratus Service Manual (Publication No. 81-270-8121) perform the Repair Procedure.

PARTS REQUIRED:

1	05011395AA	Kit, AC Condenser
		Contains: AC Condenser
		Foam Seals, Radiator to Condenser Label,
		Refrigerant Charge Level
1	04796282AB	Kit, Retaining Strap Transmission Cooler
5	06502625	Retainer, Fascia
AR(1)	04886129AA	SP-15 PAG Oil
AR(1)	04883308	Air Seal, Radiator Right Side
AR(1)	04883308	Air Seal, Radiator Left Side

POLICY: Reimbursable within the provisions of the warranty.

1997—A low-frequency rumble heard while at highway cruising speed can be silenced by replacing the front hub bearing assemblies. **1997–98**—Excessive cold crank time, start die-out, or weak run-up may be corrected by replacing the powertrain control module (PCM) under warranty, according to TSB #18-18-98. **1998–99**—Poor AC performance or compressor failure will be repaired under warranty or under "goodwill." **1999**—A metallic noise heard from the rear doors can be silenced by modifying the window regulator channel. **1999–2000**—No-starts and stalling may be caused by a malfunctioning sentry key immobilizer system.

Breeze, Cirrus, Stratus Profile

	1995	1996	1997	1998	1999	2000
Cost Price ($)						
Breeze	—	18,200	18,865	19,505	21,090	—
Cirrus	22,115	23,235	24,125	24,765	22,180	22,365
LXi	24,555	25,695	26,465	26,465	24,840	25,050
Stratus	17,895	18,200	18,865	19,505	21,090	—
V6	19,750	20,100	24,060	24,475	25,025	—
Used Values ($)						
Breeze ▲	—	4,000	5,000	6,000	7,000	—
Breeze ▼	—	3,500	4,500	5,500	6,000	—

Cirrus A	5,000	5,500	6,000	6,500	7,500	8,500
Cirrus V	4,500	5,000	5,500	6,000	6,500	8,000
LXi A	5,500	6,000	6,500	7,500	9,000	10,000
LXi V	5,000	5,500	6,000	7,000	8,000	9,000
Stratus A	5,000	5,500	6,000	6,500	7,500	—
Stratus V	4,500	5,000	5,500	6,000	6,500	—
V6 A	5,500	6,000	6,500	7,500	9,000	—
V6 V	5,000	5,500	6,000	7,000	8,000	—
Reliability	❷	❷	❷	❷	❷	③
Crash Safety	③	③	③	③	③	⑤
Side	—	—	③	③	③	③
Offset	❶	❶	❶	❶	❶	❶
Head Restraints						
Avenger	❶	—	❷	—	❷	—
Stratus (F)	❶	—	❶	—	❷	—
Stratus (Rear)	—	—	—	—	❶	—

Note: Crash ratings are applicable to all models.

Ford

CONTOUR, MYSTIQUE ★

RATING: Not Recommended (1995–99). One of the most failure-prone, hazardous vehicles you can buy—industry insiders call the Mystique the "Mistake." The only reason this car is an even worse buy than the Taurus and Sable is that it has been taken off the market—drying up a miniscule parts supply and driving up part prices (one owner told of paying $700 for an alternator). Although discontinued in Canada, the Contour continued to be sold in the States through the 2001 model year. **Maintenance/Repair costs:** Higher than average. Most repairs are dealer dependent. **Parts:** Higher-than-average cost, and body parts are sometimes hard to find. **Best alternatives:** The Ford Escort wagon, Honda Accord, Hyundai Elantra wagon or Sonata, Nissan Altima or Stanza, and Toyota Camry. Mazda's 626 is a particularly worthwhile alternative to the Contour and Mystique—it's a more stylish, reasonably priced, highway-proven sedan with a better reliability record. **Online help**: For the latest owner reports, service bulletins, and money-saving tips, look at *www.contour.org/FAQ*; *www.tgrigsby.com/views/ford.htm* (The Anti-Ford Page); and *www.autosafety.org/autodefects.html.*

Strengths and weaknesses: These front-drive, mid-sized twin sedans (the Contour has a more angular nose and a different dashboard) are based on the European-designed Mondeo. They are set on a wheelbase slightly larger than that of the Taurus and come with a choice of two engines and transmissions: a base 16-valve 125-hp, 2.0L 4-cylinder or an optional 24-valve 170-hp, 2.5L V6. Either engine may be hooked to a standard 5-speed transaxle or an optional 4-speed automatic.

The main advantages of the Contour and Mystique are exceptional handling and a powerful V6 engine. Their drawbacks are a plethora of safety-related defects; an inadequate parts supply; cramped rear seating; a wimpy, oil leaking, noisy 4-banger; and atrocious quality control that is highlighted by powertrain failures, electrical system shorts, poor body assembly, and ineffective, noisy brakes that are costly to maintain. Owners also report chronic steering and transmission failures, frequent computer module failures, and a long wait for parts—even those parts needed to carry out safety-related recall campaigns.

> Phil, we are having issues with our '98 Contour accelerating without us touching the gas pedal. I can go from 0–50 without my foot being on the accelerator. I replaced a mass air-flow sensor, the throttle position sensor, O2 sensor, and the idle air control…. Nothing worked.
>
> Phil, Contour.org is back and doing its darndest to keep our beloved Contours (I have the SVT model) running well. Here is the proper link to the water pump failure poll, which has 15 pages! (*www.contour.org/archive*). As another point, with regard to the oiling problem I mentioned in a previous email, Ford says that there is no oiling problem, yet they have changed the crankshaft damper in newer versions of the Duratec, and they have also changed the design of the oil pan. If nothing is wrong, why fix it?"

Safety summary: All models/years: 1995–1996—NHTSA opened an official probe into front-suspension coil spring failures and engine cooling fan fires on the 1995 Contour, and headlight switch failures on 1996 models. **1995–99**—Many reports of engine fires, fuel tank leaks, fuel and oil odours permeating the interior, difficulty in filling the fuel tank, and inaccurate fuel readings. • Malfunctioning airbags that go off when they shouldn't or don't go off when they should. • Reports of serious injuries caused by airbag deployment. • Airbag light stays on for no reason. • Chronic stalling at idle or after attained cruising speed. • Complete electrical shutdown. • Lights come on or shut off unexpectedly. • Seatback often collapses for no reason or after a rear fender-bender. • Brakes often fail, make a grinding noise when applied, and often need replacing (warped rotors and prematurely worn pads). This repair doesn't ensure the brakes will work properly, or that other safety-related failings won't occur:

> Brakes failed and replaced during the first month I had my '99 Contour. After that repair, I had an accident due to lack of braking ability. During the collision, there was no deployment of the airbag and the seat belt came loose.

• Frequent engine and transmission failures. • Transmission will not hold vehicle in Park. • Check Engine light stays lit for no reason.

Secret Warranties/Service Tips/TSBs

All models: 1995–97—Transaxle fluid seepage can be corrected by servicing with a remote vent kit or by replacing the main control cover. • Parking brakes that stick or bind need a parking brake cable service kit. • Front-end accessory drivebelt slippage can be corrected by installing an upgraded FEAD belt, steel idler pulley, and splash shield kit. **1995–98**—Stall and/or exhaust sulfur smell requires a revised power control module; try to get some of the emissions warranty applied. • Stall, hooting, or moosing noise from engine compartment can be fixed by replacing the air intake duct, idle air resonator, and idle air hose with a revised duct and resonator assembly (#F6RZ-9B659-CA). **1995–99**—Upgraded front brake pads have been put into service to silence front brake groaning. • Tips for fixing windshield water leaks. • Paint delamination, peeling, and fading (see Part Two). **1995–2000**—Repeat failure of the heater core. • Automatic transmission fluid leakage. **1997–99**—Fuel pump whine heard through the speakers. **1998**—Harsh automatic shifting is likely caused by a miscalibrated PCM (powertrain control module). • Frequent shut-off when fuelling can be fixed by installing a new flapper baffle in the fuel-filler pipe. • Inaccurate fuel gauge readings may be corrected by installing either a new fuel tank or a fuel pump. **1998–99**—Water may leak through the door into the interior. **1998–2000**—Eliminate spark knock by recalibrating the PCM. • Ford suggests the catalytic converter be changed to prevent a rotten-egg exhaust smell; once again, fight for emissions warranty "goodwill" to reduce the $500 replacement cost. **1999**—Automatic transmission won't shift into any forward gear. • "Fluttering" heard from the heater area. **1999–2000**—Engine hesitation upon start-up requires the recalibration of the PCM (an emissions warranty item). • Owner Notification Program 01B78 provided for the free repair or replacement of warped instrument panel covers until August 31, 2002, regardless of mileage. Ask for a pro rata refund.

Contour, Mystique Profile

	1995	1996	1997	1998	1999
Cost Price ($)					
GL/LX	16,895	17,595	17,395	18,495	17,595
SE	19,795	18,865	19,350	19,475	19,695
Used Values ($)					
GL/LX ▲	3,000	4,000	4,500	5,000	6,000
GL/LX ▼	2,500	3,500	4,000	4,500	5,500
SE ▲	4,000	4,500	5,500	6,000	7,000
SE ▼	3,500	4,000	5,000	5,500	6,000

Reliability	❶	❶	❶	❶	❶
Crash Safety	⑤	⑤	⑤	⑤	—
Side	—	—	③	③	③
Offset	❷	❷	❷	❷	❷
Head Restraints (F)	❶	—	❷	—	❷
Rear	—	—	❶	—	❶

SABLE, TAURUS ★★

RATING: Below Average (2000–03); Not Recommended (1986–99). The worst of a bad lot; these cars are bargain priced because their owners can't wait to get rid of them. Don't look for any major quality improvements from Ford. Hoping to recapture lost sales in the car's next redesign, Ford has adopted a siege mentality, not seen since Chrysler circled its wagons as it faced bankruptcy two decades ago. An extended bumper-to-bumper warranty is a prerequisite for anyone buying a Sable or Taurus. Of course, this extra protection will wipe out any savings realized from a low selling price. The high-performance Taurus SHO (Super High Output) is a double-whammy wallet buster. New data show it has serious engine deficiencies that can cost up to $15,000 to remedy; plus it shares most of the other generic safety- and performance-related defects that have long plagued the Taurus and Sable. Supposedly improved through a 2000 redesign, the recent models continue to generate a large volume of safety- and performance-related failures. 1999 was the last model year for Sable and the Mercury brand in Canada; they're still sold in the States, however. **Maintenance/Repair costs:** Much higher than average, but repairs aren't dealer dependent. Shopping at engine, transmission, brake, and muffler shops offering lifetime warranties can prevent some repeat repair costs. **Parts:** Average cost (independent suppliers sell for much less) and very easy to find, except for the discontinued SHO engine and Taurus parts like fuel pumps and electrical components, needed to correct chronic stalling and electrical shorts. **Best alternatives:** The Honda Accord, Hyundai Elantra wagon or Sonata, Mazda 626, Nissan Sentra or Stanza, and Toyota Camry. A good alternative to the SHO and its failure-prone engine would be a Ford Mustang GT or Probe GT, or the Probe's twin, the Mazda MX-6. **Online help:** Taurus Transmission Victims: *members.aol.com/MKBradley/index.html*; *www.v8sho.com*; *www.tgrigsby.com/views/ford.htm* (The Anti-Ford Page); and *www.autosafety.org/autodefects.html*.

Strengths and weaknesses: Although they lack pick-up with the standard 4-cylinder engine, these mid-sized sedans and wagons are competent family cars, offering lots of interior room, nice handling, a good crash rating, and many convenience features. From a performance standpoint, the best powertrain combination for all driving conditions is the 3.0L V6 hooked to a 4-speed for the family sedan, and the Yamaha power plant harnessed to a manual gearbox on the high-performance SHO.

But these cars are extremely risky buys that are aging badly. To see just how badly, take a look at the "Dead Ford," and NHTSA website links listed in Appendix I. Chronic engine head gasket/intake manifold and automatic transmission failures; a plethora of hazardous airbag, fuel system, brake, suspension, and steering defects; and chronic paint/rust problems are the main reasons their rating is so low this year. Plus, owners are reporting that engine and transmission repairs don't last: some owners are routinely putting in new engines or transmissions every year or two.

I've recommended these cars in the past because Ford's "goodwill" programs usually compensated owners for most of the above-noted failures (except for self-destructing SHO engines) once the warranty had expired. Unfortunately, these refund programs have dried up as Ford puts stonewalling over integrity. Owners are routinely faced with $3,000 engine or automatic transmission repair bills, in addition to thousands of dollars in repairs for defective fuel systems, brakes, and suspension and steering assemblies.

Ford rejects many owner complaints on the grounds that repairs were done by independent agencies, the vehicle was bought used, or is no longer under the original warranty: three reasons that are often rejected by small claims court judges.

SHO

The Taurus SHO sedan, debuting in 1989, carries a Yamaha 24-valve 3.0L V6 with 220 hp; a stiff, performance-oriented suspension; and 5-speed manual transmission. As of 1993, a 4-speed automatic transmission became available. In mid-1996, a redesigned SHO debuted with a standard Yamaha 32-valve V8. Unfortunately, the manual transmission was dropped at that time, a move that turned off most die-hard performance enthusiasts. The SHO is an impressive high-performance car that, unfortunately, has its own unique Yamaha-sourced engine problems in addition to carrying Ford's failure-prone automatic transmission. Both problems were well detailed in the following recent email sent to me by David S., a Cold Lake, Alberta, resident and '97 SHO owner:

> The 3.4L V8 engine found in 1996–99 Ford Taurus SHOs seems to be failing at a high rate, mostly with camshaft failures. The information on this can be found at *www.v8sho.com*, which details fairly well the problem. The repair costs for this failure are astronomical.... Mr. Edmonston, I have to tell you my good news(?). I had to get the automatic transmission replaced (147,000 km), but using the name from your website I sent an email just to see what would happen. After a few days, I was contacted by an official who offered to pay half of the cost of the transmission. He did go through the spiel that I should have taken it to a Ford dealer, we don't usually do this, etc., but I received my cheque for $1,231 a couple of days ago.

Automatic transmission failures

Since 1991, Ford's automatic transmissions have been just as failure-prone as Chrysler's; they function erratically, and are slow to shift—an annoying drawback if you need to rock the car out of a snowbank, and fairly dangerous if you need to pull out onto a busy roadway. These problems are caused principally by a cracked aluminum forward clutch piston, although dozens of other causes, including major hardware and software components, have been linked to the above failures. Breakdowns usually occur after three years of use, around the 80,000–120,000 km mark, and can cost $3,000–$3,500 to repair at the dealer, or half that much at an independent garage, which I recommend, if no after-warranty assistance is proffered.

Engine/Transmission – Driveability Problems/DTC Set

Article No.

01-19-1

10/01/01

Driveability - Perceived cold engine long crank/hard start

Transmission - Sudder/vibration on

Deceleration in First gear - Harsh

Coasting downshifts

2000–01 Taurus and Sable

ISSUE: This problem may be caused by the miscalibration of the powertrain control module (PCM) in vehicles equipped with the 3.0L 24-valve Duratec engine.

Poor automatic transmission performance also means sudden, unintended acceleration, as this owner of a '99 Taurus points out:

> Sudden acceleration is experienced as the vehicle shifts from First to Second gear. This occurs during stop-and-go traffic or low speed (i.e. mall parking) situations, and with the foot off both the throttle and brake. This lurch is greatly increased by even slight downhill slopes. Observation of the tachometer at this point shows the engine gaining 200 to 300 rpm, and that extra power being dumped into Second gear creates the lurch experienced. This occurs at a time when the driver is expecting a constant, predictable rate of progress and necessitates immediate braking to control the car. These dynamics are particularly frightening when turning in a tight intersection. The only assurance of smooth progress is to be braking or accelerating at these low speeds.
>
> Initially, my concern was for transmission longevity, which at this shift point can respond with a loud clunk and a jerk, which is felt throughout the car. However, innumerable intimidating recurrences have led me to observe that this car is a danger to other vehicles and pedestrians. Although this sudden acceleration can be anticipated

intellectually, it nevertheless catches the driver off guard as attention is required elsewhere (i.e. looking for pedestrians, watching for traffic etc.). I would not loan this vehicle to a friend and could not in good conscience sell it privately.

Engine failures

Ford's other major powertrain problem is the 3.8L engine's chronic head gasket failures that are carried over to the 1996 and later Windstars, and intake manifold defects found on other engines carried on more recent models. Head gasket symptoms include engine overheating; poor engine performance; and a thin film deposited on the inside of the windshield, thus cutting down night driving visibility. Repairs range from $700 to $1,000, depending upon what other damage has occurred from overheating. Left untreated, the failure can "cook" your engine, requiring $3,000–$4,000 in repairs. And, even if treated in time, this defect can cause failures in emissions components (oxygen sensors and various computer modules) and other hardware malfunctions that can lead to other, expensive repairs.

These engine repairs were covered by Ford's 00M09 "goodwill" engine warranty up to 7 years/160,000 km on 1994–95 Tauruses and Sables and 1995 Windstars. Owners are still angry over this warranty extension because the free engine repair didn't last, additional engine parts were damaged and never covered (oxygen sensors, etc.), or they were never told of the free repairs. All good reasons that have been upheld in small claims court (see Part Two and Windstar section).

Paint delamination

Over the past decade, there have been frequent complaints of paint delamination, peeling, and premature rusting affecting Tauruses and Sables. Ford is the target of multiple class action paint lawsuits and is settling most small claims court cases, although more class actions may still be imminent.

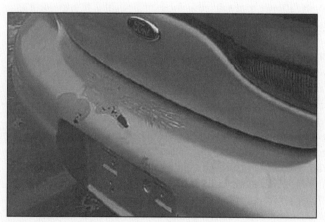

Paint delamination is easy to spot and has nothing to do with acid rain, tree sap, or bird droppings.

Other problems

The 4-cylinder engine is a dog that no amount of servicing can change. It's slow, noisy, prone to stalling and surging, and actually consumes more gas than the V6. The 3.0L 6-cylinder is noted for engine head bolt failures and piston scuffing, and is characterized by hard starting, stalling, excessive engine noise, and poor fuel economy. Transmission cooler lines leak and often lead to the unnecessary repair or replacement of the transmission.

Other things to look out for: blown heater hoses, malfunctioning fuel gauge sending units, and brakes that need constant attention—in front, they're noisy, pulsate excessively, tend to wear out prematurely, require a great deal of pedal effort, and are hard to modulate. Master cylinders need replacing around 100,000 km.

The 1988–95 models continue to have defective ignition modules, oxygen sensors, and fuel pumps, which cause rough running, chronic stalling, hard starting, and electrical system short circuits. Other problem areas include the following: biodegradable tie-rods, ball joints, coil springs, and motor mounts; an automatic transmission that is slow to downshift, hunts for Overdrive, and gives jerky performance; air conditioners that are failure-prone and can cost up to $1,000 to fix; malfunctioning heaters that are slow to warm up and don't direct enough heat to the floor (particularly on the passenger side); a defective heater core that costs big bills to replace (buy from an independent supplier); and noisy, prematurely worn rack-and-pinion steering assemblies. Front suspension components also wear out quickly.

Electrical components interfere with radio reception. The automatic antenna often sticks, electric windows short circuit, power door locks fail, and the electronic dash gives inaccurate readings. Owners report that electrical short circuits—which illuminate the Check Engine light and cause flickering lights and engine surging—are frequently misdiagnosed.

Body/trim items are fragile on all cars (did somebody mention door handles?). Paint adherence is particularly poor on plastic components, weld joints, and the underside—even with mudguards. Owners also report that water leaks into the trunk through the tail light assembly and there's an annoying sound of fuel sloshing when accelerating or stopping.

Vehicle history: 1986—Taurus and Sable debut with a wimpy 2.5L 4-cylinder, an adequately powered but failure-prone 3.0L V6, and an optional and even more unreliable 3.8L V6 (offered through 1996). **1989**—SHO high-performance model, with self-destructing Yamaha engines, is introduced. **1990**—Driver's side airbag. **1992**—Slightly redesigned with a more rigid chassis and the dropping of the 4-banger. **1993**—SHO gets an automatic transmission and engines and transmissions start breaking down on all models. **1994**—Dual front airbags; powertrain continues to self-destruct. **1995**—A watershed year for engine head gasket failures and "cooked" engines. **1996**—A terrible sales year highlighted by ugly ovoid restyling where windows look like portholes, headroom was reduced, and entry/exit became more problematic; 3.8L V6 was dropped, leaving two mediocre V6 engines to choose from. Other changes included upgraded engines, new electronic controls for the LX, better handling and ride quality, more effective soundproofing, and some transmission refinement. **1997**—SHO gets a V8 and an automatic transmission. **2000**—Slightly restyled with incremental improvements, like a more comfortable ride, a more powerful and quieter powertrain, upgraded airbags, adjustable pedals, seat belt pretensioners, and improved child safety seat anchors; the oval design was dropped and sales prices reduced, in a futile effort to win back sales lost to the Japanese. **2001–03**—Minor upgrades as the cars are phased out.

Owners of 1996–99 models still report serious safety-related deficiencies (see "Safety summary") and other performance-related problems, like engine and transmission seal leaks; the automatic transmission shifting erratically or not at all; front-end failures including the outer tie-rods, ball joints, and stabilizer bar links; power windows that fail one after the other and cost $300–$500 each to repair, and "possessed" windshield wipers.

Who needs a radio? Each Taurus and Sable provides a symphony of rattles, buzzes, whines, and moans to keep you company on long drives. The most annoying? The incessant snapping and creaking of the plastic in the centre console and dash from the plastic sections binding against each other when the body flexes, especially if the sun has been shining on it.

The reliability of year 2000 models continues to go downhill. Fuel system failures result in surging, stalling, and a gasoline smell that invades the interior; electrical shorts cause the vehicle to suddenly shut down and not start; malfunctioning ABS, airbag, and Check Engine lights stay lit; powertrain and body components have a short lifespan; and owners have found that the restyled head restraints block rear and side visibility.

The 2001–03 models use the adequate, though dated, base 3.0L Vulcan V6; however, the high-performing 24-valve V6 provides plenty of power for most driving needs. Other nice standard features include heated outside mirrors, a 60/40 split-fold rear seatback for additional cargo space, a driver's footrest, and reserve power to operate the power windows and moon roof after the engine is shut off. Wagons get four-wheel disc brakes.

These cars are generally quiet-running, provide good handling and road holding, and offer a comfortable ride, along with better-than-average crash protection. Of course, they are also heavily discounted (we know why). Some of the minuses include insufficient storage space, limited rear headroom and access, and a history of serious transmission and engine failures. Engine intake manifold defects top the list, accompanied by sudden engine shutdown. The automatic transmission often shifts out of First gear too soon, shifts slowly, constantly bangs through the gears, and frequently chooses the wrong gear. Also expect chronic warped brake rotors, AC failures, electrical system shorts (lots of blown fuses), steering, front suspension, fuel (faulty fuel pumps), and brake system deficiencies, and extremely poor fit and finish.

Getting compensation

Canadian owners still have to threaten small claims court action to get Ford Canada to accept repairs done by independent garages, repeat failures, or failures that occur in the 100,000–160,000 km ("no man's land") range, where warranty decisions are particularly inconsistent.

Anyone seeking assistance should call Ford's toll-free number, 1-800-565-3673 (1-800-565-FORD). Keep in mind what one Ford customer assistance whistle-blower whispered in my ear:

> The company has taken a harder line in reviewing customer claims. *The only thing that gets our attention is if a small claims lawsuit is threatened or has been filed.* These are kicked upstairs to Legal Affairs and are settled right away by staffers who have far more latitude and much less attitude.

Safety summary: All models/years: Tie-rod may collapse suddenly. Although the 1992 models were recalled to fix this defect, many other model years are affected and haven't been recalled. The son of a West Coast Taurus owner relates this incident:

> The right inner tie-rod, a piece of the suspension critical to the steering and thus safety of my 1992 Taurus, broke while my father was attempting to make a right turn from a stop sign. The car lost all steering control and the front wheels were seized. Fortunately, the car was barely moving, and no collision occurred.... I hope you can inform all Taurus and Sable owners of the inherent dangers lurking in their steering system.

• Front coil springs may fracture due to excessive corrosion. Ford has replaced many coils for free under a secret warranty. Interestingly, Ford's Windstars have the same problem and benefit from a 10-year extended warranty. Use that as your Taurus coil benchmark, as this Whitby, Ontario, engineer should do:

> I have a 1995 Mercury Sable that has developed two broken coil springs, on front right and rear left wheel. The fracture surfaces on the front spring show no fatigue bands and are compatible with intergranular stress corrosion or hydriding, both indicating a manufacturing defect. Microscopic examination would be required to confirm the cause of failure.
>
> This car has seen only light-duty service, is low mileage, and has always been garaged. I feel this is a significant safety issue. The failures have given no warning signs, and only the front one was detected during routine maintenance. The front spring has broken in two places, leaving a broken spring end only a quarter inch [0.6 cm]

from the tire. I cannot easily see what is stopping it [from] going right
into the tire, and suspect it would have worked its way in over the
course of a few more miles. I am also concerned that a local independent mechanic says he has seen several spring failures on the
Taurus/Sable, but that the local dealer's service rep has not. I note
from the *Lemon-Aid* website that Transport Canada is investigating
spring failures on this vehicle type.

• These vehicles eat brake rotors, calipers, and pads every 5,000 miles (8,000 km).
• Brakes produce a grinding, growling noise in addition to an acrid smell. **All
models: 1995**—Sudden windshield shattering. • AC failures. • Headlight failures. **1995–96**—Fuel pump failures. • Airbag fails to deploy or is accidentally
deployed. • Transmission slips out of Park. • Engine compartment fires. •
Defective door locks. **1995–97**—Sudden acceleration. • Stalling. • ABS failures. **1996**—Chronic stalling. • Cruise control won't slow vehicle on slopes. •
Left front wheel may separate from car. • Loss of steering when it rains. • Loss
of power steering. • Frequent engine head gasket failures. • Transmission fails
or shifts erratically. • Dash reflects into the windshield. • Faulty door lock
switch. • Defective heating/defrosting system causes excessive windshield fogging. **1997**—Transmission jumps from Park to Reverse. • Sudden steering loss.
• Wheels fly off. • Engine head gasket and automatic transmission failures.
1998—Accelerator and brake pedals are too close to each other. • Vehicle
won't slow when accelerator pedal is released. • Faulty cruise control won't slow
vehicle down. • Automatic transmission malfunctions. • Chronic brake failures. • Defective rotor and wiring assembly caused ABS failure. • Loss of
steering when steering belt pulley and pump failed. • Defective rack-and-
pinion steering spring yoke. • Sudden steering lock-up. • Trunk lid fell on
owner's head, due to defective torsion bar. • Trunk light burned garment in the
trunk. • Faulty headlights. • Headlights don't give enough light to the sides. •
Daytime running lights flicker due to defective module. • Dashboard reflects
in the windshield, causing reduced visibility. • Heater system failed. • Driver's
seat belt won't retract or lock into position. • Hatchback window suddenly
exploded while vehicle was parked. **1999**—Engine fires. • No airbag deployment and inadvertent airbag deployment. • Frequent complaints of sudden
acceleration or high idle when taking the foot off the gas pedal, at a standstill,
or when shifting into Reverse, slowly accelerating, or applying the brakes. •
Reports of accelerator sticking. • Many reports of no-starts or sudden stalling
caused by fuel pump failure. • Defective power-steering pump causes sudden
steering lock-up. • ABS brakes locked up when applied and vehicle suddenly
accelerated. • Many reports of brake pedal having been pushed to the floor
with no braking effect. One '99 Taurus owner recounts the following tragic
experience in his NHTSA complaint:

Sudden brake loss, cruise control wouldn't disengage, brakes to floor,
emergency brake pulled to no effect, death of four.

Every element of this owner's story is repeated throughout the NHTSA database from reports of other Taurus and Sable owners. • Cruise control fails to disengage when vehicle is going downhill. • Frequent automatic transmission failures that include: slipping, hesitation, lurching into gear, failure to engage First gear, and a defective fluid pump destroying the catalytic converter. • Transmission in Park position allowed vehicle to roll downhill. • Transmission may leak fluid onto the exhaust manifold. • Steering wheel and brakes vibrate excessively when braking. • Front passenger's seat belt won't retract or lock into position. • Seat belt broke. • Seat belts fail to retract in a collision. • In the morning and evening, the light tan dashboard reflects upon the windshield, causing reduced visibility. • Rear defroster/defogger works poorly. • Rear windshield exploded when defroster/defogger activated. • In another incident, rear windshield exploded while vehicle was underway. • Headlights dim when brakes are applied. • Trunk light bulb burned part of luggage. • Electrical system shorts lead to the erratic operation of power door locks (they unlock while vehicle is underway) and windows. • AC discharges a foul odour that causes eyes to water and burn. • Fuel tank leaks. • Vehicle will stall out when fuel gauge shows the tank is one-quarter full. In fact, the gauge is so inaccurate that it will vary its reading by a half a tank depending upon whether you are going uphill or downhill. **2000**—Over 300 safety failures have been recorded (50 complaints would be normal) for the first year of the Taurus' latest redesign. Most of the problems are similar to those reported for previous years: evidence that Ford doesn't want to spend the money or squeeze its suppliers to install better quality components. No airbag deployment and inadvertent activation; gas fumes in the interior (driver found it exceeded CO_2 monitor limits and caused drowsiness and headaches); constantly lit warning lights; complete electrical failure; and sudden acceleration, surging, and stalling, accompanied by brake failure, continue to be the most frequent complaints:

> I released the brake after stopping at a stop sign, and turned the wheel to the right, the vehicle suddenly accelerated to what seemed about 100 km/h in about 10 seconds. The vehicle went toward the right and struck a curb, and the brakes did not appear to work. Once the vehicle came to a rest, the engine then shut off, the windshield broke, and the driver's side door wouldn't open.
>
> I suffered minor injuries.

Whatever you do, don't ignore the Check Engine light. In another recorded incident, the car didn't run away, stall, or lose its brakes; it simply exploded:

> At start-up the intake manifold exploded, resulting in total destruction. Shrapnel was embedded in the insulation cover on the hood and found throughout the engine compartment. The windshield washer module on the right side was blown off and found approximately five feet [1.5 m] from the car.

This vehicle has been in for service for hard starting and fuel system Check Engine light for the past year.

2001—Complaints continue unabated and echo those from previous years. • When coming to a stop, vehicle continues to accelerate because foot presses brake and gas pedal at the same time. • Car accelerated while backing up. • Airbag warning light comes on for no reason. • Inadvertent airbag deployment. • Sudden brake failure. • Strong fuel odour seeps into the interior. • Power steering suddenly failed. • Warped rotors. • Rear-view mirror too low on windshield; blocks view to the right. • Dash reflects onto windshield. • Early automatic transmission replacement. • Transmission clunks and jerks into gear. • Driver-side seat belt tightens by itself while driving. • Left rear wheel came off in transit; lost control of car. **2002**—Engine compartment fire. • Airbags deploy for no reason or fail to deploy. • Airbag warning light stays lit. • Rear left wheel and rim flew off due to defective lug nuts. • Sudden acceleration; vehicle surges and then shuts off when fuel tank is filled. • Frequent stalling, hard starts, and poor idle caused by chronic fuel pump failures or a contaminated fuel pressure sensor. • Strong fuel smell comes from the air vents (see "Secret Warranties/Service Tips/TSBs"). • Fuel gauge stuck on Full. • Fuel tank is easily punctured • Engine had to be replaced because block heater was incorrectly mounted on the engine. • Engine belt tensioner shattered. • Excessive steering vibration. • Interior rear view mirror location obstructs visibility. • Dash reflects onto the front windshield. • Seat belts may not reel out or retract. • Seat belt continually tightened around child and had to be cut. • Adjustable brake and accelerator pedals are set too close together and are often too loose. • Rear brake lines rub together. • High beam lights are too dim. • Cigarette lighter pops out and falls under passenger seat. **2003**—Complete brake failure. • Airbags deploy for no reason or fail to deploy. • Airbag warning light stays lit. • Rear left wheel and rim flew off due to defective lug nuts. • Sudden acceleration; vehicle surges and then shuts off when fuel tank is filled. • Frequent stalling, hard starts, and poor idle caused by chronic fuel pump failures or a contaminated fuel pressure sensor. • Strong fuel smell comes from the air vents. • Fuel gauge stuck on Full. • Fuel tank is easily punctured. • Engine had to be replaced because block heater was incorrectly mounted on the engine. • Engine belt tensioner shattered. • Excessive steering vibration. • Interior rear-view mirror location obstructs visibility. • Dash reflects onto the front windshield. • Seat belts may not reel out or retract. • Seat belt continually tightened around child and had to be cut off. • Adjustable brake and accelerator pedals are set too close together and are often too loose. • Right rear wheel almost fell off due to faulty stabilizer bolt. • Rear brake lines rub together. • High beam lights are too dim. • Cigarette lighter pops out and falls under passenger seat. • Firestone tire blowout.

Secret Warranties/Service Tips/TSBs

All models/years: NHTSA reports that there is a service bulletin that confirms the automatic transmission torque converter clutch fails to engage (problem dates back to 1996 models and includes Windstars).

> **Technical Service Bulletins Summary**
>
> Make: Ford
> Model: Taurus
> Year: 2003
> **Service Bulletin Number:** 03123
> **Component:**
> Powertrain: automatic transmission: torque converter
> **Summary Description:**
> Torque converter clutch not engaging when commanded and/or
> diagnostic trouble codes P0741 or P1744 stored in memory. Models from 1996 to 2003. *TT

• A cracked forward clutch piston may cause Forward/Reverse problems. Install the improved clutch piston and ask Ford to cover part of the cost inasmuch as their bulletins confirm it's a design defect. • Repeated heater core leaks. • A rotten-egg odour coming from the exhaust probably means that you have a faulty catalytic converter; replacement may be covered under the emissions warranty. • A buzz or rattle from the exhaust system may be caused by a loose heat shield catalyst. • A sloshing noise from the fuel tank when accelerating or stopping requires the installation of an upgraded tank. • Paint delamination, fading, and peeling (see Part Two). **1994–98**—No Fourth gear may signal the need to install an upgraded forward clutch control valve retaining clip. **1994–99**—Service tips to silence wind noise around doors. **1995–99**—Tips for sealing windshield water leaks and reducing noise, vibration, and harshness while driving. **1995–2000**—A harsh 3–2 downshift/shudder when accelerating or turning may have a simple cause: air entering the fluid filter pick-up area due to a slightly low ATF fluid level. **1996–97**—An acceleration or deceleration clunk is likely caused by the rear lower subframe isolators allowing movement between the mounts and the subframe. • A front suspension clunk may signal premature sway bar wear. • Harsh automatic 1–2 shifting may be caused by a malfunctioning electronic pressure control or the main control valves sticking in the valve body. **1996–98**—Troubleshooting tips for a torque converter clutch that won't engage. • Hard starts or long cranks may be caused by a miscalibrated PCM, a faulty IAC, or a malfunctioning fuel pump. • Install a power-steering service kit to silence steering moan. • A rattle heard when accelerating may be corrected by replacing the exhaust pipe flex coupling. • Water leaking onto the passenger floor area is likely caused by insufficient sealing of the cabin air filter to the cowl inlet. **1996–99**—Frequent no-starts, long cranks, or a dead battery may be caused by excessive current drain or water entry in the ABS module connector. **1996–2001**—Inoperative power windows may need a new motor and lubrication of the glass run weather stripping. **1997**—Stalling or surging of 3.0L engines when shifting may signal the need to reprogram the power control module (PCM). **1997–98**—Lack of AC temperature control may be corrected by replacing the blend air door actuator. **1999**—Owner Notification Program regarding transmission rear lube tube and bracket replacement. • Engine buzz or rattle. • Slight vibration upon acceleration. • Lack of engine braking. • Excessive spark knock with the 3.0L engine. • Engine oil pan leaks. • No

Reverse engagement is likely caused by the Reverse clutch lip seals shearing or tearing during Reverse engagement in cold weather. • No 3–4 shifts; 3–4 shift shuddering. • Outer tie-rod squeaks or pops. • Excessive steering noise on vehicles equipped with the 3.0L engine. • Inoperative speed control and blower motor. • Self-activating front wipers need an upgraded multifunction switch (covered under warranty or "goodwill"). • Hard to turn ignition key. • Wagons display a false "door ajar" warning. • Intermittent loss of instrument panel illumination. • Separation between the layers of the instrument panel. • Premature deterioration of the front seat trim. • Power window binding. • Inaccurate fuel tank gauge; fuel tank causes gas pump to shut off prematurely. **2000**—Engine pan oil leaks. • Automatic transmission may operate erratically. • A hissing sound may be heard coming from the intake manifold. • A growling or scraping sound may be heard during acceleration. **2000–01**—3.0L engines may exhibit a rough start or poor idle, excessive spark knock, or backfire on start-up. • 3–4 shift shudder. • The exhaust pipe contacts the rear control arm, resulting in rear end buzzing, groaning, and rattling. • Fuel smell permeates the interior (see following bulletin).

Intake Manifold Gaskets – Fuel Smell to the Interior

Article No. 01-4-3   03/05/01

2000–01 Taurus
2001 Escape
2000–01 Sable

This article applies to 2000–01 Taurus/Sable vehicles with 3.0L 4V Duratec engine built through 4/1/2001 and 2001 Escape vehicles with 3.0L 4V Duratec engine built through 6/1/2001 only.

Issue

Some vehicles may exhibit a fuel odour noticed through the vents inside the vehicle. The odour may be noticed upon initial start-up after "Hot Soak." This condition produces a fuel odour only and does not involve visible fuel or include the presence of a combustible mixture. This may be caused by the lower intake manifold gaskets.

Action

If fuel odour condition is verified and no fuel leaks or mechanical problems are found, replace the lower intake gaskets with revised gaskets.

2000–03—No-start or hard starts (see following bulletin).

No-Start/Hard Start/Rough Idle

Article No.: 03-3-50

Date: 2/17/03

DRIVEABILITY - Idle air control (IAC) valve
2000–03 Taurus
2002 Thunderbird
2000–03 Explorer, Ranger
2001–03 Explorer's Sport Trac, Explore Sport
2000–02 LS
2000–03 Sable, Mountaineer

ISSUE: Some vehicles may exhibit driveability conditions.
These may include:
^No-start/difficult to start/stall
^Low idle
^Rough idle
^High idle
^Hesitation/surge while accelerating or at steady speed
These conditions may be intermittent with no Diagnostic Trouble Codes (DTC) and no Malfunction Indicator Lamp (MIL).

2001—Side airbag light may remain lit. • Rough idle; Check Engine light remains lit. • Automatic transmission fluid leakage from the main control cover area. • Blower motor may overheat. • Sticking/binding ignition key lock cylinder. **2002**—Frequent heater core failures. **2003**—Transmission may not go into Reverse. • Troubleshooting transmission malfunctions. • Engine cooling-fan-induced body boom. • Rough engine idle sensation, and unusual engine noise at idle. • Incorrectly installed gear-driven camshaft position sensor synchronizer assemblies may cause engine surge, loss of power, or MIL lamp to light. • Rattling, clunking front suspension. • Power window grunting noise.

Sable, Taurus Profile								
	1996	1997	1998	1999	2000	2001	2002	2003
Cost Price ($)								
Sable GS	22,595	23,595	24,395	24,595	—	—	—	—
LS Wagon	25,496	26,596	25,096	25,795	—	—	—	—
Taurus GL	22,195	23,195	—	—	—	—	—	—
Taurus LX	25,095	26,195	23,295	23,495	24,495	24,250	24,550	24,750
GL/SE Wagon	22,196	23,196	23,995	24,695	26,495	26,555	27,285	27,630
SHO	32,430	32,695	37,795	37,995	—	—	—	—
Used Values ($)								
Sable GS ⋀		3,000	4,000	5,000	6,500	—	—	—	—
Sable GS ⋁		2,500	3,500	4,500	6,000	—	—	—	—
LS Wagon ⋀		4,000	5,000	6,000	7,500	—	—	—	—
LS Wagon ⋁		3,500	4,500	5,000	7,000	—	—	—	—
Taurus GL ⋀		3,000	3,500	—	—	—	—	—	—
Taurus GL ⋁		2,500	3,000	—	—	—	—	—	—
Taurus LX ⋀		3,500	4,000	5,000	6,500	9,000	11,000	13,000	15,500
Taurus LX ⋁		3,000	3,500	4,500	6,000	8,000	10,000	12,500	14,500
GL/SE Wagon ⋀		3,000	3,500	6,500	7,500	9,500	12,000	14,000	16,000
GL/SE Wagon ⋁		2,500	3,000	5,500	7,000	9,000	10,500	13,000	15,000
SHO ⋀		5,500	6,500	8,000	9,000	—	—	—	—
SHO ⋁		4,500	5,500	7,000	8,000	—	—	—	—

Reliability	❶	❶	❶	❶	❶	❷	❷	❷
Crash Safety	④	④	④	⑤	—	⑤	⑤	⑤
Side	—	③	③	③	—	③	③	③
Offset	⑤	⑤	⑤	⑤	⑤	⑤	⑤	⑤
Head Restraints (F)	❶	❶	—	❶	③	⑤	④	③
Rear	—	—	—	—	—	—	③	③
Rollover Resistance	—	—	—	—	—	—	④	④

General Motors

ACHIEVA, ALERO, GRAND AM, SKYLARK ★★★

RATING: Average (2000–03), with the right powertrain set-up and an extended powertrain warranty; Below Average (1995–99); Not Recommended (1985–94). Only the Grand Am and its Alero twin survived the 1999 model year. Keep in mind that the 4-cylinder engines are noisy and rough-running. **Maintenance/Repair costs:** Higher than average. Repairs aren't dealer dependent. **Parts:** Higher-than-average cost, but they can be bought for much less from independent suppliers. **Best alternatives:** The Acura Integra; Honda Accord; Hyundai Elantra wagon, Sonata, or Tiburon; Mazda 626; Nissan Altima; and Toyota Camry. **Online help:** For the latest owner reports, service bulletins, and money-saving tips, look at *www.autosafety.org/autodefects.html*, or use Google to search for GM paint delamination, piston slapping, or manifold defects.

Strengths and weaknesses: These cars originally came with a failure-prone 150-hp Quad SOHC engine, a 5-speed transaxle, and ABS. The basic front-drive platform continues to be a refined version of the Sunfire (Sunbird) and Cavalier J-body. They are too cramped to be family sedans (rear entry/exit can be difficult), too sedate for sporty coupe status, and too ordinary for inclusion in the luxury car ranks.

In their basic form, these cars are unreliable, unspectacular, and provide barely adequate performance. An upgraded 3.1L V6 power plant gives you only five more horses than the base 4-banger and frequently requires intake manifold gasket repairs covered by a 6-year/100,000 km secret warranty. There's been a lot of hype about the Quad 4 16-valve engine, available with all models, but little of this translates into benefits for the average driver. A multivalve motor produces more power than a standard engine, but always at higher rpms and with a fuel penalty and excess engine noise.

These cars ride and handle fairly well but mostly share chassis components with the failure-prone J-bodies. This explains why engine, transmission, brake, and electronic problems are similar. Fortunately, manual transmissions are much more reliable and are also the better choice for fuel economy. Water leaks and body squeaks and rattles are so abundant that GM has published a six-page troubleshooting TSB that pinpoints the noises and lists fixes.

Vehicle history: 1991–95—Potentially unsafe door-mounted front seat belts. **1992**—A major redesign offered new styling and a 3.3L V6. **1994**—A revised 3.1L V6 replaces the 3.3L V6 and a driver's-side airbag was added. **1996**—Restyled and given standard AC, dual airbags and three-point seat belts; a new twin-cam engine replaced the 2.3L Quad 4. **1998**—De-powered airbags. **Grand Am: 1999**—Given better engines, a new platform, more standard equipment, and a restyled, more comfortable interior. **2002**—A quieter, more efficient 140-hp 2.2L base engine with 10 fewer horses than the engine it replaced, plus a revised console storage area.

The 2.5L 4-cylinder engine doesn't provide much power and has a poor reliability record. Avoid the Quad 4 and 3.0L V6 engines with SFI (sequential fuel injection) because of their frequent breakdowns and difficult servicing. Poor engine cooling and fuel system malfunctions are common; diagnosis and repair are more complicated than average, however. The engine computer on V6 models has a high failure rate, and the oil pressure switch often malfunctions. The electrical system is plagued by gremlins that cause gauges and controls to go haywire and result in the car shutting down on the highway. Seals and pumps in the power-steering rack deteriorate rapidly. Front brake discs, rotors, and pads need replacing every 5,000 miles (8,000 km). Locks and headlights self-activate.

Among body deficiencies, owners note that windshield mouldings fall off, water leaks into the trunk and through the doors, door panels often need replacing, the sun visor fails to stay in place, seat cushions aren't durable, and paint defects are quite common.

Alero and Grand Am (1999–2003)

These redesigned cars aren't very impressive. The best engine choice for power, smoothness, and value retention is the 207-hp 3.4L V6; it gives you much-needed power and is quite fuel efficient. Early reports indicate that the new 2.2L engine is quieter, but its lack of power is noticeable, particularly when coupled to an automatic transmission. Stay away from the Computer Command Ride option; true, it allows you to choose your own suspension setting, but the settings aren't quite what they pretend to be.

Taking their styling cues from GM's Grand Prix, the Grand Am and its Alero twin offer a roomy, comfortable interior in two- and four-door body styles. They share the same platform and mechanical components, and the base Grand Am SE uses a 140-hp 2.2L power plant, while other trim levels use the 150-hp 2.4L Quad DOHC engine; a 170-hp 3.4L V6 engine is standard on the SE2.

The upscale Alero, Oldsmobile's entry-level model, debuted in 1999 as the replacement for the slow-selling Achieva—often referred to as the "under-Achieva." The Alero shares the Grand Am's chassis and powertrains, although only the 2.2L and 3.4L V6 are offered. The V6 may be teamed with either a 5-speed manual or a 4-speed automatic transmission.

1999–2003 Grand Ams are well appointed with many standard features, including standard traction control. They have a competent V6; good steering and handling, and average quality control. Some of their disadvantages: a mediocre ride over rough terrain; excessive 4-cylinder noise; and a noisy interior. Also, expect difficult rear seat access (coupe); awkward radio controls; rear visibility obstructed by the spoiler; problematic trunk access; annoying body creaks and rattles; and doubtful long-term powertrain reliability.

Equally well equipped, Aleros give impressive V6 acceleration (even though it's the same engine found in the Grand Am, it performs better in the Alero). You'll find logical, user-friendly gauges and controls; a fairly spacious interior for cargo and passengers; standard traction control; and a quiet-running V6 powertrain. Here's the Alero's downside: excessive 4-cylinder engine noise and torque steer; steering not as crisp as the Grand Am's; difficult rear seat access (coupe); and questionable long-term durability. Alero will be dropped during the 2004 model year due to the phase-out of GM's Oldsmobile division.

Overall quality control is bad. GM's quality improvements, evident on its trucks, vans, and SUVs, weren't carried over to these passenger vehicles. Owners warn of powertrain malfunctions, including sudden transmission failure and poor shifting; engine overheating; and premature brake pad and rotor wear. The following two emails are typical of the engine and brake problems affecting recent Aleros and Grand Ams:

> I bought a '99 Alero with 55,000 km on it. After driving it for a year, I now have 95,000 km on it. Yesterday the warning light for low coolant came on and this morning I took the car to my local repair shop. He filled the reservoir (overflow) up and checked for any leaks, found none and I drove home.
>
> I quickly noticed the engine running rough, so when I got home I called him again. He checked the reservoir (overflow) again and it was already down again.... Then, he checked the oil dipstick—it was wet, steamy, and very light in colour. You probably guessed it a long time ago; all the water went into the cylinders!!!
>
> Can I not expect more than 100,000 km from the Alero's 3.4L, 6-cylinder engine!!!

•

> Phil, I have problems with the front brakes on a 2000 Alero. I have had the rotors replaced once (28,000 km), pads twice, and there is a constant rubbing sound coming from the front end that the dealer says is the result of a rust buildup on the edge of the rotors. They told me it's something I have to live with.

Owners also mention electrical problems; suspension squeaks; and substandard body assembly producing more squeaks and rattles, water leaks, and poor paint adhesion. There are reports that the sunroof may leak water into the electrical panel, causing short-circuits. Rear visibility may be obstructed by the spoiler.

Safety summary: All models/years: Airbag failed to deploy and inadvertent airbag deployment. • Sudden acceleration and stalling. • Frequent brake failures and extended stopping distance; brake caliper seizure damages pads and rotors. • Power-steering failures and fluid leakage. • Transmission jumps out of gear. • Shoulder belt rides across driver's neck. • Erratic fuel gauge operation. • Headlights suddenly shut off or don't provide enough illumination. • Head restraints block rear vision. • Dash is reflected onto the windshield. • Water leaks everywhere. **1996**—Left wheel came off after the stud that holds the wheel unbolted from the wheel. • Oxygen sensor failures cause Check Engine light to come on. • Defective master cylinder, drums, pads, and rotors. • Engine, transmission, and AC failures. • Seat belt sticks into driver's side or will not fasten properly. • Water leaks into the trunk. • Passenger-side power door lock and window lock do not work properly. **1997**—Many reports of vehicle first losing power and then suddenly accelerating. • Accelerator cable snapped, causing pedal to go to the floor. • While vehicle was being driven, the hood suddenly flipped backward, hitting the windshield. • Windshield reflection obstructs vision. • Premature brake replacements. • Seat belt improperly fitted. • Design flaw allows wheels to rub against front fender. • Mirrors aren't adjustable enough to see other vehicles, and seatbacks are too high for some drivers to see over. • Driver-side bucket seat isn't anchored properly; rocks from side to side. • Intermittent windshield wiper failures. **1998–99**—Vehicle caught fire while parked. • Premature brake pad wearout and warped rotors every 4,800–8,000 km (3,000–5,000 mi.). • Cruise control is either inoperative or fails to disengage. • Chronic hesitation and stall-out, accompanied by dash lights and other electrics going haywire. • Enhanced traction system engages when not needed. • Complete electrical system shutdown while vehicle was underway. • Rainwater leaks through the dash panel into the fuse box. • Wheel lug nuts sheared off, causing wheel to fall away. • Severe brake, steering, and body vibrations; vehicle intermittently violently jerks to one side. • Steering pump failure. • Fuel pressure regulator leaks fumes into the interior. • Sunroof exploded when side window was opened while vehicle was underway. • Windows run off their channels and shatter. • Power window motors often need replacing. • Windshield washer fluid freezes due to poor tubing design. • Headrests obstruct rear visibility. • Locks and headlights self-activate. • Faulty fuel level sensor gives a false Empty reading. • Seat belts tend to twist when retracting. **2000**—Although there aren't an unusually large number of complaints recorded, the same problems keep appearing. They include frequent brake light burnout; poor braking or the complete loss of braking; overheated, warped brake rotors and excessive vibration when braking; chronic stalling; the trunk lid opening on its own while the vehicle is underway; and water leaks through the doors and sunroof. The sunroof leaks result in the electrical system shorting out and the vehicle shutting down. **2001**—Very few complaints reported so far; however, stalling, brake rotor warpage, and sunroof leaks appear, once again. Other problems: fire ignited at the right rear of vehicle; fuel tank is easily punctured; and rear axle bent or broken, leading to loss of control. **2002**—Frequency of safety complaints has increased substantially. • Transmission suddenly failed while cruising at speeds over 100 km/h. • Chronic stalling. • Vehicle continued accelerating after passing another car on the highway. • Car constantly surges and hesitates. • • Vehicle tends to wander all over the road; pulls to one side when accelerating. • Steering shudders upon braking or acceleration; faulty power steering pump; steering feels too loose. • ABS light comes on, followed by brake failure; brake pedal set too low; parking brake failure. • Fuel pump failure. • Shoulder belts twist in their housing; in the GT two-door and they ride abnormally high on the shoulder/neck area. • Power doors lock on their own. • Headlights blink on and off. • Theft alarm sounds for no reason. • Middle rear lap seat belt is too short to secure a child safety seat and GM says an extension isn't available. • Loose driver's seat. • Windshield wipers shut off intermittently. • Rear windshield shattered when defogger was activated; side door glass shattered behind mirror for no reason. • Inside door edge is razor sharp. • Slight front impact causes the battery tray to either break off, or results in the battery sliding off the tray. **Alero:** Engine compartment fire. • Right front wheel separated because the lug nuts and bolts sheared off. • Tapped brakes to turn cruise control off and vehicle accelerated. • Rear main oil seal leak blew oil onto exhaust pipe. • Fuel tank leakage. • Water leakage onto the back of the instrument panel causes the instruments and gauges to malfunction; other electrical shorts cause instrument panel gauges and controls to fail. • Windshield water leaks cause electrical shorts. • Hard to find horn "sweet spot" in an emergency. • Side mirror spring mounts break when passing over unpaved roads. •

Secret Warranties/Service Tips/TSBs

All models/years: A rotten-egg odour coming from the exhaust may be the result of a malfunctioning catalytic converter—possibly covered by the emissions warranty. Stand your ground if GM or the dealer claims you must pay. • Tips on removing AC odours; GM has a special kit to keep AC odours at bay. • Paint delamination, peeling, or fading (see Part Two). **1990–2000**— Countermeasures for water collecting in the tail lights. **1995–97**—Intermittent loss of Drive at highway speeds may require the replacement of the control valve body assembly. • Engine popping noises can be silenced by tightening the torque strut mount bolts. **1995–98**—A steering squeak or squawk may be reduced by installing a rack-and-pinion service kit. **1996–98**—Install a seat belt webbing stop button if the seat belt latch slides to the anchor sleeve. • Passenger compartment water leaks can be plugged by applying silicone sealer to the top vent grille assembly. **1997**—No-starts may be due to an improperly routed and pinched wire from the generator to the wiring harness. • Excessive oil consumption in the 2.5L engine may be caused by one or more damaged intake valve guides. • Hard starting and engine pinging can be fixed by the installation of a new PROM module (#16121217), says TSB #88-6E-11. **1997–98**—Hard starting or a weak or dead battery may signal the need to repair the B+ stud and/or starter wiring. **1999–2000**—No Third or Fourth gear may signal a defective direct clutch piston. • Upgraded pads and rotors

will fix brake pulsation/vibration (see Malibu entry on page 229). • A wet
front or rear carpet may mean the front door water deflectors need to be
replaced. • Simply changing the radiator cap may cure your hot-running
engine. **Skylark: 1995–98**—Intermittent Neutral/loss of Drive at highway
speeds can be fixed by replacing the control valve body assembly. **Grand Am,
Alero: 1998–2003**—Automatic transmission flaring. **1999**—Hesitation or
lack of power when accelerating on vehicles equipped with the 3.4L engine
may simply require reprogramming the power control module (PCM). • Paint
chipping from the Grand Am SE's rocker panel and lower quarter panel can be
prevented by installing upgraded driver- and passenger-side rocker mouldings.
1999–2001—A front-end clunk or rattle can be silenced by replacing the
brake pedal assembly under warranty. • Water leak troubleshooting. • Wind
rush from the front windshield. **1999–2002**—Excessive pedal or steering
wheel pulsation when braking (see following bulletin).

Front Disc Brakes – Pedal/Steering Wheel Pulsation

File In Section: 05 – Brakes   Date: December 2001
Bulletin No.: 00-05-23-002A

Models:

1997–2002 Malibu

1997–99 Cutlass

1999–2002 Alero, Grand Am

Condition

Some customers may comment on a pulsation condition felt in the brake pedal and/or
steering wheel during a brake apply. In some cases, it may be noted that the pulsation
condition has reoccurred in 5,000-11,000 km (3,000-7,000 mi.) after having had the brakes
serviced, tires rotated, or any type of servicing that required wheel removal.

Cause

Pulsation is the result of brake rotor thickness variation causing the brake caliper piston to
move in and out of the brake caliper housing. This hydraulic "pumping/pulsing" effect is
transmitted through the brake system and may be felt in the brake pedal. In severe cases,
this condition may also transmit through the vehicle structure and other chassis system
components such as the steering column or wheel. The major contributor to rotor thickness
variation is excessive lateral run-out of the rotor, causing the brake pads to wear the rotor
unevenly over time.

Correction

Confirm that the brake pads have the number 1417 printed on the edge of the pad backing
plate (refer to the illustration). This indicates the correct brake pads have been previously
installed. The brake pads contained in Front Pad Kit, P/N 18044437, are the only brake pads
that should be used on these vehicles. If the number 1417 is not present, or if the number is
not legible, replace the brake pads. If the correct pads were previously installed, verify the
brake pad thickness. If the brake pad friction material thickness is 4.6 mm (0.18 in.) or
greater, re-use the pads. If the friction material thickness is less than 4.6 mm (0.18 in.), install
new brake pads contained in Front Pad Kit P/N 18044437.

If the rotor thickness is less than 25 mm (0.98 in.), install a new rotor. If rotor thickness is
greater than 25 mm (0.98 in.), refinish the rotor.

Replace existing front brake rotors and pads, if necessary, with new components indicated
in the table following the applicable Service Manual procedures and the service guidelines
contained in Corporate Bulletin Number 00-05-22-002.

• Faulty front door window glass. • Front wheel tire noise may be silenced by replacing Goodyear Eagle tires. **2000**—If the vehicle stalls, hesitates or won't start, you may need to replace the modular fuel sender strainer. **2000–01**—If the Check Engine light comes on, it may mean the fuel-sender-to-tank o-ring is defective. • Install a fuel tank sender kit under warranty if the fuel gauge gives inaccurate readings. • TSB #01-06-01-005 allows for free 3.1L engine piston replacement to cure an engine ticking noise. **2000–03**—Firm transmission shifts and shudders or transmission slips or fails to shift. • Loss of power steering. • Noisy front suspension. • Inaccurate fuel gauge readings (see following bulletin).

Inaccurate Fuel Gauge Readings

Bulletin No.: 01-06-04-008D

Date: April 2003

Inaccurate or erratic fuel gauge reading, fuel-pump-related driveability concerns (install new fuel tank sender)

2000–03 Chevrolet Cavalier, Malibu
2000–03 Oldsmobile Alero
2000–03 Pontiac Grand Am, Sunfire

Condition: Some customers may comment about inaccurate or erratic fuel gauge readings. A typical comment might be that it appears from the gauge reading that there is fuel available, yet the tank is nearly empty.

Cause: This condition may be the result of the corrosive effect of certain fuel blends on the contact surfaces of the fuel tank sender.

This is a common GM defect that affects many more than the models listed in this service bulletin. Repairs can cost over $500. Generally, GM will pay for the fix up to 7 years/160,000 km if pressured by a small claims lawsuit.

• Front door window glass comes out of run channel; and wind noise from rear of vehicle. **2002**—No-starts, harsh transmission shifts. • Transmission fluid leakage. • Premature failure of the transaxle converter pump. • A Customer Service Campaign will pay for the inspection and correction of a transaxle converter bearing failure, detailed in TSB #01031. • Remedy for suspension noise or malfunctions. • Shift indicator doesn't show correct gear selection. • Engine alerts stay lit. • Brake pedal, underbody, or suspension clunk or rattle noise. • Door creaking. • Windshield glass distortion. **2003**—Poor shifting and inaccurate gauges (see following bulletin).

Erratic Readings, Shifts, and Cruise Control Operation

Bulletin No.: 02-07-30-044

Date: November 2002

Erratic speedometer, erratic shifting, cruise control inoperative, DTCs P0502, P0758, P1860 set (repair Vehicle Speed Sensor wires and reposition harness)

2003 Oldsmobile Alero
2003 Pontiac Grand Am
with 2.2L Engine (VIN F - RPO L61), automatic transmission (RPO MN4) and non-anti-lock brakes (RPO J41)

^Erratic speedometer readings

^Erratic shifting

^Cruise control inoperative

Cause: These conditions may be caused from the extra length of Vehicle Speed Sensor (VSS) harness intermittently contacting the right axle shaft. This contact may cause a rub-through to the wires enclosed in that harness, resulting in the above conditions.

Achieva (Calais), Grand Am, Skylark Profile

	1996	1997	1998	1999	2000	2001	2002	2003
Cost Price ($)								
Achieva S	19,925	20,735	21,200	—	—	—	—	—
Grand Am	18,000	19,035	19,610	21,795	20,625	20,915	21,405	21,640
Skylark	20,035	21,220	22,965	—	—	—	—	—
Used Values ($)								
Achieva S ▲	4,000	4,500	5,000	—	—	—	—	—
Achieva S ▼	3,500	4,000	4,500	—	—	—	—	—
Grand Am ▲	4,500	5,000	6,500	8,500	10,000	11,000	13,500	15,500
Grand Am ▼	4,000	4,500	5,500	7,500	9,000	10,500	12,500	14,500
Skylark ▲	4,000	4,500	5,000	—	—	—	—	—
Skylark ▼	3,500	4,500	4,500	—	—	—	—	—
Reliability	❷	③	③	③	④	④	④	
Crash Safety								
Achieva 2d	④	—	—	—	—	—	—	—
Achieva 4d	⑤	—	—	—	—	—	—	—
Grand Am 2d	—	④	—	—	—	④	④	④
Grand Am 4d	④	⑤	—	④	④	④	④	④
Skylark 2d	—	④	—	—	—	—	—	—
Skylark 4d	④	⑤	—	—	—	—	—	—
Side								
Achieva 4d	—	❶	❶	—	—	—	—	—
Grand Am 2d	—	—	—	—	—	❶	❶	❶
Grand Am 4d	—	—	❶	❶	③	③	③	—
Skylark 4d	❶	❶	—	—	—	—	—	—
Offset	—	—	—	—	❶	❶	❶	❶
Head Restraints	❶	—	❶	—	❷	—	③	③
Alero	—	—	—	—	—	—	—	❷
Rollover Resistance	—	—	—	—	—	—	④	④

BONNEVILLE, CUTLASS, CUTLASS SUPREME, DELTA 88, GRAND PRIX, IMPALA, INTRIGUE, LESABRE, LUMINA, MALIBU, MONTE CARLO, REGAL ★★★

RATING: Average (2000–03); Not Recommended for front-drives (1988–99); Above Average for rear-drives (1984–87). Although these GM models are generally classed as medium-sized cars, some of them move in and out of the large car class as well. Overall, the Intrigue, Malibu, Monte Carlo, and Grand Prix provide the best quality at the highest depreciation rate (for used-car bargain hunters). Nevertheless, use some of the savings for extra powertrain protection, or get close to the service manager's daughter. **Maintenance/Repair costs:** Higher than average, but repairs aren't dealer dependent. **Parts:** Higher-than-average cost (independent suppliers sell for much less), but not hard to find. Nevertheless, don't even think about buying one of the front-drives without a supplementary 3- to 5-year powertrain warranty. **Best alternatives:** The Acura Integra; Honda Accord; Hyundai Elantra wagon, Sonata, or Tiburon; Mazda 626; and Toyota Camry. **Online help:** The Center for Auto Safety has a huge database of service bulletins and owner complaints at *www.autosafety.org/autodefects.html*, or, once again, you can use Google to search for GM paint delamination, engine piston slapping, or manifold defects.

Strengths and weaknesses: The following problems are common to all models: no-start or no-crank conditions caused by defective ignition and start switch assembly; hot engine idles poorly; engine oil pan leaks; harsh shifting, harsh 1–2 upshifts; poor engine performance and transmission slipping (clean out debris in valve body and case oil passages); some transmissions may produce a grinding or growling noise when engaged on an incline with the engine running and the parking brake not applied; delayed shifts, slips, flares, or extended shifts in cold weather; erratic shifting; excessive vibration on smooth roads; generator whine, hum, moan, or vibration; premature alternator failure; steering vibration, shudder, or moan during parking manoeuvres.

Body assembly on all models is notoriously poor and is no doubt one of the main reasons why GM has lost so much market share over the past decade. Premature paint peeling and rusting, water and dust leaks into the trunk, squeaks and rattles, and wind and road noise are all too common. Accessories are also plagued by problems, with defective radios, power antennas, door locks, cruise control, and alarm systems leading the pack. Premature automatic transmission failures and excessive noise when shifting have been endemic up to the 1998 model year. Since then, the company's powertrain problems have been less frequent. Engine intake manifold gaskets, though, have a high failure rate and are covered by a 6-year/100,000 km secret warranty (see confidential GM service bulletin on page 2).

Rear-drives

The rear-drives are competent and comfortable cars, but they definitely point to a time when handling wasn't a priority and fuel economy was unimportant. Nevertheless, interior comfort is impressive, overall reliability is pretty good, repairs are easy to perform, defects aren't hard to troubleshoot, and cheaper independent garages can service them quite easily.

Electrical malfunctions increase proportionally with extra equipment. The AC module and condenser and wheel bearings (incredibly expensive) also have short life spans. The rear edge of trunk lids, roof areas above doors, and the windshield and windshield posts rust through easily.

Front-drives

Front-drive technology is not GM's proudest achievement. Its front-drives, phased into the lineup in the 80s, are a different breed of car: less reliable and more expensive to repair than rear-drives, with a considerable number of mechanical (brake, steering, and suspension components, for example) deficiencies directly related to their front-drive configuration. Nevertheless, acceleration is adequate, fuel economy is good, and they're better at handling than their rear-drive cousins—except in emergencies, when their brakes frequently lock up or fail, notwithstanding ABS technology. The Detroit Big Three's front-drive designs and manufacturing weaknesses make for unimpressive high-speed performance, a poor reliability record, and expensive maintenance costs. That's why most fleets and police agencies use rear-drives when they can get them. They've seen the rear-drives' safety and operating cost advantages. Interestingly, Chrysler, Ford, and GM have announced a return to rear-drive full-sized cars by 2005.

Medium-sized front drives aren't particularly driver-friendly. Many models have a dash that's replete with confusing push buttons and gauges that are washed out in sunlight or reflect annoyingly upon the windshield. At other times, there are retro touches, like the Intrigue's dash-mounted ignition, that simply seem out of place. The keyless entry system often fails, the radio's memory is frequently forgetful, and the fuel light comes on when the tank is just below the "½" fuel-level mark. The electronic climate control frequently malfunctions and owners report that warm air doesn't reach the driver-side heating vents. Servicing, especially for the electronic engine controls, is complicated and expensive, forcing many owners to drive around with their Service Engine, airbag, and ABS warning lights constantly lit.

Other major problem areas found over the past decade: engine head gasket leaks; plastic intake manifold cracking; automatic transmission failures and clunking; leaking and malfunctioning AC systems (due mainly to defective AC modules); faulty electronic modules; rack-and-pinion steering failure; weak shocks; excessive front brake pad wear; warping rotors; seizure of the rear brake calipers; rear brake/wheel lock-up; myriad electrical failures, requiring replacement of the computer module; leaking oil pan; and suspension struts.

The base 2.3L and 2.5L engines found on pre-'95 models provide insufficient power. The more powerful 3.1L V6 is peppier, but it's seriously hampered by the 4-speed automatic transaxle. The high- performance 3.4L V6, available since 1991, gives out plenty of power, but only at high engine speeds.

One major powertrain problem found over the past decade involves the 3.4L V6 engine: specifically, engine head gasket leaks and plastic intake manifold cracking. The head gasket defect mirrors the same failures seen with GM's Saturn models and Ford's 1994–96 Taurus, Sable, and Windstar. The intake manifold problem is much more insidious due to the extensive damage that can be caused in a short period of time, as this GM service manager confirms:

> One problem that I do not see mentioned on your website involves late 1990s full-sized GM cars (LeSabre, Delta 88, Bonneville) with the 3.8L (VIN K) engine. GM has released a TSB regarding a poorly

designed intake manifold that actually melts from EGR heat. Their cure is to replace the upper and lower intake manifold at a cost of approximately $1,000 to the consumer.

What the TSB does not reveal is that by the time most consumers are aware that there is a problem, irreversible engine damage has occurred. This is because when the intake fails, coolant leaks internally into the crankcase, therefore contaminating engine oil. The only way to know that this is happening is to check the oil on a daily basis. Once enough coolant is lost, the vehicle overheats and by that time, there are several quarts of coolant in the oil (and a wiped out engine).

I know of many defects on various cars, but this one bothers me the most as the consumers have no way to protect themselves. Most of these folks (the LeSabre and Delta 88 crowd, who are mostly elderly) are driving around in mechanical time bombs.

Additionally, owners report a high number of automatic transmission failures and clunking; leaking and malfunctioning AC systems (due mainly to defective AC modules); poor engine performance and myriad electrical shorts, requiring the early replacement of various computer modules; rack-and-pinion steering failure; weak shocks; excessive front brake pad wear; warping rotors; seizure of the rear brake calipers; rear brake/wheel lock-up; leaking oil pan; and suspension struts.

Other deficiencies: The instruments and steering column shake when the car is travelling over uneven road surfaces; and lots of road and wind noise comes through the side windows, thanks to the inadequately soundproofed chassis. Seating isn't very comfortable due to the lack of support caused by low-density foam, knees-in-your-face low seating, and the ramrod-straight rear backrest. The ride is acceptable with a light load, but when fully loaded, the car's back end sags and the ride deteriorates. Owners report that 3.8L engines won't continue running after a cold start, the exhaust system booms, 3T40 automatic transmissions may have faulty Reverse gears, and the instrument panel may pop or creak.

2002–03 models do have a nice array of standard features; a good choice of powertrains; a comfortable ride; and an easily accessed and roomy interior. On the other hand, they continue to have noisy engines at high speeds; rear seating that's uncomfortable for three; bland styling; and obstructed rear visibility due to a high-tail rear end. Most importantly, these cars are hobbled by a chintzy powertrain warranty that's clearly insufficient, knowing GM's past engine and transmission deficiencies. Imagine, having to pay $3,000–$5,000 for a new engine or transmission just as your used car "bargain" passes its fifth year.

Intrigue

Strikingly similar to the Alero, the Oldsmobile Intrigue is GM's replacement for the Cutlass Supreme and represents the most refined iteration of the W-body shared by the Century, Grand Prix, Lumina, and Regal. It's more luxurious than the Lumina and performs as well as the Accord, Camry, and

Maxima. Its rigid chassis has fewer shakes and rattles than are found on GM's other models, and its 3.8L engine provides lots of low-end grunt but lacks the top-end power that makes the Japanese competition so much fun to toss around. '99 versions got a torquier 3.5L V6 coupled to standard traction control. This engine's a bit more refined, but it's still not smooth, and the automatic transmission still struggles to get past its first two gears. Year 2000 models returned unchanged, while the 2001 Intrigue was given a couple of new colours and an upgraded air filtration system.

1995–2003 Impala, Lumina, and Monte Carlo

These models are popular two- and four-door versions of Chevy's "large" mid-sized cars, featuring standard dual airbags, ABS, and 160-hp V6 power. The Monte Carlo was formerly sold as the Lumina Z34. Powertrain enhancements have increased horsepower and fuel efficiency. Each car has been given a slightly different appearance and a distinct "personality." A 3.1L V6 is the standard engine, a standard 3.4L 210-hp V6 powers the coupe and is optional with the LS Lumina, and a 3.8L V6 equips the more upscale versions.

Vehicle history: 1996—The 3.4L got a slight horsepower boost, and all-disc braking was adopted on the Monte Carlo Z34 and upscale versions of the LS. **1997**—A better-performing transmission, mated to the 3.4L engine, gives smoother shifts. **1998–99**—Few changes, except for the addition of the 3.8L V6 to the Monte Carlo Z34 and Lumina LTZ. **2000**—Lumina's standard 3.1L engine got a bit more torque and a small horsepower boost, in addition to more standard equipment. This was the Lumina's last year before it was replaced by the Impala. But the Monte Carlo soldiered on, having been reworked and brought out on the Impala platform for 2000. It was carried over unchanged.

Except for the automatic transmission upgrade, owners report that newer versions still have some of the same shortcomings seen on earlier front-drive models. For example, in spite of some noise reduction progress, body construction is still below par, with loose door panel mouldings, poorly fitted door fabric, and misaligned panels. Other common problems: fuel pump whistling, frequent stalling, vague steering, premature paint peeling on the hood and trunk, heavy accumulation of hard-to-remove brake dust inside the honeycomb-design wheels, and front tires that scrape the fenders when the wheel is turned. Despite its own recent redesign, the 3.1L engine isn't entirely problem-free. Faulty intake manifold gaskets (a chronic problem affecting the entire model lineup; see "Secret Warranties/Service Tips/TSBs"), electronic fuel-injection systems, and engine controls have created many problems for GM owners. The 4-speed automatic transmission still has some bugs. The front brakes wear quickly, as do the MacPherson struts and shock absorbers. Steering assemblies tend to fail prematurely. The electrical system is temperamental. The sunroof motor is failure prone. Owners report water leaks from the front windshield. Front-end squeaks may require the replacement of the exhaust manifold pipe springs with dampers.

1997–2003 Cutlass and Malibu

These two front-drive, medium-sized sedans are slotted in between the Cavalier and Lumina in both size and price. They are boringly styled cars that use a more rigid body structure to cut down on noise and improve handling. Standard mechanicals include a 2.4L twin-cam 4-cylinder engine or an optional 3.1L V6. There's plenty of passenger and luggage space. Although headroom is tight, the Malibu can carry three rear passengers and gives much more legroom than either the Cavalier or Lumina. 1998 was the Cutlass' last model year, while its Malibu twin continues on.

Other points to consider: The base 4-cylinder is loud, handling isn't on par with the Japanese competition, there's lots of body lean in turns, outside mirrors are too small, there's no traction control, and the ignition switch is mounted on the dash (a throwback to your dad's Oldsmobile).

In addition to the generic front-drive problems listed previously, owners also report the following: early failure of the intake manifold gasket (see "Secret Warranties/Service Tips/TSBs"); fuel-injector deposits cause chronic stalling, poor idling, or hard starts; excessive vibration occurs at any speed; transmission doesn't lock when the key is in the accessory position; steering is very loose; backfires caused by defective computer modules; premature suspension strut failures (vehicle bottoms out with four or more passengers aboard); excessive AC noise; and the high-beam light switch fails intermittently.

Safety summary: All models/years: Airbag failed to deploy. • Sudden engine failure or overheating (faulty intake manifold). • Vehicle suddenly accelerating or stalling in traffic. • Brake failures. • Dash reflection in the windshield obstructs view. • Trunk lid may fall. • Improper headlight illumination. • Horn is difficult to activate due to the hand pressure required. **1995–97**—Seating design forces driver to sit too close to the fully powered airbag housing. • Frequent cruise control failures. • Inadequate braking. • Emergency brake doesn't work properly; it won't remain locked. • Ventilation system emitted fumes that made occupants ill. • Seat belt didn't restrain passenger sufficiently in an accident. • Inoperative rear seat buckles. • Rear seat belts are too short to secure a child seat or large person. • Rear seat belt design forces user to sit on buckles; they are too close to the seat and difficult to fasten. • Many reports that door locks continually engage and disengage while driving. • Power window motor failure. • Outside rear-view mirrors positioned too far back for a clear view. • Windshield wipers operate erratically. • Water collects in the headlight lenses, causing them to fog or malfunction. • Brake lights and tail lights aren't very durable. **1998**—Sudden acceleration; faulty fuel pressure regulator suspected. • Power seat puts occupant too close to airbag. • Headrest can't be raised high enough for someone over six feet tall. • Engine hesitates when accelerating. • Ignition coil failure also causes engine to stall and backfire. • Flexible hose line from fuel pump rests against sharp metal edge of the heat shield. • Trunk popped open while driving. **1998–99**—Automatic transmission and electrical system failures. **2000–01**—Sudden electrical shutdown. • Exhaust/gas fumes in the interior. • Automatic transmission failure. • Hard, noisy shifting. • Excessive vehicle vibration while underway. • Front control arm breakage. • Blurred windshield. • Tires mounted on aluminum wheels tend to leak air. • Vehicle wanders or floats on the highway. • Heater gives out insufficient heat. • Automatic trunk flies up and falls down on one's head. • Headlight switch overheats. **Bonneville: 2000–01**—Battery located in the back of the rear seat went bad, causing sulfuric acid fumes to escape into the passenger compartment, making passengers ill. • Weak spring design allowed trunk lid to fall on person's head, causing injury. • Automatic trunk lid flies up and then comes down on driver's head. **2002**—Premature engine mount failure causes excessive vibration. • Tilt steering locks. • Outside rear-view mirror vibration. • Loose head restraints. **2003**— Defogger was activated and fire ignited. • Fire erupted in the rear deck speaker. • The sun washes out gauge readings. **Impala: 2003**—Frequent complaints of dash area and engine compartment fires. • Front harness wires overheat; excessive current load from fuel pump may burn the ignition block wire terminal; inhalation injuries caused by the melting of the wiring harness plastic. • Electrically heated seat burned the driver's back. • The connection that goes to the brake pedal piston collapsed, causing total brake failure. • Chronic stalling; engine sputters, hesitates; Service Engine and battery lights come on (dealer unable to correct problem). • When traction control is activated, wheel slip computer is also activated and security system kills the engine and prevents it from being restarted. • Driver's side wheel fell off. • Vehicle jerks when passing over rough pavement. • Car rolls back at a stop. • Excessive steering wheel vibration. • Fuel sloshes in tank when accelerating or stopping. • Brake rotors had to be replaced at 7,500 km. • Left and right control arm, lower control arm, ball joint, and steering failure. • AC refrigerant leaks into car interior. • Driver's seat adjuster failed, causing seat to suddenly move backwards, causing loss of vehicle control. • The rubber seal on the windows, which sometimes acts as a squeegee when lowering and raising the window, has been replaced with a new design, which allows road salt to enter and short-circuit the window mechanism. • Front driver's side windshield wiper doesn't clean the windshield completely; poor design allows dirty windshield washer fluid to be deflected off the windshield and cuts the view out of the side windows. • A hazy film collects on the inside of all the windows (dealer says it's normal). **LeSabre: 2000–01**—Under-hood fire erupted as driver was parking car. • When the fuel tank is full, fuel leaks from the top. • False airbag deployment injured driver. • Airbag deployment when key inserted into the ignition. • Car stalled because fuel lines leaked. • Cruise control cable disconnects from cruise control module, jamming the accelerator cable to full throttle. • Accelerator cable popped out of its bracket, causing vehicle to go to full throttle. • Brake pedal went all the way to the floor due to missing brake shaft retainer clip. • When applying brakes, pedal becomes very hard, resulting in extended stopping distance. • Sudden steering loss. • Excessive highway wander. • Shoulder belt crosses at driver's neck. • Hard-to-read speedometer. • Difficulty seeing dashboard controls due to dash-top design. • ABS and service light come on for no reason. • Engine head gasket failure. • Intermittent windshield wiper failure. • Horn is hard to operate, unless driver balled her hand into a fist and pounded on it. • Water leaks into interior through the dash. • Headlight design creates a shadow, impeding visibility. **2003**—Engine intake manifold failure (see "Secret Warranties/Service Tips/TSBs"). • Engine surging while driving on the highway. • Brake pedal goes almost to the floor without stopping the vehicle. **Monte Carlo: 1995–2001**—Under-hood fires. • Airbag deployment caused driver's shirt to catch on fire. • Side airbag flap material falls off, leaving a large hole. • Side airbag falls out of its mounting. • Extremely poor wet traction. • Frequent loss of braking and premature rotor warpage and pad wearout. • Although GM TSB asks dealers to re-weld the subframe engine cradle, owners say the fix isn't effective. • Early fuel pump and water pump failures. • Vehicle rolls downhill when parked on an incline. • Dash gauges go haywire from chronic electrical shorts. • Check Engine, ABS, and airbag lights stay lit despite dealers' best troubleshooting attempts. • Shoulder belt crosses at neck and seat belts don't retract properly. • Horn is hard to access. **2002**—Fire ignited from overheated seat heater. • Sudden steering loss; excessive steering effort. • Vehicle rolls back on an incline. • Excessive brake pulsation. • Constant headlight flickering. **2003**—Engine cradle mounting welds came apart from the steering gear, and driver and passenger seat belts tighten up progressively to the point where they are extremely uncomfortable.

Secret Warranties/Service Tips/TSBs

Keep in mind that some of the following service bulletins may apply to more than one model and to subsequent model years. **All models: 1988–96**—Frequent reports of wind noise affecting the 1990–96 Cutlass, Grand Prix, and Regal and the 1988–94 Lumina have led to the publication of TSB #53-15-16, which outlines the causes of and remedies for persistent wind noise. **1991–97**—Bulletin #83-20-06 outlines procedures for fixing prematurely rusted door bottoms. **1993–2003**—AC-induced odours can be eliminated by using a coil coating kit. • A rotten-egg odour coming from the exhaust is probably caused by a malfunctioning catalytic converter (covered by the emissions warranty). • Paint delamination, peeling, or fading (see Part Two). **1995–2001**—Troubleshooting engine oil pan leaks. **1995–2003**—Two GM service bulletins confirm a pattern of engine intake manifold defects, which are covered by a 6-year/100,000 km secret warranty:

Engine Coolant – Consumption/Leak

Bulletin No.: 01-06-01-007A   Date: July 2001

Engine Coolant Consumption or Coolant Leak (Inspect For Material Degradation/Replace Intake Manifolds)

Models

1995–97 Buick Riviera
1995–98 Buick LeSabre, Park Avenue
1996–98 Buick Regal
1998 Chevrolet Lumina, Monte Carlo
1995–96 Oldsmobile Ninety-Eight
1995–98 Oldsmobile Eighty-Eight

➤

1998 Oldsmobile Intrigue
1995–98 Pontiac Bonneville
1997–98 Pontiac Grand Prix
with 3.8L Engine (VIN K - RPO L36)

Condition

Some owners may comment on excessive engine coolant consumption, or an engine coolant leak near or under the throttle body area of the upper intake manifold.

Cause

Upper intake manifold composite material may degrade around the EGR stove pipe and could result in an internal or external coolant leak.

Correction

Follow the upper intake manifold removal instructions found in the Engine Unit Repair Section of the Service Information Manual.

Here's the second and most recent "smoking gun" GM internal service bulletin admitting to poor-quality engine intake manifolds. Note that this defect has existed over eight model years and imagine how many owners have paid to fix this defect, which GM admits here *is clearly its own fault* (see following bulletin).

Engine Oil or Coolant Leak

Bulletin No.: 03-06-01-010A

Date: April 2003

Engine oil or coolant leak
(install new intake manifold gasket)

2000–2003 Buick Century
2002–03 Buick Rendezvous
1996 Chevrolet Lumina APV
1997–2003 Chevrolet Venture
1999–2001 Chevrolet Lumina
1999–2003 Chevrolet Malibu, Monte Carlo
2000–2003 Chevrolet Impala
1996–2003 Oldsmobile Silhouette
1999 Oldsmobile Cutlass
1999–2003 Oldsmobile Alero
1996–99 Pontiac Trans Sport
1999–2003 Pontiac Grand Am
2000–03 Pontiac Grand Prix, Montana
2001–03 Pontiac Aztek
with 3.1L or 3.4L V6 engine (VINs J, E - RPOs LGB, LA1)

Condition: Some owners may comment on an apparent oil or coolant leak. Additionally, the comments may range from spots on the driveway to having to add fluids.

Cause: Intake manifold may be leaking allowing coolant, oil or both to leak from the engine.

Correction: Install a new-design intake manifold gasket. The material used in the gasket has been changed in order to improve the sealing qualities of the gasket. When replacing the gasket, the intake manifold bolts must also be replaced and torqued to a revised specification The new bolts will come with a pre-applied threadlocker on them.

Faulty engine intake manifolds afflict GM, Ford, and Chrysler models and are generally fixed for free up to 7 years/160,000 km when copies of bulletins like the one above are attached to your work order. If you miss this free repair, you could cook your engine (see page 292 for bulletin on Ford engines).

Don't break out the champagne yet over GM's apparent recognition of its engine defect. This 2003 LeSabre owner says GM's intake manifold fix is no fix at all:

> I recently received a letter from GM stating that there may be a problem with coolant leaks around gaskets at the upper intake manifold or at the lower intake manifold which might "cause high engine temperatures." The letter says it is a "voluntary customer satisfaction program." The suggested fix is to take the vehicle in to the local dealer and have them change some of the fasteners and then "add cooling system sealant" to the radiator. It seems to me that putting cooling system sealant in a brand new car (and thus reducing the life of the radiator) is an unacceptable fix for a possible gasket problem. I would think that the company needs to replace the intake manifold gaskets instead, if they are the faulty part. However, when I called the number that GM supplied they said that they would not replace the gasket and that if we did not have the repair done as stated in their letter and the gasket subsequently failed after the warranty period was over, we would have to pay the full cost of the repairs.

1996—Second-gear starts; poor 1–3 shifting. • Steering column noise. • Air conditioning odours and diagnosis of AC noises. • Whistle noise from HVAC. • Diagnosis and correction of fluttering, popping, ticking, and clunking noises. • Popping noise from the front of the vehicle when turning. **1997**—AC flutter or moan. • Cold-start rattle. • Engine cranks but will not run. • Engine oil leak at oil pan sealing flange and rear of engine near flywheel cover. • Engine oil level indicates over-full. • Excessive vibration of electrochromic mirror. • High beams are intermittent. • Inoperative power door locks. • Intermittent Neutral/loss of Drive at highway speeds. • Instrument panel buzzes and rattles when the brakes are applied. • Popping or thump noise from the left rear of vehicle is normal, according to GM. • Transmission gear whine at 40–70 km/h. **1997–98**—A rough-running engine may be fixed by merely changing the plug wires. **1997–99**—A low-speed steering shudder or vibration may be corrected by replacing the steering pressure and return lines with revised "tuned" hoses. • Front disc pads have been upgraded to reduce brake squeal. • A shaking sensation at cruising speed may be fixed by replacing the transmission mount. **1997–2000**—Front disc brake pulsation will be corrected by installing upgraded pads and rotors, says TSB #00-05-23-002. • An automatic transmission oil leak can be fixed by installing an upgraded part:

A/T – Oil Leak From Vent

Bulletin No.: 01-07-30-032A   Date: January 2002
Subject: Transmission Oil Leaking From Transmission Vent (Replace Transmission Case Cover Gasket/Channel Plate Gasket With New Design Gasket)

➤

Models:

1997–99 Buick Riviera
1997–2001 Buick Park Avenue
1998–2001 Buick LeSabre
1999–2001 Buick Regal
2000–01 Buick Century
1997–2001 Chevrolet Lumina, Monte Carlo
1999–2001 Chevrolet Venture
2000–01 Chevrolet Impala
1997–99 Oldsmobile Eighty Eight
1998–2001 Oldsmobile Intrigue
1999–2001 Oldsmobile Silhouette
2001 Oldsmobile Aurora (with 3.5L Engine)
1997–2001 Pontiac Bonneville, Grand Prix
1999–2001 Pontiac Montana
With Hydra-Matic 4T65-E Automatic Transmission (RPOs MN3, MN7, M15, M76).

Automatic transmission leaks are a factory-related problem, says this TSB.

1998—A wet right rear floor signals the need to reseal the stationary glass area. • Engine runs rough. • Power-steering shudder and vibration. • Front suspension scrunch/pop. • Reducing AC odours. • Inaccurate speedometer. **1998–99**—Power-steering shudder/vibration may be fixed by replacing the pressure pipe/hose assembly. **1999–2000**—No Third and Fourth gear may mean the direct clutch piston assembly needs to be replaced. • An engine that runs hot, overheats, or loses coolant may only need an upgraded radiator cap (check this before authorizing any expensive repairs). **2000–01**—TSB #01-06-01-005 allows for free 3.1L engine piston replacement to cure an engine ticking noise. • Reduced AC performance; AC makes a tick-tock noise. • Eliminating an air vent whistling noise or a steering vibration, shudder, or moan. **2001**—Remedies for delayed automatic transmission shifts (see bulletin found in Century "Secret Warranties"). **2001–02**—Poor engine performance and erratic shifting. • Intermittent no-start. **Cutlass and Malibu: 1997–99**—Front disc brake pulsation will be corrected by installing upgraded pads and rotors, says TSB #00-05-23-002. **1997–2003**—Inoperative tail lights due to water intrusion. • Automatic transmission flaring. **1999–2002**—Troubleshooting tips for plugging water leaks into the trunk and interior. **2000–01**—Faulty fuel gauge. **2002**—Dash rattling correction. **2003**—Firm shifts, no downshifts, shudder.

Bonneville, Cutlass, Cutlass Supreme, Delta 88, Grand Prix, Impala, Intrigue, LeSabre, Lumina, Malibu, Monte Carlo, Regal Profile

	1996	1997	1998	1999	2000	2001	2002	2003
Cost Price ($)								
Bonneville	29,440	31,175	33,255	29,000	30,740	32,065	32,365	33,430
Cutlass Supreme	25,285	26,355	—	—	—	—	—	—
Delta 88 LSS	30,190	32,185	32,950	32,515	—	—	—	—
Grand Prix	23,940	26,305	26,035	27,489	28,050	28,110	28,050	28,277
Impala	30,675	—	—	—	24,595	24,490	24,875	26,020

Intrigue	—	—	27,998	27,994	28,365	28,450	28,365	—
LeSabre	29,560	32,370	33,100	28,845	30,465	32,120	32,960	33,720
Lumina	21,455	22,340	22,980	23,074	—	—	—	—
Malibu	—	19,995	20,595	20,895	22,050	22,495	22,760	22,980
Monte Carlo	23,625	24,275	24,895	24,715	26,090	26,165	26,525	27,620
Regal	25,035	27,795	28,410	27,695	29,120	28,895	29,080	29,980
Used Values ($)								
Bonneville ʌ	5,500	7,000	9,000	11,500	13,500	16,500	19,500	22,000
Bonneville v	4,000	6,000	7,500	10,000	12,500	15,000	18,000	21,000
Cutlass Supreme ʌ	4,500	5,500	—	—	—	—	—	—
Cutlass Supreme v	3,500	5,000	—	—	—	—	—	—
Delta 88 LSS ʌ	5,500	7,500	9,000	11,500	—	—	—	—
Delta 88 LSS v	4,500	6,000	8,000	10,500	—	—	—	—
Grand Prix ʌ	4,500	5,500	6,500	9,500	11,000	14,500	17,500	20,500
Grand Prix v	4,000	5,000	6,000	8,000	9,500	13,000	16,500	18,500
Impala ʌ	—	—	—	—	10,500	13,000	15,500	17,000
Impala v	—	—	—	—	9,000	12,000	14,000	16,000
Intrigue ʌ	—	—	7,500	9,500	11,500	14,000	16,500	—
Intrigue v	—	—	6,000	8,500	10,500	12,500	15,000	—
LeSabre ʌ	5,500	7,000	8,000	11,500	13,000	16,500	20,000	22,500
LeSabre v	5,000	6,000	7,000	10,000	12,000	15,000	18,500	21,000
Lumina ʌ	3,500	4,500	5,500	7,000	—	—	—	—
Lumina v	3,000	4,000	5,000	5,500	—	—	—	—
Malibu ʌ	—	4,000	5,000	6,000	8,500	10,000	12,000	14,500
Malibu v	—	3,000	4,000	4,500	7,000	8,500	10,500	13,000
Monte Carlo ʌ	4,000	5,500	7,000	8,500	11,000	13,000	16,000	18,000
Monte Carlo v	3,500	4,500	6,000	8,000	9,500	11,500	14,500	16,500
Regal ʌ	4,500	5,500	7,000	9,500	11,000	13,500	17,000	20,000
Regal v	4,000	5,000	5,500	8,500	9,500	12,500	15,500	18,500
Reliability	❷	❷	❷	③	③	③	③	③
Crash Safety								
Bonneville 4d	⑤	⑤	⑤	—	—	④	④	④
Cutlass 4d	—	—	—	④	④	—	—	—
Cutlass Supreme 2d	④	—	—	—	—	—	—	—
Delta 88 4d	④	—	—	—	—	—	—	—
Grand Prix 4d	—	④	—	—	—	④	④	④
Impala	—	—	—	—	⑤	⑤	⑤	⑤
Intrigue	—	—	④	④	④	—	—	—
LeSabre 4d	—	④	④	④	—	—	④	④
Lumina 4d	⑤	⑤	④	④	—	—	—	—
Malibu	—	④	④	④	—	④	④	④
Monte Carlo	④	④	—	—	—	⑤	⑤	④
Regal 2d	④	—	—	—	—	—	—	—
Regal 4d	—	—	—	④	—	④	④	④
Side								
Bonneville 4d	—	—	—	—	—	④	④	④
Grand Prix	—	—	—	—	—	—	—	❷
Impala	—	—	—	—	④	④	④	④
Intrigue	—	—	—	—	—	③	③	—

LeSabre 4d	—	—	③	③	④	④	④	④
Lumina	⑤	⑤	⑤	⑤	—	—	—	—
Malibu	—	❶	❶	❶	—	❷	④	④
Monte Carlo	④	④	—	—	—	③	③	③
Regal 4d	—	—	③	③	③	③	③	③
Head restraints								
Bonneville	—	❶	—	❶	⑤	⑤	⑤	⑤
Cutlass	—	❶	—	❶	—	—	—	—
Cutlass Sup.	—	❶	—	—	—	—	—	—
Grand Prix	—	—	—	—	—	—	—	③
Intrigue	—	—	—	❶	—	❶	❶	—
LeSabre 4d	—	❶	—	❶	⑤	⑤	⑤	⑤
Lumina	—	❶	—	❶	—	—	—	—
Malibu	—	❷	—	❷	—	❷	❷	❷
Monte Carlo	—	❶	—	❶	—	❷	❷	❷
Regal 4d	—	—	—	❶	—	❶	❶	❶
Offset								
Bonneville 4d	—	—	—	—	⑤	⑤	⑤	—
Cutlass 4d	—	③	③	③	—	—	—	—
Grand Prix 4d	—	③	③	③	③	③	③	④
Impala	—	—	—	—	—	—	—	④
Intrigue	—	—	③	③	③	③	③	—
LeSabre 4d	—	—	—	—	⑤	⑤	⑤	—
Lumina 4d	⑤	⑤	⑤	⑤	⑤	⑤	—	—
Monte Carlo	—	—	—	—	—	—	—	④
Malibu	—	③	③	③	③	③	③	③
Regal 4d	—	③	③	③	③	③	③	③
Rollover Resistance								
Lumina 4d	—	—	—	—	—	④	—	—
Impala	—	—	—	—	—	④	—	—

CENTURY, CIERA ★★★

RATING: Average (1998–2003); Below Average (1997); Not Recommended (1982–96). In the early years, the same failure-prone components were used year after year. The 1996 Century isn't in the same league as the revised 1997 version, which adopted the W-platform used by the Chevrolet Lumina, Pontiac Grand Prix, and 1998 Oldsmobile Intrigue. A 1996 Ciera is cheaper, but you won't have the important mechanical and body upgrades offered by its 1998 replacement, the '98 Oldsmobile Cutlass. The new Cutlass is an upgraded mid-sized sedan similar to the new Malibu (be careful not to confuse the new Cutlass with the Cutlass Supreme, a 10-year-old model that was replaced by the Intrigue, which is equipped like the Century). **Maintenance/Repair costs:** Higher than average, but repairs aren't dealer dependent. **Parts:** Higher-than-average cost (independent suppliers sell for much less), but not hard to find. Nevertheless, don't even think about buying one of these front-drives without a 3- to 5-year comprehensive warranty. **Best alternatives:** The Acura Integra; GM Cavalier or Sunfire (Sunbird); Honda

Accord; Hyundai Elantra wagon, Sonata, or Tiburon; Mazda 626 or Protegé; Nissan Sentra or Stanza; and Toyota Camry. **Online help:** Owner reports and service bulletins can be found at *www.autosafety.org/autodefects.html*, or you can use Google to search for GM paint delamination, engine piston slapping, or manifold defects.

Strengths and weaknesses: The Century and Ciera were always outclassed by the competition due to their lack of high-quality components and fresh styling. Nevertheless, these cars have always been popular with fleet buyers and car rental agencies because they were useful as comfortable family sedans and wagons. Handling and other aspects of road performance varied considerably depending on the suspension and powertrain chosen. But overall reliability remained a constant: abysmally poor.

The 1988–96 models are particularly unreliable. The 2.5L 4-cylinder engine suffers from engine-block cracking and a host of other serious defects. The 2.8L V6 engine hasn't been durable either; it suffers from premature camshaft wear and leaky gaskets and seals, especially the intake manifold gasket, a problem carried over to GM's entire 2003 model lineup (see "Secret Warranties/Service Tips/TSBs" on pages 226–228). The 3-speed automatic transmission is weak and the 4-speed automatic frequently malfunctions. Temperamental and expensive-to-replace fuel systems (including the in-tank fuel pump) afflict all models/years, causing chronic stalling, hard starting, and poor fuel economy (use the emissions warranty as leverage to get compensation). Fuel system diagnosis and repair for the 3.0L V6 are difficult, and the electronic controls are often defective. Air conditioners frequently malfunction and the cooling system is prone to leaks.

Prematurely worn power-steering assemblies are particularly commonplace. Brakes are weak and need frequent attention due to premature wear and dangerously rapid corrosion; front brake rotors warp easily; excessive pulsation is common; and rear brake drums often lock up, particularly when damp. Shock absorbers and springs wear out quickly. Rear wheel alignment should be checked often. Electric door locks frequently malfunction. Water leaks onto carpeting. Premature and extensive surface rust—due to poor paint application, delamination, and defective materials—is common for all years. Far more disturbing are scattered reports of severe undercarriage/suspension rusting, possibly making the vehicles unsafe to drive—and costing lots of money to correct, as the owner of a 1990 Century relates:

> Recently I was doing an oil change on my car and I noticed a small divot in the engine cradle (or subframe). I poked at it and put my finger right through it! I discovered that the cradle was rotted on both sides near the idler arm. The car is only eight years old and has only 112,000 km on it. I have had it into two collision repair places and they both said they have never seen a rotted engine cradle. One man has been in the business 25 years!

Vehicle history: 1982–96—Early 125–150-hp V6 engines replaced by a 3.3L V6 in 1989. A failure-prone 4.3L diesel engine was carried from 1982–85 (beware!). A 3.1L V6 came on the scene in 1994 along with a driver-side airbag and ABS. **1997**—Given a complete make-over that included the following: a spunkier 160-hp 3.1L V6 engine; gobs of room and trunk space (rivalling that of the Taurus, Concorde, Accord, and Camry); sleeker styling; a much quieter interior; and an upgraded, standard ABS system that produces less pedal pulsation. Engine noise was also reduced, although insufficient firewall insulation means a considerable amount of noise still gets into the interior. Other new features included upgraded door seals, steering-wheel-mounted radio controls, and additional heating ducts for rear passengers. **1998**—Reduced-force airbags. **1999**— Adoption of a revised ABS system, better traction control, and an enhanced suspension to reduce body roll. **2000**—Given a small horsepower boost to 175. **2003**—Given a minor facelift and a freshened interior.

On the downside, the post-'96 Century's engine intake manifolds have a short lifespan (covered by a 6-year/100,000 km warranty), the speed-dependent power steering is too light and vague, and its suspension and handling are more tuned to comfort than performance. The front air deflector shield has also been the object of many complaints. Its low placement causes the shield to hit the roadway whenever passing over a small dip or bump. Furthermore, the bumper pulls off when passing over parking blocks.

Overall reliability has improved a bit since the 1997 model changeover glitches were corrected. However, powertrain breakdowns are still commonplace and fit and finish remain subpar, particularly when compared with the Japanese competition.

The 2000–03 models aren't much improved. They continue to have premature engine head gasket failures, "piston slap" noise, early transmission breakdowns, electrical system and computer module malfunctions, and front and rear brakes that rust easily, wear out early, with discs that warp far too often. Shock absorbers and MacPherson struts wear out or leak prematurely. The power rack-and-pinion steering system degenerates quickly after three years and is characterized by chronic leaking. Poor body fit, particularly around the doors, leads to excessive wind noise and water leaks into the interior. Door locks also freeze up easily.

Safety summary: All models/years—Vehicle suddenly accelerates on its own. • Horn buttons difficult to access and depress due to their small size; must take eyes off the road. • Dash reflection in windshield causes poor visibility. • Headlights provide poor visibility. • Head restraints won't stay in the raised position. **1996**—Cruise control speed increases upon descending a hill. • Sudden brake loss. • Chronic stalling. • Oxygen sensor failures believed to be cause of stalling problems. • Steering radius is too large, and steering response is sluggish. • Cannot read clock in daylight. • Airbag assembly on steering wheel blocks view of instrument panel. • Back windows often shatter. • Fuel pump failures. • Transmission failures. • Gearshift lever fell off in driver's hand. • Front door power motors failed. **1997**—Sudden brake loss. • Car moved forward when put into Reverse. • Battery exploded twice. • Poor design of magnetic variable steering results in difficult handling, with vehicle swaying at 60 km/h, and struts contributing to instability. • Sway bar links failure. • Fuel tank warning system activates prematurely. • Defroster system button breaks easily. • Windshield wipers fail frequently. • Defective airbag cover. • Power door lock failures. • Driver's seat belt won't fully retract. **1998**—Idle surge after releasing brake due to faulty oxygen sensor. • Leaking lower intake manifold. • Engine oil pan leakage. • Chronic stalling. • Transmission shifts erratically. • Transmission hard to put into Reverse; faulty gearshift lever. • Sudden loss of electrical power. • Climate control switch failures. • Excessive brake vibrations. • Headlight switch failure. • Windshield wiper arm failures. • Water leaks into trunk. • Horn blows on its own when car is not running. **1999**—Engine fire upon start-up. • Chronic engine hesitation when accelerating or changing gears. • Cruise control failed to disengage. • Premature transmission failure: won't go into Reverse; shift lever hangs up; Drive gear won't hold vehicle when stopped on an incline. • Seat belt trapped child around waist; had to be cut free. • Front right window suddenly exploded. • Tire jack won't hold vehicle's weight. **2000**—Engine replaced twice. • Transmission has a tendency to shift often, whether it's necessary or not. • Engine produces a metallic noise. • If vehicle is driven with the windows down, there is a loud, shaking noise and the vehicle vibrates violently. • Steering wheel heats up when the radio and headlights are on. • Driver's seat leans to the side. • Large head restraints block vision. • Low beams don't illuminate the highway adequately; the light spreads only to the side end of the front fender, resulting in poor visibility. • Air scoop/spoiler hits or scrapes the ground. • If vehicle is parked on uneven ground, the doors stick due to body flexing. • Driver-side window suddenly exploded, as from decompression, while underway. • Wipers can't be aligned. **2001**—Brakes failed. • Transmission won't hold vehicle parked on an incline. • Cannot drive car with rear windows down due to the air pressure hurting eardrum. **2002**—Sun visors are hard to use. • Gas pedal may be mounted too low for some drivers. • Key has to be jiggled in ignition to start car. • Reverse and tag lights fail due to frayed wiring at trunk hinge. **2003**—Sudden brake failure. • Car rolls backward when stopped in gear on an incline. • Passenger-side windshield wiper channels water directly in the line of vision on the upstroke, temporarily blocking driver's vision. • Vent behind shifter handle becomes very hot when heater is on. • Gear shift lever continually sticks. • Water leaks onto the interior carpet. • Air dam deflector on the front of the vehicle is mounted too low and hits the road on dips.

Secret Warranties/Service Tips/TSBs

All models/years—An upgraded low level fuel sensor will fix a fluctuating fuel gauge that bedevils GM's entire car lineup; it's an expensive repair that's covered by a GM "goodwill" warranty, if you insist. **1992–97**—Troubleshooting a grinding or growling noise that occurs when vehicle is parked on an incline.

1993–2003—A rotten-egg odour coming from the exhaust is probably the result of a malfunctioning catalytic converter; replacement cost may be covered by the emissions warranty. • Eliminate AC odours by installing an evaporator cooling-coil coating kit. • Paint delamination, peeling, or fading (see Part Two). **1995–97**—Intermittent Neutral/loss of Drive at highway speeds can be fixed by replacing the control valve body assembly. **2001**—Delayed automatic transmission shifting (see following bulletin).

A/T – 4T65E, Delayed Shifts/Flares/Extended Shifts

Bulletin No.: 01-07-30-014 Date: April 2001
Technical
Subject: 4T65-E Transmission Delayed Shifts, Slips, Flares or Extended Shifts During Cold Operation (Replace Shift Solenoid Valve Assembly)

Models:
2001 Buick Century, LeSabre, Park Avenue, Regal
2001 Chevrolet Impala, Lumina, Monte Carlo, Venture
2001 Oldsmobile Aurora, Intrigue, Silhouette
2001 Pontiac Aztek, Bonneville, Grand Prix, Montana
with 4T65-E Automatic Transmission (RPOs MN3, MN7, M76, M15)

Condition:
Some owners may comment on one of several delayed shifts, slips, flares or extended shifts during cold operation. These symptoms can affect the 1–2 shift only. The transmission won't shift out of First gear until the temperature is high enough to unstick the solenoid. This condition can last up to several shift patterns. These symptoms can return after the vehicle sits, usually six hours or more.

Century: 1994–98—A cold engine tick or rattle heard shortly after start-up may be fixed by replacing the piston/pin assembly. **1997–99**—A low-speed steering shudder or vibration may be corrected by replacing the steering pressure and return lines with revised "tuned" hoses. • Front disc pads have been upgraded to reduce brake squeal. • A shaking sensation at cruising speed may be fixed by replacing the transmission mount. • TSB #00-03-06-001 gives a comprehensive listing of common front-end noises and what's needed to silence them. • Install a new steering wheel inflatable restraint module to make it easier to sound the horn. **1997–2001**—Binding automatic transmission shift lever (see following bulletin).

A/T – Difficult Shift Lever Operation

Bulletin No.: 01-07-30-017   Date: April 2001
Technical
Subject: Transmission Shift Lever is Difficult to Move
(Replace Shift Lever)

Models:
1997–2001 Buick Century   ➤

> **Condition:**
> Some owners may comment that the transmission range selector lever is difficult to move/shift.
>
> **Cause:**
> The original shift lever may not impart enough mechanical advantage on the shift linkage to provide low enough effort when shifting gears.

1998—A wet right rear floor signals the need to reseal the stationary glass area. **1998–99**—Poor AM reception on vehicles with a windshield-mounted antenna may be improved by installing an in-line antenna jumper. **1999–2000**—Simply changing the radiator cap may cure your hot-running engine and prevent coolant loss. **2000–01**—GM's TSB says the best way to eliminate an engine ticking noise is to replace the engine's pistons (covered by a secret warranty, of course). **2000–02**—Exhaust system ping, snap. • Poor transmission performance. • No-start remedy. **2003**—Firm shifts, no downshifts, shudder.

Century, Ciera Profile

	1996	1997	1998	1999	2000	2001	2002	2003
Cost Price ($)								
Century	23,820	24,545	25,215	25,199	25,570	25,200	25,325	25,820
Ciera S/SL	23,625	—	—	—	—	—	—	—
Used Values ($)								
Century ∧	4,500	5,500	7,000	9,500	11,500	13,000	15,000	17,000
Century ∨	3,500	4,500	6,000	8,500	10,000	11,500	13,500	15,500
Ciera S/SL ∧	3,500	—	—	—	—	—	—	—
Ciera S/SL ∨	3,000	—	—	—	—	—	—	—
Reliability	❷	❷	❷	❷	③	③	③	③
Crash Safety								
Century 4d	④	④	④	—	—	④	④	④
Side (Century 4d)	—	—	—	—	③	③	③	③
Offset	—	③	③	③	③	③	③	④
Head Restraints (F)	—	❶	—	❶	—	❷	❷	❶
Rear	—	—	—	—	—	❶	❶	❶

Note: 1995 Ciera earned a four-star frontal crashworthiness rating.

Honda

ACCORD   ★★★★

RATING: Above Average (2003, 1990–99); Recommended (2000–02); Average (1985–89). With the 16-valve 4-cylinder engine or V6, the Accord is one of the most versatile compacts you can find. Think of it as a better-performing

Toyota Camry, with similar high-quality components and powertrain defects covered by extended warranties. Consequently, the 2003 model has been down-rated due to its redesign glitches. These include the powertrain problems already noted, and numerous reports of sudden acceleration and stalling, brake failures, and airbag malfunctions that cause the devices to go off when they shouldn't and not deploy when they should. **Maintenance/Repair costs:** Lower than average. Repairs aren't dealer dependent. **Parts:** Higher-than-average cost, but they can easily be found for much less from independent suppliers. **Best alternatives:** The Acura Integra; Hyundai Elantra wagon, Sonata, or Tiburon; Mazda 626; and Toyota Camry. **Online help:** Owner complaints and service bulletins can be found at *www.autosafety.org/autodefects.html* and helpful owner forums can be found at *www.kbb.com*; *www.edmunds.com*; *www.carforums.com/forums*; and *www.cartrackers.com/Forums*.

Strengths and weaknesses: Fast and nimble without a V6, this is the mid-sized sedan of choice for drivers who want maximum fuel economy and comfort along with lots of space for grocery hauling and occasional highway cruising. With the optional V6, the Accord is one of the most versatile mid-sized cars you can find. It offers something for everyone, and its top-drawer quality and high resale value mean there's no way you can lose money buying one.

The Accord doesn't really excel in any particular area; it's just very, very good at everything. It's smooth, quiet, mannerly, and competent, with outstanding fit and finish, inside and out. Other strong points: comfort, ergonomics, impressive assembly quality, reliability, and driveability. Some of its weak points: insufficient torque with the base engine on early models makes for constant highway downshifting; the automatic transmission tends to shift harshly and slowly (covered by a "goodwill" warranty); rear passenger room is tight; and the aforementioned safety-related complaints reported to NHTSA.

Despite all the foregoing praise, this hasn't always been a great car. During the '80s, Accords were beset with severe premature rusting, frequent engine camshaft and crankshaft failures, and severe front brake problems. Engines leaked or burned oil and blew their cylinder head gaskets easily, and carbureted models suffered from driveability problems through 1986.

If left untreated, rust perforations develop unusually quickly. Especially vulnerable spots are front fender seams; door bottoms; and areas surrounding side-view mirrors, door handles, rocker panels, wheel openings, windshield posts, front cowls, and trunk and hatchback lids.

Vehicle history: 1990–93—More room and additional power through a new and quieter 2.2L 4-cylinder engine. Rear seating space remains inadequate, the added weight saps the car's performance, and the automatic transmission shifts harshly at times. Owners report prematurely worn automatic transmissions, constant velocity joints, and power-steering assemblies, and numerous air and water leaks. **1994**—Redesign adds dual airbags, increases interior room and boosts 4-cylinder horsepower from 125–130 to 145. **1995**—Addition of a 175-hp 2.7L V6. The automatic transmission still works poorly with the 4-cylinder, producing acceleration times that are far from impressive, and owners still complain of excessive road noise and tire whine. Nevertheless, no significant reliability problems have been reported with that redesign. **1996**—Slightly restyled, the trunk opening was enlarged, and a rear-seat pass-through feature increased cargo space. **1998**—Substantially reworked, with more powerful engines (150–200 hp), including a new 200-hp 3.0L V6, a more refined suspension and automatic transaxle, upgraded ABS, additional interior space, and more glass; wagon version dropped. **1999**—ABS on the LX. **2000**—Side airbags with all V6-equipped models. **2001**—A restyled exterior, dual side airbags, V6 traction control, and improved sound-proofing. **2003**—This larger, totally restyled model offers a V6 and 6-speed manual tranny combo, increased 4-cylinder and V6 horsepower (160 and 240, respectively), and increased fuel economy.

Confidential technical service bulletins show that the 1994–97 models are susceptible to AC malfunctions, engine oil leaks, Check Engine light coming on for no reason, transmission glitches, power-steering pump leaks, windows falling off their channels, and numerous air and water leaks. Usually, these problems are simple to repair and Honda customer relations staff are helpful; however, Honda staffers and dealers are reluctant to admit their mistakes and may be getting a bit too arrogant in their dealings with the public. Witness the company's failure to publicly disclose its 1994–97 engine oil leak problems which have now been extended to include the 2002 Accord and 2003 Odyssey.

Bulletins and owner complaints relating to the reworked 1998–2000 models show a surprisingly large number of factory-related powertrain and body defects, undoubtedly due to the Accord's redesign. Some of those deficiencies, affecting both safety and performance: chronic lurching, hesitation, and stalling while on the highway, accompanied by the Check Engine light coming on; hard starting; frequent transmission failures; poor tracking that allows vehicle to wander; defective rear-computerized motor mounts; electrical shorts; coolant and brake master cylinder leakage; ABS and AC failures; and poor radio reception.

Body and accessory problems for these same model years include a plethora of squeaks, creaks, groans, and rattles; wind noise; water leaks; fuel gauge defects; paint chipping, bubbling, and peeling on hood, trunk, and roof (Honda blames it on bird droppings); leaky sunroof; windshield with vertical lines of distortion; driver-side mirror that shakes excessively; faulty fuel sending unit makes for inaccurate fuel readings (when full, indicates three-fourths full); speedometer off by 10 percent.

Owners of 2001 and 2002 models report that sudden, unintended acceleration remains a serious problem and can occur at any time, as the owner of this 2001 Accord relates:

> While taking the car through a car wash, vehicle accelerated and ran
> into two other cars and through a fence.

Other performance-related problems include automatic transmission break-downs, expensive and frequent servicing of the brake rotors and pads, and electrical glitches.

The 2003 redesign has made a bad situation, with over 200 safety-related complaints registered by NHTSA, when a quarter of that number would be normal. Sadder still, Honda promised us better-performing, more durable transmissions in its redesigned 2003s. The company lied (fortunately, an extended warranty now covers tranny breakdowns up to eight years).

Other problems related to this last redesign: a "rotten-egg" smell in the cabin; coolant in the engine oil pan; frequent hard starts; transmission shifts erratically; brake shuddering, grinding, and squealing; warped brake rotors; a popping noise when accelerating; a hole in the AC condenser; defective CD changer; stereo speaker hum; the windshield creaks in cold, dry weather; the moon roof doesn't close all the way; non-stop rattling; windows rattle and tick; wrinkled, bubbling, door window moulding; roof water leaks; and the headliner sags in the rear.

The aforementioned increase in engine, transmission, and brake failures is worrisome. Nevertheless, CAA surveys have shown that customer satisfaction is an impressive 88 percent, compared to 85 percent for both the Toyota Camry and Mazda 626. Keep in mind that Honda puts a "goodwill" clause in almost all of its service bulletins, allowing service managers to submit any claim to the company long after the original warranty period has elapsed.

Safety summary: All models/years: Sudden acceleration, stalling. • Airbags fail to deploy or deploy for no reason. • Check Engine light is always on. • Excessive windshield glare. • AC failure. • Premature front/rear brake wear. • Gas and brake pedals are too close together and often get pressed at the same time. • Faulty power windows. • Seat belt continually ratchets tighter. **1995–96**—Brake failures/lock-up. • Injury from airbag. • Passenger-side seatbacks won't stay upright. **1996**—Front passenger seat belt locks up. • Faulty power door locks. • The steering column separates from the shaft. **1997**—Fire caused by faulty wiring harness. • Cruise control doesn't accelerate properly and won't downshift the transmission. • Transmission shifted into Reverse and vehicle moved forward. • ABS brakes lock up. • Sudden brake failure. • Location of the oil filter allows oil to leak onto the exhaust system and catalytic converter. • Faulty brake master cylinder. • All four front brake pads cracked right down the centre. • Power-steering fluid leakage. • Oil plug fell off into the oil pan and sprayed oil everywhere. • Left side seat belt fails to retract. • Seat belt tightened and locked up; occupant had to cut belt. • When sun visor is opened, it blocks driver's vision due to its large size. • Defroster fails to defrost side windows, and actually causes them to fog up. • Door continually out of adjustment. **1998**—Defective rear computerized motor mounts on '98 and '99 models. • ABS brake light comes on continually. • Frequent brake failures. • Sudden brake lock-up. • Brake master cylinder failures. • Floormat bunches under the brake pedal. • Engine oil leakage. • Power-steering fluid leakage, causing sudden loss of steering control. • Vehicle rolled back when parked. • Automatic transmission gears disengage and make a loud noise when engaging. • Transmission fails to engage at slow speeds. • Transmission fails to fully lock up in Overdrive. • Transmission hunts for the right gear. • Clutch pedal failure. • Automatic transmission parking mechanism failure. • Due to design of dashboard lights, it's hard to read odometer, digital clock, and radio indicator. • Can't see high beam indicator light in the daytime. • Light tan dash reflects too much sunlight into the eyes. • Instrument panel lights are too bright at night and can't be dimmed enough. • To activate horn, driver must remove hand from steering wheel. • Fuel gauge shows two-thirds full when the gas tank is full, or indicates an empty tank with warning light on while 19 L (5 gal.) remain in the tank. • Poor seat belt design allows for belt to wrap around the release lever and get stuck, or causes seatback to suddenly recline. • Seat belts get trapped underneath the seatback electric switch. • Rear passenger-side door won't unlock. • Sunroofs and headliners often need replacing. **1999–2000**—Airbag deployment caused extensive neck and head injuries. • Sudden brake loss. • Emergency brakes failed to hold on hill, allowing car to roll into lake. • Brake master cylinder leakage. • Driver's seatback suddenly fell back. • Steering knuckle broke while driving. • Bolt that holds the lower control arm assembly broke away from the frame, causing wheel to come out of fender. • Many complaints of chronic lurching, hesitation, and stalling while on the highway, accompanied by Check Engine light coming on (dealers say they can't duplicate the problem). • Sudden tire tread failures (Michelin MXV4). • Engine sputters at half throttle. • Hard starting. • Frequent transmission failures. • Vehicle doesn't track well; wanders all over the road. • Engine mount makes a clunking sound. • Exhaust pipe runs under oil pan plug, causing dripped oil to burn off exhaust. • Seat belts fail to retract or continually tighten up, choking occupant. • Right front passenger window exploded while driving. • Windshield has vertical lines of distortion. • Driver-side mirror shakes excessively. **2001**—Excessive front-end vibration and wandering over the highway. • Automatic transmission leaks and jerks into gear. • Rear stabilizer bar links broke. • Vehicle rolls back when stopped on an incline. • Complete brake loss. Check Engine and airbag lights remain lit. • Incorrect fuel gauge readings. • The front windshield has a UV protective coating that gives the windshield a wavy appearance. **2002**—Car suddenly shuts down in traffic due to a defective Immobilizer system. • Automatic transmission failures. • Seat belt wouldn't retract or continually tightens; child had to be cut free. • Child safety seat can't be installed because buckle latch is located too far into the seat. • Partial brake failure, brakes fail to "catch" at first, then suddenly grab. • Vehicle pulls sharply when braking. • Electrical short caused CD player overheating and battery sparking. • Trunk lid may suddenly fall. **2003**—Sudden, unintended acceleration while car is in motion or when put into Reverse. • Axle suddenly snapped. • Front and side curtain airbags deployed for no reason. • Severe pulling to the right. • Power steering groan believe to be caused by the steering pump. • Console overheats and smells burnt. • Keys overheat in the ignition. • Complete brake failure. • ABS and traction control lights stay lit and corrective parts aren't easily found. • Frequent Michelin tire blowouts. • Rear vision is obstructed by head restraints, high rear deck, and roof pillar.

Secret Warranties/Service Tips/TSBs

All models/years: Steering wheel shimmy is a frequent problem, and is taken care of in TSB #94-025. **All models: 1994–97**—Poor radio reception may be caused by a corroded coaxial connector. • If the AC doesn't blow cold air, consider replacing both the evaporator and the receiver/dryer. • Oil seepage from the engine block requires sealing and the installation of a new exhaust manifold bracket. • Acura CL and Honda Accord, Prelude, and Odyssey models equipped with 4-cylinder engines may have defective engine oil seals that can slip, causing the engine to drain of oil and eventually seize. • Power-steering pump fluid leakage requires a new o-ring. **1995–96**—A creaking noise coming from the instrument panel can be silenced through a variety of measures outlined in a series of Honda bulletins. • Seat belt is slow to retract. **1997**—AC won't blow cold air. • Torque converter won't lock up. • Fifth gear grinds during upshift. • Leak from the power-steering pump. • Rear wheel bearing noise. • Front door glass comes out of run channel. **1998**—Trunk spoiler damages paint. • Creak from the rear shelf area, headliner, windshield, and rear window. • Front ABS wheel sensor harness rubs against wheel. • Rattle from rear stabilizer bar. • If the brake system indicator stays on, install an improved master cylinder reservoir cap float. • An inaccurate fuel gauge must be replaced with an upgraded unit. • Tips on eliminating wind noise from the top of the front windshield and a creaking noise from the rear shelf, headliner and windshield area. • Coolant leakage from the radiator drain plug may require the replacement of the drain plug/o-ring assembly. • Rear door water leaks may be plugged simply by removing excess weather stripping. **1998–99**—A clutch pedal squeak or groan is likely due to insufficient lubrication of the piston cup seal. • Noisy rear wheel bearings are covered by a "goodwill" replacement program (see following bulletin).

Noisy Rear Wheel Bearings

99-040   August 3, 1999

Applies To

1998–99 Accord

SYMPTOM

A growling or whining noise from the rear wheel bearings. The pitch changes with vehicle speed and is not affected by road surface conditions.

PROBABLE CAUSE

Water contamination in the rear hub bearing assemblies.

CORRECTIVE ACTION

Replace both rear hub bearing assemblies and spindle nuts.

WARRANTY CLAIM INFO

Failed part: #42200-S87-A51; #H/C 5436852

Out of warranty

Any repair performed after warranty expiration may be eligible for goodwill consideration by the District Service Manager or your Zone Office. You must request consideration, and get a decision, before starting work.

Pay particular attention to Honda's "goodwill" guidelines, found in almost every internal service bulletin used in Canada and in the United States. Don't let the dealer or Honda tell you that "goodwill" is applied only to American-sold vehicles. They'll never win that kind of argument in small claims court.

1998–2000—Manual transmission bangs in Reverse. • Warped, deformed windshield moulding. **1998–2001**—Tips on silencing a moon roof squeak (eligible for "goodwill" consideration). **1998–2002**—V6 engine oil leaks (an extension of a problem first noticed on 1994–97 models). • Deformed windshield moulding.

V6 Engine Oil Leaks

Bulletin No.: 01-009

Date: September 10, 2002

1998–02 Accord V6
*1999–2003 Odyssey
*2003 Pilot
SYMPTOM: An oil leak from the front, middle, or rear of the engine.

PROBABLE CAUSE: The cast aluminum engine block may be porous at the front, middle, or rear.

CORRECTIVE ACTION: Depending on the location of the leak, seal it with JB Weld or with 3-Bond-coated sealing bolts.

1999—Wrinkled rear door sash trim. • Glove box door rattles, wheels clicking, and clutch pedal and rear wheel bearing noise. • Loose AC, heater, temperature, and fan control knobs. • Inaccurate fuel gauge. **1999–2000**—Engine hard starts. • Coolant leaks from the water passage near the EGR valve. • PCM computer module needs to be recalibrated under warranty to prevent MIL (malfunction indicator light) from coming on for no reason. • TSB #00-038 says a transmission shudder or judder will be fixed for free under a "goodwill" program. **1999–2003**—Automatic transmission malfunctions and failures will be fixed or replaced under a more recent and comprehensive "goodwill" extended warranty program (see Part Two). **2001**— Windshield hum or whine. • Cracked, damaged foglight lens. • The horn plate bolts on the driver's airbag may not have been properly torqued and could cause a rattle in the steering wheel. **2003**—"Goodwill" campaigns to replace automatic transmissions and MICU units that regulate door locks, trunk alarm, etc. • Corrective action for coolant leakage into the engine oil pan; oil leaks at the cylinder head cover. • A faulty air intake air breather pipe hose may cause the engine warning light to remain lit. Its replacement is covered by a special Honda Product Update Campaign. • Engine clicking or ticking at idle. • Automatic transmission won't go into Reverse ("goodwill" campaign).

Product Update Campaign – A/T No-Reverse condition

Bulletin No.: 03-042

Date: July 31, 2003

Product Update: No-Reverse condition

BACKGROUND: If a vehicle is stuck in snow and the transmission is shifted several times between a Forward drive gear and Reverse (at wheel speeds above 12 mph [19 km/h]), a no-Reverse condition can develop.

• Automatic transmission leaks on the cooler lines. • Hard starts. • Troubleshooting calipers, rotors, and pads, following complaints of excessive brake vibration (wait a minute, weren't these the same chronic problems present before Honda's much-vaunted 2003 brake upgrade?):

> My 2003 Accord has been in the Honda dealer with problems with the front brakes (warped rotors). After having the front rotors resurfaced and pads replaced twice it was found that the front calipers were hanging up. My car just turned 17,000 miles [27,200 km] and it has had problems with the front brakes since it had 8,000 miles [12,800 km], at that time I was told by the dealer that I was "riding" my brakes and they would only take care of this problem for me at no cost just this "one time." I feel Honda is knows that 2003 Accords have brake problems and Honda puts the blame on everyone else except themselves. My vehicle has now been in the Honda dealer for two weeks because they are unable to locate new calipers. From talking with other 2003 Accord owners and reading information on other websites, [I know] I'm not alone with this problem.

• Troubleshooting ABS brake light illumination. • Inaccurate gauges and odometer. • Vehicle pulls to the right:

Steering/Suspension – Vehicle Pulls to the Right

Bulletin No.: 03-036

Date: July 1, 2003

2003 Accord

SYMPTOM: The vehicle drifts to the right at highway speeds.

PROBABLE CAUSE: The camber settings are uneven.

CORRECTIVE ACTION: Shift the front subframe to the right.

Out of warranty: Any repair performed after warranty expiration may be eligible for goodwill consideration by the District Parts and Service Manager or your Zone Office. You must request consideration, and get a decision, before starting work.

• Excessive steering vibration. • Noisy power steering countermeasures. • Investigating owner reports of cracked windshields. • Doors don't unlock in cold weather. • Poor AC cooling. • Rear shelf rattling. • Dash or pillar creaking or clicking. • Roof water leak fix. • Roof moulding channel leaks water. • Wrinkled door window molding. • Remedies for front brake noise or judder when braking. **2003–04**—Remedies for a sulfur smell in the interior.

Accord Profile

	1996	1997	1998	1999	2000	2001	2002	2003
Cost Price ($)								
LX	20,295	20,995	23,800	23,800	23,000	22,800	23,000	25,000
EXi/EX	22,995	23,495	26,800	26,801	31,300	30,800	31,100	32,500
Used Values ($)								
LX ∧	7,500	9,000	10,500	12,500	14,000	15,500	17,500	20,000
LX ∨	6,000	8,000	9,500	11,000	13,000	14,000	16,000	18,500
EXi/EX ∧	8,500	9,500	12,000	14,500	16,500	21,500	24,500	27,500
EXi/EX ∨	8,000	8,500	10,500	13,000	15,000	20,000	22,500	26,000
Reliability	④	④	④	④	④	⑤	⑤	⑤
Crash Safety (2d)	—	④	④	④	—	⑤	⑤	⑤
4d	④	④	④	④	⑤	⑤	⑤	—
Side (2d)	—	—	③	③	④	③	⑤	—
4d	❷	④	④	④	④	④	⑤	—
Offset	③	③	③	③	③	③	⑤	—
Head Restraints (F)	❷	③	③	—	③	③	④	—
Rear	❶	❷	❷	—	❷	②	③	—
Rollover Resistance	—	—	—	—	⑤	⑤	⑤	—

Hyundai

SONATA	★★★★

RATING: Above Average (1999–2003); Average (1995–98); Not Recommended (1986–93). The 1994 model year was skipped. These cars haven't registered one-tenth the number of safety complaints as the higher-rated Honda Accord. For maximum savings, I suggest you buy a 1999–2003 version, with some of the original warranty left, plan to keep it at least five years to shake off the depreciation, and put some of the savings on the purchase price into a comprehensive supplementary warranty to protect yourself when the warranty ends. **Maintenance/Repair costs:** Higher than average. Repairs aren't dealer dependent. **Parts:** Higher-than-average cost, and often back ordered. **Best alternatives:** The Acura Integra, GM Cavalier or Sunfire, Honda Accord, Hyundai Elantra wagon or Tiburon, Mazda 626, and Toyota Camry. **Online help:** For the latest owner reports, service bulletins, and money-saving tips, look at *www.autosafety.org/autodefects.html*; *www.kbb.com*; *www.edmunds.com*; *www.carforums.com/forums*; and *www.cartrackers.com/Forums*.

Strengths and weaknesses: This mid-sized front-drive sedan was built under Mitsubishi licensing, but its overall reliability isn't anywhere near as good as what you'll find with Mitsubishi's cars and trucks sold in Canada under the Chrysler and Eagle monikers. Acceleration is impressive with the manual gearbox, but only passable with the automatic. Handling and performance are also fairly good, although emergency handling isn't confidence inspiring, particularly due to the imprecise steering and excessive lean when cornering. As with other Hyundai models, the automatic transmission performs erratically, the engine is noisy, and reliability is a problem—it's way below average for the 1989–93 models; the 1995–98 models are moderately improved (remember, Hyundai skipped the 1994s).

Vehicle history: 1995—Redesigned for additional interior room, more horsepower, and an upgraded automatic transmission. Nevertheless, acceleration with the automatic is still below average with the 4-banger, and the automatic gearbox downshifts slowly. (The manual transmission is still more reliable and fuel efficient.) **1996**—More standard features, like air conditioning, power steering, a split folding rear seatback, liquid-filled engine mounts, and additional soundproofing. **1999**—Arrived with a redesigned body and suspension, side airbags, two new engines, and a huge price increase that's not reflected in its low resale value. **2000**—Side airbags and larger wheels. **2001**—A new grille and additional standard features of minor importance.

Throughout the Sonata's history, Hyundai technical service bulletins are replete with references to automatic transmissions that exhibit what Hyundai describes as "shift shock," as well as delayed shifting. In addition to the tranny problems, owners of pre-1995 models report poor engine performance (hard starting, poor idling, stalling); the engine runs hot, and when you're stopped at a traffic light, it shakes like a boiling kettle; #3 spark plug often needs replacing or cleaning; rough engine rattle; high oil consumption (1L every two to three months); excessive front brake pulsation and premature wear; steering defects (when the steering wheel is turned to either extreme, it makes a sound like metal cracking); cruise control malfunctions and electrical short circuits; battery life of only 18 months; malfunctioning lights; radio failures; falling interior roof liner; faulty hood locks; rotten-egg smell coming from the catalytic converter; broken muffler; faulty resonator; defective exhaust pipe; poor door and window sealing (water leaking into the interior when the car is washed); and premature paint peeling and rusting.

The 1995–2003 Sonatas have elicited very few quality-control and safety complaints and represent the better buys in this group, following the '95 and '99 models' redesign. However, automatic transmissions, brakes, airbags, steering, and fuel- and electrical-system components still top the list of parts most vulnerable to premature failure or malfunctioning. Airbag and Check Engine lights are constantly lit, and fit and finish continue to be only average.

Safety summary: All models/years—Airbags don't deploy when they should or deploy when they shouldn't. • Frequent automatic transmission failures. • Hyundai may not offer a seat belt extension for large occupants. **1996**—Tire fell off car. • Battery blew up while car was idling. • Airbag light is continuously lit. • Brake malfunctions. • Chronic stalling, particularly when AC is engaged. • Frequent engine valve cover gasket failures. • Poor-quality spark plugs cause sluggish acceleration. • Check Engine light is lit continuously. • Water leaks from the front of the car. **1997**—Frequent engine failures. • Transmission gearshift will not stay in place. • Power window switch failed. **1999**—Complete brake failure. • Airbag warning light comes on for no reason. • Sudden alternator failure causes entire vehicle to shut down. • **2000**—Driver-side airbag deployed when driver slammed the door. • Airbag light stays lit, and corrective parts are on national back order. • Sudden brake loss; brakes don't hold in a panic situation. • Warped front brake rotors produce excessive steering shimmy. • Stalls when in low gear or when decelerating (recall campaign didn't remedy the problem). • Power-steering leaks and early replacement. • Window often comes off its track. • Power window caught child's head and neck. • Headlights dim when AC engages. **2001**—Hood flew up and shattered windshield. • Engine sleeves can come loose, causing pistons to smash spark plugs. • Engine bucks and hesitates before rpms suddenly increase and car takes off. • Frequent stalling upon deceleration. • Faulty crankshaft position sensor is blamed for the poor engine performance. • Automatic transmission may suddenly shift into Neutral, or the shift lever sometimes pops out of gear. **2002**—Problems getting recall work done. • Axle (U-bolt) failed while car was underway. • Seat belt latch releases when jostled by passenger's elbow. **2003**—Driver-side seat belt buckle suddenly released. • Large rear-view mirror obstructs the view.

All models/years: Troubleshooting tips for delayed engagement of the automatic transmission. • Harsh shifting when coming to a stop or upon initial acceleration is likely caused by an improperly adjusted accelerator pedal switch TCU. • A faulty air exhaust plug could cause harsh shifting into Second and Fourth gears on vehicles with automatic transmission. • Brake pedal pulsation can be corrected by installing upgraded front discs and pads. • Troubleshooting tips for reducing brake noise. **All models: 1989–98**—Revised measures to reduce AC odours. **1992–95**—Difficult-to-engage Reverse gear needs an upgraded part. **1995–98**—Harsh shifting might be fixed by installing an upgraded transaxle control module (TCM) under a "goodwill" warranty. • If wind noise makes a "kazoo" sound, try installing an additional drip rail moulding. **1995–99**—Tips are offered on getting the automatic transmission to shift properly. **1999**—Shudder or vibration during acceleration can be eliminated by correcting a sticking inboard CV-tripod joint assembly. • A humping/knocking noise heard from the left front side of the vehicle on hard right turns may be caused by the left rear corner of the transaxle mounting bracket base touching the body. • Tips on silencing front wheel bearing noise. **1999–2000**—No-starts, hard starting, or erratic idling may all be caused by a canister purge valve that's stuck open. • Correcting hard manual shifting into First or Second gear and shudder on acceleration (CV joints). **1999–2001**—Correcting erratic shifts. • Key sticks in ignition cylinder. • Silencing gear whine. **2000**—Rear suspension produces a metallic rubbing noise. **1999–2002**—Harsh, delayed shifts. **2000–01**—Correcting droning or rumbling brake noise at freeway speeds. **2001–02**—Hyundai will fix a noisy rear suspension by replacing the rear stabilizer bar bushing (see following bulletin).

Suspension (Rear) – Knocking/Squawking Noise

Number: 02-50-007   05-2002

Models:
Sonata 2001–02; XG 300 2001; XG 350 2002

DESCRIPTION
Some 2001 MY and 2002 MY Sonata, XG300, and XG350 vehicles may experience a knocking or squawking noise from the rear suspension while driving the vehicle over rough road surfaces at low speeds. This noise may originate from the rear stabilizer bar and bushing rubbing together.

2002—Troubleshooting poor shifting and torque converter clutch malfunctions. • 2–3 shift flare. • Erratic operation of the automatic climate control. **2003**—Harsh shifts into Drive or Reverse. • Sticks in Second gear.

Sonata Profile

	1996	1997	1998	1999	2000	2001	2002	2003
Cost Price ($)								
Base	16,595	16,995	17,495	19,495	19,995	20,495	21,195	21,595
Used Values ($)								
Base Λ	3,500	4,500	6,000	7,000	9,500	11,000	13,000	15,000
Base V	3,000	4,000	5,000	6,000	8,500	10,000	11,500	14,000
Reliability	③	③	③	③	④	④	④	④
Crash Safety	③	③	③	—	—	—	④	④
Side	—	❶	❶	—	④	④	④	④
Offset	❶	❶	❶	③	③	③	③	③
Head restraints	❶	❶	—	③	—	③	③	③
Rear	—	—	—	❶	—	—	—	③
Rollover Resistance	—	—	—	—	—	—	⑤	—

Mazda

626, MX-6, MAZDA6   ★★★★★

RATING: Recommended (1999–2003); Above Average (1996–98); Average
(1994–95); Not Recommended (1985–93). Why a higher rating for the latest
models than the Accord? Simple. Accords aren't discounted, so you'll pay a lot
more for a used model than for a 626, which costs a lot less now that the
Mazda6 has hit the showrooms. Furthermore, the Accord's latest revision has
compromised quality, while the latest 626/Mazda6 duo seem to have no more
than an average number of first-year production snafus. Nevertheless, an
extended powertrain warranty is recommended as protection against automatic
transmission breakdowns and factory-related defects. Make sure the car fits
your size: tall drivers should be wary of the low headrests, which can be hazardous in a collision, and short drivers will want to ensure they can see
adequately without getting dangerously close to the airbag housing, particularly on pre-1998 models that carried fully powered airbags. **Maintenance/
Repair costs:** Higher than average. Repairs aren't dealer dependent. Mazda
suggests changing the engine timing chain after 100,000 km. **Parts:** Easily
found, but sometimes costly. Although Mazda has promised to cut prices, you
should still compare prices with independent suppliers. **Best alternatives:** The
Acura Integra; GM Cavalier or Sunfire; Honda Accord; Hyundai Elantra
wagon, Sonata, or Tiburon; and Toyota Camry. **Online help:** Owner reports
and service bulletins can be found at *www.autosafety.org/autodefects.html*;
www.alldata.com; *www.kbb.com*; *www.edmunds.com*; *www.carforums.com/
forums*; and *www.cartrackers.com/Forums*.

Strengths and weaknesses: Although far from being high-performance vehicles, these cars ride and handle fairly well and still manage to accommodate four people in comfort (except for the MX-6 coupe/Ford Probe). The 1988–92 versions incorporated a third-generation redesign that added a bit more horsepower to the 4-banger. Apart from that improvement, these cars have changed little over the years and are still easy riding, fairly responsive, and not hard on gas. On the downside, the automatic transmission downshifts roughly, the power steering is imprecise, and the car leans a lot in turns.

Four-wheel steering was part of the sedan's equipment in 1988, and it was added exclusively to the MX-6 a year later. Wise buyers should pass over this option and look instead for anti-lock brakes and airbags on 1992 LG and GT versions. The manual transmission is a better choice because the automatic robs the engine of much-needed horsepower, as is the case with most cars this size. A passenger-side airbag was added to all '94 models.

A mid-sport and mid-compact hybrid, the MX-6 (Ford Probe) is a coupe version of the 626. It has a more sophisticated suspension, more horsepower, and better steering response than its sedan alter ego. The 1993 model gained a base 2.5L 165-hp V6 power plant. Overall reliability and durability are on par with the 626.

The 1995–97 models offer improved performance, handling, and overall reliability, plus reasonable fuel economy. Owners still complain, though, of subpar body construction, electrical system and cruise control glitches, dim headlights, brakes and AC compressors that wear out prematurely, and automatic transmissions that shift poorly and are prone to premature failure. The Check Engine light comes on and goes off repeatedly due to oil spilling into the airflow sensor or the intake manifold gasket leaking. Expect jerky downshifts when the 4-cylinder is at full throttle. Shocks and struts (MacPherson) aren't very durable and are expensive to replace (especially when the model is equipped with the electronic adjustment feature).

Body problems include windshield mouldings that flake and fall off; door and hatch locks that often freeze up; the right side of the dash is often loose; the interior door panel pulls away; interior colours fade; headliner rattles; and the metal surrounding the rear wheelwells is prone to rust perforation, as are hood, trunk, and door seams. The paint seems particularly prone to chipping. The underbody and suspension components on cars older than five years should be examined carefully for corrosion damage. The exhaust system rarely lasts more than two years, and wheel bearings fail repeatedly within the same period.

Vehicle history: 1998—Attractive Millenia-type styling, a longer wheelbase and larger cabin, a reinforced body to keep creaks and rattles to a minimum, and more powerful engines. **1999**—A larger selection of standard accessories. **2000**—Restyled and substantially improved with a small horsepower boost, enhanced handling, steering, and interior appointments. **2001**—Improved sound system, an emergency trunk release, and user-friendly child safety seat anchors.

Owners of 1998–2002 models report malfunctioning automatic transmissions, engine head gasket failures, fuel system glitches that cause sudden acceleration and stalling, faulty airbags, and electrical shorts that result in the Check Engine light staying lit and engine stalling, or shutdown.

Other complaints point out that shifting isn't all that smooth, nor is the automatic gearbox very reliable; the car is hard-riding over uneven pavement; there's too much body lean in turns; excessive torque steer (pulling) to the right often occurs when accelerating; road noise intrudes into the cabin; the rear spoiler blocks rear visibility; and the trunk opening isn't conducive to loading large objects. As if that wasn't enough, Mazda has a history of automatic transmission and fit and finish deficiencies; and scheduled maintenance overcharges (check out the CBC *Marketplace* archives).

Mazda6

The 2003 Mazda6 is offered with two power plants: an impressive 160-hp inline 4-cylinder that equals the Accord's entry-level engine and a 220-hp V6 that trumps the Camry's 192 horses, but comes up a bit short when compared with the 240 horses unleashed by the Accord and Altima. Either engine can be hooked to a 5-speed manual or automatic transmission that also offers a semi-manual "Sport Shift" feature.

Don't get the idea that this is a warmed-over 626. It's set on an entirely new platform and carries safety and convenience features never seen by its predecessor, like two-stage airbags and a chassis engineered to deflect crash forces away from occupants. Wider than the Accord, the Mazda6's interior allows for a comfortable ride and carries an unusually large trunk.

During its first year on the market, there have been few owner complaints. However, some owners mention interior clunks that are omnipresent and a number of driveability concerns that include poor engine and transmission performance (a chronic problem), a "rotten-egg" smell that pervades the interior, and rust-like stains in the door sashes and trunk lids (see *Edmunds.com*).

Safety summary: All models/years: Interestingly, the 626's different iterations have registered far fewer complaints than their Asian, European, or American counterparts. • Head restraints may be too low. One Canadian neurologist wrote *Lemon-Aid* that early 626 head restraints are set too low and cannot extend to a safe level; he says there is an additional two inches required for a six-foot-tall occupant. The doctor maintains his '97 Mazda 626 (and other model years) cannot be safely operated by a driver over 5'10". • Inadvertent airbag deployments or airbags failed to deploy in a collision. • Frequent automatic transmission malfunctions and failures. **1997**—Several incidents where the steering failed without warning. • Frequent transmission failures. • Premature tire wear. • Brake failures and extended stopping distance. • Chronic electrical shorts. • Exhaust fumes enter into the interior. • Horn button hard to locate in an emergency. • Poor braking on wet roadways. • Headrest too low for tall drivers (think back to the neurologist's comments). • Vehicle started on its own, then fire erupted. • Hesitation or stalling while driving. **1998**—Sudden, unintended acceleration. • Front axle pulled out of the transmission. • Steering rack gear broke in two without prior warning. •

Sudden automatic transmission downshifts. • Frequent transmission failures. • Many reports of tire tread separation. • Poor braking leads to extended stopping distance. • Driver's seat is so low that it must be brought dangerously close to the airbag housing for maximum visibility. **1999**—Left lower strut bolts loose, bent, and broken, causing the driver-side wheel to fall. • Premature tire wear. • When AC engages, engine hesitates and causes car to jerk. • Automatic transmission shift shock. • Transmission fails upon deceleration, it downshifts harshly, O/D light flashes, and then engine compartment starts to fill with transmission fluid. • Headlights dim intermittently. • Excessive vibration at low speeds. • Seat belts won't properly secure a child safety seat. **2000**—Cylinder head failures at the #2 cylinder. • 4-cylinder engine stumbles badly in cold weather. • Automatic transmission jerks during 2–1 shift, lurches into gear due to sudden high revs, and sometimes won't go into gear. • Cracked passenger-side rear axle. • Check Engine light stays on. **2001**— Automatic transmission jerks into gear. • Seat belts fail to retract. **2002**—Loose front wheel bearing. • AC constantly blows cold air.

Secret Warranties/Service Tips/TSBs

All models/years: Non-turbo models that idle roughly after a warm restart could have fuel vaporizing in the distribution pipe (TSB #023/87R). • Excessive rear brake squealing can be reduced with improved brake pads (TSB #015/89-11). • Excessive vibrations felt in the brake pedal, steering wheel, floor, or seat when applying the brakes can be fixed by installing a redesigned brake assembly. • TSB #50901898 gives tips for eliminating wind noise around doors. **All models: 1993–97**—Engine camshaft noise may be corrected with a new friction gear spring and lock nut. **1995–96**—A 3–4 shift hunt is probably caused by failure in the 3–4 shift solenoid hydraulic circuit. • Front strut squeaks on turns could be caused by interference between the upper seat spring and the strut dust cover, or between the dust cover and the rubber bump stopper. **1996–97**—Unwanted 4–3 downshifts or intermittent shifting into Overdrive is covered in bulletin #015/98. **1997**—Camshaft friction noise. **1997–98**—Wind noise around doors. • Inoperative speedometer. • Steering wheel slightly off centre. • Brake pulsation repair. • Dead battery troubleshooting. • Tips on fixing faulty sunroofs, a seat belt warning buzzer that sounds for no reason, rough automatic transmission shifts, excessive idle vibration, rear brake squeal, coolant leaks, and hard-to-close trunk lid. **1998–2000**—Tips on silencing a rear end tapping noise, and preventing AC odours. **1998–2002**—Remedy for mildew odour. **2000**—Troubleshooting an MIL light that won't go off.

626, MX-6, Mazda6 Profile

	1996	1997	1998	1999	2000	2001	2002	2003
Cost Price ($)								
626	19,365	19,995	19,995	20,140	20,140	23,175	23,470	—
MX-6	22,780	23,325	—	—	—	—	—	—
Mazda6	—	—	—	—	—	—	—	24,295

Used Values ($)								
626 ▲	4,500	5,500	7,500	8,500	10,500	13,000	16,000	—
626 ▼	4,000	5,000	6,000	7,500	9,500	11,500	14,500	—
MX-6 ▲	5,000	6,000	—	—	—	—	—	—
MX-6 ▼	4,000	5,000	—	—	—	—	—	—
Mazda6 ▲	—	—	—	—	—	—	—	18,500
Mazda6 ▼	—	—	—	—	—	—	—	17,500
Reliability	❷	③	④	④	④	④	④	④
Crash Safety (626 4d)	④	—	④	④	④	④	④	⑤
Side (626 4d)	❷	③	③	③	③	③	③	③
Offset	—	—	③	③	⑤	⑤	⑤	④
Head Restraints	—	❶	—	❶	—	❶	❶	③

Nissan

ALTIMA ★★★

RATING: Average (2002–03, 1993–97); Above Average (1998–2001). Here's the Altima dilemma: up to 1997, these cars were fairly reliable, though so-so performers. Thereafter, performance was improved incrementally as prices remained quite reasonable. Then, the totally new, high-performance and stylish 2002 Altima changed everything. Sure, it's a great highway performer, but few can pay the $24,000–$30,00 entry fee. Moreover, safety- and performance-related defects are extraordinarily frequent and difficult to diagnose. Hopefully, later iterations will be better built and dealer mechanics will be more competent in servicing these rather sophisticated machines. Watch out for early model bargains: the 140-hp 4-cylinder engine barely provides the necessary versatility needed to match the competition. Although the SE gives the sportiest performance, the less expensive GXE is the better deal from a price/quality standpoint. You will need an extended powertrain warranty though to protect you from automatic transmission failures on 1998–2001 models and a more extensive warranty to protect you from post-2001 Altima defects. **Maintenance/Repair costs:** Higher than average. Repairs are dealer dependent. **Parts:** Owners complain of parts shortages on the 2002 and later versions, parts on earlier models are relatively inexpensive. **Best alternatives:** The Acura Integra; GM Cavalier or Sunfire; Honda Accord; Hyundai Elantra wagon, Sonata, or Tiburon; Mazda 626; and Toyota Camry. **Online help:** For the latest owner reports, service bulletins, and money-saving tips, look at *www.autosafety.org/autodefects.html*; *www.alldata.com*; *www.kbb.com*; *www.edmunds.com*; *www.carforums.com/forums*; and *www.cartrackers.com/Forums.*

Strengths and weaknesses: The 1993–97 Altima's wheelbase is a couple of inches longer than the Stanza's, and the car is touted by Nissan as a mid-size, even though its interior dimensions put it in the compact league. The small cabin seats only four, and rear-seat access is difficult to master due to the slanted roof pillars, inward-curving door frames, and narrow clearance.

Expect only average acceleration and fuel economy with the pre-2002 4-cylinder engine. It has insufficient top-end torque and gets buzzier the more it's pushed. In order to get the automatic to downshift for passing, for example, you have to practically stomp on the accelerator. Manoeuvrability is good around town, but twitchy on the highway. There are no reliability problems reported with the 16-valve power plant, however, the 5-speed manual transmission is sloppy and the automatic transmission's performance has been problematic through the '97 model year; later years through 2001 are a better choice from a reliability and fuel-economy standpoint. The uncluttered underhood layout makes servicing easy. Body assembly is only so-so, with more than the average number of squeaks and rattles.

The 2002–03 redesigned models are shaped like a Passat, with the heart of a Maxima and provide scintillating V6 acceleration, flawless automatic transmission operation, good braking, well laid-out instruments and controls, and better-than-average interior room and craftsmanship.

On the other hand, the 4-cylinder engine isn't as refined as the competition and is noisy when pushed, and the V6 acceleration overpowers this car and causes excessive rear-end instability and steering pull to one side. Brakes tend to lock up on wet roads; interior appointments lack panache; there's limited rear headroom; expect snug rear seating for three adults, and obstructed rear visibility; the dashboard reflects into the windshield; dash gauges wash out in sunlight; and parts are often back ordered. Quality problems multiply as these cars age.

The car's 175-hp 2.5L 4-cylinder engine is almost as powerful as the competition's V6 power plants and the optional 245-hp 3.5L V6 has few equals among cars in this price and size class. And when you consider that the Altima is much lighter than most of its competitors, it's obvious why this car produces sizzling (and sometimes uncontrollable) acceleration with little fuel penalty. Four-wheel independent suspension strikes the right balance between a comfortable ride and sporty handling. With the V6 option, drivers get 17-inch tires for more grip.

Owners report engine surging, stalling, and hard starting, possibly due to a defective engine crank sensor or throttle switch (on national back order); annoying and hazardous dash reflection onto the windshield; electrical glitches and excessive brake wear, noise, and pulsations. Snow builds up in the small wheel wells, making steering difficult and causing excessive shimmy; clutch pressure plate throw-out bearing and flywheel may fail when downshifting into Fourth gear; noisy, failure-prone rear shocks; ABS warning light stays lit; and ignition noise in radio speakers.

Vehicle history: 1993—Altima debuts with a 140-hp 2.4L 4-cylinder engine, a driver's airbag, and poorly designed, uncomfortable motorized shoulder belts. **1994**—Dual airbags and no more motorized belts. **1995**—Freshened styling. **1998**—Slightly restyled with a bit larger interior, depowered airbags, and degraded handling. **2000**—Slightly restyled again, to look longer and wider;

engine got five more horses (155 hp); and suspension/chassis enhancements improved handling somewhat and made for a quieter ride. **2002**—Completely revised with two high-performance engines (a 180-hp 2.5L 4-cylinder and an optional 240-hp 3.5L V6), a larger interior, and a more supple ride combined with sportier handling. **2003**—Inconsequential trim changes.

Altimas have always had a fairly good reliability reputation; the only problem areas with early models were prematurely worn, noisy front brakes, fuel system malfunctions, transmission and electrical system failures, and body glitches. 1998–2001 models have generated fewer complaints, but owners still report sudden acceleration and stalling; front brakes locking up or failing completely; failure of the airbags to deploy; transmission breakdowns; and poor body fit and finish, notably water leaks (trunk, mainly) and body squeaks and rattles.

Safety summary: All models: 1995–97—Fire ignited in the engine compartment while vehicle was parked. • Fire started by fuse box in passenger compartment. • Sudden acceleration. • Frequent reports that the airbag failed to deploy. • Poor braking performance. • Poor design causes electronic control unit failure. • Defective automatic transmission solenoid. • Windshield wiper fails periodically. • Water leaks into trunk area, causing premature rusting. • Automatic door lock failure. • Seat and shoulder belts lock up and don't retract. **1998**—Stalling when accelerating. • Rear seats won't lock upright. • Windows rattle excessively. • Wheel cover failure. **1999**—Several incidents where engine or electrical fires ignited while vehicle was parked. • Sudden acceleration. • Vehicle unstable on wet roadway. • Airbags failed to deploy. • Airbag light comes on for no reason. • Gearshift lever sticks in Park. • Transaxle snapped in half, taking suspension and steering knuckle with it. • Sudden tire separation; tires gradually lose air (Continental-General). • Chronic brake problems. • Driver's seat moves forward when braking. **2000**—Exhaust fumes enter vehicle. • Dashboard burst into flames while vehicle was underway. • Vehicle continues to accelerate when slowing down to a stop, or when put into Reverse. • Chronic stalling. • Automatic transmission won't stay in gear. • The rear wheelwell inner fender has sharp, jagged edges. • Firestone Affinity tire blowout. • All windows have a film on them that makes it difficult to see at night or during rainy weather. • Windshield cracks frequently. **2001**—Sudden, unintended acceleration. • Engine will suddenly shut down. • Engine motor mount failure. • Airbags failed to deploy. • Automatic transmission makes a grinding or clunking noise when shifting. • Defective sway bar bushing. • Wheel fell off, causing vehicle to slam into a wall. **2002–03**—Safety defects become more common as these cars age. Dealerships said to be aware of redesigned Altima's tendency to catch fire: fire erupted after collision; fire ignited due to a faulty fuel injection system on another occasion, and also ignited while cruising on the highway. • Airbags failed to deploy. • Vehicle was idling and then suddenly went into Reverse and accelerated as groceries were unloaded from the trunk (dash indicator showed car in "P"). • Driver run over by his own car when it slipped into Reverse. • Sudden acceleration when brakes are applied. • Transmission slips and engine hesitates when accelerating. • Chronic stalling. • Windshield distortion. • Exhaust pipe hanger pin catches debris that may ignite. • Crankshaft position sensor failure. Tail lights constantly fail. • Battery suddenly blew up. • Seat belt fails to retract. • Instrument panel gauges wash out in sunlight.

Secret Warranties/Service Tips/TSBs

All models/years: Diagnostic and correction tips for brake vibration and steering wheel shimmy. • TSB #NTB99-028 outlines the procedures necessary to fix slow-to-retract seat belts. • TSB #NTB00-037a covers possible causes of the vehicle pulling to the side. **1993–96**—No-starts or hard starts may be caused by an automatic transmission control cable that's too short; TSB #96-032 gives additional diagnostic tips. • If the transmission won't shift into Reverse, it may mean the Reverse clutch drum, snap ring, and two dish rings need replacing. • A worn differential pinion shaft may require an upgraded transmission differential case. • Rear brake squeal can be reduced by installing improved rear brake shoes. • TSB #NTB96-046 gives lots of useful tips for troubleshooting squeaks and rattles. **1998–2000**—Troubleshooting a rattling in the engine compartment. • Tips for eliminating brake vibration and shudder. **1999–2000**—A sunroof that jams when opening rearward requires a readjustment of the sunroof links. • Guidelines as to what constitutes suspension strut leakage qualifying for warranty coverage are found in TSB #NTB99-001. • Remedies for a noisy automatic transmission. **2002–03**—Hard starting:

Engine Won't Crank in Park/Will Crank in Neutral

Bulletin No.: EL02-028; NTB02-083;

Date: July 30, 2002

2002–2003 Altima (L31) - with automatic transmission

If an applied vehicle shows all of the following symptoms:

^Engine does not crank when the gear shift selector lever is in Park (P) position,

^Engine does crank when the gear shift selector lever is in Neutral (N),

^Incident usually happens if the engine is at normal driving temperature rather than cold,

The Service Procedure has two steps: Part A - Check the Park/Neutral Switch Adjustment, adjust if necessary; Part B - Adjust the Automatic Transmission Control Cable, at the Slotted Transmission Control Arm. Remove any play or "slack" in the cable.

• Chronic loss of power:

Hesitation on Acceleration

Bulletin No.: ECO3-003; NTBO3-022

Date: March 15, 2003

APPLIED VEHICLES:

2002–03 Maxima (A33) only with manual transmission
2002–03 Altima (L31) only with V6 (VQ35) engine and manual transmission

IF YOU CONFIRM: An Applied Vehicle has a momentary hesitation when accelerating between 2000 and 3000 rpm.

ACTIONS: Replace the Mass Airflow Sensor; Perform ECM reprogramming.

• Excessive engine noise:

Engine Buzz

Bulletin No.: BT02-007a; NTB02-037a

Date: November 6, 2002

2002–03 Altima, buzz noise at 2500–2700 rpm, moderate load

ACTIONS: Locate the automatic transmission breather tank and repair as shown in the Service Procedure.

• Fuel sloshing noise:

Fuel Tank Slosh/Clunk Noise

Bulletin No.: FE02-001; NTB02-103

Date: October 10, 2002

2002 and 2003 Altima (L31)

If an Applied Vehicle has "slosh" or "clunk" noise from the rear of the vehicle under the following conditions:

^ The fuel tank is 3/4 full to completely full, and

^ When braking,

^ Driving at low speeds over bumps, or

^ Accelerating at low speeds,

The Service Procedure will direct you to install the following parts:

^ Fuel Tank

^ Fuel Tank Baffle inside fuel tank

^ Shim Pads on top of fuel tank

^ Insulation Pad under the rear seat

• Suspension noise:

Intermittent Clunking Noise

Bulletin No.: FA02-003; NTB03-002

Date: January 6, 2003

CLUNK NOISE FROM FRONT SUSPENSION, 2002–03 Altima

IF YOU CONFIRM: An intermittent (difficult to duplicate) "clunk" noise coming from the front suspension area when:

^first accelerating or,

^applying the brakes or,

^going over bumps.

ACTIONS: Check/Tighten the torque on the front suspension components.

• Front door trim fabric separation. • Low power, poor running, and MIL light stays lit. • Inoperative AC/warm air flows from vents. • Poor heater performance. • AC temperature isn't adjustable:

AC compressor does not disengage when the manual selector switch is moved from the defrost position. This is covered by a service bulletin NTB03-048 dated 5-6-03 from Nissan concerning this problem. This is noted as a change in operation from earlier models and I feel it is dangerous. The only way to disengage the compressor after using the defroster is to stop the car, move the selector switch to any function that is not defroster related, turn off the ignition and restart the car. If you don't there is at least a 10 percent loss in mileage due to the fact that the AC compressor is operating and the temp selector must be adjusted up or the occupants of the vehicle will freeze.

• AC drain hose may leak into interior. Howling noise when clutch is released. • Rear suspension and radio speaker noise. • Sunroof wind noise and water leaks. • Water leakage on front floor area. • Wind noise from doors. • Sunroof won't close at highway speeds. • Faulty airbag warning light. • Wheel cover squeak, click. • Automatic transmission slips in Reverse and won't brake when in D1 range, also makes a clicking noise. • Headliner rattle. • Poor heater performance. • Fuel tank slosh noise.

Altima Profile

	1996	1997	1998	1999	2000	2001	2002	2003
Cost Price ($)								
XE/S	20,598	20,798	19,398	19,898	19,998	19,998	23,498	23,798
GXE/SE	23,498	21,398	21,998	22,698	22,698	22,698	27,698	24,675
Used Values ($)								
XE/S ▲	5,000	6,000	7,500	8,500	10,000	11,000	16,500	19,000
XE/S ▼	4,000	5,000	6,500	7,500	9,000	10,000	15,500	18.000
GXE/SE ▲	6,000	7,000	8,500	9,500	11,000	12,000	20,000	23,000
GXE/SE ▼	5,000	6,000	8,000	9,000	10,000	11,000	19,000	22,000
Reliability	④	④	④	④	④	④	❷	❷
Crash Safety	④	④	③	③	—	④	④	④
Side	—	—	③	③	③	③	③	③
Offset	—	—	—	—	③	③	⑤	❷
Head Restraints	—	❷	—	❷	❶	❶	❷	❷
Rear	—	—	—	—	—	—	❶	❷
Rollover Resistance	—	—	—	—	—	—	④	④

Toyota

CAMRY, SOLARA   ★★★★★

RATING: Recommended (2003; 1995–96); Above Average (1997–2002; 1985–94). The Solara, a two-door Camry clone, is outrageously overpriced when bought new; however, the 1999 and 2000 models are veritable bargains due to their rapid depreciation. Of the two model years, I'd go for the 2000 Solara (its second year out) for a few thousand more and a better build quality. As for Camry prices, they don't fall as dramatically as with the Solara; the 1996 LE V6 sedan is the best buy from a quality/price standpoint. Just a word of caution: 1997–2002 model Camrys and Solaras have elicited an unusually high number of safety complaints that are carried over from one model year to the next. The complaints include sudden acceleration; engine compartment fires; V6 engine failures from sludge buildup; automatic transmission breakdowns; transmission interlock failures, which allow a parked vehicle to roll away; severe wandering at highway speeds; loss of braking; and poor headlight illumination. There is nothing you can do to prevent these failures, and you may have to force Toyota to pay for their correction. **Maintenance/ Repair costs:** Higher than average, but repairs aren't dealer dependent. **Parts:** Parts can be more expensive than for most other cars in this class, making it worth your while to shop at independent suppliers. Parts availability is excellent. **Best alternatives:** The Acura Integra; Honda Accord; Hyundai Elantra wagon, Sonata, or Tiburon; and Mazda6 or 626. **Online help:** Owner feedback, service bulletins, and complaint strategies can be accessed at *www.autosafety.org/ autodefects.html; www.alldata.com; www.kbb.com; www.edmunds.com; www.carforums.com/forums; www.cartrackers.com/Forums;* and through Google, using "engine sludge" as the key word.

Strengths and weaknesses: Safety complaints aside, the Camry is a Japanese Oldsmobile (the old rear-drive kind). It's an excellent small family hauler because of its spacious, comfortable interior, good fuel economy; and impressive reliability and durability. Just make sure you change the oil more frequently than Toyota, or Lexus for that matter, suggests for its V6 engine (see engine sludge comments below).

The 1985–93 models have few problems, although they're far from perfect. Main areas of concern are failure-prone cylinder head gaskets; suspension and electrical system failures; defective starter drive and ring gear; leaking low-pressure and high-pressure power-steering lines; outer CV boots that split, causing grease to leak; premature brake wear; and some paint peeling and rusting.

Persistent problems with all Toyota vehicles up to the present are premature brake wear, and excessive noise and vibrations. Stung by consumer criticism that owners were charged for useless repairs, Toyota published a "Brake Repair" service bulletin (POL94-18) in October 1994, which set the benchmark for after-warranty assistance that can still be used today by savvy owners. Toyota states that premature brake wear and noise will be fixed under warranty for the first 12 months/15,000 miles (240,000 km), and that vibrations will be attended to, under warranty, for up to 3 years/50,000 miles (80,000 km).

Front suspension bushings wear out quickly, leading to clunking and squeaking noises when going over bumps or when stopping quickly. There's also the so-called Camry chop (exceptionally rough rides when passing over uneven roadways) reported by owners of 1992–94 models. Cruise control fails frequently on all years.

1995–96 Camrys are the most reliable and reasonably priced, but they too have their shortcomings. Owners report premature brake failures and excessive brake vibration and wear; faulty window regulators; smelly ACs; and myriad rattles, clunks, and groans that seem to come from everywhere. There is also an annoying surging and shuddering when decelerating, likely caused by a faulty PCM computer module. There are also the beginnings of automatic transmission problems (automatic transmissions that slip out of gear when parked, etc), but nowhere near the number of chronic breakdowns soon to be seen with 1997–2003 Camrys.

1994–96 model body problems include excessive wind noise coming from the front windshield, back doors, and sunroof. Trim items rust and fall off, door handles pull away, and mufflers have a short life span. No reports of rust perforation problems, but weak spots are door bottoms, rear wheel openings, and trunk and hatchback edges. There are complaints concerning premature rusting on cars painted white.

"De-contenting" hit Toyota's 1997 lineup hard, resulting in many changes that cheapened the Camry and precipitated a huge increase in owner complaints over problems that never appeared on Toyota vehicles before. One of the worst problems first showing up in 1997, and continuing through the year 2000 models, is engine sludge buildup, leading to engine failures that may cost as much as $7,000 to correct (see full report in the Sienna minivan section or go to *www.minivanreview.com/MiniVans*. Toyota has also admitted to engine head gasket leaks for the first time (see "Secret Warranties/Service Tips/TSBs").

Other changes you'll note on 1997 and later models are less expensive S-rated tires on models with 4-cylinder engines, cheaper heating/ventilation system components, no more assist handles for front occupants, no more chrome trim around the windshield, one door seal instead of three (greater chance for wind and water leaks), fewer airbag sensors, an LCD odometer, a distributorless ignition with the 4-cylinder, and a windshield-embedded antenna. Owners report the 1997 models have limited rear visibility (due to the side pillars and high trunk lid), less steering "feel," and more squeaks and rattles than previous versions.

Quality problems continue to plague the 1997–2002 models. Specifically, owners report that both the engine head gasket and automatic transmission are failure-prone (to Toyota's credit, both problems are covered by an extended "goodwill" warranty), frequent hesitation or stalling out when accelerating or braking; front power windows often run off their channel; the steering wheel vibrates excessively; brake pulsation is a constant irritant, brake components wear out early (calipers, rotors, pads, master cylinder and the ABS valve); the AC self-destructs; warning lights constantly come on; the charcoal canister needs early replacement (covered by the emissions warranty, if you insist); the suspension "bottoms out" when carrying four adults; struts leak and are noisy; and the moon roof is prone to water leaks and wind noise.

Vehicle history: 1992—No more AWD, only a hatchback and wagon are offered with a 130-hp 2.2L 4-banger or a 185-hp 3.0L V6, plus a driver's airbag. **1997**—Totally redesigned to be taller, longer, wider, more powerful, and cheaper, in both a literal and a figurative sense. Gone are the coupe and station wagon variants. The wheelbase was extended by 5 cm, giving back-seat passengers more room. Other changes: it's powered by a base 2.2L 133-hp 16-valve 4-cylinder engine (taken from the Celica) and an optional 3.0L 24-valve V6 that unleashes 194 horses. Either engine can be mated to a 5-speed manual or an electronically controlled 4-speed automatic. ABS and traction control is standard on all V6-equipped Camrys, rear seats have shoulder belts for the middle passenger, low beam lights are brighter. **1998**—Optional side airbags and an improved anti-theft system. **1999**—Debut of the Solara; adjustable front headrests; new upholstery. **2000**—Slightly restyled: given larger tires and a small horsepower boost (4-cylinder engines). The following year's models remained unchanged. **2002**—Car gets larger and now carries a 157-hp 2.4 4-cylinder engine. **2003**—Power-adjustable foot pedals are offered.

Solara

Introduced in the summer of 1998 as a '99 model, the Solara is essentially a longer, lower, bare-bones, two-door coupe or convertible Camry with a sportier powertrain and suspension and a more stylish exterior. But don't let this put you off. Most new Toyota model offerings, like the Sienna, Avalon, and RAV4, are Camry derivatives. Year 2000 models returned unchanged, except for the addition of a convertible version and three additional horses; 2001s were carried over without any significant improvements.

Relatively rare on the used-car market, a base model Solara will cost you $3,000–$4,000 more than an entry-level Camry sedan. And if you get one with the Sienna and Lexus ES 300's V6 power plant, you're looking at a few thousand dollars more.

You have a choice of either a 4- or 6-cylinder power plant. Unfortunately, vehicles equipped with a V6 also came with a gimmicky rear spoiler and a headroom-robbing moon roof. The stiff body structure and suspension, as well as tight steering, make for easy sports car-like handling, with lots of road feel and few surprises.

Safety summary: All models/years: Owners report that the Dunlop D60 A2 tire is a poor wet-weather performer and the Firestone original equipment tires fail prematurely. **1995–96**—Brake failure. • Noisy, vibrating brakes. • Premature front and rear brake wear. • Excessive engine noise. • Transmission lever can slip from Drive to Neutral. • Airbag fails to deploy or is accidentally deployed. • Sudden acceleration, stalling. • Passenger-side seatbacks won't stay upright. • Passenger seat belts over-retract. **1996**—Vehicle wanders over road. • Door bottom/undercarriage rusting. • Airbag warning light and Check Engine light always on. • Windshield film buildup. • Rocking driver and passenger seats. • Steering system leaks. **1997**—Engine compartment fire following ABS brake failure. • Airbags failed to deploy. • Violent deployment of airbag during an accident caused death. • Sudden acceleration when brakes were applied. • Tendency for car to wander all over the roadway. • Steering wheel suddenly locked up, causing an accident. • Many reports of transmission interlock system failures. • Many other reports, probably related to the interlock system, that vehicle was put in Park and keys taken out of ignition, and car then proceeded to roll away. • Seat belts continually ratchet tighter; rear seat belt was strangling child, who had to be cut free. • Plastic part fell behind the dash and lodged behind the brake pedal arm, causing an accident. • Frequent brake failures. • Premature brake pad and caliper wear or failure. • Loud grinding brake noise when braking. • Excessive noise coming from underneath the car at highway speeds. • Vehicle sits too low, has minimal ground clearance. • Driver's knee can hit the steering wheel adjuster lever, making steering wheel go up and down. On several occasions, steering wheel suddenly tilted all the way up while on the highway. • Very poor headlight illumination; headlight safety cap cover design cuts visibility severely and there's a blind spot on the driver-side headlights. • Low beam lights aren't bright enough. • Dash indicator lights are too small and low in intensity. • Inoperative rear window defroster. • Driver's seatback rocks back and forth. • Power door lock relay failure. • Car locks and unlocks on its own. • Fuel door doesn't open fully when lever is pulled. • Rear windshield exploded while car was parked overnight. **1998**—Several reports of engine fires. • Vehicle stalled, oil light came on, and fire ignited in engine compartment. • Sudden acceleration. • Many reports that airbags failed to deploy. • Frequent complaints that vehicle wanders at highway speeds and is difficult to control in a crosswind. • Overly soft suspension allows the chassis to scrape the roadway when passing over a small bump. • Frequent ABS brake failures. • Excessive brake noise and extended stopping distances. • Transmission gearshift lever went from Neutral to Drive without pressing button. • Airbag service indicator light stays on. • Engine malfunction light stays on. • Inadequate night illumination from headlights: low beam halogen headlights don't carry very far; dark spot cast from left headlight results in poor visibility; and metal deflector inside the concealed headlights blocks out all light beyond 10 m. • Electrical system failure; running lights won't shut off. • Lock design allows for occupants to be temporarily locked in vehicle if someone gets out before them and locks the doors. • Power door locks fail intermittently. • Front restraints lock up when vehicle is parked on an incline. • Sun visors are too small to block the sun, and they cut visibility. • Back windshield shattered. • Fumes from inside the vehicle fog up the windshield. • Gas tank makes sloshing noise when brakes are applied. • General Tire wears excessively on the inside tread. • Frequent complaints of moon roof leaks, which may cause electrical short. • Doors have to be slammed shut. **1999**—Incredible as it may seem, the Camry continues to have serious safety-related defects that aren't much different from what's been recorded for previous model years. They include, in order of frequency: sudden unintended acceleration; airbags not deploying during a collision; inadvertent airbag deployment, injuring occupants; complete brake failure or extended stopping distances caused by poor braking; sudden acceleration; chronic engine hesitation when accelerating or stalling; engine, airbag, and ABS warning light come on constantly; premature tire wear or blowout (Cooper and General tires); optically distorted windshield; and the transmission won't hold when stopped on a hill. **2000–01**—Safety-related incidents return unabated. • Under-hood fire (left side) while vehicle was parked overnight. • Fire ignited from underneath vehicle while driving. • Airbags failed to deploy. • Inadvertent airbag deployment. • Faulty cruise control caused vehicle to suddenly accelerate. • Sudden acceleration without braking effect. • Excessive grinding noise and long stopping distances associated with ABS braking. • Brake pedal went to floor but no braking effect. • ABS brakes suddenly locked up when coming to a gradual stop. • Defective rear brake drum. • Vehicle tends to drift to the right at highway speeds. • Excessive steering wheel vibrations at speeds over 100 km/h. • Entire vehicle shakes excessively when cruising. • Vehicle's weight is poorly distributed, causing the front end to lift up when the vehicle's speed exceeds 90 km/h. • Suspension bottoms out too easily, damaging the undercarriage. • Too-compliant shock absorbers make for a rough ride over uneven terrain. • Rear suspension noise at low speeds. • Automatic transmission slippage. • With engine running and transmission in Park position, car rolled down a hill. Two small girls inside of car jumped out, but one was run over. • Car rolled backward after it was put into Park and ignition key was removed. • Vehicle parked overnight had its rear window suddenly blow out. • Windshield distortion is a strain on the eyes. • Floor-mounted gear shift indicator is hard to read. • Seat belts are too tight on either side and tighten up uncomfortably with the slightest movement. • Shoulder belt twists and won't lie straight. • Leaking suspension struts and strut rod failure. • Trunk lid may suddenly collapse. • Faulty driver's window track. • Driver-side door latch sticks. • Sulfuric acid odour enters the interior. • Fuel tank makes a sloshing noise when three-quarters full. • Clunking noise heard from rear of vehicle when gas tank is half full. • Tire jack collapsed during change of tire. **2002**—An astounding 108 owner complaints up to December 2002. • Starter caught on fire in the parking lot; under-hood fire (left side) while vehicle was parked overnight; fire ignited from underneath vehicle while driving. • Airbags failed to deploy:

> My brother was involved in a fatal crash in a new 2002 Toyota Camry XLE. The accident occurred in North Carolina and is being investigated by the highway patrol. The car left the highway and rolled over, eventually impacting a tree. The car was equipped with front, side, and side curtain airbags. No airbag deployed in this accident. I believe the lack of airbag deployment was contributory to my brother's death.

• Inadvertent airbag deployment. • Faulty cruise control caused vehicle to suddenly accelerate. • Sudden acceleration without braking effect. • Brake pedal went to floor with no braking effect. • ABS brakes suddenly locked up when coming to a gradual stop. • Defective rear brake drum. • Many owners complain of poor brake pedal design:

> Arm that holds up brake pedal is interfering with the driver's foot. Driver stated if consumer had a large size foot, it could easily get

wedged and stuck on brake pedal. Foot gets caught between the floormat and the brake arm, needs to be redesigned.

• Front right axle broke six months after car was purchased. • Vehicle tends to drift to the right at highway speeds. • Excessive steering wheel vibrations at speeds over 100 km/h; entire vehicle shakes excessively when cruising. • Vehicle's weight is poorly distributed, causing the front end to lift up when the vehicle speed exceeds 90 km/h. • Suspension bottoms out too easily, damaging the undercarriage. • Automatic transmission slips or suddenly shifts to a lower gear; particularly poor shifting when in Overdrive. • Too-compliant shock absorbers make for a rough ride over uneven terrain. • Rear suspension noise at low speeds. • Car rolled backward after driver put it into Park and removed ignition key. • Vehicle parked overnight had its rear window suddenly blow out. • Windshield distortion is a strain on the eyes. • Floor-mounted gear shift indicator is hard to read. • Seatbelts are too tight on either side and tighten up uncomfortably with the slightest movement; shoulder belt twists and won't lie straight. • Leaking suspension struts and strut rod failure. • Trunk lid may suddenly collapse. • Faulty driver's window track. • Driver-side door latch sticks. • "Rotten-egg" exhaust smell. • Fuel tank makes a sloshing noise when three-quarters full. • Clunking noise heard from rear of vehicle when gas tank is half full. • Tire jack collapsed while changing tire. • High rear end cuts rear visibility. • Turn signal volume is too low.

Secret Warranties/Service Tips/TSBs

All models/years: To reduce front brake squeaks on ABS-equipped vehicles, ask the dealer to install new, upgraded rotors (#43517-32020). • Owner feedback over the last decade, plus dealer service managers who wish to remain anonymous, tells me that Toyota has a secret warranty that will pay for replacing front disc brake components that wear out before 2 years/40,000 km. If you're denied this coverage, threaten small claims court action. • Toyota has a special kit to reduce AC odours. **All models: 1990–2000**—Measures to eliminate front brake clicking. **1993–96**—Suspension squeaks and groans are addressed in TSB #SU95-003. **1997**—Head gasket leaks are covered by a special Toyota program that is applied only if the customer complains. • If the driver's seat rocks, Toyota has an upgraded assembly that will secure the seat. • Difficulties with moon roof operation. • Exterior rear-view mirror improvement. • Steering rack housing bushing noise. • Front shoulder belt anchor buzzes. • Front suspension groans. • Suspension rattle and popping. • Tailpipe contact with heat shield. • Headliner buzzes or rattles. • Moon roof rattles. • Manual front seat movement/noise. • Power front seat chattering. • Radio volume control too sensitive. • Rubbing noise from door trim. • Seatcover loose at lower rear corners. • Seat movement field fix procedure. • Armrest improvement. • Fuel door operation improvement. • Wind noise repair kit. **1997–98**—A front suspension groan can be fixed by replacing the front spring bumper. • Steering rack bushing noise. **1997–99**—Fuel door operation improvement. • Tips on reducing steering noise. • New front brake pad kits will reduce brake grinding or groaning, says bulletin #BR001-99. • To enhance headlight performance, the alignment process has been modified. **1997–2000**—Silencing steering rack end noise. **1997–2001**—Engine oil sludge will be corrected for free up to February 28, 2003. • Trunk leaks will be fixed under Toyota's base warranty.

Trunk Water Leaks

Bulletin No.: BO028-00

Date: November 3, 2000

Models: 1997–2001 Camry (U.S.), 1998–2001 Sienna, 1999–2001 Solara, and 2001 Avalon

A field fix is available for incidents of moisture and odours permeating into the vehicle. The Quarter Panel Air Duct flaps may have become loose or missing. Replacing the Quarter Panel Air Duct will remedy the condition.

1998–99—Door glass that runs off its channel is a common factory-related problem that Toyota admits is covered under its base warranty. Here's the catch: the dealer isn't authorized to upgrade the channel (a half-hour procedure) unless the customer asks for the service. **1999–2000**—Seat movement, or no movement of seat adjustment. **2000–01**—Wheel bearing dust deflector ticking noise. **2001**—Troubleshooting a false MIL warning. **2002**—Special Service Campaign to replace the driver-side front airbag. • Automatic transmission shift quality improvements . • Catalytic converter heat shield rattle. • Free replacement of the JBL amplifier addresses popping noise. • Gas cap sticks. • Campaigns to repair the washer reservoir tank; remove coil spring spacers. • Tips on eliminating sulfur exhaust odours. **Solara:** Water leaking into the trunk area. • Poor durability of rear-view mirrors. **2002–03**—Harsh automatic transmission shifts:

Light Throttle Second–Third Gear Shift Shock/Shudder

Bulletin No.: EG022-02

Date: December 23, 2002

2002–03 Camry

Some 2002 and 2003 model year V6 Camry vehicles produced at TMMK may exhibit a triple shock (shudder) during the 2–3 upshift under "light throttle" acceleration. Follow the repair procedure in this bulletin to adjust the condition on applicable vehicles.

• Excessive brake vibration:

Front Brake Vibration

Bulletin No.: BR006-02

Date: December 24, 2002

2002–03 Camry (V6 XLE & V6 SE)

Under certain usage conditions, some 2002–03 model year Camry vehicles may exhibit front brake vibration. The rotor and pad have been improved to correct this condition. The new rotor and pad must be installed as a set. The revised parts have been introduced into production.

• Sliding roof repair tips (TSB #BO002-03). • Power front seat feels loose (TSB #BO004-03). • Poor AC/heating:

AC – Blower Volume Gradually Diminishes

Bulletin No.: AC001-03

Date: April 15, 2003

AC PERFORMANCE & DURABILITY IMPROVEMENT

2002–03 Camry

Some 2002–03 model year Camry owners may experience a condition where the blower volume gradually decreases after about 1.5 hours of driving. It has been determined that, in hot high humidity conditions, the AC system evaporator is freezing over, blocking the airflow path. There may be some instances where this condition may affect the AC compressor and clutch assembly. An in-line thermistor resistor harness is now available to correct this concern.

Camry: 2003—Poor shift quality, can be corrected by updating the ECM calibration (TSB #TC008-03).

Camry, Solara Profile

	1996	1997	1998	1999	2000	2001	2002	2003
Cost Price ($)								
Camry Coupe	20,488	—	—	—	—	—	—	—
Base Sedan CE	21,138	21,178	21,348	21,680	22,180	24,565	—	—
LE	24,718	25,458	25,268	26,508	27,070	27,695	23,755	24,800
LE V6	29,858	—	—	—	—	—	27,585	27,070
Wagon V6	32,178	—	—	—	—	—	—	—
Base Solara	—	—	—	26,245	26,665	27,580	28,175	28,175
V6	—	—	—	29,815	30,270	33,075	33,990	34,290
Used Values ($)								
Camry Coupe ▲	6,500	—	—	—	—	—	—	—
Camry Coupe ▼	5,500	—	—	—	—	—	—	—
Base Sedan CE ▲	—	8,500	9,500	11,500	13,500	15,000	—	—
Base Sedan CE ▼	—	7,000	8,500	10,000	12,000	13,500	—	—
LE ▲	7,500	9,500	11,500	13,500	15,500	17,000	18,500	20,500
LE ▼	6,500	8,500	10,000	12,000	14,000	16,000	17,000	19,000
LE V6 ▲	7,500	—	—	—	—	—	21,000	23,500
LE V6 ▼	7,000	—	—	—	—	—	19,500	22,000
Wagon V6 ▲	8,000	—	—	—	—	—	—	—
Wagon V6 ▼	7,000	—	—	—	—	—	—	—
Base Solara ▲	—	—	—	12,500	16,000	18,500	21,500	24,000
Base Solara ▼	—	—	—	11,000	14,500	17,000	20,000	22,500
V6 ▲	—	—	—	12,500	16,500	19,500	25,000	28,500
V6 ▼	—	—	—	11,000	15,500	18,000	23,500	27,000
Reliability	⑤	④	④	④	④	④	④	④
Crash Safety	④	④	④	④	—	④	⑤	④
Side	—	③	③	④	③	④	❷	❷
Solara	—	—	—	③	③	③	③	③

Offset	③	⑤	⑤	⑤	⑤	⑤	⑤	⑤
Head Restraints	③	—	③	—	❷	④	④	④
Rear	—	—	—	—	—	—	③	—
Solara	—	—	—	③	—	③	③	③
Rollover Resistance	—	—	—	—	—	⑤	④	④

Volkswagen

NEW BEETLE ★★★

RATING: Average (1998–2003). The New Beetle is an expensive trip down memory lane carried along on a Golf/Jetta platform. Personally, I don't think it's worth it—with or without its speed-activated spoiler and dash-mounted bud vase. And, interestingly enough, I'm not alone in my opinion. Sales are down and used Beetle prices have nose-dived. Another negative is the large number of safety-related complaints registered by NHTSA involving electrical fires, chronic stalling, and transmission failures. **Maintenance/Repair costs:** Average, but only a VW dealer can repair these cars. **Parts:** Easily found, since they're taken mostly from the Golf parts bin. Body parts are harder to find. **Best alternatives:** The Acura Integra; GM Cavalier or Sunfire; Honda Accord; Hyundai Elantra wagon, Sonata, or Tiburon; Mazda 626; Nissan Sentra; and Toyota Camry. **Online help:** For the latest owner reports on their Beetle love/hate relationship, service bulletins, and money-saving tips, look at *www.myvwlemon.com*; *www.vwvortex.com*; *www.autosafety.org/autodefects.html*; *www.alldata.com*; *www.kbb.com*; *www.edmunds.com*; *www.carforums.com/forums*; and *www.cartrackers.com/Forums*.

Strengths and weaknesses: The New Beetle was a hands-down marketing and public relations winner when the model was reintroduced as a 1998 model after being absent since 1979.

Why so much emotion for an ugly German import that never had a functioning heater, was declared "Small on Safety" by Ralph Nader and his Center for Auto Safety, and carried a puny 48-hp engine? The simple answer is that it was cheap and represented the first car most of us could afford as we went through school, got our first job, and dreamed of…getting a better car. Time has taken the edge off the memories of the hardship the Beetle made us endure—like having to scrape the inside windshield with our nails as our breath froze—and left us with the cozy feeling that the car wasn't that bad after all.

But it was.

Now VW has resurrected the Beetle and produced a competent front-engine, front-drive, compact car—set on the chassis and running gear of the Golf hatchback—that's much safer than its predecessor, but oddly enough is still afflicted by many of the same deficiencies we learned to hate with the original.

Again, without the turbocharger, the 115-hp base engine is underwhelming when you get it up to cruising speed (the 90-hp turbodiesel isn't much better), there's still not much room for rear passengers, engine noise is disconcerting, radio buttons and power accessory switches located on the door panels aren't user-friendly, front visibility is hindered by the car's quirky design, and storage capacity is at a premium.

On the other hand, the powerful, optional 1.8L turbocharged engine makes this Beetle an impressive performer; the heater works fine; steering, handling, and braking are quite good; and the interior is not as spartan or tacky as it once was.

Vehicle history: 2000—Addition of a 150-hp turbocharged 4-cylinder engine, firmer suspension, and improved theft protection. **2001**—Larger exterior mirrors and a trunk safety release. **2002**—Introduction of the 180-hp Turbo S, with a new Electronic Stabilization Program (where do they get these names?). **2003**—Convertible and turbodiesel arrive.

In a nutshell, here are the New Beetle's strong points: standard side airbags; easy handling; sure-footed, comfortable, though firm, ride; impressive braking; comfortable and supportive front seats with plenty of headroom and legroom; and cargo area that can be expanded by folding down the rear seats.

On the minus side: serious safety defects have been reported by owners (see NHTSA data below), powertrain performance is unimpressive, and body construction is second-rate. Specific owner gripes: the base engine runs out of steam around 100 km/h; diesel engines lack pep and produce lots of noise and vibration; faulty O_2 sensor causes the Check Engine light to come on; frequent ECM (electronic control module) failures; axle oil pan and oil pump failures; delayed shifts from Park to Drive, or failure to shift into Fourth gear; car is easily buffeted by crosswinds; optional high-mounted side mirrors, large head restraints, and large front roof pillars obstruct front and rear visibility; limited rear legroom and headroom; difficult rear entry/exit; excessive engine and brake noise; early brake component replacement; malfunctioning dash gauges; awkward-to-access radio buttons and door panel-mounted power switches; faulty window regulators; skimpy interior storage and trunk space; interior vent louvre loosens and breaks; hatchback rattles and sometimes fails to open; AC disengages when decelerating; front lights retain water and short out; and the low-slung chassis causes extensive undercarriage damage when going over a curb.

Safety summary: 1998—Driver's head restraint sits too high and can't be lowered, seriously restricting rear visibility. • Oil pan hole leaked oil and caused vehicle to stall. • Sudden loss of power while driving at 100 km/h, forcing driver to reset computer by restarting the vehicle. • While driving at any speed, vehicle goes into emergency mode and suddenly slows down to about 20 km/h. • Instrument cluster failure. • Vehicle was smoking under the hood because a faulty hose leaked oil onto the engine. • While stopped at a traffic light, vehicle just exploded into flames and was a total loss. **1999**—

Vehicle caught fire on inside of ignition switch box. • Another fire reportedly ignited in the wiring harness behind the dashboard. • Brake and accelerator pedals are too close together. • Sudden, unintended acceleration, and steering locked up. • Cruise control wouldn't disengage when brakes were applied. • Airbags failed to deploy. • Airbag warning light often comes on for no reason. • Sudden tread separation on the low-profile sporty tires. • When brakes are applied in a panic stop, one of the rear wheels will lock up along with one of the front wheels, causing vehicle to go into a spin. • Chronic hesitation and stalling on the highway (one fatality reported). • Vehicle won't start when facing down on a slope. • Frequent automatic transmission breakdowns. • Clutch failure causes vehicle to stall. • Left-side driveshaft cracked twice. • Driver's seat broke in a collision, causing severe injuries. • Driver-side seat came off its track and fell into back seat. • Tire jack fails to hold vehicle. • Cracked battery leaked acid onto power-steering fluid reservoir. • Vehicle shakes and shudders when driven with the sunroof fully open. • Headrest cannot be adjusted down to permit driver to see through rear and side windows; it's also quite uncomfortable for short drivers. **2000–01**—Many complaints of prolonged hesitation when accelerating. • Steering suddenly locked up. • Prematurely worn rear brake pads (TSB #00-01, November 27, 2000). • Low-mounted fuel tank is easily punctured. • Mass airflow sensor and secondary air injection pump motor failures. • Back glass suddenly shattered. • Windows fall into door channel due to defective regulators. • Hard to keep rear window free of rain, snow, or dew. • Windshield distortions impede vision. • Airbags failed to deploy. • Airbag warning light stays lit constantly. • Rear seat belted passengers hit their heads on the unpadded side pillars. **2002**—ABS failure. • Window goes up and down on its own. • Brake fluid leakage. • Harsh downshifts; vehicle loses power (mass air flow sensor is suspected cause):

> Car downshifts extremely hard when coming to a stop, causing driver and passengers to be lunged forward in their seat.
> Dealer states that this is a characteristic of the car. Problem is intermittent and increases when vehicle is warmed up.
> On one occasion downshift occurred so hard that I thought I was just rear-ended by another car. I bought the car for my wife and now she is afraid to drive it.

2003—Sudden acceleration, stalling. • Side airbag deployed for no reason. • Driver-side airbag failed to deploy. • Punctured fuel tank leaked fuel. • Steering wheel lock-up; excessive shake, constant pulling to the right (torque steer). • Back glass suddenly exploded. • Rear windshield is hard to see through. • Dash warning lights come on constantly for no apparent reason. • Head restraints still sit too high to be comfortable and obstruct rear visibility. • Open sunroof sucks exhaust into the cabin. • Left front strut slipped down through the spindle, causing the spindle to hit the wheel well.

Secret Warranties/Service Tips/TSBs

All models/years: Lousy radio reception. **1998–99**—An erratic-shifting automatic transaxle is likely caused by an improper throttle angle setting. VW will correct the problem under its base warranty. • Troubleshooting tips on silencing instrument panel, front door lock/latch, and door speaker squeaks or rattles. • Possible causes and fix for wind noise or whistle coming from the instrument panel. • Diagnosing humming noise from front of vehicle when cornering. • No adjustment of air flow from centre air outlets. • Throttle pedal and shifter lever vibration or knocking vibration. **1998–2002**—Troubleshooting a noisy blower motor. • Malfunctioning instrument cluster. • Hood emblem chrome peeling off. • Faulty window regulator repair tips. **2000–01**—Prematurely worn rear brake pads. **2001**—Inoperative secondary oil pump. **2002**—Transmission appears to leak fluid. • Inoperative fresh air blower motor.

New Beetle Profile

	1998	1999	2000	2001	2002	2003
Cost Price ($)						
Base	19,940	21,500	21,950	21,950	21,950	23,210
Used Values ($)						
Base ∧	8,500	10,000	12,000	14,000	16,000	18,500
Base ∨	7,500	8,500	10,500	12,500	14,500	17,500
Reliability	③	③	③	④	④	④
Crash Safety	—	④	④	④	④	④
Side	—	⑤	⑤	⑤	⑤	⑤
Offset	⑤	⑤	⑤	⑤	⑤	⑤
Head Restraints (F)	④	④	—	④	④	④
Rear	③	③	—	—	③	③

PASSAT ★★

RATING: Below Average (1998–2003); Not Recommended (1989–97). Don't listen to the car journalists who love European cars; they don't pay for service visits. Read owner opinions and you'll see the Passat is a big disappointment. Word has gotten out that these cars are over-hyped for their performance prowess, aren't very dependable, and cost a lot to maintain. Consequently, Passats have lost their lustre to Japanese luxury cars and now depreciate quickly. But beware; their low price won't cover the extraordinarily high repair bills you'll get from Otto and Hans. But, if you're a risk-taker, protect your wallet somewhat by staying away from pre-'98s and insist upon a comprehensive extended warranty. **Maintenance/Repair costs:** Much higher than average. Most major repairs are dealer dependent. **Parts:** Parts and service are more expensive than average; long waits for parts are commonplace. **Best alternatives:** The Acura Integra, Audi A4 or A6, and the Honda Accord.

Online help: For owner feedback detailing the "dark side" of VW ownership go to *www.myvwlemon.com*; *www.vwvortex.com*; *www.autosafety.org/autodefects.html*; *www.alldata.com*; *www.kbb.com*; *www.edmunds.com*; *www.carforums.com/forums*; *www.cartrackers.com/Forums*; and through Google, using "VW coil pack stalling" in your search.

Strengths and weaknesses: This front-drive compact sedan and wagon uses a standard 2.0L engine and other mechanical parts borrowed from the Golf, Jetta, and Corrado. However, a 2.8L V6 became the standard power plant beginning with the '99 wagon. Its long wheelbase and squat appearance give the Passat a massive, solid feeling, while its styling makes it look sleek and clean. As with most European imports, it comes fairly well appointed.

As far as overall performance goes, the Passat is no slouch. The multi-valve 4-cylinder engine is adequate, and its handling is superior to that of most of the competition. The 2.8L V6 provides lots of power when revved and is the engine that works best with an automatic transmission.

Vehicle history: 1990—Debuts with a 134-hp 2.0L 4-cylinder engine. **1993**—A 172-hp 2.8L V6 powered the GLX. **1994**—4-cylinder engines were axed. **1995**—Redesigned model adopted dual airbags, a re-styled interior, rear headrests, a softened suspension, and a much-improved crashworthiness rating; 4-cylinder engine returned and a TDI wagon and sedan debuted. **1998**—Based upon the Audi A4 and A6, this model offers more usable interior space, better handling, and better engine performance with its 150-hp turbocharged 1.8L engine and 190-hp 2.8L V6. **2000**—AWD model arrives. **2001**—A restyled version debuts with a 170-hp engine alongside a new W8, 270-hp AWD luxury car.

Passats are infamous for transmission malfunctions and engine ignition coil/fuel system glitches that are hard to diagnose and costly to repair. Even when they're operating as they should, the Passat's manual and automatic gearboxes leave a lot to be desired. For example, the 5-speed manual transmission gear ranges are too far apart: there's an enormous gap between Third and Fourth gear, and the 4-speed automatic shifts poorly with the 4-banger. Also, owners report that the transmission won't shift from lower gears, as well as problems with clutch slave cylinder leaks, front brakes (master cylinder replacements, brake booster failure, rotor warpage, premature wear, and excessive noise), MacPherson struts, and fuel and electrical systems as the car ages. Owners mention defective tie-rod and constant velocity joint seals that allow debris to enter into system, effectively causing premature wearout of internal components; engines often leak oil; early replacement of the power steering assembly; and fuel and computer module problems that lead to hard starts and chronic stalling.

On the body side, there's a helicopter-type wind noise when cruising with the windows or sunroof open; sunroof rattles; front spoiler and rear trim fall off; a persistent water leak from the pollen filter; interior trim and controls are fragile; heated seats are a pain in the...well, you know; driver's seat memory feature fails; door speakers are frequently replaced; fuel gauge malfunctions, indicating fuel in tank when it's empty; windshields may be optically distorted; rear-view passenger-side mirrors are too small and cause several blind spots.

Owners report that VW dealer servicing is the pits. Cars have to be brought in constantly to fix the same problem, recall campaign repairs are often slow because parts aren't available, and warranty coverage is spotty because VW headquarters doesn't empower or pay dealers sufficiently to take the initiative. Competent servicing and parts are particularly hard to find away from the larger cities, and many of the above-mentioned deficiencies can cost you an arm and a leg to repair.

Safety summary: 1996—Many complaints that transmission slips out of Third gear into Neutral. • Vehicle suddenly accelerated forward as lever was put into Reverse. • Intermittent stalling due to electronic control module failure. • Check Engine light constantly goes on and off. • Engine-valve cover gasket failures. • Plastic shroud on top of engine rubs against the fuel line. • Leaking windshield and door seals. • Premature wheel-bearing failure on the driver's side. • Door lock failure allows door to open while under power, or makes doors difficult to open. • Instrument cluster wiring harness failures. • Repeated trunk-switch failures. • Chronic trunk water leaks. • Premature brake pad wearout. • All dash gauges suddenly stop working. **1997**—When manual transmission lever is put into Reverse, it often goes into First gear instead. • Sudden steering wheel lock-up. • Cooling fan control module failure. • Rear window defroster power button works only when held in the On position. • Door handle failures. • Frequent window regulator failures. **1998**—Engine head gasket/manifold leaks, car stalls, and turbo blows:

> I wanted to advise you of problems I am having with my VW '98 Passat. I see you have the Passat listed in your book as a good buy. I am writing to get you to consider changing your recommendation.
>
> I just got off the phone with the National Safety Transportation Board. They are racking up calls on the Passat. Seems I am not the only one who has a Passat that stalls out with no warning for no apparent reason. I now have $2,400 into trying to fix the problem, and no solution has been found. It is a miracle I have not been in and/or caused an accident. The other NHTSA complaints are identical to mine.
>
> In addition, my turbo and manifold blew out, to the tune of $1,500, due to extreme heat. I live in Maine, take great care of the car, and have been told by two dealers that the turbo and manifold should not have blown at 64,000 miles [100,000 km]. To boot, they said there is nothing I can do to prevent it from blowing again. The NHTSA also said there were a number of complaints for blown turbos. My mechanic said the folks at the VW parts warehouse in Boston have had so many calls to replace manifolds and turbos on Passats, that they have the parts list pinned up over their phones.

I don't think this is a good sign for what is becoming a number-one sedan choice in America, and hope you warn potential buyers in your next edition and on your website.

My next stop is the *myvwlemon.com* site—thanks for the link!

L.C.

Portland, Maine

• Erratic transmission performance. • Gas tank can't be filled without the pump shutting off repeatedly. • AC recirculation switch failure. • Serious blind spots caused by the small size and narrow view of the three mirrors. • Front seats move back and forth when vehicle is braking or accelerating. • Total electrical-system failure. **1999**—Electrical fire. • Airbags failed to deploy. • Airbag light comes on for no reason. • Sudden, unintended acceleration. • Cruise control doesn't disengage, or engages on its own. • Accelerator pedal fails to return after full throttle. • Chronic stalling on the highway. • Early transmission clutch failure. • Clutch depressed to the floor and gear stayed engaged. • Front suspension's lower right arm failure due to a faulty bushing. • Front left wheel came off when making a turn. • Premature failures of the Michelin MXV4 tire; when rear tires blow out, they wreck havoc on vehicle's undercarriage (wheelwell and well lining), in some cases causing the fuel tank to leak. • Other complaints of ruptured fuel tanks. • Oil line ruptured while driving. • Missing power steering cap caused fluid to leak out. • Driver's seat has excessive fore and aft movement. • Windshield cracked while vehicle was parked in direct sunlight. **2000**—More reports of fire erupting in the engine compartment. • Excess raw fuel flows out of the exhaust system. • Hard starts and chronic stalling. • Check Engine light comes on intermittently and then engine shuts down. • While cruising, vehicle speeds up; when brakes applied, it slows down, until foot is taken off the brake, then it surges again. Owners describe it this way:

> Dangerous situation. When accelerating from a complete stop, vehicle does one of three things: 1) gasps for gas and goes nowhere (dangerous when making left-hand turns), or 2) tries to move ahead like a carbureted car with vapour lock, or 3) performs normally.

• Braking doesn't disengage cruise control. • Hesitation and long delays when accelerating. • Automatic transmission suddenly drops out of gear. • Airbags failed to deploy; airbag warning light stays lit. • Many complaints of windshield distortion (there's an accordion effect where letters and objects expand and contract as they pass by). • Passenger window suddenly exploded just after being rolled up. • Windshield wipers cut out. • Plastic engine nose shield fell off. • Rear tire failure damaged the fuel-filler neck, causing a fuel leak. **2002**— An incredible number of automatic transmission malfunctions, breakdowns, and early replacements. • Transmission vibration and noise. • Premature CV joint failure. • Oil pan is easily punctured due to low ground clearance. • Some electrical and fuel system glitches cause chronic stalling; ignition coils still seem to be a primary cause of this stalling and loss of engine power. • Gas pedal remained stuck to the floor. • Brakes don't grab as well when vehicle is cold, premature brake wear, and noisy braking. **2003**—Several reports that fire ignited in the engine compartment. • Excess raw fuel flows out of the exhaust system. • Hard starts and chronic stalling. • Check Engine light comes on intermittently and then engine shuts down. • While cruising, vehicle speeds up, when brakes applied, it slows down until foot is taken off the brake, when it surges again. • Vehicle runs out of fuel despite the fuel gauge showing a quarter-tank of gas. • Braking doesn't disengage cruise control. • Hesitation, long delays when accelerating. • Automatic transmission suddenly drops out of gear; airbags failed to deploy or deploy for no reason. One VW employee told U.S. federal investigators he was fired for complaining about the airbag hazard:

> The driver-side head airbag (air curtain) of a 2003 Volkswagen Passat W8 sedan deployed spontaneously while I was driving the car...a few minutes later, when the car was stopped, the steering wheel airbag deployed spontaneously...I suffered a permanent wrist injury and am suffering from post-traumatic stress syndrome...the incident, which happened during a test drive, was reported to the management of the VW dealership for which I was working and to VW of America by the management...I sent a detailed incident report to both VW of America [VWOA] and VW AG (Germany) CEOs... A VW customer service representative admonished me to not make a fuss about the incident, saying it was a once-in-a-lifetime occurrence unlikely to happen again, and advised me that my letter to the VWOA CEO had been received but that he had not read it.... The owner of the dealership advised me in a special meeting that he had been contacted by a VWOA management representative, who was unhappy with the complaints I had made to the customer service representative about the lack of follow-up by VW and the means of alerting VW owners about the incident I was considering.... I left the meeting believing my job and future in the car business, at least selling VW products, would be in jeopardy if I took any affirmative action such as filing this complaint. A promise that I would be informed by VWOA of the reason for the spontaneous deployment has not been fulfilled and I have not been contacted by any VW representative in almost four months.... Recently, I was fired because of an incident I consider related directly to the incident.... I am filing this report because I have just learned that another person has, reportedly, experienced the spontaneous deployment of an airbag in a VW car and I am now confident that what I experienced was not a freak occurrence.

• Airbag warning light stays lit. • Many complaints of windshield distortion (there's an accordion effect where letters and objects expand and contract as they pass by). • Passenger window suddenly exploded just after being rolled up. • Windshield wipers cut out. • Plastic engine nose shield fell off. • Rear tire failure damaged the fuel-filler neck, causing a fuel leak. • Super-heated seats.

Secret Warranties/Service Tips/TSBs

All models/years: Failure-prone, malfunctioning automatic transmissions. **1992–94**—Poor 2.8L engine performance or a rough idle could be due to a misrouted EVAP vacuum hose or an improperly routed positive crankcase ventilation hose, which will cause a vacuum leak. **1995–96**—Troubleshooting tips are offered on automatic transmission fluid seepage. **1995–99**—An erratic-shifting automatic transmission may be due to an improper throttle angle setting. **1996–97**—If the transmission pops out of gear, check for a hairline crack on the selector shaft shift detent sleeve. • Transmission fluid seepage. • Shifter is hard to move or won't go into Reverse. • Knocking/vibrating shift lever. • Vehicle will not move into any forward gear. **1998–99**—Tips on fixing a door speaker rattle or vibration. • VW says a delayed upshift after a cold start is normal and a wait of 40 seconds isn't too long (typical of German logic: "Our cars are perfect, our customers aren't."). **1998–2000**—Defective fresh air control lever light affects operation of heating/AC system. **1998–2001**—Malfunctioning radio volume control and instrument cluster. **1999**—Engine cranks, but won't start. • Malfunctioning windshield wipers. • Engine misfire. **2000–01**—Airbag warning light remains lit. **2001**—Noisy sunroof. • Broken armrest lid latch. **2003**—Updates for the ECM and TCM modules.

Passat Profile

	1996	1997	1998	1999	2000	2001	2002	2003
Cost Price ($)								
Base	27,230	28,620	28,450	29,100	29,100	29,500	29,550	29,550
Used Values ($)								
Base ∧	5,500	8,000	10,000	13,000	15,500	18,000	21,000	24,500
Base ∨	4,500	6,500	9,000	12,000	14,000	16,500	19,500	23,500
Reliability	③	③	③	③	③	③	③	④
Crash Safety	④	④	—	—	⑤	⑤	⑤	⑤
Side	—	—	—	—	④	④	④	④
Offset	❶	❶	⑤	⑤	⑤	⑤	⑤	⑤
Head restraints	—	❶	❷	❷	—	③	③	❷
Rear	—	—	❶	❶	—	❷	❷	❷

LARGE CARS/WAGONS

These are the cars you're most likely to see in your rear-view mirror with their red and blue lights flashing. Quintessential highway cruisers for travelling salespeople, law enforcement agencies, large families, and retirees, the full-sized American car is an icon of a time long passed. No longer able to compete with high fuel costs and more versatile minivans and small sport-utilities, most of these "land yachts" have been axed or are being phased out, as is the case with Ford's Crown Victoria and Grand Marquis. Only Chrysler is still in the game with its spacious and attractively styled Concorde, Intrepid, and 300M sedans.

Ford's blown its five-star rating with the Crown Victoria and Mercury Grand Marquis mainly because of serious engine, transmission, and electrical problems. Plus, scary wet-weather handling is just too dangerous to ignore.

Owners once had to pay a premium for these behemoths, which usually came fully loaded with performance and convenience features, but they were happy to do so because these vehicles offer considerable comfort and stability at high speeds. They also depreciate relatively quickly (making them great used-car bargains), can seat six adults comfortably, and are ideal for motoring vacations. Repairs are a snap and can be done almost anywhere, and there's a large reservoir of reasonably priced replacement parts sold through independent agencies.

The downside?

Atrocious fuel economy, mediocre highway performance, and handling that's neither precise nor exciting. The interior is comfortable, but not as versatile as a minivan or SUV, and you don't get as commanding a view of the road as in other, taller vehicles.

LARGE CAR/WAGON RATINGS

Above Average

Ford Crown Victoria, Grand Marquis (1984–95)

General Motors Caprice, Impala SS, Roadmaster (1995–96)

Average

DaimlerChrysler Concorde, 300M, Intrepid
  (2002–03)

Ford Cougar, Thunderbird (1985–97)

Ford Crown Victoria, Grand Marquis
  (1996-2003)

General Motors Caprice, Impala SS,
  Roadmaster (1982–94)

Not Recommended

DaimlerChrysler Concorde, Intrepid,
  LHS, New Yorker, Vision
  (1993–2001)

Ford Cougar, Thunderbird (1999-2002)

Station wagons (full-sized)

If passenger and cargo space and carlike handling are what you want, a large station wagon may not be the answer—a used minivan, van, light truck, or compact wagon can fill the same need for less cost and will probably still be around a decade from now. Popular (though troublesome) wagons—like the Caprice and Roadmaster (both axed in 1996)—in which you could cram a Little League team are an endangered species, losing out to the van and minivan craze.

Some disadvantages of large station wagons: difficulty in keeping the interior heated in winter, atrocious gas consumption, sloppy handling, and poor rear visibility. Rear hatches and rear brake supporting plates tend to be rust-prone.

DaimlerChrysler

300M, CONCORDE, INTREPID, LHS, NEW YORKER, VISION ★★★

RATING: Average (2002–03); Not Recommended (1993–2001). Like most Chryslers, these poor-quality cars are more style than substance. Recent models get a better rating not because they're better built, but because they're better protected with a 7-year powertrain warranty to protect you from chronic engine failure (particularly the 2.7L Mitsubishi V6) and automatic transmission breakdowns. Although the '99 300M is bargain priced, its first year glitches can wipe away most of your savings. Stay away from the discontinued pre-1999 LHS, New Yorker, and Vision. Parts are rare and mechanics cringe when these hard-to-service cars arrive in their service bay. **Maintenance/Repair costs:** Higher than average, but most repairs aren't dealer dependent. **Parts:** Higher-than-average cost (independent suppliers sell for much less), but not hard to find. **Best alternatives:** A GM Bonneville, Caprice, LeSabre, or Roadmaster; Ford's early Cougar, T-Bird, or Crown Victoria, and Mercury Grand Marquis. **Online help:** *www.datatown.com/chrysler*; *www.wam.umd.edu/ ~gluckman/Chrysler/index.html*; *www.daimlerchryslervehicleproblems.com*; *intrepidhorrorstories.blogspot.com*; and *www.autosafety.org/autodefects.html*.

Strengths and weaknesses: These full-sized cars share the same chassis and offer most of the same standard and optional features. They provide loads of passenger space and many standard features such as four-wheel disc brakes and an independent rear suspension. Since their 1998 redesign, base models are equipped with a failure-prone 2.7L V6 aluminum engine that delivers 200 hp. Higher line variants get a more powerful 3.2L V6 225-hp power plant, or a 242-hp 3.5L V6. Earlier models also carried a 3.3L 153-hp 6-banger, but 70 percent of buyers chose the 3.5L for its extra horses. Both engines provide plenty of low-end torque and acceleration, but this advantage is lost somewhat when traversing hilly terrain: the smaller V6 power plant strains to keep up.

These cars have better handling and steering response than the Sable and Taurus or GM mid-sized front-drives, but the difference is marginal when you tote up the $3,000–$10,000 cost of powertrain, brake, and AC repairs.

Furthermore, these cars can be as unsafe as they are unreliable. Read the following owners' experiences, which are both scary and typical:

> Travelling on the freeway at 100 km/h, my 1999 Chrysler 300M's rear windshield was sucked out and flew to the side of the road. I had no prior problems with the windshield. Entire rear windshield and casing flew off.
>
> •
>
> My 2000 Concorde accelerated on its own. I had to hit a tree to stop the car. The airbags did not deploy upon impact. Tires continued spinning after impact, until I turned off the ignition.

Owner reports confirm that there are chronic problems with engine sludge gumming up the works of the 2.7L engine, leaking 3.3L engine head gaskets, and noisy lifters that wear out prematurely around 60,000 km. Water pumps often self-destruct and take the engine timing chain along with them (a $1,200 repair). Engine surging and unintended acceleration is also a frequent refrain, affecting all model years. However, the one recurring safety problem affecting almost all model years concerns the steering system. Says *www.daimlerchryslervehicleproblems.com*:

> Chrysler has been under investigation by NHTSA for more than 55,000 warranty claims for steering problems with these vehicles and 1,450 reports of steering control problems, some including complete loss of steering control....
>
> Many consumers have also paid over $1,200 (U.S.) for replacement steering assemblies.... Common symptoms of steering problems with these vehicles are typically loose steering, excessive play in the steering, vibration, wandering, steering out of alignment, clunks, rattle, rubbing, or binding.

The 4-speed LE42 automatic transmission is a spin-off from Chrysler's failure-prone A604 version—and owner reports show it to be just as unreliable.

Owners tell of chronic glitches in the computerized transmission's shift timing and other computer malfunctions, which result in early replacement and drive-ability problems (stalling, hard starts, and surging).

Body problems abound, with lots of interior noise; uneven fit and finish with misaligned doors, jagged trunk edges; poor-quality trim items that break or fall off easily; exposed screw heads; faulty door hinges that make the doors rattle-prone and hard to open; distorted, poorly mounted windshields; windows that come off their tracks or are misaligned and poorly sealed; power window motor failures; and steering wheel noise when the car is turning.

AC failures are commonplace and costly to repair. The problem has become so prevalent that Chrysler has a little-known warranty extension that will pay for the replacement of the evaporator up to seven years. Chrysler has tried to limit compensation to certain models, only, but the company is stuck with its 7-year benchmark, which owners can cite for any AC failure (see page 52).

Vehicle history: 1994—Debut of a sporty LHS and redesigned New Yorker equipped with variable-assist power steering; Concorde gets the touring suspension and a small horsepower boost (eight). **1997**—New Yorker dropped along with the 3.3L V6 on the base LX model. **1998**—Concorde and Intrepid were completely redesigned, given two new V6s (a 200-hp 2.7L and a 225-hp 3.2L), ABS, traction control (on the LXi), and dual front airbags. **1999**—Improved steering and ride. **2000**—Suspension upgrades, a freshened instrument panel, and standard variable-assist steering on the LXi. **2001**—Steering-mounted audio controls, a rear seat centre shoulder belt, and an internal trunk release. **2002**—A 300M Special performance model comes with a new grille, upgraded ABS, and more user-friendly child safety seat anchors. Concorde got the LHS' styling and most of the other LHS amenities, including a 250-hp 3.5L V6, leather trim, high-tech gauges, ABS, traction control, and 17-inch alloy wheels. The LXi acquired the 3.2L V6 with a 234-hp variant of the 3.5L V6. **2003**—Intrepid gets a 244-hp 3.5L V6, Concorde horsepower goes to 250, and the 300M's power is boosted to 255-hp. All will adopt rear drive as late-2004 models. It'll be fun watching Chrysler bad-mouthing front-drives to promote its new rear-drive models.

300M and LHS

These two models represent the near-luxury and sport clones of the Chrysler Concorde. Although they use the same front-drive platform as the Concorde, their bodies are shorter and they're styled differently. In fact, the 300M is the shortest of Chrysler's mid-sized sedans. Both cars are powered by a 253-hp 3.5L V6 and mated to Chrysler's AutoStick semi-automatic transmission. Mechanical and body deficiencies generally mirror those of the Concorde and Intrepid.

Safety summary: All models/years: No airbag deployment in a collision. • 2.7L engine suddenly self-destructs due to excess oil sludge and overheating. Owners describe the failure this way:

The primary symptom is that the car heater, for no reason, does not blow hot air. If this has been happening it is likely that your car engine has been overheating and causing sludge to buildup in the top half of the engine. Ultimately your engine will fail with very little warning. Some symptoms are: car starts to burn oil, very light traces of white smoke from exhaust, and the engine may seem to run a little rough at idle.

•

Immediately examine your oil fill cap to see if there is any buildup of a black grease-like gunk. If you see this, immediately contact your mechanic to determine if you have a sludge buildup. If sludge is present your engine will almost certainly fail with little or no warning. Cost for repairs averages $6,500 (U.S.).

• Engine surging and sudden, unintended acceleration. • Many reports of sudden transmission failures, often due to cracked transmission casings. • Transmission fluid leakage caused by defective transmission casing bolt. • Gas fumes enter the interior. • Windshields are often distorted and may fall out while vehicle is underway. • A high rear windowsill obstructs rear visibility. • Headlights may be too dim for safe motoring and cut out completely or come on by themselves. Defrosting is also inadequate, allowing ice and moisture to collect at the base of the windshield. Chrysler has a fix for these two problems that requires the installation of a new headlight lens and small foam pads into the defroster outlet ducts. • Both ABS and non-ABS brakes perform poorly, resulting in excessively long stopping distances or the complete loss of braking ability. • Brake rotors rust prematurely and warp easily, and pads have to be changed every 15,000 km. • The overhead digital panel is distracting and forces you to take your eyes from the road. • The emergency brake pedal catches pant cuffs and shoelaces as you enter or exit the vehicle. **1994–97—** The front suspension may collapse, causing the driver to lose control of the vehicle. NHTSA knows of 26 complaints and 105 warranty claims for 1994 models and another 49 complaints covering 1995–97 years that used an upgraded suspension. Broken welds or cracks where the lower control arm attaches to the front cradle may be the cause of the failures. **1996—**A sudden loss of power, the engine shuts down, power steering and brakes become inoperative, and the Check Engine light comes on. • High-pressure fuel lines between the two cylinder heads leak gas onto the engine. • When shifting into Reverse from Park, automatic transmission acts as if it's in Neutral, and the engine races when the accelerator is pressed. • Vehicle shakes violently when ABS brakes are applied. • Dashboard reflection in the windshield hampers visibility. • Horn buttons difficult to access in emergency situations. • Stuck right rear door lock won't allow door to open. • Door hinges don't hold door open securely, causing injury to occupants when door closes unexpectedly. **1997—** Fire ignited in trunk. • Fuel line hoses disconnected from the engine, spilling fuel into the engine area. • Vehicle decelerates while driving. • Steering linkage failure causes vehicle to wander all over the roadway. • Power-steering failure— extremely hard to turn. • Seat backrest failure. • Frequent windshield replacements due to distortion—particularly annoying at night when combined with poor headlight illumination. • Frequent instrument panel malfunctions: lights, gauges, AC all go out at once. **1998**—Reports of sudden acceleration when shifting into Reverse. • When transmission relay fails, it causes a harsh downshift to Second gear while at highway speeds. **1999**—Vehicle suddenly accelerated when shifted into Reverse at a car wash. • The bolt that holds the fan and engine pulley came loose, resulting in complete loss of steering ability. • Brakes continually lock up, grind when applied, and result in extended stopping distance. • Vehicle will suddenly shudder or lurch violently while underway at cruising speed. • Fuel smell invades the interior. • Shifter pin to interlock cable broke off, causing the ignition key to be removable while vehicle is in gear. • Frequent failure of the power window motors. **2000–01**—Transmission won't shift to Reverse and engine stalls. • Side seat belts don't retract. • Front and rear windshields distort view; there may be an annoying reflection on the inside of the windshield, particularly evident on vehicles with beige interiors. **2002**—Yikes, transmission malfunctions continue, unabated:

> Transmission intermittently bumps, shifts, or slams into gear. [It happens] [w]hen driving at around 40–50 mph [65–80 km/h] and flooring it to accelerate then letting off the accelerator pedal. There is sometimes a bang or bump, sometimes harsh feeling in the front end or transmission.
>
> This is sometimes so hard that passengers feel it and complain. Bump is sometimes felt on deceleration in lower gears nearing a stop.

• Steering drifts, sometimes takes undue effort, squeaks, and clunks. • Seat belt button is too sensitive; belt is easily unlatched inadvertently. **300M: 1999**—Airbags suddenly deployed for no reason when changing lanes. • Transmission jumped from Park to Reverse with engine running. • Driver's son took shifter out of Park without key in ignition, and vehicle rolled down hill. • Vehicle constantly shakes and shimmies; wobbles and bobbles on the highway. **2001**—Sudden stalling in traffic. • Unstable driver's seat. • Fuel tank easily overflows. **2002**—Brake failure, then engine surges. • No-starts. • Sunroof exploded. • Right front wheel disconnected from vehicle. **2003**—Sudden brake failure. • Surging when stopped. • Rear visibility compromised by narrow rear windows in the 300M.

Secret Warranties/Service Tips/TSBs

All models/years: A rotten-egg odour coming from the exhaust is probably caused by a malfunctioning catalytic converter; this is covered by Chrysler's original warranty *and* the emissions warranty. Don't take "no" for an answer. The same advice goes for all the squeaks and rattles and the water and wind leaks that afflict these vehicles. Don't let Chrysler or the dealer pawn these problems off as maintenance items. They're all factory related and should be covered for at least five years. **All models: 1993–98**—Delayed transaxle engagement can be corrected through upgraded hardware and software components.

1993–99—Troubleshooting tips for trunk water and dust leaks. • Paint delamination, peeling, or fading (see Part Two). **1993–2000**—If the vehicle leads or pulls at highway speeds, TSB #02-16-99 suggests a whole series of countermeasures, including replacing the engine mounts, if necessary. Chrysler will apply the base warranty to this repair. • Loose or noisy steering may be corrected by servicing the inner tie-rod bushings or simply replacing the tie-rod. • Harsh, erratic, or delayed transmission shifts can be corrected by replacing the throttle position sensor (TPS) with a revised part. **1993–2001**—More tips on fixing loose or noisy steering.

Steering – Loose Feel/Clunking on Turns

NUMBER: 19-001-01

Mar. 23, 2001

OVERVIEW: This bulletin provides service procedures and parts information for the inner tie-rod bushings.

MODELS: 1993–2001 (LH) Concorde/Intrepid/LHS/New Yorker/Vision/300M

SYMPTOM: Loose feel or clunk in the steering wheel as the wheel is moved from side to side.

DIAGNOSIS: Observe the inner tie-rod to steering gear attaching point while moving the steering wheel from side to side. If there is movement between the gear and inner tie-rod, perform the repair.

1995–99—More troubleshooting tips are offered on diagnosing and fixing trunk water leaks. **1995–97**—If the AC suction line fails, replace it and install a revised right-side engine ground strap; the original ground strap probably caused the failure. **1996–97**—If you hear a metallic popping noise coming from the front of the vehicle when you accelerate from a stop, install two new upper and two new lower cradle mounting isolators. • Rear drum brake ticking can be silenced by burnishing the rear brakes. **1998–99**—A rough idle or poor driveability may require the testing and replacing of the EGR valve and power control module (PCM). • An engine hiss noise can be silenced by replacing the throttle body assembly. • Delayed shifts and other transmission malfunctions affecting a broad range of models are addressed in TSB #21-03-98. This is proof positive that Chrysler's transmission woes are far from over. • Troubleshooting tips for no hot air or lack of cold air. • Poor heater performance may mean the PCM should simply be reprogrammed. • Window sticks in the up position. • Countermeasures for correcting excessive road noise and a variety of squeaks, rattles, and squawks. • Troubleshooting tips for correcting water leaks on top and/or under floor carpets. • Poor AM radio reception can be fixed by installing a new electronic backlight module. **1998–2000**—Poor AC performance can be fixed by first carrying out Customer Satisfaction Recall #857 and then reprogramming the power control module. • Repair procedures are outlined for reattaching the rear door trim panel. • Guidelines for silencing wind noise emanating from the sunroof and the area in front of the B-pillars. • Front suspension strut squeaking can be stopped by installing a revised front strut striker cap. **1998–2001**—Loose driver's seat. • Window sticks in the up position. **1998–2002**—Erratic AC operation:

AC – Erratic Operation

NUMBER: 24-009-01   DATE: Aug. 3, 2001

MODELS

1998 - **2002** (LH) LHS/300M/Concorde/Intrepid

NOTE: PERFORM CUSTOMER SATISFACTION RECALL NO. 857, REPROGRAM PCM, FOR 2000
MODEL YEAR VEHICLES BUILT PRIOR TO AUGUST 30, 1999 (MDH 0830XX).

SYMPTOM/CONDITION

Erratic operation of the AC and heater systems including: lack of cold air, lack of hot air,
unrequested mode change (Automatic Temperature Control [ATC] only), no control of mode
or temperature control or dithering/tapping blend door noise. These symptoms may be
accompanied by the following Diagnostic Fault Codes (DTCs): Blend Door Feedback, Blend
Door Stall, A/C Control Mode Door Input Shorted To Battery, In-Car Temp Sensor Failure,
ATC Messages Not Received, or Mode Door Stall.

1999–2002—Snapping sound when opening or closing door. **2000–01**—
Erratic engine idle. • Front strut noise. • Front suspension or steering gear
rattle. • Vehicle leads or pulls. • Speaker screw contacts door seal. **2000–04**—
Fuel tank slow to fill; note that this has been a chronic problem affecting five
model years (see following bulletin).

Fuel System – Fuel Tank Slow to Fill

NUMBER: 14-001-03

DATE: Jan. 24, 2003

2000–04 (LH)   LHS/300M/Concorde/Intrepid

OVERVIEW: This bulletin involves correcting any or all of the following items as necessary:

^Kinked/plugged fuel tank vent lines

^Replacing the fuel tank control valve

^Replacing the Leak Detection Pump (LDP) filter

^Unplugging or replacing the fuel tank fill tube assembly

2001—Troubleshooting automatic transmission surge, sag, and shift bump
complaints (TSB #18-007-01). **2002**—Transaxle limp-in, engine misfire,
engine no-start. • Discoloured window moulding. **2002–04**—Vehicles
equipped with a 3.5L engine that has a rough idle when cold may need the
powertrain control module (PCM) recalibrated or replaced; a free service
under the emissions warranty (see TSB #18-042-03). **2003**—Engine stumbling or misfire. • Defective power control module. • Delayed or temporary
loss of transmission engagement after initial start-up. • Transmission goes into
"limp" mode. • Harsh 4–3 downshift. • Headliner sag or rattle. • Front brake
noise or pulsation. • Poor AC performance. • Rear strut squeaks. • Wind noise
from sunroof or B-pillar when driving.

300M, Concorde, Intrepid, LHS, New Yorker, Vision Profile

	1996	1997	1998	1999	2000	2001	2002	2003
Cost Price ($)								
300M	—	—	—	39,150	39,675	40,900	39,900	40,335
Concorde	26,005	26,815	26,915	27,635	28,115	28,485	29,690	30,240
Intrepid	22,980	24,055	24,395	25,060	25,520	25,910	25,765	25,095
LHS	38,420	40,500	40,500	41,150	41,370	41,655	—	—
New Yorker	34,490	—	—	—	—	—	—	—
Vision	23,770	24,775	—	—	—	—	—	—
Used Values ($)								
300M ∧	—	—	—	12,500	16,000	20,000	24,000	28,000
300M ∨	—	—	—	11,000	14,000	18,500	22,500	26,000
Concorde ∧	5,000	6,000	8,000	9,500	11,500	14,000	17,500	20,000
Concorde ∨	4,000	5,000	7,000	8,000	10,500	13,000	16,000	18,500
Intrepid ∧	4,000	5,000	7,000	8,500	10,500	12,500	15,500	17,500
Intrepid ∨	3,500	4,500	6,000	7,500	9,000	11,000	14,000	16,000
LHS ∧	6,000	7,000	9,000	13,000	17,000	21,000	—	—
LHS ∨	5,000	6,000	7,500	11,000	15,000	19,000	—	—
New Yorker ∧	5,000	—	—	—	—	—	—	—
New Yorker ∨	4,500	—	—	—	—	—	—	—
Vision ∧	4,000	5,000	—	—	—	—	—	—
Vision ∨	3,500	4,000	—	—	—	—	—	—
Reliability	❶	❶	❶	❶	❶	❷	③	③
Crash Safety	④	④	—	④	④	④	④	④
300M	—	—	—	—	—	—	—	❸
Side	④	④	—	④	④	④	④	④
Offset	—	—	—	—	❷	❷	❷	③
LHS/300M	—	—	—	❶	❶	③	③	③
Head Restraints (F)	—	❶	—	③	—	❶	③	⑤
Rear	—	—	—	❷	—	—	❷	❷
300M (F)	—	—	—	❷	—	❷	③	❷
Rear	—	—	—	—	—	—	—	❷
Intrepid	—	❶	—	—	❷	④	④	⑤
Rear	—	—	—	—	—	—	③	❷
LHS	—	❶	—	❷	—	③	—	—
Vision	—	❶	—	—	—	—	—	—

Note: All these vehicles are practically identical and should have similar crashworthiness scores, even though not every model was tested each year.

Ford

COUGAR, THUNDERBIRD ★

RATING: Not Recommended (1999–2002); Average (1985–97). For readers wondering how the Cougar could go from Average to Not Recommended, remember that we are reviewing distinctly different vehicles. The early rear-drives improved over the years; however, the 1999–2002 front-drive iteration carries all of the deficiencies of Ford's front-drives, coupled to the Contour and Mystique's own sub-set of problems. Plus, as a first-year vehicle, the Cougar's quality control suffered even more (see "Safety summary" and "Secret Warranties/Service Tips/TSBs"). **Maintenance/Repair costs:** About average, and most repairs aren't dealer dependent. **Parts:** Moderately priced (independent suppliers sell for much less), and not hard to find for rear-drives. Front-drive parts, however, are more expensive and not as easily found. And they will likely become rarer, with both the Contour and Cougar taken off the market. **Best alternatives:** A GM Caprice, LeSabre, or Roadmaster; Ford's early Cougar, T-Bird, or Crown Victoria, and Mercury Grand Marquis. **Online help:** *www.autosafety.org/autodefects.html* and *www.blueovalnews.com.*

Strengths and weaknesses: These are no-surprise, average-performing, two-door, rear-drive, luxury cars that have changed little over the years. Handling and ride are far from perfect, with considerable body lean and rear-end instability when taking curves at moderate speeds or on wet roadways.

Overall reliability of these models has been average, as long as you stay away from the turbocharged 4-cylinder engine and watch out for 3.8L V6 engine head gasket failures and automatic transmission glitches.

True, these cars offer lots of power, but excessive noise and expensive repairs are the price you pay when they're pushed too hard. Front suspension components wear out quickly, as do power-steering rack seals. Owners of recent models have complained of ignition module defects, electrical system bugs, premature front brake repairs, steering pump hoses that burst repeatedly, erratic transmission performance, early AC failures, defective engine intake manifolds, numerous squeaks and rattles, faulty heater fans, and failure-prone power window regulators.

Vehicle history: 1989—Thunderbird is trimmed down and equipped with a fully independent suspension, and a 3.8L V6; a 210-hp Super Coupe (SC) model debuts. **1991**—A 200-hp 5.0L V8 arrives. **1994**—A 4.6L V8 debuts along with dual front airbags and re-styled front and rear ends. **1996**—Super Coupe is dropped and more re-styling tweaks are added. **1997**—Four-wheel disc brakes and dash/interior touch-ups.

1999–2002 Cougar

Essentially a Contour spin-off, this Cougar's main attributes are its attractive styling and pleasant handling. On the other hand, owners have to accept so-so acceleration with the base models, problematic transmission performance, a four-seater with a narrow, claustrophobic interior, limited rear-seat room, obstructed rear visibility, an ugly and superfluous trunk-lid spoiler, and excessive interior noise.

The front-drive Cougar, re-styled as a hatchback, is equipped with a 16-valve, 125-hp 2.0L inline-four and a 24-valve, 170-hp 2.5L V6, later replaced with an upgraded 200-hp power plant and optional ABS and side airbags. It shares the Contour's chassis (with 2.5 cm added), base 4-banger, and V6, but its suspension and steering are much tighter.

Emergency handling is acceptable, but not in the same league as Japanese sedans. The firm suspension and quick, responsive steering make the Cougar both nimble and stable when cornering under speed, especially with the optional Sport Group's rear disc brakes and larger wheels (you'll have to put up with a harder, noisier ride, though). The car is also quite peppy around town, with a good amount of low-end torque. Braking is also quite good, with little fading after successive stops.

Acceleration is only so-so with the base 4-cylinder or V6 engine and they both run roughly; the 4-banger is not as refined or fun to push as the Japanese competition. The 170-hp V6 lacks passing or merging power; 0–100 km/h takes about 10 seconds. The automatic transmission tends to "hunt" the proper gear when going over hilly terrain, and there's no way to lock out Overdrive in Fourth gear. The 5-speed hooked to the V6 also shifts roughly. The base suspension doesn't absorb bumps very well and the optional Sports Group tires produce a busy, jostling ride on any surface that's less than perfect. Steering is also a bit heavy in city traffic.

Owner-reported problems include chronic engine stalling; automatic transmission failures accompanied by slipping, "hunting" during the 1–2 shift; humming and clanking noises; manual transmission also hard to shift from one gear to another; electrical glitches; engine increases rpms when shifting; chronic stalling, rough running, and hard starts; premature front and rear brake wear and a low grinding noise or squeak heard when the brakes are applied; misaligned trunk, sunroof, door, and side windows jamming; door latch failures; doors that lock and unlock themselves; faulty driver-side door weather stripping that produces excessive wind noise; and water leakage into the interior (be wary of car washes).

2002–03 Thunderbird

After a brief hiatus, the Thunderbird name returned affixed to a $56,615 retro-styled, two-seat, rear-drive convertible that looks nothing like its 1955–57 namesake, or the $25,095 '97 model it replaced (now worth about $5,000). This 'bird shares variations of the engine and chassis used by the Lincoln LS and Jaguar S-Type, as well as their 5-speed automatic transmission. Power is supplied by a retuned 280-hp 3.9L V8.

The car is way overpriced. Sure, you get lots of bells and whistles for your $50,000+, but other cars offer just as much for far less money. Secondly, this is one dull-looking luxury roadster with few features that distinguish it from a half dozen cheaper imports of the same genre. Other minuses: a tiny, shallow trunk; a cheap-looking, boring instrument panel; limited headroom; an unwieldy folding top cover; and excessive air turbulence when driven with the top down.

Ford wants us to believe that the new Thunderbird iteration is true to the heritage of its classic forebears and represents good value for the money. Unfortunately, this Thunderbird proves just the opposite. Head restraints are rated "Poor" by IIHS, the official launch and delivery was delayed several times due to factory-related problems, the base MSRP is double what a Thunderbird cost just a few years ago, and the car will be discontinued in 2005.

Safety summary: 1996—Vehicle caught fire while parked for 13 hours. • Airbags failed to deploy. • Airbag indicator light comes on for no reason. • Right rear wheel came off. • During inclement weather, design of engine allows water to saturate the air filter, causing engine to die out. • PCM chip defect causes engine to cut out and the Check Engine light to come on. • Malfunctioning crankshaft and oxygen sensors may cause chronic stalling and no-starts. • Cracked intake manifold allows coolant leakage. • Frequent motor mount failures. • Transmissions are noisy, won't shift properly, and frequently won't shift at all. • Excessive driveshaft vibrations. • Power steering works poorly at low speeds and sometimes cuts out completely when cruising on the highway. • Heater and AC compressor failures. • Defective AC fan switch. • Frequent reports of sudden brake failures, front brake rotor warpage, and noisy brakes. • Brake pedal sinks below the accelerator pedal level, causing driver to depress the accelerator. • Hood struts are too weak to keep hood in open position. • Power window regulator failures. • Electric door locks are failure prone. • Headlights require constant adjustment and don't provide as much illumination as with other model years. • Seat belt doesn't release properly. • Speedometer and gauges work erratically. **1997**—Sudden acceleration while stopped at a traffic light. • Left vehicle in Park with engine running and it suddenly lurched into Reverse. • Car suddenly pulled to the left when braking, and steering locked up. • Excessive vibrations while cruising that increase in intensity when braking. • Headrests can't be raised high enough to protect the head. • Seat won't latch. • Dash reflection on the windshield obstructs visibility. **1999**—Inadvertent airbag deployment. • Driver's airbag deployed after collision and seat belt failed to lock up. • Sticking throttle causes sudden, unintended acceleration. • Cruise control wouldn't disengage. • Chronic hesitation or stalling (electrical shorts or a faulty fuel pump, fuel regulator, intake gaskets, or IAC solenoid are the prime suspects). • No-start due to faulty ignition or starter. • Transmission failures. • While driving at 110 km/h, transmission downshifted on its own. • Sudden brake failure (locked up). • Total brake failure when ABS brake master cylinder "exploded." • Brake pads, calipers, and rotors need replacing after only 32,000 km (20,000 mi.). • Power steering fails and dash lights go out when car is driven through a rain puddle. This may be caused by the serpentine belt getting wet. • Plastic fuel tank is prone to early disintegration, contributing to stalling. • Gas tank seal swells and breaks, spilling fuel. • Fuel tank wiring harness melted. • Brake lights don't come on when brakes are applied. • Electrical failures tend to blow out the fuel pump. • On another occasion, dash lights suddenly came on, engine died, and brakes and steering ability were gone. • Steering failures due to a broken suspension strut or the tie-rod bolt shearing off. • Wheel may crack, causing a tire blowout. • Frequent reports of tire tread separation at the sidewalls or prematurely wearing out (Firestone Firehawk). • Lug nut wrench doesn't work. • Trunk won't open or close, and remote release is useless. • Horn is hard to activate. • Inadequate rear windshield defogger. **2000–01**—Broken stabilizer bar bracket allowed wheel to drop under car. • Intermittent brake failure. • Automatic transmission hesitates, as it "hunts" for the correct gear and then shifts with a jerk. • Faulty seal causes fuel tank leakage. • Fuel smell in the interior comes in through the vents; fuel also leaked onto the ground. • Horn is hard to activate. • Engine hangs in higher rpms when foot is taken off the gas pedal and clutch is depressed. • Chronic stalling. • Lights flicker and loss of all electrical power. • Headlight failures. • Airbag and engine warning lights stay lit. • Cupholder spills drinks on right hand turns at speeds higher than 35 km/h (upgraded console/cupholder installed in mid-2000). • Tire sidewall failure. • Key won't work in the ignition. • Hard to find a child safety seat that fits in the rear. • The silly, non-functional rear spoiler is distracting and cuts rearward vision. **2001**—Airbags didn't deploy. • Engine compartment fire erupted while in traffic. • Gas fumes permeates interior through the air vents. • Broken rear stabilizer bar bracket. • Instrument panel light dims when braking. • Brake lights often fail.

Secret Warranties/Service Tips/TSBs

All models/years: Ford's "goodwill" warranty extensions cover engine and transmission breakdowns up to about seven years. There's nothing like a small claims court action to "focus" Ford's attention (pun intended). The same advice applies if you notice a rotten-egg odour coming from the exhaust. **All models: 1985–97**—A buzz or rattle from the exhaust system may be caused by a loose heat shield catalyst. **1989–97**—Water dripping from the floor ducts when the AC is working requires a relocated evaporator core. **1993–2002**—Paint delamination, peeling, or fading (see Part Two). **1993–2000**—Brake vibration diagnosis and correction. **1994–97**—An erratic or prolonged 1–2 shift can be cured by replacing the cast aluminum piston with a one-piece stamped steel piston that has bonded lip seals, and by replacing the top accumulator spring. • A simple solution for correcting a transmission shudder or vibration in Third or Fourth gear may be to simply change the transmission fluid or recalibrate the power control module (PCM). **1995–97**—Tips on sealing windshield water leaks and reducing noise, vibration, and harshness while driving. **1999**—Three bulletins target automatic transmission failures, suggesting that either the Overdrive/Reverse ring gear be replaced or an upgraded transaxle assembly be installed. • Front brake groaning during city driving can be silenced by installing revised brake pads under warranty, says TSB #99-8-9. **1999–2000**—Engine hesitation and a rough idle may be corrected by reprogramming the PCM. • Engine knock. • An exhaust sulfur odour evident just after highway cruising may signal the need to replace the catalytic converter under the emissions warranty. Transmission won't shift into any forward gear. • Automatic transmission fluid leaks. • Water leaks and wind noise troubleshooting tips. **1999–2001**—No forward gear (see following bulletin).

No Forward Gear Engagement

Article No. 00-18-2

09/04/00

1994–97 PROBE

1994–2000 CONTOUR

2001 ESCAPE

1994–2000 MYSTIQUE

1999–2001 COUGAR

ISSUE: Some vehicles may exhibit no forward gear ranges due to the misalignment of the forward/coast clutch cylinder snap ring with respect to the legs of the forward clutch piston.

ACTION: During assembly of the forward/coast clutch cylinder, the gap in the select fit retaining ring should be located midway (i.e., 45 degrees) between adjacent legs of the forward clutch piston.

• Rear brakes moan or groan (see following bulletin).

Rear Brakes Moaning/Groaning Noise

Article No. 00-26-5

12/25/00

1999–2001 COUGAR

ISSUE: Some vehicles equipped with rear disc brakes may exhibit a "moaning/groaning" noise on initial brake application (cold soak). This may be caused by the rear brake pads vibrating in the caliper. Braking performance is not affected by this condition.

ACTION: Install revised rear disc brake service kit.

• Brake warning light stays lit. **1999–2002**—Harsh, delayed upshifts. • Repeated failure of the heater core. **2000**—Airbag light remains lit. • Low coolant lamp on for no apparent reason. • Automatic transmission fluid leakage. • Water leak or wind noise at the upper corner of the B-pillar. **2003**—Rough-running, misfiring engine. • Harsh shifts. • Driveline vibration. • No-start due to battery drain. • Rear brake squealing.

Cougar, Thunderbird Profile

	1995	1996	1997	1999	2000	2001	2002	2003
Cost Price ($)								
Cougar	22,095	23,495	24,995	19,995	20,595	23,655	26,995	—
T-Bird	22,995	23,595	25,095	—	—	—	51,550	56,615
T-Bird SC	28,697	—	—	—	—	—	—	—
Used Values ($)								
Cougar ⋀	3,500	4,500	5,500	9,500	11,500	14,000	18,500	—
Cougar ⋁	3,000	4,000	4,500	8,000	9,500	12,500	17,000	—
T-Bird ⋀	4,500	6,000	5,000	—	—	—	37,000	42,000
T-Bird ⋁	3,500	5,000	4,500	—	—	—	34,000	39,000
T-Bird SC ⋀	5,000	—	—	—	—	—	—	—
T-Bird SC ⋁	4,000	—	—	—	—	—	—	—
Reliability	③	③	③	❷	❷	❷	❷	❷
Crash Safety	⑤	⑤	⑤	—	—	—	④	—
Side	—	—	③	—	—	③	⑤	—
Cougar	—	—	—	—	—	—	—	③
Head Restraints	❶	—	❶	—	—	—	❶	❶
Cougar (F)	❶	—	❶	❷	—	❷	❷	—
Cougar (Rear)	—	—	—	❶	—	❷	❷	—

CROWN VICTORIA, GRAND MARQUIS   ★★★

RATING: Average (1996–2003); Above Average (1984–95). Downgraded from five to three stars due to an increasing number of powertrain failures and safety-related deficiencies. Don't waste your money buying a 1998 or 1999 version if you can find a low-mileage 1995. It'll cost much less, give you most of the same features, and have a more durable engine intake manifold. The Marquis is a slightly more luxurious version that costs a bit more but gives little of consequence for the extra expense. **Maintenance/Repair costs:** Average, but some electronic repairs can be carried out only by Ford dealers. **Parts:** Higher-than-average cost (independent suppliers sell for much less), but they're not hard to find. **Best alternatives:** A Buick LeSabre, an early Ford Thunderbird or Cougar, GM Caprice or Roadmaster, and Toyota Avalon. **Online help:** *www.autosafety.org/autodefects.html; www.tgrigsby.com/ views/ford.htm; www.flamingfords.info; www.crownvictoriasafetyalert.com;* and *www.blueovalnews.com.*

Strengths and weaknesses: These cars are especially suited to people who need lots of room and oodles of convenience features. Handling, though, is mediocre, and can be downright scary on wet roads where traction is quickly lost and the car fishtails out of control. Passing over small bumps is also a white-knuckle affair as the car bounces around, barely controllable.

Both the 4.6L and 5.0L V8s provide adequate though sometimes sluggish power, with most of their torque found in the lower gear ranges. The Lincoln

Town Car shares most of the same components and afflictions as the Crown Vic and Grand Marquis.

Vehicle history: 1995—Restyled and given standard heated outside mirrors and a new interior treatment. **1997**—Improved steering and rear air suspension (a horror to diagnose and repair). **1998**—More power steering and suspension improvements. **1999**—ABS and a new stereo system. **2000**—An emergency trunk release, user-friendly child safety seat anchorages, and an improved handling package for quicker acceleration. **2001**—A small horsepower boost, minor interior improvements, adjustable pedals, seat belt pretensioners, and improved airbag systems. **2002**—Traction control to offset the car's notoriously poor wet-weather traction.

On the downside, there are a number of factory-related problems that reappear year after year. They include failure-prone fuel pump, sender, fuel filter, and fuel hose assemblies; ignition module and fuel cut-off switch malfunctions that cause hard starting and frequent stalling; brakes (rotors, calipers, and pads), shock absorbers, and springs that wear out more quickly than they should; and chronic front suspension noise when passing over small bumps. Inadequate inner fender protection allows road salt to completely cover engine wiring, brake master cylinder, and suspension components; frequent inspection and cleaning is required. Hubcaps frequently fall off. Finally, there is such a high number of safety-related complaints concerning brake and fuel lines, suspension, and steering components that an undercarriage inspection is a prerequisite to buying models three years or older. Other annoying body defects include poor fit and finish, trunk leaks, subpar interior materials, and flimsy plastic trim.

Safety summary: All models/years: Fuel line and electrical fires. • Sudden, unintended acceleration. • Airbags that fail to deploy. • ABS brake failures. **All models: 1992–2001**—Rear-end impact may puncture fuel tank; two TSB repairs already carried out. **1995-97**—NHTSA is looking into 31 brake line failures, apparently from corrosion or abrasion. **1996**—Engine surges without warning or shuts down when brakes are applied. • Cruise control won't disengage when brakes are applied. • Oil pan/gasket leaks. • Many reports that the left frame bracket broke at weld, causing vehicle to pull sharply to the right when brakes were applied. • Reports of ball joint and lower control arm failures say that the vehicle's front wheel assembly is also affected. • Police department inspectors report their vehicles have shown excessive play in the Pitman arms. • Brake lines are routed too close to the body and chafe excessively. • Brake pedal went to the floor due to failure of the stop switch and clip-on pedal. • Frequent replacement of front brake components. • Steering locks up, will not return, or is so loose it won't steer vehicle. • Cracked intake manifolds cause loss of coolant (see "Secret Warranties/Service Tips/TSBs"). • Frequent catalytic converter failures. • Inoperative rear window defroster. • Seat belt buckle doesn't stay latched. • Seat belts failed to restrain occupants during a collision. **1997**—Sudden acceleration due to a design flaw of the throttle linkage and bracket. • Floormats can shift under the gas or brake pedals, causing them to jam. • Vehicle left in Park position with engine on slipped into Reverse. • Collapsed body mounts allow undercarriage to rub flat spots on steel brake lines, causing brake failure. • Steering wheel lock-up while driving. • Front suspension ball joint failure after having recall campaign correction done. • Lower passenger-side control arm fell off when vehicle was in First gear. • Sharp door edges have injured three people. • Engine intake manifold failures that cause antifreeze to leak into the engine compartment (see "Secret Warranties/Service Tips/TSBs"). **1998**—NHTSA investigators are looking into reports that the inertia fuel cutoff switch operates when it shouldn't, stalling the vehicle. • Sudden loss of power; stalling. • Traction control engages for no reason, causing loss of power and control. • Steering too sensitive when changing lanes, making it easy to lose control. • Dome light switch is poorly designed; it can only be activated by the driver due to its location. • Loss of lighting caused by sudden electrical system failure. • Rubber hose leading from the fuel tank is easily hit when going over a bump or pothole. **1999**—Sudden stalling while underway (fuel inertia cutoff switch self-activates when vehicle hits a pothole or goes over a small bump). • Steering shaft failure when turning. • Cracked rear trailing arm assembly frames. • Transmission jumps from Park into gear. • Premature brake rotor warpage and pad wearout causes excessive brake noise (grinding), vibration, and extended stopping distance. • Sticking front calipers cause vehicle to veer to the right or left. • Premature wear of the lower control arm. • Headlights aren't bright enough. • Loose rear outer door handles. • Driver's seat misalignment places steering wheel and gas/brake pedals too far to the right. **2000**—Oversensitive steering causes vehicle to wander. • Power window failures in cold weather. • Headlights short out intermittently. **2001**—No airbag deployment. • Many reports of sudden acceleration when slowing down. • When driving in rainy weather, water gets into the engine compartment, causing the water pump to throw the fan belt and leading to loss of control of the vehicle (see TSB below). • Frequent complaints of little traction on wet roads. • ABS failure leading to brake lock-up or loss of braking ability. • Spongy brakes sink to floor with little braking effect. • Brake and accelerator pedals mounted too close together. • Vehicle moves forward when shifted into Reverse. • Vehicle rolls back when stopped on an incline. • Windshield wipers fail intermittently and easily freeze up in sleet. **2003**—Vehicle struck from behind and exploded in flames. • Tire tread separation. • Missing upper control arm bolt. • Brake booster failed. • Fan belt comes off in rainy weather, causing overheating and loss of power steering, water pump, and other accessories. • Horn "sweet spot" too small and takes too much effort to sound. • Sunlight causes a reflection of the defrost vents onto the windshield and poor dash panel illumination.

Secret Warranties/Service Tips/TSBs

All models: 1985–2002—Repeated heater core failure. **1990–2001**—Correcting a radio whine or buzz in the speakers. **1992–2001**—Measures to protect fuel tank from puncturing and fuel igniting from a rear-end collision.

1993–2001—An exhaust buzz or rattle may mean you have a loose catalyst or muffler heat shield. • Paint delamination, peeling, or fading (see Part Two). **1994–99**—Tips on preventing wind noise around the doors. **1995–97**—ABS brakes that activate on their own or produce a grinding, pulsing, fluttering effect on the brake pedal probably need upgraded wiring connectors at the ABS sensors. **1995–99**—Tips on reducing noise, vibration, and harshness, as well as plugging windshield water leaks. **1996–2001**—The following intake manifold coolant leakage bulletin traces the problem back to 1996 models and shows Ford is at fault. It can be useful to get a repair refund if Ford refuses to extend its 1998–2001 Special Service Campaign (see following bulletin) to these earlier models, or says that time period or mileage make you ineligible for compensation.

Engine Intake Manifold Leakage

Article No.: 02-2-2

Date: 02/04/02

1996–97	THUNDERBIRD
1996–2001	CROWN VICTORIA, MUSTANG
2002	EXPLORER
1996–2001	TOWN CAR
1996–97	COUGAR
1996–2001	GRAND MARQUIS

ISSUE: Some vehicles may exhibit an intake manifold crossover (first runner) coolant seepage condition. This may be caused by a crack in the intake manifold coolant crossover.

ACTION: Inspect the suspect intake manifold for a coolant leak at the first runner crossover area. If coolant seepage is found in this area, order the appropriate service kit.

1997–98—Lack of AC temperature control may require a new air door actuator. **1997–99**—Delayed upshifts may require a new 2–3 accumulator along with a revised piston. • A rough idle or exhaust system resonance can be fixed by installing an exhaust system mass damper. **1998–99**—A pull or drift when braking in rainy weather can be corrected by installing upgraded front brake linings that are less sensitive to water, says TSB #98-13-4. • A poorly performing AC that also makes a thumping noise may need a new suction accumulator and suction hose assembly. **1998–2000**—Ford Special Service Campaign 00B60 (January 31, 2002) allowed for the free installation of control arm reinforcing brackets or new control arms, regardless of mileage. Ask for a partial refund. **1998–2001**—A Ford Special Service Campaign will replace the engine mounts free of charge on vehicles in fleet service. **1998–2002**—In a separate campaign, the automaker has extended the intake manifold warranty to seven years, without any mileage limitation. This campaign is in response to complaints of coolant leakage leading to engine overheating. **1998–2002**—Inoperative shift interlock. **1999–2001**—Correcting a 2–1 shift clunk noise. **1999–2002**—Engine head gasket leakage:

Engine Oil Leak From R/H Cylinder Head Gasket

Article No.: 03-6-2

Date: 03/31/03

1999–2002	CROWN VICTORIA, MUSTANG
1999–2001	E SERIES, EXPEDITION, F-150, SUPER DUTY F SERIES
2000–01	EXCURSION
1999–2002	TOWN CAR
1998–99	NAVIGATOR
1999–2002	GRAND MARQUIS

ISSUE: Some vehicles equipped with the Romeo-built 4.6L 2V engine or 5.4L 2V Windsor and 5.4L Supercharged engine may exhibit an oil leak or oil weepage from the cylinder head gasket at the right hand rear or the left hand front of the engine. Oil weepage is not considered detrimental to engine performance or durability. An oil leak may be caused by metal chip debris lodged between the head gasket and the block, chip debris between the cylinder head and the head gasket, or by damage to the cylinder head sealing surface that occurred during the manufacturing process.

ACTION: Once an oil leak is verified with a black light test at the head gasket joint, replacement of the head gasket can be performed. If the head was damaged by chip contamination, the head should be replaced. A revised "Service-Only" gasket is now released for both of these cases.

2000–01—Troubleshooting a ticking noise in First gear. **2000–03**—Excessive engine noise:

Engine Timing Chain Grinding Noise

Article No. 03-15-7

Date: 08/04/03

2000–03	CROWN VICTORIA
2000–03	GRAND MARQUIS

ISSUE: Some 4.6L 2V engines may exhibit a grinding type noise from the timing chain area. This may be caused by excessive wear of the timing chain tensioner arms. The tensioner arm has an aluminum base with a nylon surface. Another indication of this condition may be fine nylon and/or aluminum particles present in the engine oil.

ACTION: Inspect the timing chain and arms to determine if excessive wear exists. If this condition is present, replace the timing chains, tensioners, and the tensioner arms.

2001—Correcting a 3–4 shift flare. **2001–02**—Front-end accessory drivebelt slips off water pump pulley when splashed with water (TSB #02-5-4). **2003**—Ford says rear axles "may be noisy, or exhibit rear axle shaft and/or axle bearing premature wear. This is caused by excessive load, temperature, and inadequate lubrication." Ford will replace the axle bearings under dealer operation code 030505A. • Water in the headlights and erratic headlight operation. • Inaccurate fuel gauge. • Power steering assist calibration. • Excessive power steering pump noise. • Front wheel area click or rattle. • Anti-theft system may cause the transmission to stick in Park or the steering wheel to lock. • Defective front coil springs may cause the vehicle to have a harsh ride or the suspension to sit low in the front. Ford will install free revised front coil springs:

#3W1Z-5310-EA and #3W1Z-5310-HA. • Cracked wheel rims (call 1-800-325-5621 to replace the affected wheel(s) up to five years or 240,000 km (150,000 mi.) from the vehicle's warranty start date.

Crown Victoria, Grand Marquis Profile

	1996	1997	1998	1999	2000	2001	2002	2003
Cost Price ($)								
Crown S/LTD	27,195	29,895	30,995	31,895	32,095	—	—	—
Grand Marquis GS	30,295	32,195	32,895	33,695	31,195	34,125	35,120	35,800
Used Values ($)								
Crown S/LTD ▲	6,000	7,500	9,500	12,500	14,500	—	—	—
Crown S/LTD ▼	5,000	6,500	8,000	11,000	12,500	—	—	—
Grand Marquis GS ▲	5,500	7,500	9,500	11,500	15,000	17,500	21,000	25,000
Grand Marquis GS ▼	23,000							
Reliability	③	③	③	③	③	④	④	④
Crash Safety	④	⑤	⑤	⑤	⑤	⑤	⑤	⑤
Side	—	—	④	④	④	⑤	④	④
Head Restraints	—	❶	—	❶	—	❶	❶	③
Rollover Resistance	—	—	—	—	—	⑤	⑤	⑤

General Motors

CAPRICE, IMPALA SS, ROADMASTER ★★★★

RATING: Above Average (1995–96); Average (1982–94). This is an excellent car for first-time buyers. **Maintenance/Repair costs:** Maintenance is inexpensive and easy to perform, and repairs can be done by any corner garage. **Parts:** Average parts costs can be cut further by shopping at independent suppliers, who are generally well-stocked. **Best alternatives:** An early Ford Thunderbird or Cougar, Crown Victoria or Mercury Grand Marquis, and GM LeSabre. **Online help:** *www.autosafety.org/autodefects.html.*

Strengths and weaknesses: These cars are large, comfortable, and easy to maintain. The trunk is spacious. Overall handling is acceptable, but expect a queasy ride from the too-soft suspension. Gas mileage is particularly poor. Despite the many generic deficiencies inherent in these rear-drives, they still score higher than GM's front-drives for overall reliability and durability. The Impala SS is basically a Caprice with a 260-hp Corvette engine and high-performance suspension.

Vehicle history: 1991 Chevrolet Caprice/Impala SS—Adopted a more rounded styling, a bit larger interior, ABS brakes, a driver-side airbag, and three-point seat belts; the sporty LTZ was launched with wider tires and an upgraded suspension; wagons got a roof rack, a rear wiper/washer, and a tail-gate that swung out or down. **1992**—A tilt steering wheel and a larger optional V8 (wagons). **1993**—New trim and rear lights and rounded rear wheel openings; LTZ sedan got the 5.7L V8 (180 hp). **1994**—A passenger-side airbag, a base 4.3L V8, and an optional high-performance 5.7L spun off of the Corvette's LT1 V8 (standard with the Impala SS); a redesigned dash-board including a failure-prone digital speedometer, and an improved electronic automatic transmission. **1995**—Restyled rear roof pillar, upgraded seats, and foldaway mirrors. **1996**—Impala SS gearshift lever moved to the console; a more reliable analog speedometer and a tachometer were added.

On 1988–91 models, engine problems include crankshaft and head gasket failures, cracked cylinder heads, injection pump malfunctions, and oil leaks. Engine knocking is another common problem on early models that's hard to correct inexpensively, due to the various possible causes that have to be elimi-nated. Early V8s, in particular, suffer from premature camshaft wear, and the 350-cubic-inch V8s often fall prey to premature valve guide wear caused by a faulty EGR valve. Cars equipped with the 5.7L diesel V8 should be approached with caution; they aren't very durable and cost an arm and a leg to troubleshoot and repair. The 4-speed automatic transmission was troublesome until 1991, with burnt-out clutches and malfunctioning torque converters being the most common failures.

The 1991–96 models have shown the following deficiencies: AC glitches; prematurely worn brakes (lots of corrosion damage), steering, and suspension components, especially shock absorbers and rear springs; serious electrical problems; and poor-quality body and trim items.

Body assembly is not impressive, but paint quality and durability is fairly good, considering the delamination one usually finds with GM's other models. Wagons often have excessive rust around cargo-area side windows and wheel-wells, and hubcaps on later models tend to fly off.

Safety summary: All models: 1996—Child was able to shift gear into Neutral, jumped out of car, and was run over. • Airbags failed to deploy. • Airbag light stays lit for no apparent reason. • Gas pedal sticks on initial appli-cation. • ABS brakes lock up. • Transmission torque converter/engine flywheel breakage. • Broken torque converter bolts. • Steering box loosens up despite new bolts. • Steering lock-up. • Sometimes vehicle fishtails uncontrollably while at moderate speed. • Front coil spring failure. • Premature tire wear caused by faulty suspension components that can't be fixed by repeated align-ments. • Fuel pump failure caused by wiring harness short.

Secret Warranties/Service Tips/TSBs

All models/years: A rotten-egg odour coming from the exhaust is usually the result of a malfunctioning catalytic converter. **All models: 1993–96**—Paint delamination, peeling, or fading (see Part Two). **1994**—Excessive oil con-sumption is likely due to delaminated intake manifold gaskets. Install an upgraded intake manifold gasket kit. • GM campaign 94C15 will adjust, at no charge, a misadjusted automatic transmission shift linkage that could, if left alone, burn out the Low/Reverse clutch. **1994–96**—Excessive engine noise can be silenced by installing an upgraded valve stem oil seal. • A chuggle or surge condition in vehicles with a 5.7L engine will require a reflash calibration. **Roadmaster: 1994**—Excessive oil consumption is likely due to delaminated intake manifold gaskets. Install an upgraded intake manifold gasket kit. • Poor AC performance can be improved by replacing the temperature control cable. • Delayed automatic transmission shift engagement is a common problem addressed in TSB #47-71-20A. **1995–96**—Delayed automatic transmission shift engagement may require the replacement of the pump cover assembly. **1996**—You may need to replace the transmission's reaction sun shell if you can't shift into Reverse, Second, or Fourth gear.

Caprice, Impala SS, Roadmaster Profile

	1990	1991	1992	1993	1994	1995	1996
Cost Price ($)							
Caprice	20,128	19,698	20,298	20,806	22,500	25,455	28,345
Caprice wagon	21,347	20,398	21,598	22,138	24,985	29,120	30,980
Impala SS	—	—	—	—	—	29,005	30,675
Roadmaster	—	—	25,398	26,298	29,798	32,930	34,230
Used Values ($)							
Caprice ∧	2,000	2,500	2,500	3,000	3,500	4,500	5,500
Caprice ∨	1,500	2,000	2,000	2,500	3,000	4,000	4,500
Caprice wagon ∧	2,500	3,000	3,000	3,500	4,000	4,500	5,500
Caprice wagon ∨	2,500	2,500	2,500	3,000	3,500	4,000	4,500
Roadmaster ∧	—	—	3,500	4,000	4,500	5,000	6,000
Roadmaster ∨	—	—	3,000	3,500	4,000	4,500	5,000
Reliability	❷	❷	❷	❷	③	③	③
Crash Safety	—	④	④	④	④	④	④
Head Restraints	—	—	—	—	—	❶	—

LUXURY CARS

We are being conned

Money doesn't buy you love—nor quality and reliable performance in a luxury car. Ask any Cadillac, Jaguar, Lincoln Continental, Mercedes, or Saab owner. They now know more dependable and better-performing cars can be had for half the price from other automakers. Heck, even the Germans prefer Japanese brands over their own.

Used luxury cars can be great buys, if you ignore all the hype, know how to separate symbol from substance, and are smart enough to know that most of the high-end models don't give you much more than their lower-priced entry-level versions. For example, the Lexus ES 300 is a Toyota Camry with a higher sticker price; the Audi A4 isn't much different from the Volkswagen Passat; Lincoln's front-drive Continental uses mostly Ford Taurus and Sable power-trains; and the Acura 3.2 TL, Infiniti I35 (formerly called the I30), and Jaguar X-Type are fully loaded, high-tuned versions of the Honda Accord, the Nissan Maxima, and the European Ford Mondeo, respectively.

Both high- and low-end models project a flashy cachet; come loaded with high-tech safety, performance, and comfort features; and can be bought, after three years or so, for half of what they sold for new. Furthermore, if you can get servicing and parts from independent garages, you'll save even more. On the downside, there *are* overpriced luxury lemons out there (like the Continental and the Cadillac Allanté and Catera, for example) that aren't built anymore and are known to be unreliable, with hard-to-service engines and transmissions and servicing costs that rival Neiman Marcus.

Take Mercedes-Benz, for example. A $5-million study conducted over five years by the Massachusetts Institute of Technology says the company makes lousy cars. The MIT study concluded over a decade ago that Mercedes built poor-quality vehicles and then attempted to fix its mistakes at the end of the assembly line. As one reviewer of *The Machine that Changed the World*, by James P. Womack, Daniel T. Jones, and Daniel Roos (HarperCollins, November 1991), wrote,

> This study of the world automotive industry by a group of MIT academics reaches the radical conclusion that the much vaunted Mercedes technicians are actually a throwback to the pre-industrial age, while Toyota is far ahead in costs and quality by building the automobiles correctly the first time.

Readers of my *Lemon-Aid SUVs, Vans, and Trucks* guides know, from the internal service bulletins I quote extensively, that Mercedes' M-Class sport-utilities have been plagued by serious factory defects (running the gamut from powertrain failures to fit and finish deficiencies). However, a confidential January 2002 quality survey leaked to the press confirms that Mercedes' quality problems now affect its entire vehicle lineup. The survey, commissioned by European automakers from TUV, a German auto-inspection and research association, ranked Mercedes twelfth in quality control, just behind GM's much-maligned Opel. A few weeks earlier, J.D. Power & Associates released a study of 156,000 car owners that showed five-year-old Mercedes vehicles had a higher-than-average number of problems (engine oil sludge being foremost on 1998–2001 models). Power subsequently lowered the company's rating for quality control to "fair" from "good."

Now, almost two years later, German drivers have apparently reached the same conclusion as Power. The 38,454 members of ADAC, Germany's largest automotive club, who responded to a December 2003 survey put Volkswagen as number 31, Mercedes as number 32, and Land Rover as number 33 among the 33 brands polled on overall customer satisfaction.

Automakers and Customer Satisfaction

Automakers with the highest customer satisfaction

1. Toyota	12. Daihatsu	23. Renault
2. Subaru	13. Volvo	24. Alfa Romeo
3. Honda	14. Jaguar	25. Rover
4. Mazda	15. Citroen	26. Audi
5. Nissan	16. Kia	27. Opel
6. Mitsubishi	17. Skoda	28. Chrysler
7. Suzuki	18. Lancia	29. Smart
8. Porsche	19. Daewoo	30. Fiat
9. Saab	20. Peugeot	31. Volkswagen
10. Hyundai	21. Ford	32. Mercedes
11. BMW	22. Seat	33. Land Rover

Source: ADAC 2003 survey

Industry insiders believe Mercedes' quality problems are symptomatic of a malaise affecting many luxury car builders: rushing too many new models into production and building cheaper, smaller, bare-bones knock-offs of popular models.

Traditionally, the luxury-car niche has been dominated by American and German automakers. During the past decade, however, buyers have gravitated towards Japanese models. This shift in buyer preference has forced Chrysler out of the market, made Ford drop its problem-plagued Lincoln Continental, and has GM reconsidering a return to rear-drive Cadillacs.

OK, so you're well advised to choose a Japanese model, but doesn't that mean you'll have to dig deep in your wallet, wiping out most of your expected savings from buying used? Not necessarily. You don't always have to spend a lot to get true luxury and ironclad reliability. Smart buyers can pick up a fully equipped 2000 Toyota Camry or Avalon for between $17,000 and $19,000, or about half of what these models originally cost. Or, to put it in a different perspective: each car costs less than what a new 2001 Ford Focus ZTS sold for three years ago. Similar savings are realized by the purchase of a Honda Accord, Nissan Maxima, or Mazda 929, all of which offer similar equipment, reliability, and performance to Acura, Infiniti, and Lexus models, but for much, much less.

It's sad but true. There aren't any American luxury cars that can match an equivalent Japanese model for overall reliability, durability, and value. And this isn't because Japanese products are that well made; far from it, as anyone who's purchased a quirky Saab 9000 or a transmission-challenged Lexus will attest. No, it's simply because GM, Ford, and Chrysler's vehicles are so poorly made that they make everyone else look better. A fact that's reflected in the head-spinningly high depreciation rates and plummeting market share seen with most large-*cum*-luxury cars put out by the Big Three. GM's rear-drive Cadillac DeVille and Lincoln's Town Car come closest to meeting the imports in overall reliability and durability, yet they still come nowhere near the quality level of many entry-level imports. Examples of lousy American luxury cars abound: The Chrysler front-drive New Yorker and LHS are unremarkable and are plagued by serious powertrain reliability problems, and most GM Cadillacs have been characterized by innovative, albeit unreliable, technology like variable-cylinder engines (the 4-6-8 engine), cobbled-together diesel power plants, and poorly engineered, high-maintenance, low-quality front-drive components.

What does this foretell for the future of used luxury cars? Firstly, prices for American entries will plummet as a souring economy takes its toll. Plus, a flood of off-lease cars will further cut into prices and give buyers a wider choice among imports and the Detroit Big Three. Finally, we'll likely see the renaissance of rear-drives, with Cadillac and Ford leading the parade.

LUXURY CAR RATINGS

Recommended
Acura TL (1999–2003)
BMW 5 Series (1992–2003)
BMW M Series (1997–2003)
BMW Z4 (2003)

Infiniti I30 (2000–03)
Lexus ES 300, GS 300, LS 400, SC 400 (1996–2001)

Above Average
Acura RL (1996–2003)
Acura TL (1996–98)
Audi A4, A6 (100), A8, S6
  TT Coupe (1996–99)
BMW 3 Series (1995–2003)
BMW Z3 (1996–2002)
Ford/Lincoln Mark VII, Mark VIII
  (1995–98)
General Motors Aurora (2001–03)
General Motors Cadillac Brougham,
  Fleetwood rear-drive (1993–96)

Infiniti I30 (1997–99)
Infiniti I35 (2000–03)
Infiniti J30 (1994–97)
Infiniti Q35 (2001–03; 1991–96)
Lexus ES 300, GS 300, LS 400,
  SC 400 (2002–03; 1990–95)
Nissan Maxima (1989–2003)
Toyota Avalon (1995–2003)
Volvo 900 series (1989–96)

Average

Audi A4, A6 (100), A8, S6, TT Coupe
  (2000–03)
BMW 3 Series (1994)
BMW 5 Series (1985–91)
Ford/Lincoln LS (2000–03)
Ford/Lincoln Mark VII, Mark VIII
  (1994)
Ford/Lincoln Town Car (1995–2003)
General Motors 98 Regency,
  Park Avenue (1998–2003)
General Motors Aurora (1995–99)
General Motors Cadillac Brougham,
  Fleetwood rear-drive (1984–92)
General Motors Cadillac Concours,
  DeVille, Fleetwood front-drive
  (1995–2003)

General Motors Riviera (1995–99)
Infinity I30 (1996)
Infiniti J30 (1993)
Infiniti Q45 (1997–2000)
Kia Magentis (2003)
Mercedes-Benz 300 series,
  400 series, 500 series,
  E-Class (1985–91)
Mercedes-Benz C-Class (1994–2003)
Nissan Maxima (1986–88)
Volvo 900 series, S80, S90, V90
  (1997–2003)
Volvo 850, C70, S40, S70, V40,
  V70 (1993–2003)

Below Average

BMW 3 Series (1984–93)
Ford/Lincoln Continental (1988–2002)
Ford/Lincoln Mark VII, Mark VIII
  (1986–93)
Ford/Lincoln Town Car (1988–94)
General Motors 98 Regency,
  Park Avenue (1991–97)

General Motors Cadillac Catera,
  Eldorado, Seville (1992–2003)
General Motors Concours, DeVille,
  Fleetwood front-drive (1985–94)
Kia Magentis (2001–02)
Mercedes-Benz 300 series, 400 series,
  500 series, E-Class (1992–2003)

Not Recommended

Audi 90, A6 (100), S6 (1984–95)
General Motors 98 Regency, Park
  Avenue (1985–90)
General Motors Cadillac Eldorado,
  Seville (1986–91)

General Motors Riviera (1986–93)
Infiniti G20 (1994–2002)

Acura

RL

RATING: Above Average (1996–2003). Basically a fully loaded, longer, wider, and heavier TL, equipped with a larger engine that produces less horsepower than its smaller brother. Watch out for the failure-prone, notchy 6-speed manual transmission. Resale value is high on all Acura models. **Maintenance/ Repair costs:** Average, and most repairs are dealer dependent. **Parts:** Most mechanical and electronic components are easily found and moderately priced.

Some reports that recall repairs are often delayed because corrected parts aren't available (transmission/transfer case, for example). Body parts may be hard to come by and can be expensive. **Best alternatives:** Consider the departed Acura Legend, BMW's 5 Series, Infiniti's I30 or I35, and the Lexus GS 300/400. You may want to take a look at the TL sedan: it's not as expensive, and is a better performer, though passenger room is more limited. **Online help:** *www.cbel.com/acura_cars* and *acurasucks.com/Main.htm.*

Strengths and weaknesses: Good, though not impressive, acceleration that's smooth and quiet in all gear ranges; exceptional steering and handling; comfortable ride; loaded with goodies; top-quality body and mechanical components. On the other hand, the steering can be numb, and manual and automatic transmissions are sometimes problematic.

The 3.5 RL is Honda's—oh, I mean, Acura's—flagship sedan. It's loaded with innovative high-tech safety and convenience features one would expect to find in a luxury car. These include heated front seats, front and rear climate controls, a rear-seat trunk pass-through, xenon headlights (get used to oncoming drivers flashing you their headlights), "smart" side airbags, ABS, traction control, and an anti-skid system.

The 3.5L 210-hp V6 mated to a 4-speed automatic transmission provides good acceleration that's a bit slower and more fuel-thirsty than the TL, partly due to the RL's extra pounds. The car handles nicely, with a less firm ride than the TL, although steering response doesn't feel as crisp. Interior accommodations for four occupants are excellent up front and in the rear, due to the RL's use of a larger platform than the TL.

Vehicle history: 1996—RL replaces the Legend. **1998**—A sportier suspension, alloy wheels, and a three-point rear-centre seat belt. **1999**—Side airbags, high-intensity discharge headlights, larger brakes, and a retuned suspension. **2000**—A Vehicle Stability Assist system and upgraded side airbags. **2001**—An in-trunk emergency opener. **2002**—A small horsepower boost (15), OnStar assistance, wider tires, larger brakes, and more sound deadening.

Owner-reported problems: a failure-prone, misshifting manual transmission, noisy transmission engagement, frequent stalling, malfunctioning accessories, electrical shorts, premature brake wear, and front wheel liner cracking.

Safety summary: All models/years: It's interesting to note that the RL has had remarkably few complaints registered by NHTSA. **All models: 1996**—Airbags failed to deploy in a collision. **1998**—Premature wearout of the front and rear brake pads around 24,000 km (15,000 mi.). **1999**—ABS failed to respond, resulting in rear-end collision. **2000**—Vehicle suddenly stalls when decelerating or cruising on the highway; transmission replaced, but problem returned. • Premature transmission replacements. **2001**—Transmission shifts poorly when accelerating or decelerating; vehicle stalls at slower speeds. • 6-speed manual transmission misshifts when going from Third to Fourth gear; it engages Second gear instead, causing extensive engine damage. • In cold weather, Second gear is hard to engage and produces a grinding noise. • Sometimes transmission pops out of Second gear. • Cracked front wheelwell liners. **2002**—Extensive engine damage caused by downshifting into Second gear; grinding:

> Very bad "grind" going into Second gear, when the transmission is cold. It takes about 25 minutes of driving until it starts to shift smoothly. The colder the weather is outside, the worse the problem.
>
> You can feel the gears grinding in the transmission. I have a petition with over 60 signatures from other RSX owners.
>
> This problem can be very dangerous if you are trying to get into Second gear and the transmission is grinding so bad it locks you out.

• Chronic stalling when decelerating. **2003**—Vehicle suddenly stalled while exiting a freeway. • Dashboard display is unreadable in daylight. • Seat belt did not restrain driver.

Secret Warranties/Service Tips/TSBs

All models/years: Like Honda's, most of Acura's TSBs allow for special warranty consideration on a "goodwill" basis, even after the warranty has expired or the car has changed hands. Referring to this euphemism will increase your chances of getting some kind of refund for repairs that are obviously factory defects. • Seat belts that fail to function properly during normal use will be replaced for free under the company's lifetime seat belt warranty. • Diagnostic procedures and correction for off-centre steering wheels. **All models: 1996**—Rapid rear brake pad wear can be corrected by installing upgraded pads. • Moon roof wind noise can be corrected by replacing the visor clips and mounting hardware. • If the driver's seatback piping wears out prematurely, Acura suggests it be replaced. **1996–97**—Front window wind noise can be reduced by aligning the glass and sash. • Window noise during operation can be silenced by replacing the glass stabilizers and sashes, as well as the glass, if it's scratched. • Drivers who find the footrest is positioned too far away may obtain a replacement footrest from Acura. **1996–98**—A growling or whining coming from the rear wheels can be fixed by replacing the hub bearing unit. • Brake squeal during light application can be fixed by replacing the front pads. **1996–2000**—Moon roof rattles can be silenced by replacing the moon roof glass. **1996–2002**—Intermittent electrical shorts.

Security/Electrical System – Intermittent Problems

98-028
October 1, 2001
MODELS: 1996–2001 3.5 RL; 2002 3.5 RL
SYMPTOMS: The security system sounds intermittently while the vehicle is parked.
The door locks cycle while driving. The instrument panel lights remain on.
PROBABLE CAUSE: Water is leaking into the front pillars. The water is getting into the connectors
for the under-dash fuse relay box, the driver's multiplex control unit, or the door lock actuator,
causing a short circuit.

1997–2001—Master cylinder clutch fluid leakage. **1999**—A navigation system that locks up or resets can be corrected by rewriting the unit's software; a remanufactured unit may also be considered. **1999–2000**—A squeaking, creaking driver's seat is addressed in TSB #00-010. **2000**—Troubleshooting noisy automatic transmissions. • Moon roof rattles. • Driver's seat noise. • Steering wheel clunk. **2000–01**—Stability Assist may activate too soon. • Engine starts and dies when ignition is released. **2000–02**—Low-speed stalling. **2003**—Airbag light comes on for no reason and troubleshooting automatic transmission malfunctions.

RL Profile

	1996	1997	1998	1999	2000	2001	2002	2003
Cost Price ($)								
Base	52,300	54,600	55,000	52,000	52,000	53,000	54,000	55,000
Used Values ($)								
Base ▲	10,000	12,000	15,000	19,000	23,000	30,000	37,000	42,000
Base ▼	9,500	10,000	13,000	17,000	21,000	28,000	35,000	40,000
Reliability	④	④	⑤	⑤	⑤	⑤	⑤	⑤
Crash Safety	—	—	—	④	④	④	④	④
Offset	—	—	—	—	—	—	—	③
Head Restraints	—	❷	❶	—	❷	❶	❶	❶

TL ★★★★★

RATING: Recommended (1999–2003); Above Average (1996–98). Resale value is high on all Acura models. **Maintenance/Repair costs:** Average cost, but many repairs are dealer dependent. **Parts:** Higher-than-average cost (some independent suppliers sell for much less under the Honda name), but not hard to find. **Best alternatives:** Consider the Acura Integra, Audi A4, BMW's redesigned 3 series, Infiniti's redesigned I30 or I35, the Mazda Millenia, and the Lexus ES 300. You may want to take a look at Acura's CL coupe: it's not as expensive, and is as close as you can get to the Accord with lots of standard bells and whistles thrown in. **Online help:** *www.cbel.com/acura_cars* and *www.autosafety.org/autodefects.html.*

Strengths and weaknesses: The TL has impressive acceleration, handles well, rides comfortably, and is well put-together, with quality mechanical and body components. However, the suspension may be too firm for some, and the vehicle has uncomfortable rear seating, excessive road noise, and problematic navigation system controls.

Filling the void left by the discontinued Vigor, the TL combines luxury and performance in a nicely styled front-drive five-passenger sedan that uses the same chassis as the Accord and CL coupe. Base models will likely carry an adequate, though unimpressive, 2.5L inline 5-cylinder engine. Performance enthusiasts will opt for versions equipped with the more refined 3.2L 225/260-hp V6 mated to a 4-speed automatic transmission. It provides impressive acceleration (0–100 km/h in just over 8 seconds) in a smooth and quiet manner, without any fuel penalty. Handling is exceptional with the firm suspension, but can be a bit tricky when pushed. Bumps are a bit jarring and the ride is somewhat busier than other cars in this class, but this is a small price to pay for the car's high-speed performance.

Vehicle history: 1998—TLs came with a bit more standard equipment than previous years. **1999**—2.5L engine was dropped and practically everything else was upgraded. **2000**—Enhanced performance features that include a better-performing 5-speed transmission, a free-flowing intake manifold, side airbags, and depowered frontal airbags. **2002**—A new performance version based on the CL Type S, a minor face-lift, new wheels and headlights, and more comfortable seat belts.

Interior accommodations are better than average up front, but rear occupants may discover that legroom is a bit tight and the seat cushions lack sufficient thigh support. The cockpit layout is very user-friendly, due in part to the easy-to-read gauges and accessible controls (far-away climate controls are the only exception). Standard safety features include ABS, traction control, childproof door locks, three-point seat belts, and a transmission/brake interlock.

Owners complain of chronic automatic and manual transmission failures (covered by a goodwill warranty), engine surging and stalling, malfunctioning airbags and accessories, electrical shorts, premature brake wear, and poor body fits. Owners point out that the window regulator may need replacing, the ignition switch buzzes, the trunk lock jams, and the rear bumper is often loose.

Safety summary: All models/years: Horn is difficult to locate in emergency situations. • Airbags fail to deploy in a collision. • Sudden, unintended acceleration. **All models: 1996**—Both airbags suddenly deployed for no reason while vehicle was underway. • Driveline whines upon acceleration. • Rear brake failure; brakes are frequently in need of repair. • Prematurely worn rear brake pads. • Passenger-side window suddenly shattered. **1997**—Chronic stalling as vehicle decelerates. • Steering column fire. • Complete brake loss. • Check Engine light comes on often. **1998–2001**—Clutch master cylinder fluid leakage. **1999**—Airbags deployed in a collision and severely burned driver's hands. • Seat belt failed to retract in a collision, allowing driver to hit windshield. • Transmission fails to downshift or upshift. • Front rotors warp within 160,000 km (10,000 mi.). • Door locks operate erratically. • Wiper blades leak graphite, smearing windshield. • Instrument panel is washed out in sunlight, making odometer practically invisible. **2000**—Brake pedal feels spongy, and it's easy to confuse brake and gas pedals. **2001**—Automatic transmission failures that leave the engine revving high (like when passing), but the car doesn't accelerate (it actually slows down). **2002**—Driver's seat belt unreeled during accident. • Automatic transmission failures at high speed. • Transmission grinds when shifting from First to Second gear.

Secret Warranties/Service Tips/TSBs

All models/years: Like Honda's, most of Acura's TSBs allow for special warranty consideration on a "goodwill" basis, even after the warranty has expired or the car has changed hands. Referring to this euphemism will increase your chances of getting some kind of refund for repairs that are obviously factory defects. • Seat belts that fail to function properly during normal use will be replaced for free under the company's lifetime seat belt warranty. • Diagnostic procedures and correction for off-centre steering wheels. **All models: 1996**—Rapid rear brake pad wear can be corrected by installing upgraded pads. • Moon roof wind noise can be corrected by replacing the visor clips and mounting hardware. • If the driver's seatback piping wears out prematurely, Acura suggests it be replaced. **1996–97**—Details of Acura's 14-year free engine repairs/tune-ups agreement with the United States' EPA. • Front window wind noise can be reduced by aligning the glass and sash. • Window noise during operation can be silenced by replacing the glass stabilizers and sashes, as well as the glass, if it's scratched. • Drivers who find the footrest is positioned too far away may obtain a replacement footrest from Acura. **1996–98**—A growling or whining coming from the rear wheels can be fixed by replacing the hub bearing unit. • Brake squeal during light application can be fixed by replacing the front pads (eligible for "goodwill"). **1999**—A navigation system that locks up or resets can be corrected by rewriting the unit's software; a remanufactured unit may also be considered. **1999–2000**—A squeaking, creaking driver's seat is addressed in TSB #00-014. • A wrinkled rear door sash trim will be covered under a "goodwill" policy, even if correction was done by an independent body shop. • Tips on replacing a leaking torque converter. • Troubleshooting moon roof creaks. **1999–2002**—Front, middle, or rear engine oil leaks likely caused by a too-porous cast aluminum engine block (TSB #01-041). • Loose front seat back panel. **2000**—Excessive cranking when restarting. • Faulty front and rear water passage gaskets at the cylinder head can cause a coolant leak next to the EGR valve. • Radiator/condenser fan runs continuously, discharging battery. • Vehicle clunks when going over bumps. **2000–01**—MIL (malfunction indicator light) and airbag warning light may stay lit for no apparent reason. • V6 engine oil leaks. • Speed sensor plug may be missing. • Panic alarm activates inadvertently. • Brake pedal pulsation. • Windshield wiper smearing and streaking. **2001**—A booming sound may be heard when the moon roof is opened while the car is underway. • Moon roof squeaks. • Climate control changes intermittently. **2000–03**—Honda extended its warranties to 7 years/ 100,000 miles (160,000 km) on automatic transmissions (see CL section, pages 48–49)

TL Profile

	1996	1997	1998	1999	2000	2001	2002	2003
Cost Price ($)								
Base	34,900	36,600	37,000	35,001	35,000	36,000	37,000	37,800
Used Values ($)								
Base ∧	8,500	10,000	12,500	15,500	18,500	23,000	27,000	31,000
Base ∨	7,500	9,000	11,000	14,000	17,000	21,500	25,500	29,000
Reliability	[4]	[4]	[4]	[5]	[5]	[5]	[5]	[5]
Crash Safety	[4]	[4]	[4]	—	—	[4]	[4]	[4]
Side	—	—	—	—	—	[5]	[4]	[4]
Offset	—	—	—	[5]	[5]	[5]	[5]	[5]
Head Restraints	—	[1]	[1]	[1]	[1]	[1]	[1]	[1]

Audi

90, A4, A6 (100), A8, S6, TT COUPE ★★★

RATING: Average (2000–03); Above Average (1996–99); Not Recommended (1984–95). Rating has been dropped due to poor wet weather braking performance, and serious transmission and ignition coil pack failures. The 1997 V6-equipped A4 is a price/performance bargain in this series, while the 2000 TT is an excellent buy considering it sells for about half the price ($27,000) originally charged. Try for a second series model. **Maintenance/Repair costs:** Higher than average, and almost all repairs have to be done by an Audi dealer. Long delays for recall repairs. **Parts:** Way-higher-than-average cost, and independent suppliers have a hard time finding parts. Don't even think about buying one of these front-drives without a 3- to 5-year supplementary warranty backed by Audi. **Best alternatives:** Other vehicles worth taking a look at: the Acura Integra, TL or RL; BMW 3 Series; Infiniti I30 or I35; and Lexus ES300. TT Coupe shoppers may also want to look at the BMW Z3 Series, Honda S2000, and Mazda Miata. **Online help:** *www.audiworld.com*; *www.audi-tt.org*; *www.vwvortex.com*; *MyAudiTTsucks.com*; and *www.robertfarago.com/tac* (The Truth About Cars).

Strengths and weaknesses: These cars are attractively styled and comfortable to drive, handle well, and provide a spacious interior. Yet the pre-1993 models, including the old 90 and 100, have a worse-than-average reliability record and are plagued by mechanical and electrical components that don't stand up to the rigors of driving in cold climates. Look for the better-built and more recent A4 and A6 models. The dealer body isn't strong enough to adequately service all of these vehicles when things go wrong, so owners of older models are generally left to independent garages to serve their needs.

The 1996 and later models are the pick of the Audi litter (when all-wheel drive became an optional feature on all entry-level models). The A6, the reincarnation of the 100 series, is packed with standard features, and is a comfortable, spacious, front-drive or all-wheel-drive luxury sedan that comes with dual airbags and ABS. It uses the same V6 power plant as the A4, its smaller sibling, but has 47 additional horses. Unfortunately, the engine is no match for the car's size (0–100 km/h in 13 seconds), and steering and handling is decidedly trucklike. The A8, the first luxury car with an all-aluminum body, competes with the BMW 7 Series and the Mercedes S-Class. Equipped with a WHO 174-hp 2.8L V6 or a 300-hp V8, the A8 is an above-average buy. Its only drawbacks: it comes with a high price, steering is a bit imprecise for an Audi, and its aluminum body can only be repaired by an Audi dealer.

The S6 is a solid performer with its turbocharged 227-hp 2.2L 5-cylinder engine. Its reliability is better than average and its sports performance leaves the A6 in the dust. The S6 is equipped with sports suspension, a turbocharger, and four-wheel drive.

Vehicle history: 1994—Airbags became a standard feature. **A4: 1997**—The A4 V6 sedan was renamed the 2.8 and joined a new entry-level A4 1.8T. An improved 190-hp DOHC V6 also debuted that year. **1998**—The addition of the A4 2.8 V6 wagon equipped with a 5-speed Tiptronic transmission. **1999**—Addition of an A4 1.8 wagon, and the base 1.8 model received additional insulation. **2000**—A high-performance S4 joined the A4 lineup, and A4 2.8s were given a power-assisted front passenger's seat. The S4 is a limited-production, high-performance spin-off that carries a 227-hp turbocharged rendition of the old 5-cylinder power plant. **2001**—The base 1.8L engine got 20 extra horses; an all-new 2001 S4 sedan and Avant, featuring a 250-hp 2.7L twin-turbocharged V6, also joined the lineup. **2002**—A4 was totally revamped, getting a roomier interior, a 10-hp boost to the base engine, and a 3.0L all-aluminum, 5-valve-per-cylinder, 220-hp V6 engine, hooked to a new 6-speed manual transmission. Other features: a more rigid body, an upgraded independent rear suspension, and brake assist. **2003**—Addition of a convertible. **A6: 1999**—Carried over with minor changes. **2000**—Addition of two performance sedans and side curtain airbags (standard on the 4.2). **2001**—2.7T and the 4.2 A6 models got Audi's electronic stabilization program, which prevents fishtailing and enhances traction control. **2002**—Debut of all-wheel drive, a 2.7L engine, and adjustable air suspension. **2003**—The new RS6 debuts equipped with a 450-hp 4.2L V8; the sporty S6 Avant adds a more powerful V8, sport suspension, and special trim, the 2.7T 17-inch wheels. On the debit side, front passenger-seat memory is no more, and steering-wheel shift buttons are gone. **TT: 2001**—A two-passenger softtop Roadster debuts; addition of Electronic Stability Program (ESP), a rear spoiler, and a 225-hp turbocharged 4-cylinder engine. **2002**—A new radio with in-dash CD. **2003**—All-wheel drive now only found on uplevel models; a revised grille.

These alphabetically named cars are conservatively styled, often slow off the mark (in spite of the V6 addition when hooked to an automatic), and plagued by electrical glitches. The 4-speed automatic shifts erratically (delayed and abrupt engagement), and the 2.8L V6 engine needs full throttle for adequate performance. Handling is acceptable, but the ride is a bit firm and the car still exhibits considerable body roll, brake dive, and acceleration squat when pushed. Handling is on a par with the BMW 3 Series, and acceleration times beat out those of the Mercedes. Up until the 2003 models' arrival, AWD had been extended to entry-level models at a time when most automakers were dropping the option on passenger cars.

Overall quality control improved markedly with the 1996–99 model years and then started going downhill. Through the 2003 models, there have been an inordinate number of safety- and performance-related defects reported by owners. The electrical system is the car's weakest link and it has plagued Audi's entire lineup for the past decade. Normally, this wouldn't be catastrophic; however, as the cars become more electronically complex, with more functions handled by computer modules, you're looking at some annoying glitches to say the least (particularly, chronic ignition coil pack failures, resulting in stalling or no-starts). Other "annoyances": transmission suddenly downshifting or jerking into forward gear, brake failures in rainy weather, premature brake wear and grinding when in Reverse, fuel system malfunctions leading to surging and stalling, early lower control arm replacement, steering grinds when turned, mirror memory setting doesn't work, distorted windshields, and body glitches head the list of things likely to go wrong. Furthermore, servicing is still spotty due to the small number of dealers in Canada and the fact that these cars are extremely dealer-dependent; owners report long servicing delays.

90

These cars were launched in 1988 as entry-level Audis, sharing the same wheelbase and powertrain components. Equipped with an efficient but wimpy 4-cylinder (dropped in 1991) or the more powerful 2.3L 5-cylinder engine, four-wheel disc brakes, and galvanized body panels, these small sedans are leagues ahead of Audi's mid-1980s vehicles. The 1991 models are clearly a better choice; they use an improved 4-speed automatic transmission hooked up to a more powerful engine. 1992 was basically a carryover year in which unsold 1991 models were recycled. Audi's first convertible, the Cabriolet, first appeared in 1994. It's essentially a 90 model set on a shorter wheelbase with a standard automatic transmission. The 90 was redesigned in 1995 (replacing both the 80 and the old 90) as the Sport 90, a stylish sporty version that was more show than go—it was dropped shortly thereafter. Common problems include AC, electrical system, and brake malfunctions. Although bargain-priced, these cars should be shunned due to the poor parts supply, unwillingness of mechanics to troubleshoot and service them (it takes even more skill and patience with older models), and the general poor quality of replacement parts.

TT Coupe

The best of the Audi lineup, the TT Coupe is a sporty front-drive hatchback with 2+2 seating, set on the same platform used by the A4, Golf, Jetta, and New Beetle. A two-seat convertible version, the Roadster, was launched in the spring of 2000. The base 180-hp 1.8L engine (lifted from the A4) is coupled to a manual 5-speed, while the optional engine uses a 6-speed manual transaxle. Shorter and more firmly sprung than the A4, the TT's engines are turbocharged.

More beautifully styled and better handling than the Prowler, the TT comes with lots of high-tech standard features that include four-wheel disc brakes, airbags everywhere, traction control (front-drive models), a power top (Quattro), a heated-glass rear window, and a power-retractable glass windbreak between the roll bars (convertible). An alarm system employs a pulse radar system to catch prying hands invading the cockpit area.

Problem areas reported by owners: premature transmission failures and grinding of the Second gear synchronizers, excessive brake noise, electrical shorts causing dash gauges and instruments to fail, premature wheel bearing failure, and steering wheel clunks.

Safety summary: All models/years: Extremely poor wet braking on later models, caused by water contaminating the brake rotor and disc; braking delay is almost two seconds. • Chronic stalling. • Many cases of distorted windshields. **A4: 1997**—Sudden acceleration. • Ignition switch failure causes many electrical systems to malfunction. • Premature clutch failure. • Battery exploded. **1998**—Stuck gas pedal. • Premature transmission failure; car pops out of gear. • Front and rear brake rotor and pad failed. • Premature upper and lower control arm failures (50 complaints found on *www.audiworld.com* website). • Sunroof opens by itself. **1999**—Sudden, unintended acceleration when backing up. • Vehicle will roll away even though parking brake is engaged. • Brakes suddenly locked up. • Engine loses power when shifting. • Door locks don't work. • Airbag failures. • Headlights burn out prematurely and don't provide sufficient illumination. • Booming noise heard if the sunroof or any window is open when car is underway. **2001**—Brakes fail to stop vehicle. • Headlights blind oncoming drivers. • Hood latch broke, allowing hood to smash into windshield. **2002**—Frequent coil pack failures (see *www.audiworld.com/search/index.html*).

> I have been in contact with close to 100 other 2002 Audi owners through the AudiWorld website and the coil pack problem is a serious issue.
>
> The ignition coil packs have been failing on at least 10 percent of the 2002 vehicles and Audi says they are all isolated cases. When they fail the car barely runs and can create a lot of personal safety issues.

• Sudden acceleration. • No airbag deployment. **A6 sedan: 1998–99**—During refuelling, gasoline spits back violently from the filler pipe. **2003**—Car fails to start (not coil-related, they say). • Sudden acceleration. • Airbags failed to deploy. • Numerous complaints of delayed braking; no brakes in rainy weather; parking brake failure; and premature replacement of the front brake rotors. • Sudden headlight failure. • Blue-white headlights blind oncoming drivers. **TT Coupe: 2000**—Engine compartment howling or moaning heard when accelerating. • Periodic grinding of the Second gear synchronizers is a common failure, said to affect many Audi and VW models. • Parking brake failure. • Engine exploded following a computer malfunction. • Electrical short causes vehicle to lose power. • Fuel gauge shows full, even though fuel is low. **2001**—Defective fuel gauge gives false reading (A6 models recalled for the same defect). • All windshields have some kind of visual distortion (anything viewed, especially straight lines, is distorted). Audi has a secret warranty to replace the windshields for free, regardless of mileage. • Sudden clutch failure (Audi paid half the replacement cost). • Central computer failure causes door locks to jam, trapping occupants. • Sudden windshield wiper failure. **2002**— Xenon headlights don't adequately light the roadway.

Secret Warranties/Service Tips/TSBs

All models/years: Defective catalytic converters that cause a rotten-egg smell may be replaced free of charge under the emissions warranty. • Inoperative radio, light is too dim. • Underbody wind noise. **All models: 2001–03**— Faulty ignition coils cause sudden stalling/no-starts; replacement coils will be installed free of charge without prior ownership or mileage restrictions; consequential damages (towing, alternate transport, ruined vacation, etc.) will also be refunded if you stand your ground (see following bulletin).

Ignition System – MIL ON/Engine Runs Rough/Low Power

Bulletin No: Group: 01 Date:

Date: Feb. 27, 2003; Number: 03-01
Ignition Coil, Misfire Diagnosis

Models: All with Eng. Code (AMB, AMU, ATC, 2001–2003
ATW, AWM, AWP AVK)

Condition:

^MIL light on/flashing

^Engine running rough

^Vehicle exhibits loss of power

^Diagnostic Trouble Codes (DTCs) P0300 and any of the following DTCs - P0301, P0302, P0303, P0304, P0305, or P0306 are stored in DTC memory indicating cylinder misfire.

A4, A6, S6: 1995–97—Delayed 1–2 shift on cold-start warm-ups is a normal condition resulting from the emissions control settings, according to Audi. **A4, A6: 1998–2000**—Diagnostic and repair procedures for disc brake squeal, an engine that will crank but not start, and engine misfires. **1999**—AC doesn't provide enough cooling. • Tips to silence rear window creaking or popping. **A4: 1996–99**—Audi will install upgraded front brakes on a case-by-case basis to "fix" problems related to premature corrosion (*Automotive News*, February 8, 1999). **1997**—Turbocharger failure. • Rear axle knocking, creaking noise. •

Tips on installing transmission sound-deadening shields. • Troubleshooting vehicles producing a whining, whirring noise when they're underway. **2002**— Poor AM band reception. **A6: 1997–2001**—Erratic engine idle fluctuation. **1998–2002**—Inoperative fresh air control lever. **2000**—Automatic transmission goes into limp mode and won't shift. **2001**—Inoperative self-levelling system. • Stained D-pillar trim. **2003**—Inoperative keyless entry transmitter and faulty fresh air control lever light.

90, A4, A6 (100), A8, S6, TT Coupe Profile

	1996	1997	1998	1999	2000	2001	2002	2003
Cost Price ($)								
A4	36,250	31,600	32,700	32,700	32,990	33,785	37,225	37,310
A6 (100)	48,904	49,270	48,800	48,880	49,170	49,835	54,235	51,740
A8	—	89,840	90,540	90,540	86,250	86,500	86,500	86,500
S6	61,400	63,550	—	—	—	—	—	88,500
TT	—	—	—	—	49,500	50,400	50,400	48,650
Used Values ($)								
A4 ⋏	8,500	10,500	13,500	16,000	18,500	22,000	28,500	32,000
A4 ⋎	7,000	9,000	12,000	15,000	17,000	20,000	27,000	30,500
A6 (100) ⋏	10,000	13,000	17,000	21,500	27,000	34,000	41,000	45,000
A6 (100) ⋎	9,000	11,500	15,500	19,500	25,000	32,000	39,500	43,000
A8 ⋏	—	15,500	22,000	29,000	38,000	48,000	61,000	71,000
A8 ⋎	—	13,500	20,000	27,000	36,000	46,000	58,000	68,000
S6 ⋏	12,500	16,000	—	—	—	—	—	—
S6 ⋎	11,000	14,000	—	—	—	—	—	—
TT ⋏	—	—	—	—	27,000	32,000	37,500	43,000
TT ⋎	—	—	—	—	25,000	30,000	36,500	41,000
Reliability	❷	❷	③	④	④	④	④	④
Crash Safety								
A4	④	④	—	—	—	—	④	④
A6 (100)	⑤	⑤	—	—	—	—	—	—
A8	—	—	⑤	⑤	⑤	⑤	⑤	⑤
Side (TT)	—	—	—	—	—	⑤	⑤	⑤
A4	—	—	—	—	—	—	⑤	⑤
Offset (A6)	—	—	③	③	③	③	③	③
A4	—	—	—	—	—	—	⑤	⑤
Head Restraints								
A4 (F)	—	❶	—	③	—	⑤	⑤	⑤
A4 (Rear)	—	—	—	—	—	③	③	③
A6	—	❶	—	③	—	⑤	⑤	⑤
A8	—	❶	—	❷	—	③	❷	❷
TT	—	—	—	—	—	⑤	⑤	⑤
TT (Rear)	—	—	—	—	—	—	③	③
Rollover Resistance	—	—	—	—	—	—	④	④
TT	—	—	—	—	—	—	—	⑤

BMW

3 SERIES, 5 SERIES, M SERIES, Z3

RATING: *3 Series:* Above Average (1995–2003); Average (1994); Below Average (1984–93). *5 Series:* Recommended (1992–2003); Average (1985–91); there was no 1996 version. *M Series:* Recommended (1997–2003). *Z3:* Above Average (1996–2002). *Z4:* Recommended (2003). These cars come with a reputation that far exceeds what they actually deliver, say some of the websites listed below. For example, there are a number of credible alternatives to the Z Series like the AWD 3 Series, an A4 Quattro, or a Mazda6. **Maintenance/Repair costs:** Higher than average, but many repairs can be done by independents who specialize in BMW repairs. Unfortunately, the specialists are concentrated around large urban areas. **Parts:** Higher-than-average cost, and they're often back ordered. **Best alternatives:** Acura Integra, TL, or RL; Infiniti I30 or I35; Lexus ES 300; Mazda Millenia; and the Toyota Avalon. **Online help:** *www.straight-six.com; www.mwerks.com; www.bmwnation.com; www.roadfly.org; yoy.com/auto/m3_failure_index.html; www.bmwboard.com;* and *www.bmwlemon.com.*

Strengths and weaknesses: The 3 Series vehicles exhibit great 6-cylinder performance with the manual gearbox, and ride and handling are commendable. The 318's small engine is seriously compromised, however, by an automatic transmission. The 325e is more pleasant to drive and delivers lots of low-end torque. Through 1998, rear passenger and cargo room is limited. After a redesign of the '99 models, passenger and cargo space was increased.

The 1991 and later models provide peppy 4-cylinder acceleration only with high revs and a manual transmission. Keep in mind that city driving requires lots of manual gear shifting characterized by an abrupt clutch. If you must have an automatic, look for a used model with the 6-cylinder engine. The larger 1.9L 4-cylinder that went into the mid-'96 models doesn't boost performance appreciably.

Although the 1997 models came with traction control, it is not very effective in giving these vehicles acceptable wet pavement traction. A problem since the early '90s, the rear end tends to slip sideways when the roadway is wet (much like Ford's rear-drive Mustang).

Vehicle history: 1998—3 Series given a 2.5L inline 6-cylinder and side airbags. **1999**—Revamped with a better-performing 2.5L base engine and 2.8L 6-banger, and a more refined transmission and chassis. **2000**—A redesigned lineup of coupes, convertibles, and wagons; the hatchback is gone. **2001**—Received an engine upgrade, larger brakes and wheels, and optional 4X4 capability. High-performance M3 coupe returned with a 330-hp engine. **2002**—M3 got a new 6-speed sequential manual transmission; entire lineup got recalibrated steering, reshaped headrests, and an in-dash CD player.

2003—Coupes and convertibles are restyled, along with a transmission upgrade and a new sedan performance package.

Handling is still tricky on wet roads, despite the ASC+T traction control; rear seat access is problematic; rear passenger space is limited; and styling is the essence of bland. Brakes, electrical system, and some body trim and accessories are the most failure-prone components. Engine overheating is a serious and common failure.

5 Series

Essentially a larger, more powerful 3 Series, the 5 Series has made its reputation by delivering more performance in a larger, more versatile interior. There is no problem with rear seat or cargo room with the 5 Series Bimmer. Handling and ride are superb, although these weighty upscale models do strain when going over hilly terrain if they have the automatic gearbox.

5 Series owners report numerous electrical and fuel glitches, faulty turn signal indicators, starter failures, self-activating emergency flashers, rotten-egg odours from the exhaust, and excessive steering wheel or brake vibration.

Overall reliability was very poor with early Bimmers, but has improved of late. Nevertheless, whenever a problem does arise, repair costs are particularly high due to the small number of dealers, the relative scarcity of parts, and the acquiescence of affluent owners.

Electrical and fuel system, automatic transmission, and front brake failures are the primary weak spots of 1984–93 models. Chronic engine surging at idle and a rotten-egg smell from the exhaust are also commonplace. Door seams, rocker panels, rear-wheel openings, and fender seams are particularly prone to rust. Check the muffler bracket for premature wear, and weather seals and door adjustments for leaks.

The '94 and later models still have reliability problems affecting the automatic and manual transmissions, brakes, and fuel and electrical systems. Additionally, owners report that premature brake wear causes excessive vibration and noise when the brakes are applied. Some reports of water leaks through the doors.

Year 2000–03 models are plagued by cooling fan malfunctions, leading to engine overheating and fires; airbag malfunctions; a manual transmission that's hard to shift into Second gear, pops out of gear, and grinds when shifting; automatic transmission screeches when shifting; steering degradation when braking at slow speeds; and front door water leaks.

Vehicle history: 5 Series: 1989—Based on the 7 Series, the new 5 sits on a longer wheelbase than earlier models. Two rear-drive sedans were available: the 525i with a 2.5L 6-cylinder engine, and the 535i, whose 3.4L 6-cylinder engine developed 208 hp. **1990**—A driver-side airbag arrives. **1991**—The 525i gained a more powerful engine; 535i's automatic transmission got a shorter final-drive ratio and reprogrammed management system, producing quicker acceleration; M5 came with a 310-hp 3.5L engine. **1993**—Engines got variable valve timing. **1994**—V8 engines for the 530i sedan and wagon, and 540i sedan; passenger-side airbags; the 535i and the M5 are dropped. **1997**—The redesigned model is longer and comes with an enlarged V6 or V8 engine, dual front and side airbags, anti-lock brakes, and traction control. **1998**—A head protection system. **1999**—Station wagons get both 6-cylinder and V8 power, xenon headlights, memory for power seats and mirrors, Park Distance Control that warns of obstacles when backing up, and a self-levelling rear suspension for wagons. Standard on V8 models and newly optional for 528i versions was BMW's Dynamic Stability Control. **2000**—Return of the high-performance M5 sedan; 528i versions get a standard anti-skid system; rear side airbags for the M5. **2001**—525i sedan and wagon debut. **2002**—540i's V8 got an extra 8 hp.

M Series

Launched in 1997 as a four-door model, the M3 is a high-performance coupe equipped with a potent 240-hp 3.0L engine, a manual shifter, firmer suspension, and 17-inch tires. 1999 and 2000 cars were re-designated the M Series. The 2000 M5 is mostly a renamed 540i sports sedan. 2001 M Series models received a new 315-hp inline six, Dynamic Stability Control, and a tighter suspension (watch those kidneys), while the M3 returned for the 2001 model year in a convertible and coupe format, equipped with a high-performance 333-hp engine. The 2002s came with a modified aluminum suspension, wider 18-inch tires and wheels, a new limited-slip differential, and a refreshed interior.

Overall M3 reliability is quite impressive; however, these cars have one fatal flaw: Their engines self-destruct. In fact, 112 failed engines have been registered with the *yoy.com/auto/m3_failure_index.html* website, which dubs the power plant "The Engine of Damocles."

Except for *AutoWeek* (*autoweek.com*), little has been reported about possible main bearing or connecting rod problems with M3 engines built in 2001 and 2002. Nevertheless, the problem is real, has been confirmed by BMW, and is extensively documented online at *members.roadfly.com*. Many owners have had engines replaced with no explanation of what went wrong.

Other reported problems: loud clunking from the rear end when shifting or decelerating, said to be caused by a faulty driveshaft attachment at the differential, and poor paint application and delamination.

Z3

BMW's Z3 1.9L roadster arrived on the scene for the 1996 model year (an optional 2.8L engine was added in 1997, along with standard traction control). '98s got standard rollover bars and upgraded sport seats. '99 models received standard side airbags (318Ti excepted) and were joined by a new 2.8 coupe. A 2.5L inline six replaced the 1.9L 4-cylinder engine. 2000 models got a slight restyling and standard Dynamic Stability Control; 2001 roadsters and coupes adopted a 3.0L power plant (instead of the 2.8L), and bigger brakes and wheels were added. Also, the 2.5L engine was tweaked to unleash 14 additional horses.

Z3s have plenty of power, but they're a bit outpaced by the competition (like the non-S Boxster, the 3.2L V-6 SLK, or Honda S2000), plus, you have to get the revs up past 3000 rpm to get adequate passing torque. Dynamic Stability Control, large 17-inch wheels, and Dunlop SP Sport performance tires don't enhance handling as much as BMW pretends they do: Get used to lots of steering corrections.

Owners report frequent stalling when decelerating, faulty right-side seat switches, and a squeaking, popping noise from the driver's door or in the shoulder area of the convertible top.

Safety summary: All models/years: Sudden acceleration. • Airbag malfunctions include bag deploying inadvertently, failing to go off in an accident, and a constantly lit warning light. • Transmission pops out of gear. **All models: 2002**—Many incidents where cooling fan failure caused engine to overheat, or a fire to ignite (see *www.bimmer.org*); airbag failed to deploy; and the premature replacement of the front control arms. **318: 1995**—During an accident, the driver-side seat belt and airbags failed to operate as they should. • Other reports of airbags not deploying. • Sudden steering lock-up. • AC expansion valve failures. • Noisy exhaust manifold. • Erratic automatic transmission shifting: hesitation and jerky shifts. • Transmission slips when accelerating, causing vehicle to stall. • Clutch pressure plate failures. • Electrical system malfunctions. **1996**—Sunroof motor shorts out. • AC failures. **1997**—Fire erupted near battery terminal. • Vehicle loses power and then surges. • Gas and brake pedals are too close together. **1998**—Finger was cut off when caught in the power window. • Glass came out of door channel. • Headlights provide poor illumination of the roadway. • Severe suspension hop when passing over small bumps. • Car's rear end slides out during turns. • Incorrect fuel gauge readings. **1999**—Front plastic grille piece fell off car and damaged the windshield. • Automatic transmission failures. • Seat belt doesn't retract as it should. • Horn sounds when vehicle is put in Reverse. • Headlights come on and off intermittently. • Several incidents of fire erupting when high beams were activated. • Heated seats get too hot. **2000**—Poor wet braking. • Faulty steering damper and control arms. • Seat belt warning light stays on. • Seat belt doesn't retract properly. • Drivebelts may suddenly fail. **2001**—Fire ignited due to defective fan assembly. • Defective cooling fan causes engine to overheat; seen as a widespread problem on the bulletin board at *www.roadfly.org/bmw*. • Premature replacement of the control arms. • Defective gas pedal assembly causes jerky acceleration. BMW will replace it on a case-by-case basis. **320: 2002**—Distorted windshield. **323: 2002**—Premature failure of the magnesium-alloy control arms and steering damper. • Airbag light stays on for no reason. • Poor steering when braking at slow speeds. • Sudden acceleration while cruising. • In rainy weather brakes stiffen as they are applied, leading to extended stopping distance. • Faulty sunroof. **325i:** Transmission failure within five days of purchase. • Electrical system fire. • Steering column is kinked to the left. • Right door airbag deployed even though vehicle was hit on the left. • Sunroof glass suddenly exploded (several incidents reported):

Urgent—my 2002 325i's first sunroof glass exploded on me on 1/25/02. The replacement glass has two surface hairline cracks and two hairline cracks beneath the surface of the glass. This cannot be an isolated incident. Please examine your sunroof carefully for defects. No one at BMW is taking this seriously enough.

• Doors lock without prior warning. **328: 2002**—Sudden acceleration; when accelerating, engine cuts out, then surges forward (suspected failure of the throttle assembly). • Severe engine vibrations after a cold start as Check Engine light comes on. • If driver wears a size 12 shoe or larger, when foot is flush against the accelerator pedal, the top of the shoes rubs up against the panel above the pedal, preventing full pedal access. • Rear quarter blind spot with the convertibles. **330i: 2002**—Side airbag deployed when vehicle hit a pothole. • Vehicle overheats in low gear; tires lose air. • Vehicle slips out of Second gear when accelerating. **M3: 1998**—Brake failure. • Airbags failed to deploy. • Chronic horn failures. • Rear-view mirror blocks a substantial portion of the field of vision. • Inadvertent deployment of side airbags. **1999**—ABS failure. **2001**—Rear end clunking, leading to failure of the driveshaft attachment at the differential (confirmed by other complaints on *www.roadfly.org/bmw* website). **Z3: 1998**—Defective rear stabilizer bar. • Automatic transmission jumps out of gear. • Intermittent headlight and instrument cluster failures. • Rear-view mirror creates a huge blind spot. **1999**—Seat belts don't spool out or retract as they should. **2000**—Computer keeps engine at high revs when throttle is released. • Passenger-side seat belt jams. **2000–01**—Faulty speedometer. **2001**—Engine stalls when decelerating. • Interior and exterior lights dim when AC engages. • Passenger seat belt doesn't fit snugly. • Driver's seat rocks to and fro. • Incorrect speedometer readings. • Exterior and interior lights dim and engine loses power, when AC is engaged.

Secret Warranties/Service Tips/TSBs

All models/years: Rear sway bar links may come off the sway bar. • Front brake squeal. • Steering wheel buzz. • Door brake doesn't hold. • Driver's seat is loose. **All models: 1996–99**—Frequent crankshaft position sensor failures result in chronic Check Engine light illumination. This can be corrected by changing the sensor and installing an adapter harness under warranty or under a BMW "goodwill" policy. **3 Series: 1992–95**—Automatic transmission may be slow to shift after sitting overnight because fluid has drained out of the torque converter. **1996**—Transmission shuddering requires the installation of a modified transmission control module. **1996–97**—Delayed gear engagement or adapter case leak requires the installation of a new transmission seal kit (#21-41-422-762). **1998**—A no-start condition may signal that the oil level sensor is faulty. • A "clunk" heard during downshifts, when releasing the accelerator pedal, or when shifting into Reverse is likely caused by excessive axial clearance between the transmission output shaft and the output shaft. • Inoperative sunroof. **1998–2000**—Hard shifts or no shifts can be corrected by exchanging the valve body. **1999**—Tips for improving AM radio reception. •

An inoperative cruise control may need a new brake light switch (strange but true). **1999–2000**—Guidelines for plugging manual transmission oil drain plug leaks. **2000**—Idle speed and headlight brightness fluctuate when seat heater is activated. •Low airflow through vents. •Erratic automatic transmission shifting. **2002**—Incorrect fuel gauge readings. • Rattling, tapping engine noise. •Troubleshooting navigation system malfunctions. • No 1–2 upshift. **2003**—Harsh 3–2 and 2–1 downshifts (reprogram EGS module). **5 Series: 1996**—Oil level sensor may give an incorrect reading. **1997**—Airbag light stays lit for no reason. **1998**—A no-start condition may signal that the oil level sensor is faulty. **525i: 2000**—No 1–2 upshift. **540: 1999**—Air mass meter warranty extended to 7 years/120,000 km (75,000 mi.). **2002**—Rattling, tapping engine noise. • Passenger-side airbags may not line up with the dash. • Steering groaning, and grinding. • Troubleshooting navigation system malfunctions. **M Series: 2001–03**—After a plague of self-destructing engines, BMW put out SIB #11-04-02 in June 2003 that extended the warranty to 6 years/100,000 miles on all 6-cylinder engines, initiated a Service Action to replace key components free of charge, and recalibrated software for easier cold starts. Owner repair bills were also paid retroactively, including demands for consequential damages.

3 Series, M Series, Z3 Profile

	1996	1997	1998	1999	2000	2001	2002	2003
Cost Price ($)								
318ti	25,900	26,900	27,800	27,800	—	—	—	—
318i 4d	30,900	32,300	33,300	—	—	—	—	—
Convertible	42,900	43,900	44,900	45,900	—	—	—	—
320i 4d	—	—	—	—	—	33,900	34,500	34,900
325i, 328i	43,900	46,900	47,900	50,902	44,900	37,950	41,200	39,300
Convertible	55,300	57,900	58,900	58,900	—	52,500	52,800	53,400
323 Coupe	—	—	39,900	—	—	—	—	—
M3 2d	—	61,900	62,900	62,900	62,900	69,800	73,500	73,800
M5	—	—	—	—	102,650	104,250	105,500	105,500
Z3 1.9L/2.3L	38,900	40,500	41,500	43,900	45,901	46,900	47,200	—
Z3 2.8L	—	49,900	51,900	52,900	54,900	55,900	56,200	—
Z4 2.5L	—	—	—	—	—	—	—	51,500
Z4 3.0L	—	—	—	—	—	—	—	59,500
Used Values ($)								
318ti ⋀	9,000	10,000	12,000	15,000	—	—	—	—
318ti ⋁	8,000	8,500	10,500	13,500	—	—	—	—
318i 4d ⋀	10,500	12,500	14,500	—	—	—	—	—
318i 4d ⋁	9,000	11,000	12,500	—	—	—	—	—
Convertible ⋀	15,000	16,500	19,500	22,500	—	—	—	—
Convertible ⋁	13,500	15,000	18,000	21,000	—	—	—	—
320i 4d ⋀	—	—	—	—	—	21,500	25,000	28,500
320i 4d ⋁	—	—	—	—	—	20,000	23,500	26,500
323 Coupe ⋀	—	—	17,000	—	—	—	—	—
323 Coupe ⋁	—	—	15,500	—	—	—	—	—

325i, 328i ▲	12,000	13,500	18,000	23,000	25,000	26,000	30,500	33,000
325i, 328i ▼	11,000	12,000	16,500	21,500	23,000	24,500	29,000	31,500
Convertible ▲	17,500	20,000	23,500	29,000	—	37,000	42,000	47,000
Convertible ▼	16,000	18,500	22,000	27,500	—	35,000	40,500	45,500
M3 2d ▲	—	16,500	20,500	30,500	34,000	45,000	54,000	60,000
M3 2d ▼	—	15,000	19,000	29,000	32,000	43,000	52,000	58,000
M5 4d ▲	—	—	—	—	53,000	66,000	79,000	90,000
M5 4d ▼	—	—	—	—	50,000	63,000	76,000	87,000
Z3 1.9L/2.3L ▲	15,000	17,000	20,000	23,500	27,500	33,000	38,000	—
Z3 1.9L/2.3L ▼	13,500	15,500	18,000	22,000	26,000	31,000	36,000	—
Z3 2.8L ▲	—	19,000	22,000	27,000	32,000	34,000	38,,000	—
Z3 2.8L ▼	—	17,500	20,500	25,500	30,000	32,000	36,500	—
Z4 2.5L ▲	—	—	—	—	—	—	—	44,000
Z4 2.5L ▼	—	—	—	—	—	—	—	42,000
Z4 3.0L ▲	—	—	—	—	—	—	—	50,000
Z4 3.0L ▼	—	—	—	—	—	—	—	48,000

Reliability	③	③	④	④	④	⑤	⑤	⑤
Crash Safety (3 Series)	—	—	—	—	—	—	④	④
328i	④	④	—	—	—	—	—	—
Side (3 Series)	—	—	—	—	—	—	—	③
Offset	—	—	—	—	⑤	⑤	⑤	⑤
Head Restraints (3 Series)	—	❶	—	❷	③	③	③	③
Rear	—	—	—	❶	—	—	—	—
M3	—	—	—	—	❷	❷	❷	❷
Convertible	—	—	—	❶	—	—	—	—
Z3	—	❶	—	③	—	③	③	—
Z4	—	—	—	—	—	—	—	⑤

5 Series Profile

	1996	1997	1998	1999	2000	2001	2002	2003
Cost Price ($)								
525i, 528i	—	54,900	56,200	57,200	55,500	54,700	55,200	55,500
Used Values ($)								
525i, 528i ▲	—	16,000	20,000	25,500	32,000	36,000	42,500	48,000
525i, 528i ▼	—	14,500	18,500	24,000	30,500	34,500	40,500	45,000
Reliability	⑤	⑤	⑤	⑤	⑤	⑤	⑤	⑤
Offset	—	⑤	⑤	⑤	⑤	⑤	⑤	⑤
Head Restraints (F)	—	③	—	③	—	⑤	⑤	⑤
Rear	—	❷	—	—	—	—	—	—

Note: The 5 Series hasn't been crash-tested by NHTSA.

Ford/Lincoln

CONTINENTAL, LS, MARK VII, MARK VIII, TOWN CAR

RATING: *Continental:* Below Average (1988–2002). *LS:* Average (2000–03). *Mark VII, Mark VIII:* Above Average (1995–98); Average (1994); Below Average (1986–93). *Town Car:* Average (1995–2003); Below Average (1988–94). In a nutshell: rear-drives, yes; front-drives, no. Although early front-drive Continentals are dirt-cheap, their low quality make them risky buys. Now that Ford has dropped the Continental after its 2002 model year, servicing problems will likely increase as well. The rear-drive Town Car and LS are the best choice for quality and performance, but you are still taking a substantial risk. The Mark series isn't a bad choice either, particularly in view of its incredibly low cost. **Maintenance/Repair costs:** Higher than average, and they must be done by a Ford or Lincoln dealer. **Parts:** Higher-than-average cost, but not hard to find (except for electronic components and body panels). **Best alternatives:** Acura Integra, TL, or RL; Cadillac DeVille; Infiniti I30 or I35, Lexus ES 300; and Mercedes E-Class. **Online help:** *www.autosafety.org/ autodefects.html* and *www.blueovalnews.com.*

Strengths and weaknesses: These large luxury cruisers are proof that quality isn't proportional to the money you spend. Several designer series offer all the luxury options anyone could wish for, but the two ingredients most owners would expect to find—high quality and consistent reliability—are sadly lacking, especially with the front-drive versions. All models, however, have poor-quality automatic transmissions, electrical systems, brakes, body hardware, and fit and finish. NHTSA-recorded safety complaints also target more front-drive than rear-drive Lincolns, with engine, transmission, airbag, and brake failures cropping up repeatedly over the years—and increasing in severity and frequency.

Continental (front-drive)

When the Continental went front-drive in 1988, what was a mediocre luxury car became a luxury lemon with serious safety-related deficiencies. The frequency and cost of repairs increased considerably, and parts became more complex, complicating easy diagnosis and repair. The automatic transmission tends to self-destruct, particularly on 1988–2000 models; engine head gaskets blow (see Part Two); electrical components are unreliable, with intermittent loss of all electrical power; stopping performance is compromised by premature brake wear and wheel lock-up; and body hardware continues to be an embarrassment. The redesigned 1995 Continental featured a new V8 power plant, more aerodynamic styling, and fibreglass panels. However, engine, transmission, electrical system, and brake problems actually worsened.

Vehicle history: 1991—15 additional horses (155) and an upgraded 4-speed automatic transmission. **1992**—A passenger-side airbag and five more horses (160). **1994**—A slight restyling and suspension improvements. **1995**—A new 260-hp V8 and 4-speed automatic transmission; restyled, including dual airbags, antilock braking, automatic climate control, and an air-filtration system. **1996**—Anti-theft alarm. **1997**—Traction control added and failure-prone air springs dropped. **1998**—A shorter nose and 2.5 cm less rear legroom. **1999**—Front side airbags and a 15-hp boost to 275 hp. **2000**—Rear child-seat anchors and an emergency trunk release.

These cars don't offer the kind of trouble-free driving one would normally expect in a luxury vehicle selling for over $40,000. The automatic levelling air-spring suspension system makes for a stiff ride (especially on early models), while still allowing the Continental to "porpoise" due to its heavy front end. The Continental's anemic V6 powertrain is poorly suited to a car of this heft. The engine hesitates in cold weather and the automatic transmission shifts roughly.

Mechanical defects include frequent engine flywheel and transmission forward clutch piston replacements; failure-prone ABS, electrical, suspension, and steering systems; and glitch-ridden electronic modules, causing hard starts and sudden stalling. The mass of electrical gadgets increases the likelihood of problems as the cars age. For example, automatic headlight doors fail frequently, and the electronic antenna and power windows often won't go up or down. The computerized dashboard is particularly failure prone.

Other reliability complaints concern transmission fluid leakage due to misplaced bolts, rough upshifting caused by a defective valve body, and air conditioning and heating that sometimes work in reverse order.

Town Car

The rear-drive Town Car is the best of a bad lot, sharing most of its parts with the Crown Victoria and Grand Marquis. Its only saving grace is that, thanks to its rear-drive configuration, it's relatively inexpensive to repair and parts aren't hard to find. Nevertheless, the Town Car is still afflicted by many generic problems that reappear year after year. Some of the more common problems are safety-related defects; engine head gaskets warped because a plastic part in the intake manifold has failed; transmission, AC, and electrical glitches; biodegradable tie-rod ends; and body hardware deficiencies.

Vehicle history: 1990—Restyled to look less square. **1991**—The 4.6L V8 replaced the 5.0L; a new front suspension; and four-wheel disc brakes. **1993**—Dual airbags. **1994**—Dual exhausts. **1995**—Restyled; electronically adjustable steering, and seats have extra travel. **1995**—Slightly restyled, and steering improvements. **1996**—Engine upgraded and revised climate controls. **1997**—Steering refinements, but loss of dual exhausts cuts horsepower by 20 (drops to

190 hp). **1998**—Redesigned for a faster, lower and stiffer ride. **1999**—Side airbags. **2000**—Improved child seat anchorages and a trunk emergency escape release. **2001**—Engine got 25 more horses; adjustable pedals; and seat belt pretensioners; the following model year got few changes. **2003**—Restyled; a revised frame, suspension, and steering system; and 17-inch tires. Also new: four-wheel, fully assisted ABS disc brakes, front-side airbags, an upgraded navigation system, and a 14-hp boost.

Incidentally, Ford will pay for intake manifold failures long after the warranty has expired—if you are a fleet customer (taxi, limousine, and law enforcement). Others are routinely denied after-warranty assistance. Unfair? You bet. Stupid? Absolutely!

One owner of a '97 Lincoln afflicted by this malady had this to say:

> Ford has extended a no-charge coverage for this part for seven years and no mileage limitation, and it's automatically extended to subsequent owners. This should be extended to all owners of vehicles equipped with this defective part. Ford customer service has rejected [my] claim when contacted by telephone. They have not replied to two requests [sent] by mail.

LS

Lincoln's latest iteration, the LS rear-drive sedan comes with a high-performance 200-hp variant of the Taurus 3.0L V6, mated to an optional manual or a standard automatic gearbox. Also available: a 250-hp 3.9L V8, based on that of the Jaguar XK8 coupe, coupled to a semi-automatic transmission. Both engines are identical, but the Lincoln produces 30 fewer horses than the Jag equivalent. There is very little difference between the 2000 and 2001 models, except that the 2001 carries standard traction control. The 2002s came back unchanged.

The LS offers a lot for a reasonable base price. The V6 version is priced in the range of the BMW 3 Series, Lexus ES 300, and Mercedes C-Class, while delivering standard equipment and interior space that rivals the 5 Series, GS, and E-Class.

Lincoln's return to rear-drive has opened up a Pandora's box of powertrain, AC, electrical system, and body glitches. Owners report jerky transmission shifting, excessive drivetrain and body noise and vibrations, inconsistent braking response, and erratic AC performance.

Safety summary: All models/years: Sudden, unintended acceleration; gas pedal sticks. • Loss of braking. • Inadvertent deployment of airbags or airbags don't deploy when they should. • Sudden loss of electrical power. • Severe pull and vibration when braking. • Brake failures due to premature wear of rear drums and rotor warpage. • Steering control degrades or locks up when passing through puddles. • Annoying reflections onto the front windshield. • Horn is hard to activate. • Mirrors vibrate excessively and don't adjust easily. **Continental: 1996**—While parked, vehicle suddenly jumped out of Park and rolled forward and hit another car. • Transmission jumped out of gear while driving. • Several reports that the front suspension collapsed. • Front strut failures. • Clock spring broke, causing loss of steering. • Steering wheel jams intermittently. • Power seats malfunction. **1997**—Blown engine head gaskets. • Engine suddenly stalls in traffic. • Vehicle often won't start; starter whirrs, but won't crank. • Premature failure of the tie-rod ends. • Several incidents of steering failure; cracked steering gear. • Gasoline smell permeates interior. • Broken rear side door handle disables the door. • Rear-view mirror distortions. • Speedometer is difficult to read in daylight and gas gauge is often in error. • **1998**—Cracked high-pressure plastic line on top of engine caused fuel to spew out and catch fire. • Several complaints that engine coolant leaks and bubbles up onto the engine compartment, risking a fire. • Premature engine timing chain failure. • Gas pedal set higher than brake pedal, causing unintended acceleration. • Cruise control speeds up when vehicle goes downhill. • Frequent stalling and no-starts likely caused by a sensor failure. • Sudden steering failure. • Right front wheel assembly came off as vehicle came to a stop. • Power-steering pump fails periodically. • Front suspension failed as vehicle came to a stop. • Interior lights fail, smoke. • Many complaints that the interior ventilation system leaks exhaust fumes. **1999**—Brake line ruptured. • Headlights fail to adequately light side of the road. • Visual image speedometer can't be seen by colour-blind drivers. **2000**—Warning lights come on constantly and car's central computer module often malfunctions. • Airbag deployed without warning. • Brakes don't work well; require extended stopping distance. • Side-view mirror can't be adjusted properly due to a design defect. **2001**—Car suddenly accelerated while in Reverse; brake/transmission interlock not connected. • Driver's foot can be snared by two console cables when going from gas pedal to the brakes. • Instrument panel washes out in bright sunlight. **2002**—Sudden forward acceleration when shifter placed into Reverse. • While in Park with the brakes applied, vehicle rolled back into another car. • Sticking, binding shoulder belt. **LS: 2000–01**—Sudden acceleration in forward or Reverse gear. • Airbag deployment for no reason. • Airbag failed to deploy. • Lurching, hesitating automatic transmission shifting. • Brakes fail during the first five minutes after a cold start. • Brake pedal becomes hard and resists application or turns mushy and goes to the floor. • Warning lights come on for no reason. • Defective steering causes violent swerving from side to side. • Automatic door locks engage by themselves, locking out driver. **2002**—Sudden shutdown while on the highway. **Town Car: 1996**—Vehicle fires reportedly ignited in the engine compartment wiring. • Frequent reports of sudden acceleration. • Many reports of sudden acceleration while in Reverse, leading to the replacement of the speed control servo and servo cable. • Frequent complaints of chronic stalling. • Airbag packing gets hard in cold weather, leaving horn inoperative. • Trunk lid flew open on highway. • Many incidents where seat belts either are too short for adults, won't retract, or ratchet tighter while being worn. • Two front seatbacks collapsed rearward when vehicle was rear-ended. • Excessive noise when braking. **1997**—Intake manifold failures caused by faulty plastic part. Fleet vehicles get special after-warranty assistance, but regular customers are left to slowly twist in the wind (see Part Two, "Secret Warranties"). • Shock absorbers fell off vehicle. • Repeated air spring failures. • Poorly designed sunroof switch is easily broken. • Rear suspension design leads to poor directional control. • Headlights fail when high or low beams are activated. • Water leaks through the windshield wiper motor assembly. **1998**—Traction control engages at the wrong time, making driver lose control of the vehicle. • Fuel may spit out of filler pipe when refuelling. • Easy to get foot stuck on accelerator pedal due to placement of partition. • Fuse panel location interferes with applying the brake pedal. • Rear-view mirror creates a large blind spot. • Passenger-side door won't open close to curb, due to car's low stance. **1999**—Loss of all electrical power while cruising on the highway. • Chronic stalling. • Head restraints won't lock into position. **2000**—Vehicle suddenly accelerates when cruise control is engaged and brakes are applied. The following NHTSA report is rather typical of other similar complaints:

> Driver was going 75 mph [120 km/h] with cruise control set. When approaching a curve, driver applied the brakes to slow down, and as brake pedal was pressed, vehicle speeded up. Driver was coached from limousine service on a two-way radio how to control vehicle. Driver turned off cruise control switch and vehicle returned to normal.

• Inadvertent airbag deployment. • Frequent brake failures (brake pedal will fade and not hold). • Horn is hard to activate. • Vehicle pulls hard to one side when braking. • Faulty trunk light bulb ignited clothing in trunk. • Power windows fail intermittently. **2001**—Sudden acceleration when brakes are applied. • Inadvertent airbag deployment.

> Passenger side airbag deployed at 70 mph [110 km/h] with no impact to vehicle.
>   Lost control of vehicle temporarily and crossed traffic to other side of road. Regained control after crossing back to original lane shoulder and braking hard.
>   Very frightening experience considering the noise, surprise, and dust from the airbag deploying. Only good thing was that no traffic was coming in other lane.

• NHTSA also is looking into side-impact airbags deploying for no reason. Seventy-six complaints and nine injuries reported. • Frequent brake failures. • Wheel lug studs break off at the hub. • Ignition locks up when key is inserted. • Broken driver's seat. • Headlights can't be aimed properly. • Brake and accelerator pedal set too close together. Dash reflects onto windshield. **2002**—Sudden acceleration while driving down a mountain, or upon start-up. • Airbags didn't deploy. • Repeated brake master cylinder failures. • Brake pedal not responsive, until pressure is reapplied. • Gas and brake pedal are mounted too close together. • Head restraints set too low. • While driving, sunroof blew off. **2003**—Sudden, unintended acceleration. • Complete brake failure. • Brake light causes an annoying reflection onto the rear windshield. • Hood latch snapped while driving.

Secret Warranties/Service Tips/TSBs

All models: 1985–2002—Repeated heater core leaks. **1993–99**—Paint delamination, peeling, or fading (see Part Two). **Continental: 1984–94**—A hum from the air suspension system can be corrected by replacing the compressor isolators with upgraded parts. **1994–99**—Tips on plugging door, window, and moon roof wind noise. **1995–97**—An acceleration or deceleration clunk is likely caused by the rear lower subframe isolators allowing movement between the mounts and the subframe. • A front suspension clunk may signal excessive sway bar wear. **1995–98**—No Fourth gear may mean you have a defective forward clutch control valve retaining clip. • Condensation buildup on the inside of windows may be stopped by installing an upgraded pressure cycling switch. • An intermittent shifting into Neutral or loss of forward or Reverse gear is likely caused by a defective forward clutch piston (a problem that has haunted Ford and Lincoln for over 12 years). • Front brake groaning, moaning, or squealing can be silenced by installing upgraded brake pads under the bumper-to-bumper warranty. **1995–99**—Troubleshooting tips for silencing a creak or pop while turning or braking and wind noise coming from the side doors. **1996–98**—No-starts may be due to fuel pump wire chafing. **1997–98**—Lack of AC temperature control. **1998**—Inaccurate fuel gauge readings. **1998–99**—Steering wheel vibration/moaning can be fixed by installing a longer power steering hose. **1999**—No Reverse engagement with the automatic transmission may be caused by torn Reverse clutch lip seals. Ford will cover the repair under a special "goodwill" policy (see Part Two). **1998–2002**—Hard to turn ignition switch. **1999–2002**—Engine hesitation, surging, and bucking can be fixed under warranty by reprogramming the PCM.

Engine Controls – Engine Hesitation/Surging/Bucking

Article No. 02-13-5

07/08/02

Driveability – Hesitation, bucking or surge felt during steady speeds between 40–60 mph (64–96 km/h)

MODELS: Lincoln: 1999–2002 Continental

ISSUE: Some vehicles may exhibit a hesitation, buck or surge during a steady state operation at 40–60 mph (64–96 km/h). This may be caused by the Powertrain Control Module (PCM) calibration.

LS: 2000–01—Frequent bulletin references to automatic transmission defects producing: delayed engagement (PCM module seen as likely culprit), driveline vibration and buzz/clunk/drone, and fluid leakage. • Trunk may suddenly open. • Inaccurate ambient temperature display. • Inoperative AC dual zone heater. • ABS, airbag, and Service Engine lights come on for no apparent reason. • Noisy front power windows. • Steering wheel "nibble," hum, or boom noise. • 3.9L oil leak from the bell housing area. • Poor braking on V6-equipped models. • V6 engine noise on acceleration and highway drone noise. • Hard starts or no-starts. • Instrument panel squeaks and rattles. **2000–02**—Inoperative power windows. • Oil pan drain plug leaks. • Correction for a noisy suspension. **2000–03**—Inoperative defroster. **2001–02**—A faulty cooling fan is the likely cause of engine overheating. **2003**—Harsh shifting. **Mark VII, Mark VIII: 1985–99**—An exhaust buzz or rattle may be caused by a loose heat shield catalyst. **1986–94**—The in-tank fuel pump is the likely cause of radio static. Install an electronic noise RFI filter (#F1PZ-18B925-A). **1993–94**—A squeak or chirp coming from the blower motor can be stopped by installing an upgraded blower motor. • Automatic transmissions with delayed or no forward engagement, or a higher engine rpm than expected when coming to a stop, are covered in TSB #94-26-9. **Town Car: 2001**—Rear-end impact may puncture fuel tank; two TSB repairs already carried out. **2001–04**—Engine ticking. **2003**—Premature wear of the axle shaft or axle bearing. • Erratic AC blower motor operation. • Blower motor whistling. • Inaccurate fuel gauge. • Power steering assist calibration; excessive power steering pump noise. • Front wheel area click or rattle. • Anti-theft system may cause the transmission to stick in Park or a locked steering wheel; and rear parking brake clicking. • Poor AM radio reception.

Continental Profile

	1995	1996	1997	1998	1999	2000	2001	2002
Cost Price ($)								
Continental Ex.	50,995	51,896	49,995	51,995	52,795	52,895	51,920	52,900
Used Values ($)								
Continental Ex. ⋀	6,000	7,500	8,500	11,000	14,000	19,500	26,000	32,500
Continental Ex. ⋁	4,500	6,000	7,500	9,500	12,500	18,000	24,500	31,000
Reliability	❷	❷	❷	❷	❷	❷	❷	❸
Offset	❸	❸	❸	❸	❸	❸	❸	❸
Head Restraints	❶	—	❶	—	❶	—	❷	❷

LS Profile

	2000	2001	2002	2003
Cost Price ($)				
LS	40,595	40,870	42,300	42,500
Used Values ($)				
LS ⋀	17,000	22,500	28,000	32,000
LS ⋁	15,500	21,000	26,500	30,500
Reliability	❸	❸	❸	❹
Crash Safety	❺	❺	❺	—
Side	—	❹	❹	❹
Offset	❺	❺	❺	❺
Head Restraints	❶	❷	❷	❺
Rollover Resistance	—	❺	❺	❺

Mark VII, Mark VIII Profile

	1991	1992	1993	1994	1995	1996	1997	1998
Cost Price ($)								
Mark VII, VIII	38,895	41,010	43,968	47,995	50,996	51,895	53,695	56,595
Used Values ($)								
Mark VII, VIII A	4,500	5,000	6,000	7,000	8,000	9,000	10,500	12,500
Mark VII, VIII V	4,000	4,500	5,000	6,000	7,000	8,000	9,000	11,000
Reliability	❷	❷	❷	❷	❷	③	③	③
Head Restraints	—	—	—	—	❶	—	❶	—

Note: The Mark series hasn't been crash-tested by NHTSA.

Town Car Profile

	1996	1997	1998	1999	2000	2001	2002	2003
Cost Price ($)								
Town Car	44,895	45,895	50,195	52,195	51,495	53,970	53,445	55,205
Used Values ($)								
Town Car A	8,500	10,000	13,000	16,500	21,500	27,500	35,000	40,000
Town Car V	7,500	9,000	11,500	15,000	20,000	26,000	32,000	38,000
Reliability	④	④	④	④	④	④	④	⑤
Crash Safety	④	④	—	—	④	⑤	⑤	⑤
Side	—	—	—	④	④	④	④	⑤
Head Restraints	—	❶	—	❶	—	❶	❶	③
Rollover Resistance	—	—	—	—	—	—	—	⑤

General Motors

98 REGENCY, PARK AVENUE ★★★

RATING: Average (1998–2003); Below Average (1991–97); Not Recommended (1985–90). **Maintenance/Repair costs:** Higher than average, but repairs aren't dealer dependent. **Parts:** Higher-than-average cost (independent suppliers sell for much less), but not hard to find. Nevertheless, don't even think about buying one of these front-drives without a 3- to 5-year extended warranty backed by the automaker. **Best alternatives:** Acura Integra, TL, and RL; Cadillac DeVille; Infiniti I30 and I35; Lexus ES 300; Nissan Maxima; and Toyota Avalon. **Online help:** *www.autosafety.org/autodefects.html.*

Strengths and weaknesses: Full-sized luxury sedan aficionados love the flush glass, wrap-around windshield and bumpers, and clean body lines that make for an aerodynamic, pleasing appearance. But these front-drive cars are more than a pretty package; they provide lots of room (but not for six), luxury, style, and—dare I say—performance. Plenty of power is available with the 205-hp 3.8L V6 engine and the 240-hp supercharged version of the same power plant. On the other hand, owners decry the cars' ponderous handling, caused partly by a mediocre suspension and over-assisted steering with the base model; obstructed rear visibility; hard braking accompanied by severe nosedive; and interior gauges and controls that aren't easily deciphered or accessed.

Although the 1991–96 Park Avenue and '98 Regency were improved over the years, they compiled one of the worst repair histories among large cars. Main problem areas are the engine, automatic transmission, fuel system, steering, brakes, electrical system (including defective PROM and MEMCAL modules), starter and alternator, and badly assembled, poor-quality body hardware. The 3.0L V6 engine is inadequate for cars this heavy, and the 3.8L has been a big quality disappointment.

Under-hood servicing is complicated. Other problems: automatic transmission and engine computer malfunctions are common, the fuel-injection system is temperamental, window mechanisms are poorly designed, the power-steering assembly is failure prone, there are frequent electrical failures, front brake pads and rotors require frequent replacement, and shock absorbers leak or go soft very quickly. Extensive surface corrosion has been a problem because of poor and often incomplete paint application at the factory.

Vehicle history: Park Avenue: 1991—A horsepower boost tied to a revised 4-speed automatic transmission, an updated chassis, antilock braking, a driver-side airbag, and height-adjustable seat belts. **1992**—Debut of the supercharged Ultra. **1993**—A slightly more powerful base engine. **1994**—Dual airbags were added and the Ultra's supercharged engine gained 20 hp. **1995**—Base engines boosted to 205 hp; fresh interior and exterior styling. **1996**—All models get variable-assist steering and the Ultra gains 20 more horses. **1997**—Park Avenue and Ultra were redesigned to include a reworked powertrain, a stiffer body, improved interior amenities, upgraded four-wheel disc brakes, and an upgraded ventilation system. **1998**—De-powered airbags. **2000**—StabiliTrak stability control was added.

Plenty of power is available with the 205-hp 3.8L V6 engine and the Aurora's 240-hp supercharged power plant. It does 0–100 km/h in under 9 seconds (impressive, considering the heft of these vehicles), and improves low- and mid-range throttle response. Both the Park Avenue and Ultra use a stretched version of the more rigid Riviera and Aurora platform.

The revised 1998–2003 models continue to have serious engine intake manifold and transmission problems in addition to airbag, AC, fuel, and electrical system failures. Poor fit and finish is characterized by leaks, squeaks, rattles, moans, and whines.

Safety summary: All models: 1998—Chronic stalling and loss of electrical power, particularly when braking. • Vehicle also suddenly accelerates when braking. • With cruise control engaged, vehicle picks up speed when going downhill. • Faulty fuel sending unit; fuel gauge failure. • Cracked engine head gasket. • Transmission failures. • Brakes or steering fail in rainy weather. • ABS failure may be caused by defective computer module. • Steering failure caused by broken serpentine belt. • Premature failure of brake rotors, pads, and calipers. • Goodyear tire tread separation. • Faulty air level ride filled up rear shocks so rear end sticks up high in the air. • Seat belts jam in the retractor; fail to extend or retract. • Door locks don't work properly. • Windshield dash glare. **1999**—Sudden acceleration after vehicle jumped from Park into Drive. • Frequent stalling; Check Engine light comes on. • Loss of steering due to premature steering pump failure. • Brake rotor overheating and warpage creates excessive vibration and pulling to one side when brakes are applied. • Transmission jerks when going from Reverse to Drive. • Airbag light comes on for no reason. • Shoulder belt twists in retractor. • Premature failure of Goodyear tires. • Keys won't lock or unlock the doors. • Battery often goes dead. **2000**—Airbags deploy when they shouldn't and fail to deploy when they should. • Steering may suddenly lock up. • Excessive steering wheel vibrations numb hands. • Horn is hard to activate, especially in cold weather. • Front seat lapbelts may be too short; GM will give owners a free extension if they sign a waiver of liability. • Windshield wipers suddenly quit working. **2001**— Sudden, unintended acceleration. • Delayed and extended shifts, slippage in cold weather; early replacement. • Intermittent windshield wiper shut-off. • Trunk lid fell down on driver's head. • Excessive dash reflection onto windshield. • Hard to find horn button in an emergency. • Windshield wiper malfunctions. • Driver's seat belt locks up. **2002**— Intermittent horn failure in cold weather.

Secret Warranties/Service Tips/TSBs

All models/years: The THM 44C-T4 automatic transaxles on front-drive models equipped with V6 engines are particularly failure prone. **All models: 1993–2002**—AC odours can be reduced by applying a cooling coil coating or installing a special kit. • A rotten-egg odour coming from the exhaust is probably caused by a malfunctioning catalytic converter and may be covered under GM's emissions warranty. • Paint delamination, peeling, or fading (see Part Two). **1995–96**—Wind noise around front and rear doors; diagnosis and repair. **1995–2001**—Engine oil pan leaks. **1997–99**—Excessive brake noise can be reduced by installing upgraded pads and rotors. **1997–2001**— Troubleshooting steering vibration, shudder, or moan. **1998**—Spark plug electrode erosion is the likely cause of engine knock, a rough-running engine, or lack of power. • A fuel gauge that gives inaccurate readings probably needs a new fuel level sensor. • Rattling from the rear may mean the fuel tank strap is loose or defective. **1998–99**—Low power, stalling, or stumbling when accelerating can be cured by re-calibrating the PCM. **1998–2000**—A hard-to-shift gear-shift lever may need a new cable assembly. **1999–2000**—An engine that runs hot, overheats, or loses coolant may simply need a new radiator cap. • Transmission whine in Park or Neutral may be silenced with a new drive sprocket support bearing. • Slips, harsh upshift or garage shifts, and launch

shudders have a variety of causes and corrections, says TSB #00-07-30-002. •
Diagnostic procedures for an engine that runs hot, overheats, or loses coolant
are outlined in TSB #00-06-02-001. **1999–2001**—Tips on correcting excessive engine vibration and silencing generator whine, hum, and moan.
2000–01—Inoperative power sunroof. **2001**—Delayed and extended shifts,
slippage in cold weather. **2001–02**—Poor engine performance and erratic
shifting (TSB #02-07-30-013). • Door lock falls into door panel. **2003**—
Erratic automatic transmission shifting. • Transmission grind/growl when
vehicle is parked on an incline.

98 Regency, Park Avenue Profile

	1996	1997	1998	1999	2000	2001	2002	2003
Cost Price ($)								
Park Avenue	38,150	40,865	41,850	41,060	42,075	43,000	43,700	45,790
98 Regency	36,610	—	—	—	—	—	—	—
Used Values ($)								
Park Avenue Λ	7,000	8,000	11,000	13,500	17,500	22,500	27,500	31,000
Park Avenue V	5,500	7,000	9,000	12,000	16,000	20,500	25,500	29,000
98 Regency Λ	7,000	—	—	—	—	—	—	—
98 Regency V	6,000	—	—	—	—	—	—	—
Reliability	❷	❷	③	③	③	④	④	④
Crash Safety	—	—	—	—	—	④	④	④
Side	—	—	—	—	—	④	④	④
Offset	—	⑤	⑤	⑤	⑤	⑤	⑤	⑤
Head Restraints								
Park Avenue	—	❶	—	❶	—	❶	❶	❶
Rollover Resistance	—	—	—	—	—	—	—	④

AURORA, RIVIERA   ★★★★

RATING: *Aurora:* Above Average (2001–03); Average (1995–99). There was
no year 2000 model. Now that GM is phasing out its Oldsmobile division,
Aurora resale values are falling rapidly, making the second-series, revamped
2001 and 2002 excellent used buys. *Riviera:* Average (1995–99); Not
Recommended (1986–93). GM skipped the 1994 model year and introduced
an all-new 1995 version. **Maintenance/Repair costs:** Higher than average, but
repairs aren't dealer dependent. **Parts:** Higher-than-average cost (independent
suppliers sell for much less), but not hard to find. GM's phase out won't affect
availability or costs, since these vehicles use the same generic parts found on
many other GM products. **Best alternatives:** Acura Integra, TL, or RL;
Cadillac DeVille, Fleetwood, and Brougham; Ford Crown Victoria or Mercury
Grand Marquis; Mercedes E-Class; Nissan Maxima; and Toyota Avalon.
Online help: *www.autosafety.org/autodefects.html.*

Strengths and weaknesses: Although the redesigned 1988–93 cars got performance, handling, and ride upgrades, they kept the same low level of quality control, with multiple design and manufacturing defects, including serious fuel injection, engine computer, and electrical system problems that haven't been solved to this day. One particularly poor design was the complex Graphic Control Center, which used an oversensitive video screen and small push buttons. It's both distracting and expensive to repair. The automatic transmission is notoriously failure prone, and brakes wear out prematurely and perform poorly. Surface rust and poor paint quality are the most common body complaints on all years. Shock absorbers wear out quickly, and the diesel engine seldom runs properly.

Vehicle history: 1995—Riviera was totally redesigned with standard dual airbags, ABS, a 3.8L V6, and a supercharged variant. **1997**—Additional standard features and a smoother-shifting automatic transmission. **1998**—A supercharged engine arrives. **1999**—Traction control.

Overall, 1995–99 models offer many more luxury features but continue the checkered repair history. As with many of its front-drives during the latter half of the '90s, GM improved quality somewhat, but there are still many generic deficiencies affecting the automatic transmission (torque converter constantly engages and disengages), engine, fuel and electrical systems, computer modules, AC compressor, brakes (rotor warpage and premature pad replacement), steering, suspension, and fit and finish. Trunk wheelwell leaks are common. Because of their problematic brakes, these cars usually have a pronounced low-speed shudder/vibration and severe pull that intensifies when passing over uneven terrain or when braking.

Aurora

This front-drive Olds luxury sedan is aimed at the Acura, Infiniti, and Lexus crowd. It uses the same basic design as the Riviera but doesn't share the same major mechanical features or popular styling. Because it's a relatively new entry into the Oldsmobile line, GM took more care in the selection of mechanical, electronic, and body components. This has made the Aurora more reliable and glitch-free than GM's other vehicles, which continue to be hobbled with poor-quality components and subpar fit and finish. Too bad that this progress is for naught, as Aurora folds along with the entire Oldsmobile line.

Vehicle history: 1997—Larger front brakes. **1999**—Additional engine mounts to damper vibration. **2001**—A new platform and now equipped with a 3.5 V6 or 4.0L V8 engine.

The Aurora's main advantages are its sporty handling and unusual aero-styling. In contrast to the Riviera, the Aurora seats five only and offers a 4.0L V8 derived from the Cadillac 4.6L V8 Northstar engine. Acceleration is underwhelming (this is a heavy car) but adequate for highway touring. Road and wind noise are omnipresent, and the rear trunk's small opening compromises the large trunk's ability to handle odd-sized objects.

The 1995–2000 Auroras have similar quality failings to those of the Riviera listed above, except they're not as extensive and generally become less common with the 2001 through 2003 models. Nevertheless, owners of these recent models complain of engine coolant leaks, chronic electrical and fuel supply glitches, harsh shifting, drivetrain vibration, brake failures and high mainte-nance costs, and water leaks through the front corner moulding.

Safety summary: Aurora: 1995–2001—Chronic stalling. • Horn is hard to access and operates erratically. • Headlights short out or come on inadver-tently. **1996**—Chronic stalling believed to be caused by faulty fuel pump wiring. • Fuel smell seeps into interior; fuel leaks at the fuel rail. • Car loses power steering on slow turns or when driving in the rain. • Defective headlight switch wouldn't turn lights off: $580 (U.S.) to repair. • Northstar engine alu-minum block cracked. **1996–97**—Sudden acceleration may be due to defective cruise control. **1997**—Accelerator pedal jams. • Airbags may be haz-ardous to short occupants. • Head restraints won't hold factory settings. • When battery died, occupants had to break window to get out. **1999**—Water is sucked up into engine when passing over puddles. • Power steering loses power at low speeds. • Lost all electrical power, including interior and exterior lights. • Exhaust fumes enter interior. **2001**—Total brake failure. • Will not go into First gear when cupholder is extended. • Electrical shorts cause complete electrical shutdown or erratically operating interior and exterior lights and gauges. • Reflection of the defrost grate is very distracting to short drivers. • Head restraints block rear vision. • Windshield wipers fail intermittently. **2001–03**—Loss of engine coolant. **2002**—Severe front-end vibration at 100 km/h; not tire related. • Headlights flicker. **2003**—Vehicle suddenly acceler-ated when started up and placed into Reverse. • Sudden loss of steering. • When turning, feels like tire is rubbing underbody. • High headrest obstructs rear visibility. • Interior and exterior lights go out periodically. • Rear taillights dim intermittently. • ABS and traction control warning lights come on for no reason. • Will not go into First gear with cupholder extended. • Defrost grate reflects upon the windshield. **Riviera: 1998**—Engine mount failure. • Brakes don't stop vehicle; frequent rotor replacement. • Horn won't blow at times.

Secret Warranties/Service Tips/TSBs

All models: 1993–99—AC odours can be reduced by applying a cooling coil coating. • A rotten-egg odour coming from the exhaust is likely the result of a malfunctioning catalytic converter, covered by GM's emissions warranty up to five years. • Paint delamination, peeling, or fading (see Part Two). **1995–96**—Intermittent Neutral/loss of Drive at highway speeds can be fixed by replacing the control valve body assembly. **1995–98**—A noise, growl, or vibration from the front when making a right turn or when accelerating may signal the need to replace or reposition the rear transaxle mount. **1995–99**—Floor pan corro-sion perforation in the battery compartment can be corrected for free, under the base warranty, by installing a GM repair kit. **1997–99**—Excessive front brake noise can be reduced by installing upgraded pads and rotors. • A faulty rivet in the catalytic converter heat shield may cause a popping noise heard in the passenger compartment. **1998**—A fuel gauge that gives inaccurate readings probably needs a new fuel level sensor. • Rattling from the rear may mean the fuel tank strap is loose or defective. **1998–99**—A clunk, rattle, or metal-to-metal noise coming from the front of the vehicle can be silenced by installing anti-slip/friction material between the engine frame and the stabilizer shaft insulator. **1999**—Curing front strut squeaks. **Aurora: 1995–99**—A cold engine knock or ticking may be caused by excessive carbon deposits in the engine. • A steering shudder at idle or during parking may be fixed by installing an anti-shudder power-steering outlet hose assembly. **1996–99**—GM has an enhanced crankshaft rear seal to use for complaints related to leaking or poor sealing. **1997–98**—Excessive front brake noise can be reduced by installing upgraded pads and rotors. **1998**—Harsh or delayed gearshifts may require the installation of an enhanced garage shift package. • Accessory drive noise may be caused by a misaligned accessory drive pulley. • Delayed or no engine braking in D3 may require the replacement of the forward and coast latch piston assemblies. **1998–99**—Diagnostic and repair tips for a faulty cruise control and speedometer. • Front-end clunks and rattles can be silenced by a judicious use of anti-friction materials. **1999–2000**—Overheating or coolant loss may be corrected by simply replacing the radiator cap and polishing the radiator filler neck. **2000–01**—If there's a sudden loss of power when accelerating, the transmission fluid pressure switch may be defective. **2000–02**—Seatback squeaks. • Poor shifting. **2001**—Cooler fitting coolant leaks. • Delayed Reverse engagement. **2001–02**—Shake, vibration at cruising speed. • Tilt steering sticks. • Noisy steering. • Inoperative heated seat. **2003**—Intermittent no-start, no-crank condition. • Engine overheating in cold weather. • Sudden engine shutdown. • Harsh shifting remedy. • Automatic transmission grind/growl when vehicle is parked on an incline. • Poor transmission and engine performance may be caused by debris in the transaxle valve body and case oil passages, says TSB #02-07-30-013. • Incorrect First gear ratio; delayed Reverse engagement; harsh shifting upon start-up; transmission whining noise and cooling line leaks; leakage from the quick-connect fitting at the case cover; no Fourth gear, or slipping in Fourth gear; oil leakage from the oil level sensor; and intermediate shaft clunk. • Water contamination of the ABS sensor. • Excessive vibration on smooth roads. • Broken sunroof deflectors. • Faulty windshield wipers. • Horn blows on its own, or refuses to blow. • Loose, sagging attachment arms/straps in the rear compartment seatback trim panel.

Aurora Profile

	1995	1996	1997	1998	1999	2001	2002	2003
Cost Price ($)								
Aurora	43,020	43,695	46,045	47,250	46,190	39,590	40,030	46,590
Used Values ($)								
Aurora ⋀	6,000	7,500	8,500	11,500	14,500	21,000	26,000	35,000
Aurora ⋁	5,000	6,500	7,500	10,000	12,500	19,500	24,500	33,000

Reliability	③	③	③	③	③	③	③	④
Crash Safety	③	③	③	③	③	④	④	④
Side	—	—	—	—	—	③	③	③
Offset	—	—	—	—	—	⑤	⑤	⑤
Head Restraints	❶	—	❶	—	❶	⑤	⑤	⑤

Riviera Profile

	1993	1995	1996	1997	1998	1999
Cost Price ($)						
Riviera	30,790	39,525	40,700	42,415	44,950	44,125
Used Values ($)						
Riviera ⋀	4,000	5,000	6,000	8,500	10,500	14,000
Riviera ⋁	3,500	4,500	5,000	7,000	9,000	12,500
Reliability	❷	③	③	③	③	③
Head Restraints	—	❶	—	❶	—	❶

Note: These vehicles haven't been crash-tested.

CADILLAC BROUGHAM, FLEETWOOD (RWD)   ★★★★

RATING: Above Average (1993–96); Average (1984–92). A smart choice for retirees, these cars are only slightly ahead of the Ford Crown Victoria and Grand Marquis when it comes to comfort and reliability. The '94 and later models feature the most performance for your money. **Maintenance/Repair costs:** Average, and repairs aren't dealer dependent. **Parts:** Reasonably priced (independent suppliers sell for much less) and not hard to find, despite the fact that these rear-drives were dropped in '96. **Best alternatives:** Acura Integra, TL, or RL; Cadillac DeVille; a fully loaded Ford Crown Victoria or Mercury Grand Marquis; and the Mercedes E-Class. **Online help:** *www.autosafety.org/autodefects.html.*

Strengths and weaknesses: The quintessential land yacht, these cars emphasize comfort over handling with their powerful engines and large chassis. Nevertheless, with their spacious interior and many convenience features, these large cars are ideal for vacationing and light trailer pulling.

Vehicle history: 1992—Traction control; dual airbags. **1994**—New transmission and engine (from the Corvette). **1996**—An upgraded sound system and centre storage armrest.

The most serious problem areas are the fuel-injection system, which frequently malfunctions and costs an arm and a leg to repair; engine head gasket failures; automatic transmissions that shift erratically; a weak suspension; computer module glitches; brakes that constantly need rotor and pad replacement; poor body assembly; and paint defects. From a reliability/durability standpoint, the rear-drives are much better made than their front-drive counterparts.

GM technical service bulletins show that these vehicles also have noisy power-steering units and cooling fans, the AC bi-level mode produces extreme temperature differences, the instrument panel squeaks and rattles, there are rear quarter-panel gaps and rusting at the rear side-door window moulding, and water leaks into the passenger side of the front compartment.

Safety summary: All models: 1996—Airbags failed to deploy. • Seat belts didn't restrain driver and passenger during a collision. • Chronic stalling due to fuel sending unit failure. • Transmission pounds when shifting gears. • Water pump leakage on the serpentine belt may cause steering to lock up. • Power-steering hose and pump failure. • Brakes often lock up when applied. • Excessive brake noise caused by the premature wearout of brake rotor and drum. • AC cooling switch and high-pressure hose failures. • Instrument cluster hard to read in daylight. • Power door locks and trunk lock frequently fail to operate properly. • Loose windshield moulding. • Defective keyless entry module.

Secret Warranties/Service Tips/TSBs

All models: 1993–96—Paint delamination, peeling, or fading (see Part Two). **1996**—Harsh 1–2 shift. • No Reverse, Second, or Fourth gear. • 3–2 part throttle downshift flare. • Engine noise (install new valve stem oil seal). • Transmission chuggle/surge. • Transmission fluid leak from pump body (replace bushing). • Crunch/pop noise in steering system. • AC odours. • Radio frequency interference diagnosis. • Inoperative heater.

Cadillac Brougham, Fleetwood (RWD) Profile

	1990	1991	1992	1993	1994	1995	1996
Cost Price ($)							
Brougham, Fleetwood (RWD)	39,816	37,298	37,488	39,988	41,798	46,830	46,965
Used Values ($)							
Brougham, Fleetwood (RWD)	⋀ 3,500	4,500	5,000	5,500	6,500	7,500	9,000
Brougham, Fleetwood (RWD)	⋁ 3,000	4,000	4,500	5,000	6,000	6,500	7,500
Reliability	③	③	③	③	③	④	④
Head Restraints	—	—	—	—	—	—	❷

Note: The Brougham and Fleetwood (RWD) haven't been crash-tested.

CADILLAC CATERA, ELDORADO, SEVILLE   ★★

RATING: Below Average (1992–2003); Not Recommended (1986–91). 2001 was the Catera's last model year. **Maintenance/Repair costs:** Higher than average; Catera repairs are more expensive because they are dealer dependent. Long delays for recall repairs on all models. **Parts:** Higher-than-average cost (independent suppliers sell for much less), but most parts aren't hard to find. Don't buy any of these cars without a 3- to 5-year supplementary warranty.

Best alternatives: Acura Integra, TL, or RL; Cadillac DeVille, Brougham, or Fleetwood; Ford Crown Victoria or Mercury Grand Marquis; and the Mercedes E-Class. **Online help:** *www.autosafety.org/autodefects.html* and *www.supremecourt.nm.org/pastopinion/VIEW/98ca-020.html.*

Strengths and weaknesses: The early Cadillacs are luxury embarrassments, and later models barely pass muster. Even though most use the same mechanical components with the same deficiencies as the Riviera and Toronado models, they're far more failure-prone, due to the complexity of their different luxury features and hard-to-find Catera parts.

Catera

Assembled in Germany and based on the Opel Omega, the rear-drive, mid-sized Catera comes with a 200-hp V6 engine, 4-speed automatic transmission, 16-inch alloy wheels, four-wheel disc brakes, a limited-slip differential, traction control, and standard dual front airbags. The conservatively styled Catera (the uninspired styling has Lumina written all over it) was designed to compete with the BMW 328i, Lexus ES 300, and Mercedes-Benz C280.

Vehicle history: 1998—De-powered airbags. **1999**—More complex electronics and emissions systems to meet federal standards. **2000**—Slight styling changes, side airbags, improved throttle control, and a retuned suspension.

The Catera has received good press reviews for its quiet, spacious, and comfortable interior; responsive handling; fine-tuned suspension; and almost nonexistent lean or body roll when cornering. On the downside, though, the steering system lacks balance and allows the vehicle to wander; the controls aren't easy to figure out, some gauges are hard to read, and the driver's rear view is hindered by the large rear head restraints and narrow back windshield. Furthermore, owners report chronic stalling and hard starts, possibly due to a malfunctioning idle control valve; the transmission "hunts" for the right gear; constant warning light illuminations; poor AM radio reception (requiring an additional amplifier); and loose interior panels. Body fit and finish isn't impressive: body panels are often misaligned, and door locks freeze shut. Two other performance problems reported by owners: when you pass over a large expansion joint, the floor pan vibrates annoyingly; if you drive over a bump when turning, the steering wheel kicks back in your hands.

A few other points you may wish to consider: GM dealers are notoriously bad when it comes to understanding and repairing European-transplanted cars (just ask any Saab owner). As well, low-volume cars generally don't have an adequate supply of replacement parts in the pipeline until they've been on the market for a while. Add in the Catera's European connection and the fact it has just been dropped by GM, and you'd best be ready to endure long service waits and high parts costs for those repairs not covered under warranty.

Finally, the fact that Cateras are European-built doesn't necessarily mean that these Cadillacs will be reliable. In fact, just the opposite is more likely. Based on the past performance of Big Three European imports, it's a safe bet that these cars will be less reliable and more troublesome than the competition. GM first learned that lesson with the British-built, failure-prone Vauxhall Firenza it unleashed on an unsuspecting Canadian public in the '70s. A few years later, it settled out of court on several class actions that I piloted, and paid a $20,000 fine to the federal government for misleading advertising. (On a nationally advertised road trip across Canada, GM said the cars excelled. Truth is, they were a mess. They required a team of engineers just to get started.)

Eldorado and Seville

From 1992 on, the Eldorado's styling became more distinctive, even though the vehicle shares most powertrain and chassis components with the Seville. Although the base 4.9L V8 provides brisk acceleration, the 32-valve Northstar V8, first found on the 1993 Touring Coupe, gives you almost 100 more horses, with great handling and a comfortable ride. Overall, the Touring Coupe or Sport Coupe will give you the best powertrain, handling, and braking features. Of course, you'll have to contend with poor fuel economy, rear visibility that's obstructed by the huge side pillars (a Seville problem, as well), confusing and inconvenient climate controls, and a particularly complex engine compartment.

Sitting on the same platform as the Eldorado, the Seville has European-style allure with a more rounded body than the Eldorado. Apart from that, since its redesign in 1992 its engine, handling, and braking upgrades have followed the Eldorado's improvements in lockstep fashion.

Vehicle history: Whether you buy a used Eldorado or Seville, keep in mind that the improved versions came out with the 1995 models, which carried on unchanged until their redesign for 1998. So, if you must buy one of these models, remember that the only distinguishing feature between them is styling, not performance. In fact, between the 1998 and 2001 models, the only real change was the Eldorado's Northstar engine tweaking for year 2000 models. The 2002 Sevilles were given an upgraded suspension.

These cars have generic deficiencies that fall into common categories: poorly calibrated and failure-prone engines, transmissions, and fuel and ignition systems; a multiplicity of electrical short circuits; and sloppy body assembly using poor-quality components. Specifically, engines and fuel systems often produce intermittent stalling, rough idling, hesitation, and no-starts; the Overdrive automatic is prone to premature failure; oil pumps fail frequently; front brakes and shock absorbers wear out quickly; often, paint is poorly applied, fades, or peels away prematurely; fragile body hardware breaks easily (front bumper cracks are commonplace); and there are large gaps between sheet-metal panels and doors that are poorly hung and not entirely square. Other body problems include cracking of front outside door handles, door rattles (Eldorado), poor bumper fit, loose sun visor mounting, rear tail light condensation, fading and discolouring appliqué mouldings (Seville), interior window fogging, "creaking" body mounts, water leaking into trunk from licence plate holder (Eldorado), noisy roof panels and seatback lumbar motors, and a creaking noise at the front-door upper hinge area.

Safety summary: Catera: 1997—Engine coolant leaks. • Airbag malfunctions. • Tie-rod failure. • Loss of steering and hydroplaning when driving through puddles. • Front windshield moulding flew off. **1997–2001**—Chronic stalling. • Frequent wheel alignments. • Defective brake rotors cause excessive vibration and pull. • Premature tire wear. • Vehicle wanders and pulls to one side. • Door locks don't work and key sticks in the ignition. • Windshield wipers are inadequate in heavy rain. **1998**—Engine head gasket failures. **1999**—Accelerator can be floored and vehicle will only creep forward. • Head restraints block vision. • Loss of steering. • Excessive vehicle wandering. • Door latch sticks in the closed position. **2000**—Chronic stalling. • Hesitant shifting. • Defective ignition switch. **2001**—Airbags failed to deploy. • Gas pedal sticks. • Sudden stalling. • Windshield orange peel pattern. **Eldorado, Seville: 1986–2001**—A plethora of electrical short circuits, front axle, ABS brake, and steering failures. • Sudden, unintended acceleration. • Airbag malfunctions (deploying for no reason and injuring occupants). • Brake rotors and pads always need changing. • Excessive vibration at all speeds. • Poor headlight illumination. **Eldorado: 2002**—No airbag deployment. • Front tires wore out prematurely. **Seville: 1999**—Front control arm snapped. • Tie-rod end came apart. • Loss of power steering when driving in the rain. • Front and rear lights collect water. **2000**—Seat belt retractors don't work properly. • Excessive drifting at any speed. • Brake caliper locked up. **2001**—While driving, passenger-side wheel collapsed due to a missing suspension bolt. • Steering column rubbing noise is heard when making a right turn. **2002**—Chronic stalling in traffic. • Many reports of excessive vibration (suspension, driveshaft, wheels and tires replaced). • Noisy, erratic transmission shifting.

Secret Warranties/Service Tips/TSBs

All models: 1993–99—A cold engine knock or ticking may be caused by excessive carbon deposits in the engine. • AC odours can be reduced by applying a cooling coil coating. • Defective catalytic converters that cause a rotten-egg smell in the interior may be replaced free of charge under the emissions warranty. • Paint delamination, peeling, or fading (see Part Two). **1994**—Condensation dripping from the heater duct requires the installation of a watertight dam in the HVAC case. • An inoperative cruise control or brake/transmission interlock may signal a misadjusted stop-light switch assembly. • A binding parking brake may need a new park-brake vacuum release switch. **1996–97**—A torque converter clutch buzz or moan requires the installation of an upgraded case cover assembly spacer plate and the upper control valve body. **1996–2003**—Excessive oil consumption may be caused by dirty piston rings, says GM TSB #02-06-01-009B. **1997**—Excessive front brake noise can be cured by installing upgraded front brake pads. **1997–98**—Excessive brake noise can be reduced by installing upgraded pads and rotors. **1998**—Harsh or delayed gearshifts may require the installation of an enhanced garage shift package. • Accessory drive noise may be caused by a misaligned accessory drive pulley. • Delayed or no engine braking in D3 may require the replacement of the forward and coast latch piston assemblies. **1998–99**—Diagnostic and repair tips for a faulty cruise control and speedometer. • Front-end clunks and rattles can be silenced by a judicious use of anti-friction materials. **1998–2003**—Water, musty smell in rear compartment. • Inoperative seat heater. **1999–2000**—An engine that runs hot, overheats, or loses coolant may simply need a new radiator cap. • Steering column clunk. **2000–01**—If there's a sudden loss of power when accelerating, the transmission fluid pressure switch may be defective. **2000–02**—Power steering noise. • No power when accelerating; 1–2 shift concerns. **2001**—Intermittent inoperative instrument panel (requires replacement of the I/P cluster assembly). • Cooler fitting coolant leaks. • Delayed Reverse engagement. **2001–03**—Loss of engine coolant. **2003**—Erratic transmission performance. **All models with 4.9L engines: 1991–95**—GM will install a new computer chip that reduces stalling. **Catera: 1997**—Brake squealing can be silenced by installing redesigned calipers. • Oil leakage from the engine timing cover can be corrected by installing a new oil pump gasket. **1997–2001**—Coolant loss; engine overheating. • Rear compartment noise. • Steering column squeak. • Key can't be removed from the ignition lock cylinder. **Eldorado, Seville: 1996–2003**—Excessive oil consumption can be corrected with new piston rings, if a new ring-cleaning process doesn't work (TSB #02-06-01-009C).

Cadillac Catera, Eldorado, Seville Profile

	1996	1997	1998	1999	2000	2001	2002	2003
Cost Price ($)								
Catera	—	42,690	43,250	42,310	42,635	42,485	—	—
Eldorado	50,745	52,015	53,000	52,660	53,455	56,600	57,450	—
Seville	55,635	57,000	59,900	59,195	60,195	58,710	59,450	62,045
Used Values ($)								
Catera ⋏	—	8,000	9,500	13,500	16,500	22,000	—	—
Catera ⋎	—	6,500	8,000	11,500	14,500	20,000	—	—
Eldorado ⋏	9,500	10,500	13,500	17,500	21,500	28,500	35,000	—
Eldorado ⋎	8,000	9,000	12,000	16,000	20,000	27,000	33,000	—
Seville ⋏	9,500	11,500	15,500	18,000	23,000	31,000	40,000	45,000
Seville ⋎	8,000	10,000	13,500	16,000	21,000	28,000	37,000	42,000
Reliability	❷	❷	③	③	③	③	③	④
Offset								
Catera	—	⑤	⑤	⑤	⑤	⑤	—	—
Seville	❶	❶	—	—	⑤	⑤	⑤	—
Head Restraints								
Catera	—	③	—	❷	—	③	—	—
Eldorado	—	❶	—	❶	—	❶	❶	—
Seville	—	❶	—	❶	❶	❶	❶	❶

Note: Reliability figures apply to the Eldorado and Seville only; Catera reliability information is given in the text.

CADILLAC CONCOURS, DEVILLE, FLEETWOOD (FWD)

RATING: Average (1995–2003); Below Average (1985–94). Interestingly, a new Concours sold at a $10,000 premium over the DeVille, yet the difference narrows considerably as the vehicles age. There are two major safety problems affecting 1995–99 models: inadvertent side and front airbag deployment, and chronic stalling in traffic. **Maintenance/Repair costs:** Higher than average, and most repairs must be done by a dealer. Long delay for recall repairs. **Parts:** Higher-than-average cost (independent suppliers sell for much less), but not hard to find. All of these front-drives require a 3- to 5-year supplementary warranty. **Best alternatives:** Acura Integra, TL, or RL; Infiniti I30 or I35; and the Lexus ES 300. **Online help:** *www.autosafety.org/ autodefects.html.*

Strengths and weaknesses: Although they have better handling and are almost as comfortable as older, traditional Caddies, the early models of these luxury coupes and sedans aren't worth considering because of their dismal reliability and overly complex servicing. Redesigned 1995–99 versions have posted fewer complaints; however, they are still far below the industry norm for quality and reliability. As with the Eldorado and Seville, you get the best array of handling, braking, and performance features with the post-1996 versions. They do ride more quietly and comfortably, but fuel economy is still poor, the dash controls and gauges are confusing and not easily accessible, and the rear view is obstructed by the high trunk lid and large side pillars.

Vehicle history: 1996—DeVilles were given the Northstar V8 and an upgraded automatic transmission and suspension. The Concourse received 25 additional horses along with improved steering and suspension. **1997**—Substantially reworked and given new styling, side airbags, and an upgraded interior. **1998**—De-powered airbags. **2000**—A number of high-tech improvements, including refinements to the V8 engine, Night Vision, Rear Parking Assist, and StabiliTrak traction control. **2002**—An enhanced suspension.

The 4.3L V6, 4.1L V8, and 4.5L V8 engines and 4-speed automatic transmission suffer from a variety of terminal maladies, including oil leaks, premature wear, poor fuel economy, and excessive noise. The electrical system and related components are temperamental. Steering is noisy, the suspension goes soft quickly, and the front brakes often wear out after only 18 months/ 20,000 km. Problems with the digital fuel injection and engine control systems are very difficult to diagnose and repair. Poor body assembly is characterized by premature paint peeling and rusting, excessive wind noise in the interior, and fragile trim items.

Safety summary: Concours, DeVille: 1995–96—A short circuit caused by wet carpets could cause the airbags to suddenly deploy. **DeVille: 1998**— Inadvertent side airbag deployment. • Wheel flew off car after wheel studs failed. • Vehicle suddenly accelerated, killing one person and injuring others. • Accelerator sticking. • Cruise control self-activates. • Chronic stalling while

underway. • Can't read speedometer in daylight. • Many complaints of front
and rear brake rotor warpage and premature pad and caliper failure. • Sudden
loss of power steering. • Vehicle tends to wander all over the road. • Leaking
engine oil coolant. • Windshield washer fluid doesn't pump high enough. •
Gas tank sensor failure causes inaccurate fuel readings. • Interior lights frequently malfunction. **1999**—Airbags explode when vehicle is started, idles,
accelerates, or is parked. Several occupants have been injured. NHTSA looked
into a flood of complaints of inadvertent side airbag deployment on 1998 and
1999 models and forced GM to recall these cars. • Incidents where front and
side airbags failed to deploy in a collision. • Engine overheating, loose head
bolts, and excessive oil consumption. • Stalling when coasting or coming to a
stop. • Vehicle rolls backward when in gear. • Fuel tank leaks fuel. • Premature
warpage of the front and rear brake rotors. • Failure-prone ignition and electronic control module. • Tire flew off while vehicle was underway. •
Factory-equipped jack inadequate to support vehicle. • Instrument panel
lighting hard to read in daylight. • Power door locks operate erratically. •
Windshield wipers won't come on unless turned on High. • Driver's seat belt
constantly tightens up. **2000**—Sudden, unintended acceleration and chronic
stalling. • Steering locked up. • Automatic transmission jolts when shifting. •
Airbags deploy inadvertently. • A shroud may impede accessing brake pedal. •
Frequent crankshaft sensor failure. • Digital instrument panel can't be read in
daylight. • Sun visor blocks out overhanging traffic lights. • Horn is hard to
access. **2001**—Transmission doesn't shift all the way into Drive; pops out of
gear and allows vehicle to roll down an incline. • Brake pedal goes to the floor
without braking. • Steering wheel emits a grinding sound. • Side mirror creates
a huge blind spot. **2002**—Sudden acceleration in Reverse. • Driver's side
wheel fell off. • Chronic stalling after refuelling. • Seat belts are too short for
some occupants. • Shoulder belt fits short drivers poorly. • Distorted windshield. • Airbag light stays lit. **2003**—Intermittent stalling. • Total brake
failure. • Instrument panel shuts down. • Sun visor obstructs vision. • Tire jack
collapsed.

Secret Warranties/Service Tips/TSBs

All models/years: Defective catalytic converters that cause a rotten-egg smell
in the interior may be replaced free of charge under the emissions warranty. •
Paint delamination, peeling, or fading (see Part Two). **All models: 1994**—
Condensation dripping from the heater duct requires the installation of a
watertight dam in the HVAC case. • An inoperative cruise control or
brake/transmission interlock may signal a misadjusted stop-light switch
assembly. • TSB #476003 goes into great detail about how to troubleshoot the
various engine oil leaks afflicting 1994 models. • Doors that won't stay open
on slight grades require upgraded door springs. • Noisy fuel pumps can be
silenced only by installing an upgraded fuel pump under warranty. • TSB
#476506 gives lots of tips on fixing 4.6L engines that run roughly, miss, surge,
or hesitate. • Poor heat distribution (driver's feet get cold) can be fixed by
replacing the floor outlet assembly. • Rear compartment water leaks are

addressed in TSB #311510. **1998**—Harsh or delayed gearshifts may require the installation of an enhanced garage shift package. • Delayed or no engine braking in D3 may require the replacement of the forward and coast latch-piston assemblies. **2001**—Intermittent inoperative instrument panel (requires replacement of the I/P cluster assembly). • Cooler fitting coolant leaks. • Delayed Reverse engagement. **2000–02**—Loss of power when accelerating. • 1–2 shift concerns. • Noisy steering. • Steering column rubbing noise. • Scratched door glass. • Parking brake won't release; warning lamp stays lit. **2001–03**—Loss of engine coolant. **2003**—Erratic transmission shifting. **All models with 5.7L engines: 1994–96**—A chuggle or surge condition will require a reflash calibration. • Excessive engine noise can be silenced by installing an upgraded valve-stem oil seal. **1996–97**—A torque converter clutch buzz or moan requires the installation of an upgraded case-cover assembly spacer plate and the upper control valve body. **1997–98**—Excessive front brake noise can be reduced by installing upgraded pads and rotors. **1998–99**—Diagnostic and repair tips for a faulty cruise control and speedometer. • Front-end clunks and rattles can be silenced by a judicious use of anti-friction materials. **1999–2000**—An engine that runs hot, overheats, or loses coolant may simply need a new radiator cap. **Concours, DeVille: 1996–2003**—Excessive oil consumption can be corrected with new piston rings, if a new ring-cleaning process doesn't work (TSB #02-06-01-009C). **DeVille: 2003**—Intermittent no-starts; no electrical power (align engine wiring junction block; TSB #06-03-009).

Cadillac Concours, DeVille, Fleetwood (FWD) Profile

	1996	1997	1998	1999	2000	2001	2002	2003
Cost Price ($)								
Concours	54,340	56,985	58,600	57,490	—	—	—	—
DeVille	48,125	49,400	50,495	49,710	51,995	51,895	52,555	54,925
Fleetwood (FWD)	46,965	—	—	—	—	—	—	—
Used Values ($)								
Concours ▲	9,000	10,500	14,000	17,000	—	—	—	—
Concours ▼	7,500	9,000	12,500	15,500	—	—	—	—
DeVille ▲	7,000	8,500	13,000	16,000	21,500	27,000	34,000	40,000
DeVille ▼	6,000	7,500	11,500	15,000	19,500	25,500	33,000	38,000
Fleetwood (FWD) ▲	9,500	—	—	—	—	—	—	—
Fleetwood (FWD) ▼	8,000	—	—	—	—	—	—	—
Reliability	❷	③	③	③	③	③	③	④
Crash Safety								
Concours	③	—	—	—	—	—	—	—
DeVille	③	④	④	④	③	③	—	❶
Side (DeVille)	—	④	④	④	④	④	④	④
Head Restraints (F)	—	❶	—	❷	—	❷	❷	❷
Rear	—	—	—	—	—	❶	❶	—
Rollover Resistance	—	—	—	—	—	—	—	⑤

Infiniti

RATING: *G20:* Not Recommended (1994–2002). *I30:* Recommended (2000–03); Above Average (1997–99); Average (1996). *I35:* Above Average (2002–03). *J30:* Above Average (1994–97); Average (1993). *Q45:* Above Average (2001–03, 1991–96); Average (1997–2000). The 1997–99 Q45s were "de-contented" by Infiniti, meaning they sold for less because they were made more cheaply, came with fewer standard features, and were equipped with a smaller, less powerful engine. The 2002 I35 exhibits a disturbingly high number of performance- and safety-related defects; other Infinitis, though, demonstrate impressive reliability and quality control. 2002 is the G20's last model year. **Maintenance/Repair costs:** Higher than average, and repairs must be done by either an Infiniti or a Nissan dealer. **Parts:** Higher-than-average cost, but not hard to find (except for body panels). **Best alternatives:** The fully equipped Honda Accord, Mazda Millenia or 929, Nissan Maxima, and Toyota Camry or Avalon are better buys from a price/quality standpoint, but they don't have the same luxury cachet. Also consider the Acura Integra, Legend, TL, or RL, and the Mercedes E-Class. **Online help:** *www.carsurvey.org/ manufacturer_Infiniti.html.*

Strengths and weaknesses: With its emphasis on sporty handling (diluted somewhat with the '97 and later model years), the Infiniti series takes the opposite tack from the Lexus, which puts the accent on comfort and luxury. Still, the Infiniti comes fully equipped and offers owners the prestige of driving a comfortable and nicely styled luxury car that's more reliable than what's offered by Lexus, but not quite as refined.

G20

The least expensive Infiniti, the 1994–96 G20 is a front-drive luxury sports sedan that uses a base 2.0L 140-hp 16-valve, twin-cam, 4-cylinder power plant to accelerate smoothly, albeit noisily, through all gear ranges. Dual airbags came on line midway through the 1993 model year, and ABS is standard. Towing capacity is 1,000 lb. (450 kg). Cruise control is a bit erratic, particularly when traversing hilly terrain. Unlike the engine, the automatic transmission is silent, and power is reduced automatically when shifting. Steering is precise and responsive on the highway. However, the rear end tends to swing out sharply following abrupt steering changes. Early Infiniti G20s rode a bit too firmly, which led to the suspension being softened on the 1994 model. Now drivers say that the suspension tends to bounce and jiggle occupants whenever the car goes over uneven pavement or the load is increased.

Vehicle history: Returning after a three-year hiatus, the '99 G20 wasn't worth the wait. It's basically a package of unfulfilled expectations with its wimpy 2.0L

140-hp engine, firm ride, and ordinary styling. On the positive side, the car does handle well. Year 2000 models got a bit more horsepower and an upgraded transmission and 2001s returned with standard leather seats and a power sunroof.

Infiniti G20s aren't as refined as their entry-level Lexus counterparts in interior space, drivetrain, or convenience features. Owners have complained that the engine's lack of low-speed torque means that it has to work hard above 4000 rpm—while protesting noisily—to produce brisk engine response in the higher gear ranges. The automatic transmission shifts roughly, particularly when passing (a problem corrected in the 1994 models); the power steering needs more assist during parking manoeuvres; and the dealer-installed fog lights cost an exorbitant $500 to replace. Poorly thought-out control layout is best exemplified by the hard-to-reach heat/vent controls, an armrest-mounted trunk and filler release that's inconvenient to operate, and centre console–mounted power window switches that are difficult to find while driving. Tall drivers will find the legroom insufficient. The trunk is spacious, but its small opening is limited by the angle of the rear window.

Owner complaints target failure-prone brake rotors, prematurely worn brake pads, and excessive noise when braking.

J30

Introduced as an early 1993 model and dropped in 1997, the rear-drive, four-door J30 and its high-performance variant, the I30, are sized and priced midway between the G20 and the top-of-the-line Q45. The J30 uses a modified version of the Nissan 300ZX's 3.0L 210-hp V6 engine. Although the vehicle is replete with important safety features and it accelerates and handles well, its engine is noisy, passenger and cargo room have been sacrificed to styling, and fuel economy is underwhelming.

The J30 comes with a standard airbag (or dual airbags, depending on the model year), ABS, and traction control. It's changed very little over the years, meaning that there's no reason to choose a more recent model over a much cheaper older version.

Quality problems include airbag malfunctions (inadvertent deployment and failure to deploy), cracked exhaust manifold, leaking fuel injection system, and excessive vibration when accelerating.

I30/I35

Introduced as an early '96 model, the I30 is a sport sedan spin-off of the Nissan Maxima with additional sound-deadening material and a plusher interior. The car has a roomy interior, but its ride is unimpressive and handling is compromised by excessive body lean when cornering. Engine and road noise is omnipresent. The redesigned year 2000 model adds rear seatroom and reduces body lean considerably.

Vehicle history: I30s come loaded with standard safety, performance, and comfort features, notably a 190-hp 3.0L V6 engine with dual camshafts and anti-lock brakes. **1996–99**—Models changed little, except for front side airbags and new headlights and tail lights added to the '98s. **2000**—Represents the best value from a price/performance perspective. It was entirely revamped with more conservative styling, 37 more horses, and a larger cabin. Head restraints were also upgraded, suspension improved, larger wheels were added, and high-intensity headlights adopted. **2002**—Renamed the I35 and given a larger V6 engine, new styling, and more standard features.

Incredible, but true, the recently minted I35 has elicited more performance-related complaints than its I30 predecessor, which was no paragon of quality control. This same phenomenon has been noted with Nissan's new Altima models, which continue to have serious factory-related glitches three years after the model's launch.

I35s are known for hesitation when accelerating, electrical shorts, excessive front-end play, vibration, drivetrain noise, loose steering, rattling noises, incorrect fuel gauge reading, and inoperative seat memory buttons.

On the other hand, owners report that earlier versions had chronic suspension failures; drivetrain vibration and clunking; faulty steering; and defective transverse links, springs and struts.

Q45

Faster and glitzier than other cars in its category, this luxury sedan provides performance, while its chief rival, the Lexus ES400, provides luxury and quiet. Up to the '96 model, the Q45 used a 32-valve 278-hp 4.5L V8 tire-burner not frequently found on a Japanese luxury compact. It accelerates faster than the Lexus, going 0–100 km/h in 7.1 seconds without a hint of noise or abrupt shifting. Unlike the base engine of the G20, though, the Q45's engine supplies plenty of upper-range torque as well. The suspension was softened in 1994, but the car still rides much more firmly than its Lexus counterpart. The four-wheel steering is precise, but the standard limited-slip differential is no help in preventing the car's rear end from sliding out on slippery roads, due mainly to the original equipment "sport" tires, designed mainly for 190 km/h autobahn cruising. There's not much footroom for passengers, and cargo room is disappointing. Fuel economy is nonexistent. ABS is standard, but a passenger-side airbag wasn't available before 1994.

Vehicle history: 1994—Redesigned, including a restyled front end, a chrome grille, and an updated instrument panel. **1997**—A downsized 4.1L V8 set on a smaller platform, effectively changing the character of the car from a sporty performer to a highway cruiser. **1998**—Front seat belt pretensioners. **2002**—A new 4.5L V8 producing 340 hp (up from 266). The transmission is a 5-speed automatic with a manual shift mode. High-end electronics are standard, including traction control (TCS), Vehicle Dynamic Control (VDC), Electronic Brake Force Distribution (EBD), tire pressure monitors, high-intensity xenon headlights, and Voice Control for the climate control and eight-speaker Bose 300-watt audio system, including a six-disc CD changer. **2003**—A rear-axle upgrade for faster and smoother acceleration.

The Q45 has been exceptionally reliable throughout its model run, despite some reports of premature AC failures, power steering problems, excessive wind noise around the A-pillars, sunroof wind leaks, tire thumping, cellular telephone glitches, faulty CD players, and a popping sound from the radio. Owners say that the paint scratches and flakes off so easily that it has to be constantly touched up.

Technical service bulletins list the following defects affecting the 1994–96 models: AC not blowing cold, front brake pad noise, low or rough idle, doors locking/unlocking themselves, and windshield cracking. You may also be interested in reviewing other helpful bulletins that contain troubleshooting tips for AC compressor leaks and noise, brake clunking noises and pedal pulsation, booming/drone noise and vibration, cold-weather hard starts, rough idle, suspension noise, Code 45 driveability alerts, and brake shudder and steering-wheel shimmy.

Bulletins for the 1997 model don't cover much that's new, concerning themselves principally with clunking noises and pedal pulsation, cold-weather starting tips, hard starting, and rough idle and suspension noise diagnostic tips. The 1998 bulletins contain no useful tips, and the 1999–2003 TSBs are integrated into the "Secret Warranties/Service Tips/TSBs" section.

Safety summary: G20: 1996—Violent deployment of airbag during collision resulted in permanent eye damage. • Brakes were applied to disengage cruise control and vehicle suddenly accelerated. • Noisy brakes; dealer cannot fix the problem. • Oil pressure switch failure. **1999**—Carbon monoxide poisoning. • When car is put into Reverse, driver's seat reclines without warning. **2001**—Foul odour emitted by AC. • Brake failure. • Brake rotors glaze over and need turning. • Airbags failed to deploy. **J30: 1995**—Airbag failed to deploy. • Airbags deployed during low-speed (11 km/h) fender-bender, causing extensive injuries to occupants. • Rear end swings out when accelerating. • Fuel injector system leaks fuel. • Excessive vibrations when accelerating make vehicle difficult to steer. • Driver's seat belt won't retract. **1996**—Cracked exhaust manifold. • Door locks lock and unlock on their own. **1997**—Sudden acceleration. • Leaking fuel injectors. **I30/I35: 1996**—Sudden, unintended acceleration. • Sunroof blew off vehicle. **1997**—Brakes failed. • Vehicle wouldn't decelerate. • Chronic stalling. **1998**—Airbag malfunctions. • Side window blew out. • Brake failure. **1999**—When using the turn signal, it's easy to turn off the headlights. • Airbag light stays on continuously. • Water seeps inside the vehicle from beneath. **2000**—Sudden, unintended acceleration. • Transmission jerks when shifting. • Premature wear of brake rotors. • Sunlight washes out gauges. • Headlight aimed too low. **2001**—Rear suspension failed. • Sudden, unintended acceleration. • Cruise control wouldn't disengage when brakes were applied. **2002**—Airbags failed to deploy. Steering wheel pulls sharply to one side when accelerating. • Poor braking. • Stalling. **Q45: 1995**—Sudden acceleration when coming to a stop. • Gas and brake pedals are set too close together. • Failure of driver's power seat adjuster motor. • Hood flew up while driving along the highway at about 100 km/h. **1996**—Airbag indicator flashes due to ECM failure. • Premature failure of the shock absorber and power window. **1997**—Owner alleges that vehicle design causes the vehicle to hydroplane where other cars wouldn't. • Airbag warning light comes on for no reason. • When car is put into Reverse, driver's seat reclines without warning. • Severe front-end vibration continued after tires were replaced. **1998**—Airbag failed to deploy. • Accelerator pedal stuck while vehicle was stopped. **2000**— Excessive vibration starts at 100 km/h. **2001**—Sudden acceleration when vehicle was shifted into Reverse gear. **2002**—Excessive vibration caused by bent original-equipment wheels.

Secret Warranties/Service Tips/TSBs

All models/years: Troubleshooting tips to correct hard starts. • Vehicles with sunroofs may have wind noise coming from the sunroof area because of a small pinhole in the body sealer at the rear C-pillar. • Windshield cracking. • Erratic operation of the power antenna requires that the antenna rod be replaced. • Slow retraction of the front seat belt can be fixed by wiping off any residue found on the seat belt D-ring. **G20: 1999**—Excessive blower noise can be reduced by installing a new cover. • Coolant leakage may be caused by a defective intake manifold expansion plug. • Replace the window glass run rubber if window makes a popping sound when opened. **1999–2000**— Countermeasures for front-end clunks when turning or braking. **1999–2001**—Power seat won't move or makes a grinding noise. • Shock absorbers that clunk will be replaced under warranty. **2000**—Engine lacks power; stuck in Third gear. • Correcting a brake judder. • Cloudy, scratched instrument cluster lens. • Parcel shelf rattle or buzz. • Low idle or dies when put into gear. • Preventing a rotten-egg smell emitted by the exhaust. **2001–02**—Rear brake caliper clunk, rattle, or knock. • Defroster not flush, rattles. **I30/I35: 1996–1998**—If either one of the front power seats won't move, check for a broken power seat drive cable. **1996–2000**—Excessive blower noise can be reduced by installing a new cover. **2000–01**— Transmission slippage. **2001–02**—Rear brake caliper clunk, rattle, or knock. **2002**—Faulty sunroof. • Radio ignition static. **2002–03**—Upgraded brake pads to reduce brake judder or other anomalies. **Q45: 1994–96**—Doors that intermittently lock by themselves require the installation of countermeasure front door lock actuators (TSB #NTB96-027). **1997–99**—A lumbar support mechanism that's inoperative should be replaced with an upgraded support mechanism. • If either one of the front power seats won't move, check for a broken power seat drive cable. • Excessive blower noise can be reduced by installing a new cover. • TSB #ITB98-062 gives an exhaustive listing for a variety of squeak and rattle repairs. **1997–2000**—TSB #ITB00-010 gives a detailed list of brake judder countermeasures. **1998–99**—An automatic transmission that produces a "double thump" noise when coming to a stop likely needs a new transmission control module (TCM). **2002**—Engine hesitation. • Steering pull to the right; excessive vibration. • Difficult to move shift lever. • Front suspension noise. • Rear power seat grinding noise. • Door sash rusting. Inoperative rear sunshade. • Trunk lid hard to close. • Hard to read oil gauge and smoke from tailpipe. • Airbag light stays lit. • Loose driver's seat cushion. • Poor AC performance. • Inoperative headlight low beam. **2002–03**—Incorrect shifting. • Navigation system stuck in "please wait" mode. • Upgraded brake pads to reduce brake judder or other anomalies.

G20, I30/I35, J30, Q45 Profile

	1996	1997	1998	1999	2000	2001	2002	2003
Cost Price ($)								
G20	31,440	—	—	29,950	29,950	29,900	29,900	—
I30/I35	40,600	40,600	41,000	41,350	41,950	39,900	39,500	39,700
J30	51,600	52,600	—	—	—	—	—	—
Q45	72,000	65,000	66,500	71,000	71,000	70,000	73,000	74,900
Used Values ($)								
G20 ∧	6,500	—	—	12,000	14,500	17,000	21,000	—
G20 ∨	5,000	—	—	10,500	13,000	15,500	19,000	—
I30/I35 ∧	8,000	12,000	12,500	16,000	19,500	24,000	29,000	33,500
I30/I35 ∨	6,500	8,500	11,000	14,500	18,000	22,500	27,500	32,000
J30 ∧	8,500	10,500	—	—	—	—	—	—
J30 ∨	7,500	9,000	—	—	—	—	—	—
Q45 ∧	9,500	12,000	14,500	19,000	25,000	35,000	46,000	54,000
Q45 ∨	8,500	9,500	13,000	17,000	23,000	33,000	44,000	52,000
Reliability	④	⑤	④	④	④	④	⑤	⑤
Crash Safety (I30/I35)	—	—	④	—	④	④	④	④
J30	④	—	—	—	—	—	—	—
Side (I30/I35)	—	—	④	—	④	④	④	④
Offset								
I30/I35	❶	③	③	③	③	③	③	③
J30	—	—	—	—	③	③	—	—
Q45	—	❷	❷	❷	❷	❷	—	⑤
Head Restraints								
G20	—	—	—	❷	—	❶	❶	—
I30/I35	—	❷	—	❷	⑤	⑤	⑤	⑤
J30	—	❶	—	—	—	—	—	—
Q45	—	❶	—	❶	⑤	⑤	⑤	⑤
Rollover Resistance (I35)	—	—	—	—	—	—	④	④

Kia

MAGENTIS ★★★

RATING: Average (2003); Below Average (2001–02). Consider buying a competitor with more refinement and a proven history for reliability and good quality control. **Maintenance/Repair costs:** Too early to tell. **Parts:** Average cost, but parts aren't widely available, yet. **Best alternatives:** A loaded Honda Accord, Nissan Maxima, or Toyota Camry. **Online help:** *www.mycarstats.com/ auto_complaints/KIA_complaints.asp* and *steviaonlinesales.com/KIA.html.*

Strengths and weaknesses: Sold in the States as the Optima, this front-drive, five-passenger sedan was launched several years ago in Canada as the Magentis. Essentially a Hyundai Sonata without traction control, the Magentis comes with a twin-cam 138-hp 2.4L 4-cylinder or optional 170-hp 2.7L V6 hooked to a 4-speed automatic transmission (V6s have the Sonata's separate gate for manual shifting and four-wheel ABS). Other standard features: front seat belt pretensioners, a tilt steering column, independent double wishbone front suspension and independent multi-link rear suspension, 60/40 split folding rear seat, and tinted glass.

The Magentis is nicely appointed, provides good V6 performance, handles well, and rides comfortably. There's also plenty of front headroom and better-than-average fuel economy with regular fuel. The car is a bit better built than Kia's other models, but fit and finish is still inferior to other Asian makes. Still, performance and reliability are expected to be similar to the Sonata.

Unfortunately, this car has some major weaknesses that include: a weak 4-cylinder engine, a poorly performing 4-speed automatic transmission, mediocre braking, average rear headroom, considerable body lean when turning, excessive wind and tire noise; a small trunk opening; and a weak dealer network.

Owner complaints deal primarily with poor servicing, sudden acceleration, stalling, brake failure, premature brake pad and rotor wear, and subpar fit and finish.

Magentis

	2001	2002	2003
Cost Price ($)			
LX	20,995	21,295	22,250
LX V6	23,995	24,295	25,750
SE V6	27,995	29.095	28,750
Used Values ($)			
LX ⋀	11,000	13,000	15,000
LX ⋁	9,500	11,500	13,500
LX V6 ⋀	12,500	15,000	17,500
LX V6 ⋁	11,000	13,500	16,000
SE V6 ⋀	14,500	17,500	20,000
SE V6 ⋁	13,000	16,000	18,500
Reliability	③	③	③
Crash Safety	—	—	④
Side	—	—	⑤
Offset	③	③	③
Head Restraints	③	③	③
Rollover Resistance	—	—	⑤

Lexus

ES 300, GS 300, 430, LS 400/430, SC 400/430 ★ ★ ★ ★

RATING: Above Average (2002–03; 1990–95); Recommended (1996–2001). A bit more refined than the Infinitis, Lexus' lineup offers first-class performance and better-than-average reliability, with the exception of recent powertrain defects.

The two latest model years have been downgraded due to serious design deficiencies relating to sudden acceleration, chronic engine/transmission stumble, shudder, and surge, and dash gauges that are unreadable during daylight hours. **Maintenance/Repair costs:** Higher than average, and repairs must be done by either a Lexus or a Toyota dealer. **Parts:** Higher-than-average cost, but not hard to find (except for body panels). **Best alternatives:** A fully equipped Legend, Honda Accord, Nissan Maxima, or Toyota Camry will provide airbags, comparable highway performance, and reliability at far less initial cost, but you don't get the Lexus *cachet*. If you do pay top dollar for a used Lexus, its slow rate of depreciation virtually guarantees that you'll get much of your money back. **Online help:** *us.lexusownersclub.com*; *us.lexusownersclub.com/ forums/index.php?act=ST&f=7&t=3584&*; *www.carsurvey.org/manufacturer_ Lexus.html*; and *yotarepair.com/Automotive_News.html* (for Lexus engine sludge and other repair hints search for "Toyota engine sludge" on Google).

Strengths and weaknesses: These are benchmark cars known for their impressive reliability and performance. Sports cars, they're not. But if you're looking for your father's Oldsmobile from a Japanese automaker, these luxury cars fill the bill. Like the Acuras and Infinitis, Lexus models all suffer from some automatic transmission failures, engine sludge buildup (*www.autooninfo.info/ VCC200310ToyotaEngineReliability.htm*), early rear main engine seal and front-strut replacement (front-struts often replaced under a secret warranty), front brake, electrical, body, trim, and accessory deficiencies, most of which are confirmed by confidential technical service bulletins.

ES 300

Resembling an LS 400 dressed in sporty attire, the entry-level ES 300 was launched in 1992 to fill the gap between the discontinued ES 250 and the LS 400. In fact, the ES 300 has many of the attributes of the LS 400 sedan for much less money. A five-passenger sedan based on the Camry but 90 kg (200 lb.) heavier and with a different suspension and tires, it comes equipped with a standard 3.0L 24-valve engine that produces 181–210 horses, coupled to either a 5-speed manual or a 4-speed electronically controlled automatic transmission. Unlike the Infinitis, the ES 300 accelerates smoothly and quietly, while averaging about 14L/100 km in mixed driving. The suspension is soft and steady. Passenger and cargo room are plentiful, with lots of legroom and headroom (except on sunroof-equipped versions).

Vehicle history: 1994—Dual airbags and a new 3.0L 6-cylinder that boosted horsepower (3) to 188. **1995**—A new front air intake, standard foglights, and new brake/signal lights. **1997**—A restyled interior and exterior, increased interior dimensions, improved centre rear seat belt, and horsepower increased (12) to 200. **1998**—De-powered airbags, along with side airbags and an upgraded anti-theft system. **1999**—Horsepower increased (10) to 210, upgraded automatic transmission, and traction control. **2000**—Restyled front ends and tail lights, and improved child safety seat anchors. **2001**—An emergency trunk release. **2002**—A longer, taller body; new 5-speed automatic transmission; improved brakes, steering, and suspension; and more standard luxury features; no more standard traction control.

On April 3, Toyota issued a press release admitting it has an engine sludge problem and will cover claims with an extended warranty.

Surprisingly, for a vehicle this well made, government-reported safety-related defects are surprisingly omnipresent. These include airbag-induced injuries; sudden acceleration; an unreliable powertrain that surges, stumbles, stalls, and shifts erratically; ABS and Goodyear tire failures; excessive vibration when underway; interior window fogging; unreadable dash gauges; and poor AC performance.

GS 300

The rear-drive GS 300 is a step up from the front-drive ES 300 and just a rung below Lexus' top-of-the-line LS 400. It carries the same V6 engine as the ES 300, except it has 20 more horses. This produces sparkling performance at higher speeds, though the car is disappointingly sluggish from a start. Fuel economy is sacrificed for performance, however, and the base suspension and tires pass noisily over small bumps and ruts. Visibility is also less than impressive, with large rear pillars and a narrow rear window restricting the view. There's not much usable trunk space, either, and the liftover is unreasonably high.

Vehicle history: 1996—A light rear-end restyling and a 5-speed automatic transmission. **1998**—Restyled once again and given an upgraded V8. **2000**—A new brake assist system and more user-friendly child safety seat anchors. **2001**—Substantially upgraded with a 300-hp 4.3L V8, upgraded transmission controls, standard side curtain airbags, smart airbags, an emergency trunk release, and a host of other convenience features.

Owner complaints have centred upon brake failures, electrical and fuel system malfunctions resulting in unintended sudden acceleration and hesitation, electrical shutdown, wheel bearings, excessive front-end vibration, and fragile wheel rims.

LS 400, LS 430

The Lexus flagship, the LS 400 rear-drive arrived in 1990 with a 250-hp 4.0L V8. It outclasses all other luxury sedans in reliability, styling, and function. Its powerful engine provides smooth, impressive acceleration and superior highway passing ability at all speeds. Its transmission is smooth and efficient. The suspension gives an easy ride, without body roll or front-end plow during emergency stops, thereby delivering a major comfort advantage over other luxury compacts. Other amenities: antilock brakes, a driver-side airbag, and automatic temperature control.

Vehicle history: 1993—A passenger-side airbag and interior/exterior restyling. **1995**—Increased interior and exterior dimensions, a more powerful engine, and a better-performing drivetrain for quicker acceleration. **1997**—Side airbags. **1998**—An improved V8, a new 5-speed automatic transmission, Vehicle Skid Control (VSC), and a host of interior upgrades. **2001**—Totally redesigned with a sleeker body, a 4.3L V8, an upgraded suspension, and a more spacious, reworked interior. Additional safety and comfort features have also been added.

The brakes don't inspire confidence, owing to their mushy feel and average performance. Furthermore, there's limited rear footroom under the front seats, and the rear middle passenger has to sit on the transmission hump. This car is a gas-guzzler that thirsts for premium fuel.

Owner complaints deal mainly with sudden, unintended acceleration; stalling due to a faulty throttle sensor; traction control causes vehicle to swerve (usually to the left) unexpectedly; failure of the VSC to activate; main computer failures; spongy brakes; electrical glitches; and door locks that stick shut, trapping occupants.

SC 300, SC 400

These two coupes are practically identical, except for their engines and luxury features. The cheaper SC 300 gives you the same high-performance 6-cylinder engine used by the GS 300 and Toyota Supra, while the SC 400 uses the 4.0L V8 engine found in the LS 400. You're likely to find fewer luxury features with the SC 300 because they were sold as options. Nevertheless, look for an SC with traction control for additional safety during poor driving conditions. On the downside, V8 fuel consumption is horrendous, rear seating is cramped, and trunk space is unimpressive. Also, invest in a good anti-theft device, or your Lexus relationship will be over almost before it begins.

Vehicle history: 1993—A passenger airbag. **1995**—Slightly restyled. **1996**—Given the LS 400's V8. **1998**—SC got the 4.0L V8 engine, while the SC 300 continued to use the previous year's inline-six, but ditched its 5-speed manual transmission. Other upgrades: variable valve timing, a more refined 5-speed automatic transmission, a new anti-theft system, and de-powered airbags. **1999**—American-sold models got larger brakes.

Safety summary: ES 300: 1996—Fire in the engine compartment. • Frequent reports that the airbag failed to deploy. • Weak seatback collapsed rearward in a collision. • Entire vehicle shimmies. • Sudden steering failure when turning.

1997—Vehicle left in Park rolled backward and hit another car. Same thing occurred with a vehicle parked in a garage, but this time cause was isolated to a failure of the shift lock actuator fuse. • Owner says airbags are a hazard for short people. • Also, floor pedals are located too high and are too far apart for short people. • Middle rear shoulder belt locks up, making it very difficult to get occupant out; owner had to cut the belt. • Instrument cluster lights aren't bright enough for night driving. **1998**—Vehicle accelerated as brakes were applied. • **1999**—Rear seat belts don't hold a child safety seat firmly. • Vehicle suddenly swerves from one lane to another. • Excessive oil consumption, blue smoke comes from the tailpipe, PCV valve is clogged up, and head gasket has failed (all symptomatic of Toyota's "oil sludge" problem, covered in the Sienna section). **2000**—Sudden, unintended acceleration when in Reverse. • Engine stalls or won't accelerate in traffic. • Vehicle suddenly downshifts from Fourth to First in heavy traffic; jerky shifting. • Rolls backward when transmission is in Drive. • Swerves left on a straight road. • Rear-view mirror doesn't move, resulting in poor visibility. **2001**—Engine fire erupted from what investigator said was fuel leaking from a rubber hose that had disconnected from the fuel filter. • Car suddenly accelerated as driver slowed coming to a stop sign, and again when pulling into a parking space. • Traction control engages much too easily when merging into traffic. • Vehicle started up and began moving down the street in Reverse, despite the fact that there was no key in the ignition cylinder and vehicle was left in Park. • Vehicle hesitates when applying accelerator after decelerating; computer replacement is said to be on national back order. **2002**—Sudden, unintended acceleration. • Airbags failed to deploy. • Impossible to read speedometer and other gauges in sunlight; they have red needles against a black background. • Won't go into gear properly. • Fuel cap won't screw off. • Warped brake rotors. • Defective Goodyear Eagle tires (side-wall bubbling). **2002–03**—Chronic engine/transmission surging and stalling not fixed by computer module recalibration, switching to premium fuel, etc. (see NHTSA complaint below):

The transmission of the Lexus 2003 ES 300 is subject to major hesitation, particularly in crowded intersections and with lack of acceleration. Very noticeable when traveling about 27 mph [43 km/h] and then needing to move, there is major delay in the signal telling the engine and transmission to work together and move the car. This vehicle is new with about 1,000 miles [1,600 km]. It cannot make up its mind to upshift or downshift and this delay will mean a major crash someday. Around 40 mph [64 km/h] it wants to upshift to the Fifth gear, and just below that hunts to go back to Fourth.

The manufacturer says, as he did for the 2002 models, that a software fix is being prepared. They stated the problem from the 2002 was fixed. Evidently that is not the case. They now tell me that a fix is coming year-end. How many accidents will occur by then? Dealer says that the car will learn from the driver, but that is not working, and hesitation from 0–5 mph [0–8 km/h], from 27–45 [43–72 km/h], etc. Is very pronounced. If you "floorboard" it from slow speeds, its hesitation is great, and car almost dies. Lexus says "don't do that", but from car creation to now, car movement meant add more gas, not the reverse. My safety depends on it.

GS 300: 1998—Vehicle surges or suddenly accelerates. • After yaw sensor replacement, as per recall, yaw sensor failure caused an accident. • Rear brake caliper plate for brake pads fell off after brake pins dislodged. • Poor low beam illumination. • Trunk lid falls down unexpectedly. **1999**—Sudden, unintended acceleration and unexpected delayed acceleration. • Airbags failed to deploy. Wheels break under normal driving conditions. Complete brake failure. • Excessive vibration at highway speeds. **2002**—Fire ignited from fuel filter leak. • Sticking accelerator. • Sudden, unintended acceleration. • Vehicle started without key. • Traction control engages too easily. • Inadequate headlight illumination. • Digital dash indicator washes out in sunlight.

Secret Warranties/Service Tips/TSBs

All models: 1990–2000—Eliminating brake clicking when changing direction of travel (requires a special grease recommended by Toyota/Lexus). **ES 300: 1996–99**—A knocking noise from under the floor in the rear of the car can be fixed by following the field fix outlined in TSB #SU005-96. **1997–99**—New front brake pads have been developed to reduce brake grind and groan. Toyota will install them at a reduced price under its "goodwill" policy. **1997–2000**—Front suspension noise may be silenced by installing an upgraded suspension support, says TSB #SU002-99. **1997–2001**—Turn signal flashes erratically. **1999**—Excessive engine noise when idling at normal operating temperature. • If the vehicle shudders during a 2–3 shift, try changing the transaxle valve body under warranty, before moving on to other repairs. • Rear suspension squeaks and groans. • Front brake groaning and grinding. • New, improved brake pads will reduce rear brake squeaks. • Tips on troubleshooting a false MIL alert. **1999–2001**—Information on correcting automatic transmission fluid leaks. **2000–01**—Procedures for obtaining a free seat belt extender. **2002**—Harsh 2–3 shift. • Tilt steering hard to move from down position. • Troubleshooting steering pull and interior squeaks and rattles. • Coil spring creaking. • Heat shield rattles. • No sound from amplifiier. • Gas cap sticks. **2002–03**—TSB No. #TC004-03, issued August 4, 2003 gives recalibration instructions for correcting erratic shifting. This free repair is in effect for 96 months or 80,000 miles [128,000 km], and is limited to the correction of a problem based upon a customer's specific complaint. • Unreadable dash gauges will be corrected free of charge under TSB # EL001-03, issued January 23, 2003. • A shim kit will reduce front brake vibration says TSB # BR002-02, issued December 24, 2002. • A gas cap sticking fix is detailed in TSB #EG003-02, issued February 8, 2002. • Body creak or snap from top of front windshield. **GS 300: 1998–2000**—Front window wind noise. • Noisy seat belt retractor. **1998–2001**—Glove box rattling. **2000–02**—Front stabilizer bar noise. **2001–02**—Front coil spring clicking. **2002**—No sound from amplifier. • Steering pull troubleshooting. **LS 400, LS 430: 1998–99**—An upgraded blower motor that is better at maintaining blower speed will be installed under warranty. **1999–2000**—Countermeasures to reduce steering noise and improve smoothness. **2000**—Moon roof water leaks. **2001**—Moon roof rattle and rear corner air leak. • Instrument panel rattling. • Rear seat and luggage compartment creaking. • False illumination of the MIL (malfunction indicator light). **2002**—No sound from amplifier. • Steering pull troubleshooting.

ES 300, GS 300, LS 400/430, SC 400/430 Profile

	1996	1997	1998	1999	2000	2001	2002	2003
Cost Price ($)								
ES 300	45,600	42,960	43,820	44,235	43,995	44,000	43,400	43,800
GS 300	71,400	71,400	58,900	59,220	59,420	60,700	60,700	61,700
LS 400/430	78,700	78,700	78,300	78,690	78,950	80,000	81,900	82,800
SC 400/430	85,500							
Used Values ($)								
ES 300 ʌ	11,500	13,500	15,500	18,000	23,500	27,000	33,000	37,000
ES 300 v	10,000	12,000	14,000	16,500	21,500	25,500	31,000	35,000
GS 300 ʌ	13,000	16,000	19,000	24,500	30,500	36,000	43,500	49,000
GS 300 v	47,000							
LS 400/430 ʌ	65,000							
LS 400/430 v	15,000	18,000	24,000	30,000	37,000	46,000	56,000	62,000
SC 400/430 ʌ	19,500	23,500	31,000	—	—	—	60,000	67,000
SC 400/430 v	16,000	21,000	28,000	—	—	—	58,000	64,000
Reliability	④	④	⑤	⑤	⑤	⑤	⑤	⑤
Crash Safety								
ES 300	⑤	—	④	④	—	—	—	⑤
GS 300	③	③	—	—	—	—	—	—
Side (ES 300)	—	—	⑤	⑤	—	⑤	—	⑤
Offset								
ES	—	—	—	—	—	—	⑤	⑤
GS	—	—	—	⑤	⑤	⑤	⑤	⑤
LS	⑤	⑤	⑤	⑤	⑤	⑤	⑤	⑤
Head Restraints								
ES 300	—	③	—	③	—	③	③	③
GS 300	—	—	—	③	—	⑤	⑤	⑤
LS 400/430	—	❷	—	③	—	⑤	⑤	⑤
SC 400/430	—	—	—	❶	—	—	⑤	⑤
Rollover Resistance								
(ES 300)	—	—	—	—	—	—	—	④

Mercedes-Benz

300 SERIES, 400 SERIES, 500 SERIES, E-CLASS ★★★

RATING: Below Average (1992–2003); Average (1985–91). **Maintenance/ Repair costs:** Higher than average, but many repairs can now be done by independent garages. Beware of engine oil sludge. **Parts:** Higher-than-average cost and limited availability. **Best alternatives:** Acura Integra, TL, or RL; Cadillac DeVille; Ford Crown Victoria or Mercury Grand Marquis; Infiniti I30 or I35; Lexus ES 300; Mazda Millenia; and Toyota Avalon. **Online help:** *benzworld.org; www.mercedes-benz-usa.com; www.mercedesproblems.com; mbspy.bacosys.be /mbquality.htm; www.troublebenz.com; www.lemonmb.com; www.carsurvey.org;* and *www.oil-tech.com/32million.htm.*

Strengths and weaknesses: These cars are ideal mid-sized family sedans. They're relatively reliable, depreciate slowly, and provide all the interior space that the pre-1994 190 series and present-day C-Class leave out. Their only shortcomings are a high resale value that discourages bargain hunters and a weak dealer network that limits parts distribution and drives up parts costs.

If, ironically, you'd like to drive one of these cars but are of an economical frame of mind, choose the 260E—it offers everything the 300 does, but for much less. The 300CE is a coupe version, appealing to a sportier crowd, while the 300TE is the station wagon variant.

Vehicle history: 1997—A new 5-speed automatic transmission, and the E420 got a V8 engine. **1998**—The addition of a station wagon and all-wheel drive. The 300D added a turbocharger for extra power; the E320 came with a new 3.2L V6. Other additions: a BabySmart child protection system, Brake Assist, and an electronic Smart Key feature. **1999**—A new side-impact head protection feature. **2000**—Diesel dropped; a new all-wheel-drive E430 with standard side airbags was added. All models got new wheels, Touch Shift (an automanual device), and Electronic Stability. **2001**—One-touch opening sunroofs.

Quality control has traditionally been better than average with the 300 and higher series; however, it is trending downward. Owners point out recurring problems with the fuel and electrical systems, causing lights, instruments, and gauges to shut off and the trunk lid to open when the engine is shut down. Other common problems: premature rusting of the doors, engine won't shut off; stalling and engine surging; engine problems caused by a stretched timing chain; 1998–2001 oil sludging (see "Secret Warranties/Service Tips/TSBs"); computer module failures (for both engine and transmission); erratically performing and noisy transmission; leaking transmission transfer case; excessive power steering; and front window noise.

Safety summary: 300 series: 1997—Airbag deployed for no reason. • Airbags failed to deploy in a collision. • Brakes locked up, causing extended stopping distance. • Premature failure of the automatic transmission, AC compressor, and hatch door release. • Single windshield wiper doesn't clear windshield adequately. • Instrument gauge cluster doesn't light gauges sufficiently. • Double-pane windows, rear windshield, and rear-view mirrors blur images. **1998**—Sudden, unintended acceleration while on the highway. • Airbag failed to deploy in a collision. • While parking, steering went out and car caught on fire. • Total loss of braking; pedal went to floor. • Premature failure of the automatic transmission, tie-rod, belt tensioner, fuel pump, fuel level sensor, oxygen sensor, windows, power-assisted sunroof, electric seats, turn signal switch, and brake lights. • Power seat suddenly moved back and reclined while vehicle was in traffic. **1999**—Sudden acceleration when turning or decelerating to exit the freeway. • Engine fuel line leakage. • Sunroof electrical fire. • Fuel pump failures. • Inaccurate fuel gauge says tank is full, but almost five more gallons (23L) can be pumped. • Sudden stalling while underway, especially when going over a bump in the road. • Excessive vibration when decelerating. • Transmission leaks oil, disengages, and then suddenly locks up. • ABS suddenly activated, throwing vehicle to side of the road. • Self-activating door locks. • Severe window hazing in rainy weather. **2000**—Panic stops may produce a brake pedal stiffness and loss of braking ability. • Premature brake booster failure. • Poor acceleration said to be caused by fuel injection control module. • Fuel gauge still gives false low readings. • Horn blows on its own, and warning lights are constantly lit. **2001**—Side airbags deploy inadvertently. The following owner of a 2001 300E recounts his surprise at the time:

> While driving down the highway, my passenger side curtain and rear side door airbags deployed for no reason at all.... It scared the hell out of me and nearly caused me to crash the car.

• Water enters the automatic transmission control module, preventing the transmission from changing gears. • Vehicle hesitates when accelerating with gas pedal halfway depressed, then it lurches forward. **2002**—Steering locked up while turning. • Total electrical failure in traffic leading to vehicle shutdown. • Stalling when accelerating. • Windows don't stay up. **2003**—Faulty gateway module and software cause failure in the braking system, supplementary restraints telephone, and tire pressure feedback. • Electrical failures can leave the vehicle with no rear brakes and limited use of the front brakes. • Erratic transmission shifts.

Secret Warranties/Service Tips/TSBs

All models/years: Engine surges at full load. • Vacuum pump oil supply modified through the introduction of a second bore in oil spray nozzle. This helps reduce complaints that engine won't shut off. • Airbag Service Campaign. **All models: 1986–98**—Fuel pump relay failures. **1997**—Engine fails to start due to faulty DAS system. **1998**—Engine rattle countermeasures. **1998–2001**—

Free engine repairs or replacement due to engine oil sludge, following the O'Keefe class action settlement in April 2003. **2000**—A Special Service Campaign will replace, free of charge, side airbags that may deploy if the vehicle is left in the sun. **2003**—Piston slap engine noise.

300 series, 400 series, 500 series, E-Class Profile

	1996	1997	1998	1999	2000	2001	2002	2003
Cost Price ($)								
300ED	58,500	59,950	59,950	59,950	—	—	—	—
320E 4d	64,750	65,900	66,450	66,750	67,150	67,900	68,350	69,950
420E, 430	—							
500E, 500S	132,500	132,950	117,900	122,900	112,851	114,650	116,950	118,450
Used Values ($)								
300ED ⋀	15,000	18,500	21,000	27,000	—	—	—	—
300ED ⋁	13,500	17,000	19,000	25,000	—	—	—	—
320E 4d ⋀	16,500	18,000	24,000	29,000	37,000	45,000	54,000	61,000
320E 4d ⋁	15,500	17,000	22,500	27,000	35,000	43,000	52,000	58,000
420E, 430 ⋀	19,000	21,000	26,000	31,000	40,000	48,000	58,000	—
420E, 430 ⋁	17,000	19,500	24,500	29,000	38,000	46,000	55,000	—
500E, 500S ⋀	24,000	28,000	37,000	45,000	53,000	70,000	84,000	94,000
500E, 500S ⋁	22,000	26,000	34,000	42,000	50,000	65,000	80,000	90,000
Reliability	③	③	③	④	④	④	④	④
Offset	—	③	③	③	⑤	⑤	⑤	⑤
Head Restraints (4d)	—	⑤	—	③	—	⑤	⑤	⑤
Wagon	—	—	—	—	—	③	③	—

C-CLASS   ★★★

RATING: Average (1994–2003). Although these cars beat out the Detroit Big Three in reliability and comfort, they've had a free ride by an automotive press that has ignored their quality and safety shortcomings when compared with the Asian competition. Keep in mind that you'll have to keep your car much longer to amortize its higher cost. **Maintenance/Repair costs:** Higher than average, and most repairs must be done by a Mercedes dealer if you don't live in an area where independent shops have sprung up. Look out for engine oil sludge (see page 298) **Parts:** Higher-than-average cost. Parts are highly dealer dependent and relatively expensive. **Best alternatives:** Acura Integra, TL, or RL; BMW 3 Series; Infiniti I30 or I35; Lexus ES 300; and Toyota Avalon. **Online help:** *forums.mbnz.org/forums; www.mercedesproblems.com; www.troublebenz.com; www.lemonmb.com;* and *www.carsurvey.org.*

Strengths and weaknesses: Replacing the failure-prone 190-series, the 1994 C-Class gained interior room and two new engines: a base 147-hp 2.2L and a 194-hp 2.8L 6-cylinder—a real powerhouse in this small car, when coupled to the manual 5-speed transmission. The 4-speed automatic is a big disappointment—it requires a lot of throttle effort to downshift and prefers to start out in Second gear. The 1994 versions add much-needed horsepower, but lack the manual 5-speed transmission that would set those extra horses free. Rear seat-room is limited, and a lot of road noise intrudes into the passenger compartment.

Vehicle history: 1997—C-Class replaced the standard 2.2L engine with the more robust 2.3L (C230) and revised headlamps. **1998**—A new 2.8L engine (C280), BabySmart car seats, Brake Assist, and side airbags. **1999**—Models got the SLK's 2.3L supercharged engine, replacing the C230's normally aspi-rated power plant, a better-performing drivetrain, and standard leather upholstery. **2000**—A Touch Shift auto-manual transmission, stability control, and Tele-Aid, a communications system for calling for assistance. **2001**—Completely revamped, gaining two new engines, additional safety features, and more aerodynamic styling. **2002**—Additional rear room and storage space, more high-performance features, a wagon, and an AWD sedan and wagon.

Keep in mind that owner surveys give the entry-level C-Class cars a *just* better-than-average rating, while the 300 and higher series have always scored way above average in owner satisfaction. The 1994 model C-Class is the better buy from a quality and reliability standpoint; nevertheless, owners report fre-quent problems with sudden, unintended acceleration; drivetrain noise and vibration; and slipping or soft shifts. Engines (oil sludge), brakes, AC, and the electrical system are also failure-prone.

Safety summary: 1996—Airbags failed to deploy. • Airbag light stays on for no apparent reason. • After parking the vehicle and turning off the ignition, the vehicle lurches forward or rocks backward. • In another incident, vehicle was put in Park on an incline and keys were removed; vehicle rolled backward down the hill. • Brakes are noisy when applied and don't brake well. • Complete electrical system failure. **1997**—While in Reverse, vehicle suddenly accelerated backward. **1998**—Airbag warning light came on and then airbag suddenly exploded. • Transmission fluid leakage. • Faulty gas gauge sensor. • Rear suspension bouncing makes it difficult to maintain directional control. • Inoperative windshield wipers. • Car is very vulnerable to side-wind buffeting. • Window failures. **1999**—Vehicle suddenly accelerated and brakes couldn't stop it. • Brakes failed on incline. **2000**—Sudden acceleration when pulling into a parking space. • Automatic transmission slips when the vehicle is cold, sticks in gear, and shifts abruptly. **2001**—Unintended acceleration. • Vehicle suddenly stopped by the highway as engine self-destructed. **2002**—Many reports of sudden loss of power; stalling. • Airbags failed to deploy. • Wide rear quarter panel blind spot (C240). • Multiple electrical short circuits. • Differential failure. • Vehicle wanders over highway. • Driver seat and side rear-view mirror fail to return to preset position. **2003**—Sudden engine surging. •

Fuel gauge failure and loss of power. • Faulty fuel tank causes engine warning light to stay lit. • No throttle response and strong fuel smell pervades the interior. • Vehicle jerks when accelerating. • Weak wheels are easily bent.

Secret Warranties/Service Tips/TSBs

All models/years: Excessive engine valve train noise may be caused by a stretched timing chain. After 48,000 km, the camshaft and timing chain drive should be checked carefully, especially if excessive noise is heard. • Water in the oxygen sensor connector in the front passenger wheelwell. • Ignition key difficult to remove. • Clicking from the front door lock trim. **All models: 1998–2001**—Free engine repair or replacement for oil sludge. **1999**—Hesitation after a cold start and rough 1–2 and 2–3 shift during warm-up. **1999–2000**—If the brake pedal is hard to apply, replace the brake booster and crankcase vent hoses. **2001**—Troubleshooting hard starts and poor engine performance.

C-Class Profile

	1996	1997	1998	1999	2000	2001	2002	2003
Cost Price ($)								
220	35,995	—	—	—	—	—	—	—
230	—	36,950	37,550	37,950	38,450	—	33,950	34,450
240	—	—	—	—	—	37,450	37,950	38,450
280	49,995	50,995	49,950	49,950	49,950	—	—	—
Used Values ($)								
220 ▲	11,000	—	—	—	—	—	—	—
220 ▼	9,500	—	—	—	—	—	—	—
230 ▲	—	13,000	15,000	17,000	20,000	—	24,000	28,000
230 ▼	—	11,500	13,500	15,500	18,500	—	22,000	26,000
240 ▲	—	—	—	—	—	23,000	27,000	32,000
240 ▼	—	—	—	—	—	22,000	25,000	31,000
280 ▲	15,000	17,500	19,500	23,000	28,000	—	—	—
280 ▼	14,000	16,000	18,000	21,000	26,000	—	—	—
Reliability	③	③	③	③	③	③	③	④
Crash Safety								
(C220, C230)	④	④	—	—	—	—	—	—
Side								
(C230)	—	③	③	③	—	—	—	—
Offset	—	—	—	—	—	⑤	⑤	⑤
Head Restraints (F)	—	❷	—	③	—	⑤	⑤	⑤
Rear	—	—	❷	—	—	—	—	—

Nissan

MAXIMA	★★★★

RATING: Above Average (1989–2003); Average (1986–88). The redesigned 1995–99 version offers a peppier engine, more rounded styling, and a bit longer wheelbase; it apparently has fewer factory-related problems, as well. **Maintenance/Repair costs:** Higher than average, but repairs can be done practically anywhere. **Parts:** Higher-than-average cost, but easy to find. Xenon headlights are frequently stolen from the car because they are easily accessed and can cost $800 each to replace. **Best alternatives:** Acura Integra, TL or RL; Infiniti I30 or I35; Lexus ES300; Mazda Millenia; and Toyota Avalon. **Online help:** *www.mycarstats.com/auto_complaints/NISSAN_complaints.asp* and *www.consumeraffairs.org/automotive/nissan.html.*

Strengths and weaknesses: These front-drive sedans are very well equipped and nicely finished, but cramped for their size. Although the trunk is spacious, only five passengers can travel in a pinch (in the literal sense). The 6-cylinder, 190-hp engine, borrowed from the 300ZX in 1992, offers sparkling performance; the fuel injectors, however, are problematic. The '93 models got standard driver-side airbags, and the Maxima remained unchanged until the 1995 model's redesign and a second redesign of the year 2000 version.

Early Maximas are less expensive to buy, but more costly to maintain—for example, the exhaust manifold, a component that commonly fails, will set you back $300–$500 to replace on 1993–96 models. Owners report that the '95 Maxima's suspension was cheapened, to the detriment of both the ride and the handling.

Minor electrical and front suspension problems afflict early Maximas. Brakes and engine timing belts need frequent attention in all years. Newer models have a weak automatic transmission and the ignition system can malfunction. There have also been reports of "cooked" transmissions. This is due to a poorly designed transmission cooler. Mechanics say that this breakdown can be avoided by installing an externally mounted transmission cooler with a filter and replacing the transmission filter cooler at every oil change.

Owners report that the V6-equipped Maxima is sometimes hard to start in cold weather, due to the engine's tendency to flood easily. The cruise control unit is another problematic component. When it's engaged at moderate speeds, it hesitates or "drifts" to a lower speed, acting as if the fuel line were clogged. It operates correctly only at much higher speeds than needed. Incidentally, owners say that a new fuel filter will *not* correct the problem. Additionally, though warped manifolds were once routinely replaced under a "goodwill" warranty, Nissan now makes the customer pay. The warpage causes a manifold bolt to break off, thereby causing a huge exhaust leak. Most fuel-injector malfunctions are caused by carbon clogging up the injectors; there are additives you can try that might reduce this buildup. There have also been internal problems with the coil windings on the fuel-injectors. Your best bet is to replace the entire set.

Nissan has had problems with weak window regulators for some time. If the window is frozen, don't open it. The rubber weather stripping around the window is also a problem. It cuts easily and causes the window to go off track, which in turn causes stress on the weak regulators. Driver-side window breakage is common and can cost up to $300 to repair. Costly aluminum wheels corrode quickly and are easily damaged by road hazards. There have been a few reports of surface rust and paint problems. Pre-1990 Maximas suffer from rust perforation on the sunroof, door bottoms, rear wheelwells, front edge of the hood, and bumper supports. The underbody should also be checked carefully for corrosion damage. Premature wearout of the muffler is a frequent problem; it's often covered by Nissan's "goodwill" warranty, wherein the company and dealer will contribute 50 percent of the replacement cost.

Vehicle history: 1995—A longer wheelbase (adding to interior room), a new 3.0L engine, and more rounded styling. They compete well with fully equipped Camrys, entry-level Infinitis, and Lexus models. Nevertheless, tall passengers will find the interior a bit cramped, and the automatic transmission is often slow to downshift and isn't always smooth. **1997**—Models got a new front-end restyling. **2000**—Version was redesigned to offer more power, interior space (particularly for rear-seat passengers), and safety/convenience features. **2001**—Carried over relatively unchanged, except for an Anniversary edition equipped with a 227-hp 3.0L V6, taken from the Infiniti I30. **2002**—Were completely revamped, featuring a 260-hp 3.5L V6 coupled to a 6-speed manual or 4-speed automatic transmission; revised interior trim, larger front brakes, new front-end styling, a power driver's seat, xenon headlights, and 16-inch wheels.

Quality control and overall reliability are apparently much better with these more recent iterations. Nevertheless, owners still report a variety of safety-related deficiencies, in addition to brake, electrical system, fuel system, and body glitches.

Redesign glitches abound and include difficulty controlling the engine speed with the gas pedal; engine popping and knocking when accelerating; stalling when braking or decelerating; transmission malfunctions; premature front brake pad wear and rotor warpage; a choppy, jarring suspension; and excessive front-end vibrations. Faulty ignition coils and inadequate headlight illumination continue to be major problems.

Safety summary: All models: 1996—Fire ignited from shorted wires under the passenger-side seat. • Airbag failed to deploy. • ABS failures. • Vehicle constantly pulls to the right. • Sudden loss of power, resulting in inoperative brakes and steering. • Chronic stalling. • Power-steering failure. • Erratic transmission performance. • Hard to shift transmission out of Park. • Key can be taken out of ignition while vehicle isn't in Park. • Power door locks failed. • Several reports of headlight explosions. **1997**—Door latch won't engage in cold weather. • Front wheel suddenly locked up while driving. • Power steering leaks fluid. • Trunk lid opened while driving. • Pedal went to the floor when brakes were applied, resulting in extended stopping distance. **1998**—Vehicle intermittently accelerates while braking. • Frequent windshield wiper failures. **1999**—Airbags failed to deploy. • Throttle "shock" and transmission hesitation. • Frequent ignition coil failures. • Vehicle pulls constantly to the left. • Cruise control resume feature doesn't work. • Power door locks cycle from lock to unlock. **2000**—ABS brake failure. • Transmission may not shift. • Airbag failed to deploy. • Early replacement of the catalytic converter (alerted by Check Engine light) and #6 ignition coil. • Poor headlight illumination. • A chlorine-type smell permeates the interior. **2001**—Engine compartment fire. • Steering lock-up, loss of brakes, and failure of the airbag to deploy. **2002**— Vehicle suddenly swerved to the right. • Vehicle accelerated in Reverse while shifter indicated Drive. • Many other scenarios where vehicle suddenly accelerated, especially when brakes were applied. • Vehicle may also suddenly shut down on the highway. • Brake and steering failure. • Windshield washer fails in cold weather. • Sunroof opens and closes on its own. • ABS light stays lit. • Intermittent front wheel lock-up, then traction slowly comes back. • Right wheel buckled when brakes were applied. • Steering wheel overheats. Water leaks into the trunk. **2002–03**—Xenon headlights are easily stolen and expensive to replace. **2003**—Hard to read instrument panel lights. • Passenger-side airbag deployed on its own. • Paint chips easily.

Secret Warranties/Service Tips/TSBs

All models/years: Defective catalytic converters that cause a rotten-egg smell may be replaced free of charge under Nissan's emissions warranty; the same principle applies to EVAP canister charcoal leakage. • TSB #P195-006 looks at the many causes and remedies for excessive brake noise. • Troubleshooting MIL light alerts. **All models: 1995–96**—Timing chain rattling noise can be silenced by replacing the timing chain tensioner and slack guide. • Brake squeak or squeal can be corrected by installing front and rear brake kits. **1995–98**—An inoperative power seat may require a new drive cable. **1995–99**—Blower motor noise can be cured by installing a new blower motor cover. • A front brake groan when stopping is addressed in TSB #99-032. • A rear brake groan or hum can be fixed by readjusting the parking brake cable. • If the rear brakes squeak or squeal when cold, replace the rear brake pads with upgraded ones. • Guidelines for correcting steering pull or drift. • Tips on eliminating a foul odour emanating from the sunroof sunshade. **1996–99**— Diagnostic tips for fixing a front seat belt that's slow to retract. **1998–99**—An On-Off transmission throttle shock can be attenuated by installing an upgraded ECM. **1999**—Guidelines for correcting rocker panel creaking or popping. **2000**—Low idle or stalling in gear. • Excessive brake vibration countermeasures. • Right front strut noise. • Rear bumper scratched by trunk lid. • Tips on silencing interior squeaks and rattles and front brake groan. **2000–01**—Automatic transmission gear slippage. **2000–02**—Doors may intermittently lock by themselves. **2000–03**—Driver's seat won't go forward or backward. **2001–02**—Rear brake caliper clunk, rattle, or knock. • Rear suspension bottoms out (also an Infiniti problem). • Hood vibration. **2002**—Erratic sunroof operation. • Radio ignition static. • Driver's power seat won't move forward or backward. • Clutch howling. **2002–03**—Hesitation upon acceleration. • Lack of engine power. • Sunroof operates on its own. **2003**—Navigation screen stuck on "please wait". • Troubleshooting brake noise and judder.

Maxima Profile								
	1996	1997	1998	1999	2000	2001	2002	2003
Cost Price ($)								
Base	27,998	27,998	27,998	28,598	28,598	29,000	32,900	32,900
Used Values ($)								
Base Ʌ	7,500	9,000	11,000	13,000	16,000	18,500	22,000	25,000
Base V	6,000	7,500	9,500	12,000	14,500	17,000	20,500	23,000
Reliability	④	④	⑤	⑤	⑤	⑤	⑤	⑤
Crash Safety	④	④	④	④	—	④	④	④
Side	—	④	④	④	—	④	④	④
Offset	❶	③	③	③	③	③	③	③
Head Restraints (F)	—	❷	❷	③	③	⑤	⑤	⑤
Rear	—	—	—	❷	—	—	—	—
Rollover Resistance	—	—	—	—	—	—	④	④

Toyota

AVALON ★★★★

RATING: Above Average (1995–2003). Sorry, Toyota, but your Avalon also suffers from the same "less for more" philosophy we have seen since 1997 with most of your lineup, with a few exceptions like the Echo and Celica. Shame— like Brando in *On the Waterfront*, you, "coulda been a contender." The Avalon has exhibited an unusually large number of safety-related defects, in addition to charges that its engines are often sidelined by engine oil sludge. It's a good idea to make sure that headlight illumination is adequate for your driving needs, "green glow" dash reflections onto the windshield aren't too distracting, and windshield visibility is adequate for rainy weather. **Maintenance/Repair costs:** Average. **Parts:** Higher-than-average cost and limited availability. **Best alternatives:** A fully loaded Camry; if you want a more driver-involved experience in a Toyota, consider a Lexus ES 300 or GS 300. Other good choices: the Acura Integra, TL, or RL; BMW 3 Series; Infiniti I30 or I35; Mazda Millenia; and Nissan Maxima. **Online help:** *www.carsurvey.org/model_Toyota_Avalon.html*; *yotarepair.com/Automotive_News.html*; and *www.consumeraffairs.com/automotive/*

toyota_avalon.html; or look under "Toyota engine sludge" with the Google browser.

Strengths and weaknesses: This near-luxury four-door offers more value, interior space, and performance than do other cars in its class that cost thousands of dollars more. A front-engine, front-drive, mid-sized sedan based on a stretched Camry platform, the six-passenger Avalon is bigger than the rear-drive Cressida it replaced and similar in size to the Ford Taurus. Sure, there's a fair amount of Camry in the Avalon, but it's quicker on its feet than the Camry, better attuned to abrupt manoeuvres, and 5 cm (2 in.) longer. In fact, there's more rear-seat legroom than you'll find in either the Taurus or the new Chevrolet Lumina. It's close to the Dodge Intrepid in this respect.

Vehicle history: 1997—More power, torque, and standard features. **1998**—Seat belt pretensioners, side airbags, new headlamps and tail lights, and a new trunk lid and grille. **2000**—Restyled and considerably improved. It's more powerful, roomier, and full of more high-tech safety and convenience features.

Quality control is better than average, though steering, suspension, and fuel system components are failure-prone, and many owners have complained of engine sludge forcing them to spend thousands of dollars for engine repairs (now covered by a "goodwill" extended warranty, shown below in 1997 "Secret Warranties/Service Tips/TSBs" section). Owners also have some performance gripes that include numerous electrical system glitches, premature front brake repairs and suspension strut failures, power steering that's a bit too light, hydroplaning, excessive body lean, and under-steer when cornering. Body construction and assembly are fairly good, although rattles are commonplace for all model years (see *www.carsurvey.org/viewcomments_review_35534.html*), trunk leaks have been reported on the '99 models, and paint flaking has afflicted some 2001–03 models. Except for some engine sludge complaints, premature brake wear, and body and accessories glitches (wind noise, AC, and audio system malfunctions), the 2002–03s have had few problems.

Safety summary: All years: Airbags failed to deploy in an accident. • Sudden, unintended acceleration. • Bridgestone/Firestone, Dunlop, and Michelin tire failures. **1997**—Airbags deployed while stopped at a light. • Sudden engine failure; engine leaks oil. • Engine cylinder failure. • Fuel damper and fuel pump failed twice; leaking fuel. • Brakes failed due to freezing vacuum hose. • ABS controller failure. • Frequent complaints of steering fluid leaks. • Many reports of premature failure of the steering assembly (upper steering knuckle) and front strut support. • Front suspension bar suddenly broke. • Transmission failure caused by loss of internal pressure. • Vehicle hydroplanes on the slightest wet pavement; Bridgestone tires don't help. • Driver's seat moves when vehicle turns. • Wind blew trunk lid shut on driver's neck. • Tail light bulbs have a short lifespan. **1998**—Vehicle caught fire at fuel filler neck when getting gas. • Gas tank fuel hose leaks fuel. • Airbag deployment caused severe chest and chin injuries. • Front seat reclined suddenly when vehicle was hit from the rear. • Engine surges and drops rpms rapidly and unexpectedly when engaging cruise control or when taking foot off the gas pedal. • Power-steering pump failure and fluid reservoir leakage. • Early replacement of brake pads, calipers, and rotors. • Front suspension bangs and clanks when going over a bump of any size and rear suspension bottoms out. • Constant vibration in steering wheel and accelerator while driving caused by fuel pressure regulator. • Loose driver's seat. • Kick panel falls off repeatedly. **1999**—Airbag warning light comes on for no reason. • Cruise control operates erratically. • Brake pedal went to floor with little effect. • Car shifts poorly (hesitates and jerks) when you let off the gas and then accelerate, or do a rolling stop. **2000**— Automatic transmission slippage. • Brake pedal went to the floor with no braking effect. • Driver's seat rocks back and forth. • Steering wheel off-centre. • Airbag light stays lit. • Dash lights and gauges reflect onto windshield. • Inadequate headlight illumination. • Horn failure. **2001**—Excessive highway wandering. • Engine surging at idle. • Flex hose came off the charcoal canister, causing warning light to come on when refuelling. • Front and rear suspension bottoms out when carrying four adults. • Insufficient steering feedback. • Jerky acceleration. • Sudden failure of the instrument and information panel lighting and headlights. • Driver's side-view mirror has a small viewing area. • At night, the instrument panel lights and gauges reflect a green glow onto the windshield. **2002**—Cruise control doesn't slow car when going downhill. • Vehicle veers to the left at high speeds; vehicle wanders left and right. • Driver-side seat belt doesn't retract. • Dash lights reflect onto the windshield. • Vehicle emits a strong sulfur odour, which Toyota bulletins claim is normal. **2003**— Extended braking distance caused by improperly installed brake lines. • Front brakes appear to apply themselves. • Steering wheel blocks view of speedometer; hard to read gearshift position gauge at night. • Panel glass over-heats while driving. • Incorrect readings from the fuel range finder.

Secret Warranties/Service Tips/TSBs

All models: 1990–2000—Brake pad clicking may be corrected by use of a special Toyota-recommended grease; however, some owners say it's not very effective. **1995–96**—To reduce wind noise from the front door A-pillar area, consult TSB #B0010-97. **1995–2000**—A power-steering squeak can be silenced by installing a new rack end shaft. **1996**—Tips on reducing engine noise, front door wind noise, and front suspension and rear popping noise. **1997**—AC odour troubleshooting. • Fixing front suspension crunch. **1997–99**—Front suspension noise can be eliminated by changing the suspension support. **1997–2002**—Extended warranty will pay for engine sludge damage up to eight years, without any mileage limitation. **2000**—Roof water leaks. • Sliding roof and door mirror noise. **2000–01**—Measures to reduce instrument panel luminosity. • Wheel bearing ticking noise. • Door popping and creaking. **2003**—Blank navigation screen.

Avalon Profile

	1996	1997	1998	1999	2000	2001	2002	2003
Cost Price ($)								
XL	33,368	33,718	34,688	35,605	36,595	36,370	38,365	—
XLS	35,778	36,188	37,868	42,515	43,800	44,710	45,135	45,560
Used Values ($)								
XL ▲	8,500	10,000	12,500	15,000	19,000	23,000	27,000	—
XL ▼	8,000	8,500	10,500	13,000	17,500	21,500	25,000	—
XLS ▲	9,500	11,000	13,000	16,500	21,000	26,000	30,000	35,000
XLS ▼	8,500	10,000	11,500	14,500	19,000	24,500	28,000	33,000
Reliability	④	⑤	⑤	⑤	⑤	⑤	⑤	⑤
Crash Safety	④	④	④	—	③	③	④	④
Side	—	⑤	⑤	—	④	④	④	④
Offset	❷	❷	③	③	⑤	⑤	⑤	⑤
Head Restraints (F)	❶	❶	③	③	③	③	③	③
Rear	—	—	❶	❶	—	—	—	—
Rollover Resistance	—	—	—	—	—	—	④	④

Volvo

850, C70, S40, S70, V40, V70 ★★★

RATING: Average (1993–2003). Surprisingly, for a car company that emphasizes its commitment to safe cars, the 850 and 70 series have quite a few safety-related defects reported by owners, including engine and seat fires, loss of steering, sudden acceleration, transmission failures, electrical shorts, light failures, and tire blowouts. As if this weren't bad enough, Ford's cost-cutting and sadistic customer relations have left many new and used buyers leery of getting a Volvo. Sure, prices are depressed, but quality is problematic and the dealer support is shaky. **Maintenance/Repair costs:** Higher than average, and repairs must be done by a Volvo dealer. **Parts:** Higher-than-average cost and limited availability. **Best alternatives:** Don't waste your money on a 1997 850; the 1996 models are virtually identical The 1998 model 850s were renamed the C70, S70, and V70; they also have a disappointingly high number of safety-related deficiencies reported to the federal government. Interestingly, new Volvo sales have been very poor since Ford took over, resulting in much lower prices on the entire used lineup. Other choices: Acura Integra, TL, or RL; BMW 3 or 5 Series; Infiniti I30 or I35; Lexus ES 300; Mazda Millenia; Nissan Maxima; and Toyota Avalon. **Online help:** *www.volvospy.com*; *www.consumeraffairs.com/automotive/volvo.htm*; *www.consumeraffairs.com/automotive/volvo_fires.html*; and *www.carsurvey.org*.

Strengths and weaknesses: Bland, but practical to the extreme, with plenty of power, good handling, and lots of capacity. For 1997, the 850 GLT got a bit more lower-end torque, while the turbo version was upgraded with electrically adjusted front passenger seats and an in-dash CD player. The base 850 sedan uses a 2.4L 24-valve, 168-hp 5-cylinder engine hooked to a front-drive power-train. (An all-wheel-drive version is available only in Canada and Europe.) Wagons use the same base power plant, hooked to a 5-speed manual or optional 4-speed electronic automatic. GLTs have a torquier, turbo variant of the same power plant that boosts horsepower to 190.

The "sports" sedan T5 is a rounder, sportier-looking Volvo that delivers honest, predictable performance but comes up a bit short on the "sport" side. Volvo's base turbo boosts horsepower to 222, but its new T-5R variant uses an upgraded turbocharger that boosts power to 240 horses—for up to seven seconds.

Passenger space, seating comfort, and trunk and cargo space are unmatched by the competition. Braking on dry and wet pavement is also exemplary. The ride of both the sedan and the wagon deteriorates progressively as the road gets rougher and passengers are added. Turbo versions are particularly stiff, and passengers are constantly bumped and thumped.

The 850 hasn't escaped the traditional AC, electrical system, and brake problems that afflict its predecessors. Additionally, owners have complained that the early models have uncomfortable seat belts, insufficient rear travel for the front seats, and many body hardware deficiencies.

70 series and 90 series

Making its debut for the 1998 model year, the 70 series is basically the discontinued 850 using a nom de plume. The letters S, V, and C preceding the numerical designation stand for sedans, wagons, and coupes. The 90 series is a re-designated rear-drive 960, and, as with the 70 series, sedans are indicated by an S and wagons by a V. Both the 70 and 90 series are carried over relatively unchanged, except for their names.

With the front-drive 70 series, all-wheel drive is offered with the wagons, and the base 2.4L 5-cylinder engine comes with three horsepower ratings: 168, 190, and 236 hp. Only two transmissions are available: a manual 5-speed (relatively rare) and an automatic 4-speed.

Handling is superb, with the suspension dampened somewhat for a more comfortable ride than what many European imports offer. AWD performs flawlessly, road and body noise are muted, and the cars are well appointed with a full array of standard safety features, with the exception of traction control, which is optional.

On the downside, rear seating is cramped for three adults, and the instrument panel appears to be overly busy, with a confusing array of gauges, instruments, and controls on the centre console. Plus, the three rear head restraints induce claustrophobia while severely restricting rear visibility.

The 90 series has plenty of room for three rear seat passengers and its 181-hp V6 performs very smoothly and fairly quietly, providing plenty of power for passing and merging. The car's tight turning circle makes parking a snap, and the suspension has been tuned for comfort rather than performance. Still, handling is quite good. Once again, the large rear head restraints obstruct rear visibility.

As far as quality control and dealer servicing are concerned, Volvo technical service bulletins and owner complaints indicate that factory defects on all models have been on the rise for the past five years. For example, the cars' electrical system may shut down in rainy weather or when passing over puddles; headlights, turn signal lights, and other bulbs burn out monthly; dash lights suddenly go berserk when passing through puddles; power window switches and locks fail constantly; wheels are easily bent; the turn signal lever doesn't return; airbags deploy for no reason; and springs are noisy.

The above defects clearly show that there's less stringent quality control at the factory level since Ford acquired the company and that Volvo is counting on Ford and Volvo dealers to repair their engineering mistakes. On the other hand, Volvo *has* improved service and warranty relations by accelerating service training programs. But the effort may be too little, too late: Volvo sales have plummeted and many dealers are trying to bail out before Ford's mismanagement ruins them.

C70

The C70's strong points: good acceleration with lots of torque, exceptional steering and handling, first-class body construction and finish, and predicted better-than-average reliability. Its weak points: difficult rear seat entry/exit, some engine turbo lag, excessive engine noise, a jarring suspension, and an uncertain future.

Seating four comfortably, this luxury coupe and convertible is based on the 850 (pardon, S70) platform, and marketed as a high-performance Volvo. It comes with two turbocharged engines: a base 2.4L 190-hp inline 5-cylinder and a 2.3L 236-hp variant. Either engine can be hooked to a 5-speed manual or a 4-speed automatic transmission. Of the two engines, the 190-hp appears to offer the best response and smoothest performance.

Acceleration is impressive, despite the fact that the car feels underpowered until the turbo kicks in at around 1500 rpm—a feature that drivers will find more frustrating with a manual shifter than with an automatic. Steering and handling are first class, fit and finish above reproach, and mechanical and body components are top quality.

The only things not to like are turbo lag, tire thumping caused by the high-performance tires, excessive engine and wind noise, and power-sliding rear seats that require lots of skill and patience.

S40 and V40

Volvo's latest small sedan and wagon come with a 1.9L 150-hp turbocharged 4-cylinder engine coupled to an automatic transmission. Two side airbags, anti-lock brakes, air conditioning, cruise control, and power windows are also standard. The 2001 model got a minor facelift, an upgraded engine and 5-speed automatic transmission, side-curtain airbags, and some handling improvements; 2002s were carried over unchanged.

These models have generated an unacceptably high number of complaints concerning chronic brake repairs, automatic transmission failures, fuel system malfunctions leading to poor driveability, and myriad electrical shorts and body defects.

Safety summary: All models: 1996—A handful of reports that while vehicle was being driven, it suddenly lost all power and the engine compartment caught fire. • Inadvertent airbag deployment injured driver. • ABS brake failures. • Vehicle suddenly downshifts while cruising on the highway. • Transmission slipped out of Park, rolled down incline, and hit a house. • During rainy periods, the steering wheel locks up or the dashboard suddenly lights up. • Repeated tire blowouts. • Premature failure of the engine cooling fan and the evaporator pump fan relay for the exhaust manifold. Owners also cite cruise control, power-steering pump, and front seat belt failures. • Electrical glitches affect the speedometer, radio cassette player, and battery. • Broken driver-side door hinge. **1997**—Heated seat caught on fire. • Driver's seatback frame broke when vehicle accelerated. • Sudden acceleration, spinning wildly when backing up. • Pirelli (205/45-17) tires blew out; the design and size is inappropriate for this vehicle. • Original equipment tires bubble. • Total brake loss in rainy weather. • Rain also causes vehicle to shut down, without steering control. • Vehicle drifts left when being driven, even after the steering mechanism was replaced. • Gas odour in the interior after driving a short distance. • Driver's seat belt retractor locks up. • Steering locks up in rainy weather. • Air pump and AC compressor failures. **1998**—Passenger-side airbag suddenly deployed while vehicle was parked. • Frontal and side airbags failed to deploy in a collision. • Right front wheel assembly disengaged from car while vehicle was underway, causing loss of control and an accident. • Vehicle suddenly accelerated; brakes locked up. • Stalling while underway caused by defective air mass sensor. • A piece of the vacuum brake system came loose, causing engine rpms to surge and spontaneously locking up the brakes. • Transmission randomly fails to engage in Reverse gear, or kicks strongly when going into Reverse. • Frequent battery failures due to battery not holding its charge. • Headlights and other lights burn out frequently. • Two incidents where the front turn signal socket smouldered and charred. • Driver's seat belt doesn't retract when disconnected. • Continental tires tread separation. • Frequent tire blowouts. • Wheels are easily bent, causing excessive vibration. • Defective door lock pin makes it difficult to open or close door. • Weak trunk lid struts allow lid to fall. • Dashboard causes excessive glare on windshield. • Tall front seats and head restraints obstruct visibility. **1999**—Sudden acceleration when applying brakes. • Vehicle shuts down when making a left turn. • Airbags failed to deploy. • While underway, driver seat suddenly moved backward. • Fuel fumes leak into interior. • Brake pedal locks up. • Chronic light failures. • Automatic door locks and trunk lock fail to open. • Automatic gas tank door jams shut. • Tailpipe extends beyond bumper, burning occupant. •

Inside door handles pinch fingers. **C70: 2001**—Power window noise. **S40, V40: 2001**—Under-hood electrical fire. • Cracked fuel regulator pump spilled fuel onto hot engine and spread fumes into the interior. • Sudden, unintended acceleration when vehicle put into Drive. • Chronic stalling attributed to faulty idle control valve and air mass meter. • Complete loss of braking. • Brake pedal hard to depress, reducing brake effectiveness. • Brakes don't stop vehicle in a reasonable distance. • Brake pedal is too close to the gas pedal. • Brake pedal snapped, went to the floor while going downhill. • When applying the brakes in cold weather, pedal won't depress, causing extended stopping distance (dealer confirmed vacuum pump motor was defective). • Premature replacement of the front and rear rotors and pads:

> I have a 2001 S40 with 30,000 miles [48,000 km] on it. I have had nothing but problems with the brakes and headlamps. I have replaced the front brakes and rotors three times. I have replaced the rear rotors once and the pads twice. The headlamps constantly blow out. I wrote Volvo and they tell me the brakes go because of the material they use. Apparently it is soft. Too bad they did not tell me I would incur these expenses before I leased it.

• Vehicle pulls to the left when accelerating or coming to a stop. • Repeated automatic transmission failures. • Airbag light stays lit. • Faulty forward/backward seat adjustment. • Noisy engine and sunroof. **V40:** More complaints that the pedal won't depress, causing total brake loss or extended stopping distance and premature wearout of the front brake pads (around 20,000 km). • A new wiring harness is available to extend the life of low-beam headlight bulbs. • Under a special program, Volvo will replace the front door window to prevent excessive noise. This replacement is contingent upon a customer complaint. • Correction for front seat whining or creaking. **2002**—Poor braking with ABS. • Dash reflects onto windshield. **S70, V70: 2000**—Airbags failed to deploy. • Vehicle suddenly pulls to one side while cruising. • Unexpected total loss of power. • Engine sputters and then shuts off. • Prematurely worn front stabilizer link rod. • Considerable brake fade at start-up. • Driver's window stuck in the down position. • AC allows exhaust fumes into the vehicle. • Chronic light failures. **V70: 2001**—Excessive reflection of beige dash onto windshield. • Engine stalls in traffic; dealer says problem is caused by a "weak" fuel pump. • Engine mounts broke. • Manual transmission clutch sticks in cold weather. • Vehicle can roll away when parked on an incline. • Brake pedal is too close to gas pedal. • Front door indent doesn't hold door open. • Sunroof blew in while going through a car wash. • Rear tailgate door won't lock. • Coffee spilled from cupholder and shorted airbag computer. • Frequent bulb failures. **2002**—Shoulder belt crosses at neck. • Sunroof broke and fell into roof liner. **2003**—Emergency brake bracket comes apart. • Tires continually wear out prematurely.

Secret Warranties/Service Tips/TSBs

All models/years: Check the valve cover nuts at every servicing interval to prevent oil leakage. • Free front seat belt extenders available. **All models: 1992–97**—Upgraded parts have been produced to correct a steering column knocking noise. • Tips on silencing an automatic transmission whining noise. **1993–97**—A number of bulletins have been issued to reduce cargo compartment and interior noise and trim rattles. **1996–99**—Automatic transmission final drive whining sound can be eliminated by putting a damper on the driveshaft. **1997**—Measures to correct high oil consumption. • New shims will minimize low-speed braking vibrations. • Tips on correcting hard starting. • AC odour troubleshooting tips. • Measures for improved ventilation and defrosting. • Engine may run too lean. **1997–99**—Rear axle whining countermeasures. • Automatic transmission final drive whining correction tips. **1998–2000**—Installation of protective door lock covers. **1999**—Measures to reduce upper windshield moulding noise. **2000**—Special Service Campaign to service the engine oil filler grate. **850, S70, V70: 1997**—Tips for eliminating upper windshield moulding noise. **1997–99**—There are at least a half-dozen bulletins addressing water leaks affecting the C70. • Rear axle whining countermeasures. **1997–2000**—Automatic transmission final drive whining correction tips. • **1998–2000**—Power-window noise can be silenced by following the procedures outlined in TSB #8330033. • Poor FM reception (static) can be improved by modifying the ground strap. **1998–2001**—Upgraded rear brake pads will be installed under warranty for more efficient and quieter braking. • Service Campaign provides for the free replacement of the headlight wiper stop lug. **2001**—Special Service Campaign to upgrade service life of headlights; free bulb replacement. **C70: 2001**—Rough cold start; long cranking time, tachometer jump, and engine warning light activated. **S40, V40: 2000**—Engine oil filler neck may be faulty. • Ticking noise may be heard from the canister purge valve. • The malfunction light (MIL) stays on while driving. **2001**—Exhaust manifold retaining nuts may be loose or missing. • Engine oil filler neck may be faulty. • A ticking noise may be heard from the canister purge valve. • The malfunction indicator light (MIL) stays on while driving. **2002**—Uneven idle. **S70, V70, C70: 1997–2000**—Reducing power seat lateral movement. **1998–2000**—Special Service Campaign to upgrade service life of headlights; free bulb replacement. • Another campaign provides for the free replacement of the headlight wiper stop lug. **C70: 1998–2002**—Uneven idle. **S60, V70: 2001**—Uneven idle.

850, C70, S40, S70, V40, V70 Profile

	1996	1997	1998	1999	2000	2001	2002	2003
Cost Price ($)								
850	29,995	31,995	—	—	—	—	—	—
Turbo	41,695	43,995	—	—	—	—	—	—
TLA/AWD	48,695	48,495	—	—	—	—	—	—

C70	—	—	54,675	49,995	50,595	52,995	49,995	59,595
S40	—	—	—	—	—	31,400	31,495	31,495
S70	—	—	33,995	34,994	35,195	—	—	—
V40	—	—	—	—	—	32,400	32,495	32,495
V70	—	—	33,295	36,295	36,495	37,495	37,995	37,995
Used Values ($)								
850 ▲	9,000	10,500	—	—	—	—	—	—
850 ▼	7,500	9,000	—	—	—	—	—	—
Turbo ▲	10,000	11,000	—	—	—	—	—	—
Turbo ▼	8,500	10,000	—	—	—	—	—	—
TLA/AWD ▲	10,000	12,000	—	—	—	—	—	—
TLA/AWD ▼	8,500	11,000	—	—	—	—	—	—
C70 ▲	—	—	15,000	19,500	24,500	29,000	35,000	50,000
C70 ▼	—	—	13,500	18,000	23,000	27,000	33,000	48,000
S40 ▲	—	—	—	—	—	19,000	22,000	25,000
S40 ▼	—	—	—	—	—	17,500	21,000	23,000
S70 ▲	—	—	13,000	15,500	18.500	—	—	—
S70 ▼	—	—	11,500	14,000	17,000	—	—	—
V40 ▲	—	—	—	—	—	19,000	23,000	26,000
V40 ▼	—	—	—	—	—	17,500	21,500	24,500
V70 ▲	—	—	13,000	16,000	18,000	22,500	26,000	30,000
V70 ▼	—	—	11,500	14,500	16,500	21,000	24,000	28,500
Reliability	⑤	⑤	④	④	④	④	④	④
Crash Safety								
850	⑤	—	—	—	—	—	—	—
S70	—	⑤	⑤	⑤	—	—	—	—
Side								
850	④	—	—	—	—	—	—	—
S40	—	—	—	—	—	—	⑤	⑤
S70	—	④	④	④	—	—	—	
Offset (850/S70)	⑤	⑤	⑤	⑤	⑤	—	—	—
Head Restraints								
850	—	⑤	—	—	—	—	—	—
C70	—	—	—	⑤	—	⑤	—	⑤
S70	—	—	—	⑤	—	—	—	—
S40/V40	—	—	—	—	—	⑤	⑤	⑤
V70	—	—	—	⑤	—	⑤	⑤	⑤

900 SERIES, S80, S90, V90 ★★★

RATING: Average (1997–2003); Above Average (1989–96). The 1998 model 900s were renamed the S90 and V90, and have apparently inherited similar brake and electrical deficiencies. The model was renamed the S80 for the 1999 model year. It's interesting to note that the 960 series becomes cheaper to acquire than the 940 as the years progress. Unfortunately, as the revamped Volvos have aged, their reliability and safety have become more problematic. **Maintenance/Repair costs:** Higher than average, and repairs must be done by a (Ford) Volvo dealer. Yikes! **Parts:** Higher-than-average cost and limited availability. **Best alternatives:** Acura Integra, TL, or RL; BMW 3 Series; Infiniti I30 or I35; Lexus ES 300; Mazda Millenia; Nissan Maxima; and Toyota Avalon. **Online help:** *www.volvospy.com*; *www.consumeraffairs.com/automotive/volvo.htm*; and *www.carsurvey.org*.

Strengths and weaknesses: Practical to the extreme, with plenty of power, good handling, lots of carrying capacity, many standard safety features, and impressive crashworthiness ratings and accident injury claim data. On the other hand, weak points include a jarring ride with vehicles equipped with 16- and 17-inch wheels; limited rear visibility; excessive engine, wind, and road noise; fuel-thirstiness (turbo models); declining quality control and increased frequency of safety-related deficiencies; and limited availability, causing soaring resale prices for recent reworked models, with little room for negotiating.

Having debuted as essentially repackaged 760s, the flagship 900 series rear-drive sedans and wagons have a much better reliability record than do the 240 and 700 series, and have been on par with the 850, S70, and V70 over the last few model years. Both the 940 and 960 offer exceptional roominess and comfort, and are capable of carrying six people with ease. The wagon provides lots of cargo space and manages to do it in great style. Some owner gripes: the base 114-hp 2.3L engine is overpowered by the car's weight, excessive fuel consumption with the turbo option, and excessive road and wind noise at highway speeds.

The 1996 960s were given front seat side-impact airbags and upgraded door locking.

Most of the 900 and 90 series' deficiencies are identical to the S70's, with some exceptions, like miscalibrated engine computer modules that cause random misfiring; rotten-egg and other exhaust odours that permeate the interior even after the catalytic converter is replaced; ignition switch, rear spring, and climate control unit failures; excessive on-road shudder/vibration, drifting, and hard steering; frequent fuel leaks; children suffering burns from the extended tailpipe; battery boiling over, causing acid to spray into engine compartment; and seat belts that catch in the door after failing to retract properly. Drivers also report that the front bumper is too low; it hits the wheel stop in parking lots, causing extensive bumper and wheelwell damage. Also, brakes continue to require frequent and expensive maintenance due to the poor durability of front and rear pads and the premature warpage of the brake rotors (15,000–30,000 km).

Vehicle history: 1999—The S80 is a redesign of the S90 and offers several interesting new features like a powerful 268-hp, transverse inline 6-cylinder engine and a sophisticated automatic transmission called the Geartronic—a 4-speed automatic with a feature for manually changing gears, if one so desires. Additionally, the car is chock-full of safety features, has the largest interior of any Volvo, gives impressive performance and handling, and is attractively styled. **2001**—Dual-stage airbags and 16-inch wheels.

Unfortunately, the S80s' defects closely resemble the problems reported on prior years' models (see "Safety summary") and seriously undermine Volvo's much-touted safety claims.

Safety summary: All models: 1991–95—Airbags deploy for no reason. **1998**—Engine fire. • Airbags didn't deploy in a collision. • Fuel system leak (T-junctions and clamps replaced). • Other fuel leaks reported where owners claim problem may relate to the fuel expansion tank or its hoses. • Vehicle suddenly accelerated. • Tire tread separation. Premature failure of the headlight, taillight, turning signal, driveshaft, front and rear brake pad and rotor, tailgate struts, window switches, and door locks. • Turn signal bulbs are scorched and plastic melted. • Total loss of braking ability. • Inappropriate placement of the tailgate handle causes one to pull the tailgate close to one's face, causing nose injury. • Brakes didn't work on an incline after vehicle stalled out. **1999**—Electrical short caused under-hood fire. • Another fire occurred as vehicle was backing into a parking space. • Airbags deployed inadvertently while car was in Park. • Vehicle suddenly accelerated while parking. • Accelerator pedal became stuck when passing another vehicle on the highway. • Several incidents where electrical switches continually malfunction, console and console knobs are hot to the touch, and tapes have melted in the tape deck. • Chronic short circuits of headlights and turn signal lights, leading to lights constantly burning out; wires melted in turn signal socket. • Engine wire harness cracked and fell apart; shorted out near engine and radiator. • Fuel pump leaks and other unspecified leaks from the gas tank area. • Fuel tank wouldn't accept fuel. • Fuel line sprayed small amounts of fuel from impact with a rock. It should have some kind of protective shield. • Tire tread separation. • Transmission grinding and vibration when underway. • Suddenly stalled while turning. • Steering wheel locks up when making a left turn. • Total brake failure and excessive brake fade after successive braking. • Defective steering rack replaced by dealer. • Front wheel fell off the axle. • Sudden ball joint failure also causes premature tire wear. • Chronic front end shimmy. • Subframe bushing problem. • Clunking sound when automatic transmission is put into Reverse. • Power windows operate erratically. **2000**—Severe glare onto windshield from beige dash. • Airbags failed to deploy. • Chronic stalling; refuses to accelerate on turns. • Signal light blown; housing melted. • Excessive front-end vibration, accompanied by a thumping or humming sound. • Broken right front ball bearing. • Brakes fail to stop car when applied shortly after start-up. • When stopped on an incline, vehicle will roll back even though transmission is set in Drive. • Front head restraints block view, and front seat belt retractor locks unexpectedly. • Poorly anchored fuel filler could spill fuel in an accident. **2001**—Engine compartment electrical fire. • Fuel tank leakage. • Vehicle doesn't track in a straight line. • Rough terrain causes vehicle to bounce and veer off in one direction. • Vehicle jolts forward when accelerator pedal is depressed.

Secret Warranties/Service Tips/TSBs

All models/years: Check the valve cover nuts at every servicing interval to prevent oil leakage. • New steering components will reduce power steering knocking. • AC evaporator odours can be controlled by installing a new fan control module. • Tips on silencing noise from the manual front seats. **All models: 1992–98**—Oil pump leaks are usually due to loose pump retaining screws. **1997–99**—Rear axle whining countermeasures. • Automatic transmission final drive whining correction tips. • Upgraded rear brake pads to reduce grinding. • Upgraded weather stripping to reduce upper windshield moulding noise. • Installation of protective covers for door locks. • Improvements for door handle operation in cold weather. **1998**—Service Campaign #83 provides for the free replacement of faulty AC compressors. Service Campaign #83A and 83B provide for the free replacement of the front panel to prevent it from interfering with the AC. **S80: 1999**—Uneven throttle. **1999–2000**—Automatic transmission shudder during upshift. **1999–2001**—New rear brake pads have been developed to reduce vibration. • Power seat movement on acceleration and deceleration. • Loose A-pillar trim. • Subframe bushing knocking noise. **2000**—Free engine oil grate inspection.

900 series, S80, S90, V90 Profile

	1996	1997	1998	1999	2000	2001	2002	2003
Cost Price ($)								
960	46,400	47,400	—	—	—	—	—	—
S90	—	—	47,400	—	—	—	—	—
V90	—	—	49,075	—	—	—	—	—
S80	—	—	—	49,995	55,995	54,395	54,395	54,895
Used Values ($)								
960 A	12,000	15,500	—	—	—	—	—	—
960 Y	10,000	13,000	—	—	—	—	—	—
S90 A	—	—	19,500	—	—	—	—	—
S90 Y	—	—	17,000	—	—	—	—	—
V90 A	—	—	20,000	—	—	—	—	—
V90 Y	—	—	17,500	—	—	—	—	—
S80 A	—	—	—	17,000	21,500	29,000	36,000	42,000
S80 Y	—	—	—	15,500	19,500	27,000	34,500	40,000
Reliability	④	③	③	③	③	④	④	④
Crash Safety								
960	—	④	—	—	—	—	—	—
S80	—	—	—	—	—	⑤	⑤	⑤
Side (S80)	—	—	—	—	—	⑤	⑤	⑤
Offset (S80)	—	—	—	—	⑤	⑤	⑤	⑤
Head Restraints								
960/S90	—	⑤	—	—	—	—	—	—
S80	—	—	—	⑤	⑤	⑤	⑤	⑤
Rollover Resistance	—	—	—	—	—	—	—	⑤

SPORTS CARS

There are two kinds of cars in this category: the traditional two-seater roadster, styled much like the MGB of the early '70s, Mazda's Miata, or, in the extreme, the Chevrolet Corvette; and sporty cars, such as coupes and hatchbacks, that offer sportier styling, performance, and handling than their entry-level versions. Plus, they are often more versatile and cheaper to maintain than "pure," traditional sports cars. Honda's Si and the Ford Mustang GT are two examples of this kind of sporty car. Other notable examples covered elsewhere in this guide: the Audi TT (a stylish Golf in drag); BMW Z3 (a looker that lacks the precise steering of a Miata); BMW Z4 (better steering and an upgraded suspension that equals the Boxster); Mazda6 (plenty of horsepower to challenge VW's Passat and throws in a stick-shift not found with Accord and Camry); and Jaguar X-Type (stiff-riding, doesn't handle as well as an Audi A4, hampered by a low-grade engine, and uses poor-quality parts).

The Internet offers a comprehensive forum that goes into numbing detail as to what makes a good sports car at *www.sportscarforums.com*. Different cars are rated, service tips are given, and the age-old feud between Camaro/Firebird and Mustang owners is omnipresent.

Having owned a Mustang, I feel the Camaro or Firebird (above) is a much better starter sports car. It's more forgiving in its handling and has fewer quality issues. Plus, the "rust gremlins" won't snack on your GM as much.

Most sports cars, or "high-performance vehicles" as they're euphemistically named, don't offer the comfort or reliability of a Hyundai Tiburon or Toyota Celica. Instead, they sacrifice reliability, interior space, and a comfortable suspension for speed, superior road handling, and attractive styling. They also need a whole slew of expensive high-performance packages, because many entry-level sports cars aren't very sporty in their basic form. Remember, too, that sports cars often have serious accident damage that may not have been repaired properly, resulting in serious tracking problems because of a bent chassis.

You should find many fully loaded sporty cars at a fraction of their original cost. Sports cars, on the other hand, will probably still cost much more than they're worth. Remember, most models that have been taken off the market—like the Toyota Supra, Nissan 300ZX, and Chevrolet Corvette ZR1—aren't likely to become collectors' cars with soaring resale values. In fact, discontinued Japanese sports cars like the Nissan 1600 haven't done nearly as well as some of the British roadsters taken off the market at about the same time.

The recently dropped 2002 GM Camaro and Firebird are a special case. Not only are they relatively reliable and cheap to maintain, but their resale prices have remained reasonable and there's plenty of used stock to choose from. But, don't expect them to appreciate in value anytime soon (although the early muscle versions are holding their own).

Why do they do it? Mazda's Miata and RX-8 horsepower ratings didn't need to be "boosted" to snare shoppers.

Horsepower hijinks

Sports car buffs usually equate performance thrills with high horsepower ratings, even though there are many other handling features that need to be considered. Nevertheless, automakers are just as fixated upon horsepower and aren't above falsifying the figures to get a leg up on the competition. In 1999, Ford suckered over 5,000 Mustang SVT Cobra owners with 270-hp Cobras that they claimed had 320 horses. Two years later, Ottawa's Competition Bureau found Hyundai had boosted its ratings between 4 and 9 percent on its entire lineup for over a decade and that Kia (owned by Hyundai) 2001–02 model figures were suspect, as well. Again, in 2001, Mazda claimed that the Miata's horsepower had jumped from 140 to 155. When owners found the 2001 version was no quicker than the 2000 model, Mazda quickly revised its numbers down to 142.

But, Mazda is still playing with horsepower figures: Its 2004 RX-8 is less powerful than originally thought. First presented as having a 250-hp engine, the number was dropped slightly, to 247. Then, Mazda restated its horsepower rating to a still-optimistic 238 and offered customers $500 and free basic maintenance for four years or 80,465 km (50,000 mi.), or a refund.

SPORTS CAR RATINGS

Recommended

General Motors Camaro, Firebird,
 Trans Am (1997–2002)
Honda Prelude (1993–2001)

Hyundai Tiburon (2000–03)
Mazda Miata (1990–2003)
Toyota Celica (2001–03; 1995–99)

Above Average

DaimlerChrysler Avenger, Sebring
 (2002–03)
Honda Prelude (1985–92)

Hyundai Tiburon (1997–99)
Toyota Celica (2000; 1986–94)

Average

DaimlerChrysler Avenger, Sebring
 (2000–01)
DaimlerChrysler Laser, Talon
 (1996–98)

Ford Mustang (1996–2003)
General Motors Camaro, Firebird,
 Trans Am (1994–96)
General Motors Corvette (1997–2003)

Below Average

DaimlerChrysler Avenger, Sebring
 (1995–99)
Ford Mustang (1980–95)

General Motors Camaro, Firebird,
 Trans Am (1992–93)
General Motors Corvette (1994–96)

Not Recommended

DaimlerChrysler Laser, Talon
 (1990–95)
Ford Cobra (1999–2003)

General Motors Camaro, Firebird,
 Trans Am (1982–91)
General Motors Corvette (1977–93)

DaimlerChrysler

AVENGER, SEBRING

RATING: Above Average (2002–03); Average (2000–01); Below Average (1995–99). The Avenger and its more luxuriously appointed Sebring twin have had fewer factory-related defects than other new Chrysler designs, though this is faint praise indeed. Drive a hard bargain, because the money you save will be eaten up in transmission, engine head gasket, and AC evaporator repair bills, unless you get the 7-year powertrain warranty, threaten small claims court action, or use your service manager successfully in getting "goodwill" assistance. The Sebring convertible is an attractively styled bargain ragtop. **Maintenance/Repair costs:** Average. Avenger repairs must be done by a Chrysler dealer. **Parts:** Average cost and availability. **Best alternatives:** Ford Mustang or Probe, GM Camaro or Firebird, Hyundai Tiburon, Mazda Miata, Nissan 240SX, and Toyota Celica. **Online help:** *www.autosafety.org/ autodefects.html; www.datatown.com/chrysler; www.wam.umd.edu/~gluckman/ Chrysler/index.html; www.daimlerchryslervehicleproblems.com;* and *intrepidhorrorstories.blogspot.com.*

Strengths and weaknesses: These coupes, sedans, and convertibles are good buys mainly because they've had fewer new-model "teething" problems than other Chrysler-built vehicles. Sebring is a reasonably priced luxury model equipped with standard amenities, including AC, bucket seats, and a tilt steering wheel, while the Stratus fills the sporty coupe niche with standard tinted glass and an awesome sound system.

These front-drives use powertrains and platforms from Mitsubishi's Eclipse and Galant and also share most safety features and mechanical components, including standard dual airbags and a 150-hp 2.4L 4-banger along with an optional 200-hp 3.0L V6.

Vehicle history: 1995–99—Minor restyling touches and the dropping of the 4-cylinder engine in mid-1999. **2000**—Sebring convertible's suspension was retuned to give a more comfortable ride, and the same year's base Avenger was given additional standard equipment—notably, the ES's 2.5L V6 and automatic transmission. **2001**—The redesigned Sebring added a sedan, a more powerful V6, and a premium sound system. The Avenger was dropped. **2002**—Sebrings were joined by a 200-hp 2.7L, V6 R/T sedan equipped with a manual 5-speed gearbox. **2003**—Addition of four-wheel disc brakes.

Acceleration is fairly good, though noisy, with the base 140-hp engine and a manual transmission; however, the optional V6 power plant is the engine of choice to overcome the power-hungry automatic transmission and to avoid a persistent 4-cylinder engine head gasket defect affecting all model years through 1999. Handling is better than average, and the ride is generally comfortable, except for a bit of choppiness due to the firm suspension.

Mitsubishi quality control, although much better than Chrysler, has slipped a bit as of late and is compounded by the increased use of poor-quality generic Chrysler parts and poor sales. Now that Mitsubishi has set up its own dealer network in Canada, parts availability and servicing should improve.

Owners single out the automatic transmission failures, grinding when shifting, shuddering from a stop, and defaulting to Second gear; 4-cylinder engine head gasket failures; engine oil leaks caused by broken plastic guard; loss of steering and a clanking or rattling heard when turning over rough pavement; premature suspension replacement, brake wear and brake failures; ignition, electrical system, and power control module (PCM) glitches; sunroof malfunctions; and sloppy body construction (water leaks and lots of wind noise) as the areas most needing attention. Would you believe the driver's seat motor burns out because it doesn't have a fuse? Replacement cost: $2,000!

The convertible top is prone to fly off on early models, leaks water and air, and operates erratically. A faulty window regulator allows the window to run off its track. Poor design and sloppy construction allows water into the vehicle when window is partly opened; rear windshield sealant lets water leak into vehicle; wheel rims are easily bent and leak air from normal driving; there's excessive brake dust; a black goo oozes from body panels and the undercarriage; side door mouldings melt; and the airbag coating peels.

Safety summary: All models: 1995–99—Mitsubishi-built Avengers have had few safety-related incidents reported to NHTSA. Sebring safety failures over the same period were frequent and serious. **Sebring: 1996–1999**—Upgraded engine head gasket. **1996**—Frequent reports of the convertible top flying off, fires igniting inside the driver and passenger doors and shift console, key trapped in ignition, and transmission jumping out of gear while in Park with key removed. • Engine head gasket failure reports are more frequent, as are transmission defects, ABS failures, brake rotor warpage, and sudden failure of suspension and steering components. • New problems: water leaks into the interior and collects under the back seat cushion and on the floor; carpeting may cause the steering to lock up; horn doesn't blow; digital mileage and gearshift screen goes blank; rotten-egg smell; electrical shorts cause the car to suddenly shut down. **1997**—Transmission failures have increased, sudden acceleration due to the throttle jamming is still a danger, brake failures and frequent rotor and pad replacement continue, seat belts frequently lock up, and owners report the transmission still permits the vehicle to roll away even though the lever was put into Park. • Trunk leaks, noisy steering, and an inadequate and hard-to-find spare tire also make this year's list. • Interestingly, head gasket failure reports have tapered off (too early to tell?). **1998**—More of the same old complaints. However, virtually no engine failures have been reported, but most of the same electrical short circuits, brake, and airbag complaints, as enumerated above, have continued. • There has also been a greater number of reports concerning sudden acceleration, loss of steering control due to the floormat blocking the steering column, bent wheel rims causing tire blowouts, seat belt lock-up, and alternator/battery failures. • One new item: an unusually large number of complaints that the side door panel cladding falls off while cruising. **1999**—Vehicle caught fire after hitting bumper of other car at 8 km/h (5 mph). • Other fire reported from a leaking fuel hose. • Front airbags failed to deploy upon impact. • Many incidents where the throttle stuck while engaging Reverse. • Premature replacement of the lower lateral sway bar. • Automatic transmission rebuild after 61,000 km (38,000 mi.). • Split transmission line. • Delayed, noisy transmission shifting. • Slipped into Reverse and rolled downhill, despite being in Park with ignition off. • Constant velocity joint flew off in heavy traffic on Interstate. • Brakes don't grab sufficiently; complete loss of braking due to loss of vacuum. • Defective rear defroster clip. • Windshield wipers suddenly stop working. • Convertible boot flew off while vehicle underway. • Brake failure and extended stopping distance caused by defective wheel speed sensor, modulator, or master cylinder and brake pad disintegrating, causing rotor scoring. • Automatic transmission slipped out of gear while vehicle was cruising at 120 km/h; suddenly went to 50 km/h. • Transmission fluid leakage through a crack in the transmission case. • Driver's seat belt often unlatches and seatback side latch may fail. **2001**—Brake failure accompanied by sudden, unintended acceleration. • Brake caliper bolt fell off. • Brake and accelerator pedals are too close to each other. • Window shattered when convertible top was lowered. **2002**—When putting vehicle into Reverse, it sometimes surges forward. • Engine stalls out after fill-ups. • Sudden brake failure. • Suspension feels loose at higher speeds when passing over bumps or potholes. • Steering wheel catches and pulls right when turning. • Back windows suddenly exploded. • Brake and gas pedals are too close together. • Coupes have the driver's seat set at an angle that's disorientating. **2003**—Sudden loss of steering. • Driver's airbag deployed for no reason. • Tapping brakes lock them up. • Rodents can get into the heater blower area. • Headlights dim and shut off intermittently.

Secret Warranties/Service Tips/TSBs

All models: 1995–97—Engine compartment popping or knocking may require an upgraded EGR valve. **1995–98**—Delayed transaxle engagement can be corrected by installing an upgraded trailing arm bushing. **1995–2001**—Front coil spring creak, pop, or squeak can be silenced by putting in coil spring insulators. • Intermittent loss of speed control can be prevented by installing new speed sensors. • Wind noise coming from the front windshield area is caused by wind lifting the windshield moulding at the glass. • Tips on reducing excessive front brake pulsation or shudder. • Paint delamination, peeling, or fading (see Part Two). **1997–99**—New software will prevent the transmission from shifting erratically or falling into a Second gear "limp" mode. **Sebring: 1996–99**—Upgraded engine head gasket. **1996–2000**—Steering wheel clunk or rattle. • Wet carpet (convertible). **1996–2001**—Inoperative rear window defogger. **2001**—Rough 2.7L engine idle. • Automatic transmission bump, sag, and surge. Rear suspension squawk. **2001–02**—Moderate to severe highway engine surge. • Exhaust rattle, vibration. • Low or no cabin heat. • Loose, warped front door trim panel. **2001–03**—Erratic AC operation. **2001–04**—Suspension, body pop, or clunk noise. • Windows fogging. **2002**—Hard to remove fuel cap. **2003**—Horn blows on its own. • Rear brake clunk. **2003–04**—Delayed gear engagement. • Harsh downshifts.

Avenger, Sebring Profile

	1996	1997	1998	1999	2000	2001	2002	2003
Cost Price ($)								
Avenger	18,954	18,780	19,280	20,360	—	—	—	—
Avenger V6	22,544	23,820	24,320	23,545	—	—	—	—
Sebring	19,514	21,420	21,500	23,380	26,525	—	—	—
Sebring V6	25,538	24,135	24,360	28,675	26,525	30,095	27,380	27,795
Convertible	25,210	27,030	27,530	—	32,585	33,595	33,580	—
Used Values ($)								
Avenger Ʌ	4,500	5,000	6,500	8,000	—	—	—	—
Avenger V	4,000	4,500	5,500	7,000	—	—	—	—

Avenger V6 ʌ	5,000	5,500	7,000	8,500	—	—	—	—
Avenger V6 v	4,500	5,000	6,000	7,500	—	—	—	—
Sebring ʌ	4,500	5,500	7,000	9,000	—	—	—	—
Sebring v	4,000	4,500	6,000	7,500	—	—	—	—
Sebring V6 ʌ	5,000	6,000	7,500	9,500	11,500	14,500	16,000	18,000
Sebring V6 v	4,500	5,500	6,500	8,000	10,000	13,500	14,500	16,500
Convertible ʌ	7,000	8,500	10,500	—	16,500	19,000	22,000	—
Convertible v	6,000	7,000	9,000	—	15,000	17,000	20,000	—

Reliability	❷	❷	③	③	③	③	④	④
Crash Safety (Avenger)	⑤	e	—	—	—	—	—	—
Sebring	—	(⑤)	—	—	—	④	④	④
Sebring 4d	—	—	—	—	—	⑤	⑤	⑤
Sebring cvt.	—	④	—	—	—	③	③	③
Side (Sebring)	—	—	—	—	—	③	③	③
Sebring 4d	—	—	—	—	—	③	③	③
Sebring cvt.	—	—	—	—	—	③	③	③
Offset	—	—	—	—	—	③	③	③
Head Restraints (Avenger)	—	❷	—	❷	—	—	—	—
Sebring (F)	—	❶	—	③	—	❷	③	③
Sebring (Rear)	—	—	—	❷	—	❶	❷	❷
Rollover Resistance	—	—	—	—	—	⑤	⑤	⑤
2d	—	—	—	—	—	—	—	④

LASER, TALON   ★★★

RATING: Average (1996–98); Not Recommended (1990–95). **Maintenance/ Repair costs:** Higher than average, but routine repairs can be done practically anywhere. Make sure the engine timing chain is inspected regularly and check for head gasket failures—I've received about a dozen reports of owners having to pay huge repair bills for new engines. **Parts:** Good parts availability. Dealers have had some trouble adequately servicing high-tech components, and parts are a bit more expensive than other cars in this class. **Best alternatives:** Ford Mustang or Probe, GM Camaro or Firebird, Hyundai Tiburon, Mazda Miata, and Toyota Celica. **Online help:** *www.autosafety.org/autodefects.html* and *www.daimlerchryslervehicleproblems.com.*

Strengths and weaknesses: These sporty Mitsubishi-made cars combine high performance, low price, and reasonable durability. The base 1.8L engine is adequate and the suspension is comfortable, although a bit soft. The optional 16-valve, turbocharged 2.0L comes with a firmer suspension and gives more horsepower for the dollar than most other front-drive sports coupes, without much turbo lag. The 16-valve Talon and its 4X4 variant are at the top of the trim list and provide five more horses than the turbocharged TSi. The 5-speed manual is the gearbox of choice. Torque steer makes the car appear to try to twist out of your hands when all 195 turbocharged horses are unleashed.

Vehicle history: Talon: 1992—Restyled. **1993**—Underpowered (93 hp) base DL debuts. **1995**—More power (140–210 hp), dual airbags, and restyled. **1996**—Upgraded sound system. **1997**—New front and rear ends. **1998**—Depowered airbags. **Laser: 1992**—Restyled front and rear ends.

Beginning with the 1990–94 models, owners report glitches with the 1.8L engine and electrical system, driveline vibrations, premature brake wear and excessive noise, and poor fit and finish that includes water leakage into the interior and paint delamination. Some problems reported with 1995–98 versions were unstable idling, poor idling, and reduced rpm when the AC is running; hard starts and stalling in cold weather; cold-weather transmission shift delays (2–3 and 3–4) that take up to two minutes; transmission defaults into Second gear (limp-in mode); frequent wheel alignments; a tendency to drift or lead to the right; speed control undershoot or overshoot; chronic electrical system, brake, and transmission failures; false theft alarm; centre exhaust pipe heat shield buzz; door buzz and rattle; misadjusted door glass and poor windshield sealing, causing water leaks and wind noise; noisy clutch pedal; interior window film buildup; headliner sagging; power seat switch sticking; stress marks on the quarter trim panel; buzz or rattle from the rear quarter trim; inoperative, noisy, and jerky sunroof operation; faulty lever latch pin; and the sunroof may open by itself.

Safety summary: All models/years: Standard brakes often lock up or require long stopping distances. Choose the optional ABS. • Head restraints block rear visibility. • Airbags often fail to deploy. **All models: 1995–98**—Most of the following problems reappear each year in NHTSA records: engine and fuel tank fires; fuel leakage after recall repairs; sudden acceleration due to jammed throttle; chronic transmission failures that include transfer case leakage after recall repairs (automatic and manual transaxles), causing sudden wheel lock-up; wheels fall off; engine timing belt breakage (100,000–120,000 km); loss of steering caused by going through a puddle of water or the steering belt slipping off the pulley; collapse of suspension and steering components (front control arms and ball joints); frequent replacement of brake pads and warped rotors; electrical system failures; faulty door locks and windows; water leakage into interior; horn won't work or self-activates; ABS and Check Engine lights come on for no reason.

Secret Warranties/Service Tips/TSBs

All models: 1993–99—Paint delamination, peeling, or fading (see Part Two). • A rotten-egg odour coming from the exhaust may be the result of a malfunctioning catalytic converter, which may be covered by the emissions warranty. **1995–97**—Engine compartment popping or knocking may require an upgraded EGR valve. **1995–98**—Front coil spring creak, pop, or squeak can be silenced by putting in coil spring insulators. • Delayed transaxle engagement can be corrected by installing an upgraded trailing arm bushing. **1995–99**—Intermittent loss of speed control can be prevented by installing new speed sensors. • Wind noise coming from the front windshield area is caused by wind lifting the windshield moulding at the glass. • Tips on reducing excessive front brake pulsation or shudder. **1997–99**—A light knocking noise from the rear shock area may mean you need to install various upgraded rear shock components. • New software will prevent the transmission from shifting erratically or falling into a Second-gear "limp" mode. **1998**—Erratic automatic transmission performance can be corrected by installing new software.

Laser, Talon Profile

	1991	1992	1993	1994	1995	1996	1997	1998
Cost Price ($)								
Laser	13,000	13,735	14,145	14,145	—	—	—	—
Turbo RS	14,900	15,820	16,310	16,310	—	—	—	—
Talon	15,505	16,205	14,475	16,000	19,425	20,695	19,885	20,290
Talon TSI	18,100	19,365	19,365	19,975	28,360	29,985	30,225	30,675
Used Values ($)								
Laser ▲	2,500	3,000	3,500	4000	—	—	—	—
Laser ▼	2,000	2,500	3,000	3,500	—	—	—	—
Turbo RS ▲	3,000	3,500	4,000	4,500	—	—	—	—
Turbo RS ▼	2,500	3,000	3,500	4,000	—	—	—	—
Talon ▲	2,500	3,000	3,500	4,000	4,500	5,000	6,500	8,000
Talon ▼	2,500	2,500	3,000	3,500	4,000	4,500	6,000	7,000
Talon TSI ▲	3,500	4,500	5,000	5,500	6,500	7,500	9,000	10,500
Talon TSI ▼	3,000	4,000	4,500	5,000	5,500	6,500	8,000	9,000
Reliability	❷	❷	❷	❷	❷	❷	④	⑤
Crash Safety	—	—	—	—	—	—	④	—
Side	—	—	—	—	—	—	—	❶

Ford

MUSTANG, COBRA ★★☆

RATING: *Mustang:* Average (1996–2003); Below Average (1980–95); *Cobra:* Not Recommended (1999–2003). Here's the problem: Ford has alienated its parts suppliers and reduced reliability through unrealistic price-cutting and last-minute, poorly thought-out component changes. Furthermore, Mustangs don't perform well on wet roadways and they have had a frighteningly high number of safety-related mechanical failures (chronic stalling, especially). Additionally, new crash data indicates the vehicles may be fire prone following a collision at moderate speeds. GM's Camaro and Firebird are the Mustang's traditional competition as far as performance is concerned and represent the better buy. Ford has the price advantage, with a base Mustang costing a bit less than the cheapest Camaro, but it lags from a performance standpoint. The GM models also offer more sure-footed acceleration, crisper handling, standard ABS, a 6-speed transmission, and more comfortable rear seats. All 4-cylinder Mustangs should be shunned. **Maintenance/Repair costs:** Average, particularly because repairs can be done anywhere. **Parts:** Average cost, and parts are often sold for much less through independent suppliers. Some parts are continually back ordered, particularly if involved in recall repairs (cruise control components, for example). **Best alternatives:** Ford Probe, GM Camaro or Firebird, Hyundai Tiburon, Mazda Miata, and Toyota Celica. **Online help:** *www.autosafety.org/autodefects.html; forums.mustangworks.com; www.flamingfords.info; www.tgrigsby.com/views/ford.htm; www.antiauthority.com/cobra/service/#links; www.flatratetech.com;* and *www.blueovalnews.com.*

Strengths and weaknesses: This is definitely not a family car. For example, a light rear end makes the car dangerously unstable on wet roads or when cornering at high speeds. But for those who want a sturdy and stylish second car, or who don't need room in the back or standard ABS, the 1999–2000 Mustang is a pretty good sports car buy.

Base models come equipped with a host of luxury and convenience items, which can be a real bargain once the base price has sufficiently depreciated—say, after the first three or four years. Off-lease models are particularly good buys these days.

1990–93

There are three body styles to choose from—a coupe, a coupe hatchback, and a ragtop—and two engines were offered—a wimpy 2.3L 4-banger and a 5.0L V8. A driver-side airbag was a standard feature. 1991 models added 15 more horses to the base engine (105 hp), upgraded convertible tops, and a brake/shift interlock. The following year's models were unchanged carryovers; however, the '93 model year saw the debut of the high-performance Mustang Cobra, sporting a 245-hp V8 and marketed in limited numbers in Canada.

Mustangs have never been very reliable cars, and the 1990–93 models were particularly troublesome. Yet when failures do occur, they aren't difficult or expensive to fix. The first Mustang, launched in 1964 and now worth more than $30,000, had serious rusting, electrical, and suspension problems. And guess what? Over four decade later, Mustangs still have glitch-plagued electrical systems and electronic modules that are constantly malfunctioning, transmissions that jump from Park to Reverse, and a base suspension and front brakes that wear out in the blink of an eye.

The less said about the infamous 2.3L 4-cylinder engine, the better. The V6 is also failure-prone (head gaskets, again), leaving the V8 engine with a definite performance and reliability edge. Turbocharged models aren't recommended because of their frequent and expensive mechanical breakdowns. If you want high-performance action, you'll have to pay a premium—and be prepared for some monstrous repair bills and white-knuckle acceleration on wet roadways. Sport trim models feature an upgraded suspension and wheel package that improves handling considerably.

Keep in mind that the 3.8L 6-cylinder engine has begun to tally up a record number of head gasket failures around the 150,000 km mark. Other problem areas: The front brakes, fuel pumps, and front suspension remain consistent weak spots, and MacPherson struts and various steering components are likely to wear out before their time. The parking brake cable also seizes easily. The EEC IV engine computer can be temperamental, and electrical problems are common. Assembly quality is still not on par with Japanese vehicles.

1994–2003

These models got more powerful engines, better brakes, additional airbags, and a more rigid chassis to reduce rattles and water leaks (didn't work).

Unfortunately, Ford's performance- and safety-related problems continue to be carried over year after year (see "Safety summary"). Engines and transmissions are even more unreliable than before: Both the V6 and V8 have a propensity for chronic surging and stalling; blowing engine intake manifold and head gaskets; failed motor mounts; ticking and rattling at 3000 rpm until car shifts into Second gear; automatic transmission shifts poorly, especially from First to Second gear; differential howling or whining (ring and pinion failure); engine dies when decelerating; fuel system glitches, highlighted by frequent fuel injector malfunctions; faulty differential carrier bearings; and prematurely worn clutch pressure plates. Owners also frequently complain of electrical short circuits causing instrument panel shutdown; the early replacement of brake rotors, pads, and calipers; and unbelievably poor fit and finish highlighted by paint defects, premature rusting, wind noise, water leaks, and clunks and rattles.

Vehicle history: 1993—Cobra debuts. **1994**—The 4-banger replaced with a V6, four-wheel disc brakes, dual airbags, a more rigid chassis. No more hatchbacks. Mustangs now carry a base 3.8L V6 and an optional 4.6L V8. In addition, the high-performance limited edition Cobra variation delivers 90 more horses than the stock 4.6L V8 offers. The single and twin cam V8 options make the Mustang a powerful—if a bit unsophisticated—street machine. V6 models are an acceptable compromise, even though the engines fail to deliver the gobs of power most performance enthusiasts expect. **1996**—A 4.6L V8 with upgraded spark plugs, and the Cobra received a 305-hp variant of the same power plant. **1998**—GT got a 10-hp performance boost. **1999**—Got fresh styling and another horsepower boost. That year, the V6 models also got suspension and steering gear upgrades; Ford also admitted that its 1999 SVT Cobra delivered up to 50 hp less than the 320-hp advertised. **2000**—Improved child safety seat anchoring. **2001**—GT models received hood and side scoops and larger wheels. All models got an upgraded centre console, blacked-out headlights, and spoilers. **2002**—New 16-inch alloy wheels; sporty Cobra stays home this year. **2003**—Three 4.6L V8 models: the GT with 260 hp, the new Mach 1 with 305 hp, and the 390-hp supercharged SVT Cobra.

Safety summary: All models/years: Regularly equipped Mustangs, like most rear-drive Fords, don't handle sharp curves or wet pavement very well. The rear end swings out suddenly, and the car tends to spin uncontrollably. Traction is easily lost and braking is hardly reassuring. • Serious doubts have also been raised regarding the Mustang's fuel system failing safety integrity standards and the convertible's doors tendency to jam shut in a 57 km/h frontal collision. • Transmission allows vehicle to roll away when parked on an incline; emergency brake disengages. • Airbag failed to deploy; inadvertent airbag deployment. • Sudden acceleration due to a stuck throttle. • Brake failure and premature replacement of the brake master cylinder. • Excessive vehicle vibration when accelerating. • Side windows fall off their tracks. **1996**—Carried-over defects include mostly braking, automatic transmission, and engine cooling problems (many allegations that the plastic intake manifold ruptures under pressure from the cooling system and may be a causative agent for an increase in head gasket failures). • Other repeats: airbag problems, stalling, sudden acceleration (now appears to be cruise control-related), ABS failures, frequent brake rotor and pad replacement, fuel tank leakage and fuel line fire, sudden steering loss, and water leaking into lights. • New problems: broken rear sway bar behind rear mounting bolt, excessive front-end vibrations, timing chain and fan belt failures, and Check Engine light coming on due to a defective evaporator canister solenoid. • Some airbag injuries traced to the use of sodium azide, the airbag propellent; apparently, it changes to the very toxic sodium hydroxide (caustic soda) when detonated. **1997**—Returning defects: engine overheating caused by a defective intake manifold; many more reports of manual and automatic transmission failures (popping out of gear, grinding, clutch vibrations, no reverse of 2–3 gear shift); ABS and parking brake failures; power-steering pump; seat belt fails to retract; sway bar breakage; sudden acceleration; and fuel leakage at fuel tank connection. • New problems: differential rear ring and pinion gear; AC compressor; hood pops open; front brake line separation; and front lower control arm/ball joint separation. **1998–99**—Fuel tank leaks. • Engine compartment fires. • Hood flew up unexpectedly while underway. • Frequent stalling, hesitation, and loses power. • No airbag deployment; airbag-induced injuries. • Parking brake doesn't hold (traced to a broken ratchet assembly). • Brake pedal goes to floor without braking. • Steering system failure. • Right ball joint fractured, causing wheel to turn inward. • Tire sidewall tread separation. • Seat belt tightens up continually. • Other repeats of '97 problems: transmission, braking, and engine failures. • New problems: fire ignited in the centre console and dash areas, defective seat belt retractor and poor design allows belt to slip out of guide, stalling caused by fuel pump or fuel relay cut-off switch failure, and original equipment tire blowouts (sidewall splits). **2000**—There's an unusually large number of safety complaints recorded by NHTSA for year 2000 models. • Fumes from airbag deployment made passengers ill and temporarily blinded them. • Alternator melted battery wires; car caught on fire. • Automatic transmission sticks in Reverse. • Convertible top unlatches and flips up while underway. • Hood flew up. • Head restraints sit too low. • Many reports of rear axle failures. • Brake calipers and lines were replaced to correct brake fluid leakage. • Multiple function switch failure causes headlights to suddenly go out. **2001**—Lower control arm came off. • Sudden brake lock-up. • Loose brake rotor responsible for collision. • Foot hits fuse box when engaging clutch pedal. • Seat belt retracted unexpectedly, nearly choking occupant, who had to be cut free. • Driver's seat rocks back when driving. **2002**—Fire ignited in the wiring harness under dash area. • Chronic stalling when coasting, braking, or when clutch is depressed. • Serpentine belt came off causing loss of power steering and brakes. • Wheel lug nuts fell off. • Sudden acceleration. • Sudden loss of steering when making a left-hand turn. • Car left on an incline with transmission in Park and motor shut off rolled down after 10 minutes and hit a tree. • Airbags failed to deploy in a frontal collision. • Emergency brake ratchet assembly broke, making mechanism inoperable. • Gas spills out of fuel tank due to clamps not sufficiently tightened. • Left front wheel fell off when the lower control arm and ball joint became loose. • Defective transmission spider gear. • Stuck gas pedal. • Seat belt continually tightens up when worn. • A light rear end makes the car dangerously unstable on wet roads or when cornering at moderate speeds. **2003**—Poorly designed speaker wires caused rear seat fire. • Airbags failed to deploy. • Gas pedal sticks. • Chronic stalling when decelerating. • Automatic transmission failures. • Loss of brakes. • Seat belt ratchets tighten. • Premature Goodyear tire blowout. • Water leaks through side windows.

Secret Warranties/Service Tips/TSBs

All models/years: Paint delamination, peeling, or fading (see Part Two). • Ford 7-year "goodwill" warranty extensions usually cover engine and transmission components. • Cold hesitation when accelerating, rough idle, long crank times, and stalling may all signal the need to clean out excessive intake valve deposits. These problems also may result from the use of fuels that have low volatility, such as high-octane premium blends. • Excessive oil consumption is likely caused by leaking gaskets, poor sealing of the lower intake manifold, defective intake and exhaust valve stem seals, or worn piston rings; install new guide-mounted valve stem seals for a better fit, as well as new piston rings with improved oil control. • A buzz or rattle from the exhaust system may be caused by a loose heat shield. • A thumping or clacking heard from the front brakes signals the need to machine the front disc brake rotors. **All models: 1985–2002**—Repeated heater core failures. **1994–97**—An erratic or prolonged 1–2 shift is likely caused by a defective aluminum piston. **1994–98**—Loose rocker panel mouldings. **1994–2000**—Hood may be difficult to close. **1996**—Stalling or hard starts may be due to the idle air control valve sticking. **1996–97**—The engine's lower intake manifold side and front cover gaskets might leak coolant, a problem that can cause overheating and severe engine damage (see following letter).

Director   Ford Motor Company
Vehicle Services and Programs   P.O. Box 1904
Ford Customer Service Division   Dearborn, MI 48121-1904

January, 2000

Ford Motor Company is providing a no-charge Service Program, Number 99B29, to owners of certain 1996 and 1997 model year Mustang, Thunderbird, Cougar, and 1997 F-Series vehicles equipped with 3.8L or 4.2L engines.

What Is The Reason For This Program?	The affected vehicles may experience engine coolant leaks at the engine front cover gasket; this could cause severe engine damage if not corrected. To avoid engine damage, you should make an appointment to have this service performed on your vehicle at your Ford or Lincoln Mercury Dealer as soon as possible.
No Charge Service:	At no charge to you, your dealer will replace the engine from cover gasket with a redesigned gasket and change the engine oil and filter. This service will reduce the likelihood of coolant leaks at the engine front cover, and will help avoid the potential inconvenience of breakdowns and costly engine repairs.
	Your vehicle is eligible for this program until March 31, 2001, regardless of mileage.

Ford asks owners to call their dealers immediately to have the gasket replaced, even if they have not experienced any problem. Consumers who have already had the repair will be reimbursed for their expenses.

1996–2001—Manual transmission may stick in Reverse, or pop out of Reverse. **1997–99**—Delayed or no 2–3 upshift may be caused by a leaking accumulator seal. • Road noise or dust/water leaks in the luggage compartment can be fixed by sealing the wheelhouse flange. **1997–2000**—Automatic transmission fluid leaks at the radiator can be stopped by installing an o-ring on the transmission oil cooler fitting. **1998–99**—Tips for spotting abnormal ABS braking noise. **1999–2000**—An erratically operating front windshield wiper probably has a faulty multifunction switch. Replace it under warranty, says TSB #00-9-6. • Same thing goes for an inaccurate speedometer. **1998–2002**—Guidelines for replacing defective ignition lock cylinders. **1999–2001**—Troubleshooting a downshift clunk and a driveline whine upon coastdown. **1999–2003**—Cracked roof ditch material. **2000–01**—First gear ticking. **2001–02**—Some vehicles may exhibit a FEAD belt jump-off toss with vehicles equipped with a 4.6L engine (see following bulletin).

Accessory Drive Belt—Slips Off Pulley When Wet

Article No. 02-5-4

03/01/02

MODELS: 2001–02 CROWN VICTORIA, MUSTANG, GRAND MARQUIS, AND TOWN CAR

ACTION: Verify condition. Replace the Water Pump Pulley and/or Tensioner assembly as necessary.

2001–03—Wind noise from the A-pillar area. **2002**—Service tips for reports of premature engine failure. • Air leaks in the intake manifold or engine. • Ford has found that engine cylinder heads often still leak after having been repaired. • Engine runs roughly after stopping. • 4.6L engine oil leaks from the head gasket area. • Oil pressure gauge shows low oil or no oil. • 3.8L engine may run roughly at idle; same engine may cause AM radio speaker interference. • Automatic transmission fluid leak near the radiator. • Manual transmission clashes or grinds. • Transmission ticking heard when First gear is engaged. • Rear whine heard during coastdown from 100 km/h. • Vehicles equipped with a 5-speed manual transmission may stumble or hesitate when cold. • Driveline vibration; electrical problems include erratic operation of turn signals, hard starting, and illuminated ABS warning lamp. • A shorted coil/open PCM fuse may result in no-starts or rough running. • Climate control stays in the defrost mode. • Inoperative door window due to faulty window regulator; inoperative door glass. • Defective ignition switch lock cylinder. **2003–04**—Ford will install four revised hood scoop insulators (#2L7Z-9P686-AA) to eliminate a rattle noise emanating from the hood of the vehicle. **Cobra: 2003**—Defective engine cylinder heads or valve guides (replacement cylinder head part number is 3R2Z-6049-GA).

Mustang Profile

	1996	1997	1998	1999	2000	2001	2002	2003
Cost Price ($)								
Mustang LX/Coupe	18,595	19,795	22,595	20,995	21,195	22,275	22,795	22,990
Convertible	25,895	26,795	29,295	24,995	25,195	26,945	27,465	27,760
Used Values ($)								
Mustang LX/Coupe ▲	5,500	6,500	7,500	8,500	10,500	12,500	14,500	16,000
Mustang LX/Coupe ▼	4,500	5,500	6,500	7,500	9,000	11,000	13,000	15,000
Convertible ▲	7,500	8,500	10,500	13,000	14,500	16,500	19,000	22,000
Convertible ▼	7,000	7,500	9,000	11,500	13,000	15,000	18,000	20.500
Reliability	❷	❷	③	③	③	③	③	④
Crash Safety	④	④	⑤	④	④	⑤	⑤	⑤
Convertible	⑤	⑤	—	—	—	—	—	—
Side	—	—	③	③	③	③	③	③
Convertible	—	—	—	—	—	❷	❷	❷
Head restraints	—	❶	—	❶	—	❶	❶	③
Rear	—	—	—	—	—	—	—	❶
Rollover Resistance	—	—	—	—	—	—	—	⑤

General Motors

CAMARO, FIREBIRD, TRANS AM

RATING: Recommended (1997–2002); Average (1994–96); Below Average (1992–93); Not Recommended (1982–91). Camaro and Firebird were dropped for the 2003 model year. Dammit, GM should have axed its money-losing Saturn and Saab divisions and kept Oldsmobile and the Camaro and Firebird. Although more reliable than the Mustang, these cars have also elicited many safety-related complaints, including airbag deployment injuries, sudden acceleration, brake failures, and steering loss. Be especially wary of brake rotor warpage, requiring rotor replacement every two years (about a $300 job). Bargain hunter alert: The 1996 Camaro and Firebird are essentially the same as the more expensive 1997 versions. A V8-equipped Camaro or convertible is the best choice for retained value a few years down the road. But you can do quite well with a used base coupe equipped with the performance handling package and high-performance tires. GM's decision to stop production after the '92 model year isn't unlikely to affect the cars' resale values or parts supply. **Maintenance/Repair costs:** Average, and repairs can be done by any independent garage. **Parts:** Reasonably priced and easy to find. **Best alternatives:** Ford Mustang or Probe, Hyundai Tiburon, Mazda Miata, and Toyota Celica. **Online help:** *www.autosafety.org/autodefects.html* and *www.sportscarforums.com*.

Strengths and weaknesses: When compared with the Mustang, Camaros and Firebirds are better-performing rear-drive muscle cars that produce excellent crash protection scores and high resale values. They also take the lead over the Mustang with their standard ABS and slightly better reliability record. The Camaro and Firebird's overall performance varies a great deal depending on the engine, transmission, and suspension combination in each particular car. Base models equipped with the V6 power plant accelerate reasonably well, but high-performance enthusiasts will find them slow for sporty cars. Handling is compromised by poor traction on wet roads, minimal comfort, and a suspension that's too soft for high-speed cornering and too bone-jarring for smooth cruising. The Z28, IROC-Z, and Trans Am provide smart acceleration and handling, but at the expense of fuel economy.

Vehicle history: 1987—Relatively unchanged since its last redesign in 1982, a convertible was added. **1990**—A driver-side airbag, tilt steering wheel, tinted glass, intermittent wipers, and halogen headlamps. The IROC-Z debuted with a standard limited-slip differential and 16-inch alloy wheels. **1991**—V8-equipped Z28 returned after a 3-year hiatus and the IROC-Z was axed. **1993**—Totally redesigned and given a more aerodynamic body style. Dimensions were slightly enlarged, weight was added, power boosted, and the dashboard was reworked. Dual airbags and ABS also became standard safety features. Convertible dropped. **1994**—Convertible returned with an upgraded top and 6-speed gearbox. **1995**—Added a 3.8L V6 engine. **1996**—3.8L engine used as the base power plant, the 5.7L V8 gained 10 extra horses, and a new high-performance SS option was offered for the first time on the Z28. **1997**—GM offered a 30th birthday styling package for the Camaro and some interior upgrades, V6 engine dampening for smoother running at high speeds, optional Ram Air induction, and racier-looking ground-effects body trim for the Firebird. **1998**—Got a minor facelift, and the Z28 and SS both received a slight horsepower boost. **1999**—Electronic throttle control on V6-equipped versions and a new Zexel Torsion differential used in the limited-slip rear axle. **2000**—Camaros and Firebirds got alloy wheels and an improved throttle response for cars equipped with the manual transmission. **2001**—Z28 and SS models were given five more horses and restyled chrome wheels.

During this period, performance and reliability problems are commonplace. Much like Ford's embarrassing 4-banger, the puny and failure-prone 2.5L 4-cylinder power plant was the standard engine up to 1986—part of the legacy of an earlier fuel crisis and the subsequent downsizing binge. The turbocharged V8 offered on some Trans Am models should be viewed with caution because of its many durability problems.

Body hardware is fragile, poor paint quality and application are common and lead to premature rusting, and squeaks and rattles are legion. Body integrity is especially poor on cars equipped with a T-roof. Areas particularly vulnerable to rusting are the windshield and rear wheel openings, door bottoms, and rear quarter panels. The assorted add-on plastic body parts found on sporty versions promote corrosion by trapping moisture along with road salt and grime. Also note that the Camaro's flat seats don't offer as much support as the better-contoured Firebird seats.

These cars are also plagued by chronic fuel-system problems, especially on the Cross-Fire and multi-port fuel-injection controls. Automatic transmissions, especially the 4-speed, aren't durable. The standard 5-speed manual gearbox has a stiff shifter and a heavy clutch. Clutches fail frequently and don't stand up to hard use. The 2.8L V6, used through 1989, suffers from leaky gaskets and seals and premature camshaft wear. The larger 3.1L 6-cylinder has fewer problems. However, malfunctioning dash gauges and electrical problems are common, and exhaust parts rust quickly. Dual outlet exhaust systems on V8 engines are expensive to replace. Front suspension components and shock absorbers wear out very quickly.

Of this grouping, you should stick with the 1996–2003 models for the best performance and price. All of these cars are much better overall performers than previous models, and additional standard safety features are a plus.

These sporty convertibles and coupes are almost identical in their pricing and in the features they offer (the Firebird has pop-up headlights, a more pointed front end, a narrower middle, and a rear spoiler). As noted above, both cars got a complete make-over in 1995, making them more powerful and aerodynamic, with less spine-jarring performance.

As one moves up the scale, overall performance improves considerably. The V8 engine gives these cars lots of sparkle and tire-spinning torque, but there's a fuel penalty to pay. A 4-speed automatic transmission is standard on the 5.7L-equipped Z28; other versions come with a standard 5-speed manual gearbox or an optional 6-speed. Many of these cars are likely to have been ordered with lots of extra performance and luxury options, including a T-roof package guaranteed to include a full assortment of creaks and groans.

Not everything is perfect, however. Owners report premature automatic transmission failures, a noisy base engine, and excessive oil consumption with the larger engine. Fuel economy is unimpressive, the AC malfunctions, front brakes (rotors and pads, mostly) and MacPherson struts wear out quickly, servicing the fuel-injection system is an exercise in frustration, electrical problems are common, gauges operate erratically, and body problems are common. These include: door rattles, misaligned doors and hatch, a sticking hatch power release, and poor fit and finish. Owners also complain that the steering wheel is positioned too close to the driver's chest, the low seats create a feeling of claustrophobia, visibility is limited by wide side pillars, and trunk space is sparse with a high liftover.

Safety summary: All models/years: Early brake rotor warpage and pad replacement. One dealer mechanic explains the problem this way:

> The rotors are not thick enough and have insufficient air to cool them. ASE-certified independent mechanics and dealership employees (unofficially) buy slotted "racing" rotors or use ceramic non-metal pads from other sources. This has apparently gone on since 1998 on both Firebirds and Camaros.

• Airbag malfunctions. • Seat belts fail to lock up. **All models: 1995–96—** Many reports that car caught fire near the fuel tank. • Fuel line retaining clamp could fail, causing the plastic fuel lines to come into contact with the exhaust manifold cover. • Other fires ignited near the radio and in the engine compartment. • Many reports claiming sudden acceleration. • Airbag failed to deploy. • Frequent ABS brake failures; pedal goes to the floor. • ABS is particularly ineffective in rainy weather. • Rear brake caliper failure. • Emergency brake fails frequently, allowing car to roll away even though shift lever is placed in Park. • In wet conditions or when passing over a puddle, the power-steering pump fails, resulting in steering lock-up. • Frequent transmission failures while driving. **1996—**Transmission jumps out of gear. • Traction control fails in cold weather. • Right rear axle broke. • Rear main oil seal leakage and failure. • ABS light remains lit due to defective jumper. • Seat belts slip off their guides and their anchorages may break. • Faulty ignition control module. • Windshield wipers stay on one speed, don't clean enough of the right side, and their placement blocks right-side visibility. **1997—**Fire caused by a short in the defroster wiring. • Engine intake manifold gasket and valve cover failure. • Faulty power-steering pumps. • Stalling in the rain. **1997–98—**Four recurring problems are prematurely worn brake pads and warped or cracked rotors, sudden acceleration, no airbag deployment, and failure of the emergency brake to hold. **1998—**Dash fire. • Axle seal, tie-rod, serpentine belt, fuel pump, brake caliper bolt, AC blower motor, fuel gauge, and wiper failures. **1999**—Interestingly, both the Camaro and Firebird have about one-third fewer safety-related complaints registered against them by NHTSA than does the Ford Mustang. • Airbags failed to deploy upon impact. • Cracked fuel tank leaks fuel. • Accelerator pedal sticks. • Prematurely warped front brake rotors jerk to one side when brakes are applied and cause pulsation, excessive noise, and extended stopping distance. • Many incidents of clutch slippage at low mileage. • Frequent complaints that the stock shifter causes misshifts. • Electrical system shorts cause instrument panel and assorted gauges and lights to operate erratically. • Turn signal lights don't flash, headlights often dim to about 50 percent of their intended brightness, heater slows down, and power windows run slowly. **2000**—Engine surging and stalling. • Electrical wires melted. • Emergency brake failed to hold vehicle; came off in driver's hand. • Rear brake lock-ups and chronic pad and rotor failures. • T-top flew off vehicle. • Seat belt failed to retract in an emergency stop. • Headlights flicker or suddenly go out. • Horn collects water, which muffles sound. • Front end pulls to the right. • Headrests are set too low (same complaint heard from Mustang owners). • Replacement windshields are seriously distorted along the bottom edge. • Windows leak water. • Premature power-window motor failures. • Severe vibration when accelerating. **2001**—Premature automatic transmission failure. **2002**—Airbags failed to deploy. • Premature brake rotor wear causes excessive shudder, vibration. • Design causes front windshield distortion. • Early headlight failures.

Secret Warranties/Service Tips/TSBs

All models/years: Eliminate AC odours by applying an evaporator core cooling coil coating. • A rotten-egg odour coming from the exhaust is probably the result of a malfunctioning catalytic converter, which may be covered by the emissions warranty. • Paint delamination, peeling, or fading (see Part Two). • GM guidelines to dealers on troubleshooting exterior lamp condensation complaints. • Oil leaks between the intake manifold and engine block are most often caused by insufficient RTV bonding between the intake manifold and cylinder block. **All models: 1993–96**—Uneven rear brake pad wear or premature wear can be corrected by replacing the caliper anchor bracket, guide pins, and the brake pads with upgraded parts. **1993–2002**—GM has a special kit to prevent AC odours in warm weather. **1994–98**—GM guidelines for repairing front brake problems. **1995–96**—Delayed automatic transmission shift engagement may require the replacement of the pump cover assembly. **1997**—Fixing automatic transmission slippage. • Engine oil leak diagnosis. • Theft alarm sounds when vehicle gets wet. • Diagnosing engine miss and poor driveability. **1997–2002**—Radio speaker buzz or rattle. **1998**—Tips on eliminating roof panel ticking. **1998–2000**—An engine that loses coolant or runs hot may simply need a new radiator cap or the radiator filler neck polished. • Install upgraded disc pads to eliminate rear brake chirp or groan and front brake squeal when braking. • Silence accessory drive belt chirping or squeaking by installing a new double row idler pulley, generator bracket, and serpentine

belt. **1998–2002**—Water runs out of front lower corners of rear hatch. •
Engine spark knock remedy. **1999**—If the convertible top closes with difficulty, it may be because the headliner is too short. **1999–2001**—Excessive oil
consumption (see Corvette "Secret Warranties/Service Tips/TSBs"). • Steering
wheel squeaks when turning. • Windshield moulding squeaks. **2000**—Repair
tips for fixing an inoperative or erratically operating antenna. **2001–02**—
Slipping or missing Second, Third, or Fourth gear. • Rear brake rattling.
2002—Erratic radio operation. • Intermittent no-start caused by fuel pump
and fuel gauge wiring harness short. • Harsh automatic transmission shifts. •
Automatic transmission pump leaks. • Quarter trim panels pull away. •
Troubleshooting guide for correcting wind noise and water leaks. • Exhaust
ping. • Radiator cap may not hold sufficient vacuum. • Rattling door handles.
• Noisy, faulty clutch pedal.

Models with 2.5L engines/all years—Spark knock can be fixed with a new
PROM module (#12269198), if the emissions warranty applies. • Frequent
stalling may require a new MAP sensor (TSB #90-142-8A). **3.8L V6:
1996–98**—These engines have a history of low oil pressure caused by a failure-
prone oil pump. A temporary remedy is to avoid low-viscosity oils and use
10W-40 in the winter and 20W-50 for summer driving.

Camaro, Firebird, Trans Am Profile

	1995	1996	1997	1998	1999	2000	2001	2002
Cost Price ($)								
Camaro/RS	18,995	20,195	22,075	22,790	23,100	26,065	26,120	26,995
Z28	23,650	25,530	27,270	27,840	28,670	31,630	29,540	30,785
Convertible	26,045	28,365	29,080	29,795	30,105	38,270	38,585	39,225
Firebird	19,795	20,955	23,120	24,580	24,865	27,605	26,915	27,695
Trans Am	27,390	28,755	30,780	34,080	34,750	35,505	35,815	36,365
Used Values ($)								
Camaro/RS ⋀	5,000	6,000	7,500	8,500	10,500	12,000	14,500	17,000
Camaro/RS ⋁	4,500	5,000	6,000	7,500	9,500	10,500	13,000	15,500
Z28 ⋀	5,500	6,500	7,500	10,500	12,000	14,500	17,500	20,000
Z28 ⋁	5,000	5,500	6,500	9,000	10,500	13,000	16,000	18,500
Convertible ⋀	8,000	10,000	11,000	13,000	15,000	19,000	22,000	26,000
Convertible ⋁	7,000	8,500	10,000	11,500	13,500	17,000	20,000	24,000
Firebird ⋀	5,500	6,500	7,000	8,500	10,500	13,500	14,500	16,500
Firebird ⋁	5,000	6,000	6,000	7,500	9,500	12,500	13,000	15,000
Trans Am ⋀	6,500	8,000	9,000	10,500	13,000	16,500	20,000	23,000
Trans Am ⋁	6,000	6,500	7,500	9,000	11,500	14,500	18,000	21,000
Reliability	③	④	④	④	④	④	⑤	⑤
Crash Safety (Camaro)	⑤	⑤	⑤	④	④	④	④	④
Side (Camaro)	—	—	③	③	③	③	③	③
Head Restraints	❶	—	❶	—	❶	—	❶	❶

CORVETTE   ★ ★ ★

RATING: Average (1997–2003); Below Average (1994–96); Not Recommended (1977–93). The cheaper 1996 Corvette won't have the cachet or the mechanical and body refinements of the redesigned 1997 version. If you choose the 1997 model, try to get a second-series car that was made after June 1997. Keep in mind that premium fuel and astronomical insurance rates will further drive up your operating costs. Plus, don't discount the serious safety-related problems you're likely to experience on 1997–2001 models. They run the gamut of sudden steering lock-up when underway, electrical shorts causing vehicle shutdown, a non-functioning parking brake, brake failures due to premature rotor warpage (around 16,000 km), and seat belts that jam in the retractor. The locked-up steering is particularly scary because it apparently has carried over to year 2001 models, and traffic accident investigators may simply conclude that a resulting accident was due to driver inexperience or unsafe driving. **Maintenance/Repair costs:** Higher than average, although most repairs can be done by any independent garage. Long waits for recall repairs. **Parts:** Pricey, but easy to find. Surprisingly, it is often easier to find parts for older Corvettes, through collectors' clubs, than to find many of the high-tech components used today. **Best alternatives:** Ford Mustang or Probe, GM Camaro or Firebird, Mazda Miata, and Toyota Supra. **Online help:** *www.corvetteforum.com* and *www.carreview.com*.

Strengths and weaknesses: Corvettes made in the late '60s and early '70s are acceptable buys, due mainly to their value as collector cars and their uncomplicated repairs. Unfortunately, the Corvette's overall reliability and safety have declined over the years as its price and complexity have increased. This is due in large part to GM's updating its antiquated design with high-tech, complicated add-ons rather than coming up with something original. Consequently, the car has been gutted and then retuned using failure-prone electronic circuitry. Complicated emissions plumbing, braking, and suspension systems have also been added in an attempt to make the Corvette a fuel-efficient, user-friendly, high-performance vehicle—a goal that General Motors has missed by a large margin.

The electronically controlled suspension systems have always been plagued by glitches. Servicing the different sophisticated fuel-injection systems is a nightmare—even (especially) for GM mechanics. The noisy 5.7L engine frequently hesitates and stalls, there's lots of transmission buzz and whine, the rear tires produce excessive noise, and wind whistles through the A- and C-pillars. These, and the all-too-familiar fibreglass body squeaks and paint delamination (yes, fibreglass delaminates), continue to be unwanted standard features throughout all model years. The electronic dash never works quite right (speedometer lag, for example).

On the other hand, Corvette ownership of more recent models does have its positive side. For example, the ABS vented disc brakes, available since 1986, are easy to modulate and fade-free. The standard European-made Bilstein FX-3 Selective Ride Control suspension can be preset for touring, sport, or performance. Under speed, an electronic module automatically varies the suspension setting, finally curing these cars of their earlier endemic over-steering, wheel spinning, breakaway rear ends, and other nasty surprises.

All used Corvettes are high-risk buys, but the 1977–93 models have been particularly troublesome. These models are notorious for experimenting with complicated and failure-prone safety, emissions, and performance "innovations" that were routinely brought in one year and dropped shortly thereafter—making for difficult troubleshooting and hard-to-find parts. There's also a greater chance you'll get stuck with a turned-back odometer or an accident-damaged car, written off by the insurance company and then resold through wholesalers, auctions, body shops, or their employees. All these scams can be detected by running a Carfax check online or by fax (see Part One).

Another precaution: Get a GM-backed supplementary warranty, or look for a recent model that has some of the original warranty left. The frequency of repairs and the high repair costs make maintenance outrageously expensive. Following are some of the things that can put a large dent in your wallet if they haven't been fixed already.

1984–90

These model years are incredibly difficult to service. One *Lemon-Aid* reader had a faulty engine bearing at 16,000 km and spent $2,500 to remove the engine. It takes half a day to change the spark plugs on the passenger side. Likely mechanical problem areas are the emission control system (injectors, computer-controlled sensors, fuel injection, and engine gaskets), AC, and ignition/distributor. Owners also experience engine and drivetrain failures, Bosch radio malfunctions, and the need to make frequent wheel alignments. Fragile body hardware, poor fit and finish, wind/road noise, and water intrusion into the interior are still major weaknesses. Owners complain of faulty controls and window lifts, defective paint (base coat comes through the finish), interior/exterior parts and trim, glass and weather stripping, instruments, lights, door locks, upholstery, and carpeting.

1991–2003

Though the restyled 1991 Corvette remained the same mechanically, all models got the convex tail and square tail lights previously used only on the upscale ZR-1 coupe. Acceleration Slip Regulation on 1992–96 models effectively reduces the horrendous wheelspin that threw many Corvettes out of control when accelerating on slippery surfaces. A new LTI engine with 55 more horses came on the scene with the 1992 'Vette, and the following year the ZR-1 got a 405-hp variant of the same power plant, shortly before the model was replaced in the spring of 1995 by the Grand Sport. Incidentally, the super-powered ZR-1's depreciated price makes the car a bargain when one totes up the cost of its standard performance features.

A more substantial redesign was carried out in mid-1997. The transmission was moved back, creating a roomier cockpit; the interior was made much more user-friendly; structural improvements reduced body flexing (a problem with most convertibles) and made for a more rigid hatchback; and a new aluminum 340-hp LSI V8 engine arrived on the scene. The '98 and '99 versions are pretty much carryovers of the redesigned '97 and aren't worth a higher price. A high-performance hardtop model was launched for the '99 model year. Year 2000 models returned unchanged; however, the 2001 Corvette got a horse-power boost, an Active Handling performance upgrade, and was joined by a high-performance Z06 variant. For 2002, the Z06 got a 20-hp boost to 405 hp, enhanced rear shocks, aluminum front stabilizer bar links, high-performance brake pads, and new aluminum wheels.

Owners admit the redesigned '97 models offer improved performance, better handling, and additional safety features, but they still find fault with the stiff ride, poor fuel economy, and excessive interior noise. From a relia-bility standpoint, these 1997 and later models are more refined, with the most serious problems being excessive engine oil consumption and an oily black buildup on the exhaust tips and catalytic converter failures. Defective steering columns on 1977 through 2001 models lock while underway or parked, a widespread problem, says the following Corvette owner:

> This item has failed on an estimated 3,000 Corvettes throughout the U.S. Please see Internet site *www.corvetteforum.com*. As a safety pro-fessional, I see this as a hazard that Chevrolet needs to address with more severity. The loss of steering control because the steering wheel locks can lead to property loss, as well as death.

The active handling system often malfunctions and makes their car veer into traffic or spin out of control; faulty electronic and electrical systems cause the car to suddenly shut down; the brake, suspension and AC system are unre-liable; and body fit and finish is subpar.

Other deficiencies: engine chirping; excessive cabin heat, even with AC set to MAX; driver's seat moves while driving; warped trunk door; seat belts twist easily and tend to pull down uncomfortably against the shoulder; passenger seat belt jams and won't extend or retract; smelly fumes enter the cabin, causing watery eyes and dizziness; excessive heat buildup from catalytic con-verters deforms rear bumper assembly and makes interior unbearable; the glass rear-view window limits rear vision; and front and rear wheel weights may fly off the wheels.

Servicing the different sophisticated fuel-injection systems isn't easy and may be the primary reason why so many owners complain of having to take their Corvettes back to the shop repeatedly to correct poor engine performance.

Safety summary: 1996—Fire started in the engine computer system. • Faulty front wheel bearing hub, fuel pump, intake manifold, and tire pressure sensor (no parts available). • Transmission failures and fluid leakage. • Excessive vibra-tion when top is taken off. **1997–98**—Sudden loss of power, engine shuts down, and warning lights come on everywhere. • Defective throttle control module, parking brake, brake rotors and pads, seat belt retractors, fuel line clips, and Check Engine light. **1997–2001**—NHTSA is looking into 350 complaints, 24 crashes, and 10 injuries related to steering column lock-ups; GM admits it has processed 24,000 warranty claims and sent its dealers three bulletins about the problem. • **1998**—Fuel tank leakage. • No airbag deployment. • Transmission failure, leaks. • Emergency brake won't hold. • Excessive vibrations when driving. • Poor headlight illumination. **1999**—Sudden, unintended acceleration. • Fuel tank leaks when gassing up; vehicle caught fire as raw fuel was ignited by the catalytic converter. • Fuel pump failures. • Parking brake won't hold car. • Chronic premature warpage of the brake rotors. • Front lap belts jam in the retractor. • Electrical shorts caused headlights to stick open, melted rear-view mirror assembly, and a plethora of other electronic glitches, leading to vehicle shutdown. • Engine serpentine belt and tensioner failures. • Poorly anchored driver's seat and warped trunk door. **2000–01**—Catalytic converter caught fire. • When fuel tank is full, full leaks from the top of the vent. • Fuel leaks from the fuel lines near the firewall inside the engine compartment. • Chronic stalling; fuel-injector failures cause vehicle to shudder and stall. • Engine dies while driving in the rain and brakes don't work. • Early failure of the engine serpentine belt and tensioner. • If one wheel loses traction, the throttle closes, starving the engine. • Brakes drag and lock up; brake pedal doesn't spring back; overheated rotors are common. • Car is nearly uncontrollable at time of brake lock-up. • Seat belt doesn't retract properly when reeling it out and tightens up progressively when driving. • Driver's seat rocks. • Foot easily slips off clutch and brake pedals. **2002**—Sudden stalling on the highway accompanied by brake failure. • Erratic transmission performance (shifts to Fourth before entering Second gear; won't shift into Second when going uphill). • Horn is hard to access since it's just a small indentation on the steering wheel.

Secret Warranties/Service Tips/TSBs

All models/years: A rotten-egg odour coming from the exhaust is probably caused by a defective catalytic converter, which may be covered by the emissions warranty. • Clearcoat paint degradation, whitening, and chalking, long a problem with GM's other cars, is also a serious problem with the fibreglass-bodied Corvette, says TSB #331708. It too is covered by a secret warranty for up to six years (see Part Two). **All models: 1992–96**—Oil leaks between the intake manifold and engine block are most often caused by insufficient RTV bonding between the intake manifold and cylinder block. **1993–2002**—GM has a special kit to prevent AC odours in warm weather. **1995–96**—Delayed automatic transmission shift engagement may require the replacement of the pump cover assembly. **1995–2000**—Guidelines for repairing brake rotor warpage. **1997**—Correcting water leaks into the rear compartment. • Inadequate heating, defrosting. • Correcting drivebelt noise. **1997–98**—What to do when the Low Engine Coolant light comes on. • Silence a muffler insulator rumble noise by installing upgraded insulators. • Countermeasures to eliminate water leaks above the door glass and door glass rattles. **1997–99**—A no-start condition can be corrected by reprogramming the power control module (PCM). • TSB #99-06-02-016 has the remedy for a low coolant light that comes on at start-up. • Shift boot squeaking can be silenced by installing a new shift boot assembly. • Accessory drive squeaks can be corrected by installing a new idler pulley assembly. **1997–2000**—Repair tips for an inaccurate fuel gauge. **1997–2001**—Sound system speakers make the door panel rattle or buzz. **1997–2002**—Tips on correcting water leaks in various areas. • Loose driver's seat. **1997–2003**—Inoperative AC. **1998–2000**—Tips on correcting a faulty rear window defogger. • An inoperative or noisy window motor can be corrected by replacing the window regulator and motor assembly. **1998–2002**—Engine spark knock remedy. **1999**—Rattling from the left fuel tank area can be silenced by installing a fuel tank foam insulator pad. **1999–2000**—An engine that runs hot or loses coolant may simply need a new radiator cap or polishing of the radiator filler neck. **1999–2001**—Wind noise around the B-pillar. **1999–2002**—Poor transmission performance; SES light lit. • Excessive oil consumption (see following bulletin).

Higher Than Normal Oil Consumption

Bulletin No.: 01-06-01-023A

Date: June 2002

MODELS: 1999–2001 Camaro, Firebird; 1999–2002 Corvette with 5.7L engine.

CONDITION: Some owners may comment on higher than expected oil consumption. When checked, the oil consumption could be in the range of 700–1000 km/L (400–600 miles per quart). On the LS6 engine only, the technician may find oil behind the engine throttle plate and in the intake manifold.

CORRECTION: Replace the engine valley cover if oil is found behind the throttle body or in the intake manifold before replacing the piston ring.

2000—Reducing exhaust boom. • Repair tips on fixing an inoperative or erratically operating antenna. • Left headlamp door may not remain closed. **2001**—Incomplete brake pedal return can be fixed by replacing the vacuum brake booster. **2001–02**—Slipping or missing Second, Third, or Fourth gear. **2002**—Engine knock. • Erratic fuel gauge or radio operation. • False Service Engine lamp illumination. • Harsh transmission shifts; 2–4 band and 3–4 clutch damage; transmission pump leaks. • Light brake drag; brake light remains lit. • B-pillar wind noise. **2001–03**—Engine knock or lifter noise. **2002–03**—Exhaust system jingle noise.

Corvette Profile								
	1996	1997	1998	1999	2000	2001	2002	2003
Cost Price ($)								
Base	48,080	48,895	50,430	53,870	60,050	61,400	62,400	68,120
Convertible	56,335	—	58,430	60,850	66,965	68,315	69,665	74,120
Used Values ($)								
Base ⋀	20,000	27,000	31,000	34,000	38,000	42,000	48,000	55,000
Base ⋁	18,000	25,000	29,000	31,000	35,000	39,000	45,000	50,000

Convertible ▲	22,000	—	35,000	39,000	42,000	45,000	53,000	60,000
Convertible ▼	20,000	—	33,000	36,000	39,000	42,000	50,000	56,000
Reliability	❷	❷	③	③	③	③	③	③
Head Restraints (F)	—	—	—	③	—	③	③	③
Rear	—	—	—	—	—	❷	❷	❷

Honda

PRELUDE	★ ★ ★ ★ ★

RATING: Recommended (1993–2001); Above Average (1985–92). These are reliable used sporty cars that cost far too much; cheaper, almost as reliable makes should be checked out first. **Maintenance/Repair costs:** Average. Repairs aren't dealer dependent. To avoid costly engine repairs, check the engine timing belt every 2 years/40,000 km and replace it every 96,000 km ($300). **Parts:** Higher-than-average cost, but independent suppliers sell parts for much less. **Best alternatives:** Ford Mustang or Probe, GM Camaro or Firebird, Mazda Miata, and Toyota Celica. **Online help:** *www.hpoa.org*; *www.92lude.com/forum*; *www.preludeonline.com*; and *www.winnipegpreludeclub.com/links.html.*

Strengths and weaknesses: Unimpressive as a high-performance sports car, the Prelude instead delivers a stylish exterior, legendary reliability, and excellent resale value.

The 1978–87 first-generation Preludes were described as luxury sporty cars, but didn't offer much of either. They should be inspected carefully for engine problems and severe underbody corrosion, particularly near the fuel tank. They're also prone to extensive rusting around wheel openings, door bottoms, the trunk lid, fenders, rear tail lights, bumper supports, chassis members, and suspension components. Noisy front brakes, premature disc warpage, high oil consumption, and worn engine crankshaft/camshaft lobes are the main problem areas with these models.

The 1988–91 models offer more and smoother engine power, excellent handling, and improved reliability. There are some generic complaints that continue to crop up, including rapid front brake wear, scored and warped front brake rotors, automatic transmission failures, defective constant velocity joints, premature exhaust system rust-out, and a warping hood.

The 1992–96 models are shorter, wider, and heavier. They're not very fast. The four-wheel steering found on the 1992 4WS version is more gimmick than anything else. It was dropped after 1994. The automatic transmission is smoother, although it still saps some of the Prelude's power. Both the rear seating and tiny trunk are inadequate for most people. You can expect fewer but all-too-familiar glitches, including engine oil leaks (covered by a secret warranty), minor electrical problems, body and accessory defects, brake squealing, and prematurely warped front brake rotors. Most independent mechanics can now service these cars because Preludes haven't changed that much over the years.

1997–2001

The year for big Prelude changes was 1997, while 1998–2001 models just coasted along with minor improvements. The '97 was restyled, re-powered, and given handling upgrades that make it a better-performing, more comfortably riding sports coupe. It got an additional five horses for the base 2.2L VTEC engine, a new Automatic Torque Transfer System (ATTS), an upgraded suspension, and standard ABS, AC, 16-inch wheels, and a CD player with six speakers. The Sequential SportShift automatic transmission (a variation of the one used in the NSX) equips the base Prelude. Overall, the car is roomier (the extended wheelbase gives added stability and provides more room in the rear seating area), has a more solid body structure, and includes a totally redesigned, user-friendly dash with analogue gauges.

On these more recent models, owners report that the engine tends to leak oil and crank bolts often loosen (causing major engine damage). AC condensers frequently fail after a few years and often need cleaning to eliminate disagreeable odours. Other problems include minor electrical glitches, brake squealing, and prematurely warped front brake rotors. A host of new technical features adds to the Prelude's complexity and guarantees that you'll never stray far from the dealer's service bay. In fact, most corner mechanics are poorly equipped to service these cars, and the Automatic Torque Transfer System (ATTS) won't make their job any easier.

Safety summary: All models: 1999—Sudden tire tread separation. • Power-steering loss; steering failure after steering pump replaced. • Airbags failed to deploy upon impact. • Engine loses power in cold weather or at cruising speeds. **2000**—Poor throttle response on hot days with AC engaged while passing through the lower gears. • Airbag deployed three seconds after collision. • Premature failure of Fifth gear. • Excessive carbon buildup leads to chronic stalling. **2001**—Sudden brake failure caused collision. • Poorly designed clutch causes harsh shifting.

Secret Warranties/Service Tips/TSBs

All models/years: Steering wheel shimmy can be reduced by rebalancing the wheel/tire/hub/rotor assembly in the front end. • Seat belts that fail to function properly during normal use will be replaced for free under Honda's lifetime seat belt warranty. • Honda will also repair or replace defective steering assemblies, constant velocity joints, and catalytic converters free of charge up to 5 years/80,000 km on a case-by-case basis. • Honda TSBs allow for special warranty consideration on a "goodwill" basis for most problems even after the warranty has expired or the car has changed hands. **All models: 1992–97**— You may have to change the Fifth gear shift fork if the transmission grinds when going into Fifth gear. **1994–96**—Silence rear headliner rattling by applying EPT sealer 5T to the rear headliner where it contacts the wiring harness. **1994–97**—Engine oil leaks will be fixed for free under a Honda "goodwill" program. **1997**—A squeaking seat may need a new seat pivot bushing. **1997–98**—Power-window clunking can be stopped by changing the motor. **1997–99**—A rear suspension clunk can be fixed by replacing the coil springs. • Doors that are hard to open from the inside may simply require a new inner door handle rod. • A rattling moon roof may need new guide rails and a readjustment of the glass brackets ("goodwill"). • A trunk clunking noise may be silenced by replacing the trunk spring clip. **1997–2000**—Deformed upper windshield mouldings are addressed in TSB #00-064. **1997–2001**—Rear suspension clunks may be silenced by replacing the upper collars in both rear damper assemblies. **1998–2001**—Corrective measures to apply to a warped or deformed windshield moulding. **1999–2000**—Try replacing the power-steering pump bearing and seals to silence a noisy power-steering pump. **2000–01**—Automatic transmission warranty extension.

Prelude Profile

	1994	1995	1996	1997	1998	1999	2000	2001
Cost Price ($)								
Base/SR	21,895	26,995	27,395	27,300	27,600	27,800	27,900	28,300
VTEC	28,295	29,695	29,995	—	—	—	—	—
Used Values ($)								
Base/SR ⋀	5,000	6,500	8,000	9,500	12,000	14,000	16,500	19,000
Base/SR ⋁	4,000	6,000	7,000	8,000	10,500	13,000	15,000	17,500
VTEC ⋀	5,500	7,500	9,000	—	—	—	—	—
VTEC ⋁	4,500	6,500	8,000	—	—	—	—	—
Reliability	⑤	⑤	⑤	⑤	⑤	⑤	⑤	⑤
Head Restraints	—	❷	—	❷	—	❷	—	❷

Hyundai

TIBURON ★★★★★

RATING: Recommended (2000–03); Above Average (1997–99). A high-performance Elantra. Keep in mind that for about $1,000–$1,500 more you can get the better-performing FX model. **Maintenance/Repair costs:** Higher than average, although most repairs can be done by any independent garage. **Parts:** Average cost and good availability. **Best alternatives:** Ford Mustang or Probe, GM Camaro or Firebird, Mazda Miata, Nissan 200SX, and Toyota Celica. **Online help:** *www.automotiveforums.com/vbulletin/f741*; *www.newtiburon.com/yabbse/index.php*; and *groups.msn.com/HyundaiTiburon/ messageboard.msnw*.

Strengths and weaknesses: This is a fun-to-drive, budget sport coupe that's based on the Elantra sedan and has earned a good overall reliability record. On early models, the base 16-valve 1.8L 4-cylinder engine is smooth, efficient, and adequate when mated to the 5-speed manual transmission. Put in an automatic transmission and performance suffers somewhat, and engine noise increases proportionally. Overall handling is crisp and predictable, due mainly to the Tiburon's long wheelbase and sophisticated suspension.

Vehicle history: Since its debut as a '97 model, the Tiburon has changed little. **1997**—The FX got a more sprightly 2.0L engine. **1998**—Addition of a 145-hp 2.0L across the lineup. **2000**—Four-wheel disc brakes and a restyled interior and exterior. **2001**— Redesigned wheels and a rear spoiler. **2003**— Restyled, larger, and a new 2.7L V6 (GT).

Standard brakes are adequate, though sometimes difficult to modulate. As with most sporty cars, interior room is cramped for average-sized occupants. Tall drivers, especially, might find rearward seat travel insufficient, making headroom a bit tight. Although no serious defects have been reported, be on the lookout for body deficiencies (fit, finish, and assembly), harsh shifting, slipping with the automatic transmission, frequent clutch failures, oil leaks, brake glitches (premature front brake wear and excessive brake noise), seat belt twisting and jamming in its housing, and extensive paint flaking.

Safety summary: All models/years: No airbag deployment. **1999**—Brake failure on wet pavement. • Car jolts when accelerating. • Transmission slippage. • Tires won't hold air. • Original-equipment jack won't support vehicle. • Seat belt webbing jams in retractor. **2000**—Inadvertent airbag deployment. Sudden acceleration caused by faulty cruise control. • Shoulder belt twists and jams at door post and is hard to latch. • Premature wheel bearing failure. • Headlight illumination is inadequate with lowbeams. • Headlights and tires fail prematurely. **2001**—Seatback failure from rear-end collision. • Seat belts are hard to latch. **2002**—Airbag deployed when it shouldn't have. • Reflection of the sun on the dash distracts vision. • Horn controls may be hard to find in an emergency. • Rear head restraints appear to be too low to protect occupants. • Front seat belts are difficult to latch and tighten or loosen on their own; and the rear seat belt configuration complicates the installation of a child safety seat. • The rear spoiler is distracting and cuts rearward vision. **2003**—Airbag deployed for no reason. • Under-hood fire. • Steering assembly spindle snapped off. • Sunroof malfunctions. • Inoperative side windows. • Hood suddenly popped up.

Secret Warranties/Service Tips/TSBs

All models/years: Hyundai brake pad kit #58101-28A00 may eliminate squeaks and squeals during light brake application. • Hyundai suggests that you replace the oil pump assembly if the engine rpm increases as the automatic transmission engages abruptly during a cold start. • Harsh automatic transmission shifting, no Fourth gear engagement, and a lit MIL light may all point to the need for a new automatic transaxle oil temperature sensor or transaxle solenoid. **1997**—A tip on eliminating clutch pedal squeaking and drag is offered. **1997–98**—DOHC timing chain noise can be stopped by installing an upgraded timing chain. • Park–Reverse or Park–Drive harsh shifting may require an upgraded TCM. **1997–99**—Poor automatic transmission performance is addressed in TSB #97-40-031. • Automatic transmission drain hole oil leak and fluid leak behind the torque converter. • Delayed engagement into Drive or Reverse is addressed in TSB #99-40-006. **1997–2001**—Correction for an erratic-shifting or slipping automatic transmission that often flares or sticks in gear. **1999**—Tips on dealing with a hard-to-fill fuel tank. **1999–2003**—Erratic shifting remedies. **2000**—Timing belt noise may be caused by the belt rubbing against the front dust cover. **2002**—Malfunctioning automatic transaxle solenoid. • MIL lamp troubleshooting guide. **2003**—Sunroof leaks.

Tiburon Profile

	1997	1998	1999	2000	2001	2002	2003
Cost Price ($)							
Base	16,996	17,895	17,895	18,995	19,195	19,995	19,995
FX/SE	18,895	19,895	19,895	21,295	21,495	22,395	22,395
Used Values ($)							
Base ⋏	5,000	6,000	7,500	8,500	10,500	13,000	15,500
Base ⋎	4,500	5,000	6,500	7,000	9,500	11,500	14,000
FX/SE ⋏	16,500						
FX/SE ⋎	5,000	6,000	7,000	8,500	10,500	13,500	15,500
Reliability	④	④	④	⑤	⑤	⑤	⑤
Head Restraints (F)	❶	—	❷	—	③	③	⑤
Rear	—	—	❶	—	—	—	—

Mazda

MIATA ★★★★★

RATING: Recommended (1990–2003). There was no 1998 model. An almost-perfect sports car, except for its poor braking performance on rain-slicked roadways. **Maintenance/Repair costs:** Below-average costs, and most repairs aren't dealer dependent. **Parts:** Average cost, with good availability. **Best alternatives:** Ford Mustang or Probe, GM Camaro or Firebird, Hyundai Tiburon, Nissan 200SX, and Toyota Celica. **Online help:** *www.miata.net*, *www.straight-six.com*, and *www.miataforum.com*.

Strengths and weaknesses: The base 1.6L engine delivers adequate power and accelerates smoothly. Acceleration from 0 to 100 km/h is in the high 8-second range. The 5-speed manual transmission shifts easily and has well-spaced gears; the 6-speed adds 27 kg (60 lb.) and doesn't impress that much. The vehicle's lightness, precise steering, and 50/50 weight distribution make this an easy car for novice drivers to toss around corners.

Vehicle history: 1995–98—The Miata changed very little. **1999**—Some handling upgrades and additional standard features. **2001**—A slight horsepower boost, a restyled interior and exterior, 15-inch wheels, seat belt pretensioners, improved ABS, and an emergency trunk release. **2003**—16-inch V-rated tires and strut-tower braces.

Owners' top performance gripes target the same characteristics that make other sports car enthusiasts swoon: inadequate cargo space, cramped interior for large adults, excessive interior noise, and limited low-end torque, which makes for frequent shifting.

Owners also say it's important to change the engine timing chain every 100,000 km. Other reported problems: crankshaft failures, leaky rear end seals and valve cover gaskets, rear differential seal failure, a leaking or squeaky clutch, hard starts and stalling, torn drive boots, transmission whining in upper gear ranges, engine and exhaust system rattles, electrical system glitches, brake pulsation, valvetrain clatter on start-up (changing oil may help), prematurely worn-out shock absorbers and catalytic converter, the softtop cover comes off or breaks, and minor body and trim deficiencies.

Safety summary: All models/years: Used Miatas will likely have some collision damage; make sure you run a Carfax check online or by fax (see Part One). **1995–97**—Engine and horn failures. • Roof leaks. • Accelerator pedal cut a slit in the carpet, allowing the gas pedal to jam. **1997**—Airbag failed to deploy. • Convertible hardtop flew off. • Gas tank expansion puts too much stress on the metal. **1999**—Airbags failed to deploy upon impact. • While passing another car on the highway, accelerator cable and the cable adjuster assembly disengaged from the horseshoe bracket that holds the cable. •

Transmission suddenly failed, causing both rear wheels to seize. • Keizer aluminum wheel cracked, damaging brake caliper, rotor, and fender. • Performs poorly on wet roads. • At highway speeds, vehicle tends to wander all over the roadway. **2000**—In heavy rain, stepping on the brakes results in a 2-second delay before braking; must continually pump the brakes. • Airbags deployed two minutes after collision. • Convertible top latches may inadvertently open while vehicle is underway. • Hard shifting and stiff shifter at Neutral causes gear "hunting," grinding, and rattling. • Gas pump shuts off before tank is filled. **2001**—Vehicle rolled down hill despite being parked with emergency brake engaged. **2002**—Interior can heat up to 130 degrees because exhaust system is mounted too close to the centre console. **2003**—Poor headlight illumination.

Secret Warranties/Service Tips/TSBs

All models/years: TSB #006/94 gives all of the possible causes and remedies for brake vibration. • TSB #N00198 addresses complaints that the steering wheel is off-centre. • Other bulletins address the issue of musty AC odours. **All models: 1990–95**—Dirt and debris can clog up side sill drain holes, allowing water to collect and corrosion to occur; drill larger drain holes. **1990–99**—Paint damage caused by the trunk rubber cushions will be repaired under the base warranty. Ask for pro-rata compensation if the warranty has expired. **1996–97**—An inoperative AC may need a new power-steering pressure switch; believe it or not, they are related. • Tips for troubleshooting power window glitches. **1999**—A hard-to-start engine may have debris accumulated at the fuel pressure regulator valve area, causing the valve to stick open. • Engine rattling may be caused by premature wear of the engine thrust bearing or the engine harness clips rubbing against the car's frame. • Muffler rattling may be silenced by installing an upgraded unit. **1999–2002**—Additional tips on reducing AC odours. **1999–2003**—Clutch chatter upon cold start-up. **2002**—Clutch chatter during cold takeoff on manual transmission-equipped vehicles. • Fuelling difficulty due to gas pump shutting off early. • The 6-speed manual transmission won't shift into Fifth gear or Reverse.

Miata Profile

	1995	1996	1997	1999	2000	2001	2002	2003
Cost Price ($)								
Base	21,820	24,210	24,695	26,025	26,995	27,605	27,695	27,695
Used Values ($)								
Base ʌ	7,000	9,000	10,000	12,000	14,000	16,000	20,000	23,000
Base v	6,500	7,500	8,500	10,500	13,000	14,500	18,000	21,000
Reliability	④	⑤	⑤	⑤	⑤	⑤	⑤	⑤
Crash Safety	④	④	—	—	—	④	④	④
Side	—	—	—	—	—	③	③	③
Head Restraints (F)	—	❶	—	❶	—	③	③	③
Rear	—	—	—	—	—	❷	❷	❷
Rollover Resistance	—	—	—	—	—	—	—	⑤

Toyota

CELICA   ★★★★★

RATING: Recommended (2001–03, 1995–99); Above Average (2000, 1986–94). The 1996 and 1997 models are practically identical; choose the cheaper version. The reworked 2000 model has been downgraded due to its many factory-related deficiencies. Keep in mind that the 1989–96 GTS is far superior to the GT, with its 135-hp DOHC 2.0L engine, firmer suspension, better equipped interior, ABS, and a more sporting feel. All handle competently and provide the kind of sporting performance expected from a car of this class. The extra performance in the higher-line versions does come at a price, but this isn't a problem, given the high resale value and excellent reliability for which Celicas are known. Few safety-related complaints or recalls. **Maintenance/Repair costs:** Average, and most repairs can be done at any garage. **Parts:** Reasonably priced and easy to find. **Best alternatives:** Ford Mustang or Probe, GM Camaro or Firebird, Hyundai Tiburon, and Nissan 200SX. **Online help:** *www.celica.net/main.asp* and *www.toyotanation.com.*

Strengths and weaknesses: The pre-1986 Celicas weren't very sporty. Their excessive weight and soft suspension compromised handling and added a high fuel penalty. With the 1986 make-over, Celicas gained more power and much better handling—especially in the GT and GTS versions—but the GT is still more show than go, with limited rear passenger room.

Redesigned 1994 models are full of both show and go, with more aerodynamic styling, an enhanced 1.8L that gives more pickup than the ST's 1.6L, and better fuel economy. Among the upgraded models available, smart buyers should choose a used 1994 ST for its more reasonable price, smooth performance, quiet running, and high fuel economy.

Owner gripes target the excessive engine noise, limited rear seat room, and inadequate cargo space. Pre-1994 models get the most complaints regarding brakes, electrical problems, AC malfunctions, and premature exhaust wearout. The 1994 models may have a manual transmission that slips out of Second gear, as well as hard starts caused by a faulty air flow meter (#22250-74200). Areas vulnerable to early rusting include rear wheel openings, suspension components, the area surrounding the fuel-filler cap, door bottoms, and trunk or hatchback lids.

Vehicle history: 1995—A GT convertible debuts. **1996**—Extra sound insulation and add-on skirts. **1997**—GT given five more horses and the notchback GT is axed. **1998**—ST dropped and GT given more standard features. **1999**—GT Sport Coupe is dropped. **2000**—Crisper handling, a new 180-hp engine, and a 6-speed gearbox (GT-S). **2003**—Hatchback coupes are slightly restyled.

All late-model Celicas offer decent reliability and durability, with three major exceptions: engine sludging; an engine-blowing, self-destructing 6-speed gearbox; and premature, costly brake repairs:

> Toyota has a big problem with their 6-speed in the new Celica. They even told me about it at Toyota. The malfunction is that when trying to shift from Third to Fourth gear, the transmission will slip into Second instead of Fourth. This then causes the engine to be blown.
>
> This is a very dangerous situation if trying to merge with traffic on Interstate at around 70–75 mph [113–120 km/h] and suddenly your car decelarates instantly to around 50 mph [80 km/h]. They need to do something about it before someone gets seriously hurt....

Servicing and repair are straightforward, and parts are easily found. The front-drive series performs very well and hasn't presented any major problems to owners. Prices are high for Celicas in good condition, but some bargains are available with the base ST model.

Some common problems over the years include engine failure caused by engine oil sludge (1997–2001 models), a problem covered by Toyota "goodwill" (see Sienna); brake pulsation and pulling to one side; rear defroster terminals breaking on convertibles; sunroof leaks; erratic CD changer performance; and smelly AC emissions.

On the redesigned 2000 and later models, another subset of problems is found. This includes: engine failures while driving ("weak" valves blamed); stalling after a cold start; engine knocking; excessive oil consumption; early replacement of the belt tensioner and airflow meter; the aforementioned failure-prone 6-speed transmission; insufficient AC cooling; lights dim and heater lags when shifted into idle; seat belt tabs that damage door panels; interior panels separating; driver's window catches and doesn't go all the way up; drive belt squeaks when turning; a squeaking gear shift lever; a grinding noise emanating from the front wheels and brakes; paint peeling; and limited rearward visibility. The audible reverse alarm isn't Toyota's brightest idea. Audible only inside the vehicle, it adds a forklift cachet to your Celica.

Safety summary: All models/years: Even if your vehicle has 4X4 capability, it's imperative that snow tires be fitted in order to avoid dangerous control problems on snow and ice. **All models: 1996**—Sudden brake failure. • Broken brake caliper bolt. • Clogged-up idle control valve makes for hard starts. **1997**—Convertible rear window glass shattered as top was lowered. • Headlights and instrument lights dim when brakes are applied. **1999**—Convertible top and sunroof leaks. **2000**—A huge increase in safety-related complaints. • Fuel leak caused by a broken hose. • No airbag deployment. • Seat belts didn't hold driver in place in a frontal collision. • Cruise control suddenly slows car down without warning. • Constant stalling. • Won't shift into Overdrive. • Clutch and accelerator pedal stick to the floor. • Excessive steering wheel play. • At 100 km/h, vehicle pulls to one side. • Passenger-side wheel suddenly locked up, causing an accident. • Shield protecting wires and fuel lines came off and caused extensive AC valve damage. • Spoiler fell off due to loose bolts. **2000–01**—Without a lockout on the 6-speed gear shift, car can be inadvertently shifted from Fifth to Second gear. **2001**—Engine failures. **2002**—Airbags failed to deploy. **2003**—Hood latch failure.

Secret Warranties/Service Tips/TSBs

All models/years: Remember, *www.celica.net/main.asp* has lots of info on common problems and solutions, including a copy of Toyota TSB # TC002-01, confirming misshifts with the 6-speed tranny. • Troubleshooting updates for steering pulling complaints are found in TSB #ST005-01. • Older Toyotas with stalling problems should have the engine checked for excessive carbon buildup on the valves before any more extensive repairs are authorized. • Owner feedback and dealer service managers (who wish to remain anonymous) confirm the existence of Toyota's secret warranty that will pay for replacing front disc brake components that wear out before 2 years/40,000 km. • The decade-old problem of brake pulsation/vibration is fully outlined and corrective measures are detailed in TSB #BR94-002, issued February 7, 1994. • To reduce front brake squeaks on ABS-equipped vehicles, ask the dealer to install new, upgraded rotors (#43517-32020). **All models: 1990–2000**—Toyota has put out a special grease to minimize brake clicking. **2000**—GT-S automatic transmission fluid leaks. • Loose outer door handle. • Sunshade improvements. • Cruise control shock can be attenuated by replacing the ECU. • Moon roof creaking. • Squeak and rattle service tips. **2000–01**—Drivebelt and engine squealing. • Enhanced sunroof durability. **2000–02**—Insufficient rear hatch support. **2003**—Throttle body motor malfunctions. • Fuel tank check valve Special Service Campaign.

Celica Profile

	1996	1997	1998	1999	2000	2001	2002	2003
Cost Price ($)								
Base	27,968	28,528	34,138	34,475	23,980	24,140	24,645	24,645
Used Values ($)								
Base ▲	9,500	11,000	13,000	15,000	14,500	16,500	18,000	21,000
Base ▼	8,500	10,000	12,000	14,000	13,000	15,000	16,500	19,000
Reliability	④	⑤	⑤	⑤	⑤	⑤	⑤	⑤
Crash Safety	—	—	—	—	—	④	④	④
Side	—	—	—	—	—	③	③	③
Head Restraints (F)	—	❷	—	③	—	⑤	⑤	⑤
Rear	—	—	—	❷	—	—	—	—
Rollover Resistance	—	—	—	—	—	—	—	⑤

MINIVANS

Part car, or part truck?

Not all minivans are alike. Like sport-utilities, minivans fall into two categories: upsized cars and downsized trucks. The upsized cars are "people-movers." They're mostly front-drives, handle like a car, and get great fuel economy. The Honda Odyssey and Toyota Sienna are the best examples of this kind of minivan. In fact, their road performance and reliability surpass the front- and rear-drive minivans built by DaimlerChrysler, Ford, and General Motors.

GM's Astro and Safari and Ford's Aerostar, on the other hand, are downsized trucks. Using rear-drive, 6-cylinder engines, and heavier mechanical components, these minivans handle cargo as well as passengers. On the negative side, fuel economy is no match for the front-drives, and highway handling is also more trucklike. Interestingly, rear-drive GM and Ford minivans are much more reliable performers than the front-drive Ford Windstar or Chrysler minivans. As AWDs, though, they'll keep you in the repair bay for weeks.

GM's minivans, like the Venture shown above, are the best Detroit offers—which is no compliment. They're marginally better than the Chrysler Caravan and Ford Windstar, but have nowhere near the quality or reliability of Honda, Mazda, Nissan, or Toyota.

Rear-drive vans are also better suited for towing trailers in the 1,600–2,950 kg (3,500–6,500 lb.) range. Most automakers say their front-drive minivans can pull up to 1,600 kg. (3,500 lb.) with an optional towing package (often costing almost $1,000 extra), but don't you believe it. Owners report white-knuckle driving and premature powertrain failures caused by the extra load. It just stands to reason that Ford and Chrysler front-drives equipped with engines and transmissions that blow out at 60,000–100,000 km under normal driving conditions are going to meet their demise much earlier under a full load.

Quality not Job 1

Quality control has always been a serious problem with minivans and vans. In the '60s, VW minivans were seen as unreliable, rust-catching boxes that spent more time in the service bay than on the road. And to this day, the VW EuroVan is more a curiosity than a credible people-mover.

But Chrysler minivans did catch on from their debut in 1984. Yet they were just as failure-prone as VW's offerings, with one key difference: Chrysler's 7-year warranty took much of the sting out of repair costs. So, for over 20 years, owners have grown accustomed to biodegradable engines and automatic transmissions, brakes, and air conditioners. When you look at the Caravan's latest service bulletins, you'll be amazed at how little Chrysler's defect patterns have changed during the past two decades.

Ford's minivans have gone from bad to worse. Its first minivan, the rear-drive 1985 Aerostar, wasn't all that dependable, with serious brake, suspension, and body flaws, but at least its engines and transmissions lasted a reasonable period of time. Then the company brought out the front-drive 1995 Windstar—one of the poorest-quality minivans ever built. Renamed the Freestar in 2003, its failure-prone powertrain, suspension, electrical, fuel, and braking systems can put both your wallet and your life at risk.

Fortunately, there's been a flood of Canadian small claims court decisions that say Ford must pay for engine and transmission repairs, even if the original warranty has expired (see pages 428–432).

One exception to Ford's quality decline is the Mercury Villager, a co-venture that also produced the Nissan Quest. Better built than most front-drive minivans, the Villager/Quest duo lasted through the 2000 model year; then Nissan decided to go it alone.

GM's minivans run in the middle of the pack, offering more dependability than Chrysler and Ford, but not quite as much as the Asian competition. Plagued by engine intake manifold, brake, fuel system, and fit and finish glitches, repair costs can quickly add up.

Asian competitors aren't perfect machines either, as a quick perusal of NHTSA-registered safety complaints, service bulletins, and online complaint forums will quickly confirm. Asian companies, looking to keep costs down, have also been bedevilled by chronic engine and automatic transmission failures, sliding door malfunctions, catastrophic tire blowouts, and electrical malfunctions. In fact, their apparent decline in quality since 1997 and high MSRP over the past few years have actually boosted the attractiveness of GM, Nissan, and Mazda minivans, which, until recently, were only mediocre contenders.

MINIVAN RATINGS

Recommended
No models are recommended.

Above Average

DaimlerChrysler PT Cruiser (2002–03)	Honda Odyssey (1999–2003)
Ford Villager/Nissan Quest (1997–2002)	Mazda MPV (2002–03)

General Motors Astro, Safari
(2001–03)

Toyota Sienna (1998–2003)

Average

DaimlerChrysler Caravan, Voyager,
Grand Caravan, Grand Voyager,
Town & Country (2002–03)
DaimlerChrysler PT Cruiser (2001)
Ford Villager/Nissan Quest (1995–96)
General Motors Astro, Safari
(1996–2000)

General Motors Montana, Silhouette,
Trans Sport, Venture (1997–2003)
Honda Odyssey (1996–98)
Kia Sedona (2002–03)
Mazda MPV (2000–01)
Toyota Previa (1991–97)

Below Average

DaimlerChrysler Caravan, Voyager,
Grand Caravan, Grand Voyager,
Town & Country (1998–2001)

Mazda MPV (1988–98)

Not Recommended

DaimlerChrysler Caravan, Voyager,
Grand Caravan, Grand Voyager,
Town & Country (1984–97)
Ford Villager/Nissan Quest
(1993–94)

Ford Windstar (1995–2003)
General Motors Astro, Safari
(1985–95)
General Motors Lumina, Lumina APV,
Trans Sport (1990–96)

DaimlerChrysler

CARAVAN, VOYAGER, GRAND CARAVAN, GRAND VOYAGER, TOWN & COUNTRY ★★★

RATING: Average (2002–03); Below Average (1998–2001); Not Recommended (1984–97). Not to be bought without Chrysler's 7-year power-train warranty, or similar protection offered through an independent company. Major generic defects and a cheapskate warranty make the 1984–2001 models very risky buys. **Maintenance/Repair costs:** Repair costs are average during the warranty period and rise dramatically after the warranty expires. **Parts:** Higher-than-average costs, especially for paint, AC, transmission, and ABS components, which are covered under a number of "goodwill" warranty programs and numerous recall campaigns. Independent garages offer cheaper parts, provide longer warranties, and will often give expert testimony when the replaced component is found to be poorly manufactured. **Best alternatives:** The red-hot Honda Odyssey and Toyota Sienna minivans only cost a bit more, effectively dealing a severe blow to Chrysler's hopes to capture additional minivan sales without additional discounts and rebates. A new upscale Town & Country may cost up to $13,000 more than a base Caravan, yet only cost a few thousand more after five years on the market. Mazda's 2002 MPV is a good alternative; however, Nissan's Quest has been deep-discounted, reducing prices on used versions. Some full-sized GM or Chrysler rear-drive cargo vans, ripe for conversion, might be a more affordable and practical buy if you intend to haul a full passenger load, do some regular heavy hauling, use lots of accessories, or take frequent motoring excursions. **Online help:** *www.geocities.com/plumraptor, www.autosafety.org/autodefects.html, www.data-town.com/chrysler, www.wam.umd.edu/~gluckman/Chrysler/index.html,* and *www.daimlerchryslervehicleproblems.com.*

Strengths and weaknesses: Cheap and plentiful, Chrysler's minivans continue to dominate the new- and used-minivan market, though they're quickly losing steam, due to a cooling of the market and better product quality from GM and Japanese and South Korean automakers. They can carry up to seven passengers in comfort and also ride and handle better than most truck-based minivans. The shorter-wheelbase minivans also offer better rear visibility and good ride quality, and are more nimble and easier to park than truck-based minivans and larger front-drive versions. Cargo hauling capability is more than adequate, with a 1,225–1,600 kg (2,700–3,500 lb.) maximum towing range.

Caravans also give you a quiet and plush ride, excellent braking, lots of innovative convenience features, user-friendly instruments and controls, a driver-side sliding door, and plenty of interior room. Depreciation is slower than average, but much faster than pickups, SUVs, and Japanese minivans.

Don't make the mistake of believing that Chrysler's Mercedes connection means you'll get a top-quality minivan. You won't. In fact, owner complaints and service bulletins tell me that the 2004 minivans will likely have similar powertrain, electrical system, brake, suspension and body deficiencies as previous versions. The following *Lemon-Aid* reader's email is rather typical:

> My 2003 Dodge Caravan is a piece of garbage. My new Caravan had a recall for a part in the transmission. It is noisy, rough running, and it doesn't get the 21–27 mpg [8–11 km/L] as advertised. 12 mpg [5 km/L] is more realistic.
>
> Be warned! This van is terrible. Look at the other vans. Do not buy or lease this vehicle.

Acceleration with the base engine and handling with the extended versions is fairly mediocre. Both automatic transmissions perform poorly in different ways, but the 3-speed is decidedly the worst of the two. Most model years carry a chintzy base warranty that's overwhelmed by the enormity of chronic powertrain, ABS, and body defects, and is undermined by the automaker's hard-nosed attitude in interpreting its warranty obligations.

These minivans pose maximum safety risks, due to their chronic electronic, mechanical, and body component failures. Owners report bizarre "happenings" with their minivans, suggesting that these vehicles require the services of an exorcist rather than a mechanic (seat belts that may strangle children, airbags that deploy when the ignition is turned on, or sudden stalling on the highway when within radar range of airports or military installations).

If the above mechanical problems were concentrated only upon pre-'96 models, later models would be an acceptable buy. But that's not the case. Astoundingly, recently launched minivans continue to exhibit an array of serious mechanical deficiencies that belie Chrysler's so-called commitment to quality improvement. Some of the more serious and most common problems include the premature wearout of the engine tensioner pulley, automatic transmission speed sensors, engine head gaskets, motor mounts, starter motor, steering column glitches, front brake discs and pads (the brake pad material crumbles in your hands), front rotors and rear drums, brake master cylinder, suspension components, exhaust system components, ball joints, wheel bearings, water pumps, fuel pumps and pump wiring harnesses, radiators, heater cores, and AC units. Fuel injectors on all engines have been troublesome, the differential pin breaks through the automatic transmission casing, sliding doors malfunction, engine supports may be missing or not connected, tie-rods may suddenly break, oil pans crack, and the power-steering pump frequently leaks. Factory-installed Goodyear tires frequently fail prematurely at 40,000–65,000 km.

Since 1996, Chrysler's V6 engines have performed quite well—far better than similar 3.0L and 3.8L engines equipping Ford's Taurus, Sable, and Windstar minivan. Nevertheless, some owners have reported early engine head gasket failures, hard starts, stalling, serpentine belt failures, and power-steering pump hose blowouts (causing loss of power steering).

Chrysler's A604, 41TE, and 42LE automatic transmissions built over the past decade are a nightmare from a reliability standpoint (see "Safety summary"): Imagine having to count to three in traffic before Drive or Reverse will engage, "limping" home on the highway in Second gear at 50 km/h, or experiencing a catastrophic failure, like the following reader relates:

> My '99 Grand Voyager had a complete differential failure at 104,000 km. The retaining pin sheared off, which allowed the main differential pin to work its way out and smash the casing and torque converter.
>
> The cause of the failure is simple. Spinning the tires and having the differential components load up on torque when they acquire traction. This causes the pinion gears to spin on the pin. This would be fine but somehow since the differentials' conception no one has designed the system to properly lubricate between the gear and the pin. With the spinning there is excessive friction and heat, causing the components to score. Eventually, one of the gears will either bite into or fuse to the pin, causing the pin to spin.
>
> It doesn't take an engineer to determine that the small retaining pin can't withstand all that torque. In our case this is what happened. The gear bit, the pin spun, shearing the retaining pin off. With the centrifugal force the main pin worked its way out of the housing and smashed a 2" x 4" [4 cm x 10 cm] hole through the bell housing and nearly punctured the torque converter. In my opinion this is a design

flaw that should have been corrected 10 years ago. From my research I have determined that the transaxle identification number matches the original A604 transaxle. I was shocked that they would still use these in 1999.

Over the past decade, fit and finish has gotten worse, not better. In fact, some of the 1996–2000 models left the factory with wavy roof panels and assorted panel dents that dealers were asked to repair (see "Secret Warranties/Service Tips/TSBs"). Body hardware and interior trim are fragile and tend to break, warp, or fall off (door handles are an example).

Chrysler minivans are a self-contained orchestra of clicks, clunks, rattles, squeaks, squeals, and chattering, with noisy brakes, suspensions, and steering assemblies combined with poorly anchored bench seats and body panels. Finish problems can be summed up in three words: paint, paint, paint. The paint will likely discolour or delaminate on horizontal panels (roof and hood) after the third year. Chrysler knows about this problem and often tries to get the owner to pay half the cost of a repainting job (about $1,500 on a $3,000 job), but will eventually agree to pay the total cost if the owner stands fast, or threatens small claims court action.

Vehicle history: 1991—Restyled second generation models offered all-wheel drive, ABS, and a driver-side airbag (all optional); body was rounder and the glass area was increased. **1992**—Standard driver-side airbag. **1993**—Upgraded front shoulder belts and bucket seat tilts forward to ease entry/exit. **1994**— Passenger-side airbag, side door guard beams, a redesigned dash, new bumpers, and mouldings. **1996**—Third generation models have more aerodynamic styling, a driver-side sliding door, roll-out centre and rear seats, a longer wheelbase, standard dual airbags and ABS (ABS later became optional on base models), and a more powerful 150-hp 2.4L 4-cylinder engine. **1998**—The 3.0L V6 engine was paired with a better-performing 4-speed automatic transmission and the 3.8L V6 got 14 additional horses (180). **2000**—A new AWD Sport model (it was a sales flop) and standard cassette player and AC. **2001**— A small horsepower boost for the V6s, front side airbags, adjustable pedals, upgraded headlights, and a power-operated rear liftgate. **2002**—Fuel tank assembly redesigned to prevent post-collision fuel leakage, a tire air-pressure monitor, and a DVD entertainment system,

True, there's an abundance of used Chrysler minivans on the market selling at bargain prices; however, very few have any of their original warranty coverage left, and "goodwill" repair refunds are spotty and guidelines are vague. Don't even consider the 4-cylinder engine—it has no place in a minivan, especially when hooked to the inadequate 3-speed automatic transmission. It lacks an Overdrive and will shift back and forth as speed varies, and it's slower and noisier than the other choices. The 3.3L V6 is a better choice for most city-driving situations, but don't hesitate to get the 3.8L if you're planning lots of highway travel or carrying four or more passengers. Since its introduction, it's been relatively trouble-free, and it's more economical on the highway than the 3.3L, which strains to maintain speed. The sliding side doors make it easy to load and unload children, install a child safety seat in the middle, or remove the rear seat. On the downside, they expose kids to traffic and are a costly, failure-prone option. Child safety seats integrated into the rear seatbacks are convenient and reasonably priced, but Chrysler's versions have had a history of tightening up excessively or not tightening enough, allowing the child to slip out. Try the seat with your child before buying it. You may wish to pass on the tinted windshields; they seriously reduce visibility. Be wary of models featuring all-wheel drive and ABS brakes: The powertrain isn't reliable and is horrendously expensive to repair, and Chrysler's large number of ABS failures is worrisome. Ditch the failure-prone Goodyear original equipment tires and remember that a night drive is a prerequisite to check out headlight illumination, called inadequate by many.

Safety summary: All models/years: Owners report that cruise control units often malfunction, accelerating or decelerating the vehicle without any warning; brakes wear out prematurely, or fail completely; and that sudden stalling and transmission failures create life-threatening situations. **1995–96—** No steering. • Seatbacks fall backward. • Fuel tank is easily damaged. • Park won't hold vehicle. • Transmission fails, suddenly drops into low gear, won't go into Reverse, delays engagement, or jumps out of gear. • Rear windows fall out or shatter. • Power window and door lock failures. • Sliding door jams, trapping occupants. • Weak headlights. **1996—**3.3L and 3.8L lower engine oil leaks. • Coolant seepage from rear heater hose connections. • Cold-start stumble. • Rough idle, hesitation, or sags after fuel tank is filled (see "Secret Warranties/Service Tips/TSBs"). • Intermittent driveability problem near radar (again, explained more fully in "Secret Warranties/Service Tips/TSBs"). • Intermittent powertrain shudder. • Transmission limp-in caused by a faulty speed sensor. • Excessive transmission downshifting/upshifting in cruise control; dealers will install an upgraded overdrive clutch hub. • Difficulty going into Second gear or Reverse after a cold start. • Upshift shuddering. • ABS activates below 16 km/h. • Front wipers activate while driving or will not turn off. • Vehicle drifts or leads at high speeds. • Integrated child safety seat seatbelt retractor may restrict seat belt travel; dealer will replace assembly at no charge under Customer Satisfaction Note #650. • Child seat shoulder harness won't pull out. • False info on fuel tank capacity and inaccurate fuel gauge. • Faulty sliding door locks. • Inoperative sliding door and liftgate power lock motor; the sliding door may be difficult to open from the outside. • Unexplained theft alarm activation or dead battery. • Flying hubcaps (see "Secret Warranties/Service Tips/TSBs"). • Broken steering belt tensioner causes the sudden loss of power steering and power brakes. • Sliding door falls off. • Faulty power door locks. • Cracked axle/drive shaft. • Cruise control drops speed and then surges to former setting. • With AC engaged, vehicle stalls, then surges forward. • Power-steering failure, excessive noise. • Vehicle, parked with transmission in Park and with emergency brake applied, rolled into a lake. **1996–97—**Dashboard interior light switch started burning when ignition switch was turned on. • Numerous complaints of 4-cylinder head gasket failures. • When driving through water, air breather intake ingests water and engine seizes. • Sluggish acceleration after cold starts. • Slipping engine serpentine belt causes immediate steering loss. • Transmission hesitates and stumbles at highway speeds. • Constant stalling, often due to failure of the power control module (PCM) and oxygen sensor. • Chronic transmission failures. • Transmission allows vehicle to roll away when in Park. • One can move automatic transmission shift lever without applying brakes. • Several incidents where ignition was turned and vehicle went into Reverse at full throttle, although transmission was set in Park. • PRNDL indicator suddenly goes blank, comes back on only after vehicle restart. • ABS failure caused an accident. • Brakes activated by themselves while driving. • Prematurely warped rotors and worn-out pads cause excessive vibrations when stopping. • Steering may suddenly lock up. • Loss of steering control after running through a puddle. • No standard head restraints on the second- and third-row seats. • Seatback collapsed in collision. • Right front door latch failures, and sliding door often opens while vehicle is underway. • Driver- and passenger-side locks failed on sliding doors. • Distorted windshields and exterior rear-view mirror. • Inadequate windshield defrosting caused by poor design. • Early burnout of the AC compressor clutch. • Inoperative blower motors caused by a defective resistor. **1996–2002**—Steering may emit a popping or ticking noise. **1997**—1–2 shift shudder fix. • Delayed transaxle engagement. • Engine sags, hesitates, stumbles, stalls, or is hard to start. • Faulty speed control. • Momentary loss of power steering. • Low-speed tire wobble. • Smooth-road shake, vibration, or wobble. • Wipers won't park or wipe in intermittent mode. • Water leaks onto floor from HVAC housing. **1998**—Engine overheating. • Delayed transaxle engagement. • Transmission desensitization. • Intermittent loss of speed control or power-assisted steering. • Sags, hesitation, stumble, hard starts, or stalling. • Right rear tail light caught fire. • Slipping engine serpentine belt causes immediate steering loss. • Defective engine head gaskets, rocker arm gaskets, and engine mounts. • Chronic stalling caused by camshaft or oxygen sensor failures. • Surging and hesitation at highway speeds, especially with AC engaged. • Multiple transmission failures. • Vehicle rolled away while parked. • Many reports of vehicle suddenly jumping from Park into Reverse and speeding away. • Transmission fluid leaks due to defective front pump housing oil seal. • Sudden steering or brake loss. In one incident, the steering wheel separated from the steering column. • Frequent replacement of the steering column and rack and pinion. • Front suspension strut failure. • Many reports of defective liftgate gas shocks. • Many incidents reported of electrical short circuits and total electrical system failure. • Difficult to see through windshield in direct sunlight. • Defroster vent reflects in the windshield, obscuring driver's vision. • Poor steering-wheel design blocks the view of instruments and indicators. • Rear-view mirror often falls off. • Horn hard to find on steering hub. **1999**—Van rolled away while in Park. • Transmission failures. • When put into Reverse, vehicle may accelerate or brakes may lock up. • Sliding power door opens when vehicle passes over a bump. • Instrument panel fire. • Sudden, unintended acceleration. • When cruising on the highway, vehicle will suddenly shut down completely; problem also occurs at traffic lights. • Premature engine head gasket and automatic transmission failures. • Faulty

speed sensors cause the automatic transmission to shift erratically and harshly.
• With cruise control engaged, transmission won't downshift when going
uphill. • Five-year-old was able to pull shift lever out of Park into Drive
without engaging brakes. • Sudden tie-rod breakage, causing loss of vehicle
control. • Chronic steering pump and rack failures. • Poor braking performance: brake pedal depressed to the floor with little or no effect; excessive
vibrations or shuddering when braking. • Rusted-through front brake rotors
and rear brake drums. • Original equipment Goodyear Conquest tires leak air
or fail prematurely, with sidewall defects most evident; don't last half of their
expected mileage rating. • Sudden Goodyear Conquest blowout and split
wheel after passing over a small bump in the road. • Sliding power door opens
when vehicle passes over a bump. • Power side windows fail to roll up. • Horn
often doesn't work. • Dash gauges all go dead intermittently. **2000**—Gas tank
rupture. • Engine camshaft failure. • Sudden acceleration as vehicle being
parked; no airbag deployed in ensuing collision. • Many incidents where children were able to shift transmission without applying brakes. Although the
owner's manual says vehicle should have a transmission/brake interlock, the
feature is lacking (see "Secret Warranties/Service Tips/TSBs"). • Excessive
transmission noise, fluid leak, and then premature transmission failure. •
Cruise control malfunctions. • ABS brake failure. • Frequent premature rotor
and pad replacements; brake rotors often found to be out-of-round and pads
show signs of heat damage. Both components are usually replaced under a
secret warranty. • Parking brake lock-up. • Sudden blowout, premature wear,
and sidewall bulging of Goodyear tires (often replaced under a secret warranty). • Sudden steering lock-up. • Steering column replacement. • Two front
seatbacks collapsed from rear impact. • In a collision, third rear seat flew forward, injuring children seated on it. • Broken door latch. • Several incidents
where side windows exploded for no apparent reason. • Carbon monoxide
intrudes into the cabin area. • Front passenger seat metal bar may cause leg
burns when heated by sun radiation. **2000–01**—Sudden loss of engine power,
accompanied by fuel leakage from the engine compartment. • Emergency
parking brake may not release, due to premature corrosion. • Right front brake
locked up while driving, causing the vehicle to suddenly turn 90 degrees to the
right; same phenomenon when braking. • Vehicle pulls to the left or right
while driving. • When driving about 60 km/h up an incline, transmission suddenly slips into low gear and the vehicle stops. • Defective clock spring causes
airbag light to remain lit. • Transmission shift lever blocks the driver's right
knee when braking. • Excessive engine and steering wheel noise. • Carbon
monoxide comes through air vents. • Fifth-wheel assembly fell off while
vehicle was underway. • Back sliding door popped open while cruising. •
Instruments are recessed too deep into the dash, making it hard to read the
fuel gauge and speedometer, especially at night. **2001–02**—Engine camshafts
may have an improperly machined oil groove. • Engine hesitation or stalling. •
Vehicle may surge at 80–100 km/h. • Front-end grinding, clicking, or
knocking. • Snow and water ingestion into rear brake drum. • Faulty power-
sliding door. • Inaccurate fuel tank gauge drops one-quarter to one-half while
driving. • Faulty power seat adjuster. • Difficult to remove fuel cap (install a

new seal); this free repair applies to all of the 2002 vehicle lineup. **2002**—
Adults cannot sit in third-row seat without neck smashing into roof as vehicle
passes over bumps. • Airbags deployed for no reason. • Airbag light comes on
randomly and clock spring defect disabled the airbag. • Power-steering fluid
leakage. • Middle-seat seat belt unbuckles on its own. • Rear side vent window
exploded while driving. • Headlights come on and off on their own. **2003**—
Automatic transmission won't shift or suddenly drops into Reverse. • Exposed
electrical wires under the front seats. • Excessive steering vibration. • Seat belts
unlatch themselves. • Missing suspension bolt caused the right side to collapse.
• Wiper blades stick together.

Secret Warranties/Service Tips/TSBs

All models/years: If pressed, Chrysler will replace the AC evaporator for free
up to seven years. Other AC component costs are negotiable. **1993–2000**—
Paint delamination, peeling, or fading (see Part Two). • A rotten-egg odour
coming from the exhaust may be the result of a malfunctioning catalytic converter, probably covered under the emissions warranty. **1995–98**—Possible
causes of delayed transmission engagement (TSB #21-07-98). **1996**—Poor
engine performance near military installations or airports is caused by radar
interference. Correct by installing a "hardened" crankshaft position sensor
and/or reprogramming (flashing) the PCM with new software calibrations. •
Rough idle, hesitation, or sags after the fuel tank is filled can only be corrected
by the installation of a new fuel tank, according to TSB #18-28-95. • Steering
noise during parking lot manoeuvres may be fixed by installing a new power-
steering gear and left-side attaching bolt. **1996–99**—A serpentine belt that
slips off the idler pulley requires an upgraded bracket. • Upgraded engine head
gasket. • Oil seepage from the cam position sensor. **1996–2000**—Strut tower
corrosion (see following bulletin).

Suspension/Body – Strut Tower Corrosion

Number: 23-044-02
Date: Oct. 14, 2002
SUBJECT: NS Strut Tower Corrosion
OVERVIEW: This bulletin involves correcting a corrosion staining, surface corrosion, or corrosion
perforation condition at the top of the strut tower(s).
MODELS: 1996–2000 NS Town & Country/Voyager/Caravan
SYMPTOM/CONDITION: Cosmetic corrosion or perforation at upper strut tower(s) usually
between the strut and upper load path beam inner panel (inner fender).

• Cruise control that won't hold the vehicle's speed when going uphill may
have a faulty check valve. • Countermeasures detailed to correct a steering
column click or rattle. • Airbag warning light stays lit. **1996–2001**—AWD

models *must* be equipped with identical tires; otherwise, the power transfer unit may self-destruct. • A suspension squawk or knock probably means the sway bar link needs replacing under Chrysler's "goodwill" policy (5 years/ 100,000 km). **1996–2003**—Rusted, frozen rear brake drums (see following bulletin).

Brake Drums (Rear) – Snow/Water Ingestion

Number: 05-001-02

Date: Mar. 4, 2002

OVERVIEW: This bulletin involves installing a revised rear drum brake support (backing) plate and possible replacement of the rear brake shoes and drums.

MODELS: 1996–2003 (RS) Town & Country/Voyager/Caravan

SYMPTOM/CONDITION: While driving through deep or blowing snow/water, the snow/water may enter the rear brake drums causing rust to develop on the rear brake drum and shoe friction surfaces. This condition can lead to temporary freezing of the rear brake linings to the drums. This symptom is experienced after the vehicle has been parked in below freezing temperatures long enough for the snow/water to freeze inside of the rear brake drums. When the parking brake has been applied the symptom is more likely to occur.

• Roof panel wavy or has depressions. **1997–98**—Engines that run poorly or stall may need the PCM reprogrammed under the emissions warranty. **1997–2000**—If the ignition key can't be turned or cannot be removed, TSB #23-23-00 proposes four possible corrections. **1997–2001**— Rear brake noise (see following bulletin).

Rear Brake Howl/Moan

Number: 05-003-01

Date: Apr. 20, 2001

OVERVIEW: This bulletin involves replacing the rear disc brake adapters.

MODELS: 1997–2001 Voyager/Caravan/Town & Country

SYMPTOM/CONDITION: During low speed and/or low speed turns such as a parking lot manoeuvre, with no brake pedal pressure applied, a low frequency howl/moan noise is heard from the rear brake area.

1998—A faulty radiator fan relay may cause the engine to overheat; replace it with a new relay and reprogram the powertrain control module under Customer Satisfaction Notice #771. **1998–99**—Front brakes continue to wear out quickly on front-drive minivans. Owners report that Chrysler pays half the cost of brake repairs for up to 2 years/40,000 km. • Silence a chronic squeaking noise coming from underneath the vehicle by installing a new strut pivot bearing. **1998–2000**—Troubleshooting AC compressor failure (see following bulletin).

AC Compressor – Locks Up At Low Mileage

Number: 24-15-99

Date: Jul. 9, 1999

OVERVIEW: This bulletin involves determining the extent of AC compressor lock-up and either working the compressor loose or replacing it.

MODELS: 1998–2000 Town & Country/Caravan/Voyager
1998–2000 Chrysler Voyager (International Market)
1998–2000 (PL) Neon

SYMPTOM/CONDITION: The AC compressor may lock up, causing the drive belt to slip in the AC clutch pulley, producing a squealing noise at initial start-up.

1999–2000—Measures to prevent the right-side sliding door trim panel from hitting the quarter panel when the door is opened. • Tips for eliminating radio speaker static. **2000**—Delayed shifts. **2000–01**—Poor starting, • Rear disc brake squeal. • AC compressor failure, loss of engine power when switching on the AC, serpentine belt chirping, and spark knock can all be traced to a miscalibrated PCM. • No heat on front right side, due to a defective blend air door. • AC compressor squeal. • Rear bench seat rattle or groan. • Hood hinge rattle. • Noisy Michelin tires (for a free replacement, dealer must refer to Chrysler TSB #22-003-01 and call Michelin Canada Public Relations at 1-888-871-4444, or for Quebec: 1-800-565-7638). • Centre console won't hold a cellular phone. • Inoperative overhead reading lamp and rear wiper. • Noisy roof rack. • Noisy power-sliding door. **2001–02**—Engine surging at highway speeds. • Engine knocking. • Engine sag and hesitation caused by a faulty throttle position sensor (TPS). • Engine mount grinding or clicking. • Steering wheel shudder; steering column popping or ticking. • Poor rear AC performance. • AC leaks water onto passenger side carpet. • Wind or water leaks at the rear quarter window. • High-pitched belt-like squeal at high engine RPMs. • Sliding door reverses direction. • Incorrect fuel gauge indicator. • Loose tail lamp. Flickering digital display. **2001–03**—Rear brake rubbing sound. • Oil filter leaks with 3.3L and 3.8L engines (confirmed in TSB # 09-001-03).

> On February 25, 2003, my 2002 Grand Caravan lost almost all of its engine oil which resulted in engine failure. At no time did the vehicle's warning sensors indicate any problem with the engine. The failure was the result of a leak in the filter gasket of the FE292 Mopar oil filter. Documentation from the oil filter manufacturer indicates that the oil filter gasket overhangs the inside diameter of the adapter head by .1 cm/side [.045 in./side].

2002—Transmission slips in First or Reverse gear. • Airbags deployed for no reason. • Airbag light comes on randomly and clock spring defect disabled the airbag. • Power-steering fluid leakage. • Middle-seat seat belt unbuckles on its own. • Rear side vent window exploded while driving. • Erratically operating power sliding door or liftgate. • Headlights come on and off on their own. •

Noisy engine and transmission. **2002–03**—Sliding door or liftgate malfunctions. **2003**—Troubleshooting water leaks. • Three bulletins relating to automatic transmission malfunctions: delayed gear engagement; harsh 4–3 downshift; and excessive vibration and transfer gear whine.

Caravan, Voyager, Grand Caravan, Grand Voyager, Town & Country Profile

	1996	1997	1998	1999	2000	2001	2002	2003
Cost Price ($)								
Caravan	18,840	19,885	20,255	24,230	24,970	24,885	25,430	25,430
Grand Caravan	20,320	21,465	23,160	25,890	26,665	29,505	28,875	29,295
Town & Country	38,280	40,350	41,040	41,260	41,815	41,150	40,815	42, 705
Used Values ($)								
Caravan ⋏	5,000	6,500	8,000	10,000	12,000	14,000	19,000	21,000
Caravan ⋎	3,500	5,500	6,500	8,500	11,000	13,000	17,000	19,000
Grand Caravan ⋏	5,500	7,500	9,000	11,000	13,000	16,000	20,000	23,000
Grand Caravan ⋎	4,000	6,500	8,000	9,500	12,000	14,000	18,500	21,000
Town & Country ⋏	7,000	8,500	11,000	13,500	17,000	21,000	26,000	32,000
Town & Country ⋎	6,000	7,500	9,000	12,000	15,500	19,500	24,000	30,500
Reliability	❶	❶	❷	❷	❷	❷	③	③
Crash Safety (F)								
Caravan	—	④	③	—	④	④	④	④
Grand Caravan	③	③	③	④	④	④	④	④
Town & Country	—	④	③	—	—	—	—	④
Town & Country LX	③	③	③	④	④	④	④	④
Side								
Caravan	—	—	—	⑤	⑤	④	④	④
Grand Caravan	—	—	—	⑤	⑤	④	⑤	⑤
Town & Country LX	—	—	—	⑤	⑤	④	⑤	⑤
Offset (G. Caravan)	❷	❷	❷	❷	❷	❶	❷	❷
Town & Country	❷	❷	❷	❷	❷	❶	❷	❷
Rollover Resistance	—	—	—	—	—	③	③	③

Note: Voyager and Grand Voyager prices and ratings are almost identical to those of the Caravan and Grand Caravan.

PT CRUISER ★★★★

RATING: Above Average (2002–03); Average (2001). The 2002+ models' powertrain warranty makes a big difference in the Cruiser's rating. Nevertheless, despite its hot-rod flair, this Neon spin-off's popularity is waning with sales down 25 percent. Similar hard times have hit other "nostalgia" cars like the VW New Beetle and resurrected Ford Thunderbird. **Maintenance/ Repair costs:** Average, until the 5-year mark, when poor durability, first-year glitches, and the warranty's expiration will likely hike maintenance and repair costs. Another reason to buy a supplementary powertrain warranty or choose a 2002 version protected by Chrysler's 7-year warranty. **Parts:** Reasonably priced, since many parts come from the Neon generic parts bin. Body parts are another matter. Expect long delays and high costs. **Best alternatives:** In a pinch, you may wish to consider the Kia Sedona minivan (third year on the market), or the following wagons: VW's Jetta wagon, the Subaru Legacy Outback Limited, or the Volvo V40. Sport-utilities worth considering are the Subaru Forester, Honda CR-V EX, GM Tracker, Hyundai Santa Fe, and Suzuki Grand Vitara. Both Ford's Escape and Jeep's Liberty are risky SUV alternatives. The Escape is unproven and the Liberty is both unproven and rollover prone, say *Autoweek* and Germany's *Auto Bild* magazine ("Wie gefahrlich ist der Jeep?" or "How dangerous is the Jeep?"). **Online help:** *www.ptcruiser.org, www.ptcruiserlinks.com, www.datatown.com/chrysler, www.wam. umd.edu/~gluckman/Chrysler/index.html, www.daimlerchryslervehicleproblems.com,* and *www.autosafety.org/autodefects.html.*

Strengths and weaknesses: Cobbled together with Neon parts and engineering, the PT Cruiser is essentially a fuel- and space-efficient hatchback mini-minivan. It's noted for excellent fuel economy (regular fuel), nimble handling around town, good braking, lots of interior space, easy access, a versatile cargo area, many thoughtful interior amenities, slow depreciation, and unforgettable hot-rod styling.

Forget about hot-rod power, though. The 2.4L 150-hp, 4-cylinder engine is not very smooth running and, when matched to the automatic transmission, struggles when going uphill or merging with freeway traffic. This requires frequent downshifting and lots of patience—accelerating to 100 km/h takes about 9 seconds. The automatic transmission doesn't have much low-end torque, either, forcing early kickdown shifting and deft manipulation of the accelerator pedal. High-speed handling is competent, but not impressive; hard cornering produces an unsteady, wobbly ride due to the car's height. Count on a firm ride with lots of engine, wind, and road noise in the cabin area. ABS braking is acceptable, when the system functions as it should.

Reliability has been decent, although there have been some drivetrain complaints that include excessive oil consumption due to a faulty valve cover gasket, and automatic transmission failures or erratic transmission performance (gears down to "limp mode") due to a faulty transmission control module:

> I have had my transmission go out twice now. The first time the whole tranny had to be replaced, second time it just lost all its fluid. The 41TE transmission is one of the worst transmissions ever made. Go to any search engine and type in 41TE and all the websites talking about the problems with the tranny will come up. DC has known of the problems since 1989 and doesn't care.

Writes another owner of a 2001 PT Cruiser:

> Transmission control unit went out on the freeway in stop-and-go traffic. Tranny went into failsafe (Second gear) so I drove it to the dealership for repairs. Took one day (they had the part in stock). Two days later, my wife's Dodge Caravan had the *same* part go out on her.

Premature failure of the power-steering pump and the steering unit are also frequent problems that can result in costly repairs once the warranty expires.

Windshield stress cracks are another PT Cruiser specialty reported on the Internet by owners in Australia, Canada, and the United States. Chrysler is replacing the windshields under a "goodwill" program, while insisting that the poor windshields just happen to be "rock prone."

Other owner concerns: annoying wind noise when driving with the rear window or sunroof open; drivetrain whine; moisture between clearcoat and paint turns the hood a chalky white colour; and water leaks through the side passenger window.

Safety summary: 2001—Some side wind instability. • Tall drivers beware: The windshield is uncomfortably close, and its styling makes it difficult to see overhead traffic lights. • The three small and recessed instrument pods are difficult to read in the daylight. • Wide pillars obstruct one's view. • When parked, transmission slipped out of gear and vehicle rolled down driveway. • Hot exhaust may melt the rear bumper. • Oil blows through tailpipe. • Engine suddenly shuts down when vehicle passes over a large puddle. • Sudden loss of all electrical power. • Chronic stalling due to a faulty ignition coil. • Defective powertrain control module (PCM). • Steering wheel loosens on its shaft. • Excessive vibration caused by out-of-round tires or a too-loose suspension. • Steering column popping or cracking sound. • Head restraints won't stay in position, tend to drift up. • Headlights flicker from bright to dim. • Low-beam headlight may suddenly go out. • Only part of the headlight beam illuminates the roadway. **2002**—Sudden, unintended acceleration. • Gas pedal went to floor with no acceleration. • Airbags deployed for no reason, or failed to deploy. • Suddenly shifts into First gear while cruising. • Sudden brake lock-up. • Headrests are too high, block vision. • Optima battery leaks acid. • White powder leaks from airbag. • Hard-to-read speedometer. **2003**—Airbags failed to deploy. • Chronic engine overheating. • Sudden front axle/bearing seizure threw car out of control and caused $7,000 damage to the drivetrain. • Other automatic transmission failures while car was underway. • Premature failure of the clutch assembly. • Headlights flicker when braking. • Chrysler misleads buyers that the car has a rear stabilizer bar when really it's just a beefed-up axle (see *www.petitiononline.com/2003stab/petition.html*). • Sudden, unintended acceleration while stopped at a traffic light or when braking. • Self-activating door locks and seat heater. • Third brake light gasket doesn't sit flush to the windshield. • Goodyear Eagle tire sidewall blew out.

Secret Warranties/Service Tips/TSBs

All models/years—2001—Hard starting due to a faulty fuel pump module. • Hard starting in cold weather due to the 5-volt regulator failure in the SBEC PCM module. • A faulty transmission control module (TCM) may cause harsh shifting. • MIL (malfunction indicator light) comes on due to a faulty TCM harness connector or a defective evaporator purge flow monitor. • Poor acceleration and spark knock. • Due to a delamination problem, the accessory drive belt for the power steering pump and AC compressor may need replacement. • Left or right floor latch on rear seat won't release. • Fuel gauge won't indicate full. • Missing or loose roof luggage rack stanchion. • Airbag pads fall off. • Airbag rattles. • Ticking noise caused by faulty rear body exhauster. • Discoloured B- and C-pillar door appliqués. • Wind buffeting with the windows and/or sunroof open or partially opened. • The front door water dam may contact the speaker and create a buzzing or humming. **2001–02**—Highway speed surge. **2001–03**—Alarm sounds for no reason. • Transmission slips in Reverse or First gear. • Moisture accumulation in headlights. • High-speed engine surging. **2002–03**—Steering column clicking. **2003**—Turbo engine hesitation, loss of boost, and screeching. • Delayed gear engagement. • Harsh 4–3 downshift. • Rear windshield washer nozzle leak. • Warning lights come on for no reason. • Warped rear bumper.

PT Cruiser Profile

	2001	2002	2003
Cost Price ($)			
Base	23,665	23,850	22,500
Limited	27,180	27,305	27,420
Turbo	—	—	27,700
Used Values ($)			
PT Cruiser ⋀	14,000	15,500	18,000
PT Cruiser ⋁	12,500	14,500	16,000
Limited ⋀	15,500	18,000	21,000
Limited ⋁	14,000	16,500	19,000
Turbo ⋀	—	—	21,500
Turbo ⋁	—	—	20,000
Reliability	④	④	④
Crash Safety (F)	❷	④	④
Side	④	④	④
Head Restraints (F)	⑤	⑤	⑤
Rollover Resistance	④	④	④

Ford

WINDSTAR ★

RATING: Not Recommended (1995–2003), noted for atrocious quality control at the factory and supplier level. **Maintenance/Repair costs:** Average while under warranty; outrageously higher than average thereafter, due primarily to powertrain breakdowns not covered by warranty or insufficiently covered by parsimonious "goodwill" gestures. **Parts:** Reasonably priced parts are easy to find, mainly due to the entry of independent suppliers, lured by attractive profits sustained by parts that apparently have a high failure rate, like brake master cylinders and speedometers. Digital speedometers can be exceptionally expensive. **Best alternatives:** Still can't beat the Japanese for minivan reliability and performance. Honda's Odyssey and the Toyota Sienna are the best choices if you don't mind spending a few thousand dollars more. You can cut costs and get fairly good reliability from the Ford Villager; a recent GM Venture, Montana, Astro, or Safari; Mazda's MPV; and the discontinued Nissan Axxess or Quest. Some full-sized GM (Chevy Van and Vandura) or Chrysler rear-drive cargo vans might be a more affordable and practical buy if you intend to haul a full passenger load, do some regular heavy hauling, use lots of accessories, or take frequent motoring excursions. Even an older Ford Aerostar rear-drive minivan may fill the bill if the automatic transmission, electrical system, and brakes check out OK. **Online help:** *www.tgrigsby.com/ views/ford.htm*; *www.notjobone.com*; *ca.geocities.com/windstarwoes*; and *www.autosafety.org/autodefects.html.*

Strengths and weaknesses: The Windstar is built on a modified Taurus platform, and as such, has some of the carlike handling characteristics of Chrysler's minivans. On the other hand, you'll also encounter many of the horrific engine, automatic transmission, electrical, suspension, and brake system problems experienced by Taurus and Sable owners.

Vehicle history: 1996—45 more horses added to the 3.8L engine (200), a smaller 3.0L V6 powers the GL, upgraded seat belts, and a tilt-slide driver-side seat to improve rear seat access. **1998**—A wider driver's door, easier rear seat access, and new front styling. **1999**—A bit more interior space; the third-row bench got built-in rollers; improved steering and brakes (compromised by rear drums, though); ABS; an anti-theft system; new side panels; a new liftgate; larger headlights and tail lights; and a revised instrument panel. **2001**—The base 3.0L V6 is gone, an upgraded automatic transmission, a low-tire-pressure warning system, "smart" airbags, new airbag sensors, and a slight restyling. **2002**—Dual sliding doors. **2003**—Freestar debuts as a 2004 model.

Base models may not have head restraints for all seats, and the digital dash can be confusing and expensive ($500) to replace. Optional adjustable pedals help protect drivers from airbag injuries. Be careful, though; some drivers have found that they are set too close together and say they often felt loose. Other nice safety features: airbags that adjust deployment speed according to occupant weight and a sliding door warning light.

Engine and transmission failures

Engine and transmission failures are commonplace. The 3.0L engine is overwhelmed by the Windstar's heft and struggles to keep up, but opting for the 3.8L V6 may get you into worse trouble. Even when it's running properly, the 3.8L knocks loudly when under load and pings at other times. Far more serious is the high failure rate of 3.8L engine head gaskets shortly after the 60,000 km mark. Ford's 7-year/ 160,000 km Owner Notification Program only covers '95s, so owners are asked to pay $1,000 to $3,000 for an engine repair, depending upon how much the engine has overheated. Transmission repairs seldom cost less than $3,000.

Early warning signs are few and benign: the engine may lose some power or overheat; the transmission pauses before downshifting or shifts roughly into a higher gear. Owners may also hear a transmission whining or groaning sound, accompanied by driveline vibrations. There is no other prior warning before the transmission breaks down completely and the minivan comes to a sudden banging, clanging halt.

> I just want to thank you for saving us at least $1,500. The transmission in our '98 Windstar went *bang* with only 47,300 miles [75,700 km]. After reading about Ford's goodwill adjustment on your site, we were told by our local Ford dealer that owner participation would be $495. We received a new rebuilt Ford unit installed. Believe it or not, I am a fairly good mechanic myself and this came with no warning! We even serviced the transmission at 42,000 miles [67,200 km] and found no debris or evidence of a problem.

Apparently, automatic transmission glitches also affect Ford's 2001 Taurus, Sable, Windstar, and Continental. In a March 2001 Special Service Instruction (SSI) #01T01, Ford authorized its dealers to replace all defective transaxles listed in its TSB, which describes the defect in the following manner:

> The driver may initially experience a transaxle "slip" or "Neutral" condition during a 2–3 shift event. Extended driving may result in loss of Third gear function and ultimately loss of Second gear function. The driver will still be able to operate the vehicle, but at a reduced level of performance.

Ford's memo states that owners weren't to be notified of the potential problem.

Brakes are another sore point with Windstar owners. They aren't reliable, and calipers, rotors, and the master cylinder often need replacing. Other frequent Windstar problems concern no-starts and chronic stalling, believed to be caused by a faulty fuel pump or powertrain control module (PCM); electrical system power-steering failures; hard steering at slow speeds; excessive steering wheel vibrations; sudden tire tread separation and premature tread wear; advanced coil spring corrosion, leading to spring collapse and puncturing of the front tire (only 1997–98 models were recalled); rear shock failures at 110 km/h; left-side axle breakage while underway; exploding rear windshields; power-sliding door malfunctions; and failure-prone digital speedometers that are horrendously expensive to replace. There have also been many complaints concerning faulty computer modules; engine oil leaks; AC failures; and early replacement of engine camshafts, tie-rods, and brake rotors and calipers.

Getting compensation

Since 1997, I've lobbied Ford to stop playing cat and mouse with its customers and set up a formal 7-year/160,000 km transmission warranty similar to its 3.8L engine extended warranty. I warned the company that failure to protect owners would result in huge sales losses by Ford as word spread that its vehicles were lemons.

As of March 2000, Ford of Canada used my suggestion as a benchmark in settling owner claims in Canada. Unfortunately, Ford USA got wind of it and squashed the Canadian initiative. Interestingly, the three top Ford Canada executives who pleaded the Canadian case have since left the company. Jac Nasser, the Ford USA CEO who rejected additional protection for owners, was fired shortly thereafter.

> Hi Phil: I just wanted to let you know that I did have to go to small claims court to nudge Ford into action. In pretrial settlement proceedings, the Ford representative at first gave me an offer of $980 for my troubles. I countered with the actual cost of $2,190 to replace my '96 Windstar's transmission. He did not like that idea, and we went back into the court setting. After instruction from the judge, I began to copy my 200+ pages (for the judge as evidence) of documentation for why this is a recurring problem with Ford transmissions (thank you, by the way, for all the great info).
>
> I think it made him a little scared, so I asked if he would settle for $1,600 (a middle ground of our original proposals) to which he accepted. My transmission costs were $2,190, so I basically paid about $600 for a new transmission (*not* a Ford replacement, either).
>
> Anyway, I figured a guaranteed $1,600 was better than not knowing what would happen in court. Thanks for your help!

Ford's denial of owner claims has been blasted in small claims court judgments across Canada during the past few years. Judges have ruled that engines and transmissions must be reasonably durable long after the warranty expires, whether the vehicle was bought new or used, notwithstanding that it was repaired by an independent, or had the same problem repaired earlier for free.

The three most recent engine judgments supporting Ford owners are:

Dufour v. Ford Canada Ltd, Quebec Small Claims Court (Hull), No. 550-32-008335-009, April 10, 2001, Justice P. Chevalier. Money refunded for 1996 Windstar engine repairs (see page 82) or download from *lemonaidcars.com).*

Schaffler v. Ford Motor Company Limited and Embrun Ford Sales Ltd., Ontario Superior Court of Justice, L'Orignal Small Claims Court, Court File No. 59-2003, July 22, 2003, Justice Gerald Langlois. Plaintiff bought a used 1995 Windstar in 1998. Engine head gasket was repaired for free three years later under Ford's 7-year extended warranty. In 2002 at 109,600 km, head gasket failed, again, seriously damaging the engine. Ford refused a second repair. Justice Langlois ruled that Ford's warranty extension bulletin listed signs and symptoms of the covered defect that were identical to the problems written on the second work order ("persistent and/or chronic engine overheating; heavy white smoke evident from the exhaust tailpipe; flashing 'low coolant' instrument panel light even after coolant refill; and constant loss of engine coolant.") Judge Langlois concluded "the problem was brought to the attention of the dealer well within the warranty period; the dealer was negligent." The Plaintiffs were awarded $4,941, plus 5 percent interest. This includes $1,070 for two months' car rental.

John R. Reid and Laurie M. McCall v. Ford Motor Company of Canada, Superior Court of Justice, Ottawa Small Claims Court, Claim No: #02-SC-077344, July 11, 2003, Justice Tiernay. A 1996 Windstar bought used in 1997 experienced engine head gasket failure in October 2001 at 159,000 km. Judge Tiernay awarded the Plaintiffs $4,145 for the following reasons: "A Technical Service Bulletin dated June 28, 1999, was circulated to Ford dealers. It dealt specifically with 'undetermined loss of coolant' and 'engine oil contaminated with coolant' in the 1996–98 Windstar and five other models of Ford vehicles. I conclude that Ford owed a duty of care to the Plaintiff to equip this vehicle with a cylinder head gasket of sufficient sturdiness and durability that would function trouble-free for at least seven years, given normal driving and proper maintenance conditions. I find that Ford is answerable in damages for the consequences of its negligence."

The Ford TSB that Judge Tiernay cited is found in the Windstar's "Secret Warranties/Service Tips/TSBs" section.

Automatic transmission lawsuits have also been quite successful. They are often settled out of court because Ford frequently offers 50–75 percent refunds, if the lawsuit is dropped. Alan MacDonald, a *Lemon-Aid* reader who won his case in small claims court, gives the following tips on beating Ford:

I want to thank you for the advice you provided in my dealings with
the Ford Motor Company of Canada, Limited and Highbury Ford Sales
Limited regarding my 1994 Ford Taurus wagon and the problems with

the automatic transmission (Taurus and Windstar transmissions are identical). I also wish to apologize for not sending you a copy of this judgment earlier that may be beneficial to your readers. (*MacDonald v. Highbury Ford Sales Limited*, Ontario Superior Court of Justice in the Small Claims Court London, June 6, 2000, Court File #0001/00, Judge J. D. Searle).

In 1999 after only 105,000 km the automatic transmission went. I took the car to Highbury Ford to have it repaired. We paid $2,070 to have the transmission fixed, but protested and felt the transmission failed prematurely. We contacted Ford, but to no avail: their reply was we were out of warranty period. The transmission was so poorly repaired (and we went back to Highbury Ford several times) that we had to go to Mr. Transmission to have the transmission fixed again nine months later at a further $1,906.02.

It is at that point that I contacted you, and I was surprised, and somewhat speechless (which you noticed) when you personally called me to provide advice and encouragement. I am very grateful for your call. My observations with going through small claims court involved the following: I filed in January of 2000, the trial took place on June 1 and the judgment was issued June 6.

At pretrial, a representative of Ford (Ann Sroda) and a representative from Highbury Ford were present. I came with one binder for each of the defendants, the court and one for myself (each binder was about 3 inches thick—containing your reports on Ford Taurus automatic transmissions, ALLDATA Service Bulletins, Taurus Transmissions Victims (Bradley website), Center for Auto Safety (website), Read This Before Buying a Taurus (website), and the Ford Vent Page (website).

The representative from Ford asked a lot of questions (I think she was trying to find out if I had read the contents of the information I was relying on). The Ford representative then offered a 50 percent settlement based on the initial transmission work done at Highbury Ford. The release allowed me to still sue Highbury Ford with regards to the necessity of going to Mr. Transmission because of the faulty repair done by the dealer. Highbury Ford displayed no interest in settling the case, and so I had to go to court.

For court, I prepared by issuing a summons to the manager at Mr. Transmission, who did the second transmission repair, as an expert witness. I was advised that unless you produce an expert witness you won't win in a car repair case in small claims court. Next, I went to the law school library in London and received a great deal of assistance in researching cases pertinent to car repairs. I was told that judgments in your home province (in my case Ontario) were binding on the court; that cases outside of the home province could be considered, but not binding, on the judge.

The cases I used for trial involved *Pelleray v. Heritage Ford Sales*

Ltd., Ontario Small Claims Court (Scarborough) SC7688/91 March 22, 1993; *Phillips et al. v. Ford Motor Co. of Canada Ltd. et al.*, Ontario Reports 1970, 15th January 1970; *Gregorio v. Intrans-Corp.*, Ontario Court of Appeal, May 19, 1994; *Collier v. MacMaster's Auto Sales,* New Brunswick Court of Queen's Bench, April 26, 1991; *Sigurdson v. Hillcrest Service & Acklands* (1977), Saskatchewan Queen's Bench; *White v. Sweetland*, Newfoundland District Court, Judicial Centre of Gander, November 8, 1978; *Raiches Steel Works v. J. Clark & Son*, New Brunswick Supreme Court, March 7, 1977; *Mudge v. Corner Brook Garage Ltd.*, Newfoundland Supreme Court, July 17, 1975; *Sylvain v. Carroseries d'Automobiles Guy Inc.* (1981), C.P. 333, Judge Page; *Gagnon v. Ford Motor Company of Canada, Limited et Marineau Automobile Co. Ltée.* (1974), C.S. 422–423.

In court, I had prepared the case, as indicated above, had my expert witness and two other witnesses who had driven the vehicle (my wife and my 18-year-old son). As you can see by the judgment, we won our case and I was awarded $1,756.52, including prejudgment interest and costs.

Mental Distress

Canadian courts have become more generous in awarding plaintiffs money for mental distress experienced when defects aren't repaired properly under warranty. In *Sharman v. Formula Ford Sales Limited, Ford Credit Limited, and Ford Motor Company of Canada Limited,* Ontario Superior Court of Justice, No: 17419/02SR, 2003/10/07, Justice Sheppard awarded the owner of a 2000 Windstar $7,500 for mental distress resulting from the breach of the implied warranty of fitness, plus $7,207 for breach of contract and breach of warranty. Problems: Windstar sliding door wasn't secure and leaked air and water after many attempts to repair it. Interestingly, the judge cited the *Wharton* decision (see page 36) as support for his award for mental distress.

> The plaintiff and his family have had three years of aggravation, inconvenience, worry, and concern about their safety and that of their children. Generally speaking, our contract law did not allow for compensation for what may be mental distress, but that may be changing. I am indebted to counsel for providing me with the decision of the British Columbia Court of Appeal in *Wharton v. Tom Harris Chevrolet Oldsmobile Cadillac Ltd.*, [2002] B.C.J. No. 233, 2002 BCCA 78. This decision was recently followed in *T'avra v. Victoria Ford Alliance Ltd.*, [2003] B, CJ No. 1957.
>
> In *Wharton*, the purchaser of a Cadillac Eldorado claimed damages against the dealer because the car's sound system emitted an annoying buzzing noise and the purchaser had to return the car to the dealer for repair numerous times over 2.5 years. The trial court awarded damages of $2,257.17 for breach of warranty with respect to

the sound system, and $5,000 in non-pecuniary damages for loss of enjoyment of their luxury vehicle and for inconvenience, for a total award of $7,257.17. The Court of Appeal upheld the decision of the trial judge and Levine J.A. spent considerable time reviewing the law, but in particular the law relating to damages for breach of implied warranty of fitness: "The principles applicable to an award of damages for mental distress resulting from a breach of contract were thoroughly and helpfully analyzed in the recent judgment of the House of Lords in *Farley v. Skinner*, [2001] 3 W.L.R. 899, [2001] H.L.J. No. 49, affirming and clarifying the decision of the English Court of Appeal in *Watts v. Morrow*, [1991] I W.L.R. 142 1. Both of those cases concerned a claim by a buyer of a house against a surveyor who failed to report matters concerning the house as required by the contract. In Watts, the surveyor was negligent in failing to report defects in the house, and non-pecuniary damages of $6,750 were awarded to each of the owners for the inconvenience and discomfort experienced by them during repairs. In *Farley*, the surveyor was negligent in failing to discover, as he specifically undertook to do, that the property was adversely affected by aircraft noise. The House of Lords upheld the trial judge's award of non-pecuniary damages of $610,000, reversing the Court of Appeal, principally on the grounds that the object of the contract was to provide 'pleasure, relaxation, peace of mind, or freedom from molestation' and also because the plaintiff had suffered physical discomfort and inconvenience from the aircraft noise."

This Court applied the "peace of mind" exception to the breach of a liability insurance contract in *Warrington*. The Court upheld the award of non-pecuniary damages of $10,000 for the plaintiff's mental distress resulting from the insurer's delay in paying benefits.

This Court upheld an award of damages of $1,000 in *Wilson v. Sooter Studios* (1988), 42 B.L.R. 89 (C-A.), where a photographer arrived late to take wedding photographs, instead of 102 photographs contracted for, only 10 photographs of acceptable quality were produced. The award was for the bride's "direct and inevitable" (p. 92) disappointment resulting from the breach of contract.

In *Farley* (at para. 19), Lord Steyn described the "peace of mind" cases as "not the product of Victorian contract theory but the result of evolutionary developments in case law from the 1970s." He cited *Jarvis v. Swans Tours Ltd.*, [1973] Q.B. 233 (C.A.) and *Jackson v. Horizon Holidays Ltd.*, [1975] 1 W.L.R. 1468 (C.A.), in which damages were awarded to "disappointed vacationers" (as described by Newbury J.A. in Warrington at para. 13); *Heywood v. Wellers* (a fimi), (1976) 1 All E.R. 300 (Q.B.), where solicitors failed to take action, as instructed, to bring proceedings to refrain molestation (also cited in Warrington at para. 14); and significantly for this case, *Jackson v. Chrysler Acceptances Ltd.*, [1978] R.T.R. 474. As described by Lord

Steyn (at para. 19).

In Jackson's case the claim was for damages in respect of a motor car which did not meet the implied condition of merchantability in section 14 of the Sale of Goods Act. The buyer communicated to the seller that one of his reasons for buying the car was a forthcoming touring holiday in France. Problems with the car spoilt the holiday. The disappointment of a spoiled holiday was a substantial element in the award sanctioned by the Court of Appeal.

Lord Steyn rejected the argument made on behalf of the surveyor that to fall within the "peace of mind" category of cases, the "very object of [the] contract" (as stated by Bingham L.J. in *Watts*) had to be pleasure, relaxation, and peace of mind." He rejected a narrow reading of those words, pointing out that in *Watts*, the Court of Appeal did not consider the contract in issue to be of that kind. Citing *Jackson v. Chrysler Acceptances Ltd.*, where a spoiled holiday was only one object of the contract, he held (at para. 24), "It is sufficient if a major or important part of the contract is to give pleasure, relaxation, or peace of mind."

Lord Scott started his analysis by reference to the principles laid down in *Hadley v. Baxendale*, (1 8S4) 9 Exch. 341 (at para. 75–76): "The basic principle of damages for breach of contract is that the injured party is entitled, so far as money can do it, to be put in the position he would have been in if the contractual obligation had been properly performed. He is entitled, that is to say, to the benefit of his bargain: see *Robinson v. Harmon*, (1848) 1 Exch. 850, 855."

Lord Scott characterized the claim in *Watts* as "a case where the recovery of damages for consequential loss consisting of vexation, anxiety, or other species of mental distress had to be considered" (at para. 80). He made two qualifications to the proposition set out in *Watts* that damages "for physical inconvenience and discomfort caused by the breach" are recoverable. First, he pointed out (at para. 84): "Consequential damage, including damage consisting of inconvenience or discomfort, must in order to be recoverable, be such as, at the time of the contract, was reasonably foreseeable as liable to result from the breach: see *McGregor on Damages*, 16th ed. (1996), para. 250, pp. 159–160."

Second, he explained the phrase "physical inconvenience and discomfort" as referring to the cause of the inconvenience or discomfort (at para. 85): "If the cause is no more than disappointment that the contractual obligation has been broken, damages are not recoverable even if the disappointment has led to a complete mental breakdown. But, if the cause of the inconvenience or discomfort is a sensory (sight, touch, hearing, smell, etc) experience, damages can, subject to the remoteness rules, be recovered."

The reasons for judgment in *Farley* provide a summary and survey of the law as it has developed, in England, to date. They are helpful in analyzing and summarizing the principles derived from *Watts*, which are, in my view, applicable to the case at bar. In summary they are (borrowing the language from both *Watts* and *Farley*):

(a) A contract-breaker is not in general liable for any distress, frustration, anxiety, displeasure, vexation, tension, or aggravation which the breach of contract may cause to the innocent party.

(b) The rule is not absolute. Where a major or important part of the contract is to give pleasure, relaxation or peace of mind, damages will be awarded if the fruit of the contract is not provided or if the contrary result is instead procured.

(c) In cases not falling within the "peace of mind" category, damages are recoverable for inconvenience and discomfort caused by the breach and the mental suffering directly related to the inconvenience and discomfort. However, the cause of the inconvenience or discomfort must be a sensory experience as opposed to mere disappointment that the contract has been broken. If those effects are foreseeably suffered during a period when defects are repaired, they sound in damages even though the cost of repairs not recoverable as such.

Application of law to the facts of this case:

In the *Wharton* case, the respondent contracted for a "luxury" vehicle for pleasure use. It included a sound system that the appellant's service manager described as "high end". The respondent's husband described the purchase of the car in this way: "[W]e bought a luxury car that was supposed to give us a luxury ride and be a quiet vehicle, and we had nothing but difficulty with it from the very day it was delivered with this problem that nobody seemed to be able to fix.... So basically we had a luxury product that gave us no luxury for the whole time that we had it."

It is clear that an important object of the contract was to obtain a vehicle that was luxurious and a pleasure to operate. Furthermore, the buzzing noise was the cause of physical, in the sense of sensory, discomfort to the respondent and her husband. The trial judge found it inhibited listening to the sound system and was irritating in normal conversation. The respondent and her husband also bore the physical inconvenience of taking the vehicle to the appellant on numerous occasions for repairs. The inconvenience and discomfort was, in my view, reasonably foreseeable, if the defect in the sound system had been known at the date of the contract. The fact that it was not then known is, of course, irrelevant.

The award of damages for breach of the implied warranty of fitness satisfies both exceptions from the general rule that damages arc not awarded for mental distress for breach of contract, set out in *Watts* as amplified in *Farley*.

The justice continued and said at para. 63 "...awards for mental distress arising from a breach of contract should be restrained and modest."

The court upheld the trial judge's award of $5,000 in *Wharton* where the issue was a buzzing in the sound system.

In my view, a defect in manufacture which goes to the safety of the vehicle deserves a modest increase. I would assess the plaintiff's damage for mental distress resulting from the breach of the implied warranty of fitness at $7,500.

Judgment to issue in favour of the plaintiff against the defendants, except Ford Credit, on a joint and several basis for $14,707, plus interest and costs.

Safety summary: All models/years: I'm both amazed and disgusted at the large number of safety complaints registered against recent-model Windstars; '98 Windstars, for example, have over 600 complaints in the NHTSA database, compared to 100 or so for the imported competition. And it gets worse the further back you go. **All models: 1995–98**—The following is a short summary of problems carried over, year after year; unfortunately, I don't have the space to list many other reported defects. Nevertheless, you can easily access NHTSA's website (see Appendix I) for the details of thousands of other Windstar complaints. • Airbag failed to deploy. • Severe injuries caused by airbag deployment. • Sudden acceleration and chronic stalling. • Control arm and inner tie-rod failures cause the wheel to fall off. • Sudden steering lock-up or loss of steering ability. • Engine head gasket failures. • Loose or missing front brake bolts could cause the wheels to lock up or a loss of vehicle control. • Chronic ABS and transmission failures. Roger McCoy, a tenacious and persistent Columbus, Ohio, CBS investigative reporter, discovered that '95 Windstar sales represented 17 percent of the market, but 77 percent of NHTSA's combined '95 minivan transmission complaints. He interviewed an NHTSA spokesman in early 2001 and was told that NHTSA knew Windstar transmissions were "less robust and more failure-prone than the competition." McCoy's analysis is bolstered by *Consumer Reports* and CAA member surveys highlighting the tranny problem. ALLDATA service bulletins show the same automatic transmission defect is factory-related and is a widespread problem for Windstar, Taurus, and Sable. • Almost a dozen reports that the vehicle jumps out of Park and rolls away when on an incline, or slips into Reverse with the engine idling. • Transmission and axle separation. • Faulty fuel pump, sensor, and gauge. • Built-in child safety seat is easy to get out of, yet securing seat belts are too tight; child almost strangled. • Faulty rear liftgate latches; trunk lid can fall on one's head. • Horn doesn't work properly. **1999**— This is a faithful summary of the several hundred complaints in the NHTSA database. Keep in mind that many of these defects have been found in previous model-year Windstars, but may not have been included due to space limitations. • Airbag failed to deploy. • While parked, cruising, turning on the ignition, or when brakes are applied, vehicle suddenly accelerates. • Stuck accelerator causes unintended acceleration. • Chronic stalling caused by fuel vapour lock or faulty fuel pump. • Check Engine light constantly comes on, due to a faulty gas cap or over-sensitive warning system. • Front passenger-side wheel fell off when turning at a traffic light; in another reported incident, dealer found the five lug nuts had broken in half. • Vehicle pops out of gear while parked and rolls away. • Frequent transmission failures, including noisy engagement, won't engage forward or Reverse, slips, or jerks into gear. • Transmission jumped from Park to Reverse and pinned driver against tree (this is a common problem affecting Ford vehicles for almost three decades). • Sudden loss of power steering, chronic leakage of fluid, and early replacement of steering components, like the pump and hoses. • Excessive brake fade after successive stops. • When brake pedal is depressed, it sinks below the accelerator pedal level, causing the accelerator to be pressed as well—particularly annoying for drivers with large feet. • ABS module wire burned out. • Complete electrical failure during rainstorm. • Horn button "sweet spot" is too small and takes too much pressure to activate; one owner says, "Horn doesn't work, unless you hit it with a sledgehammer." • Windshield suddenly exploded when car was slowly accelerating. • Sliding door opens and closes on its own, sticks open or closed, or suddenly slams shut on a downgrade. • Sliding door closed on child's arm. • Door locks don't stay locked; passenger-side door opened when turning, causing passenger to fall out. • Many complaints that the side or rear windows suddenly exploded. • Rear defogger isn't operable (lower part of windshield isn't clear) in inclement weather when windshield wipers are activated. • Windshield wipers fail to clear windshield. • Water pours from dash onto front passenger floor. • Floor cupholder trips passengers. • Continental General tires lose air and crack between the treads. • Unspecified original equipment tires have sudden tread separation. • Large A-pillar (where windshield attaches to door) seriously impairs forward visibility, hiding pedestrians. • Seat belts aren't as described in owner's manual (supposed to be automatic retractable). • Two incidents where flames shot up out of fuel tank filler spout when gassing up. **2000**—Vehicle caught on fire while parked. • Sudden, unintended acceleration while stopped. • Chronic stalling; engine shuts down when turning. • Sometimes cruise control won't engage or engages on its own. • Right passenger-side wheel came off due to lug nut failure. • One Ingersoll, Ontario, owner of a year 2000 Windstar recounts the following harrowing experience:

> Last week, as my wife was running errands, the support arm that goes from the rear crossmember (not an axle anymore) up under the floor, broke in half. The dealer replaced the whole rear end as it is one welded assembly. If she had been on the highway going 80 km/h she would probably have been in a bad accident.

• Check Engine light constantly comes on for no reason. • Driver heard a banging noise and Windstar suddenly went into a tailspin; dealer blamed pins that "fell out of spindle." • Transmission jumped out of gear while on highway. • Many reports of premature transmission replacements. • Transmission lever can be shifted without depressing brake pedal (unsafe for children). • After several dealer visits, brakes still spongy, pedal goes to floor without braking, and emergency brake has almost no effect. • When braking, foot also contacts the accelerator pedal. • Emergency brake is inadequate to hold the vehicle. • Dealers acknowledge that brake master cylinders are problematic. • Joints aren't connected under quarter wheel weld; one weld is missing and three aren't properly connected. • Passenger door opened when vehicle hit a pothole. • While underway, right-side sliding door opens on its own and won't close (see "mental distress" judgment on pages 432–436). • When parked on an incline, sliding door released and came crashing down on child. • Hood suddenly flew up on the freeway. • Steering failed three times. • Power-steering pump whines and lurches. • Steering wheel is noisy and hard to turn. • Rear side windows, liftgate window, and windshield often explode suddenly. • When the interior rear-view mirror is set for night vision, images become distorted and hard to see. • Windshield wipers are unreliable. • Second-row driver-side seat belt buckle wouldn't latch. • Original equipment tire blowouts and sidewall bulging. • Driver must hunt for right place to push for horn to work. **2000–01**—Harsh 3–2 shifting when coasting then accelerating. • Transmission fluid leakage. • 3.8L engine hum, moan, drone, spark knock, and vibration. • Vibration under light acceleration. • Power-steering grunt or shudder during slow turns. • Power-steering fluid leaks. • Faulty self-activating wipers and door, trunk, and ignition locks. • Centre storage bin binds, and door glass may bind or travel slowly. • Discharged battery after extended parking. • Vehicles equipped with PATS anti-theft device may not crank or start. **2001**—Airbag may suddenly deploy when the engine is started. • Vehicle may not start. • Transmission shudder during 3–4 shifts. • Transmission fluid leaks from the main control cover area. • Power-steering grunt or notchy feel when turning. • Drifting or pulling while driving. • Steering fluid leaks. • Rear drum brakes drag or fail to release properly when operated in wet conditions or in below-freezing temperatures. • Warning lamps may continually flash. • Fogging of the front and side windows. • Twisted seatback frame. **2002**— Airbags failed to deploy. • Sudden automatic transmission failure. • Gas and brake pedal are set too close. • Back door won't open or close properly. • Both sliding doors won't retract. • Child can shift transmission without touching brake pedal. **2003**—Engine surging. • Sudden, unintended acceleration when braking. • Brake and gas pedals are mounted too close together. • Stalling caused by faulty fuel pump fuse. • Tire jack collapsed.

Secret Warranties/Service Tips/ TSBs

1995–98—Replace the seat belt retractor if the integrated child safety seat's belt twists or binds. • A driver's seat that chucks or squeaks may need a seat track repair kit. • Ford says a clunking noise when shifting out of Park is normal. • A parking brake that won't release needs a new parking pawl actuating rod. • Power door locks that grind or won't work may need a new front door lock actuator. • Tips on finding and silencing instrument panel buzzing, rattling, squeaking, chirping, and ticking. • The front-end accessory drive belt (FEAD) slips in wet weather, causing a reduction in steering power-assist; Ford suggests the belt be replaced. • A whistling noise from the front AC heater plenum requires a tighter seal. • Getting rid of AC odours requires a new moisture purge module and "disodorizer." • Water leakage onto carpet or headliner in rear cargo area is a factory-related defect covered in TSB #98-5-5. **1995–99**—Tips for correcting excessive noise, vibration, and harshness while driving; side door wind noise; and windshield water leaks. • An exhaust buzz or rattle may be caused by a loose catalyst or heat shield. **1995–2000**—A harsh 3–2 downshift/shudder when accelerating or turning may simply mean the transmission is low on fluid. • Diagnostic tips on brake vibration, inspection, and friction material replacement. **1995–2001**—Buzzing noise in speakers caused by fuel pump. **1995–2002**—Silencing suspension noise (see following bulletin).

Suspension (Front) – Grunting/Popping Noise on Turns

Article No.: 02-13-2

07/08/02

1995–2002 WINDSTAR

ISSUE: Some vehicles may exhibit a grunting/popping noise coming from the front suspension at speeds below 20 mph (32 km/h) when turning. This may be caused by contact between the rubber-coated outer rim of the upper spring seat bearing and seal assembly at the underside of the shock tower sheet metal. Colder weather could result in this rubbing noise being more noticeable.

ACTION: Install 2F2Z-18A027-BA spacers between the front strut assembly mounting bracket and the strut tower.

1995–2003—Engines that have been repaired may have an incorrectly installed gear driven camshaft position (CMP) sensor synchronizer assembly. This could cause poor fuel economy, loss of power, and engine surge, hesitation, and rough running. **1996–98**—Harsh automatic 1–2 shifting may be caused by a malfunctioning electronic pressure control or the main control valves sticking in the valve body. • Unwanted airflow from the AC vents can be stopped by replacing the evaporator case baffle. • An intermittent Neutral condition when coming to a stop signals the need to replace the forward clutch piston and the forward clutch cylinder. • Black soot deposits on the right rear quarter panel can be avoided by installing an exhaust tailpipe extension under Ford's base warranty. • Engine oil mixed with coolant or coolant loss signals the need for revised 3.8L engine lower intake manifold side gaskets and/or front cover gaskets. The TSB printed below can go a long way in getting a repair refund since it shows the defect is factory-related.

Engine – Coolant Loss/Oil Contamination

Article No.: 99-20-7

10/04/99

^COOLING SYSTEM - 3.8L - UNDETERMINED LOSS OF COOLANT

^COOLING SYSTEM - 4.2L - UNDETERMINED LOSS OF COOLANT

^ENGINE - 3.8L - ENGINE OIL CONTAMINATED WITH COOLANT

^ENGINE - 4.2L - ENGINE OIL CONTAMINATED WITH COOLANT

1996–97 THUNDERBIRD
1996–98 MUSTANG, WINDSTAR
1997–98 E-150, E-250, F-150
1996–97 COUGAR

ISSUE: Engine coolant may be leaking into the engine oil on some vehicles. The internal coolant leak may be difficult to identity. This may be caused by the lower intake manifold side gaskets and/or front cover gaskets allowing coolant to pass into the cylinders and/or the crankcase.

ACTION: Revised lower intake manifold side and front cover gaskets have been released for service.

1997–98—A rattling or clunking noise coming from the front of the vehicle may be caused by a loose front tension strut bushing retainer. **1998**—Lack of AC cooling may be caused by refrigerant leak at the P-nut fitting. • AC may have a loose auxiliary climate control fan switch. • A Low Fuel light lit for no reason signals the need for an upgraded fuel tank and sender assembly. • A malfunction indicator light (MIL) lit for no reason may simply show that the gas cap is loose. • An inaccurate metric speedometer requires a new speedometer gear. • An overhead console that's loose or hangs down needs a revised bracket. • Sliding-door rattles and squeaks when passing over bumps require adjusting and silicone. • Squeaks and creaks from the left rear of the driver's seat can be silenced by lubricating the lateral stability bracket. • Stalling when stopping, parking, coasting, or during slow turns can be corrected by reprogramming the PCM. • An upper radiator hose leak requires an upgraded hose or protective sleeve. • Excessive vibration at highway speeds may require new rear brake drums. **1998–99**—Tips on spotting abnormal ABS braking noise, although Ford says some noise is inevitable. **1998–2001**—Remedy for a power-steering fluid leak (see following bulletin).

Steering Rack – Fluid Leaks

Article No. 01-5-6

March 19, 2001

FORD:

1998–2001 WINDSTAR

ISSUE

Some vehicles may exhibit a power steering fluid leak from the end seals of the steering rack and pinion. This may be caused by fluid leaking past the main shaft at the end seals.

ACTION

Replace the power steering rack with a revised steering rack (-3504-).

This problem is caused by defective shaft end seals, which places the responsibility for paying for the repair squarely on Ford's shoulders.

1999—No Reverse engagement may be caused by torn Reverse clutch lip seals. • To improve the defogging of the driver-side door glass, install a revised window demister vent. • A squeaking or rattling noise coming from the rear of the vehicle is likely caused by a poorly insulated parking brake cable. **1999–2000**—If the power-sliding door won't close, replace the door controller; if it pops or disengages when fully closed, adjust the door and rear striker to reduce closing resistance. • Front wipers that operate when switched off need a revised multi-function switch (service program and recall). **1999–2003**—Inoperative rear window defroster. **2001–02**—Service tips for reports of premature engine failures. • Vacuum or air leaks in the intake manifold or engine system causing warning lamps to light. • Concerns with oil in the cooling system. • Engine cylinder heads that have been repaired may still leak coolant or oil from the gasket area. • Hard starts; rough running engines. • Shudder while in Reverse or during 3–4 shift. • Transmission fluid leakage. • Power-steering fluid leaks. • Brake roughness and pulsation. • Rear brake-drum drag in cold weather. • Fogging of the front and side windows. • False low tire warning. • Repeated heater core failures. • Troubleshooting MIL warning light. • Hard-to-fill fuel tank. **2001–03**—Remedy for a slow-to-fill fuel tank. **2002**—Automatic transmission fluid leaking at the quick connect for the transmission cooler lines. • MIL light comes on, vehicle shifts poorly, or vehicle won't start. • Instrument panel beeping. • Buzz, groan, or vibration when gear selector lever is in Park. • Some vehicles may run roughly on the highway or just after stopping. • A clunk is heard when shifting from Park to another gear. • Defective ignition switch lock cylinders. • Erratic dome light operation. • Anti-theft system operates on its own. • Battery may go dead after extended parking time. • Sliding doors rattle and squeak. • Steering system whistle/whine. • Slow, hard-to-fill fuel tank. • Loose rear wiper arm. **2003**—Front-end grinding popping noise when passing over bumps or making turns. • Sliding door malfunctions. • Airbag warning light stays lit. • Inoperative rear window defroster.

Windstar Profile

	1996	1997	1998	1999	2000	2001	2002	2003
Cost Price ($)								
GL/Base	23,495	24,495	24,495	24,295	—	—	—	—
LX	27,495	28,995	28,995	28,195	25,995	26,750	25,995	26,195
SEL	—	—	—	36,195	36,195	33,190	33,685	37,015
Used Values ($)								
GL/Base ⋀	5,000	6,000	8,000	10,000	—	—	—	—
GL/Base ⋁	4,500	5,500	6,500	8,500	—	—	—	—
LX ⋀	6,000	7,000	9,000	12,000	12,000	14,000	16,500	21,000
LX ⋁	5,000	5,500	8,000	10,500	10,500	12,500	15,000	20,000
SEL ⋀	—	—	—	11,000	14,000	16,000	20,000	30,000
SEL ⋁	—	—	—	9,500	13,000	14,500	18,500	29,000
Reliability	❶	❶	❶	❶	❷	❷	❷	❷
Crash Safety (F)	⑤	⑤	⑤	⑤	⑤	⑤	⑤	⑤
Side	—	—	—	⑤	④	④	④	④

Offset	5	5	5	3	3	3	3	3
Head Restraints (F)	1	1	—	3	—	5	5	5
Rear	—	—	—	1	—	3	3	3
Rollover Resistance	—	—	—	—	—	3	4	4

Ford/Nissan

VILLAGER, QUEST ★★★★

RATING: Above Average (1997–2002); Average (1995–96); Not Recommended (1993–94). Best used for city commuting, rather than long highway journeys. Still sold in the States, the Villager was dropped in Canada (along with the Mercury franchise) after the 2000 model year. 2002 was the old Quest's last model year. **Maintenance/Repair costs:** Higher than average. Costs can be kept down by frequenting independent repair agencies. **Parts:** Both Ford (Mercury dealers were closed down) and Nissan dealers carry parts, and parts are less expensive than those of most other minivans in this class. The exception to this rule: broken engine exhaust manifold studs (a frequent problem through 1995), AC, and electrical components. **Best alternatives:** Since there's little difference between the last three model years, choose an off-lease used 1999 or 2000 version (the redesigned '99 will likely have a few more first-series glitches). The Quest, engineered by Nissan and built by Ford, is practically identical to the Villager, except for some slight styling differences, more standard equipment, and a slightly lower rate of depreciation. By choosing a Villager cargo van over a wagon, you can save between $1,500 and $2,000. Other minivans worth considering are the GM Venture, Honda Odyssey, a 2002 Mazda MPV, or a Toyota Sienna. **Online help:** *www.mycarstats.com/auto_complaints/MERCURY_complaints.asp* and *www.autosafety.org/autodefects.html.*

Strengths and weaknesses: Smaller and easier to handle than most rear-drive minivans, the Villager and Quest were built by Ford at its truck factory in Avon Lake, Ohio, and sized comfortably between the regular and extended Chrysler minivans. These front-drive, five- or seven-passenger minivans are the most fun to whip around the city in.

These minivans' strongest assets are a 170-hp 3.3L V6 engine that gives them carlike handling, ride, and cornering; modular seating; and reliable mechanical components. Nissan borrowed the powertrain, suspension, and steering assembly from the Maxima, mixed in some creative sheet metal, and left the job of outfitting the sound system, climate control, dashboard, steering column, and wheels to Ford. This has resulted in an attractive and not overly aero-styled minivan.

These fuel-thirsty minivans are quite heavy, though and the 3.0L and 3.3L engines have to go all out to carry the extra weight. Surprisingly, GM's 2.8L engines produce more torque and the Villager/quest powertrain set-up trails the Odyssey in acceleration and passing. Other minuses: a cheap-looking interior; the control layout can be a bit confusing; suspension is too soft; and rear-seat access can be difficult.

Most owner-reported problems involve excessive brake noise and premature brake wear, door lock malfunctions, interior noise, and driveline vibrations. There have also been many reports of engine exhaust manifold stud and crankshaft failures (through 1996) costing up to $7,000 to repair. Other problems include electrical shorts; brake failures due to vibration, binding, or overheating; premature wear of the front discs, rotors, and pads; chronic stalling, possibly due to faulty fuel pumps or a shorted electrical system; and loose steering and veering at highway speeds. Other common problems include film buildup on windshield and interior glass; a sulfur smell from the exhaust system; poor AC performance or compressor failures, accompanied by musty, mildew-type AC odours; and recurring fuel-pump buzzing heard through the radio speakers.

Vehicle history: 1996—Annoying motorized shoulder belts were dropped, a passenger-side airbag was added, and the dash and exterior were slightly restyled. **Villager: 1999**—The Pathfinder's 3.3L V6 debuts, giving the Villager and Quest an additional 19 horses; the Villager gained a fourth door; more interior room; a revised instrument panel that's easier to reach; restyled front and rear ends; and improved shifting, acceleration, and braking. The suspension was retuned to give a more carlike ride and handling, the old climate control system was ditched for a more sophisticated version with air filtration. Mercury's top-of-the-line model, the Nautica, was dropped. **Quest: 1999**—A larger platform, standard ABS brakes, a driver-side sliding rear door, upgraded headlights, and rear leaf springs. The second row of seats can be removed and the third row is set on tracks. **2000**—An improved child safety seat anchoring system. An entertainment centre with a larger screen is standard on all Quest models, as well as a stabilizer bar on the GLE.

Safety summary: 1994–96—Vehicle suddenly accelerated forward. • Inadvertent airbag deployment. • Sudden stalling due to faulty fuel pump. • Both steering and brakes failed when turning into an intersection. • Steering wheel locked up while making a right turn. • Chronic ABS failures; brake pads and rotors need replacing every 5,000 km, and drums often need turning. • Alarm system will lock and unlock the doors on its own. • Remote-control door locks often won't respond, trapping occupants inside. • Faulty rear door latch and lock allow the door to come open while driving. • The sliding door opens for no apparent reason. • Power windows often jam. • Seat belts don't retract properly and ratchet too tightly. • Shoulder belt got caught around child's neck and had to be cut away. • Frequent rear windshield wiper failures. • Solar window at certain angles distorts vision by reflecting images. **1997–99**—Airbags fail to deploy. • Power door locks self-activate. • Gas fumes leak into the interior. • Gas pedal sticks. • Sudden acceleration. • Brake failures (extended stopping distance, noisy when applied). **2000**—Gas and brake pedals are too close together. • Frequent brake repairs and failures. • Some steering wander and excessive vibration. • Vehicle tends to lurch forward when the AC is first engaged. • Weak tailgate hydraulic cylinders. • Instrument panel's white face hard to read in daylight hours. **2000–01**—Front brake grind/groan. • Cycling or self-activating front door locks. • Missing seat belt latch plate stopper button. • Broken shift lock cable plate causes shift indicator to be misaligned. • ABS failures. • Complete brake loss. • Brake and accelerator pedals are the same height, so driver's foot can easily slip and step on both at the same time. • 22-month-old child was able to pull the clasp apart on integrated child safety seat. • Seat belts don't retract properly. • Rear window on liftgate door shattered for unknown reason (dealer was aware of problem and replaced window under warranty). • Power-steering fluid leakage due to o-ring at rack gear splitting. • Electric door lock and power window failures have trapped occupants in their vehicles. **2002**—Stuck accelerator pedal. • Leaking front and rear struts degrade handling. • Steering wheel is off-centre to the left. • Continental tire tread separation.

Secret Warranties/Service Tips/TSBs

1993–96—A crunch/grunt noise from the rear suspension may be caused by rear shackle bushings that need lubrication. **1993–97**—Front door windows that bind may have the glass rubber improperly installed in the door sheet metal channel. **1993–98**—Automatic transmission whining when accelerating may be caused by a faulty transaxle support bracket and insulators. **1993–2000**—Paint delamination, peeling, or fading (see Part Two). **1993–2002**—Repeat heater core failure. **1995–99**—Tips for correcting windshield water leaks and excessive noise, vibration, and harshness. **1996–2002**—Power door locks that intermittently self-activate are a common occurrence that's covered in TSB #98-22-5. **1997–98**—Tips on silencing rattles and creaks. • Hard starts, no-starts, stalling, or an exhaust rotten-egg smell can all be corrected by replacing the power control module (PCM) under the emissions warranty. **1997–99**—An exhaust buzz or rattle may be caused by a loose catalyst or muffler heat shield. **1999–2002**—Side windows pop open. • Rear AC blows warm air.

Villager, Quest Profile

	1995	1996	1997	1998	1999	2000	2001	2002
Cost Price ($)								
Villager GS	22,595	23,695	24,295	24,595	24,595	24,595	—	—
Villager LS	27,095	28,095	29,195	29,495	29,495	29,495	—	—
Quest XE/SE	29,598	30,598	30,898	30,898	27,798	30,498	30,498	30,698
Quest GXE	24,598	25,598	25,598	25,598	32,498	33,498	35,198	35,198
Used Values ($)								
Villager GS ▲	4,000	5,500	7,000	9,000	11,000	13,000	—	—
Villager GS ▼	3,000	4,500	6,000	8,000	10,000	11,500	—	—
Villager LS ▲	5,000	6,000	8,000	10,000	12,500	14,500	—	—
Villager LS ▼	4,500	5,500	7,500	9,000	11,000	13,000	—	—

Quest GXE Λ	5,000	6,000	8,500	9,500	12,500	15,000	18,000	22,000
Quest GXE V	4,500	5,500	8,000	8,500	11,500	13,500	16,500	20,500
Quest XE/SE Λ	5,500	7,000	7,500	10,500	13,000	16,000	19,500	23,000
Quest XE/SE V	4,000	6,500	7,000	9,000	12,000	14,500	18,000	22,000
Reliability	③	③	④	④	④	④	④	④
Crash Safety (F)	④	④	④	—	—	④	⑤	⑤
Side	—	—	—	—	—	⑤	⑤	⑤
Offset	—	❷	❷	❷	❶	❶	❶	❶
Head Restraints	③	—	❷	—	❶	❶	❶	❶
Rollover Resistance	—	—	—	—	—	—	④	④

General Motors

ASTRO, SAFARI ★★★★

RATING: Above Average (2001–03); Average (1996–2000); Not Recommended (1985–95). These vehicles are more mini-truck than minivan. Believe it or not, these run-of-the-mill minivans are beginning to look quite good when compared to the problem-plagued Chrysler and Ford minivans and the overpriced Asian competition (VW? Not even in the running). They have fewer safety-related problems reported to the government, are easy to repair, and cost little to acquire. Stay away from the unreliable all-wheel-drive models; they're expensive to repair and not very durable. **Maintenance/Repair costs:** Average. Any garage can repair these rear-drive minivans. **Parts:** Good supply of cheap parts. A large contingent of independent parts suppliers keeps repair costs down. Parts are less expensive than they are for other vehicles in this class. **Best alternatives:** As with the Aerostar, the classified ads are jam-packed with sellers wanting to unload their Astros and Safaris simply because their vehicles have high mileage or the owners are small businesses whose needs have moved up to a larger van. Whatever the reason, you can find some real bargains if you're patient. Front-drive minivans made by Nissan and Toyota have better handling and are more reliable and economical people carriers; unfortunately, they lack the Astro's considerable grunt, essential for cargo hauling and trailer towing. Also consider getting a later-model Ford Aerostar (watch the tranny, though), or a GM Montana or Venture, if hauling isn't a high priority. **Online help:** *www.autosafety.org/autodefects.html.*

Strengths and weaknesses: More a utility truck than a comfortable minivan, these boxy, rear-drive minivans are built on a reworked S-10 pickup chassis. As such, they offer uninspiring handling and relatively high fuel consumption. Both Astro and Safari come in a choice of either cargo or passenger van. The cargo van is used either commercially or as an inexpensive starting point for a fully customized vehicle. The Safari is identical to the Astro, except for a slightly higher base price.

With the right options, the Astro and Safari have the advantage of being versatile cargo haulers when equipped with a heavy-duty suspension. In fact, Astro's 2,500 kg (5,500 lb.) trailer-towing capability is 900 kg (2,000 lb.) more than that of the front-drive Venture. The base 4.3L V6 gives acceptable acceleration, but the High Output variant of the same engine (first available in the 1991 model) is a far better choice, particularly when it's mated to a manual gearbox. The full-time AWD versions aren't very refined, have a high failure rate, and are expensive to diagnose and repair.

Vehicle history: 1991—A more powerful V6; and lap/shoulder belts. **1993**—Base engine gained 15 hp. **1994**—Driver-side airbag, side-door guard beams, plus a centre-mounted rear stop lamp was installed in the roof. **1995**—Lightly restyled front end, extended bodies, and a 190-hp engine. **1996**—Passenger-side airbag, a new dash, engine torque cut by 10 lb.-ft., and more front footroom. **1997**—Upgraded power steering. **1998**—An improved automatic transmission. **1999**—A reworked AWD system. **2000**—Only seven- and eight-passenger models available; engine made quieter and smoother, while the automatic transmission was toughened up to shift more efficiently when pulling heavy loads; and a larger fuel tank was installed. **2001**—A tilt steering wheel; cruise control; CD player; remote keyless entry; power windows, mirrors, and locks. **2002**—A rear heater on cargo models. **2003**—Upgraded four-wheel disc brakes.

The 1985–95 versions suffer from failure-prone automatic transmissions, poor braking systems, failure-prone AC compressors, and fragile steering components. The early base V6 provides ample power, but also produces lots of noise, consumes excessive amounts of fuel, and tends to have leaking head gaskets and failure-prone oxygen sensors. These computer-related problems often rob the engine of sufficient power to keep up in traffic. While the 5-speed manual transmission shifts fairly easily, the automatic takes forever to downshift on the highway. Handling isn't particularly agile on these minivans, and the power steering doesn't provide the driver with enough road feel. Unloaded, the Astro provides very poor traction, the ride isn't comfortable on poor road surfaces, and interior noise is rampant. Many drivers find the driving position awkward (no left legroom) and the heating/defrosting system inadequate. Many engine components are hidden under the dashboard, making repair or maintenance awkward. Even on more recent models, highway performance and overall reliability aren't impressive. Through the 2000 model year, the 4-speed automatic transmissions are clunky and hard shifting, though they're much more reliable than Ford or Chrysler gearboxes.

Other owners report that the front suspension, steering components, computer modules, and catalytic converter can wear out within as little as 60,000 km. There have also been lots of complaints about electrical, exhaust, cooling, and fuel system bugs; inadequate heating/defrosting; failure-prone wiper motors; and axle seals wearing out every 12–18 months.

Body hardware is fragile, and fit and finish is the pits. Water leaks from windows and doors are common, yet hard to diagnose. Squeaks and rattles are legion and hard to locate. Sliding-door handles often break off and the sliding door frequently jams in cold temperatures. The hatch release for the Dutch doors occasionally doesn't work, and the driver-side vinyl seat lining tears apart. Premature paint peeling, delamination, and surface rust are fairly common.

The 1995–99 models are a bit improved, but they still have problems carried over from earlier years, with stalling, hard starts, and expensive and frequent automatic transmission, power-steering, wheel bearing, brake pad, caliper, and rotor repairs heading the list. Year 2000–03 models are more reliable and better performing, inasmuch as they underwent considerable upgrading by GM. Nevertheless, buyers should be aware that extra attention is merited in the following areas: excessive vibration transmitted through the AWD; automatic transmission clunk; poor braking performance (brake pedal hardens and brakes don't work after going over bumps or rough roads) and expensive brake maintenance; electronic computer modules and fuel system glitches that cause the Check Engine light to remain lit; hard starts, no-starts, or chronic stalling, especially when going downhill; heating and AC performance hampered by poor air distribution; electrical system shorts; and sliding door misalignment and broken hinges.

Safety summary: 1995–98—Vehicle continues to accelerate after foot is removed from accelerator. • Frequent stalling. • Erratic engine performance due to blocked catalytic converter. • Engine leaks oil. • Power-steering fluid leaks. • Vehicle jerks to one side when braking. • Front wheels lock up when turning the steering wheel to the right from a stop while in gear. • Steering stuck when turning. • Fresh-air ventilation system allows fumes from other vehicles to enter interior compartment. • With jack almost fully extended, wheel doesn't lift off ground. • Spare tire not safe for driving over 60 km/h. • Design of horn makes it difficult to use. • Horn buttons require excessive pressure to activate. • Driver-side window failure. • Sliding door suddenly fell off. • Faulty door hinges allow the door to fall off. • Front passenger door won't close. • Passenger-side door glass fell out. • Rear hatch latch release failed. • Rear hatch hydraulic rods are too weak to support hatch. • Front passenger's seat reclining mechanism failed. • Poor traction. • Parked in gear and rolled downhill. • Transmission failures. • Left rear axle seal leaks, causing lubricant to burn on brake lining. • Sudden wheel bearing failure. • AC clutch fell apart. • Alternator bearing failure. **1999**—Difficult starting. • Hard shifting between First and Second gear; transmission slippage. • Delayed shifting or stalling when passing from Drive to Reverse. • Leaking axle seals. • Rear cargo door hinge and latch slipped off, and door opened 180 degrees. • Floormat moves under brake and accelerator pedals. • Brake pedal set too close to the accelerator. • Fuel gauge failure caused by faulty sending unit. **2000**—Brake and gas pedals are too close together. • When brakes are applied, rear wheels tend to lock up while front wheels continue to turn. • Vehicle stalls when accelerating or turning. • Astro rolls back when stopped on an incline in Drive. • Sliding door slams shut on an incline or hinges break. • Extensive damage caused to bumper and undercarriage by driving over gravel roads. **2001**—Sudden acceleration. • Chronic stalling. • Hard starts. • Sudden total electrical failure, especially when going into Reverse. • Brake pedal set too high. • Differential in transfer case locked up while driving; defective axle seals. • Vehicle rolls backward on an incline while in Drive (dealer adjusted transfer case to no avail). • Fuel gauge failure. • Faulty AC vents. • Water can be trapped inside the wheels and freeze, causing the wheels to be out of balance. **2002**—Airbag failed to deploy. • Sticking gas pedal. • Brake pedal goes to floor without braking. • Seat belts in rear are too long; don't fit children or child safety seats. • Driver-side window failures. • Sliding-door window blew out. • Uniroyal spare tire sidewall cracks. **2003**—Harsh, delayed shifting. • On a slight incline, sliding door will unlatch and slam shut. • Intermittent windshield wiper failure.

Secret Warranties/Service Tips/TSBs

All models: 1993–99—Tips on getting rid of AC odours. • Defective catalytic converters that cause a rotten-egg smell may be replaced free of charge under the vehicle's emissions warranty. **1993–2003**—GM says that a chronic driveline clunk can't be silenced and is a normal characteristic of its vehicles. • Paint delamination, peeling, or fading (see Part Two). **1995–2000**—Dealer guidelines for brake servicing under warranty. **1995–2004**—Booming interior noise at highway speeds:

Drivetrain – Booming Noise at Highway Speeds

Bulletin No.: 00-03-09-001A

Date: July 29, 2003

Rolling boom noise inside vehicle (install pinion nose damper and/or new rear leaf spring dampers)

1995–2004 Chevrolet Astro Van models
1995–2004 GMC Safari Van models

Condition: Some owners may comment about a "boom" noise inside the vehicle while driving at speeds ranging between 97–105 km/h (60–65 mph). This condition is most noticeable from behind the driver's seat.

Cause: The condition may result from an engine-firing harmonic, which becomes noticeable at torque converter clutch (TCC) lock-up.

Correction: A new rear leaf spring damper kit (one per spring) has been developed, to be used in conjunction with a pinion nose damper tuned to 86 Hertz (Hz), to reduce the resultant noise level.

1996–98—Rough engine performance may be caused by a water-contaminated oxygen sensor, and a rough idle shortly after starting may be caused by sticking poppet valves. **1996–2000**—Hard start, no-start, backfire, and kickback when starting may be corrected by replacing the crankshaft position sensor. • Silence a boom-type noise heard during engine warm-up by installing an exhaust dampener assembly. • A rough idle after start and/or a Service Engine light that stays lit may mean you have a stuck injector poppet valve ball that needs cleaning. **1996–2001**—Poor heat distribution in driver's area of vehicle (install new heat ducts). • Exhaust rattle noise. **1997–98**—An engine ticking noise that appears when the temperature falls may require an EVAP purge solenoid valve. **1997–99**—A hard start, no-start, and rough idle can be fixed by replacing the fuel tank fill pipe assembly and cleaning the SCPI poppet valves.

1999—Steering column squeaking can be silenced by replacing the steering wheel SIR module coil assembly. **1999–2000**—If the engine runs hot, overheats, or loses coolant, try polishing the radiator filler neck or replacing the radiator cap before letting any mechanic convince you that more expensive repairs are needed. • A popping or snapping sound may emanate from the right front door window area. **2001**—Harsh automatic transmission shifts. • 2–4 band and 3–4 clutch damage. • Steering shudder felt when making low-speed turns. • Excessive brake squeal. • Wet carpet/odour in passenger footwell area (repair evaporator case drain to cowl seal/open evaporator case drain). • Delayed shifts, slips, flares, or extended shifts during cold operation (replace shift solenoid valve assembly). **2002**—Automatic transmission slips, incorrect shifts, and poor engine performance. • Service Engine Soon light comes on, no Third or Fourth gear, and loss of Drive. • Slipping or missing Second, Third, or Fourth gear. • Inadequate heating. • Roof panel has a wavy or rippled appearance. • Water leak in the windshield area. **2002–03**—Engine runs rough or engine warning light comes on. • Sliding door difficult to open. **2003**—Hard starts, rough idle, and intermittent misfiring. • Transfer case shudder. • Right rear door handle breakage.

Astro, Safari Profile

	1996	1997	1998	1999	2000	2001	2002	2003
Cost Price ($)								
Cargo	23,475	25,110	25,110	23,290	24,015	24,465	—	—
CS/base	25,285	26,920	26,920	23,839	25,675	26,440	27,255	27,600
Used Values ($)								
Cargo ▲	4,000	5,000	7,500	9,000	11,500	13,500	—	—
Cargo ▼	3,000	4,000	6,000	7,500	10,000	12,000	—	—
CS/base ▲	5,000	6,000	8,500	10,000	12,500	15,000	17,000	19,500
CS/base ▼	4,000	5,000	7,000	9,000	11,500	13,500	16,000	18,000
Reliability	❷	❷	③	③	③	④	④	④
Crash Safety (F)	③	③	③	③	③	③	③	③
Offset	❶	❶	❶	❶	❶	❶	❶	❶
Head Restraints (F)	❷	❷	—	❷	—	❷	❷	❶
Rear	❶	❶	—	—	—	—	—	—
Rollover Resistance	—	—	—	—	—	③	③	③

LUMINA, LUMINA APV, MONTANA, SILHOUETTE, TRANS SPORT, VENTURE ★★★

RATING: Average (1997–2003); Not Recommended (1990–96). **Maintenance/ Repair costs:** Average. Engine head gasket, automatic transmission, ABS, and electrical malfunctions will likely cause maintenance costs to rise after the third year of ownership. Engine head gaskets and intake manifolds are also failing around the fifth year of use. **Parts:** Engine parts are generic to GM's other models, so they should be reasonably priced and not hard to find. Body parts are likely to be more problematic and costly. **Best alternatives:** Honda

Odyssey, Mazda MPV (1992), Nissan Quest or Axxess, and Toyota Sienna.
Online help: *www.gm-v6lemons.com* and *www.autosafety.org/autodefects.html.*

Strengths and weaknesses: These minivans use the Chevrolet Lumina platform and therefore have more carlike handling than GM's Astro and Safari.
Seating is limited to five adults in the standard models (two up front and three
on a removable bench seat), but this can be increased to seven if you find a
vehicle equipped with optional modular seats. Seats can be folded down flat,
creating additional storage space.

Be wary of vehicles equipped with a power-assisted passenger-side sliding
door; it's both convenient and dangerous—despite its override circuit that prevents the door from closing on a hand, a number of injuries have been
reported. Furthermore, with most sliding doors, mechanical and electronic
glitches allow the doors to open when they shouldn't, and they are difficult to
close. Overall, this convenience feature is overpriced, failure-prone, and a bit
slow in operation.

Pre-1997 models had serious reliability problems—notably, engine head
gasket and intake manifold defects; electronic module (PROM) and starter
failures; premature front brake component wear, brake fluid leakage, and noisy
braking; short circuits that burn out alternators, batteries, power door lock
activators, and the blower motor; AC evaporator core failures; premature
wearout of the inner and outer tie-rods; automatic transmission breakdowns;
abysmal fit and finish; chronic sliding door malfunctions; and faulty rear seat
latches. Other problems include a fuel-thirsty and poor-performing 3-speed
automatic transmission; a poorly mounted sliding door; side door glass that
pops open; squeaks, rattles, and clunks in the instrument panel cluster area
and suspension; and wind buffeting noise around the front doors. The large
dent- and rust-resistant plastic panels are robot-bonded to the frame, and they
absorb engine and road noise very well, in addition to having an impressive
record for durability.

Vehicle history: 1994—A shortened nose, APV designation is dropped,
driver-side airbag arrives. **1996**—3.4L V6 debuts, and the Lumina was
replaced by the Venture at the end of the model year. **1997**—Dual airbags and
ABS. **1998**—The sliding driver-side door is available on more models.
1999—A 5-hp boost to the base V6 engine (185), de-powered airbags, an
upgraded automatic transmission, a rear-window defogger, and heated rear-
view mirrors. **2000**—Dual sliding rear side doors. **2001**—A slight restyling
and a fold-flat third-row seat.

By the way, don't trust the towing limit listed in GM's owner's manual.
Automakers publish tow ratings that are on the optimistic side—and sometimes they even lie. Also, don't be surprised to find that the base 3.1L engine
doesn't handle a full load of passenger and cargo, especially when mated with
the 3-speed automatic transmission. The ideal powertrain combo would be the
4-speed automatic coupled to the optional "3800" V6 (first used on the 1996
versions). These minivans use a quiet-running V6 power plant similar to

Chrysler's top-of-the-line 3.8L 6-cylinder, providing good mid-range and top-end power. The GM engine is hampered by less torque, however, making for less grunt when accelerating, and frequently downshifting out of Overdrive when climbing moderate grades. The electronically controlled 4-speed automatic transmission shifts smoothly and quietly—a clear advantage over Chrysler and Ford.

The 1997 and later models are less rattle-prone, due to a more rigid body structure than that of their predecessors. However, fit and finish is still not up to the Asian competition. The front windshield is particularly prone to leak water from the top portion into the dash instrument cluster (covered by a secret warranty). Owner-reported problems on post-'97s include chronic plastic intake manifold/head gasket failures (covered by a 6-year/100,000 km secret warranty), EGR valve failures, transmission fluid leaks, electrical glitches shorting out dash gauges and causing difficult starting, excessive front brake noise and frequent repairs (rotors and pads), and assorted body deficiencies, including water leaks in the jack well:

> Our 2002 Venture has a poorly fitted windshield and a misaligned dash and hood, as well as quarter panels, front doors, and the sliding rear door on the passenger side. I have inspected other 2002 and 2003 Chevrolet Ventures and have seen the same windshield fit errors.

Safety summary: All models/years: Watch out for excessive brake fading. • Other common problems: sudden steering loss in rainy weather or when passing over a puddle (serpentine belt slippage); ABS brake failures; ABS light stays on for no reason; airbags fail to deploy; sliding doors suddenly open, close, come off their tracks, jam shut, stick open, injure children, and rattle (1997–2001 models recalled); fire may ignite around the fuel filler nozzle or within the ignition switch; tie-rod failures may cause loss of control; during highway driving, transmission slips from Drive into Neutral. • Some front door-mounted seat belts cross uncomfortably at the neck, and there's a nasty blind spot on the driver's side that requires a small stick-on convex mirror to correct. **All models: 1995–99**—Recurrent safety complaints: transmission won't hold gear on a grade; headlight assembly collects moisture, burns bulb, or falls out; seatback suddenly collapses; windshield wipers fail intermittently; accelerator and brake pedals are too close together; fuel slosh/clunk when vehicle stops or accelerates (new tank useless); self-activating door locks lock occupants out or in; door handles break inside the door assembly; horn is hard to access; window latch failures. **2000**—The year 2000 models still have scattered automatic transmission failures and hard, noisy shifting; AC glitches; frequent replacement of front brake calipers, pads, and rotors; and door and window problems. **2001**—Fire ignited under driver's seat. • Windshield suddenly exploded outward while driving with wipers activated. • Firestone tire blowout. • Brakes activate on their own, making it appear as if van is pulling a load. • Steering idler arm fell off due to missing bolt. • Loose fuel tank due to loose bolts/bracket. • Fuel tank cracked when passing over a tree branch. •

Plastic tube within heating system fell off and wedged behind the accelerator pedal. • Bracket weld pin that secures the rear split seat sheared off. • Faulty fuel pump causes chronic stalling, no-starts, surging, and sudden acceleration. • Vehicle suddenly lost power while going uphill, slid back, and stalled. • Van will roll back while in gear on an incline. • Service Engine light comes on constantly. • Service Engine light remains on, due to transmission bearing assembled backward in the transmission box. • Premature transmission failures. • Centre rear lap seat belt isn't long enough to secure a rear-facing child safety seat. • Children can slide out of the integrated child safety seat. • Electrical harness failures result in complete electrical shutdown. • Headlights, interior lights, gauges, and instruments fail intermittently (electrical cluster module is the prime suspect). • Excess padding around horn makes it difficult to depress horn button in an emergency. • Weak-sounding horn. • Loud noise emanating from under the vehicle. • Frequent windshield wiper motor failures. • Heater doesn't warm up vehicle sufficiently. • Antifreeze smell intrudes into interior. • Intermittent no-starts or hard starts. • Premature failure of the transmission's Fourth clutch. • Some transmissions may produce a grinding or growling noise when engaged on an incline with the engine running and the parking brake not applied. • Delayed shifts, slips, flares, or extended shifts in cold weather. • Poorly performing rear AC. • Flickering interior and exterior lights. • Airbag warning lamp stays lit. • Windshield glass distortion. • Exterior light condensation. **2002**—Rear hatch handle broke, cutting driver's hand. • Vehicle jumped out of Park and rolled downhill. • Vehicle suddenly shuts off in traffic. • Windshield water leaks short out dash gauges. **2003**—Rear seat belts failed to release. • Weld holding the lift wheel pin is not adequate to support weight of trailer.

Secret Warranties/Service Tips/TSBs

All models: 1990–98—An oil odour coming from the engine compartment may be eliminated by changing the crankshaft rear main oil seal. **1993–2000**—GM says that a chronic driveline clunk can't be silenced and is a normal characteristic of its vehicles. • Paint delamination, peeling, or fading (see Part Two). **1995–2000**—Dealer guidelines for brake servicing under warranty. **1996–2001**—Poor heat distribution in driver's area of vehicle (install new heat ducts). **1996–2003**—Engine intake manifold/head gasket failures:

> I just wanted to let you know that after contacting you back in January regarding our 2001 Chevy Venture head gasket problem, I have just received my judgement through the Canadian Arbitration Program.
>
> I used the sample complaint letter as well as the judgment you have posted in the *Ford Canada vs. Dufour* court case. This combined with an avalanche of similar Chevy Venture complaints that are posted on the Internet helped us to win a $1,700 reimbursement of the $2,200 we were looking for.

The reason for us not receiving the full amount is that the arbitrator stated that GM Canada would have only replaced one head gasket instead of replacing both as we had done, and that a dealer would have supplied us with a car free of charge and therefore did not allow us the car rental expense we incurred.

We are still extremely happy with the results and thank you for your books and website, you have a fan for life.

D.W.

1997—Brakes that don't work, drag, heat up, or wear out early may have a variety of causes, all outlined in TSB #73-50-27. • A rear suspension thud or clunk may be silenced by installing upgraded rear springs. **1997–98**—A fuel tank thud or clunk noise may require new fuel tank straps and insulators. • Loose lumber noise coming from the rear of the vehicle when it passes over bumps means upgraded rear shock absorbers are required. • Poor rear windshield wiper performance may require that the fluid line be purged. • Windshield wiper blade chatter can be reduced by changing the wiper arm. • Insufficient windshield clearing in defrost mode requires the installation of new seals. **1997–99**—Upgraded front disc pads will reduce brake squeal. **1997–2000**—Front door windows that are inoperative, slow, or noisy may need the window run channel adjusted or replaced, in addition to new weather stripping. **1997–2002**—Pssst! GM minivans may show premature hood corrosion and blistering. A dealer whistleblower tells me that dealers have been authorized to repair the hoods free of charge (refinish and repaint) up to six years under a GM "goodwill" program. • Mildew odour; water leaks. • Wind noise at base of windshield. **1997–2003**—Poor-quality engine intake manifolds (see TSB on page 227). **1997–2004**—Defective catalytic converters that cause a rotten-egg smell in the interior may be replaced free of charge under the emissions warranty. **1998**—No-start, engine miss, and rough idle may indicate that melted slush has contaminated the fuel system. **1998–99**—An inoperative sliding door may have a defective control module. **1998–2000**—Poor AC performance in humid weather may be caused by an undercharged AC system. **1999**—Diagnostic tips for an automatic transmission that slips, produces a harsh upshift and garage shifts, or causes acceleration shudders. **1999–2000**—If the engine runs hot, overheats, or loses coolant, try polishing the radiator filler neck or replacing the radiator cap before considering more expensive repairs. • Before taking on more expensive repairs to correct hard starts or no-starts, check the fuel pump. • An automatic transmission that whines in Park or Neutral, or a Service Engine light that stays on, may signal the need for a new drive sprocket support bearing. **1999–2003**—Incorrect fuel gauge readings caused by a contaminated fuel-tank sensor/sender. If a fuel "cleaner" doesn't work, GM says it will adjust or replace the sensor/sender for free, on a case-by-case basis (*Toronto Star*, June 13 and 14 and December 20, 2003). This failure afflicts GM's entire lineup and could cost up to $800 to repair. **2000–02**—Service Engine Soon light comes on and automatic transmission is harsh shifting. • Hard start, no-start, stall, and fuel gauge inoperative. **2001**—Customer Satisfaction Program (read: secret warranty) to correct the rear HVAC control switch. **2001–02**—Poor engine and automatic transmission operation (see following bulletin):

A/T – 4T65E Poor Performance/Incorrect Shifts/SES On

File In Section: 07 – Transmission/Transaxle

Bulletin No.: 02-07-30-013

Date: April 2002

TECHNICAL

Subject:

Incorrect Transmission Shifts, Poor Performance of Engine, Transmission Slipping, SES Lamp Illuminated, DTC P0756, P0757 (Clean Transaxle Valve Body and Case Oil Packages of Debris)

Models:

2001–02	Buick Century, LeSabre, Park Avenue, Regal
2002	Buick Rendezvous
2001	Chevrolet Lumina
2001–02	Chevrolet Impala, Monte Carlo, Venture
2001–02	Oldsmobile Aurora, Intrigue, Silhouette
2001–02	Pontiac Aztek, Bonneville, Grand Prix, Montana

with 4T65E Transmission (RPOs M15, MN3, MN7, M76)

Condition

Some owners may comment on any one or more of the following conditions:

^ The SES lamp is illuminated.
^ The transmission slips.
^ The transmission does not shift correctly, is very difficult to get the vehicle to start moving or the engine lacks the power to move the vehicle.

Cause

The most likely cause of the various conditions may be chips or debris:

^ Plugging an orifice on the case side of the spacer plate.
^ Restricting the movement of the 2–3 shift valves in the valve body.
^ Restricting the movement of the 3–4 shift valves in the valve body.

2001–03—Water in jack compartment. **2003**—Shudder, chuggle, hard shifting, and transmission won't downshift.

Lumina, Lumina APV, Montana, Silhouette, Trans Sport, Venture Profile

	1996	1997	1998	1999	2000	2001	2002	2003
Cost Price ($)								
Lumina Cargo	20,110	—	—	—	—	—	—	—
Passenger	22,730	—	—	—	—	—	—	—
Montana	—	—	—	25,130	26,625	26,755	27,870	28,520
Silhouette	—	—	29,410	29,955	30,630	31,105	33,060	35,695
Trans Sport/SE	23,475	23,690	24,650	—	—	—	—	—
Venture	—	23,185	24,145	24,725	24,895	25,230	25,195	25,865
Used Values ($)								
Lumina Cargo ʌ	3,500	—	—	—	—	—	—	—
Lumina Cargo ꓦ	3,000	—	—	—	—	—	—	—

Passenger ▲	5,500	—	—	—	—	—	—	—
Passenger ▼	4,000	—	—	—	—	—	—	—
Montana ▲	—	—	—	9,500	12,000	15,000	18,000	22,000
Montana ▼	—	—	—	8,500	11,000	13,500	16,000	21,000
Silhouette ▲	—	—	9,000	10,000	13,000	17,000	20,000	29,000
Silhouette ▼	—	—	7,000	9,000	12,000	15,500	19,000	27,000
Trans Sport/SE ▲	5,000	6,000	8,000	—	—	—	—	—
Trans Sport/SE ▼	4,000	5,000	6,500	—	—	—	—	—
Venture ▲	—	6,500	9,000	10,000	12,500	15,000	17,000	21,000
Venture ▼	—	5,500	7,500	9,000	11,000	14,000	16,000	20,000
Reliability	❷	③	③	③	③	③	③	③
Crash Safety (F)	⑤	④	④	④	④	④	④	④
Side	—	—	—	⑤	⑤	⑤	⑤	⑤
Offset	—	❶	❶	❶	❶	❶	❶	❶
Head Restraints (F)	—	❶	—	③	—	③	③	③
Rear	—	—	—	❶	—	—	—	—
Rollover Resistance	—	—	—	—	—	③	③	③

Honda

ODYSSEY ★★★★

RATING: Above Average (1999–2003), but not as well built as the latest Toyota Sienna; Average (1996–98). Quality has slipped since 1996, as evidenced by the disturbingly frequent reports of safety- and performance-related failures. Of particular concern are airbag malfunctions, automatic sliding door failures, engine failures, transmission breakdowns and erratic shifting, and sudden brake loss. Early Odysseys get only an Average rating due to their small engine and interior—identical shortcomings to those of Mazda's early MPV minivan. The redesigned '99 model offers better performance and a larger interior, but it suffers from many first-year glitches. **Maintenance/Repair costs:** Average; any garage can repair these minivans. **Parts:** Moderately priced parts; availability is better than average because the Odyssey uses many generic Accord parts. **Best alternatives:** If you want something cheap, but still reliable, consider a used Mercury Villager or the Nissan Axxess (see Appendix II) and Quest. If you want better handling and reliability, the closest competitor to the Odyssey is Toyota's Sienna minivan, although the redesigned 2002 Mazda MPV has lots of potential. The Pontiac Montana and Chevrolet Venture from GM are good front-drive choices—they're only a bit less reliable (engine head gasket and intake manifold), but are still acceptable. If you're looking for lots of towing "grunt," then the rear-drive GM Astro, Safari, or full-sized vans would be best. **Online help:** *consumeraffairs.com/automotive/honda_van.html*; *www.mycarstats.com/auto_complaints/HONDA_complaints.asp*; and *www.autosafety.org/autodefects.html*.

Strengths and weaknesses: When it was first launched in 1995, the Odyssey was a sales dud, simply because Canadians and *Lemon-Aid* saw through Honda's ruse in trying to pass off an underpowered, mid-sized, four-door station wagon with a raised roof as a minivan. However, in 1999 the Odyssey was redesigned, and it now represents one of the better minivans on the Canadian market.

It's easy to see what makes the Odyssey so popular: strong engine performance; carlike ride and handling; easy entry/exit; a second driver-side door; quiet interior; most controls and displays are easy to reach and read; there's lots of passenger and cargo room; an extensive list of standard equipment; and a willingness by Honda to compensate owners for production snafus.

This minivan does have its drawbacks, though, foremost being a recent decline in quality and a high resale price, making bargains rare. Owners report that front-seat passenger legroom is marginal due to the restricted seat travel; third-row seating is only suitable for children; power sliding doors are slow to retract; there's some tire rumble, rattles, and body drumming at highway speeds; premium fuel is required for optimum performance; and rear-seat head restraints impede side and rear visibility.

One can sum up the strengths and weaknesses of the 1996–98 Odyssey (and its American twin through the 1998 model, the Isuzu Oasis) in three words: performance, performance, performance. You get carlike performance and handling, responsive steering, and a comfortable ride, offset by slow-as-molasses-in-January acceleration with a full load, a raucous engine, and limited passenger/cargo space due to the narrow body.

Despite the above-mentioned drawbacks, the 1996–98 Odysseys have proven to be cheaper to acquire, more reliable, and offer better handling than American rear-drive, truck-inspired minivans. But their weak 2.2L 4-cylinder engine and small dimensions can't compete with GM's front-drives or most rear-drive competitors. The upgraded 1999 models have powerful 6-cylinder engines and a larger interior, wiping out most of the previous model's deficiencies.

Vehicle history: 1997—Small improvements. **1998**—A new 2.3L engine adds 10 horses (not enough!), and a restyled grille and instrument panel debut. **1999**—A new, more powerful engine and increased size make this second-generation Odyssey a more versatile highway performer; still, steering requires fully extended arms and power sliding doors operate slowly. **2001**—User-friendly child safety seat tether anchors, upgraded stereo speakers, and an intermittent rear window wiper. **2002**—A slight restyling, 30 additional horses, disc brakes on all four wheels, standard side airbags, and additional support for front seats.

Reliability for all models is much better than average, but Honda still has a few problems to work out. One notable and hazardous example: failure-prone sliding doors. Imagine, they open when they shouldn't, won't close when they should, catch fingers and arms, get stuck open or closed, are noisy, and frequently require expensive servicing. The Check Engine light may stay lit due to a defective fuel filler neck. There's a fuel sloshing noise when accelerating or coming to a stop, and the transmission clunks or bangs when backing uphill or when shifted into Reverse. There are also reports of rattling and chattering when put into forward gear. Owners note a loud wind noise and vibration from the left side of the front windshield, along with a constant vibration felt through the steering assembly and front wheels. Passenger doors may also require excessive force to open. And owners have complained of severe static electricity shocks when exiting. Other potential problem areas are frequent and high-cost front brake maintenance (see "Secret Warranties/Service Tips/ TSBs"), and trim and accessory items that come loose, break away, or malfunction. Automatic transmission failures continue to be a major shortcoming.

Transmission breakdowns; when shifting into Fourth gear, engine almost stalls out and produces a noise like valve clattering; transmission gear whine at 90 km/h or when in Fourth gear (transmission replaced under new 'goodwill' warranty). One owner reported the following noisy annoyances with his 2000 model Odyssey:

> At 10,000 miles [16,000 km] I complained to the dealer about the torque converter rattle and was told it was not there. I have since taken it in four times to make sure it's documented and I was told last week that Honda is aware of the annoying rattle but is not willing to make any repairs at this time. As you know, Honda is experiencing other transmission "concerns" and has extended its warranty on certain transmissions....

Front-end clunking caused by welding breaks in the front subframe; exhaust rattling or buzzing; loud fuel splashing sound in the fuel tank when coming to a stop; vehicle pulls to the right when underway; premature front brake wear; excessive front brake noise; sliding side door frequently malfunctions; electrical glitches; defective remote audio controls; leather seats split, crack, or discolour; and accessory items that come loose, break away, or won't work. Plastic interior panels have rough edges and are often misaligned.

The comprehensive base warranty has lots of "wiggle room" that the service manager can use to apply "goodwill" adjustments for post-warranty problems. However, dealer servicing has come in for a great deal of criticism from *Lemon-Aid* readers. Owners complain that recall repairs take an eternity to perform due to parts shortages, and dealers may be reluctant or unable to perform the required tasks competently.

Safety summary: 1996—While backing the vehicle out, occupant turned AC on, and vehicle shot forward with no brakes. • Cruise control failed while vehicle was going uphill. **1997–98**—Sudden acceleration upon brake application. • Minivan was put in Drive, and AC was turned on; vehicle suddenly accelerated, brakes failed, and the minivan hit a brick wall. **1999**—Sudden, unintended acceleration due to stuck accelerator. • Fire erupted in the electrical harness. • Another fire erupted as vehicle was getting fuel. • Plastic gas tank cracks, leaks fuel. • Gasoline smell when transmission is put into Reverse. • Side window exploded while driving. • Check Engine light comes on and vehicle loses all power. • Engine and electrical shutdown when coming to a stop. • When driving, all the instrument panel lights will suddenly go out (faulty multiplex controller suspected). • When parked on a hill, vehicle may roll backward; transmission doesn't hold vehicle when stopped at a light on a hill and foot is taken off accelerator or brake. • Complete loss of power steering due to a pinhole in the power-steering return hose. • Poor power-steering performance in cold weather. • Many incidents of sudden tire tread separation (Firestone). • Power door locks lock and unlock on their own. • Design of the gear shifter interferes with the radio controls. • Child unable to get out of seat belt due to buckle lock-up. • Faulty fuel gauge. • Inconvenient cell phone jack location. **2000**—During fuelling, fuel tank burst into flames. • Many incidents where driver-side sliding door opened onto fuel hose while fuelling, damaging gas flap hinge and tank. • Sudden, unintended acceleration when slowing for a stop sign. • On cold days, accelerator pedal is hard to depress. • Catastrophic failure of the right-side suspension, causing wheel to buckle. • Vehicle continually pulls to the right; dealers unable to correct problem. • Excessive steering wheel vibration at 105+ km/h. • Electric doors often inoperative. • As child slept in safety seat, seat belt tightened progressively to point that fire department had to be called; other similar incidents. • Chronic automatic transmission problems: won't shift into lower gears, suddenly loses power, torque converter failure, makes a loud popping sound when put into Reverse. • Two incidents where vehicle rear-ended due to transmission malfunction. • Van's transmission doesn't hold when stopped on a hill; gas or brakes have to be constantly applied. • Power seatback moves on its own. • Dash lights don't adequately illuminate the dash panel. • Driver's seatback suddenly reclines, hitting rear passenger's legs, even though power switch is off. • Protruding bolts in the door assembly are hazardous. • Seat belt buckle fails to latch. • Driver-side mirror breaks away; mirror glass fell out due to poor design. **2001**—While fuelling, fuel tank exploded. • In a frontal collision, van caught fire due to a cracked brake fluid reservoir. • Sudden acceleration when approaching a stop sign. • While travelling at 90 km/h, accelerator jammed. • Chronic stalling (transmission replaced). • Many reports of sudden transmission and torque converter failure. • While stopped on an incline of about 35 degrees, van rolled backward. • When Reverse is engaged, car makes a popping or clunking sound. • Cracked wheel rim. • Check Engine light constantly on (suspect faulty gasoline filler neck). • Engine knocks when vehicle reaches 90 km/h. • Entire vehicle shakes excessively at highway speeds and van pulls to the right (dealer said some type of bar adjustment was needed). • Passenger-side door window suddenly exploded while driving on the highway. • Driver's seatback collapsed from rear-end collision. • Driver's power seat will suddenly recline on its own, squeezing rear occupant's legs and falling on child. • Rear seat belt tightened up so much that a child had to be cut free. • Too much play in rear lapbelts, which won't tighten adequately, making it difficult to install a child safety seat securely. • Inoperative driver seat belt buckle. • Faulty speedometer and tachometer. • Remote wouldn't open or lock vehicle. •

Placement of the gear shift lever interferes with the radio's controls. • Unable to depress accelerator pedal on cold days. • Can hear gasoline sloshing in tank while driving. • Frequent static electricity shocks. • Many owners report that the rear head restraints seriously hamper rear and forward visibility and that it was difficult to see vehicles coming from the right side. **2002**—Over 100 complaints registered, where, normally, a couple dozen would be expected. • Wife injured when side airbags deployed inadvertently. • No airbag deployment. • Breakage of engine timing belt bolt. • Owners say many engines have faulty timing chain defect. • Engine oil leaks. • Transmission suddenly shifted from Fourth gear to First. • Loose strut bolt almost caused wheel to fall off. • Axle bearing wheel failure caused driver-side wheel to fall off. • Left to right veering and excessive drivetrain vibration. • Automatic transmission replaced. • Loud popping sound heard when brakes are applied. • Many complaints that the brake pedal went to floor with no braking capability. • Sticking sliding door. • Head restraints are set too low for tall occupants. • Rear windshield shattered from area where wiper is mounted. • Rear seat belt unlatched during emergency braking. • Brake line freezes up in cold weather. • Abrupt downshift upon deceleration. • Driver-side door came off while using remote control. • Dashboard lights come on and off intermittently. • Passenger window exploded. • Airbag light comes on for no reason. **2003**—Fire ignited in the CD player. • Passenger seatbacks collapsed when vehicle was rear-ended. • Child injured from a side collision because second-row seat belt failed to hold her in due to gap caused by door attachment. • Rear seat belts lock for no reason. • Seat belt extenders aren't offered. • Defective speed sensor caused vehicle to suddenly lose power when merging into traffic. • Vehicle suddenly shut down in traffic. • Hard starts and engine misfiring. • Many automatic transmission malfunctions. • Faulty steering causes wander. • Sudden brake failure. • Driver often shocked when touching door handle. • Fuel spits out when refuelling. • Inaccurate fuel gauge readings. • Sliding door closed on driver's hand.

Secret Warranties/Service Tips/TSBs

All models/years: Most of Honda's TSBs allow for special warranty consideration on a "goodwill" basis by the company's District Service Manager or Zone Office, even after the warranty has expired or the vehicle has changed hands. Referring to this euphemism will increase your chances of getting some kind of refund for repairs that are obviously factory defects. **All models: 1995–97**— Rear wheel bearing noise can be silenced by replacing the hub bearing assembly and hubcaps. • If the driver's seat makes a clicking noise, you may need to install a stop in the rear seat rail. **1997**—If the tailgate-open indicator light stays on, you may need to replace the tailgate latch assembly. • Distorted sound from the front speakers can be corrected only by installing new speakers. **1997–98**—If the blower motor works only on high speed, try replacing the blower motor and resistor. **1999**—Insufficient EGR flow causing poor engine performance or a DTC PO401 code reading has prompted Honda to carry out a free service campaign whereby the company will replace, at no charge, the rear intake manifold end plate and gasket, the PCV hose, and the intake manifold cover. • Excessive front brake noise will be silenced under a "goodwill" repair, if you get Honda's permission first, says TSB #99013. • There's an incredibly large number of sliding door problems covered by a recall and a plethora of service bulletins that are simply too numerous to print here. Ask Honda politely for the bulletins or "goodwill" assistance. If refused, subpoena the documents through small claims court. Normally, ALLDATA would supply the data for $30, but Honda USA has enjoined the company from giving out bulletin information to its customers. Shameful! • Problems with the fuel tank pressure sensor are covered in TSB #99-056 and could call for the installation of an in-line orifice in the two-way valve vacuum hose. • AC knocking may require the installation of a new compressor clutch set. • Front windows that bind or are noisy when activated require that a mechanic inspect the window regulator guide rail for proper lubrication, and possibly replace the glass run channel and adjust the glass channels. • An inaccurate fuel gauge is likely caused by a faulty sending unit. **1999–2001**—Extended warranty coverage on Odysseys with defective 4- and 5-speed automatic transmissions to 7 years/100,000 miles (160,000 km) to fix erratic or slow shifting. **2000–01**—Third-row seat won't unlatch. • Clunk or bang when engaging Reverse. • Bulletin confirms Honda USA is currently investigating complaints of pulling or drifting (Service Bulletin Number: 99165, Bulletin Sequence Number: 802, Date of Bulletin: 9909, NHTSA Item Number: SB608030). • Excessive front brake noise. • Dash ticking or clicking. • Information relating to closing sliding door with care to prevent outward dents or avoid damaging the slide motor gears. **1999–2003**—Engine oil leaks.

V6 Engine Oil Leaks

No: 01-009

September 10, 2002

1998–2002 Accord
1999–2003 Odyssey
2003 Pilot

SYMPTOM: An oil leak from the front, middle, or rear of the engine.

PROBABLE CAUSE: The cast aluminum engine block may be porous at the front, middle, or rear.

CORRECTIVE ACTION: Depending on the location of the leak, seal it with JB Weld or with 3-Bond-coated sealing bolts.

• Sliding door noise when passing over bumps. • Deformed windshield moulding. **2002**—Hesitation when accelerating. • Diagnosing automatic transmission problems. • No-starts; hard start in cold weather. • Driver's seat heater may not work. • Thump at cold start. • Loose rear wiper arm. • AC can't be turned off while in defog setting. • Sliding door creak or rattle. **2003**—Engine cranks, but won't start. • Troubleshooting ABS problems. • Power steering pump noise. • Warning lights blink on and off. • Exhaust rattling, buzzing. • Remote audio control troubleshooting. • Leather seat defects.

• Homelink range is too short; hard to program. • Factory security won't arm. • Faulty charging system; electrical shorts. • Front door howls in strong cross-wind. • Squealing from rear quarter windows and window motors. Fuel tank leak. • Front damper noise. • Steering wheel bent off-centre. • Manual sliding door is difficult to open.

Odyssey Profile

	1996	1997	1998	1999	2000	2001	2002	2003
Cost Price ($)								
LX	28,796	28,995	29,800	30,600	30,600	30,800	31,900	32,200
EX	—	—	—	33,600	33,600	33,800	34,900	35,200
Used Values ($)								
LX ∧	7,500	9,500	12,000	15,000	17,000	20,000	25,500	28,000
LX ∨	6,500	8,000	11,000	13,500	16,000	18,500	24,000	27,000
EX ∧	—	—	—	16,500	20,000	23,000	26,500	29,000
EX ∨	—	—	—	15,500	18,500	21,500	25,000	28,000
Reliability	③	③	③	④	⑤	⑤	⑤	⑤
Crash Safety (F)	④	④	—	⑤	⑤	⑤	⑤	⑤
Side	—	—	—	—	⑤	⑤	⑤	⑤
Head Restraints (F)	❷	❷	—	❷	—	❷	❷	❷
Rear	—	—	—	❶	—	—	—	—
Offset	❷	❷	—	❷	—	❷	❷	❷
Rollover Resistance	—	—	—	—	—	④	④	④

Kia

SEDONA   ★★★

RATING: Average (2002–03). Sedona is a very user-friendly, roomy, practical, versatile, and comfortable mid-sized minivan. **Strong points:** Reasonably priced; well appointed; transmission shifts smoothly and quietly; low ground clearance adds to stability and helps access; low step-in; comfortable ride; convenient "walk-through" space between front seats; well laid-out, user-friendly instruments and controls; lots of storage areas; good visibility; fairly well built; minimal engine and road noise; good braking; head restraints for the 2002 model are rated "Good" up front, "Acceptable" in the rear; "Acceptable" crashworthiness scores; and comprehensive base warranty. **Weak points:** Engine power is drained by the Sedona's heft; 10–20 percent higher fuel consumption than V6-equipped Dodge Caravan and Toyota Sienna; subpar, vague steering and handling; excessive engine and wind noise; and weak dealer network. Quality control is its weakest link. **Maintenance/Repair costs:** Average. **Parts:** Likely to be back ordered and cost more than average. **Best alternatives:** Check out the GM Venture, Honda Odyssey, Mazda MPV, or Toyota Sienna.

Online help: *www.autosafety.org/autodefects.html*; *members.tripod.com/ aiki_joe/i_hate_kia*; and *townhall-talk.edmunds.com.*

Strengths and weaknesses: Used Sedonas range in price from $18,000 to $19,500 for the LX—several thousand dollars less than comparable minivans. Embodying typically bland minivan styling, the front-drive, seven-passenger Sedona is 18 centimetres (7 in.) shorter than a Honda Odyssey and 11 centimetres (4.5 in.) longer than a Dodge Caravan. It comes with a good selection of standard features, including a 195-hp 3.5L V6 engine hooked to an automatic 5-speed transmission, a low step-in height, and a commanding view of the road. For convenience, there are two sliding rear side doors (automatic doors aren't available); folding, removable second- and third-row seats; a flip-up hatchback; standard front/rear air conditioning; and a large cargo bay. Other standard amenities: 15-inch tires, AM/FM/CD stereo, power steering, power windows, power door locks, power heated mirrors, tilt steering, rear defroster and wiper, dual airbags (side airbags not offered), and six adjustable head restraints.

Safety summary: 2002—Fuel tank design could spray fuel on hot muffler in a collision. • Oil leaks onto the hot catalytic converter. • Fuel leaks from the bottom of the vehicle. • Loose fuel line to fuel pump clamp. • Fuel tank filler hose vulnerable to road debris. • Fuel spits back when refuelling. • Vehicle continues to accelerate when brakes are applied. • Intermittent stalling. • Brake failure; pedal simply sinks to the floor. • Excessive brake shudder when slowing going downhill. • ABS brake light comes on randomly. • Power steering pulley broke. • Windshield may suddenly shatter for no apparent reason. • Windshields have distortion at eye level. • Second- and third-row seats don't latch as easily as touted. • Oil leaks onto the catalytic converter. • Electrical shorts cause lights, windows, and door locks to fail. • Sliding doors won't retract if object is in their way. • Stuck rear hatch door. • Child safety seat can't be belted in securely. • Child door safety lock failure. • Inoperative back-seat seat belts. • Seat belt holding child in booster seat tightened progressively, trapping child. • Kumho tire tread separation. **2003**—Under-hood fire ignited while car was underway. • Airbags failed to deploy. • Sudden, unintended acceleration. • Stuck accelerator pedal. • Brakes fail due to air in the brake lines. • Fuel odour in cabin. • Broken window regulator. • Rear seat removal instructions can throw your back out. • Tires peeled off the rim. • When reclined, passenger seatback is released upright and slams a young child forward. • AC condenser vulnerable to puncture from road debris. • Electrical shorts cause door lock malfunctions.

Secret Warranties/Service Tips

2002—Correction for engine hesitation after cold starts. • Free replacement of seat belt buckle anchor bolts. **2002–03**—Changes to improve alternator output to prevent hard starts or battery drain.

Sedona Profile

	2002	2003
Cost Price ($)		
LX	24,595	24,995
EX	27,595	28,295
Used Values ($)		
LX ⋀	15,000	17,500
LX ⋁	13,500	16,000
EX ⋀	17,500	20,000
EX ⋁	16,000	18,500
Reliability	③	③
Crash Safety (F)	⑤	⑤
Side	⑤	⑤
Head Restraints (F)	⑤	⑤
Rear	③	③
Offset	③	③
Rollover Resistance	④	④

Mazda

MPV   ★★★★

RATING: Above Average (2002–03); Average (2000–01); Below Average (1988–98). Mazda has accomplished an amazing turnaround in the past two years; its MPV is now smaller, sportier, and more nimble than its more space- and comfort-oriented counterparts. Early models were underpowered, lumbering, undersized, and overpriced. There was no '99 model. The redesigned 2000–01 model is still hampered by a wimpy powertrain and is just too small for most tasks. **Maintenance/Repair costs:** Average; independent garages can service these minivans more cheaply than Mazda dealers. **Parts:** Likely to be back ordered and cost more than average, despite Mazda's best efforts to cut prices. **Best alternatives:** The MPV is still best suited for owners not wanting the biggest family-hauler on the block, those who prefer sporty handling, and who don't mind spending less to get less. When the MPV's compared with Honda's Odyssey, the value equation gets a little murkier. With the price reduction, the base MPV LX gains a competitive advantage over the base Odyssey. When compared with the more expensive Odysseys, there's not enough savings to make up for the MPV's smaller size and less powerful engine. And the Odyssey is already available with a DVD entertainment system. Go for a cheaper 2002 model, but make sure it's a second-series version to keep factory-induced glitches to a minimum. There are plenty of reasonably priced 2- and 3-year-old MPVs on the market that have just come off lease, but they don't measure up to the better-performing 2002–03 versions.

Other models to consider: a late-model GM front-drive, Honda Odyssey, Ford Mercury Villager, Nissan Axxess or Quest, or Toyota Sienna. **Online help:** *townhall-talk.edmunds.com/direct/view/.ee93de8; forums.mazdaworld.org/index.php?showforum=35;* and *www.autosafety.org/autodefects.html.*

Strengths and weaknesses: Manufactured in Hiroshima, Japan, this small minivan offers a number of innovative features, like "theatre" seating (rear passenger seat is slightly higher) and a third seat that pivots rearward to become a rear-facing bench seat—or folds into the floor for picnics or tailgate parties. Another feature unique among minivans is Mazda's Side-by-Slide removable second-row seats, which move fore and aft as well as side-to-side while a passenger is seated. Sliding door crank windows are standard on the entry model and power-assisted on the LS and ES versions.

Mazda's only minivan quickly became a bestseller when it first came on the market in 1989, but its popularity fell just as quickly when larger, more powerful competitors arrived. Mazda sales have bounced back recently as a result of price cutting and the popularity of the automaker's small cars and pickups. This infusion of cash has allowed the company (34 percent owned by Ford) to put additional money into its 2002 redesign, thus ending a sales slump that has plagued the company for over a decade. Early MPVs embodied many of the mistakes made by Honda's first Odyssey—its 170 horses weren't adequate for people-hauling and it was expensive for what was essentially a smaller van than buyers expected—a foot shorter than the Ford Windstar and a half foot shorter than the Toyota Sienna and Nissan Quest.

Vehicle history: 1992—5-speed manual transmission deleted and the 3.0L V6 got a 5-horsepower boost. **1993**—A driver-side airbag. **1994**—A centre brake light and side-door impact beams. **1995**—Seven-passenger seating and a 155-horsepower, 3.0L engine. **1996**—A passenger-side airbag, four-wheel ABS, and four doors. **2000**—A new model with front-drive and sliding side doors. **2002**—A 200-hp V6 and 5-speed automatic transmission, power sliding side doors, revised suspension settings, and 17-inch wheels. **2003**—More standard features (LX) that include power-sliding rear side doors, 16-inch wheels, a flip-up side table, and doormat.

The MPV uses a new 3.0L Duratec V6 found in the Taurus. That means horsepower is up 35 to 200 hp and a similar number of pound-feet are also available, though some refinements produce a lower torque peak—3000 rpm versus 4400 rpm—giving the Mazda engine better pulling power at lower speed. Making better use of that power is a new 5-speed automatic transmission, which should cut fuel consumption a bit. One immediate benefit: The 3.0L is able to climb hills without continuously downshifting, and Mazda's "slope control" system automatically shifts to a lower gear when the hills get very steep.

Torque is still less than the Odyssey's 3.5L or the 3.8L engine in top-of-the-line Chryslers, though comparable with lesser Chrysler products and GM's Venture and Montana. The engine operates more smoothly than its predecessor, though it's not as quiet as Honda's 3.5L V6. The suspension has been firmed up to decrease body roll, enhancing cornering ability and producing a sportier ride than other minivans. This firmness may be too much for some.

I've been tougher on the MPV than have *Consumer Reports* and others due to the price-gouging, poor servicing, small size, underpowered drivetrain, and reliability problems (all too common on pre-2000 models). Presently it looks like most of these concerns have been met, although I'm still worried that the 3.0 Duratec may not hold up.

On more recent models, engine overheating and head gasket failures are commonplace with the 4-banger, and the temperature gauge warns you only when it's too late. Some cases of chronic engine knocking in cold weather with the 3.0L have been fixed by installing tighter-fitting, Teflon-coated pistons. Valve lifter problems are also common with this engine. Winter driving is compromised by the MPV's light rear end and mediocre traction, and low ground clearance means that off-road excursions shouldn't be too adventurous. The last couple of model years are much improved; nevertheless, expect some transmission glitches, ABS malfunctions, a rotten-egg exhaust, stalling and surging, and some oil leakage. Owners report that the electronic computer module (ECU), automatic transmission driveshaft, upper shock mounts, front 4X4 drive axles and lash adjusters, AC core, and radiator fail within the first three years. Cold temperatures tend to "fry" the automatic window motor, and the paint is easily chipped and flakes off early, especially around the hood, tailgate, and front fenders. Premature brake caliper and rotor wear and excessive vibration/pulsation are chronic problem areas (repairs are needed about every 12,000 km). Premature paint peeling afflicting white-coloured MPVs is quite common.

Safety summary: 1998—Rear anti-sway bar brackets snapped off from rear axle housing. • ABS brake failure. • Defective gas cap causes the false activation of the Check Engine light. **2000**—Fixed seat belt anchors and buckle placement prevent the safe installation of child safety seats. • Vehicle windshield and side glass suddenly shattered while parked. • Excessive vibrations while cruising. • Rear hatch door flew open when rear-ended. **2000–01**—Engine valve failure. • Cupholders will spill drink when making a sharp turn; holders were redesigned in 2002. **2000–03**—Airbags failed to deploy. **2001**—Engine surging. • Malfunctioning #1 spark plug causes chronic engine hesitation. • Tranny lever can be shifted out of Park without key in ignition; sometimes it won't shift out of Park when you want it to. • Brake failure. • Brake caliper bolt fell off, causing vehicle to skid. • Sliding doors don't lock in place. • Rear visibility obstructed by high seatbacks. **2002–03**—Engine oil leakage, sudden stalling, shifter obscures dash and is easily knocked about. **2003**—Child's neck tangled in seat belt. • Rotten-egg exhaust smell.

Secret Warranties/Service Tips/TSBs

All models/years—TSB #006-94 looks into all the causes and remedies for excessive brake vibrations, and TSB #11-14-95 gives an excellent diagnostic flow chart for troubleshooting excessive engine noise. • Serious paint peeling and delaminating will be fully covered for up to six years under a Mazda secret warranty, say owners. • Troubleshooting tips for correcting wind noise around doors. • Tips for eliminating a musty, mildew-type AC odour. **1996–98**—Tips for correcting water leaks from the sliding sunroof. • Brake pulsation repair tips. • Front power window noise. • Wind noise around doors. • Steering wheel a bit off-centre. **1997–98**—Front power window noise can be silenced by installing a modified window regulator. **2000–01**—Hard starts caused by inadequate fuel system pressure, due to a fuel pressure regulator that's stuck open. • Front brake clunking can be silenced by replacing the eight brake guide plates under warranty (TSB #04-003/00). • Insufficient airflow at bi-level setting. • Door key difficult to insert or rotate. **2000–03**—Rotten-egg exhaust smell. • Remedy for a mildew odour. • A corroded rear heater pipe may leak coolant; Mazda will fix it for free (see TSB #07-004/03). **2001**—Rear brake popping, squealing, or clicking. • Tips for eliminating a musty, mildew-type odour from the AC. **2002**— Engine tappet noise. **2002–03**—Cargo net hooks detach.

MPV Profile

	1996	1997	1998	2000	2001	2002	2003
Cost Price ($)							
Base	27,330	—	—	—	—	—	—
DX	—	—	—	25,505	25,095	25,975	26,090
LX	30,900	27,845	25,199	29,450	29,450	29,150	29,090
Used Values ($)							
Base ⋀	4,500	—	—	—	—	—	—
Base ⋁	4,000	—	—	—	—	—	—
DX ⋀	—	—	—	13,000	15,500	17,000	20,000
DX ⋁	—	—	—	12,000	14,000	16,000	19,000
LX ⋀	5,500	6,500	9,000	14,000	17,000	20,000	22,500
LX ⋁	5,000	6,000	7,500	13,000	16,000	18,500	21,000
Reliability	③	③	③	④	④	④	④
Crash Safety (F)	④	④	—	④	④	⑤	⑤
Side	❷	❷	❷	⑤	⑤	⑤	⑤
Offset	❷	❷	❷	③	③	③	③
Head Restraints (F)	❷	❶	—	③	❷	❷	❷
Rear	—	—	—	—	❶	❶	❶
Rollover Resistance	—	—	—	—	③	③	③

Note: 4X4 models cost about $500 more; there was no MPV.

Toyota

SIENNA, PREVIA ★★★☆

RATING: *Sienna:* Above Average (1998–2003). Mazda and Nissan's minivans are catching up to Honda and Toyota. Earlier Toyotas are still outclassed by the brawnier, more innovative Odyssey. *Previa:* Average (1991–97). As with the Honda Odyssey, Sienna owners also report some serious safety-related failures, including poor headlight illumination, transmission breakdowns, brake malfunctions, and faulty sliding doors. This said, the number of Toyota complaints are far less than what one finds with Chrysler, Ford, GM, and Honda. The Previa has high-priced reliability, mediocre road performance, and limited interior amenities. Nevertheless, it's far better than any of Toyota's earlier LE minivans. **Maintenance/Repair costs:** For the Sienna, like the Camry, much lower than average. The only exception is engine sludge, requiring expensive repairs. Previas aren't afflicted by the sludge problem, but their maintenance costs are still higher than average. Only Toyota dealers can repair these minivans, particularly when it comes to troubleshooting the supercharged 2.4L engine and All Trac. **Parts:** Excellent supply of reasonably priced Sienna parts taken from the Camry parts bin. Previa parts are in limited supply, but they're reasonably priced. Automatic transmission torque converters on 1998–2000 models are frequently back-ordered due to their poor reliability. **Best alternatives:** The best all-around choices are the Honda Odyssey and Nissan Quest. Mazda's MPV is a small minivan that's more reliable than the top-rated models, but pre-2002s lack power, interior room, and ride comfort. The GM minivans are fair performers, but like the Ford Windstar and Chrysler minivans, are plagued by serious powertrain reliability problems. As with most minivans and vans, you can save money by buying the cargo version, but you won't get as many features. Siennas equipped with 4X4 capability will cost about $1,000 more than the equivalent front-drive version. Be wary of the power sliding door. As with the Odyssey and GM minivans, these doors can injure children and pose unnecessary risks to other occupants. **Online help:** *www.autosafety.org/ autodefects.html*; *yotarepair.com/Sludge_Zone.html*; and *www.cartrackers.com/Forums/live/MiniVansEnthusiastDiscussionGroup/ page8.html*.

Strengths and weaknesses: The Sienna, Toyota's Camry-based front-drive minivan, replaced the Previa for the 1998 model year and abandoned the Previa's futuristic look in favour of a more conservative Chevrolet Venture styling. The Sienna seats seven, and offers dual power sliding doors with optional remote controls and a V6 power plant. It's built in the same Kentucky assembly plant as the Camry and comes with lots of safety and convenience features that include side airbags, anti-lock brakes, and a low-tire-pressure warning system.

Some of the Sienna's strong points: standard ABS and side airbags (LE, XLE); a smooth-running V6 engine and transmission that's a bit more refined and capable than what the Odyssey offers; a comfortable, stable ride; a fourth door; a quiet interior; easy entry/exit; and better-than-average fit and finish reliability. Its weak areas: V6 performance is compromised by AC and the automatic transmission powertrain and it lacks the trailer-towing brawn of rear-drive minivans:

> We have just leased a 2004 Toyota Sienna CE. As we mentioned many times to the salesperson (and sales manager), it was our intention to use this vehicle for towing our Coleman tent trailer. The trailer weighs about 1,700 lb. [770 kg] empty and we were assured by the dealership that since the Sienna '04 is rated for 3,500 lb. [1,590 kg] it would be ideal for our needs. They even arranged for the installation of a class III hitch prior to our taking possession.
>
> Imagine our surprise when we discovered within the owner's manual a "Caution" stating that one must not exceed 72 km/hr [45 mph] while towing a trailer (full text below). This limit is not stated in the promotional literature we were provided, or on the *Toyota.ca* website, or in any trailer towing rating guide. This limit was also not mentioned at any time during our purchase negotiations. Alarmingly, Toyota defines a "Caution" as a ""warning against anything which may cause injury to people if the warning is ignored." As it turns out, the dealer was not aware of this speed limit....

Although the rear seats fold flat to accommodate the width of a 4' x 8' board, the tailgate won't close, the heavy seats are difficult to reinstall (a two-person job, and the centre seat barely fits through the door), and rear visibility is obstructed by the middle roof pillars and rear head restraints. There's also no traction control, less-efficient rear drum brakes, mediocre fuel economy (premium fuel), the low-mounted radio is hard to reach, and third-row seats lack a fore/aft adjustment to increase cargo space.

Reliability is still problematic on 1997–2002 models. Although mechanical and body components are generally reliable, there's been a disturbing increase in factory-related defects reported by owners during the past few years. The most serious reliability problems concern self-destructing, sludge-prone engines (1997–2002 models) and defective automatic transmissions on 1998–2000 Siennas.

Toyota Canada advises owners who notice the telltale signs of engine sludge formation to take their vehicle to their local dealer to have the engine inspected. These signs may include the emission of blue smoke from the tailpipe and/or excessive oil consumption, which may cause overheating, rough running, or the Check Engine light to come on.

Other recent model problems reported by owners include automatic transmission failures; a clunk or banging in the driveline; when at a stop, the car will jolt or creep forward, forcing you to keep your foot firmly on the brake; stalling when the AC engages; electrical shorts; premature brake wear and excessive brake noise (mostly screeching); a chronic rotten-egg smell; distracting windshield reflections and distorted windshields; sliding door defects; window suddenly shatters; paint is easily chipped; and various other body glitches, including a hard-to-pull-out rear seat, water leaks, and excessive creaks and rattles (seat belt, sun visor).

Vehicle history: 1995—DX models get a supercharged engine. **1996**—Supercharged engine is the only power plant offered. **1997**—Extra soundproofing. **1998**—Introduction of the Sienna; no more Previa. **2001**—A rear defroster, some additional horsepower and torque, and a driver-side sliding door.

Previa

The redesigned 1991 Previa's performance and reliability are so much improved over its LE predecessor that it almost seems like a different vehicle. Roomier and rendered more stable thanks to its longer wheelbase, equipped with a new 2.4L engine (supercharged as of the 1994 model year), and loaded with standard safety and convenience features, 1991–97 Previas are almost as driver-friendly as the Chrysler and Mazda competition. Still, they can't match Ford, GM, or Chrysler front-drive minivans for responsive handling and a comfortable ride, and Toyota's small engine is overworked and doesn't hesitate to tell you so. Previa owners have learned to live with engine noise, poor fuel economy, premature front brake wear, excessive brake vibration and pulsation, electrical glitches, AC malfunctions, and fit and finish blemishes. The 4X4 models with automatic transmissions steal lots of power from the 4-cylinder power plant, though they have fewer reliability problems than similar drivetrains found on competitors, especially Chryslers.

Safety summary: Almost every model year has had serious sliding door malfunctions confirmed by owner complaints and a torrent of internal service bulletins. • Many complaints that the steering wheel locks up when making a turn, won't return to centre without extreme effort, or simply no longer responds. • Owners have also complained that the vehicle pulls sharply to one side or another when driving at moderate speeds. **Previa: 1996**—Middle right bench seat lapbelt is impossible to adjust due to its poor design. • Speed sensor failure. **Sienna: 1998**—Sudden acceleration, due to a defective throttle cable; vehicle hit a wall. • Shape and design of the Sienna creates severe blind spots. • Headlights give poor illumination. • Windshields are distorted, exhibiting a "melted" image. • Rear door doesn't shut tightly. • Poor visibility due to the tinted window design. • Headrests and third-row seats are loose and vibrate. • Shoulder belts in the middle row lock up instantly when first put on and stay locked up, binding the passenger. **1999**—Wheel lug nuts broke and allowed wheel to fall off. • Window exploded at stoplight. • Rear brake drums may overheat and warp. • Distracting dashboard reflection onto the windshield. • Windshield distortion. • Faulty fuel cap causes the Check Engine light to come on. **2000**—Check Engine light continues to come on due to a defective transmission torque converter. • Sudden acceleration during rainstorm. • Premature tire blowouts (Dunlop and Firestone). • Chronic transmission failure due to faulty torque converter. • Wheel lug nuts sheared off. • Driver's seat belt anchor bolt on door pillar unscrewed and fell to the floor. • Right rear passenger window suddenly exploded. • Annoying dash/windshield reflection also impairs visibility (very bad with black and beige colours). **2001**—Automatic transmission suddenly went into Neutral while on the highway. • Defective transmission torque converter causes the engine warning light to come on. • Sudden, unintended acceleration. • Sudden stalling when the AC is turned on • Vehicle rolled away, with shifter in Park on a hill and ignition shut off. • Reflection of the dashboard on the windshield impairs visibility. • Rear seat belts can't be adjusted. • Centre rear seat belt doesn't tighten sufficiently when children are restrained. • Slope of the windshield makes it hard to gauge where the front end stops. • Rear window exploded as front door was closed. • Sunroof flew off when opened while Sienna was underway. **2002**—Several electrical fires in the engine compartment. • Neither front nor side airbag deployed in a collision. • Defective power steering. • Loss of steering. **2003**—Unsafe transmission Overdrive design. • Child safety seat second-row tethering is poorly designed. • Vehicle jerks to one side when accelerating or stopping.

Secret Warranties/Service Tips/TSBs

All models/years: Sliding door malfunctions are a veritable plague affecting many model years. Owner feedback confirms that front brake pads and discs will be replaced under Toyota's "goodwill" policy if they wear out before 2 years/ 40,000 km. Improved disc brake pad kits are described in TSB #BR94-004. Brake pulsation/vibration, another generic Toyota problem, is fully addressed in TSB #BR94-002, "Cause and Repair of Vibration and Pulsation." **1997–2002**—Free engine overhaul or replacement due to engine sludge buildup. The program is for 3.3 million 1997 through 2002 Toyota and Lexus vehicles with 3.0L, V-6, or 2.2L 4-cylinder engines. There is no mileage limitation. **1998**—Upgraded brake pads and rotors should reduce brake groan and squeak noises. **1998–99**—To reduce sliding door creaks, the control junction materials have been upgraded. **1998–2000**—An 8-year/160,000 km warranty extension for automatic transmission failure. Says Toyota:

> We have recently become aware that a small number of Sienna owners have experienced a mechanical failure in the automatic transaxle, drive pinion bearing. This failure could result in slippage, noise, or a complete lack of movement.

> To ensure the continued satisfaction and reliability of your Sienna, Toyota has decided to implement a Special Policy Adjustment affecting certain 1998–2000 Sienna models....This Special Policy will extend the warranty coverage of the automatic transaxle to 8 years or 160,000 km, whichever occurs first, from the original warranty registration date....

• Outline of various diagnostic procedures and fixes to correct vehicle pulling to one side. • Power steering squeaks can be silenced by installing a countermeasure steering rack end under warranty. • Power steering "feel" can be improved by replacing the steering rack guide. • False activation of the security alarm can be fixed by modifying the hood latch switch. • Power window rattles can be corrected by installing a revised lower window frame mounting bracket. **1998–2003**—A new alternator has been adopted to improve charging; customers complained of a low battery charge or no-starts after running the engine at idle or low rpm for an extended period (see TSB #EL013-03). **1999–2000**—If the power- sliding door is inoperative or won't close properly, Toyota says the cable should be adjusted. **1999–2001**—Tips on fixing power seat motor cable to prevent a loose seat or inoperative seat adjustment. • Power sliding door transmitter improvements. **1999–2002**—Sliding door malfunctions. **2000**—Toyota has field fixes to correct washer fluid leakage from the rear washer nozzle and eliminate moisture and odours permeating the vehicle interior. • Correction for an inoperative spare tire lift. • Speedometer or tachometer troubleshooting. **2001**—Power sliding door malfunctions (troubleshooting tips). • False activation of the security alarm. • Power windows rattling. • Entertainment system hum. • Faulty speedometer and tachometer. • Inoperative third-row sliding seat. • Special service campaign to inspect or replace the front subframe assembly on 2001 models. • Water leaking into the trunk area. • Troubleshooting interior moisture or odours. • Loose sun visor. • Front wheel bearing ticking. **2001–02**—Inoperative power sliding door. **2002**—Troubleshooting complaints that vehicle pulls to one side. **2002–03**—Steering angle sensor calibration. • Loose sun visor remedy.

Sienna, Previa Profile

	1996	1997	1998	1999	2000	2001	2002	2003
Cost Price ($)								
Previa	35,908	36,998	—	—	—	—	—	—
Sienna Cargo 3d	—	—	24,438	24,570	24,570	—	—	—
Sienna CE 4d (16%)	—	—	26,808	26,940	27,770	29,535	29,335	29,060
Sienna LE 4d (17%)	—	—	29,558	29,980	30,705	31,900	32,985	31,925
Used Values ($)								
Previa △	5,000	6,500	—	—	—	—	—	—
Previa ▽	4,500	5,500	—	—	—	—	—	—
Sienna Cargo 3d △	—	—	8,000	11,500	13,500	—	—	—
Sienna Cargo 3d ▽	—	—	7,500	10,500	12,000	—	—	—

Sienna CE 4d Λ	—	—	11,000	12,000	15,500	19,000	22,000	25,000
Sienna CE 4d V	—	—	9,500	10,500	13,000	18,000	21,000	23,000
Sienna LE 4d Λ	—	—	12,500	15,000	17,000	20,500	24,000	27,000
Sienna LE 4d V	—	—	11,000	14,000	15,500	18,500	22,000	25,500
Reliability	③	③	④	④	④	④	④	⑤
Crash Safety (F)	④	④	⑤	⑤	⑤	⑤	⑤	⑤
Side	—	—	—	④	④	④	④	④
Offset	❶	❶	⑤	⑤	⑤	⑤	⑤	⑤
Head Restraints	③	③	❶	❶	—	❷	❷	❷
Rear	❷	❷	—	—	—	—	—	—
Rollover Resistance	—	—	—	—	—	④	④	④

INTERNET HOT SPOTS

Many of the best websites have already been listed in this guide's detailed model ratings. Nevertheless, the following sites may have more current ratings, service bulletins, safety info, owner complaints, and jurisprudence. Some of these sites are also helpful guides to setting up your own protest/gripe website.

Automobile companies have helpful, though self-serving websites, and most feature detailed sections on history, research and development, and all sorts of information of interest to car enthusiasts. They can easily be accessed through Google's browser under the automaker's name followed by .com or .ca. For extra fun and a more balanced presentation, put in the car model or manufacturer's name, followed by "lemon."

Consumer Protection

Automobile Consumer Coalition (*www.carhelpcanada.com*)
Founded by the former director of the Toronto Automobile Protection Association, Mohamed Bouchama, the ACC provides many of the same services as the APA (see below); however, it has been refined for its Ontario members. You can also reach them by telephone (416-651-0555), fax (416-651-5465), or email (*acchelp@interlog.com*).

Automobile Protection Association (*www.apa.ca*)
This Montreal-based consumer group fights for safer vehicles and has exposed many scams associated with new-vehicle sales, leasing, and repairs; for a small fee it will send you the invoice price for most new vehicles.

CBC TV's *Marketplace* (*cbc.ca/consumers/market/files/cars/index.html*)
Marketplace has been the Canadian Broadcasting Corporation's premier national consumer show for almost three decades. Its site has extensive links and in-depth reports on Chrysler paint delamination (Shadow/Sundance in Nova Scotia), ABS brake failures, airbag dangers, and a host of other automotive topics.

Consumer Reports (*consumerreports.org*)
This independent monthly magazine is published in the States by the non-profit Consumers Union. Smart consumers will pay $3.95 for one month online, and then download all the comparison tests and product or service reviews they need.

Metro Credit Union (*www.metrocu.com*)
A unique credit union that puts a car broker (Dave Lawrence or Robert LoPresti) at its members' disposition to negotiate new- or used-vehicle sales. (Tel.: 905-831-3783 or 1-800-777-8507.)

The Truth About Cars (*www.robertfarago.com*)
British journalist Robert Farago's site has biting comments on everything from German automakers' quality decline ("German Brands Sluts") to auto show models ("Motor Show Hookers"):

> You could almost forgive Rover and Ford for their crass exploitation of the female form. The former sells downmarket motors redesigned for boy racers, and the latter currently carries more debt than Paraguay.... Everyone is well aware that Motor Show babes know less about cars than a Congolese banana grower. An army of midriffs, breasts, and legs protects the PR flacks from punters' probing questions about new gear ratios and the wisdom of clear indicator lenses.

U.S. Class Actions (*www.bigclassaction.com*)
This site lists pending complaints, lawsuits, judgments, and settlements. Pending actions and investigations: **Audi** defective windshields and TT electronic malfunctions; **Cooper Tire**; **DaimlerChrysler** engine oil sludge, minivans rolling away; **Neon** engine head gaskets, paint delamination, and faulty seat belt buckles; upper ball joint defects in 1998–2003 **Dodge Durangos**; **Ford/Lincoln** faulty heater blend door; **GM Dex-Cool** coolant which may corrode the heating system; **Astro** van rear axle failures; **Aztek** defects; **"Detroit 500" 12.7L diesel truck engines** with oil leakage problems; **GMC trucks** that stall without warning; **Hyundai** horsepower misrepresentation; **Kia** horsepower misrepresentation with 2001–02 models; **Optima; Sephia** stalling; **Mazda** defective transmissions; **Mercedes-Benz** price-fixing; **Nissan Pathfinder** engine manifold studs; **Ontario auto insurers** who may have withheld insurance deductibles for written-off cars; **Saturn** defective timing chains; **Toyota** engine sludge; and **VW New Beetle** dash fires.

Incidentally, **Mercedes-Benz** has reached a $32-million settlement with plaintiffs in the class action lawsuit filed against them by owners of some 1998 through 2001 models. The suit claims that the company failed to inform car owners that non-synthetic motor oil could case engine wear and damage. There were 351,439 plaintiffs in the action, and they will receive $35 worth of vouchers to be used toward an oil change. The company has also agreed to extend the warranty coverage on plaintiffs' vehicles, to cover costs related to the damage.

Auto Safety

Center for Auto Safety (*www.autosafety.org*)
Consumers Union and Ralph Nader founded the Center for Auto Safety (CAS) to provide consumers with a voice for auto safety and quality.

Crashtest.com (*www.crashtest.com/netindex.htm*)
This site takes National Highway Traffic Safety Administration (NHTSA) figures and compares them with other tests from around the world.

You can access the recall database for 1970–2002 model vehicles, but it's not always current, and, unlike NHTSA's website (see below), owner complaints aren't listed, defect investigations aren't disclosed, and service bulletin summaries aren't provided.

U.S. National Highway Traffic Safety Administration
(*www.nhtsa.dot.gov/cars/problems*)
This free database lists owner complaints, recall campaigns, crashworthiness and rollover ratings, defect investigations, service bulletin summaries, and safety research papers. See also Transport Canada's site at *www.tc.gc.ca/roadsafety/Recalls/search_e.asp*. A list of vehicles admissible for import to Canada is available at *www.tc.gc.ca/roadsafety/importation/menu.htm*, or by calling the Registrar of Imported Vehicles at 1-800-511-7755.

Insurance Institute for Highway Safety (*www.hwysafety.org*)
A dazzling site that's long on crash photos and graphs that rate vehicles for offset crashworthiness and head restraint protection.

Information/Mediation/Protest

Chrysler Products' Problem Web Page (*www.wam.umd.edu/~gluckman/Chrysler*)
A resource for Chrysler owners who have had problems in dealing with Chrysler, including issues with peeling paint, transmission failure, the Chrysler-installed Bendix-10 ABS, and other maladies. See also Dodge Caravan Transmission Problems at *www.dodge-caravan.com*.

Chrysler, Plymouth, and Dodge Car Information (*www.allpar.com*)
This is an excellent website that's jam-packed with historical information, tips on fixing common problems inexpensively, and advice on how to deal with Chrysler representatives and dealer service managers.

Dead Ford Owners' Page (*modena.intergate.ca personal/djk*)
Dead Ford is a play on the acronym F.O.R.D.: "Found On the Road, Dead," or, when read backward, "Driver Returns On Foot." The site is a useful gathering place for Ford car, truck, sport-utility, minivan, and van owners, who discuss problems and solutions.

Ford Insider Info (*www.blueovalnews.com*)
This website is the place to go for all the latest insider info on Ford's quality problems.

GM Intake Manifold Defects (*www.gm-v6lemons.com*)

A 1999 GM Venture owner's campaign against leaky plastic intake gaskets affecting 1995–2002 3.1L, 3.4L, and 3.8L V6 engines as well as the V-8 used in the Tahoe, trucks, and Suburbans. Good links and technical info. A related site at *www.geocities.com/b_gillie/dexcool_problems* details TSBs, photos, and other sites related to the 4.3L engine defects caused by GM's Dex-Cool coolant.

GM Piston Slap (*www.pistonslap.com*)

Owners of 1999–2002 vehicles with 3.1L, 3.4L, 4.8L, 5.3L, 5.7L(LS1), 6.0L or 8.1L engines may be eligible for a "goodwill" secret warranty repair to eliminate this noise.

Neon Enthusiasts (*www.neons.org*)

Lots of technical info and service tips from owners and mechanics. A good place to find Chrysler TSBs relating to engine head gasket failures and other problems afflicting Neons.

Taurus Transmission Victims (*members.aol.com/MKBradley/index.html*)

A great site for learning about Ford's biodegradable automatic transmissions (1991–99) from Lincoln Continental, Taurus, Sable, and Windstar owners. Expert mechanics give the why and how.

Information/Services

ALLDATA Service Bulletins (*www.alldata.com/consumer/TSB/yr.html*)

Free summaries of recalls, secret warranties, and technical service bulletins, but you can't see the contents of individual bulletins. Subscribe, for about $25 (U.S.), and you'll get a CD-ROM or a password to download 1972–2004 bulletins from the Internet.

Canadian Driver (*www.canadiandriver.com*)
An exceptionally well-structured and current Canadian website for new- and used-vehicle reviews, MSRP prices, and consumer reports prepared by Canadian journalists.

Carfax (*www.carfax.com*)
If you suspect a used vehicle is a rebuilt wreck, use Carfax (Tel.: 1-888-422-7329) to carry out a background check to see if the vehicle has been "scrapped," had flood damage, is stolen, or shows incorrect mileage on the odometer. There's a fee of $14.95 (U.S.) if the order is placed via the Internet.

Car Reviews by Owners (*www.carreview.com*)
Thousands of owner reports are presented to give prospective buyers a realistic idea of how each vehicle performs after many years, when driven by average owners.

Cartrackers (*www.cartrackers.com*)
This is a large site that has a nice balance of the pros and cons of vehicle ownership. Its technical resources are impressive, and there are experts to advise you on everything from secret warranties to simple maintenance.

Consumer's Guide to Insurance (*www.insurancehotline.com*)
This free service can yield big savings by giving you comparison quotes for a wide range of insurance plans through its website and 24-hour telephone number (416-686-0531).

Kelley Blue Book and Edmunds (*www.kbb.com, www.edmunds.com*)
Good reviews of almost every vehicle sold in North America, plus an informative readers' forum.

Phil Bailey's Auto World (*www.baileycar.com*)
Phil Bailey owns his own garage and specializes in the diagnosis and repair of foreign cars, particularly British ones. He's been advising Montreal motorists for years on local radio shows and has an exceptionally well written and comprehensive website.

Vehicle Information Centre of Canada (*www.vicc.com/english/MeasureUp.htm*)
Part of the Insurance Bureau of Canada. VICC's "How Cars Measure Up" compares the insurance claims experience of 1998–99 model vehicles for collision, personal injury, and theft losses.

"BOTTOM-FISHING" FOR BARGAINS

Good "Beaters" and Friendly "Orphans"

Few people can afford to pay $30,000 for the average new car or minivan. Yet millions of Canadians must have a vehicle that's safe, cheap, and reliable, capable of taking them to school, work, or the shopping mall. Fortunately, there are plenty of cheap used choices on the market that will cost less than $3,000.

Here's what to look for:

1. **The "family car".** Sure, you'll risk a family squabble somewhere down the road, but you'll likely get a good buy for next to nothing. Plus, you will have a good idea of how it was driven and maintained, and you can use the same repair facilities that have been repairing your family's vehicles for years. Don't worry if a vehicle is almost 10 years old—that's becoming the norm for Canadian ownership, particularly the farther west you go.
2. **End of season models.** Delay your purchase from a dealer until mid-2004, when automaker and dealer clearance rebates bring lots of inexpensive trade-ins on the market.
3. **Relatively new high-mileage vehicles** sold by fleets or rental agencies like Budget—a company that offers honest, money-back guarantees and reasonably priced extended warranties.
4. **No extra fees.** Refuse "administration," "acquisition," or "title" fees.
5. **No Detroit Big Three front-drives.** Steer clear of these. They are unreliable and expensive to service.
6. **No cheap, discontinued front-drive American models.** The Lincoln Continental and Plymouth minivans are especially bad buys.
7. **No European models**—parts and servicing can be a problem, and quality has declined.
8. **Three-year-old Hyundais.** But stay away from Excels, early Sonatas, and all Kias and Daewoos. Also look for 5- to 10-year-old, one-owner Japanese models.
9. **Rear-drive, full-sized American wagons or vans**, like the Chevrolet Caprice or GMC Vamdura.
10. **More than just fuel economy.** A 4-cylinder minivan is cheap to run, but highway merging will be a white-knuckle affair. A Honda Civic isn't as fuel efficient as a Honda Insight hybrid or Toyota Prius, but servicing and performance are less problematic.

Honda Insight

Finding bargains

If an independent mechanic gives you the green light, and if you have the time, knowledge, and parts suppliers to do your own maintenance and repairs, you will likely save a ton of money buying an old beat-up-looking car or minivan. Look for one of the following Recommended vehicles; avoid those that are Not Recommended.

If you have a bit more money to spend and want to take less of a risk, look up the Recommended vehicles found at the beginning of each vehicle category in Part Three.

"Beaten" beaters (cars that won't get you through the next month)

American Motors—Hornet, Gremlin, Concord, Spirit, Pacer, and **Eagle 4X4.** Faulty engines, transmissions, and steering.

Audi—Fox, 4000, and **5000.** Engine, transmission, and fuel system problems; a combination of sudden acceleration and no acceleration.

British Leyland—Austin Marina, MG, MGB, and **Triumph.** Electrical system, engine, transmission, and clutch problems; chassis rusting.

Chrysler—Cricket, Omni/Horizon, Volaré/Aspen. Engine, brakes, and steering problems; chassis rusting. **Charger, Cordoba,** and **Mirada.** Brakes, body, and electrical system problems. The 1985–89 **Lancer** and **LeBaron**

GTS may only cost $500–$750, but they're no bargain. In fact, they suffer from many of the same problems as the **Aries** and **Reliant K** cars and their 1989 replacements, the **Spirit** and **Acclaim**. Poor reliability; turbo models are especially risky buys. Engine head gaskets leak and shock absorbers, struts, and brakes wear out quickly. Crash test scores are below average.

Although they don't cost much—$500–$1,200, depending on the year— steer clear of 1983–89 **Aries** or **Reliants**. Uncomplicated mechanical components and a roomy interior made these cars attractive buys when new, but they quickly deteriorate once in service. Both cars use low-tech components that break down frequently. They have also performed poorly in crash tests. Serious corrosion along the trunk line, rear wheel wells, and front fenders.

Be wary of the 1987-94 **Shadow** and **Sundance**. These front-drive subcompact hatchbacks and convertibles came with 2.2L and 2.5L 4-cylinder engines, and an optional, extremely expensive, and unreliable turbocharger. A failure-prone Mitsubishi-built V6 engine arrived in 1992. A driver-side airbag became standard for 1990. Main problem areas: turbos, engine head gaskets, brakes, premature rusting, and paint delamination (see CBC TV *Marketplace* link in Appendix I). 1993 Shadow given a four-star frontal crash protection rating.

Datsun/Nissan—210, 310, 510, 810, F-10, and **240Z**. Electrical system and brake problems; rusting; no parts.

Eagle—Medallion, Monaco, and **Premier**. These bargain-priced French imports—$500–$600 for the **Medallion** and $800–$1,300 for the **Premier**— had a 1988–1992 model run. Sold through Chrysler's Renault connection, they are two of the most failure-prone imports to ever hit our shores. Powertrain, fuel system, electrical system, AC, suspension, and brakes are the worst offenders. Parts are *introuvables*.

Fiat—"Fix it, again, Tony." All Fiat models and years are known for temperamental fuel and electrical systems and biodegradable bodies. Alfa Romeos have similar problems.

Ford—Cortina, Pinto, Festiva, Fiesta, Bobcat, and **Mustang II**. Watch out for electrical system, engine, and chassis rusting; fire-prone **Pintos** and **Bobcats** are mobile Molotov cocktails.

The German import **Fiesta** and the **Festiva** built in South Korea are two small imports that only survived a few years in Canada. Parts are practically unobtainable for both vehicles.

The 1994–97 Korean-built **Aspire's** size, engine, and drivetrain limitations restrict it to an urban environment, and its low quality control restricts it to the driveway. Be wary of brake, electrical, and fuel system failures. Parts are also hard to find. This said, you can pick up an Aspire dirt-cheap— $2,000–$3,000. The car has consistently posted higher-than-average crash-test scores.

General Motors—Vega, Astre, Monza, and **Firenza.** Engine, transmission, body, and brake problems. **Cadillac Cimarron** and **Allanté.** Overpriced, with poor-quality components; all front-wheel drives suffer engine, automatic transmission, electronic module, steering, and brake problems, not to mention rust/paint peeling. **Citation, Skylark, Omega,** and **Phoenix.** Engine, brake, and electronic module problems; severe rust canker.

The **Pontiac Fiero,** sold from 1984 to 1988, snares lots of unsuspecting first-time buyers through its attractive, sports-car styling, high-performance pretensions, and $700–$1,300 price. However, one quickly learns to both fear and hate the Fiero as it shows off its fiery disposition (several safety recalls) and "I'll start when I want to" character.

Hyundai—Pony and **Stellar.** Two of the worst South Korean small cars ever imported into Canada. Their most serious problems involved electrical and fuel system failures causing fires, no-starts, stalling, and chronic engine stalling. Stellars have irreparable suspension, steering, and brake deficiencies that make them dangerous to drive.

The **Excel** is a low-tech and low-quality economy car that was orphaned in 1995. Resale prices are low ($500 for an '88; $2,000 for a '94). Likely problem areas are defective constant velocity joints, water pumps, oil-pan gaskets, oil pressure switches, front struts, and leaking engine head gaskets.

An Excel cross-dressing as a sports car, the 1991–95 **Scoupe** (for $2,500 to $3,000) is essentially a cute coupe with an engine more suited to high gas mileage than hard driving.

Isuzu/Passport—The I-Mark, Stylus, and **Optima** compacts were sold from 1988 until 1992 and can be bought for $1,500–$2,000. Repair costs are higher than average due to the cars' mediocre reliability and the difficulty in finding parts. Be especially wary of transmission defects, front brake rotor warpage, and poor body construction. The 1988–89 models garnered below-average crash test scores, while the last three model years (1990–92) did quite well.

Jaguar—Chronic fuel and electrical system shutdowns. Other problems: powertrain failures, lousy body construction, poor parts supply, and few mechanics who want to repair these machines. Servicing is spotty and prices are way too high.

Renault—French for Yugo, or rather, you don't go. Fuel and electrical system failures, poor-quality CV joints and brakes, no parts, and few mechanics. The Renault 10, 12, 18, and Fuego were the worst of a bad lot. The Renault 5, the last model sold in North America, wasn't as bad as its predecessors.

Saab—900, 9000, 9-3, and **9-5** models sold from 1985 through 2003 are very poor buys. Maintenance and repair costs can be quite high and must be done by a GM or Saab dealer. 1996–2003 used prices range from $6,000–$24,000.

The 900 and 9000 series have similar deficiencies affecting the engine, cooling (biodegradable water pumps) and electrical systems, brakes, automatic transmission (clutch o-rings), and body hardware. Interestingly, the upscale 9000 series isn't as crashworthy as the cheaper 900 versions, nor is it more reliable, exhibiting similar generic deficiencies to its entry-level brother. The 9-5 model has garnered a five-star crash protection rating.

On more recent models, chronic stalling can make these vehicles extremely dangerous to drive. Short circuits are legion and run the gamut from minor annoyances to fire hazards. Electrical glitches in the traction control system's relay module give a false reading that the tires are spinning, which shuts the engine down.

Turbo-equipped models should be approached with caution because owner abuse or poor maintenance can make them wallet busters. Air conditioners and exhaust-system parts have a short life span, and leaky seals and gaskets are common. Rust perforations tend to develop along door bottoms and the rocker panels.

Volkswagen—The original **Beetle** was cheap to own but deadly to drive. Its main deficiencies: poorly anchored, unsafe front seats; a heater that never worked (fortunately, we were young, and promiscuous enough in those days to generate our own heat); fuel tank placement that was dangerous in collisions; and poorly designed wheels, and seat tracks). A pre-1998 Beetle in good condition is worth $4,000-$5,000 (CDN).

The VW **Camper** minivan was safer, but less reliable, with engine, transmission, fuel system, and heater failings. **Rabbit/Dasher** and **411/412** models are known for unreliable powertrain, electrical, cooling, and fuel systems, ineffective and poor-quality brakes, hard-to-find parts, and non-existent servicing.

Sold during 1987–93, and now costing $1,500–$2,000, the **Fox**, with its old design, can't offer the mechanical or interior efficiency that newer small cars provide, plus parts are rare. Crashworthiness is way below average.

VW's **Scirocco** is fun to drive, but risky to own. Chronic breakdowns, parts shortages, and poor crashworthiness are just the beginning. Electrical short circuits, chronic fuel supply problems, premature front brake wear, and fragile body parts are common owner complaints. Expect to pay $1,500–$2,000.

Selling for $4,000 to $8,500, the 1990–95 **Corrado** gives good all-round performance, with emphasis on smooth acceleration, a firm but not harsh ride, and excellent handling with little body roll. So why is it not recommended? Poor reliability, an unacceptably high selling price, hard-to-find parts, limited servicing outlets, and undetermined crashworthiness.

Recommended '80s to mid-'90s vehicles ($500–$5,000)

Chrysler—All rear-drives and the Colt import
Ford—All rear-drives; Escort ('91 and later) and Probe
GM—All rear-drives; Caprice, Roadmaster, Malibu, Astro, Safari, Savana, and Express
Honda—Civic, Accord, and Odyssey

Hyundai—Accent, Elantra, and Tiburon
Mazda—MX-3, Precidia, MX-6, Miata, Millenia, and 929
Mercury—Grand Marquis and Villager
Nissan—Sentra, Stanza, Axxess, and Quest
Subaru—All front-drives, Justy, and post-'95 Impreza, Legacy, and Forester
Toyota—Celica, Corolla, Supra, Avalon, Camry, and Sienna

Alternative used choices

Acura—The 5-cylinder **Vigor**, a 1992–94 spin-off of the Honda Accord sedan, sells for $5,500–$7,000. This compact has power to spare, handles well, and has an impressive reliability/durability record. Problem areas: excessive brake noise and premature brake wear, in addition to fit and finish deficiencies. The 1992 Vigor turned in below-average crash test scores.

The **Legend** is an above-average $3,000–$6,000 buy (1989–95); although it's not recommended for the 1986–88 model years. Resale value is high on all Legend models, and especially so on the coupe. Shop instead for a cheaper 1989 or later base Legend with the coupe's upgraded features and fewer reports of unintended, sudden acceleration.

Pre-1990 Legends were upscale, enlarged Accords that were unimpressive performers with either of the two 6-cylinder power plants. The 3.2L V6 that appeared in 1991 is by far a better performer. Ride quality is improved, power steering is more responsive, and rear seating is more spacious. 1992 L and LS models got seat belt pretensioners and dual front airbags, but base models didn't get a passenger airbag until the 1993 model year. The '93s also got a smoother-shifting automatic transmission, while coupes were given a new 6-speed manual tranny, 30 extra horses, traction control, and high-performance tires. The '94 GS sedan was given many of the coupe's high-performance features, including a 230-hp engine and 6-speed gearbox.

Chrysler—**Dart, Valiant, Duster, Scamp, Diplomat, Caravelle, Newport**, rear-drive **New Yorker Fifth Avenue**, and **Gran Fury**. Problem areas: electrical system, suspension, brakes, body and frame rust, plus constant stalling when humidity is high. The **Caravelle, Diplomat,** and **New Yorker Fifth Avenue** are reasonably reliable and simple-to-repair throwbacks to a time when rear-drive land yachts ruled the highways. Powered with 6- and 8-cylinder engines, they will practically run forever with minimal care. The fuel-efficient "slant 6" power plant was too small for this type of car and was changed to a gas-guzzling but smooth and reliable V8 after 1983. Handling is vague and sloppy, though, and emergency braking is often accompanied by rear-wheel lock-up. Still, what do you want for $1,500–$2,000 for a 1984–89 "retro rocket"? Problem areas are the carburetor, ignition, electrical system, brakes, and suspension (premature idler-arm wear). All the above models had severe rusting in the rear quarter panels and chronic dashboard water leaks.

Wet weather no-starts are cured by replacing the $7 ballast resistor—a white piece of ceramic mounted to the firewall near the windshield wiper motor—with two sets of wires going into it. Stalling and idle problems can be fixed by using a high-quality distributor cap and rotor (e.g. Blue Streak), distributor cap gasket (Standard PN AL-483G), silicone covered lifetime-warranty wires, and by putting weather strip foam over the ignition and voltage regular modules.

Chrysler's 1991–93 **2000GTX** is an above-average buy that may cost $3,000–$3,500, depending upon the model year. It's a reliable Japanese-built sedan that has a competitive price, modern styling, and high-performance options that put it on par with such benchmark cars as the Honda Accord and Toyota Camry. Problem areas are the front brakes, which need more attention than average.

The Chrysler **Stealth** is a competent, reasonably priced sports car that's as much go as show. Although 1995 was its last model year in Canada, it's still sold in the United States as the Mitsubishi 3000GT. Prices range from $4,500 to $5,000 for the 1991–93 base or ES model. A '95 high-performance R/T will go for about $7,500—not a bad price for an "orphan" sports car, eh? Problem areas: engine, transmission, front brake, and electrical failures. The 1993 model excelled in crash tests.

Ford—Maverick, Comet, Fairmont, Zephyr, Tracer, Mustang, Capri, Cougar, Thunderbird V6, Torino, Marquis, Grand Marquis, LTD, and LTD Crown Victoria.

Problem areas: trunk, wheelwell, and rocker panel rusting; brakes; steering; and electrical system failures.

Through its Mazda connection with the **MX-6**, the 1989–97 **Probe** escaped much of Ford's decade of mindless cost-cutting, resulting in an above-average reliability and performance rating for both companies' 1993–97 models. The 1989–92 models were more glitch-ridden and are considered below-average buys.

Available only as a two-door hatchback, there are two models, each with its own power plant: a 2.0L 4-cylinder and a 2.5L V6 engine. Both engines are exceptionally smooth and quiet. Early models are beset by severe "torque steer," a tendency for the chassis to twist when the vehicle accelerates. Nevertheless, overall handling is precise and predictable on all models without sacrificing ride quality.

The Probe's overall mechanical reliability is fairly good, but like its Mustang cousin, body assembly is the pits (no surprise here—Mazda did most of the mechanicals; Ford did the body work). Many reports of excessive ABS noise and vibrations when braking, and the front brakes tend to wear out very quickly. AC components have a short lifespan of five years at best.

Excellent frontal crash protection: 1994–97; fair protection: 1993; and above-average protection: 1991–92. Probe prices are a bit less expensive than the MX-6's, varying from $2,000 for an '89 model up to $5,000 for a '97 version. The GT model usually costs about $500 more.

General Motors—Chevette and Acadian

are cheap, rear-drive city runabouts. Problem areas: steering system defects, and brakes you have to stand on to stop. Rear-drive **Nova, Ventura, Skylark**, and **Phoenix**. Problem areas:

undercarriage, steering system, and suspension rust-out. Other recommended rear-drives: **Camaro, Firebird, Malibu, LeMans, Century, Regal, Cutlass, Monte Carlo,** and **Grand Prix.** Problem areas: rear brake backing plate rust-out and steering failures. **Bel Air, Impala, Caprice, Roadmaster, Laurentian, Catalina, Parisienne, LeSabre, Bonneville,** and **Delta 88.** Be wary of undercarriage, suspension component, and rear brake backing plate rust-out.

The Geo **Storm** was GM's Japanese-made small car that only had two model years in Canada (1992–93). Owners report serious body hardware deficiencies (not paint or rust, however), in addition to brake, exhaust, electrical, and ignition problems. Prices vary between $3,000 and $4,000, depending on the model chosen.

Mazda—Sports car thrills, minus the bills: the 1992–96 **MX-3's** base 1.6L engine supplies plenty of power for most driving situations, plus it's reasonably priced at $3,000–$4,000. When equipped with the optional 1.8L V6 power plant (the smallest V6 on the market at the time) and high-performance options, the car transforms itself into a 130-hp pocket rocket. In fact, the MX-3 GS easily outperforms the Honda del Sol, Toyota Paseo, and Geo Storm on comfort and high-performance acumen. It does fall a bit short of the Saturn SC due to its limited low-end torque, and fuel economy is disappointing. Reverse gear is sometimes hard to engage. Brake and wheel bearing problems are commonplace. Crash safety ratings have been average. Also consider the **MX-6** and its Ford Probe twin (see above).

The key word for the 1988–95 **929** is understatement: The engine is unobtrusive, the exterior is anonymous, and the interior is far from flashy. In spite of its lack of pizzazz and imprecise power steering, the 929 will accelerate and handle curves as well as the best large European sedans, and it has proven to be fairly reliable. For these advantages, you can expect to pay $3,500–$6,000 for a 1988–93 model. The '94s and '95s are priced in the $8,000–$10,000 range. Owners report some problems with premature disc brake wear, electrical glitches, exhaust system rust-out, electronic shock absorber durability (particularly with the 1989–91 models), and fit and finish deficiencies. The only real safety negative is the 929's consistently poor crash-test scores since the '88 model was first tested.

Selling for $3,000–$4,000 for a base 1988–91 model, the **RX-7** is an impressive performer with a ride that can be painful on bad roads, due primarily to the car's stiff suspension. The GSL and Turbo models are very well equipped and luxuriously finished. Except for some oil burning problems, apex seal failures, and leaking engine o-rings, the RX-7 has served to dispel any doubts concerning the durability of rotary engines.

Nevertheless, careful maintenance is in order, since contaminated oil or overheating will easily damage the rotary engine. Clutches wear quickly if used hard. Disc brakes need frequent attention paid to the calipers and rotors. The MacPherson struts get soft more quickly than average. Fuel, exhaust system, electrical glitches, and AC malfunctions are also common. Be wary of leaky sunroofs. Radiators have a short life span. Rocker panels and body seams are prone to serious rusting. The underbody on older cars should also be inspected carefully for corrosion damage. Fuel economy has never been this car's strong suit and crash-test scores were below average.

For more info, check out the Mazda RX-7 Lemon Site at *scuderiaciriani.com/ rx7/lemon_site/sources.htm*. It's a treasure trove of maintenance tips, common defects, copies of service bulletins, and specific buying and selling information.

The 1995–2002 **Millenia** is an excellent luxury car buy with lots of power and sophisticated engineering. Prices range from $5,000–$20,000—unusually rapid depreciation making for plenty of bargains—as long as the engine and transmission are OK. Nevertheless, maintenance and repair costs are higher than average, and repairs must be done by a Mazda dealer who may have great difficulty getting parts for the Miller-Cycle engine.

Launched as a '95 model and smaller than the Mazda 929, the front-drive Millenia carries the same 2.5L 170-hp V6 used by the 626. An optional turbo-charged 2.3L Miller-Cycle "S" 6-cylinder engine manages to pump out 210 horses. Both engines use a standard 4-speed automatic transmission that shifts a bit harshly when pushed. As with all luxury cars, the Millenia comes with a wide array of standard features that would normally cost thousands of dollars more. Although billed as a five-passenger car, the middle occupant in the rear seat is cramped and has to sit on a hump. The 2001 model was restyled, given substantial handling improvements, larger brakes, a revised ABS system, standard side airbags, and an upgraded interior. Frontal crash test protection has been judged better than average on 1995-98 models.

Assembly and component quality are fairly high; however, there have been some reports of Miller-Cycle engine failures and front brake, AC, fuel system, and electrical glitches. Among the powertrain problems, owners cite transmission failures and defective engine head gaskets with the base 2.5L power plant.

Nissan—The **Pulsar** and **NX** models are good small-car buys ($1,500–$2,500, depending upon the year), as long as you pick the right years and stay away from failure-prone and expensive-to-repair turbo models. The **Pulsar** was replaced by the 1991 **NX**, a similar small car that also shares Sentra components. For 1983–86 models, overall reliability is poor to very poor. As with other discontinued Nissans, the 1987–93 models have shown remarkable performance improvement and are all the more attractive due to their depreciated prices. Crash-test scores were below average for the 1990 and earlier models, while the 1991 and later versions scored quite well. Pulsars are known for minor AC malfunctions, premature wearout of front brakes and suspension components, and exhaust systems that don't last very long (two years, tops).

The 1990–92 **Stanzas** are roomy, reasonably priced ($2,000–$3,000), four-passenger compacts that offer peppy performance, more responsive steering, nimble handling, and good fuel economy. Overall reliability has been fairly good over the years. Some transmission malfunctions and a biodegradable exhaust system.

Owners complain of premature front brake wear and rust perforations, problems that are common for all years. Especially prone to rust perforation are wheel openings, the front edge of the hood, the rear hatch, and door bottoms. 1990 models produced below-average crashworthiness scores, but the 1991 and 1992 models did better than average.

The 1995–98 **200SX** is an above-average buy, if you're not a real high-performance enthusiast. The '98 SE-R offered standard AC and ABS in addition to its competent 140-hp 2.0L engine. Most repairs can be done by any garage, but parts can be hard to find.

The 200SX has sports-car flair without the substance. The interior is unnecessarily cramped, and you get only average power and handling with the base power plant. Later models are much sportier and have more passenger room.

All engines have performed reasonably well, although the SE-R's 2.0L has been the most suitable for hard-driving thrills. The clutch and clutch cable, axle seal assembly, and AC pressure hose connector have been the source of some complaints, along with occasional electrical malfunctions. Rapid front brake wear and rotor damage are common problems. Body construction is much better than average. Airbags tend to deploy when they shouldn't and not deploy when they should. Expect to pay between $3,000–$5,000. The '97 model performed quite well in government-run frontal crash tests.

The **240SX** is another recommended Nissan sporty car, produced from 1989 through 1998. Most repairs can be done by any garage and parts are reasonably priced and generally easy to find, except for body panels.

This rear-drive sport coupe carried a 2.4L 4-cylinder engine to differentiate it from its 2.0L-equipped predecessor, the 200SX. The 140-hp base engine provides more than enough torque to handle most driving needs—just don't expect fast acceleration times, or a comfortable ride. A more powerful, though noisy, twin-cam engine debuted with the '91 model. Handling is impressive, thanks to the car's independent suspension. A convertible appeared in 1992 and became the only body style available in 1994. The redesigned 1995 model arrived as a notchback coupe with a longer wheelbase and shorter overall length. It still provides a harsh ride and poor traction on slippery roadways. Headroom remains limited and cargo space is limited.

This car doesn't have any serious shortcomings, apart from a cramped interior and excessive engine noise. The few deficiencies reported concern engine timing belt failures, transmission leaks, noisy brakes that wear out quickly, and fit and finish deficiencies. Prices range from $2,500 for the first-year models to $6,000 for a '98 version. Safety complaints involve ABS brake failures and faulty airbags. 1990–93 models turned in excellent frontal crash scores, while the '95–'97s were rated as average performers.

Nissan's answer to the Corvette, the 1989–96 **300ZX** has everything: high-performance capability, a heavy chassis, complicated electronics, and average depreciation resulting in a price range of $5,000–$12,000. Turbocharged 1990 and later models are much faster than previous versions and better overall buys. This weighty rear-drive offers a high degree of luxury equipment along with a potent 300-hp engine. Traction is poor on slippery surfaces, though, and the rear suspension hits hard when going over speed bumps. Crashworthiness scores have been average.

The complexity of all the bells and whistles on the 300ZX translates into a lot more problems than you'd experience with either a Mustang or a Camaro—two cars that have their own reliability problems, but are far easier and less costly to repair. The best example of this is the electrical system, long a source of recurring, hard-to-diagnose shorts. Fuel injectors are a constant problem and lead to poor engine performance. The manual transmission has been failure-prone, clutches don't last long, front and rear brakes are noisy and wear out quickly, and the aluminum wheels are easily damaged by corrosion and road hazards. The exhaust system is practically biodegradable. The glitzy digital dash, with three odometers, and weird spongy/stiff variable shock absorbers are more gimmicky than practical. Body assembly is mediocre.

Subaru—Sold from 1988 to 1995, the **Justy** does everything reasonably well for an entry-level Subaru. Pairing smooth and nimble handling with precise and predictable steering, the 4X4 system is a boon for people who often need easy-to-engage extra traction and an automatic transmission. Price range: $1,500–$2,500. The Justy's reliability record has been about average from the 1991 model onward. Some owners complain about poor engine idling and frequent cold-weather stalling, manual and automatic transmission malfunctions, premature exhaust system rust-out, catalytic converter failures, and paint peeling. With the exception of the CVT, servicing and repairs are made easy due to a very straightforward design.

Toyota (late '80s and early '90s)—**All models**, except the LE Van, which has a history of chronic brake, chassis, and body rusting problems. Chassis rusting and V6 engine head gasket failures are common problems with the 1988–95 sport-utilities and pickups (Toyota has paid for the engine repairs up to eight years). **Celicas** are an especially fine buy, combining smooth engine performance and bulletproof reliability with sports car thrills.

Selling for $3,000 to $4,000, the 1987–93 **MR2** is a mid-engine, rear-drive, 4-cylinder sports car that's both reliable and fun to drive. On the downside, you have to put up with a cramped interior, quirky turbo handling, inflated insurance premiums, and undetermined crashworthiness. In order of frequency, the most common complaints on all MR2s are as follows: the brakes, transmission, electrical glitches, and body hardware (fit and finish) deficiencies.

The **Cressida** ages well and offers an excellent combination of dependable, no-surprise, rear-drive performance, comfort, and luxury. All this in a price range from $3,000 to $4,500 for a 1985–92 model. There is little to fault when it comes to overall reliability, and the engine is a model of smooth power. The 1990–93 models are more crashworthy, reliable, and trouble-free than earlier versions, but they're also much more expensive. Complaints heard throughout the years: engine head gasket failures, premature front brake wear and excessive brake pulsation/vibration, AC glitches, electrical short circuits, and a quirky Panasonic sound system.

From its humble beginnings in 1979, the **Supra** became Toyota's flagship sports car by 1986 and took on its own unique personality—with the help of a powerful 3.0L DOHC V6 power plant. Supra prices range from a low of $9,000 for a '90 model up to $25,000 for a '97. It's an attractively styled, high-performance sports car that had been quite reliable up until it caught the Corvette/Nissan 300ZX malady in 1993: cumulative add-ons that drove up the car's price and weight, and drove down its reliability. The 6-cylinder engines are smooth and powerful, and handling is sure and precise—better than the Celica because of the independent rear suspension. Additionally, crashworthiness has never been determined.

Early models (pre-'93) are more reasonably priced and are practically trouble-free, except for some premature front brake wear and vibrations. On later models, owners report major turbocharger problems; frequent rear differential replacements; electrical short circuits; AC malfunctions; and premature brake, suspension, and exhaust system wear. The 3.0L engine is an oil burner at times, and cornering is often accompanied by a rear-end growl. Seat belt guides and the power antenna are failure-prone. Body deficiencies are common.

Volvo—The 1989–93 **240 Series** is an average buy, costing $2,000–$3,000. Avoid the turbocharged 4-cylinder engine and failure-prone AC. Diesels suffer from cooling system breakdowns and leaky cylinder head gaskets. The brakes on all model years need frequent and expensive servicing, and exhaust systems are notorious for their short lifespan.

The 1992–93 models produced excellent NHTSA crashworthiness scores.

Selling for $3,000 to $4,000, the 1986–92 **700 Series** models are more spacious, luxurious, and complicated to service than the entry-level 240. The standard engine and transmission perform well, but aren't as refined as the 850. The 700 Series suffers from some brake, electrical, engine cooling, air conditioning, and body deficiencies. Brakes tend to wear rapidly and can require expensive servicing. The 1988 model performed poorly in crash tests, while the 1991–92 versions did quite well.

Minivans and wagons

Assuming you can't afford the big bucks for a Honda Odyssey or Toyota Sienna, you have a number of cheaper, old minivans to choose from: **Chrysler's Colt/Summit/Vista wagons**; the **Ford Aerostar**; **GM's Astro** and **Safari**; and **Nissan's Axxess**.

Recommendations: Chrysler's Colt, Summit, and **Vista**. Priced from about $700 for an '88 version to about $2,000 for a '95 (wagons are worth about $500–$1,000 more), these are three of the best small cars and wagons that Chrysler doesn't make (they're all Mitsubishi imports). The only exceptions are the 1985–88 models, which were quite troublesome.

On post-1990 Colts and Summits, the 2.4L head gasket may fail prematurely. Shocks aren't very durable, braking isn't impressive, and the front brakes have a short lifespan. Emission components, like the oxygen sensor, often fail after two years of use. A few owners have reported automatic transmission failures. Be especially wary of the troublesome 4X4 powertrain on 1989–91 wagons and the 16-valve turbo, dropped in 1990. Owners of the 1993 wagon complain of poor heating and defrosting. Surface rust is common, as are rust perforations on door bottoms, the front edge of the hood, and the rear hatch.

The 1995–97 **Ford Aerostar** isn't a bad choice, though 1986–94 models are risky buys. A 1992 XL would cost about $3,000, while a fully equipped 1997 version (the Aerostar's last year) should cost between $3,000 and $3,500. These primitive rear-drives are brawnier and more reliable than Chrysler's or Ford's front-drive minivans (exception made for the failure-prone 4X4 system), and they've posted impressive crashworthiness scores since 1992.

The 1986–94 models are at the bottom of the evolutionary scale as far as quality control is concerned. However, the last three model years showed lots of improvement. Repair costs are reasonable (except for high automatic transmission, AC, and computer module costs), and many of the Aerostar's myriad mechanical and body defects can be fixed quite easily by independent garages. The Aerostar's modern, swoopy shape belies its limited performance capabilities: the 3.0L and 4.0L engines are unreliable through the 1991 model year, and the 3.0L is a sluggish performer. Older 2.3L and 2.8L engines can barely pull their own weight. The failure-prone 4-speed automatic transmission often has a hard time deciding which gear to choose, and the power steering transmits almost no road feel to the driver. The ride is bouncy, handling is sloppy, and braking performance is poor. Reliability problems on all models make early Aerostars risky buys, especially if the previous owner has been less than fastidious in maintenance and repairs.

Valve cover and rear main oil seal leaks are frequent, and leaks from the front axle vent tube often require the replacement of the front axle assembly. Even oil pans, which you wouldn't normally associate with leaks, tend to leak as a result of premature corrosion (a big-buck repair). Fuel injectors are either faulty or plugged. A grinding/growling coming from the rear signals that the in-tank electric fuel pump is defective. Other problems include expensive electronic and electrical system glitches; power-steering, suspension, and brake defects; and premature and chronic air conditioner condenser and compressor breakdowns.

Nissan's 1991–95 **Axxess** minivan is a good choice. It's fairly reliable, easily serviced, and has posted respectable crash-safety ratings. You get carlike handling and ride comfort and as much space as the higher-priced Honda Odyssey. As with most minivans equipped with a full load and a small engine, acceleration isn't confidence inspiring on the highway. However, the Axxess is ideal for city-to-suburb commuting. What further sets the Axxess apart is its reasonable price and better-than-average reliability. Prices have remained stable, ranging from $3,000 to $4,000 for the top-of-the-line SE. You may have trouble finding one. But it's worth the wait.

Avoid: Stay away from bargain-priced minivans that require frequent and costly repairs. Chief among these are **Chrysler minivans**, **Ford Windstars**, and the **Mercury Villager/Nissan Quest** (1993–96). Chrysler models had